MUSIC
AN APPRECIATION

BY THE AUTHOR

The Norton Scores: An Anthology for Listening

McGRAW-HILL BOOK COMPANY

New York St. Louis San Francisco Auckland Bogotá Hamburg Johannesburg London Madrid Mexico Montreal
New Delhi Panama Paris São Paulo Singapore Sydney Tokyo Toronto

MUSIC
AN APPRECIATION

Roger Kamien
Queens College of the City
University of New York

Second Edition

This book was set in Baskerville by York Graphic Services, Inc.
The editors were Richard R. Wright and James R. Belser;
the designer was Jo Jones;
the production supervisor was Dominick Petrellese.
The photo editor was Inge King.
R. R. Donnelley & Sons Company was printer and binder.

MUSIC: AN APPRECIATION

567890   DODO   8321

Library of Congress Cataloging in Publication Data

Kamien, Roger.
    Music.

    Bibliography: p.
    Includes index.
    1. Music—Analysis, appreciation. I. Title.
MT6.K22M9   1980   780'.15   79–16464
ISBN 0-07-033279-7

*See Acknowledgements on pages 570–571. Copyrights included on this page by reference.
Front cover photograph by Fred J. Maroon/Photo Researchers, Inc. Back cover photograph by
Jerry Cooke/Photo Researchers, Inc.*

For Anita, David, Joshua, and Adina

CONTENTS

Preface   xxiii

I ELEMENTS

[1] SOUND: PITCH, DYNAMICS, AND TONE COLOR   2

Pitch: The Highness or Lowness of Sound   2

Dynamics   4

Dynamic Indications   5

Tone Color   5

Listening Outlines   6

Lohengrin, Prelude to Act III, by Richard Wagner   6

LISTENING OUTLINE: *Lohengrin,* Prelude to Act III,
    by Richard Wagner   7

Prelude in C Minor for Piano, Op. 28, No. 20,
    by Frédéric Chopin   7

LISTENING OUTLINE: Prelude in C Minor for Piano, Op. 28,
    No. 20, by Frédéric Chopin   7

Firebird Suite, Finale, by Igor Stravinsky   7

LISTENING OUTLINE: *Firebird Suite,* Finale,
    by Igor Stravinsky   8

"Hotter Than That," by Louis Armstrong and His Hot Five   8

LISTENING OUTLINE: "Hotter Than That,"
    by Louis Armstrong and His Hot Five   9

[2] PERFORMING MEDIA: VOICES AND INSTRUMENTS   9

Voices   9

Musical Instruments   11

String Instruments   14

Woodwind Instruments   18

Brass Instruments   23

Percussion Instruments   24

Keyboard Instruments   28

Electronic Instruments   31

A Young Person's Guide to the Orchestra, Op. 32,
    by Benjamin Britten   33

vii

[3] RHYTHM   35
    Beat   36
    Meter   37
    Accent and Syncopation   38
    Tempo   39
    Unsquare Dance, by Dave Brubeck   40

[4] MUSIC NOTATION   41
    Notating Pitch   41
    Notating Rhythm   44
    Silence (Rests)   46
    Meter   47

[5] MELODY   47
    "Yesterday," by John Lennon and Paul McCartney 51

[6] HARMONY   52
    Consonance and Dissonance   53
    The Triad   54
    Broken Chords (Arpeggios)   55
    Prelude in E Minor for Piano, Op. 28, No. 4,
      by Frédéric Chopin   55

[7] KEY   56
    The Major Scale   57
    The Minor Scale   59
    The Key Signature   60
    The Chromatic Scale   60
    Modulation: Change of Key   61
    Tonic Key   62

[8] MUSICAL TEXTURE   62
    Monophonic Texture   62
    Polyphonic Texture   63
    Homophonic Texture   64
    Changes of Texture   65
    Farandole from *L'Arlésienne Suite No. 2,* by Georges Bizet   65
    LISTENING OUTLINE: *Farandole* from *L'Arlésienne
    Suite No. 2,* by Georges Bizet   66
    "Hallelujah Chorus" from *Messiah,* by George Frideric Handel   67

Contents

[9] MUSICAL FORM 68

Techniques That Create Form 68

Repetition 69

Contrast 69

Variation 69

Types of Musical Form 69

Three-part (Ternary) Form: A B A 70

Dance of the Reed Pipes from the *Nutcracker Suite*, by Peter Illyich Tchaikovsky 70

LISTENING OUTLINE: *Dance of the Reed Pipes* from the *Nutcracker Suite*, by Peter Ilyich Tchaikovsky 71

Two-part (Binary) Form: A B 71

Prelude in C Minor from *The Well-Tempered Clavier*, Book 2, by Johann Sebastian Bach 71

LISTENING OUTLINE: Prelude in C Minor from *The Well-Tempered Clavier*, Book 2, by Johann Sebastian Bach 72

Listening for Form 72

[10] PERFORMANCE 73

The Performer 73

The Conductor 75

Recorded and Live Performance 77

Judging Performance 78

[11] MUSICAL STYLE 79

II
MIDDLE
AGES

[1] MUSIC IN THE MIDDLE AGES (450–1450) 84

[2] GREGORIAN CHANT 87

The Church Modes 88

Alleluia: Dominus dixit 88

[3] SECULAR MUSIC IN THE MIDDLE AGES 91

Danse Royale 91

[4] THE DEVELOPMENT OF POLYPHONY: ORGANUM 93

The School of Notre Dame: Measured Rhythm 94

Alleluya Nativitas, by Perotin 95

[5] FOURTEENTH-CENTURY MUSIC: THE "NEW ART" IN FRANCE AND ITALY   96

    Tosto che ll'alba, by Gherardello da Firenze   96

    Guillaume de Machaut   97

      Je puis trop bien   98

      The Notre Dame Mass   98

III
THE
RENAISSANCE

[1] MUSIC IN THE RENAISSANCE (1450–1600)   102

    Music and Renaissance Society   102

    Words and Music   105

    Renaissance Texture   105

    Renaissance Rhythm and Melody   106

[2] SACRED MUSIC IN THE RENAISSANCE   106

    Josquin des Prez and the Renaissance Motet   106

      Ave Maria . . . virgo serena   107

    Palestrina and the Renaissance Mass   108

      Pope Marcellus Mass   109

[3] SECULAR MUSIC IN THE RENAISSANCE   110

    Vocal Music   110

    The Renaissance Madrigal   112

      "As Vesta Was Descending," by Thomas Weelkes   112

    The Renaissance Lute Song   113

      "It Was a Lover and His Lass," by Thomas Morley   113

    Instrumental Music   114

      Ricercar in the Twelfth Mode, by Andrea Gabrielli   115

IV
THE
BAROQUE
PERIOD

[1] BAROQUE MUSIC (1600–1750)   118

    Baroque Unity of Mood   121

    Baroque Rhythm   121

    Baroque Melody   121

    Terraced Dynamics   121

    Baroque Texture   122

    Chords and the Basso Continuo (Figured Bass)   122

    The Baroque Orchestra   123

    Words and Music   124

    Baroque Forms   124

[2] MUSIC IN BAROQUE SOCIETY   125

Contents

[3] THE CONCERTO GROSSO AND RITORNELLO FORM   128

First Movement from Brandenburg Concerto No. 5 in D Major,
by Johann Sebastian Bach   129

LISTENING OUTLINE: Brandenburg Concerto No. 5 in D Major,
First Movement, by Johann Sebastian Bach   130

[4] THE FUGUE   131

Organ Fugue in G Minor ("Little" Fugue), by Johann Sebastian Bach   133

[5] THE ELEMENTS OF OPERA   135

[6] OPERA IN THE BAROQUE ERA   139

[7] CLAUDIO MONTEVERDI   141

Orfeo   142

[8] HENRY PURCELL   143

Ground Bass   144

Dido and Aeneas   144

[9] THE BAROQUE SONATA   148

[10] ARCANGELO CORELLI   148

Trio Sonata in E Minor, Op. 3, No. 7   149

[11] ANTONIO VIVALDI   150

Concerto Grosso in A Minor, Op. 3, No. 8   150

[12] JOHANN SEBASTIAN BACH   152

Bach's Music   155

Brandenburg Concerto No. 5 in D Major   157

Mass in B Minor   158

[13] THE BAROQUE SUITE   160

Suite (Overture) No. 3 in D Major, by Johann Sebastian Bach   161

[14] THE CHORALE AND THE CHURCH CANTATA   162

The Church Cantata   163

Cantata No. 140: *Wachet auf, ruft uns die Stimme,*
by Johann Sebastian Bach   163

[15] THE ORATORIO   172

[16] GEORGE FRIDERIC HANDEL   172

Handel's Music   174

Messiah   176

V
THE
CLASSICAL
PERIOD

[1] THE CLASSICAL STYLE (1750–1820)   184

Classical Contrast of Mood   187

Classical Rhythm   188

Classical Texture   188

Classical Melody   188

Classical Dynamics and the Piano   188

The End of the Basso Continuo   189

The Classical Orchestra   189

Classical Form   190

[2] COMPOSER, PATRON, AND PUBLIC IN THE
CLASSICAL PERIOD   191

Vienna   193

[3] SONATA FORM   194

Exposition   195

Development   195

Recapitulation   196

Coda   196

Fourth Movement from Symphony No. 40 in G Minor, K. 550,
by Wolfgang Amadeus Mozart   196

LISTENING OUTLINE: Symphony No. 40 in G Minor, K. 550,
Fourth Movement, by Wolfgang Amadeus Mozart   197

[4] THEME AND VARIATIONS   199

Second Movement from Symphony No. 94 in G Major
("Surprise"), by Joseph Haydn   199

LISTENING OUTLINE: Symphony No. 94 in G Major
("Surprise"), Second Movement, by Joseph Haydn   199

Contents

[5] MINUET AND TRIO   201

Third Movement (Minuet) from *Eine kleine Nachtmusik,* K. 525, by Wolfgang Amadeus Mozart   202

LISTENING OUTLINE: *Eine kleine Nachtmusik,* K. 525, Third Movement, by Wolfgang Amadeus Mozart   202

[6] RONDO   203

Fourth Movement (Rondo) from String Quartet in C Minor, Op. 18, No. 4, by Ludwig van Beethoven   203

LISTENING OUTLINE: String Quartet in C Minor, Op. 18, No. 4, Fourth Movement, by Ludwig van Beethoven   204

[7] THE CLASSICAL SYMPHONY   205

[8] THE CLASSICAL CONCERTO   206

[9] CLASSICAL CHAMBER MUSIC   207

[10] JOSEPH HAYDN   208

Haydn's Music   212

Symphony No. 103 in E-flat Major ("Drum Roll")   213

[11] WOLFGANG AMADEUS MOZART   216

Mozart's Music   219

Don Giovanni   221

Symphony No. 40 in G Minor, K. 550   230

LISTENING OUTLINE: Symphony No. 40 in G Minor, K. 550, First Movement   231

Piano Concerto in D Minor, K. 466   234

LISTENING OUTLINE: Piano Concerto in D Minor, K. 466, First Movement   235

[12] LUDWIG VAN BEETHOVEN   238

Beethoven's Music   242

Piano Sonata in C Minor, Op. 13 ("Pathétique")   244

Symphony No. 5 in C Minor, Op. 67   247

LISTENING OUTLINE: Symphony No. 5 in C Minor, Op. 67, First Movement   249

LISTENING OUTLINE: Symphony No. 5 in C Minor, Op. 67, Second Movement   252

xiii

VI
THE
ROMANTIC
PERIOD

[1] ROMANTICISM IN MUSIC — 258

The Romantic Period in Music (1820–1900) — 262

Individuality of Style — 263

Expressive Aims and Subjects — 263

Nationalism and Exoticism — 263

Program Music — 264

Expressive Tone Color — 264

Colorful Harmony — 265

Expanded Range of Dynamics, Pitch, and Tempo — 265

Form: Miniature and Monumental — 266

[2] ROMANTIC COMPOSERS AND THEIR PUBLIC — 267

[3] THE ART SONG — 269

Strophic and Through-composed Form — 269

The Song Cycle — 270

[4] FRANZ SCHUBERT — 270

Schubert's Music — 271

"The Erlking" — 273

Heidenröslein — 276

Fourth Movement from Piano Quintet in A Major ("Trout") — 278

LISTENING OUTLINE: Piano Quintet in A Major ("Trout"), Fourth Movement — 278

[5] ROBERT SCHUMANN — 279

Schumann's Music — 280

Träumerei from Scenes of Childhood — 282

[6] FRÉDÉRIC CHOPIN — 283

Chopin's Music — 285

Nocturne in E-flat Major, Op. 9, No. 2 — 285

Étude in C Minor, Op. 10, No. 12 ("Revolutionary") — 286

Polonaise in A-flat Major, Op. 53 — 287

[7] FRANZ LISZT — 288

Liszt's Music — 290

Concerto No. 1 for Piano and Orchestra in E-flat Major — 291

Contents

xiv

✓ [8] FELIX MENDELSSOHN   295

    Mendelssohn's Music   297

    Concerto for Violin and Orchestra in E Minor, Op. 64   297

        LISTENING OUTLINE: Concerto for Violin and Orchestra in E Minor, Op. 64, First Movement   298

[9] PROGRAM MUSIC   301

[10] HECTOR BERLIOZ   303

    Berlioz's Music   305

    Fantastic Symphony   305

[11] NATIONALISM IN NINETEENTH-CENTURY MUSIC   311

    "The Russian Five"   312

    Boris Godunov by Modest Mussorgsky   313

✓ [12] PETER ILYICH TCHAIKOVSKY   316

    Tchaikovsky's Music   318

    Romeo and Juliet, Overture-Fantasy   319

        LISTENING OUTLINE: *Romeo and Juliet,* Overture-Fantasy   320

[13] BEDŘICH SMETANA   322

    The Moldau   323

        LISTENING OUTLINE: *The Moldau*   324

[14] ANTONIN DVOŘÁK   325

    Symphony No. 9 in E Minor, "From the New World"   326

        LISTENING OUTLINE: Symphony No. 9 in E Minor, "From the New World," First Movement   326

        LISTENING OUTLINE: Symphony No. 9 in E Minor, "From the New World," Second Movement   328

[15] JOHANNES BRAHMS   332

    Brahms's Music   334

    Variations on a Theme by Haydn for Orchestra, Op. 56a 335

[16] GIUSEPPE VERDI   338

    Verdi's Music   340

    Rigoletto   341

XV

[17] GIACOMO PUCCINI   346

    La Bohème   348

[18] RICHARD WAGNER   357

    Wagner's Music   359

    The Twilight of the Gods   360

[19] GUSTAV MAHLER   365

    Mahler's Music   366

    Symphony No. 1 in D Major: Third Movement (Funeral March)   367

      LISTENING OUTLINE: Symphony No. 1 in D Major, Third Movement   368

VII THE TWENTIETH CENTURY

[1] MUSICAL STYLES: 1900–1950   372

    1900–1950: An Age of Musical Diversity   373

    Tone Color   378

    Harmony   379

      Consonance and Dissonance   379

      New Chord Structures   379

    Alternatives to the Traditional Tonal System   380

    Rhythm   382

    Melody   384

[2] MUSIC AND MUSICIANS IN SOCIETY   384

[3] IMPRESSIONISM AND SYMBOLISM   387

    French Impressionist Painting   387

    French Symbolist Poetry   387

[4] CLAUDE DEBUSSY   389

    Debussy's Music   390

    Prelude to "The Afternoon of a Faun"   393

      LISTENING OUTLINE: *Prelude to "The Afternoon of a Faun"*   393

    The Sunken Cathedral from *Preludes* for piano   395

[5] NEOCLASSICISM   396

[6] IGOR STRAVINSKY   397

Stravinsky's Music   400

Petrushka   401

    LISTENING OUTLINE: *Petrushka*, Opening Scene   403

The Rite of Spring   405

Symphony of Psalms   409

[7] EXPRESSIONISM   413

[8] ARNOLD SCHOENBERG   415

Schoenberg's Music   417

  Atonality   417

  The Twelve-tone System   418

Five Pieces for Orchestra, Op. 16   421

    LISTENING OUTLINE: *Yesteryears* from *Five Pieces for Orchestra*, Op. 16   423

A Survivor from Warsaw, Op. 46   424

[9] ALBAN BERG   427

Wozzeck   427

[10] ANTON WEBERN   438

Webern's Music   439

Five Pieces for Orchestra, Op. 10   440

    LISTENING OUTLINE: *Third Piece* from *Five Pieces for Orchestra*, Op. 10   441

[11] BÉLA BARTÓK   442

Bartók's Music   444

Concerto for Orchestra   445

    LISTENING OUTLINE: *Concerto for Orchestra*, First Movement   446

    LISTENING OUTLINE: *Concerto for Orchestra*, Second Movement   448

[12] CHARLES IVES   450

Ives's Music   452

The Unanswered Question for Chamber Orchestra   453

Putnam's Camp, Redding, Connecticut from *Three Places
in New England*   454

[13] AARON COPLAND   456

Appalachian Spring   458

xvii

[14] MUSICAL STYLES SINCE 1950   461

    Increased Use of the Twelve-tone System   461

    Extensions of the Twelve-tone System: Serialism   463

    Chance Music   463

    Electronic Music   464

    "The Liberation of Sound"   465

    Mixed Media   466

    Rhythm and Form   467

[15] MUSIC SINCE 1950: SIX REPRESENTATIVE PIECES   467

    Sonata for Flute, Oboe, Cello, and Harpsichord,
      by Elliott Carter   467

    Threnody for the Victims of Hiroshima,
      by Krzysztof Penderecki   469

        LISTENING OUTLINE: *Threnody for the Victims of Hiroshima,*
        by Krzysztof Penderecki   470

    Poème électronique by Edgard Varèse   470

        LISTENING OUTLINE: *Poème électronique,*
        by Edgard Varèse   472

    Composition for Synthesizer, by Milton Babbitt   473

    Questions on Nature, by Miriam Gideon   474

    Ancient Voices of Children, by George Crumb   475

VIII JAZZ

[1] JAZZ STYLES: 1900–1950   480

    The Roots of Jazz   480

    Jazz in Society   482

    The Elements of Jazz   482

      Tone Color   482

      Improvisation   484

      Rhythm, Melody, and Harmony   485

[2] RAGTIME   485

    Scott Joplin   487

    Maple Leaf Rag   487

[3] THE BLUES   488

    "Lost Your Head Blues," by Bessie Smith   490

[4] NEW ORLEANS STYLE   493

    Dippermouth Blues, by King Oliver's Creole Jazz Band   495

LISTING OUTLINE: *Dippermouth Blues,* by King Oliver's
Creole Jazz Band   459

    Louis Armstrong   496

[5] SWING   497

    "Blue Skies," by Irving Berlin; as performed by the
Benny Goodman Band   499

    Duke Ellington   499

      Concerto for Cootie   501

        LISTENING OUTLINE: *Concerto for Cootie,* by Duke Ellington   501

[6] BEBOP   502

    Bebop Style   503

    Charlie "Bird" Parker   503

      LISTENING OUTLINE: *Perhaps,* by Charlie Parker   504

[7] JAZZ STYLES SINCE 1950   505

    Cool Jazz   506

    Free Jazz: Ornette Coleman and John Coltrane   506

IX
ROCK

[1] ROCK STYLES   512

    Rock Tone Color   515

    Rock Rhythm   516

    Rock Form, Melody, and Harmony   517

[2] ROCK MUSIC IN AMERICAN SOCIETY   517

    Rock Music and Recordings   520

    Rock Music and Dancing   520

[3] THE BEATLES   522

    Sgt. Pepper's Lonely Hearts Club Band   523

X
NON-WESTERN
MUSIC

[1] MUSIC IN NON-WESTERN CULTURES   528

    Oral Tradition   528

    Improvisation   529

    Voices   529

    Instruments   529

    Melody, Rhythm, and Texture   530

Interaction between Non-Western and
Western Music   531

[2] MUSIC IN SUB-SAHARAN AFRICA   532
    Music in Society   532
    Rhythm and Percussion   533
    Vocal Music   535
    Texture   535
    African Instruments   535
        Idiophones   535
        Membranophones   536
        Aerophones and Chordophones   541
    Song from Angola   541
    Mitamba Yalagala Kumchuzi   542
    Hinganyengisa masingita   542

[3] THE CLASSICAL MUSIC OF INDIA   542
    Indian Performers   543
    Improvisation   544
    Elements of Indian Classical Music   544
        Melodic Structure: Raga   544
        Rhythmic Structure: Tala   545
    Instruments   547
    Maru-Bihag, by Ravi Shankar   547

[4] KOTO MUSIC OF JAPAN   549
    The Koto   549
    Historical Background   550
    Koto Music   552
        "Song of the Plovers," by Yoshizawa Kengyō   553
        Godan-Ginuta, by Mitsuzaki Kengyō   553

APPENDIXES   [I] CHRONOLOGY   556
             [II] READING LIST   561
             [III] TONE COLOR AND THE HARMONIC SERIES   568
             [IV] KEY SIGNATURES   569

             Acknowledgments   570
Contents   Index   573

xx

Color Plates 1–8 appear between pages 292–293

Plates 1 and 2: The Renaissance
Plates 3 and 4: The Baroque Period
Plate 5: The Classical Period
Plate 6: The Romantic Period
Plates 7 and 8: The Twentieth Century

 PREFACE

Why another music appreciation text? Twenty years' experience with music appreciation courses and college students has shown me the need for an accurate, clear, and engaging book that takes students' interests and knowledge into account. My goal was to write a book that is useful both for study and in the classroom. This text provides an approach to perceptive listening and an introduction to musical elements, forms, and style periods. Its discussions of composers' lives, individual styles, and representative works aim to stimulate curiosity and enthusiasm, not merely to impart facts. The book was written to heighten a reader's love of music as well as to develop listening skills. The key features outlined below have proved attractive to students and teachers alike.

Listening Outlines

A distinctive feature of this text is the use of "listening outlines" to enrich the discussion of many pieces. Meant to be followed while the composition is heard, each outline focuses attention on musical events as they unfold. The outlines can be followed easily and therefore are useful for outside listening assignments as well as for classroom work. However, since the text offers a general discussion of each composition represented, the listening outlines may be omitted.

Opera

The study of opera is aided in this book by extended excerpts from librettos, making it unnecessary for teachers to supply them. Opera texts appear with brief marginal notes that indicate the relationship between words and music and help readers follow the drama.

New Features in the Second Edition

Virtually every part of the book contains new representative compositions that are attractive to students and effective for teaching. The discussion of musical elements now includes Britten's *A Young Person's Guide to the Orchestra,* Brubeck's *Unsquare Dance,* Lennon and McCartney's "Yesterday," and the *Farandole* from Bizet's *L'Arlésienne Suite No. 2.* Other additions include *Danse Royale* (thirteenth century), *Tu se' morta* from Monteverdi's *Orfeo,* Beethoven's Sonata in C Minor, Op. 13 ("Pathétique"), *Heidenröslein,* and the Fourth Movement of the "Trout" Quintet by Schubert. New to this second edition is a section on Gustav Mahler's life and music, with the Third Movement (Funeral March) of his First Symphony as a representative work. The section on music since 1950 now includes *Questions on Nature,* a song cycle by contemporary American composer Miriam Gideon. In this edition, theme-and-variation form and the Second Movement of Haydn's "Surprise" Symphony are discussed in Part V, "The Classical Period."

The parts dealing with jazz, rock, and non-Western music have been rewritten to include more listening outlines and representative pieces. These sections offer valuable supplementary material for the study of musical elements. The jazz section traces the development of various substyles, and the rock section considers trends of the late 1970s as well as the role of music in American society. The discussion of non-Western music begins with an overview of music in cultures around the world. Traditional music of sub-Saharan Africa, India, and Japan is studied as a small sample of the vast wealth of non-Western music. This survey introduces students to a wide range of fresh and fascinating listening experiences and provides insights into other cultures.

This second edition also includes many new illustrations throughout the book. The following basic features of the original remain characteristic of *Music: An Appreciation.*

Organization

In addition to a comprehensive discussion of the musical style and sociological aspects of each historical period, the lives, individual styles, and representative works of many composers are examined in detail. Through repeated exposures to a variety of musical compositions, students are encouraged to listen for basic forms (such as A B A and theme and variations) as well as for elements of music (dynamics, tone color, rhythm, texture).

Part I of the book examines the elements of music both in general terms and with reference to illustrative pieces that are attractive, brief, and from a variety of style periods. Notation is used sparingly in this part—usually in connection with familiar tunes like "Home On the Range" that allow students first to analyze music they have known since childhood. Parts II through VII deal with specific periods of music history from the Middle Ages to the present. Each part opens with a discussion of the period's style characteristics, its cultural trends, and the roles of music and musicians in society. Jazz and rock are considered in Parts VIII and IX, and non-Western music is surveyed in Part X.

Four appendixes provide an overall chronology, a reading list, a discussion of tone color and the harmonic series, and a list of key signatures.

Flexibility

Music: An Appreciation takes a chronological approach but can adapt easily to individual teaching methods. Each style period is subdivided into short, relatively independent sections that can be studied in any order or even omitted.

While music examples are offered throughout the book, discussions of pieces require no knowledge of music notation. The examples provide visual aids for those who want them; students may prefer simply to read the text and skip the details of notation.

Readability

The biographical sketches and the descriptions of composers' individual styles attempt to give the flavor of each composer's personality and music. Anecdotal material and quotes from composers enliven the discussion.

Clarity of expression was a chief goal. This is a book that students can feel comfortable with. They will recognize that it was written for them by a musician who loves music and who wants to convey its essentials without confusion or boredom. Musical terms are defined simply and appear in bold type. Important terms and concepts are listed at the end of each section.

Supplementary Materials

This edition is accompanied by an improved set of eight records containing many of the compositions discussed. In the margins of the text, next to the titles of works or movements, there are references to record sides and bands. Other supplementary materials are a Study Guide and Student Workbook and an Instructor's Manual.

Acknowledgments

Many musicians, teachers, and students kindly read sections of the manuscript in rough draft and have earned my deep gratitude. Professors Lorna Adams, Benjamin Boretz, Andrew J. Broekema, Raoul F. Camus, Margaret Cawley, James Coleman, Gordon F. Crain, Peter Gano, Barbara Jackson, Israel Katz, Henry J. Keating, James Kurtz, Robert Morgan, William V. Porter, Robert Van Voorhis, Piero Weiss, and Franklin Zimmerman all contributed valuable suggestions.

Colleagues in the music department of Queens College were extraordinarily generous and helpful. I am particularly indebted to Anthony Nwabuoku and Professor Henry Burnett for their help with the sections about sub-Saharan

 Preface

Africa and Japan. Professors Alan Buechner, Charles Burkhart, Lawrence Eisman, Raymond Erickson, Hubert Howe, Joel Mandelbaum, Arbie Orenstein, Carl Schachter, David Walker, Robert White, and Helen Wright all read portions of the text. I am especially grateful for the help of the following experts: David Loeb (Japanese music), Teddy Rosenthal (jazz), Professors Elise Barnett (Indian music), Alvin Fosner (jazz), and Raymond F. Kennedy (rock and non-Western music). Susan Hellauer kindly provided editorial help, and Grazia Lopez assisted with a translation. My deep thanks go to many colleagues around the country whose valuable suggestions were incorporated in this edition. I am also grateful for the expert assistance of James Belser and his coworkers at McGraw-Hill.

I wish to thank Professor Raoul Camus for the fine Instructor's Manual, and Study Guide and Student Workbook that accompany this text.

My wife, Anita Kamien, contributed to every aspect of this book. She clarified ideas, helped choose representative pieces, and improved the listening outlines tirelessly. Her advice and encouragement were essential to the completion of *Music: An Appreciation.*

Roger Kamien

MUSIC
AN APPRECIATION

ELEMENTS

1 Sound: Pitch, Dynamics, and Tone Color

2 Performing Media: Voices and Instruments

3 Rhythm

4 Music Notation

5 Melody

6 Harmony

7 Key

8 Musical Texture

9 Musical Form

10 Performance

11 Musical Style

(Blair Seitz / Editorial Photocolor Archives)

1 | SOUND: PITCH, DYNAMICS, AND TONE COLOR

Sounds bombard our ears every day—the squeaks and honks of traffic noises, a child's laugh, the bark of a dog, the patter of rain. Through them we learn what's going on; we need them to communicate. By listening to the speech, cries, and laughter of others, we learn what they think and how they feel. But silence, an absence of sound, also communicates. When we hear no sound in the street, we assume no cars are passing. When someone doesn't answer a question or breaks off in the middle of a sentence, we quickly notice it, and we draw conclusions from the silence.

Sounds may be perceived as pleasant or unpleasant. Fortunately we can direct our attention to specific sounds, shutting out those that don't interest us. At a party we can choose to ignore the people near us and focus instead on a conversation across the room. We shut out most sounds, paying attention only to those of interest. The composer John Cage (b. 1912) may have meant to show this with his "composition" entitled *4'33"*, in which a musician sits at a piano for four minutes and thirty-three seconds—and does nothing. The silence forces the audience to direct attention to whatever noises, or sounds, they themselves are making. In a sense, the audience "composes" this piece. To get the effect, listen to the sounds that fill the silence around you right now.

What are these sounds that we hear? What *is* "sound"? What causes it, and how do we hear it?

Sound begins with the vibration of an object, say a table that is pounded or a string that is plucked. The vibrations are transmitted to our ears by a *medium,* which usually is air. As a result of the vibrations, our eardrums start vibrating too, and *impulses,* or signals, are transmitted to our brains. There the impulses are selected, organized, and interpreted.

Music is part of this world of sound, an art based on the organization of sounds in time. We distinguish music from other sounds by recognizing the four main properties of musical sounds: *pitch, dynamics* (loudness or softness), *tone color,* and *duration.* We'll look now at the first three of these properties of musical sound. Duration—the length of time a musical sound lasts—is discussed in section 3, "Rhythm."

Pitch: The Highness or Lowness of Sound

Pitch is the relative highness or lowness that we hear in a sound. No doubt you've noticed that most men speak and sing in a lower range of pitches than women or children do. And when you sing the beginning of "The Star-Spangled Banner," the pitch on *see* is higher than it is on *say.*

see,

Oh,

you

can

say!

Without differences of pitch, speech would be boring, and—worse—there would be no music as we know it.

The pitch of a sound is decided by the frequency of its vibrations. The faster the vibrations, the higher the pitch; the slower the vibrations, the lower the pitch. Vibration frequency is measured in cycles per second. On a piano the highest frequency tone is 4,186 cycles per second, while the lowest is about 27 cycles per second.

In general, the smaller the vibrating object, the faster its vibrations and the higher its pitch. All other things being equal, plucking a short string produces a higher pitch than plucking a long string. The relatively short strings of a violin produce higher pitches than do the longer strings of a double bass ("bass fiddle").

In music, sound that has a definite pitch is called a **tone.** It has a specific frequency, such as 440 cycles per second. The vibrations of a tone are regular and reach the ear at equal time intervals. On the other hand, noiselike sounds (the squeaking of brakes or a clash of cymbals) have an indefinite pitch and are produced by irregular vibrations.

Two tones will sound different because they have different pitches. The "distance" in pitch between any two tones is called an **interval.** When tones are separated by the interval called an **octave,** they sound very much alike. Sing the opening of "The Star-Spangled Banner" again. Notice that the tone you produce on *see* sounds like your tone on *say,* even though it's higher. (Sing the *say* and *see* tones several times.) An octave lies between them. The vibration frequency of the *say* tone is exactly half that of the *see* tone. If the *say* tone were 440 cycles per second, the *see* tone—an octave higher—would be 880 cycles per second. A tone an octave lower than the *say* tone would be half of 440, or 220 cycles per second. When sounded at the same time, two tones an octave apart blend so well that they almost seem to merge into one tone.

The interval of an octave is important in music. It is the interval between the first and last tones of the familiar scale:

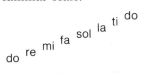

do re mi fa sol la ti do

Sing this scale slowly and notice that you fill the octave with seven different pitches before arriving at the high *do,* which "duplicates" the low *do* you start on. You do not slide up as a siren does; you fill the octave with a specific number of

 Pitch

3

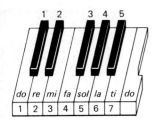

pitches. If you start from the higher *do* and continue the scale upward, each of your original seven tones will be "duplicated" an octave higher. This group of seven tones was the basis of music in Western civilization for centuries. The seven are produced by the white keys of the piano keyboard.

As time passed, five pitches were added to the original seven. They are produced by the black keys of the keyboard. These twelve tones, like the original seven, are "duplicated" in higher and lower octaves. Every tone has "close relatives" one, two, three, or more octaves away. (In non-Western music, the octave may be divided into a different number of tones, say seventeen or twenty-two.)

The distance between the lowest and highest tones that a voice or instrument can produce is called its **pitch range** or, simply, range. The range of the average untrained voice is between one and two octaves, while a piano's range is over seven octaves. When men and women sing the same melody, they usually sing it an octave apart.

The organization of pitch is a composer's first resource. In sections 5 and 6, where melody and harmony are discussed, we will look at how pitch is organized. For now we'll simply observe that composers can create a special mood in their music by using very low or high pitches. For example, low pitches can intensify the sadness of a funeral march, while high pitches can make a dance sound lighter. And a steady rise in pitch often increases musical tension.

Though most music we know is based on definite rather than indefinite pitches, noiselike sounds—such as those made by a bass drum or cymbals—figure strongly in the rhythmic life of music. In parts of Africa, the indefinite pitches of drums are very important. And with recent electronic developments, indefinite pitches have come to play a vital role in Western music as well.

Dynamics

Degrees of loudness or softness in music are called **dynamics.** Loudness is related to the amplitude of the vibration that produces the sound. The harder a guitar string is plucked (the farther it moves from the fingerboard), the louder its sound. When instruments are played more loudly or more softly, or when there is a change in how many instruments are heard, a dynamic change results which may be either sudden or gradual. A gradual increase in loudness often creates excitement, particularly when the pitch rises, too. On the other hand, a gradual decrease in loudness can convey a sense of calm.

A performer emphasizes a tone by playing it more loudly than the tones around it. We call this a **dynamic accent.** Skillful, subtle changes of dynamics add spirit and mood to performances. Often these changes are not written in the music but are inspired by the performer's feelings about it.

Improvements in making musical instruments during the last 150 years have vastly increased our range of dynamics. In fact, today's electronic equipment has expanded it to the point where loudness can cause pain. Probably no culture has used so wide a dynamic range as ours does today.

Elements

4

Dynamic Indications

When notating music for others to read, composers traditionally have used Italian words and abbreviations to indicate dynamics. The usual abbreviations and their meanings are:

pp	*pianissimo*	very soft
p	*piano*	soft
mp	*mezzo piano*	moderately soft
mf	*mezzo forte*	moderately loud
f	*forte*	loud
ff	*fortissimo*	very loud

For extremely soft or loud dynamic levels, a composer sometimes will use *ppp* or *pppp* and *fff* or *ffff*.

To show gradual changes in dynamics, the following symbols and words are used:

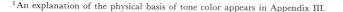

	decrescendo (decresc.)	
	or	gradually softer
	diminuendo (dim.)	
	crescendo (cresc.)	gradually louder

Like many elements of music, a dynamic indication is not absolutely precise. A tone has a dynamic level—is soft or loud—in relation to other tones around it. The loudest sound of a single violin is tiny compared with an entire orchestra's, and even further from an amplified rock group's. But it can be considered fortissimo (very loud) within its own context.

Tone Color

We can tell a trumpet from a flute even when they play the same tone at the same dynamic level. The quality of sound that distinguishes them is called **tone color,** or **timbre** (pronounced "tam'-ber"). Tone color is described by words like *bright, dark, brilliant, mellow,* and *rich.*[1]

As with dynamics, changes of tone color create variety and contrast. When the same melody is played by one instrument and then by another, it takes on different expressive effects because of each instrument's tone color. A contrast in tone color may be used to highlight a new melody: After violins play a melody, an oboe may present a contrasting one.

Tone colors also build a sense of continuity; it is easier to recognize the return of a melody when the same instruments play it each time. Specific instruments can reinforce a melody's emotional impact: The brilliant sound of a trumpet is

[1]An explanation of the physical basis of tone color appears in Appendix III.

 Tone Color

suited to heroic or military tunes, while the soothing tone color of a flute fits the mood of a calm melody. In fact, composers often invent a melody with a particular instrument's tone color in mind.

A practically unlimited variety of tone colors is available to composers. Combining different instruments—violin, clarinet, and trombone, for example—results in new colors. And tone color can be changed by varying the number of instruments or voices that perform a melody. Finally, new colors can be invented, as is the case with recent electronic developments.

Listening Outlines

Reading about pitch, dynamics, and tone color without hearing music is too abstract. To understand and recognize the properties of sound, we must *listen for them*. In this book listening outlines will help focus your attention on musical events as they unfold. These outlines must be read *as you listen to the music;* otherwise, their value to you is limited.

Each item in a listening outline describes some musical sound. It may point out dynamics, instruments used, pitch level, or mood. (Remember that indications of mood in music are subjective. What one person calls "triumphant" another may call "determined.")

Before listening to a piece of music, it's helpful to glance over an entire listening outline. Then, while hearing one item, look ahead to learn what's next. For example, in the listening outline for the Prelude to Act III of Richard Wagner's opera *Lohengrin,* the first item (1*a*) is "Full orchestra, very loud (*ff*), main melody in violins, cymbal crashes." While listening to the music described by item 1*a*, glance at item 1*b*: "Brass melody, pulsating accompaniment in strings."

Sometimes not all the instruments playing are listed; instead, only those that are prominent at a given moment are shown. For example, item 2 in the *Lohengrin* listening outline reads "Soft (*p*), contrasting oboe melody. Melody repeated by flute. Clarinet and violins continue." While other instruments can be heard, this focuses attention on the instruments that play the melody.

Each listening outline is preceded by a description of the music's main features. Instrumentation, approximate duration, and recording notes (where important) are given also.

Side 11, band 2

Lohengrin, Prelude to Act III, by Richard Wagner

Wagner makes wide and brilliant use of dynamic contrasts in this Prelude to set the scene for the wedding of the opera's hero and heroine. The Prelude opens with a feeling of exultation—great energy is conveyed by the massive sound of the full orchestra. Later the music suddenly becomes calm and gentle as we hear fewer instruments, playing softly. This is followed by another sudden contrast when Wagner again employs the full orchestra.

Elements

LISTENING OUTLINE
To be read while music is heard

Lohengrin, Prelude to Act III (1848), by Richard Wagner (1813–1883)[2]

3 flutes, 3 oboes, 3 clarinets, 3 bassoons, 4 French horns, 3 trumpets, 3 trombones, bass tuba, timpani, triangle, cymbals, tambourine, violins 1, violins 2, violas, cellos, double basses

(About 3½ min)

1   *a.* Full orchestra, very loud (*ff*), main melody in violins, cymbal crashes.
     b. Brass melody, pulsating accompaniment in strings.
     c. Full orchestra, main melody in violins, cymbal crashes.
2   Soft (*p*), contrasting oboe melody. Melody repeated by flute. Clarinet and violins continue.
3   *a.* Full orchestra, very loud (*ff*), main melody in violins, cymbal crashes.
     b. Brass melody, pulsating accompaniment in strings.
     c. Cymbals. Becomes softer (decrescendo). Becomes very loud, brass proclamation at end.

Prelude in C Minor for Piano, Op. 28, No. 20, by Frédéric Chopin   *Side 8, band 5*

In this Prelude, dynamic change is produced by a single instrument, the piano. A decrease in volume from very loud (*ff*) to soft (*p*), to very soft (*pp*) contributes to a feeling of emotional progression within this miniature lasting only a minute and a half; it's as though a majestic funeral march becomes increasingly personal.

LISTENING OUTLINE
To be read while music is heard

Prelude in C Minor for Piano, Op.[3] 28, No. 20 (1839), by Frédéric Chopin (1810–1849)

(About 1½ min)

1 Heavy chords, very loud (*ff*).
2 New section, soft (*p*).
3 Very soft (*pp*) repeat of preceding section. Slows down toward the end.

***Firebird Suite,* Finale (1919 version), by Igor Stravinsky**   *Side 12, band 3*

In the Finale of the *Firebird Suite,* Stravinsky repeats one melody over and over, creating variety and contrast through changes in dynamics, tone color, and

---

[2]With concert ending, as performed on Columbia MS 6442.
[3]The abbreviation "Op." stands for *opus,* Latin for "work." An opus number is a way of identifying a piece or set of pieces. Usually, within a composer's output, the higher a composition's opus number, the later it was written.

Listening
Outlines

7

rhythm. The *Suite* is a set of dances from *The Firebird* (1910), a ballet in which the hero marries a beautiful princess during the music of the Finale.

The Finale begins softly but becomes increasingly grand as the music gradually gets louder (crescendo), more instruments play, and the melody is repeated at higher pitches. After this slow build-up to a climax, there's a sudden quiet as all instruments but the strings stop playing. A quick crescendo then leads to a brilliant concluding section.

LISTENING OUTLINE
To be read while music is heard

Firebird Suite, Finale (1919 version[4]), by Igor Stravinsky (1882–1971)

piccolo, 2 flutes, 2 oboes, 2 clarinets, 2 bassoons, 4 French horns, 2 trumpets, 3 trombones, tuba, timpani, bass drum, triangle, cymbals, harp, violins 1, violins 2, violas, cellos, double basses

(About 3½ min)

1 *a.* Melody in French horn, soft (*p*), quivering string accompaniment.
   b. Violins, soft, melody an octave higher. Flutes join.
   c. Gets louder (crescendo) as more instruments enter.
   d. Violins and woodwinds, loud, melody at an even higher octave, crescendo to
   e. Full orchestra, melody extremely loud (*fff*).
   f. Suddenly very soft (*pp*), strings, quick crescendo to
2 *a.* Brasses, very loud (*ff*), melody in quick detached notes, timpani (kettledrums). Melody slows down, full orchestra, *fff*, timpani.
   b. Cymbals, sustained brass chords, extremely loud (*fff*). Dynamic swell at end.

Side 15, band 6

"Hotter Than That"
by Louis Armstrong and His Hot Five

A succession of different tone colors contributes to the variety within this music for jazz band. After an introduction played by the full band, we hear solos by the trumpet, clarinet, voice, guitar, and trombone. Louis Armstrong performs both as trumpeter and vocalist. His singing is like his trumpet playing in sound and style. Instead of lyrics he sings nonsense syllables like "dat-a bat-a dip-da." In one section the guitarist, Lonnie Johnson, imitates the melodic phrases sung by Armstrong, whose voice takes on a guitarlike twang.

Unlike the preceding compositions by Wagner, Chopin, and Stravinsky, this music was improvised by the performers. Their point of departure was the tune "Hotter Than That" by Lil Hardin, the band's pianist.

Within item 2 of the listening outline, the trumpet is momentarily heard

Elements

[4] Stravinsky composed three different versions of the *Firebird Suite.*

8

alone, without its accompaniment of piano and guitar. This unaccompanied solo should not be mistaken for the entrance of the clarinet (item 3), which sounds like a high-pitched whine.

LISTENING OUTLINE
To be read while music is heard

"Hotter Than That" (1927),
by Louis Armstrong and His Hot Five[5]

Voice, clarinet, trumpet, trombone, piano, banjo, guitar

(About 3 min)

1   All instruments, trumpet predominates.
2   Trumpet accompanied by piano and guitar. Trumpet briefly alone, piano and guitar rejoin.
3   Clarinet, high-pitched whine, piano and guitar accompany.
4   Voice, guitar accompaniment.
5   Voice imitated by guitar. Piano leads into
6   *a.* Muted trombone accompanied by piano and guitar.
    b. Trumpet, all instruments join. Guitar, trumpet, guitar at end.

Basic Terms

sound	pitch range
pitch	dynamics
tone	dynamic accent
interval	tone color (timbre)
octave	

PERFORMING MEDIA: VOICES AND INSTRUMENTS
Elements **2**

Voices

Throughout history, singing has been the most widespread and familiar way of making music. Ancient Greek drama included chanting choruses, and the Bible

[5] Recorded on Columbia LP CL 851, *The Louis Armstrong Story,* Vol. 1, side 2, band 5, and *The Smithsonian Collection of Classic Jazz,* side 2, band 8.

Voices

records that Moses and the Israelites sang to glorify the Lord. Singers seem always to have had a magnetic appeal, and even today adoring audiences imitate the looks and lifestyles of their favorites.

The exchange between singer and audience contains a bit of magic, something direct and spellbinding. Probably because the singer becomes an instrument, we identify with him or her especially—a human body like our own expressing emotions through sounds and words.

The voice's unique ability to fuse a word with a musical tone is the reason that poetry and singing have been inseparable in many cultures. Singing can make words easier to remember and heighten their emotional effect.

For many reasons it is difficult to sing well. In singing we use wider ranges of pitch and volume than in speaking. And we hold vowel sounds longer. Singing demands a greater supply and control of breath. Air from the lungs is controlled by the lower abdominal muscles and the diaphragm. The air makes the vocal cords vibrate, and the singer's lungs, throat, mouth, and nose come into play to produce the desired sound. The pitch of the tone varies with the tension of the vocal cords; the tighter they are, the higher the pitch.

The range of a singer's voice depends both on training and on physical make-up. Professional singers can command two octaves or even more, while an untrained voice is usually limited to about an octave and a half. Men's vocal cords are longer and larger than women's, and this difference produces a lower range of pitches. The classification of voice ranges for women and men follows, arranged from highest to lowest. (The four basic ranges are shown in bold type.)

Women	*Men*
soprano	**tenor**
mezzo soprano	baritone
alto (or contralto)	**bass**

Because of differences in taste, methods of singing vary widely from culture to culture. Oriental singing, for example, is more nasal than that of the West. While classical singers in our culture stand erect, singers in West Africa stand bending forward; and in India they sit on the floor. In fact, there are differences in performing styles in the West alone: classical, popular, jazz, folk, and rock music are all sung differently. Classical singers, for example, normally don't rely on microphones, but rock gets its point across partly by amplification.

Until the late 1600s, most music of Western culture was vocal. But by the end of the seventeenth century, instrumental music rivaled vocal music in importance. Since then, composers have continued to write vocal works—both solo and choral—with and without instrumental accompaniment. There are compositions for male chorus, female chorus, and mixed chorus, which usually combines sopranos, altos, tenors, and basses. Accompaniments to vocal works range from single instruments like guitar or piano to entire orchestras.

Throughout history, singing has been the most widespread way of making music. Two leading opera singers of our time are Shirley Verrett, soprano, and Luciano Pavarotti, tenor (J. Heffernan).

Musical Instruments

People around the world use musical instruments that vary greatly in construction and tone color. An instrument may be defined as any mechanism—other than the voice—that produces musical sounds. Western musicians usually classify instruments in six broad categories: **string** (such as guitar and violin); **woodwind** (flute, clarinet); **brass** (trumpet, trombone); **percussion** (bass drum, cymbals); **keyboard** (organ, piano); and **electronic** (synthesizer).

 Musical
Instruments

11

An instrument often is made in different sizes that produce different ranges. For instance, the saxophone family includes soprano, alto, tenor, baritone, and bass saxophones.

An instrument's tone color may vary with the **register** (part of the total range) in which it is played. A clarinet sounds dark and rich in its low register, but its high register is brilliant and piercing.[6]

Instrumental performers try to match the beautiful, flexible tone of a singer's voice. Yet most instruments have a wider range of pitches than the voice does. While a trained singer's range is about two octaves, many instruments command three or four octaves, and some have six or seven. And instruments usually produce tones more rapidly than the voice does. When writing music for a specific instrument, composers have to consider its range of pitches and dynamics and how fast it can produce tones.

Instruments provide entertainment and accompany singing, dancing, religious rites, and drama. But they have served other functions, too. In some cultures, instruments are thought to have magic powers. Bells are worn to guard against harm, and rattles are witch-doctors' tools. In parts of Africa, drums are so sacred that religious rites are not performed without them, and special ceremonies and sacrifices are sometimes enacted when making them.

Instruments have been used for communication as well. Detailed messages were sent by drumbeats; hunters blew horns for signals; and musicians announced the time by sounding brass instruments from towers. Trumpets were used for military signals and to bolster soldiers' courage in battle. For centuries, trumpets and kettledrums announced kings and queens.

Musical instruments have even been status symbols. During the nineteenth and early twentieth centuries, the piano was a fixture in any home that aspired to be middle-class. "Proper" young ladies were expected to learn the piano as one of many "accomplishments." Such ideas lost their currency when women began to move more freely in the world (around the time of World War I), and when the radio and phonograph began to replace the piano as a source of home entertainment. Still, even today there are status implications in the type of record-playing equipment someone owns. Though a stereo is not a musical instrument, a connection can be made between the "parlor piano" of 1900 and the elaborate "home entertainment centers" found in many middle-class homes.

Today only a fraction of all known instruments are used. Their popularity rises and falls with changing musical tastes and requirements. However, twentieth-century interest in music of earlier times has led to the resurrection of long-forgotten instruments like the harpsichord, an ancestor of the piano, and the recorder, a relative of the flute. Modern replicas of ancient instruments are being

[6]The scientific classification of instruments, based on the way sound is made, has five categories: *chordophones* (a stretched string is the sound generator—our "string" category); *aerophones* (a column of air is the sound generator—our "woodwind" and "brass" categories); *idiophones* (instruments whose own material is the sound generator, such as cymbals, gongs, and bells—part of our "percussion" category); *membranophones* (instruments with a stretched skin or other membrane for the sound generator, such as drums—part of our "percussion" category); and *electrophones* (instruments generating their sounds by means of electricity—our "electronic" category).

Elements

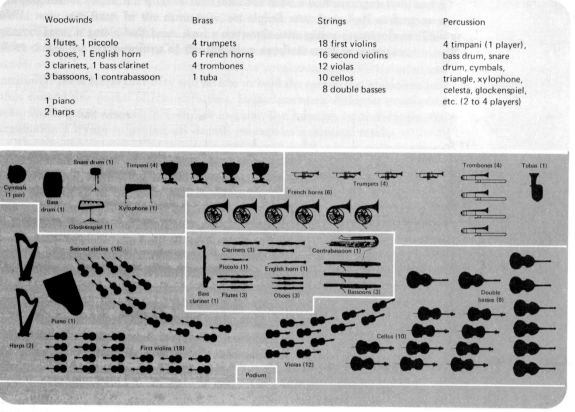

Distribution of Instruments in a Modern Orchestra
(About 100 instrumentalists)

Woodwinds	Brass	Strings	Percussion
3 flutes, 1 piccolo	4 trumpets	18 first violins	4 timpani (1 player),
3 oboes, 1 English horn	6 French horns	16 second violins	bass drum, snare
3 clarinets, 1 bass clarinet	4 trombones	12 violas	drum, cymbals,
3 bassoons, 1 contrabassoon	1 tuba	10 cellos	triangle, xylophone,
		8 double basses	celesta, glockenspiel,
1 piano			etc. (2 to 4 players)
2 harps			

Distribution of Instruments in a Modern Orchestra (about 100 instrumentalists).

built and played. In fact, modern musicians are flexible and far-ranging in their choice of instruments. Rock composers have used non-Western instruments such as the Indian *sitar* (a plucked string instrument). Jazz musicians are turning to classical instruments like the flute, while classical composers are using instruments associated with jazz, such as the vibraphone.

Compositions are written for solo instruments, for small groups, and for orchestras with over one hundred musicians. Whatever the group, it may include instruments from only one category (say strings) or from several. Modern symphony orchestras contain string, woodwind, brass, and percussion instruments. (A typical seating plan for a large orchestra is shown above, and a photograph of the New York Philharmonic is shown on page 14.) Keyboard instruments also find their way into the modern orchestra as needed. Bands consist mainly of brass, woodwind, and percussion instruments.

 Musical Instruments

13

Seating plan of the New York Philharmonic orchestra (The Friends of the New York Philharmonic).

Instruments commonly used for Western music are described in this chapter, by categories. Non-Western instruments are discussed in Part X.

String Instruments

The **violin, viola, cello** (violoncello), and **double bass** ("bass fiddle") form the symphony orchestra's string section. They vary in tone color as well as in size and range: The violin is the smallest and has the highest range; the double bass is the largest and has the lowest range. For symphonic music the strings usually are played with a **bow,** a slightly curved stick strung tightly with horsehair (see illustration). Symphonic strings are also plucked with the finger.

Of all the instrument groups, the strings have the greatest versatility and expressive range. They produce many tone colors and have wide ranges of pitch and dynamics. String players can produce tones that are brilliant and rapid or slow and throbbing; they can control tone as subtly as a singer. Orchestral works tend to rely more on the string instruments than any other group. Even with differing tone colors, the four string instruments blend beautifully. Here it will be helpful to consider the strings' construction and tone production; the violin can represent the entire family.

The hollow wooden body of the violin supports four strings made of gut or wire. The strings stretch, under tension, from a *tailpiece* on one end over a wooden *bridge* to the other end, where they are fastened around wooden *pegs.* The bridge holds the strings away from the *fingerboard* so that they can vibrate freely; the bridge also transmits the strings' vibrations to the *body,* which amplifies and colors the tone. Each string is tuned to a different pitch by tightening or loosening the pegs. (The greater the tension, the higher the pitch.)

Elements

14

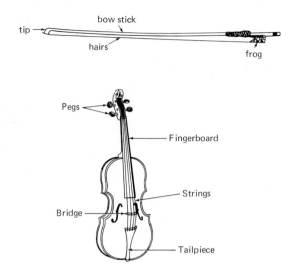

The musician makes a string vibrate by drawing the bow across it with the right hand. The speed and pressure of the bow-stroke control the dynamics and tone color of the sound produced. Pitch is controlled by the musician's left hand. In pressing a string against the fingerboard, the player varies the length of its vibrating portion and so changes its pitch. This is called *stopping* a string (because the vibrations are stopped at a certain point along the string's length). Thus a range of pitches can be drawn from each of the four strings.

Basically the viola, cello, and double bass are made in the same manner and produce sound by similar means. How the string instruments are played—the string performance techniques—increases the musical effects that they can produce. The most frequently used techniques are listed here:

Pizzicato (plucked string): The musician plucks the string, usually with a finger of the right hand. In jazz, the double bass is played mainly as a plucked instrument, rather than being bowed.

Double stop (two notes at once): By drawing the bow across two strings, a string player can sound two notes at once. And by rotating the bow rapidly across three strings (**triple stop**) or four strings (**quadruple stop**), three or four notes can be sounded almost—but not quite—together.

Vibrato: The string player can produce a throbbing, expressive tone by rocking the left hand while pressing the string down. This causes small pitch fluctuations which make the tone warmer.

Mute: The musician can veil or muffle the tone by fitting a clamp (mute) onto the bridge.

 String Instruments

15

Top—Violin. The violin is often used as a solo instrument. In the orchestra, the violins are divided into first and second violins, with the former frequently playing the main melody (Suzanne Szasz).

Above—Viola. The viola's body is about two inches longer than the violin's, and its range is thus somewhat lower. Its tone color is darker, thicker, and a little less brilliant than the violin's (Sybil Shackman/Monkmeyer).

Right—Cello. While eighteenth-century composers generally used the cello in its bass and baritone registers, composers later exploited its upper registers as well (Sybil Shackman/Monkmeyer).

Above left–Double bass. The double bass (or bass) has a very heavy tone and is less agile than other string instruments. It is often heard with the cello, but an octave lower (© Gabriele Wunderlich).

Above right–Harp. With the fingers of both hands, the harpist plucks forty-seven strings stretched on a triangular frame. The harp has a wide range of 6½ octaves (Randy Matusow).

Left–Guitar. The guitar's six strings are plucked with the fingers of the right hand. Frets mark the places where strings are pressed by fingers of the left hand (© Gabriele Wunderlich).

 String Instruments

17

Tremolo: The musician rapidly repeats tones by quick up-and-down strokes of the bow. This can create a sense of tension, when loud, or a shimmering sound, when soft.

Harmonics: Very high-pitched tones, like a whistle's, are produced when the string player lightly touches certain points on a string. (See Appendix III.)

Though the violin, viola, cello, and double bass are similar, as in any family they have their differences. The photographs and captions in this section show why each adds something distinctive to the orchestra's total sound.

Some string instruments are not played with a bow but are plucked instead. The most important of these are the **harp** and the **guitar.** The harp is the only plucked-string instrument that has gained wide acceptance in the symphony orchestra.

Woodwind Instruments

The woodwind instruments are so named because they produce vibrations of air within a tube that traditionally was made of wood. During the twentieth century, however, piccolos and flutes came to be made of metal. All the wood-winds have little holes along their length that are opened and closed by the fingers or by pads controlled by a key mechanism. By opening and closing these holes, the woodwind player changes the length of the vibrating air column and so varies the pitch.

The woodwind instruments of the symphony orchestra are listed below, arranged from highest (piccolo) to lowest (contrabassoon) in range. (The pairing indicates closely related instruments; the most important one of each pair is starred.)

{ **piccolo**
{ **flute***

{ **oboe***
{ **English horn**

{ **clarinet***
{ **bass clarinet**

{ **bassoon***
{ **contrabassoon**

Woodwind instruments are great individualists and much less alike in tone color than the various strings. The flute, with its silvery tone, differs more from the nasal-sounding oboe than the violin does from the viola (see illustrations). These unique tone colors result largely from the different ways in which vibrations are produced. Flute and piccolo players blow across the edge of a mouth hole much as one makes sounds by blowing across the top of an empty bottle.

Elements

18

Left—Piccolo. "Piccolo" is short for *flauto piccolo* ("small flute"). It plays an octave higher than the flute and is half its size. The piccolo's high register is shrill and whistlelike (Costa Manos, Magnum).

Below—Flute. The flute has a high range and is extremely agile, capable of producing rapid successions of tones. Its tone is full and velvety in the low register and bright and sparkling in the top (© Gabriele Wunderlich).

Below left—Oboe. The oboe's tone is nasal, intense, and expressive. Because the instrument's pitch is difficult to adjust, the entire orchestra is tuned to the oboe's A (High School of Performing Arts).

Bottom—English horn. The English horn is neither English nor a horn, but simply a low, or alto, oboe (© Gabriele Wunderlich).

Woodwind Instruments

Right–Clarinet. The clarinet can produce tones very rapidly and has a wide range of dynamics and tone color. The clarinetist shown here is Benny Goodman.

Above–Bass clarinet. The bass clarinet is larger than the clarinet and has a much lower range (Randy Matusow).

Above right–Bassoon. The bassoon's tone is deeply nasal (J. Schefler/High School of Performing Arts).

Above left–Contrabassoon. The contrabassoon can produce the lowest pitch in the orchestra (© Gabriele Wunderlich).

Above right–Saxophone. The saxophone has a single-reed mouthpiece like a clarinet's, but its tube is made of brass. Its tone is rich, husky, and speechlike (© Gabriele Wunderlich).

Left–Recorder. Like the flute and piccolo, the recorder has no reed. The recorder's tone resembles a flute's, but it is softer and gentler. Its five main sizes are sopranino, soprano, alto, tenor, and bass (Katrina Thomas/Photo Researchers).

 Woodwind Instruments

(Players of the **recorder,** a relative of the flute, blow through a "whistle" mouthpiece.) The rest of the woodwind instruments rely on a vibrating reed. A **reed** is a very thin piece of cane, about $2\frac{1}{2}$ inches long, that is vibrated by a stream of air. There are single- and double-reed woodwinds. In **single-reed woodwinds** the reed is fastened over a hole in the mouthpiece and vibrates when the player blows into his or her instrument. The clarinet and bass clarinet are single-reed woodwinds. The **saxophone,** too, has a single reed. Used mainly in bands, it is a cross between a woodwind and a brass instrument.

In **double-reed woodwinds** two narrow pieces of cane are held between the musician's lips. The oboe, English horn, bassoon, and contrabassoon are double-reed woodwinds.

Heard by itself, a reed produces only a squawklike sound. While the tone color of reed woodwinds is mainly determined by the bore of the instrument's tube, the reed does affect the tone color somewhat. Professional woodwind players spend much time soaking and shaping their supply of reeds to ensure the best possible tone.

Above–Trumpet and mute. The trumpet sounds brilliant, brassy, and penetrating. (© Gabriele Wunderlich).

Right–French horn. Its tone is less brassy, more mellow and rounded than the trumpet's (Randy Matusow).

Opposite page, left–Trombone. Its tone combines the trumpet's brilliance with the French horn's mellowness (© Gabriele Wunderlich).

Opposite page, right–Tuba. Its thick heavy tone is used to add weight to the lowest orchestral register (Randy Matusow).

Tone colors also differ greatly among the various registers of each woodwind instrument. In general, low registers tend to be breathy and thick, and top registers are more penetrating. Unlike the strings, which can double stop, the woodwinds can produce only a single note at a time. In symphonic music they frequently are given melodic solos. Woodwind instruments are well suited for outdoors (shepherds have played simple woodwinds for thousands of years). They are often featured in music that evokes a rustic mood.

Brass Instruments

Ranging from high to low in register, the **trumpet, French horn, trombone,** and **tuba** are the main instruments of the symphony orchestra's brass section. Trumpets and trombones are often used in jazz and rock groups.

The vibrations of brass instruments come from the musician's lips as he or she blows into a cup or funnel-shaped *mouthpiece.* The vibrations are amplified and

colored in a tube that is coiled (to make it easy to carry and play). The tube is flared at the end to form a *bell*. While modern brass instruments are made of brass, earlier ones were made of hollow animal horns, elephant tusks, wood, and even glass.

Some brass instruments, such as the cornet and baritone horn, are used mainly in concert and marching bands. The **cornet** is similar in shape to the trumpet, but its tone is more mellow. The **baritone horn** looks like a tuba and has the same range as the trombone.

Pitch of brass instruments is regulated both by varying the lip tension and by using *slides* and *valves* to change the length of the tube through which the air vibrates. The trombone uses a slide, a U-shaped tube that fits into two parallel straight tubes (see photograph). By pulling the slide in or pushing it out, the player changes the length of tube and makes it possible to play different pitches. The trumpet, French horn, and tuba use three or four valves to divert air through various lengths of tubing (see illustrations). The longer the length of tubing through which air is diverted, the lower the possible pitch. Valves came into common use around 1850. Before then, French horn and trumpet players would insert additional curves of tubing (called *crooks*) into their instruments to change the range of available pitches. When valves came into use these instruments could produce many more tones and became much more flexible. Brass players can also alter the tone of their instruments by inserting a **mute** into the bell. A mute is a hollow, funnel-shaped piece of wood or plastic.

Brasses are powerful instruments; when played loudly they can almost drown out the rest of the orchestra. Brasses are used at climaxes and for bold and heroic statements. They cannot play as rapidly as most of the string or woodwind instruments and serve less often as soloists. We often think of the brasses in terms of military marches or outdoor ceremonies. For many centuries they were simple instruments capable of producing only a few pitches and were used mainly for military signals, religious rites, or hunting calls.

Percussion Instruments

Most percussion instruments of the orchestra are struck by hand, with sticks, or with hammers. Some are shaken or rubbed. They are subdivided into instruments of definite and indefinite pitch, depending on whether they produce a tone or a noiselike sound.

Definite Pitch		*Indefinite Pitch*	
timpani	xylophone	side drum	triangle
(kettledrums)	marimba	(snare drum)	cymbals
glockenspiel	celesta	bass drum	gong
vibraphone	chimes	tambourine	(tam-tam)

The vibrations of percussion instruments are set up by stretched membranes, like the calfskin of the kettledrum, and by plates or bars made of metal, wood, or

Above—Timpani (kettledrums). The timpani are the only orchestral drums of definite pitch. A calfskin *head* is stretched over a copper, hemispherical *shell*. The pitch of the timpani is changed by varying the tension of the head. Screws around the shell's rim are tightened or loosened by hand or by a foot pedal. One percussionist generally plays two to four timpani, each tuned to a different pitch (Ludwig Industries).

Above left—Side drum (snare drum). The dry rattling sound of this drum—used a lot in marches—is produced by the vibration of *snares,* or strings, which are tightly stretched against the bottom head (Debbie Feingold).

Top—Bass drum. The largest of the orchestral drums, a bass drum is almost three feet in diameter (Cynthia Copple).

Above left–Chimes. A set of metal tubes hung from a frame, chimes are struck with a hammer and sound like church bells (Cynthia Copple).

Above right–Glockenspiel (orchestral bells). The glockenspiel's metal bars are struck with two hammers to produce a tone that is bright and silvery (Randy Matusow).

Above–Xylophone. A set of wooden bars are struck with two hard hammers to produce a dry, wooden tone (Randy Matusow).

Right–Celesta. The celesta looks like a small upright piano, but its sounding mechanism is like a glockenspiel's. Metal bars are struck by hammers that are controlled by a keyboard. The celesta's tone is tinkling and graceful (Photo by Brill/Interlochen Center for the Arts).

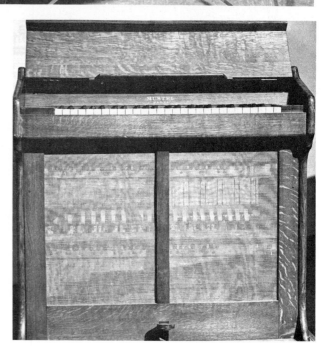

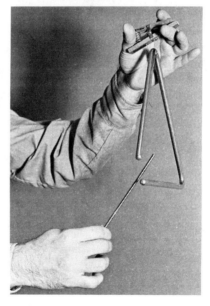

Top left–Cymbals. Cymbals are round brass plates. They usually are struck together with a sliding motion, and their sound penetrates like a sharp crash (Randy Matusow).

Top right–Gong (tam-tam). When struck by a bass drum's stick with a soft head, the gong produces long-lasting sounds that can seem solemn, mysterious, or frightening (Randy Matusow).

Right–Triangle. Struck with a metal beater, the triangle makes a tinkling bell-like sound (Randy Matusow).

Above–Tambourine. Often used to create Spanish or gypsy effects, the tambourine is played by shaking or by striking the head with the knuckles (Randy Matusow).

Musical Instruments

other sonorous materials. Extremely loud sounds may be drawn from percussion instruments like the bass drum or cymbals. However, percussion sounds die away more quickly than those of other instruments. In a symphony orchestra, one percussionist may play several different instruments during a composition.

Percussion instruments have long been used to emphasize rhythm and to heighten climaxes. But until about 1900, they played a far less important role than strings, woodwinds, or brasses. Composers of our century have been more willing to exploit the special colors of the percussion group and have occasionally written entire pieces to show it off, such as *Ionisation* (1931) by Edgard Varèse. Jazz and rock musicians have, of course, made good use of percussion instruments. Yet, for all these recent explorations, Western musicians barely approach the incredibly varied use of percussion found in Africa and Asia, where subtle changes of tone color and dynamics are used with great imagination.

Keyboard Instruments

The **piano, harpsichord, organ,** and **accordion** are the best-known keyboard instruments. A keyboard permits the performer to play several tones at the same time with ease and rapidity. This capacity in common justifies grouping instruments that are otherwise quite different: The piano and harpsichord produce sounds through vibrating strings; the organ uses vibrating air columns. The piano and, to a lesser extent, the organ are sometimes used in modern symphony orchestras for coloristic effects. All keyboard instruments are played solo, as well.

During the last two centuries, more great music has been written for the **piano** than for any other solo instrument. It is exceptionally versatile. A pianist can play many notes at once, including both a melody and its accompaniment. The piano commands a wide range of pitches. Its eighty-eight keys span more than seven octaves. The dynamic range is broad, from a faint whisper to a powerful *fortissimo*. Because of its dynamic flexibility, the Italians named it *pianoforte* ("soft-loud").

When a pianist's finger strikes a key, a felt-covered hammer swings up against a string. The greater the force on the key, the more powerful the hammer's blow on the string, and the louder the tone produced. When the pianist releases the key, a felt *damper* comes down on the string to stop the vibrations and end the tone. The steel strings are held under tension by an iron frame. Below the strings is a wooden sounding board which amplifies and colors the strings' vibrations.

There are usually three pedals on a piano. Most important is the *damper pedal,* on the right, which allows a pianist to sustain tones even after the keys are released. The pedal on the left, commonly known as the *soft pedal,* veils the sound. The middle pedal is rarely used (and is often missing from upright pianos); it allows the pianist to sustain some tones without sustaining others.

Invented in 1709, the piano came into fairly wide use in the 1780s and was mechanically perfected by the 1850s. Today it is among the most popular instruments and is used for solos, for accompaniments, and in combination with one or many other instruments.

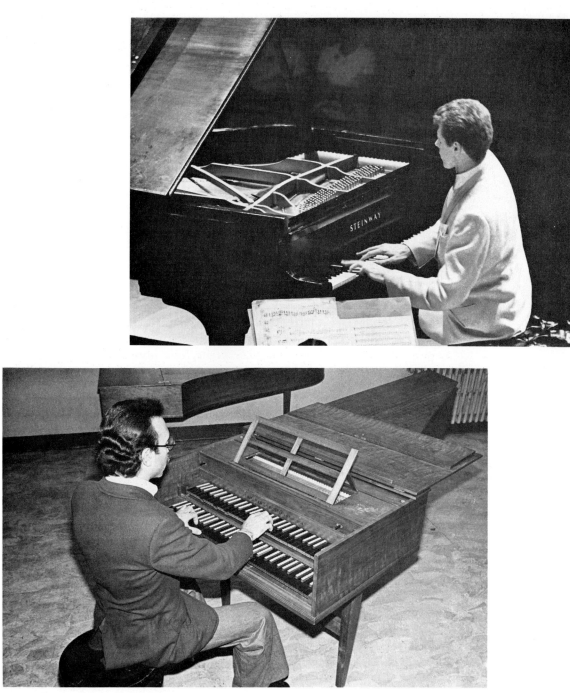

Top–Piano. One of America's best-known pianists is Van Cliburn (M. E. Warren/Photo Researchers).
Bottom–Harpischord (Randy Matusow).

 Keyboard Instruments

Pipe organ (The Bettmann Archive).　　　　Accordion (David Seymour/Magnum).

The **harpsichord** has strings that are plucked by a set of *plectra* (little wood, horn, leather, or plastic quills). These are controlled by one or two keyboards.

Pipe organs have many sets of pipes controlled from several keyboards, including a pedal keyboard played by the organist's feet. The keys control valves from which air is blown across or through openings in the pipes. Various sets of pipes are brought into play by pulling knobs called *stops*. Each set of pipes has a particular tone color which the organist uses alone or with others. The larger the organ, the more tone colors available. Organists, unlike pianists, cannot make subtle changes of dynamics by varying finger pressure. Instead, dynamic change is produced by adding or reducing the number of pipes being played or by opening and closing shutters (much like Venetian blinds) which surround some groups of pipes. The organ has a greater range of pitch, volume, and tone color than any other traditional instrument. Its tones last for as long as a finger or foot is held on a key or pedal.

The greatest period of organ music and organ building was from 1600 to 1750, when it was known as the "king of instruments." Although mostly connected with religious services, today the organ is found in many auditoriums and is used in concerts.

Elements

30

Electronic Instruments

An electronic instrument is one that produces or amplifies sound through electronic means. Invented as early as 1904 electronic instruments have had a great impact on music only since 1950.

Among the electronic instruments widely used in popular music and rock are the electric piano, organ, and guitar. A musician performs on these in public much as he or she would on a traditional nonelectronic concert instrument. Other electronic instruments are *not* usually played for an audience but are used by composers to produce sounds on audiotape. The three tools for creating such electronic music are the tape studio, the synthesizer, and the computer.

In a **tape studio,** the raw material consists of recorded sounds—definite pitches (tones) or indefinite pitches (noises). These sounds are either of electronic origin—from audio generators—or from such nonelectronic sources as flutes, jet engines, water drips, bird calls, etc. The composer manipulates these raw materials in several ways: by speeding the sounds up or slowing them down, or altering their pitch and duration. Thus a flute can be made to have the register of a bassoon. The tape can be played backwards, producing novel sound effects. A piano tone, for example, might consist of a gradual crescendo followed by a startling percussive sound, instead of the normal sharp attack followed by a gradual fading away. A sound may be given an echo, or it may be electronically filtered to change its tone color. The composer can place different sounds against each other by using several tape recorders or multitrack tape. Since audiotape

RCA sound synthesizer (The Electronic Music Center of Columbia and Princeton Universities).

can be cut and spliced, sounds can be played in any desired order. Rhythm can be fully controlled, too, since the duration of a sound depends only on the length of a tape segment.

Originating around 1951, the tape studio became the main tool of the electronic music composer of the 1950s. However, tape splicing and re-recording is a laborious and time-consuming process; as a result, many composers of the 1960s turned to synthesizers, which appeared around 1955.

Synthesizers are systems of electronic components which generate, modify, and control sound. They vary in size and capacity. The vacuum-tube RCA Sound Synthesizer is enormous, occupying an entire wall of the Columbia-Princeton Electronic Music Center in New York City. It remains one of a kind because—as composer Milton Babbitt has observed—"Nobody's going to build these monsters that cost about a quarter of a million dollars each." During the 1960s and 1970s, when transistor technology came into being, smaller, less expensive synthesizers such as the Moog and Buchla were developed and installed in electronic music studios at universities throughout the United States. They also appear in live concerts of electronic music and are used to create scores for movies and television shows. Their use in rock music is well known.

Synthesizers can generate a practically limitless variety of sounds, both musical tones and noises. They can simulate a group of conventional instruments

Buchla synthesizer (The Electronic Music Center of Columbia and Princeton Universities).

or produce weird sounds that suggest outer space. The composer has complete control over pitch, tone color, loudness, and duration. Unlike the mechanisms of the tape studio, most synthesizers can be "played" by means of a keyboard. Usually, though, only one note can be played at a time. To get two melodies at once, a composer must combine two different recordings. Some rock groups, however, use synthesizers with keyboards that can produce several tones at the same time.

Computers are the third and most recently developed means of producing sounds on audiotape. To understand this function of the computer, recall that any sound—musical tone, noise, or speech—is produced by vibrating waves. The characteristics of these waves can be represented by a series of numbers. With a computer program, a composer can feed musical specifications—numbers, words, and letters typed onto punch cards—into a computer. The computer then changes these specifications into a series of numbers that represent the final sounds. Later, these numbers are passed through a converter so that the music may be heard or recorded on audiotape. Of all electronic instruments, the computer gives composers the most precise control of sound. But since a computer does not directly produce sound—only numbers that are converted to sound on additional electronic equipment—a composer at present cannot instantly hear music he or she has programmed.

A Young Person's Guide to the Orchestra, Op. 32 (1946), by Benjamin Britten (1913–1976)

Benjamin Britten, an English composer, wrote this attractive work in 1946 as an introduction to the instruments of the orchestra. He used a theme, or main melody, by Henry Purcell, a great English composer of the seventeenth century. The majestic theme is first presented as follows:

Theme
    a. Full orchestra
    b. Woodwind section
    c. Brass section
    d. String section
    e. Percussion section
    f. Full orchestra

Thirteen variations, or varied repetitions of the theme, are then heard. Each highlights a different instrument. Together, they vary in dynamics, speed, and tone color, as well as mood. The variations follow each other without pause and range from about thirty seconds to a minute in length. (Variation 13, which features many percussion instruments, lasts almost two minutes.) Within each instrumental group, instruments are generally presented from highest to lowest in range, as follows:

 Electronic Instruments

Woodwinds	*Variation 1:*	Flutes and piccolo
	Variation 2:	Oboes
	Variation 3:	Clarinets
	Variation 4:	Bassoons
Strings	*Variation 5:*	Violins
	Variation 6:	Violas
	Variation 7:	Cellos
	Variation 8:	Double basses
	Variation 9:	Harp
Brasses	*Variation 10:*	French horns
	Variation 11:	Trumpets
	Variation 12:	Trombones and tuba
Percussion	*Variation 13:*	Timpani (kettledrums), bass drum and cymbals, tambourine and triangle, side drum and Chinese block (a hollow wooden block that is struck with a drumstick), xylophone, castanets and gong, whip (two hinged pieces of wood that are slapped against each other), entire percussion section, xylophone and triangle

Variation 13 is followed immediately by a lively new tune played by an unaccompanied piccolo. Then, other instruments enter, each playing the same tune. After woodwind, string, brass, and percussion instruments have had their turn, the brasses bring back the main theme and provide an exciting conclusion.

Basic Terms

Voices
soprano   tenor
alto   bass

Musical Instruments
register

String Instruments
violin   vibrato
viola   mute
cello   tremolo
double bass   harmonics
bow   harp
pizzicato   guitar
stop (double, triple, quadruple)

Woodwind Instruments

piccolo	contrabassoon
flute	recorder
oboe	saxophone
English horn	reed
clarinet	single-reed woodwinds
bass clarinet	double-reed woodwinds
bassoon	

Brass Instruments

trumpet	cornet
French horn	baritone horn
trombone	mute
tuba	

Percussion Instruments

timpani (kettledrums)	side drum (snare drum)
glockenspiel	bass drum
vibraphone	tambourine
xylophone	triangle
marimba	cymbals
celesta	gong (tam-tam)
chimes	

Keyboard Instruments

piano	organ
harpsichord	accordion

Electronic Instruments

tape studio
synthesizer
computer

Elements

RHYTHM ‖ **3** ‖

Rhythm is basic to life. We see it in the cycle of night and day, the four seasons, the rise and fall of tides. More personally, we feel rhythm as we breathe. We find it in our heartbeats and our walking.

The essence of rhythm is a recurring pattern of tension and release, expectation and fulfillment. This rhythmic alternation seems to pervade the flow of time. Time, as we live it, has fantastic diversity; each hour has sixty minutes, but how different one may seem from another!

 Rhythm

35

Rhythm forms the lifeblood of music, too. In its widest sense, **rhythm is the ordered flow of music through time**. Musical time is like lived time in its endless variety. It also seems to pass at varying speeds and intensities. Yet there is an essential difference between music and life. A composer can control the passage of time in music. In life, such order eludes us. We delight in surrendering to a musical time world that is ordered yet somehow related to our feelings and moods. We also enjoy letting the rhythm of music stimulate movement in our bodies.

Just as rhythm pervades our lives, so we find it everywhere in music—in pitch, tone color, and volume. How these elements change in time, and their rate of change, are concerns of rhythm. The many interrelated aspects of rhythm will be considered one at a time.

Beat

When you clap your hands or tap your foot to music, you are responding to its beat. The **beat** is a regular, recurrent pulsation that divides the music into equal units of time. Beats can be represented by marks on a time-line:

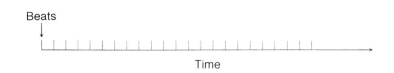

In music, such beats may occur as often as every quarter second or as seldom as every second and a half. Sometimes the beat is powerful and easy to feel, as in march or rock music. Or it may be barely noticeable, suggesting feelings like floating or aimlessness.

The pulse of music is communicated in different ways. Sometimes the beat is explicitly pounded out, by a bass drum in a marching band, for instance. At other times the beat is sensed rather than actually heard. Sing the beginning of "America" up to the words *Land where my fathers died:*

My	coun-	try,	'tis		of	thee,	Sweet	land	of	lib-	er-	ty,
|	|	|	|	|	|	|	|	|	|	|	|	|
Of	thee	|	sing.				Land (etc.)					
|	|	|	|	|	|	|						

Each of the marks represents a beat. Did you notice that you held *sing* for three beats automatically? You *sensed* the beat because you were aware of it and expected it to continue.

Beats form the background against which the composer places notes of varying lengths. Beats are basic units of time by which all notes are measured.

Notes last either a fraction of a beat, an entire beat, or more than a beat. In the excerpt from "America," for example, each of the three syllables, *My coun-try,* lasts a beat; *'tis* lasts one beat and a half; and *of* lasts only a half beat. We already noted that *sing* is held for three beats. So in this song we have notes ranging in length from a half beat to three beats.

When we talk about the combination of different note lengths in "America," we are considering its rhythm. Earlier, rhythm was broadly defined as the ordered flow of music through time. More specifically, **rhythm** can be defined as the particular arrangement of note lengths in a piece of music. The rhythm of a melody is an essential feature of its personality. Indeed, we might recognize "America" merely by clapping out its rhythm without actually singing the tones. "America"'s *beat* is an even, regular pulsation. But its *rhythm* flows freely, sometimes matching the beat, sometimes not.

Meter

In singing "America," some beats feel stronger or more stressed than others. The stress comes regularly on the first of every three beats:

My	coun-	try,	'tis		of thee,
beat	beat	beat	**beat**	beat	beat

Therefore we count the beats of "America" as 1–2–3, 1–2–3:

My	coun-	try,	'tis		of	thee,
1	2	3	**1**	2		3

Sweet	land	of	lib-		er-	ty,
1	2	3	**1**	2		3

Of	thee	I	sing.		
1	2	3	**1**	2	3

In much music we find a repeated pattern of a strong beat plus one or more weaker beats. The organization of beats into regular groups is called **meter.** Such a group containing a fixed number of beats is called a **measure.** Based on the number of beats in a measure, there are several types of meter.

When a measure has two beats, it is in **duple meter;** we count 1–2, 1–2, etc.:

Ma-	ry	had	a	lit-	tle	lamb,	lit-	tle	lamb,	lit-	tle	lamb,
|**1**	2		|**1**	2		|**1**	2		|**1**	2		|

Meter

37

The vertical lines mark the beginning or end of the measure. The first, or stressed, beat of the measure is known as the **downbeat.**

A pattern of three beats to the measure is known as **triple meter.** As we have seen in "America," we count 1–2–3, 1–2–3, etc. All waltzes are in triple meter.

Another basic metrical pattern is **quadruple meter,** which contains four beats to the measure. As usual, the downbeat is strongest; but there is another stress on the third beat, which is stronger than the second and fourth beats, and weaker than the first: 1–2–*3*–4, 1–2–*3*–4. In the following example of quadruple meter the first word is on the **upbeat,** an unaccented pulse preceding the downbeat:

Mine	eyes	have	seen	the	glo-	ry	of	the	com-	ing	of	the	Lord;	He	is	
1		2		3		4			**1**		2		3		4	

March, jazz, and rock music are usually in quadruple meter. Both duple and quadruple meter reflect the left-right, left-right pattern of walking or marching.

Sextuple meter contains six rather quick pulses to the measure. The downbeat is strongest, and the fourth beat also receives a stress: 1–2–3–*4*–5–6. For example:

Oh,	give	me	a	home		where the	buf-	fa-	lo	roam,		where the	
1	2	3	4	5	6		**1**	2	3	4	5	6	

Note that the measure is subdivided into two groups of three beats each: 1–2–3/*4*–5–6. Thus sextuple meter is a combination of duple and triple meter. Melodies in sextuple meter often create a feeling of smooth flow, as in "Silent Night."

Quintuple meter, with five beats to the measure, and **septuple meter,** with seven beats to the measure, occur frequently in twentieth-century music and occasionally in earlier music. These meters combine duple and triple meter. In quintuple meter, for example, the measure is subdivided into groups of two and three beats: 1–2–3/*4*–5 or 1–2/*3*–4–5.

Accent and Syncopation

An important aspect of rhythm is the way individual notes are stressed—how they get "special emphasis." A note is emphasized most obviously by being played louder than the notes around it, that is, by receiving a dynamic **accent.** A note is sometimes especially accented when it is held longer or is higher in pitch than those near it. In "The Star-Spangled Banner," *see* is naturally accented by being longer and higher in pitch than *Oh, say can you.* In speech as well, we stress individual words through loudness, length, and pitch.

When an accented note comes where we normally would *not* expect it, the effect is known as **syncopation.** There is a syncopation when an "off-beat" note is accented, when the stress comes *between* two beats. In the following example, syncopation occurs on the accented *my,* which comes between beats 1 and 2:

Give	**my**	re-	gards	to	Broad-		way		
1	2	3	4		1	2	3	4	

A syncopation also occurs when a weak beat is accented, as in 1–2–3–4 or 1–2–3–**4.** Such contradictions of the meter surprise the listener and create rhythmic excitement. Syncopation is one of the most characteristic features of jazz.

Tempo

We've seen that the speed of the beat may be fast or slow. This speed of the beat is known as **tempo,** the basic pace of the music. A fast tempo is associated with a feeling of energy, drive, and excitement. A slow tempo often contributes to a solemn, lyrical, or calm mood. Such associations are rooted in the way we feel and act. When we're excited our hearts beat more rapidly than when we're calm; we tend to move and speak more quickly.

A **tempo indication** is usually given at the beginning of a piece. As in the case of dynamics, the terms that show tempo are in Italian:

largo	very slow, broad
grave	very slow, solemn
adagio	slow
andante	moderately slow, a walking pace
moderato	moderate
allegretto	moderately fast
allegro	fast
vivace	lively
presto	very fast
prestissimo	as fast as possible

Qualifying words are sometimes added to these indications to make them more specific. The two most commonly used are *molto* ("much") and *non troppo* ("not too much"). We thus get phrases like *allegro molto* ("very fast") and *allegro non troppo* ("not too fast").

As with dynamics, all these terms indicate only approximate tempos; they are relative. A piece marked *andante,* for example, might be played faster by one musician than by another. With the markings as a guide, each performer chooses the tempo that seems appropriate for a piece. But there is no one "right" tempo. A piece can sound equally convincing at slightly different speeds.

The same tempo is not always used throughout a piece. A gradual quickening of tempo may be indicated by writing *accelerando* ("becoming faster"), and a gradual slowing-down of tempo by *ritardando* ("becoming slower"). An *accelerando,* especially when combined with a rise in pitch and volume, increases excitement,

 Tempo

while a *ritardando* is associated with less tension and a feeling of conclusion.

Since about 1816, composers have been able to indicate their preferred tempos by means of a **metronome,** an apparatus which produces ticking sounds or flashes of light at any desired musical speed. The metronome setting indicates the exact number of beats per minute. For example, *andante* might be represented by the metronome number 60 and *allegro* by the number 116.

Side 16, band 2

Unsquare Dance (1961), by Dave Brubeck (b. 1920)

Brubeck's *Unsquare Dance* is in septuple meter, with seven quick beats to the measure. The composer writes that this unusual meter makes *Unsquare Dance* "a challenge to the foot-tappers, finger-snappers, and hand-clappers. Deceitfully simple, it refuses to be squared." The piece is performed by a small jazz group consisting of piano, double bass, and percussion. It begins with only a pattern of beats and then becomes more active rhythmically and melodically. The meter is established by pizzicato bass tones on beats 1, 3, and 5, and by hand claps on beats 2, 4, 6, and 7:

	Clap		Clap		Clap	Clap
1	2	3	4	5	6	7
Bass		Bass		Bass		

(This septuple meter combines duple and triple meter. Each measure is subdivided into groups of two and three beats: 1–2, 3–4, 5–6–7.) Exciting syncopations occur when weak beats 2 and 4 are accented by hand claps.

After the opening six measures, the piano enters with an introductory musical idea that begins on the upbeat and emphasizes the first beat of each measure. Soon the piano part becomes more tuneful and rhythmically intricate. After the piano solo, the bass and hand claps are joined by percussive sounds in a rhythm that is faster than the beat. The final piano solo rounds off *Unsquare Dance* on a comic note.

Basic Terms

rhythm	measure
beat	downbeat
meter	upbeat
duple meter	accent
triple meter	syncopation
quadruple meter	tempo
quintuple meter	tempo indication
sextuple meter	metronome
septuple meter	

MUSIC NOTATION

We use written words to express our thoughts and communicate with others when we can't be with them. In music, ideas are also written down, or *notated*, so that a performer can play a piece unknown to him or her. **Notation** is a system of writing down music so that specific pitches and rhythms can be communicated.

Notation will be discussed here primarily to help you follow the music examples from this book that may be played in class. The aim is to help you recognize rising or falling melodic lines and long or short notes. It will be helpful for you to review pitch (section 1) and rhythm (section 3).

Notating Pitch

One way to indicate the general rise and fall of pitch is to "notate" the words of a familiar melody:

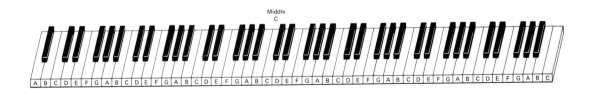

But this is not exact. With music notation we can indicate *exact pitches* by the upward or downward placement of symbols.

Seven of the twelve pitches, or tones, that fill the octave in Western music are named after the first seven letters of the alphabet: A, B, C, D, E, F, G. This sequence of letters is repeated over and over to represent the "same" tones in higher or lower octaves (remember that one octave "duplicates" the tones in another octave). These seven tones correspond to the white keys of the piano keyboard:

The C nearest to the center of the keyboard is called **middle C.** This pitch is close to the middle of the piano's range.

Notating Pitch

41

Pitches are notated by the placement of *notes* on a *staff.* A **note** is a black or white oval to which a *stem* and *flags* can be added:[7]

A **staff** is a set of five horizontal lines:

Notes are positioned either on the lines or between them, in the spaces:

The higher a note is placed on the staff, the higher its pitch.

A **clef** is placed at the beginning of the staff to show the exact pitch of each line and space. The **treble clef** is used for relatively high pitch ranges, such as those played by a pianist's right hand.

The **bass clef** is used for relatively low pitch ranges, such as those played by a pianist's left hand.

If a pitch falls above or below the range indicated by the staff, short horizontal **ledger lines** are used:

Keyboard music calls for a wide range of pitches to be played by both hands. When writing such music, composers use the **grand staff,** a combination of the treble and bass *staves* (plural of staff):

[7]Whether a note is black or white or has a stem and flags determines its duration, which is explained under the next heading, "Notating Rhythm." For now, a note is an oval symbol that shows pitch by its position on a staff.

Notes on the grand staff are shown here in relation to their position on the piano keyboard:

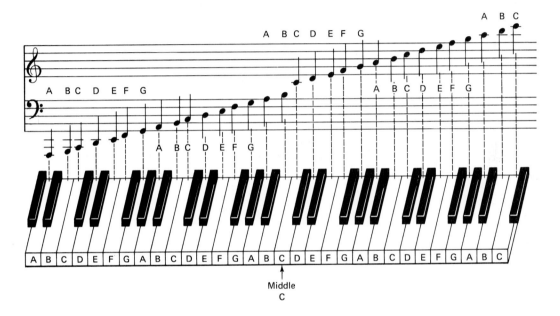

Middle
C

To show how notation is applied, here are the pitches of "Mary Had a Little Lamb" as they might be sung by women and men at the same time, an octave apart (the rhythm is not shown):

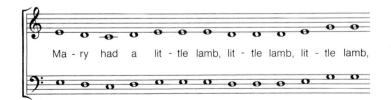

Ma - ry   had   a   lit - tle lamb, lit - tle lamb, lit - tle lamb,

Notes placed exactly underneath one another mean that the pitches are heard at the same time.

So far, only seven tones within the octave have been named, those produced by the white keys of the piano. The other five tones, played on the black keys of the piano, are indicated by one of the same seven letters plus a **sharp sign** (♯) or

Notating
Pitch

43

a **flat sign** (♭). For example, the pitch between C and D may be called either C sharp (C♯)—higher than C—or D flat (D♭)—lower than D. The same is true of the other black keys.

Here are these additional five tones in music notation:

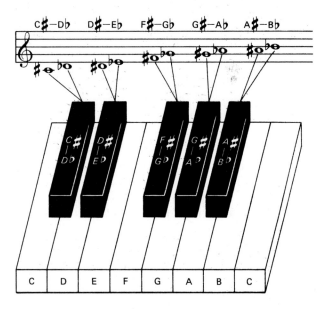

A **natural sign** (♮) is used in notation to cancel a previous sharp or flat sign (see above).

All twelve tones within the octave have now been shown in music notation.

Notating Rhythm

Music notation does not indicate the absolute duration of tones; instead, it shows how long one tone lasts in relation to others in the same piece. Under the preceding head, we have seen that the position of notes on a staff indicates their exact pitches. Now we will look at the notation system that indicates how long an exact pitch is to last compared with those around it.

A single note on the staff lasts longer or shorter depending on how it looks. It may be simply a white oval; or a white oval with a **stem** (vertical line); or a black oval with a stem; or a black oval with a stem and one or more **flags** (flying from the stem). Like any symbols, notes are easier to look at than to explain. Here are five duration symbols arranged from longest (left) to shortest (right):

Each note lasts half as long as the note to its left, or twice as long as the note to its right. For example, if a quarter note lasts one beat, a half note gets two, and a whole note gets four. In the same way, an eighth note lasts half as long as a quarter note; it gets a half beat. And a sixteenth note gets a quarter beat. This chart shows the relationships of the duration symbols used in notation:

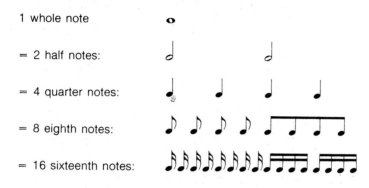

From the chart we see that one whole note lasts as long as two half notes, or as long as four quarter notes, and so on. To make it easier to read crowded notation, the flags of several eighth notes or sixteenth notes that follow each other are usually joined by a horizontal **beam**, as the chart shows.

Having looked at the notation of both pitch and duration, we can apply it and get rhythm:

Baa, baa, black sheep, have you an - y wool? Yes sir, yes sir, three bags full.

Notice that the longer notes on *wool* and *full* are half notes; the quicker notes on *have you any* are eighth notes; the other notes are all quarter notes.

To lengthen the duration of a tone (and add rhythmic variety), we can make it a **dotted note.** By adding a dot (·) to the right of a note, we increase its duration by half. Ordinarily a quarter note equals 2 eighth notes:

But a dotted quarter note equals 3 eighth notes:

In "America," the longer notes on *'tis* and *lib-* are dotted quarter notes:

My coun-try, 'tis   of thee, Sweet land   of   lib - er - ty,

Notating
Rhythm

45

Frequently, a dotted note is followed by one that is much shorter. For example, at the beginning of "The Battle Hymn of the Republic" each dotted eighth note is followed by a sixteenth note (♪.♪):

Mine eyes have seen the glo - ry of   the com - ing of   the Lord;   He   is

This long-short pattern is called **dotted rhythm.** Because the short note seems to rush to the next note on a beat, the dotted rhythm strongly emphasizes that beat. (This is why marches often use dotted rhythm.)

Another way to lengthen the duration of a note is by a **tie** (⌒). When two notes in a row are the same pitch and connected by a tie, the first note is lengthened by the duration of the second. In "The Farmer in the Dell," the two notes on *dell* are tied:

The farm - er   in   the dell,   The farm - er   in   the dell,

Thus the tone on *dell* lasts as long as a dotted quarter note plus a quarter note. The two tied notes become one continuous sound.

We can add rhythmic variety to music by shortening the duration of a note, too. We do this with a **triplet:** Three notes of equal duration are notated as a group within a curved line and the number 3 (♩♩♩). Such a three-note group lasts only as long as two notes of equal value usually do.

Silence (Rests)

Remember that silence in music can be as important as sound. We notate the duration of silence by using a symbol called a **rest.** Rests are pauses; their durations correspond to the types of notes we've already looked at:

whole rest   half rest   quarter rest   eighth rest   sixteenth rest

Meter

To show the meter of a piece, composers use a **time signature** (or **meter signature**). This is stated as two numbers, one over the other, that appear at the beginning of the staff. (If the meter changes within the piece, two new numbers are given.) Don't confuse these numbers with fractions, though they look alike. In a time signature, the upper number tells how many beats fall in a measure; the lower number tells what kind of note gets the beat (a 2 = a half note; a 4 = a quarter note). A $\frac{2}{4}$ time signature, for example, shows that there are two beats to the measure (duple meter), and a quarter note gets one beat. Duple meter may also be shown by $\frac{2}{2}$ (or by its symbol, ₵). The most common triple meter is $\frac{3}{4}$. Quadruple meter is usually $\frac{4}{4}$ (or **C**). Compound meters, which contain groupings of three beats, are indicated by $\frac{6}{8}$, $\frac{9}{8}$, $\frac{12}{8}$. A $\frac{6}{8}$ meter, for instance, is counted 1–2–3–4–5–6, with each eighth note having a beat.

Basic Terms

The Notation of Pitch	*The Notation of Rhythm*
notation	stem
middle C	flag
note	beam
staff	dotted note
clef (treble and bass)	dotted rhythm
ledger lines	tie
grand staff	triplet
sharp sign (♯)	rest
flat sign (♭)	time signature
natural sign (♮)	

MELODY ‖ 5 ‖

For a lot of us, music means melody. We've sung in schools, cars, camps, and the shower. After hearing music, we usually remember its melody best. Familiar melodies have the power to recall past emotions and experiences. Words and instruments aren't required, we don't need singers and large orchestras—just a few notes.

Melody is easier to recognize than to define. Yet it must have something special; melody is common to music of all times and all peoples. Probably the elusive "something" that evokes so much feeling will never be trapped for a

 Melody

47

dictionary. We do know that a **melody** is a series of single tones that add up to a recognizable whole. A melody begins, moves, and ends; it has direction, shape, and continuity. The up and down movement of its pitches conveys tension and release, expectation and arrival. This is the melodic curve, or line.

A melody moves by small intervals called **steps** or by larger ones called **leaps.** A step is the interval between two adjacent tones in the *do-re-mi* scale (from *do* to *re, re* to *mi,* etc.). Any interval larger than a step is known as a leap (*do* to *mi,* for example). Besides moving up or down by step or leap, a melody may simply repeat the same note. A melody's range, or the distance between its lowest and highest tones, may be wide or narrow. "Mary Had a Little Lamb" moves mostly by step within a narrow range; "Rock-a-Bye Baby" has a wider range and lots of leaps as well as steps. Melodies written for instruments tend to have a wider range than those for voices, and they often contain wide leaps and rapid notes that would be difficult to sing.

The specific order of a melody's long and short notes is important. A well-known melody can be almost unrecognizable if it is not sung in proper rhythm. Note durations, as well as pitches, contribute to the distinct character of a melody. For example, the smooth, even rhythm of "Twinkle, Twinkle, Little Star" is calm, while the snappy dotted (long-short) rhythm of "The Battle Hymn of the Republic" is exciting. Try reversing these rhythms: the first melody will lose its calmness, and the second will lack excitement.

How the tones of a melody are performed can vary its effect, too. Sometimes they are sung or played in a smooth, connected style called **legato.** Or they may be performed in a short, detached manner called **staccato.**

Many melodies are made up of shorter parts called **phrases.** These short units may have similar pitch and rhythm patterns that help unify a melody. On the other hand, contrasting phrases can furnish variety. Phrases often appear in balanced pairs; a first phrase of rising pitches may be followed by a second phrase of falling pitches. The second phrase may partly repeat the first one but have a more conclusive ending, a point of arrival. Such a resting place at the end of a phrase is called a **cadence.**

As you get further into the music explored in this book, you'll find a wealth of melodies: vocal or instrumental, long or short, simple or complex. To help sort them, let's see how some basic melodic principles apply to four familiar tunes. These are short melodies, easy to sing and remember.

"Row, Row, Row Your Boat" is first. Sing the tune only up to the word *stream.*

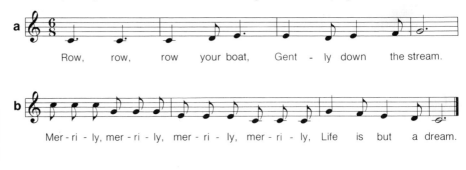

Notice that on *stream* the melody comes to a point of arrival, a resting place. This ends the first phrase of the melody. But the melody seems incomplete, as though it posed a question. Now sing the rest of the melody, the second phrase, beginning on *Merrily*. It ends conclusively and seems to answer the question. Each phrase has a point of arrival, a cadence. The first phrase ends with an **incomplete cadence** that sets up expectations; the second phrase ends with a **complete cadence** that gives an answer, a sense of finality.

Each phrase of "Row, Row, Row Your Boat" is the same length, a formula typical of many melodies called tunes. The two phrases create a feeling of symmetry and balance. The first begins with repeated notes (C–C–C—"Row, row, row") and then moves upward by step (D–E–F–G—"your boat, Gently down the stream"); the second moves downward by leap (C–G–E–C—"Merrily, merrily, merrily, merrily"); and finally by step (G–F–E–D–C—"Life is but a dream"). Often the highest tone of a melody will be the **climax,** or emotional focal point. In this song the climax comes on the first *Merrily* at the beginning of the second phrase. The leaps create a carefree quality in the quick notes on the repeated *merrily.*

The two contrasting phrases of the song can be symbolized by the letters *a* and *b*. In discussing music it's helpful to let letters represent various sections of a piece. Lowercase letters (a, b, etc.) are used for phrases and relatively short sections while capital letters (A, B, etc.) are used for longer sections. When the phrases or sections of the music differ significantly, as in this song, we use different letters: a b. When one section exactly repeats another, the letter is repeated: a a. When a section is a varied repetition of a previous one, the previous letter is repeated but with a prime mark: a a'.

Now sing the entire nursery tune "Mary Had a Little Lamb":

As in "Row, Row, Row Your Boat," this melody has two balancing phrases, the first ending up in the air with an incomplete cadence, and the second ending conclusively with a complete cadence. However, the two songs also differ from each other. In "Mary" the second phrase begins exactly like the first. It starts over again but proceeds to a different, more conclusive ending. This partial repetition serves to unify the melody. "Mary Had a Little Lamb"'s phrases may be symbolized as a a'. We will see that melodic repetition, both exact and varied, plays an important unifying role in all kinds of music.

Both repeated and contrasting phrases can be heard in the cowboy song "Home on the Range":

Melody

49

a Oh, give me a home where the buf-fa-lo roam, where the deer and the an-te-lope play,

a' Where sel-dom is heard a dis-cour-ag-ing word, and the skies are not cloud-y all day.

b Home, home on the range, where the deer and the an-te-lope play,

a' Where sel-dom is heard a dis-cour-ag-ing word, and the skies are not cloud-y all day.

A yearning quality is projected here through a longer and more complex form than that of the two other tunes. There are four phrases, and, as in "Mary Had a Little Lamb," the second phrase is a repetition of the first but has a more conclusive ending. (Sing the first two phrases a few times, comparing the note on *play* with that on *day.*) The first two phrases may be outlined a a' (varied). Contrast is introduced in the third phrase of the melody, the climactic refrain "Home, home on the range." This phrase begins in a new way—on the highest pitch of the melody—and may be labeled b. The concluding fourth phrase ("Where seldom is heard") is a repetition of the beginning but with a final ending. Thus the song as a whole is outlined a a' b a'. The principle of *statement* (a a'), *departure* or *contrast* (b), and *return* (a') that governs "Home on the Range" is an essential one in the creation of form in music.

Our final example, "America," differs from the other songs in that its phrases are not of equal length:

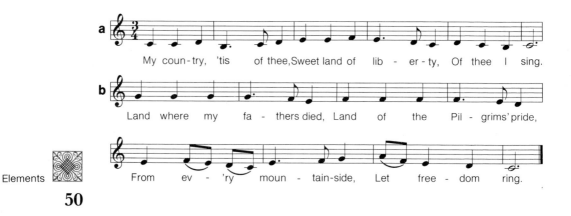

a My coun-try, 'tis of thee, Sweet land of lib-er-ty, Of thee I sing.

b Land where my fa-thers died, Land of the Pil-grims' pride,

From ev-'ry moun-tain-side, Let free-dom ring.

The second phrase (starting from *Land*) is longer than the first and creates a feeling of continuation rather than one of balance or symmetry. An interesting aspect of "America" is the way a repeated rhythmic pattern is used to unify the melody. The rhythmic pattern for "My country 'tis of thee" is repeated for "Sweet land of liberty," "Land where my fathers died," and "Land of the Pilgrims' pride."

Notice that the melody for "Land of the Pilgrims' pride" is simply a repetition a little lower of the preceding "Land where my fathers died." Such a repetition of a melodic pattern on a higher or lower pitch is called a **sequence.** This is an impelling device of varied repetition that gives a melody a strong sense of direction.

We've considered tunes that are complete in themselves. Frequently, a melody will serve as the starting point for a more extended piece of music and, in stretching out, will go through all kinds of changes. This kind of melody is called a **theme.**

The concepts and vocabulary introduced in this chapter can be used to study melodies of any style. Try using them to examine your favorite songs. You may pinpoint parts that you like and, consequently, enjoy the melodies a bit more because you know what makes them tick.

"Yesterday" (1965), by John Lennon (b. 1940) and Paul McCartney (b. 1942)

Side 16, band 3

A beautiful melody conveys a feeling of longing in "Yesterday," one of the Beatles' most haunting ballads. The solo voice is accompanied by acoustical guitar and string quartet (two violins, viola, and cello), a performing group not usually associated with rock music.

The song's vocal phrases can be outlined a a b a b a. Phrase a is irregular in length, containing seven rather than the typical eight measures. The melody moves mostly by step within a fairly wide range. It begins on a low note, rises quickly to a climax on "far away," and then descends to an inconclusive ending that expresses yearning. All of phrase a grows out of the opening repeated-note idea ("Yes-ter-day"): a long note ("day") preceded by two shorter ones ("Yes-ter"). This idea appears four times with changes of pitch and rhythm:

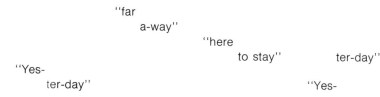

There is a syncopated quality to the rhythm, since the long notes on "(a)-*way*," "*stay*," "(be)-*lieve*," and "(yester)-*day*" are sung *before* the beat, rather than on it.

Phrase b, which begins with long repeated notes on "Why she," grows out of phrase a. Yet phrase b creates contrast because it uses slower rhythms and

"Yesterday" by Lennon and McCartney

51

emphasizes a higher register of the singer's voice. Together, phrases a and b produce a satisfying feeling of balance.

Basic Terms

melody	cadence
step	incomplete cadence
leap	complete cadence
legato	climax
staccato	sequence
phrase	theme

|6| HARMONY

When folk singers accompany themselves on a guitar, they add support, depth, and richness to the melody. We call this "harmonizing." Most music in Western culture is such a blend of melody and harmony.

Harmony refers to the way chords are constructed and how they follow each other. A **chord** is a combination of three or more tones sounded at once. Essentially, a chord is a group of simultaneous tones, while a melody is a series of individual tones heard one after another. As a melody unfolds, it provides clues for harmonizing—some of the tones of the melody are usually included in the chords of the accompaniment. But a melody does not always dictate a specific series, or **progression,** of chords. A melody may be harmonized in several musically convincing ways. A musician such as a folk singer will experiment and choose the chords that best fit a melody's mood. Chord progressions will enrich a melody by adding emphasis, surprise, suspense, or finality. In today's popular music, a song writer often composes the melody, while an arranger supplies the accompanying chords. Composers of classical music create both the melody and harmony, often at the same time.

There is a tendency to think that a melody is composed first and that the chords are added later. Actually, it's often the other way around. For centuries repeated chord progressions have given rise to improvised melodies. In jazz, for example, a pianist may play the same basic progression of chords over and over again while a trumpet player invents a continually changing melody to fit the piano's pattern. When several jazz musicians improvise different melodies at once, their music is held together by the organized chordal background—by the harmony.

Folk singer Joan Baez blends melody and harmony by accompanying herself on the guitar (Suzanne Szasz).

As different as Bach, Beethoven, jazz, folk, and rock may seem, some of the same chord progressions can be heard in all. While new chords and new progressions continually enter the language of music, the basic chordal vocabulary has remained fairly constant. We'll look now at a few principles of harmony that have proved so useful for so long.

Consonance and Dissonance

Some chords have been considered stable and restful, others unstable and tense. A tone combination that is stable is called a **consonance.** Consonances are the points of arrival, rest, and resolution. (Whoever coined the phrase "living in harmony with others" had consonance in mind.) A tone combination that is unstable is called a **dissonance.** Its tension demands an onward motion to a stable chord. A dissonance has its **resolution** when it moves to a consonance. When this resolution is delayed or accomplished in unexpected ways, a feeling of drama, suspense, or surprise is created. In this way a composer plays with the listener's sense of expectation. Dissonant chords are active and move music forward. Traditionally they have been considered harsh and have colored music that expresses pain, grief, and conflict.

Having defined consonance and dissonance, it's well to warn that they have various degrees. Some consonant chords are more stable than others, just as

 Consonance and Dissonance

53

dissonant ones vary in the levels of their tension. Dissonant chords have been used with increasing freedom over the centuries, so that a chord considered intolerably harsh in one period may seem rather mild in a later one.

The Triad

A great variety of chords have been used in music. Some consist of three different tones, others have four, five, or even more. Depending on their make-up, chords sound simple or complex, calm or tense, bright or dark.

The simplest, most basic chord is the **triad** (pronounced "try-ad"), which consists of three tones. To indicate that a triad's three tones are played at one time, it is notated:

A triad built on the first, or tonic, note of the scale (*do*) is called the **tonic chord** (*mi*), and fifth (*sol*) tones. The bottom tone is called the root; the others are a third and a fifth above the root. (From *do* to *mi* in the scale is an interval of a third, while from *do* to *sol* is the interval of a fifth.)

A triad built on the first, or tonic, note of the scale (*do*) is called the **tonic chord** (*do-mi-sol*); it is the main chord of a piece, the most stable and conclusive. Traditionally, the tonic chord would usually begin a composition and almost always end it.

The triad built on the fifth note of the scale (*sol*) is next in importance to the tonic. It is called the **dominant chord** (*sol-ti-re*). The dominant chord is strongly pulled toward the tonic chord. This attraction has great importance in music. A dominant chord sets up tension that is resolved by the tonic chord. The progression from the dominant to the tonic gives a strong sense of conclusion, and that's why it is used so often at the end of a phrase, melody, or entire piece. In "America," for example, the next to last syllable is harmonized by a dominant chord, while the last word is harmonized by the tonic chord:

A progression from the dominant chord to the tonic chord is called a **cadence.**
The word *cadence* means both the resting point at the end of a melodic phrase (as
we said in section 5) and a chord progression that gives a sense of conclusion.

Broken Chords (Arpeggios)

We have described a chord as a group of tones played together, as a block of
sound. But the tones of a chord may be presented in other ways, too. When the
individual tones of a chord are sounded one after another, it is called a **broken
chord,** or **arpeggio.** Arpeggios may appear in the melody or in the accompaniment. "The Star-Spangled Banner" is a melody that begins with such a broken
chord, or arpeggio. The notes of the tonic chord are heard one after another
instead of together:

As we go on with our study of music in this book, the importance of harmony
will become more and more apparent. You'll see that chord progressions can
produce powerful emotional effects and be more than simply a background for
melody. Sometimes a melody depends on the accompanying harmony for its
expressiveness, as in Chopin's Prelude in E Minor, discussed below.

Harmony helps give music variety and movement. There's a relaxation of
tension when a dissonant chord resolves to a consonant chord, a sense of conclusion when the dominant chord moves to the tonic. The effects of harmony are
endless, varying with the style of a particular era and the desires of individual
composers.

Prelude in E Minor for Piano, Op. 28, No. 4 (1839), by Frédéric Chopin

Side 8, band 4

Chopin's harmony makes a vital contribution to the brooding quality of this
miniature lasting less than two minutes. Without the pulsating chords of its
accompaniment, the melody might seem aimless and monotonous. It hardly
moves, alternating obsessively between a long note and a shorter one right above
it. But the returning long note seems to change in color because each time there is
a different dissonant chord below it. The dissonant chords underscore the
melancholy of this Prelude, which is meant to be played *expressivo* ("expressively").

Prelude in
E Minor
for Piano

55

Toward the end of the piece, a mildly dissonant chord is followed by a brief pause. This silence is filled with expectancy, as we wait for the dissonance to resolve. Finally the tension is released in the three solemn chords of the closing cadence.

Basic Terms

harmony	triad
chord	tonic chord
progression	dominant chord
consonance	cadence
dissonance	broken chord (arpeggio)
resolution	

Elements

7 KEY

Practically all familiar melodies are built around a central tone. The other tones of the melody gravitate toward this central one. Since the central tone is especially stable and restful, a melody usually ends on it. To feel the gravitational pull of a central tone, sing "America" and stop after the next-to-last word, *freedom;* then, after a few seconds, sing the ending tone of *ring.*

My coun-try, 'tis of thee,Sweet land of lib - er - ty,

Of thee I sing. Land where my fa - thers died,

Land of the Pil - grims'pride, From ev - 'ry

moun - tain-side, Let   free - dom   ring.

You probably felt uneasy until you supplied that last tone. This central tone is the **keynote,** or **tonic,** of the melody. When a piece is in the key of C, for example, C is the keynote, or tonic. The keynote can also be E, A, or any of the twelve tones that fill the octave in Western music.

   Key involves not only a central tone, but a central scale and chord as well. A piece in the key of C has a basic scale, *do-re-mi-fa-sol-la-ti-do,* with C as its *do,* or tonic. And the basic chord of a piece in C is a tonic triad with C as its root, or bottom tone. As we've seen in section 6, the tonic triad is made up of *do-mi-sol,* or the first, third, and fifth tones of the basic scale. Just as familiar melodies generally end on the keynote, compositions traditionally end with the restful tonic chord. Key, then, refers to the presence of a central note, scale, and chord within a piece. All other tones of a composition are heard in relationship to the central ones. Another term for key is **tonality.** After 1900, some composers abandoned the traditional system, but even today much of the music we hear is built around a central tone, chord, and scale.

The Major Scale

So far, we've referred to the *do-re-mi-fa-sol-la-ti-do* scale as a main element of key, but have not actually defined what a scale is. A **scale** is made up of the basic pitches of a piece of music arranged in order from low to high or from high to low. Many different scales have been used in various eras and cultures. The basic scales of Western music from the late 1600s to 1900 were the *major* and *minor.* And these scales have continued to be widely used during our own century.

   Let's first consider the **major scale,** the familiar *do-re-mi-fa-sol-la-ti-do.* Sing this scale and note that you produce seven different pitches and then arrive at the high *do*—the eighth note—which is really a duplication of the first tone an octave higher. As we've seen in section 1, the octave is the distance or interval between the first and eighth tones of the major scale. The major scale has a specific pattern of intervals between its successive tones. Two kinds of intervals are found in the scale: *half steps* and *whole steps.* The **half step** is the smallest interval traditionally used in Western music. The **whole step** is twice as large as the half step. Here is the pattern of whole and half steps that makes up the major scale:

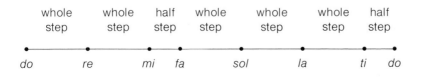

whole step	whole step	half step	whole step	whole step	whole step	half step
do	re	mi	fa	sol	la	ti	do

There is an especially strong pull from *ti* to *do* because the interval is small, a half step. You'll feel this pull when you sing the scale and stop on *ti.*

The Major Scale

Here is a major scale with C as the beginning tone:

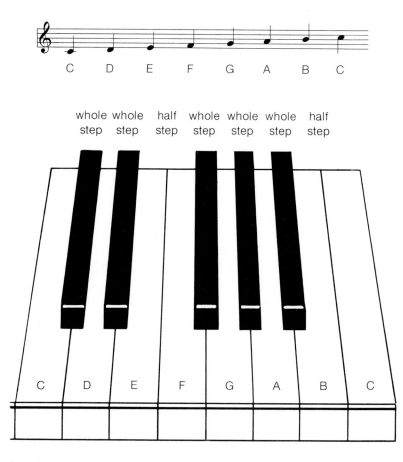

The C-major scale uses only the white keys of the piano. There are half steps between E and F, and between B and C; these pairs of tones are not separated by black keys. As notated above, "America" is based on the C-major scale; it is in the key of C major.

We can construct similar major scales by starting on any one of the twelve tones that fill an octave. The same pattern of intervals can begin on any of these tones, so there are twelve possible major scales. To understand this better, imagine the major scale as a ruler on which eight marks are spaced irregularly (as shown in the *do-re-mi* diagram on page 57). The pattern of marks stays the same no matter where the "ruler" is placed. Similarly, the pattern of whole and half steps that makes up a major scale sounds the same even when the scales start on different keynotes.

To us the important point is not the technicality of half and whole steps but the idea of a scale as a pattern of intervals. Also important is the idea of the keynote (or beginning, or tonic) of the major scale; it is the scale's central tone toward which all others seem to pull. The conclusive quality we hear in the keynote is not a result of any law of nature—it's rooted in cultural conditioning.

The Minor Scale

Along with the major scale the minor scale is fundamental to Western music. "Joshua Fought the Battle of Jericho" is a tune based upon a minor scale.

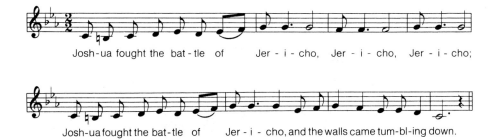

Josh-ua fought the bat-tle of   Jer - i - cho, Jer - i - cho, Jer - i - cho;

Josh-ua fought the bat-tle of   Jer - i - cho, and the walls came tum-bl-ing down.

The **minor scale**—like the major—consists of seven different tones and an eighth tone that duplicates the first an octave higher; but it differs from the major scale in its pattern of intervals. The minor scale's pattern can also begin on any of the twelve tones in an octave, so there are twelve possible minor scales. As notated above, "Joshua Fought the Battle of Jericho" is based upon a minor scale beginning on C; it is the key of C minor. Here is a comparison between a major and a minor scale both starting on C:[8]

C-major scale	whole step		whole step		half step	whole step		whole step		whole step		half step
		C		D	E	F		G		A		B C

C-minor scale	whole step		half step	whole step		whole step		half step	whole step		whole step
		C		D	E♭		F		G	A♭		B♭ C

The crucial difference between major and minor is that in the minor scale there is only a half step between the second and third tones. A major scale has a whole step here. This small difference greatly changes the sound of a scale and the mood of music using that scale. Music based on minor scales tends to sound

---

[8]The minor scale shown in this example is the *natural minor,* one of three kinds of minor scales. The other two kinds are the *harmonic minor* and the *melodic minor* scales. The three types of minor scales have slight variations in their patterns of intervals, but all can begin on any tone of the octave, and all will produce a sound that contrasts with the major scale as described above.

The Minor Scale

59

serious or melancholy. Almost all funeral marches, for example, are in minor keys. Also, the tonic triad built from a minor scale is a minor chord, while one built from a major scale is a major chord. Minor chords sound darker than major ones. Composers use the differences between minor and major to create contrasts of mood. A serious or agitated melody in C minor may be followed by a brighter tune in C major. We learn to tell the difference between minor and major as we learn to distinguish one color from another, by repeated exposure.

The Key Signature

When a piece of music is based on a major scale with D as its keynote, we say that the piece is in the key of D major. Similarly, if a composition is based on a minor scale with the keynote F, the composition is in the key of F minor. Each major and minor scale has a specific number of sharps or flats ranging from none to seven. To indicate the key of a piece of music, the composer uses a **key signature,** sharp or flat signs immediately following the clef sign at the beginning of the staff. To illustrate, here is the key signature for D major, which contains two sharps:

By using a key signature a composer avoids the problem of having to write a sharp or a flat sign before every sharped or flatted note in a piece. (The seven sharps in the key of C-sharp major and the seven flats in the key of C-flat major would otherwise make notation very complicated!) Appendix IV shows the key signatures for the different major and minor scales.

The Chromatic Scale

The twelve tones of the octave—*all* the white and black keys in one octave on the piano—form the **chromatic scale.** Unlike the major or minor scales, the chromatic scale's tones are all the same distance apart. Each tone is a half step away from the next one:

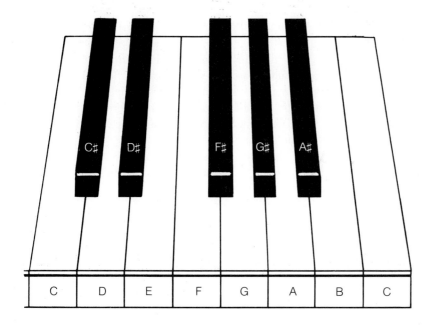

The word *chromatic* comes from the Greek word *chroma,* "color." Its derivation provides a clue to the chromatic scale's traditional function, which is to color or embellish the tones of the major and minor scales. The chromatic scale is not like the major and minor: It does not define a key. Its tones contribute a sense of motion and tension. Composers throughout history have used it to evoke strong feelings of grief, loss, and sorrow. We'll see that in the twentieth century it has become independent of major and minor scales and is used as the basis for entire compositions.

Modulation: Change of Key

Most short melodies we know remain in a single key from beginning to end. However, in longer pieces of music, variety and contrast are created by using more than one key. A composition may begin in the key of C major, for example, and then proceed to G major. A shift from one key to another within the same piece is called a **modulation.** A modulation is like a temporary shift in the center of gravity. When the music starts out in the key of C major, C is the central tone, and the C-major scale and chord predominate. With the modulation to G major, G temporarily becomes the central tone, and the G major scale and chord are now the main ones. Though modulations are sometimes subtle and difficult to spot, they produce subconscious effects that increase the listener's enjoyment of the music.

Modulation: Change of Key

Tonic Key

No matter how often a piece changes key, there usually is one main key, called the **tonic** or **home key.** The tonic key is the central key around which the whole piece is organized. Traditionally, a piece would usually begin in the home key and practically always end in it. A composition in the key of C major, for example, would begin in the home key, modulate to several other keys—say, G major and A minor—and finally conclude in the home key of C major. The other keys are subordinate to the tonic.

Modulating away from the tonic key is like visiting: We may enjoy ourselves during the visit, but after a while we're glad to go home. In music, modulations set up tensions that are resolved by returning to the home key. For centuries, the idea of a central key was a basic principle of music. But after 1900, some composers wrote music that ignored the traditional system. The results of this revolutionary step are explored in Part VII, The Twentieth Century.

Basic Terms

keynote (tonic)	half step	chromatic scale
key (tonality)	whole step	modulation
scale	minor scale	tonic key (home key)
major scale	key signature	

8 ‖ MUSICAL TEXTURE

At a particular moment within a piece, we may hear one unaccompanied melody, several simultaneous melodies, or a melody with supporting chords. To describe these various possibilities, we use the term **musical texture**; it refers to how many different layers of sound are heard at once, to what kind of layers they are (melody or harmony), and to how they are related to each other. Like fabric, musical texture is described as transparent, dense, thin, thick, heavy, or light. Composers can vary the textures within their music to create contrast and drama. We'll look now at the three basic musical textures—*monophonic, polyphonic,* and *homophonic.*

Monophonic Texture

The texture of a single melodic line without accompaniment is **monophonic,** meaning literally "one sound." If you sing alone, you would make monophonic music. Performance of a single melodic line by more than one instrument or voice is playing or singing in **unison** and results in a fuller, richer-sounding monophonic texture. Examples of unison singing, where men and women sing the same notes in different octaves, appear in the "Hallelujah Chorus" by George Frideric Handel, analyzed on pages 67–68.

Polyphonic Texture

Simultaneous performance of two or more melodic lines of relatively equal interest produces the texture called **polyphonic,** meaning "many-sounding." In polyphony several melodic lines compete for attention. (When several jazz musicians improvise different melodies at once, they produce polyphony.) Polyphony adds a dimension that has been compared to perspective in painting: Each line enriches and heightens the expression of the other. This mutual enhancement points up a difference between music and speech. If many people are saying different things at one time, the result can be confusing. But when several different melodies are sung together, highly expressive sounds may be created. This technique of combining several melodic lines into a meaningful whole is called **counterpoint.** (The term *contrapuntal texture* is sometimes used in place of polyphonic.)

To fully enjoy the simultaneous flow of several melodic lines you may have to hear a piece of music a few times. Repeated hearings lead to a satisfying awareness of how the whole is woven from its parts. It's often helpful to listen first for the top line, then for the bottom, and then for the middle lines. Such selective listening increases our appreciation of contrasting rhythms and melodic shapes and gives us a chance to hear how different lines are emphasized at any given moment.

Polyphonic music often contains **imitation,** which occurs when a melodic idea is presented by one voice or instrument and then restated immediately by another voice or instrument. It's as though different lines of texture play "follow the leader." Imitation is familiar to anyone who has sung "Row, Row, Row Your Boat."

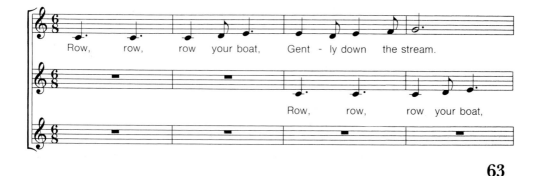

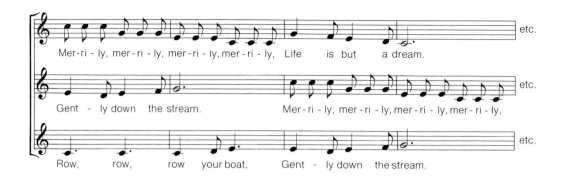

This familiar tune is a *round,* a song in which several people sing the same melody, but each starts at a different time. By the time the first singer has reached *Merrily, merrily,* etc., the second singer is only at *Gently down the stream,* and the third is just beginning *Row, row, row your boat.* At any one time, all the voices are singing different parts of the same tune.

A round like "Row, Row, Row Your Boat" is an example of strict imitation; the different voices play "follow the leader" with exactly the same melody. But imitation is usually freer—the imitating line begins like the first one but then goes off on its own. A delightful feeling of give-and-take results when a short melodic idea is quickly passed from one voice or instrument to another. This happens often in polyphonic texture.

Homophonic Texture

When we hear one main melody accompanied by chords, the texture is **homophonic.** Attention is focused on the melody, which is supported and colored by sounds of subordinate interest. Homophonic texture is familiar to anyone who has heard a folk singer accompany himself or herself on a guitar. Though the accompaniment may be quite distinctive, it is there primarily to help carry the sound and meaning of the melody. "Row, Row, Row Your Boat," when harmonized by chords, is an example of homophonic texture.

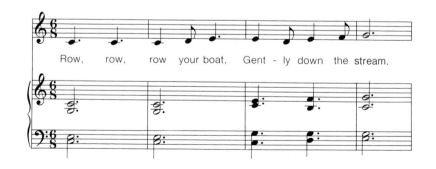

Mer-ri-ly, mer-ri-ly, mer-ri-ly, mer-ri-ly, Life is but a dream.

A hymn is another example of homophony. The hymn's tune is sung by the voice on top, while other voices have lower lines that harmonize, or blend, with the tune but are less individual. Generally, these lower voices sing notes that are different from the main tune but move in the same rhythm. All the voices moving together produce a progression of chords, one for each syllable of the hymn's text.

Accompaniments in homophonic music vary widely in character and importance. They range from subdued background chords to surging sounds that almost hide the main melody. An expressive quality in the melody can be strengthened by the rhythm or harmony that accompanies it. Sometimes a subordinate line may assert its individuality briefly and compete for the listener's attention. At such times the texture is probably best described as being between homophonic and polyphonic.

Changes of Texture

A composer can create variety and contrast by changing textures within a composition. He or she might begin with a melody and a simple accompaniment and later weave the melody into a polyphonic web. Or the composer might create drama by contrasting a single voice with massive chords sung by a chorus. Good examples of textural variety are Georges Bizet's *Farandole* and George Frideric Handel's "Hallelujah Chorus," analyzed here.

Farandole from *L'Arlésienne Suite No. 2* by Georges Bizet

Side 10, band 3

The *Farandole* comes from Bizet's music for the play *L'Arlésienne* ("The Woman from Arles"), which is set in southern France. Two contrasting themes are heard in this exciting orchestral piece. The first, in minor, is a march theme adapted from a southern French folk song. The lively second theme, in major, has the character of the *farandole,* a southern French dance.

Many changes of texture contribute to the *Farandole's* exciting mood. The piece contains two kinds of homophonic texture: In one, the accompaniment and melody have the same rhythm; in the other, the rhythm of the accompaniment

Changes of Texture

65

differs from that of the melody. The *Farandole* opens with the march theme and its accompaniment in the same rhythm. But when the lively dance theme is first presented, its accompanying chords do not duplicate the rhythm of the melody; instead, they simply mark the beat.

The *Farandole* also includes two kinds of polyphony: with and without imitation. Soon after the opening, the march theme is presented by the violins and then is imitated by the violas. At the end of the piece, polyphony results when the march and dance themes—previously heard in alternation—are presented simultaneously. In this concluding section, both themes are in major.

The *Farandole* also contains monophonic texture, which sets off the homophony and polyphony. Monophony is heard when the march theme is played by the strings in unison.

LISTENING OUTLINE
To be read while music is heard

Farandole from the *L'Arlésienne Suite No. 2* (1879), by Georges Bizet (1839–1875)[9]

Allegro deciso (forceful allegro), march tempo, quadruple meter ($\frac{4}{4}$), D minor

piccolo, 2 flutes, 2 oboes, 2 clarinets, 2 bassoons, 4 French horns, 2 trumpets, 2 cornets, 3 trombones, timpani, tambourine, bass drum, cymbals, violins 1, violins 2, cellos, double basses

(About 3 min)

1   a. Full orchestra, *ff,* march theme; homophonic (accompaniment in same rhythm as melody), minor.

     b. Violins imitated by violas, march theme; polyphonic, minor.
2   a. High woodwinds, *ppp,* dance theme; faster tempo, homophonic (accompanying chords on beat), major; decorative rushes in violins, long crescendo to *ff* as dance theme is repeated.

[9] *L'Arlésienne Suites No. 1* and *No. 2* are sets of pieces from the theater music composed by Bizet. *Suite No. 2* was arranged by Bizet's friend Ernest Guiraud after the composer's death.

    b. Full orchestra, *fff,* dance theme.
3   *a.* Strings only, *ff,* march theme in faster tempo; monophonic, minor.
    b. High woodwinds, *ppp,* dance theme; homophonic.
    c. Strings only, *ff,* continue march theme; monophonic, then homophonic as lower strings accompany melody.
    d. High woodwinds, *ppp,* dance theme; homophonic. Crescendo to
4 Full orchestra, *fff,* dance and march themes combined; polyphonic, major. Homophonic ending.

"Hallelujah Chorus" from *Messiah* (1741), by George Frideric Handel (1685–1759)

Side 3, band 7

One of the world's famous choral pieces is the "Hallelujah Chorus" from *Messiah* by Handel. In this vigorous chorus Handel offers sweeping variety by sudden changes among monophonic, polyphonic, and homophonic textures. The monophonic texture is very full-sounding as all the voices and instruments perform in unison at the proclamation "for the Lord God Omnipotent reigneth." The texture becomes polyphonic when this majestic proclamation is set against joyful repeated exclamations of *Hallelujah* in quick rhythms. Polyphony gives way to homophony as the chorus sings "The kingdom of this world . . ." to hymnlike music.

In the "Hallelujah Chorus," words and phrases are repeated over and over, as has been common practice in choral music for several centuries. (In the following text, brackets connect lines which are sung at the same time.) Handel took his text from the Revelation of St. John, which celebrates God as the Almighty and Everlasting Ruler.

	Orchestral introduction
Hallelujah!	Chorus joins, homophonic, quick exclamations
for the Lord God Ominpotent reigneth;	Monophonic, longer notes
Hallelujah!	Homophonic, quick exclamations
for the Lord God Omnipotent reigneth;	Monophonic, longer notes
Hallelujah!	Homophonic, quick exclamations
⌠for the Lord God Omnipotent reigneth; ⌡Hallelujah!	Longer-note melody against quick exclamations, polyphonic
The kingdom of this world is become the Kingdom of our Lord and of His Christ:	Hymnlike in longer notes, homophonic
and He shall reign for ever and ever,	
⌠King of Kings, and Lord of Lords. ⌡for ever and ever, Hallelujah, Hallelujah!	Bass melody, monophonic Other voices imitate, polyphonic Long repeated tones against quick exclamations; phrases repeated at higher pitches
and He shall reign for ever and ever,	Polyphonic, imitation
⌠King of Kings, and Lord of Lords, ⌡for ever and ever, Hallelujah, Hallelujah!	Long repeated tones against quick exclamations

Changes of Texture

67

and He shall reign for ever and ever,	Polyphonic
King of Kings, and Lord of Lords.	Homophonic
and He shall reign for ever and ever,	Polyphonic
{ King of Kings, and Lord of Lords,	Quick exclamations
{ for ever and ever, for ever and ever,	
Hallelujah, Hallelujah, Hallelujah,	
Hallelujah!	
	Pause
Hallelujah!	Sustained chords, homophonic

Basic Terms

musical texture	counterpoint
monophonic texture	imitation
unison	homophonic texture
polyphonic texture	

|9|| MUSICAL FORM

The word *form* is associated with shape, structure, organization, and coherence. Form calls to mind the human body or the balanced arrangement of figures in a painting.

Form in music is the organization of musical ideas in time. Music exists only in time; there its sounds begin, vary, repeat, and end. In this time flow, a composer creates something cohesive out of all the musical elements we've looked at in the previous sections—pitch, tone color, dynamics, rhythm, melody, harmony, and texture. In a logically organized piece of music one thought grows from another, and all the parts are interrelated. Our memories let us perceive the overall form by recalling the various parts and how they relate. As awareness and recall of these parts are developed through repeated listening, the form becomes clearer and takes on an emotional meaning of its own.

Techniques That Create Form

Form has already been discussed in connection with simple tunes like "Mary Had a Little Lamb" and "Home on the Range" (see section 5). These tunes have phrases that are repeated—exactly or with variation—and phrases that are contrasted. *Repetition, contrast,* and *variation* are essential techniques in short tunes as well as in compositions lasting much longer. **Repetition** creates a sense of unity; **contrast** provides variety; and **variation,** in keeping some elements of a musical thought while changing others, gives a work unity and variety at the same time.

Repetition

Musical repetition appeals to the pleasure we get in recognizing and remembering something. In a play, a scene or act is rarely repeated, but in music the repetition of melodies or extended sections is a technique widely used for binding a composition together. Through repetition a melody is engraved in the memory.

The passage of time in music, as in life, influences the way we react to events. When a musical idea returns during a piece, the effect produced is not duplication but balance and symmetry.

Contrast

Forward motion, conflict, and change of mood all come from contrast. Opposition—of loud and soft, strings and woodwinds, fast and slow, major and minor—propels and develops musical ideas. Sometimes a common element will exist between the opposing ideas to establish a sense of continuity. At other times the contrast will be complete. (The contrast between black and white is different from the contrast between black and gray.) The separate identities of such contrasting ideas are heightened by being near each other. A composer can emphasize the power and excitement of a musical idea by contrasting it with one that is calm and lyrical, much as a photographer can show the height of a building by including a human figure in the photograph.

Variation

In the variation of a musical idea, some of its features will be retained while others are changed. For example, the melody might be restated with a different accompaniment. Or the pitches of a melody might stay the same while its rhythmic pattern is changed. A whole composition can be created from a series of variations on a single musical idea.

Types of Musical Form

In discussing form as the organization of musical ideas in time, it was mentioned that a composition is made up of ideas that are interrelated. And we looked at the basic techniques for combining these ideas into a coherent whole—repetition, contrast, and variation are used constantly in music of different styles and times. In section 5 you studied several such patterns. (Remember that lowercase letters represented phrases or relatively short sections, and capital letters represented longer sections.) "Home on the Range," for example, was outlined as a a' b a'.

 Types of Musical Form

Other songs could be outlined by the same pattern of letters. (Think of "Oh, Susanna" or "Deck the Halls with Boughs of Holly.") These songs are said to have the same form, or to be of the same formal type. It's important to note, however, that two compositions having the same form may be different in every other respect.

Composers have used certain forms or patterns to organize their musical ideas. As listeners, we can respond more fully to music when we appreciate its form. We'll look now at two of the basic types of musical form.

Three-part (Ternary) Form: A B A

During the last few centuries **three-part form, A B A,** has probably been used most frequently. This form can be represented as *statement* (A); *contrast* or department (B); *return* (A). When the return of A is varied, the form is outlined A B A′. Wagner's Prelude to Act III of *Lohengrin,* analyzed in section 1, is in A B A′ form. In the Prelude, the A and A′ sections are very loud, played by full orchestra (items 1 and 3 in the outline), while the B section (item 2 in the outline) is softer, played by fewer instruments. But contrast can be of *any* kind. The A section might be softer than the B, not louder, as in Wagner's Prelude. Or the relative lengths of the three sections might vary; section B might be shorter or longer than A.

The way in which A returns after B also differs from piece to piece. Sometimes, as in the Prelude by Wagner, A returns suddenly; it's unexpected. More often, the return of A is clearly signaled. The B section will come to a definite end with a cadence and pause. The listener is thus alerted for what happens next. Or a transition might smoothly link B with A and lead into the return.

The sections of a composition in A B A form can be subdivided. One possible subdivision might be:

A	B	A
a b a	c d c	a b a

In this case, each large A section is divided into three subsections, a b a. And the large B section is divided into c d c. Depending on the piece, a listener might mistake the subsection b within the first large A section for the arrival of B. But as the music progresses, the greater contrast one hears with B will make it clear that b is a subsection within A.

Dance of the Reed Pipes from the *Nutcracker Suite,* by Peter Ilyich Tchaikovsky

The *Nutcracker Suite* is a set of dances from Tchaikovsky's fairy tale ballet, *The Nutcracker.* The *Dance of the Reed Pipes* is a particularly clear example of A B A′ form. Section A features three flutes playing a staccato melody which conveys a light, airy feeling and is repeated several times. The B section contrasts in tone

Elements

70

color, melody, and key—it features a trumpet melody accompanied by brasses and cymbals. This melody moves by step within a narrow range, in contrast to the opening flute melody, which has a wide range and lots of leaps as well as steps. The F-sharp minor key of the middle section contrasts with the D major key of the opening section. The concluding A' section, in D major, is a shortened version of the opening A section.

LISTENING OUTLINE
To be read while music is heard

Dance of the Reed Pipes from the *Nutcracker Suite* (1892), by Peter Ilyich Tchaikovsky (1840–1893)

Three-part (ternary) form: A B A'

Moderato assai (very moderate), duple meter ($\frac{2}{4}$), D major

3 flutes, 2 oboes, English horn, 2 clarinets, bass clarinet, 2 bassoons, 4 horns, 2 trumpets, 3 trombones, tuba, timpani, cymbals, violins 1, violins 2, violas, cellos, double basses

(About 2½ min)

A	1	*a.*	Low pizzicato strings, *p*, introduce
		b.	3 flutes, staccato melody in major, pizzicato strings accompany. Melody repeated.
		c.	English horn melody, legato, flutes accompany, staccato.
		d.	3 flutes, staccato melody in major, pizzicato strings accompany. Melody repeated. Cadence.
B	2	*a.*	Trumpet melody in minor, brasses and cymbals accompany.
		b.	Strings repeat trumpet melody. Flutes lead back to
A'	3		3 flutes, staccato melody in major, strings accompany. Melody repeated. Cadence.

Two-part (Binary) Form: A B

A composition subdivided into two large sections is in **two-part form, A B.** Two-part form gives a sense of *statement* (A) and *counterstatement* (B). A composition in A B form might be represented by A A B or A B B or A A B B if either or both of its large sections are immediately repeated. For example, Chopin's Prelude No. 20 in C Minor, analyzed in section 1, is in two-part form and is outlined A B B (items 1, 2, and 3 in the outline). Again, differences between A and B may be of any kind, and the two sections may be equal or unequal in length. Like three-part form, the large sections of two-part form may be divided into subsections. The B section almost always returns to the home key and gives a sense of finality.

Prelude in C Minor from *The Well-Tempered Clavier*, Book 2; by Johann Sebastian Bach

Side 2, band 2

Bach's Prelude in C Minor is in two-part (binary) form. It is outlined A A B B because each part is repeated. Parts A and B are similar in rhythm and texture

71

but differ in key. Both sections feature a continuous rhythmic flow and two-voice texture. The first part begins in C minor and then modulates to E-flat major, while the second part begins in E-flat major and then modulates back to the tonic key of C minor. Section B opens with the same rhythmic pattern as section A but is slightly higher in pitch. Each section is rounded off by a complete cadence.

This short piece was originally written for either harpsichord or clavichord (a stringed keyboard instrument). Today, it is often played on the piano as well.

LISTENING OUTLINE
To be read while music is heard

Prelude in C Minor from *The Well-Tempered Clavier,* Book 2 (1744), by Johann Sebastian Bach (1685–1750)

Two-part (binary) form: A A B B

Quadruple meter ($\frac{4}{4}$)

Harpsichord, clavichord, or piano

(About 2½ min)

A   1   Minor key, continuous rhythmic flow, two-voice texture. Cadence in major key. Section A repeated.

B   2   Major key, beginning higher in pitch than A, continuous rhythmic flow, two-voice texture. Cadence in minor key. Section B repeated.

Listening for Form

The musical patterns discussed in this section fall into clearly defined units. But music is continuous in its flow, and sometimes can't be subdivided quite so easily. Short pieces often fall into this elusive category. And some music seems to fit none of the frequently used patterns. Such music is not without form; it has a unique form that the listener can discover through repeated hearings.

Again, it's important to lean on memory when listening to music. Spotting musical ideas when they occur is fine, but it's only the beginning. The goal is to put the related ideas together by recognizing and remembering them and by finding their relationships. Through alert, repeated listening their overall shape will be made clear, and your response to music will be more satisfying.

Basic Terms

form	variation
repetition	three-part form (A B A)
contrast	two-part form (A B)

Elements

72

PERFORMANCE

Music would remain soundless on a page without a performer. Unlike books and paintings, music speaks to us through a re-creator, a musician who makes the printed music sound. A composition, even a familiar one, can be a fresh experience each time it's performed.

It's the job of the **performer** to bring life to the printed symbols laid out by a composer. Just how loud is a chord marked *f*? How fast is a section labeled *allegro*? No matter how many specific indications of rhythm, dynamics, or accent are on a page, much is left to the performer. Like that of an actor, his or her interpretation is full of subtle timings and inflections. Performers project to an audience a mixture of their own feelings and the composer's intentions. Critics sometimes say about a particularly convincing interpretation that a performer is "identified" with a work and its composer. That's how close their relationship can be.

Music created at the same time it's performed is called **improvisation.** Bach at the organ and Beethoven at the piano were brilliant improvisers; their musical ideas flowed instantly from brain to fingers. Improvisation today is a vital aspect of jazz and non-Western music.

Before the nineteenth century, performers were expected to add certain *ornaments,* or *embellishing notes,* not indicated in the printed music. Such **embellishments** offered variety and a sense of the performer's individuality. The many musicians today who perform music of the seventeenth and eighteenth centuries have made a point of learning these devices from the past. With such knowledge they can play the music as the composer intended it to be played. Music composed before 1600 presents the challenge of deciding what instruments to use. Often these were not specified by early composers, and to make things more difficult, some of the original instruments are not readily available today.

Performance styles change from generation to generation. Some performers today believe in making a work sound as it did when composed; a keyboard artist will play Bach on the harpsichord rather than on the piano. The size of an orchestra or chorus will be reduced to what was available to a church in 1630, or to a castle in 1760. Others believe that we need now to reinterpret a past work in a contemporary spirit. Today's audiences are used to a much wider range of dynamics, and they listen in larger concert halls. These performers choose to use all our modern resources to make the composer's message come alive.

The Performer

Outstanding performers of music, nearly always, have had special talents since childhood—a beautiful voice, unusual manual dexterity, an excellent ear for

 The Performer

73

Virtuoso violinist Isaac Stern, an artist of extraordinary technical mastery (Henri Cartier-Bresson/Magnum).

pitch, or a keen memory. Like athletes, they have exceptional coordination, strength, and competitive drive. Most pianists and violinists play professionally before the age of ten. Singers and woodwind players wait longer for serious training because their bodies need to mature.

Natural gifts are not enough. A developing performer studies for years with fine teachers, practices many hours a day, and cultivates musical taste and a sense of style. Out of all this may come a **virtuoso,** an artist of extraordinary technical mastery. The great solo performers are a breed alone. Above and beyond their natural gifts and training, they project a personal magnetism that can draw cheers from an audience. These rare few are constantly renewed by the challenge of performance and can make their hundredth playing of a work as exciting as the first. Discomforts of constant travel and the drain on their energies are minor matters—they thrive on communication through music.

What happens to the many fine instrumentalists who are not among the "rare few"? They teach, or play in orchestras, or both. Until fairly recently, wages for orchestral musicians were notoriously low. After lengthy and expensive training, instrumentalists were making less than sanitation workers. The musicians formed

Conductor Sarah Caldwell, Artistic Director of the Opera
Company of Boston (Jack Mitchell).

orchestral committees and improved their lives through collective bargaining.
But even with higher pay and increased benefits, players must engage in additional free-lance work. Many feel that they're subsidizing their art, but they're
willing to do so. As a member of their audience, one does well to appreciate that
performers today—however glamorous they may seem—do not have an easy life.

The Conductor

A leader of musicians, the **conductor** represents responsibility and authority. The
conductor's "instruments" are the orchestra, band, and chorus. He or she holds
performers together and makes them translate the piece into a meaningful whole.
Many, but not all, conductors use a thin stick called a **baton** to beat time and
indicate pulse and tempo. With the other hand they control the balance among
the instruments or voices so that the most important musical ideas will be
brought out. Conducting styles vary greatly among these powerful individuals,
but usually a conductor will use the left hand to indicate expression and to cue
musicians.

A page from the orchestral score of Tchaikovsky's *Romeo and Juliet.*

Most of the conductor's work is done in rehearsal, where technical problems and expressive possibilities are worked over to his or her satisfaction. When a hundred instruments or voices sound at once, the conductor must be able to detect mistakes and performers who are out of tune. Conductors read, and "hear" in their minds, an orchestral **score** that may show more than twenty different staves of notation, one for each instrumental or vocal category. Often conductors memorize the score so that they will be free to hold the eyes of the musicians and thus control fine points of interpretation. In performance, different conductors seem flamboyant, reserved, graceful, or angular. But however he or she looks, the conductor is trying to project an overall concept of a musical work.

The experience of most conductors includes mastery of at least one instrument and extended study of orchestration, music theory, and composition. Conductors are, as needed, diplomats, dictators, and teachers; their role traditionally has been thought of as the most glamorous in the music profession. In the early nineteenth century, composers began to write increasingly complex music that demanded more and more musicians. This trend fostered the rise of the virtuoso conductor—one who can hold all the forces together and make interpretive sense of their sounds.

Before the nineteenth century, the time beat was given either by the first violinist or by the keyboard player, or both. From this early custom came a title still used today—*concertmaster*. In a modern symphony orchestra the **concertmaster** is the principal first violinist, who sits on the conductor's immediate left. Solo violin music that occurs in symphonic works is played by the concertmaster. He or she also serves as the conductor's assistant by seeing that the players' music contains special markings and by checking the tuning of the orchestra before the conductor appears.

Recorded and Live Performance

Recorded performance is a sensational innovation of our time. Our homes resound with medieval music, rock, Beethoven, and Indian *ragas*. The living room is a new kind of concert hall where we can hear and repeat what we want. Performances heard on record may never have existed "live," played through from beginning to end. Instead, they are often made up of spliced tape from several performances. It's understandable that performers who have smudged some notes would like them cleaned up by the splicing process. However, too much cleaning of a tape results in a loss of natural vitality, and the long interpretive line can be destroyed.

Through **dubbing,** records have made available new listening experiences not possible in live performance. Beeps, clangs, whistles, never-ending gongs, etc., can be added to music at a composer's electronic whim. Echo chambers and other equipment have given a new dimension to tone.

It's only in the last two hundred years or so that concert-hall listening developed. Before that, music was heard in church or palace, street or home.

 Recorded and Live Performance

Much music was intended for amateurs to enjoy around their fireplaces. In church, at dances, or on ceremonial occasions, the listener often was also a performer.

In a live performance artists put themselves on the line; training and magnetism must overcome technical difficulties to involve the listeners' emotions. What is performed, how it sounds, how the artist feels about it that evening—all can never be repeated; they exist for a fleeting moment. An audience responds to the excitement of such a moment, and in responding, feelings are exchanged between stage and hall.

Despite the special electricity of a live performance, there are those who object to coughs and sneezes, the price of tickets, and the fact that seats don't recline in a concert hall. They prefer the living room, where they can choose in comfort from a staggering variety of music and performers on records. But in the living room, recorded music can become background sound. Carried to extremes, this can lessen the ability to concentrate. Total satisfaction from music requires that we focus attention as we would at a live performance.

Although records have wooed some people away from concert halls, it's also true that they have helped to build audiences for live performances. Enthusiasm for a record has filled innumerable seats in concert halls. So even though it's a very individual matter, most alert listeners will try to strike a happy balance between the voltages offered by the concert hall and by the wall socket.

Judging Performance

If you have listened to two music lovers arguing after a concert about the merits of what they had just heard, you know how much heat can be generated. Our response to a musical composition or an artist is subjective to a large extent and is rooted in deep feeling. Even professional critics can differ strongly in their evaluations of a performance. One will be bowled over by how clearly an artist has revealed the structure of a piece, and another will find the performance cold and unrewarding. There is no one "truth" about what we hear and feel.

Is a concept, an overall idea, projected by the performer? Do some sections of a piece communicate something to you, while others do not? Can you figure out why? Subtle effects of phrasing, dynamics, tone color, and tempo become more noticeable after listening to a number of performers. Listen to the same work played by three different musicians—say, pianists. At first, you may like the second pianist best, but by the third hearing you may decide that it was the first pianist who made the most of what the composer tried to say. All three pianists have played the same notes and yet made three different statements. This is what "molding an interpretation" means.

To a large extent, it's up to us as listeners to evaluate the performance of music. We can do that in the most sensitive way by being alert and open-minded. These qualities will enhance our ability to compare performances and judge music so that we can get full enjoyment from it.

Basic Terms

performer   baton
improvisation   score
embellishments   concertmaster
virtuoso   dubbing
conductor

MUSICAL STYLE   Elements 11

We use the word "style" in reference to everything from clothing to cooking, automobiles to paintings. In music **style** refers to a characteristic way of using melody, rhythm, tone color, dynamics, harmony, texture, and form. The particular way these elements are combined can result in a total sound that's distinctive or unique. When we hear an unfamiliar piece on the radio and identify it as jazz, Italian opera, or as a symphony by Beethoven, we are responding to its style. We speak of the musical style of an individual composer, a group of composers, a country, or a particular period in history. Compositions created in the same geographical area or around the same time are often similar in style. Yet, composers using the same musical vocabulary can create a personal manner of expression just as people dressed in a similar style can have an individual look.

Like most other things, musical styles change from one era in history to the next. These changes are continuous, so any boundary line between one style period and the next can only be an approximation. Though sudden turning points do occur in the history of music, even the most revolutionary new styles are usually foreshadowed in earlier compositions. And few changes of style sweep away the past entirely. Even after a new style has become established, elements of the previous style are usually preserved in the musical language.

The history of Western art music can be divided into the following style periods:

Middle Ages (450–1450)
Renaissance (1450–1600)
Baroque (1600–1750)
Classical (1750–1820)
Romantic (1820–1900)
Twentieth Century to 1950
1950 to the Present

In the following chapters, we'll describe the general features of each style period and show how it differs from the preceding one. An awareness of the character- Musical Style

79

istics of a style helps you to know what to listen for in a composition written in that particular period. And by knowing the common practice of a period, we can better appreciate the innovative or unique features of a particular composition.

Music is not created in a vacuum. To fully understand the style of a composition, one has to be aware of its function in society. Is a piece meant to provide entertainment in a nobleman's castle, a concert hall, or a middle-class home? Is it designed to accompany singing, dancing, religious rites, or drama? Musical style is shaped by political, economic, social, and intellectual developments as well. And often, similar features of style can be found in different arts of the same period.

The history of music is probably as old as the history of mankind itself. There is pictorial evidence of musical activity in Egypt as early as 3000 B.C. We know that music played an important role in the cultures of ancient Israel, Greece, and Rome. But hardly any notated music has survived from these ancient civilizations. The first style period to be considered in this book is the European Middle Ages, from which notated music has come down to us. Through the power of notation, music created over a thousand years ago can come alive today.

MIDDLE AGES

MIDDLE AGES

1 Music in the Middle Ages
 (450–1450)

2 Gregorian Chant

3 Secular Music in the Middle
 Ages

4 The Development of
 Polyphony: Organum

5 Fourteenth-century Music:
 The "New Art" in France
 and Italy

Though sacred music was dominant during the Middle
Ages, there was much secular music as well. This detail
of girls dancing is by Andrea de Bonaiuto, a painter of
the mid-fourteenth century (Scala/Editorial Photocolor
Archives).

1 | MUSIC IN THE MIDDLE AGES (450–1450)

A thousand years of European history are spanned by the phrase "Middle Ages." Beginning around 450 with the disintegration of the Holy Roman Empire, this era witnessed the "Dark Ages," a time of migrations, upheavals, and wars. But the later Middle Ages (until about 1450) was a period of cultural growth: Romanesque churches and monasteries (1000–1150) and Gothic cathedrals (1150–1450) were constructed, towns grew, and universities were founded.

During the Middle Ages a very sharp division existed among three main social classes: nobility, peasantry, and clergy. Nobles were sheltered within fortified castles surrounded by moats. During wars, these knights in armor engaged in combat, while in peacetime they amused themselves with hunting, feasting, and tournaments. Peasants—the vast majority of the population—lived miserably in one-room huts. Many were serfs, bound to the soil and subject to feudal overlords. All segments of society felt the powerful influence of the Roman Catholic Church. In this age of faith, hell was very real, and heresy was the gravest crime. Monks in monasteries held a virtual monopoly on learning; most people—including the nobility—were illiterate.

Just as the cathedral dominated the medieval landscape and mind, so was it the center of musical life. Most important musicians were priests and worked for the church. An important occupation in thousands of monasteries was liturgical singing. Boys received music education in schools associated with churches and cathedrals. With this preeminence of the church, it's no surprise that for centuries only sacred music was notated.

Most medieval music was vocal, though a wide variety of instruments served as accompaniment. Few music manuscripts of the time indicate specific instruments, but from paintings and literary descriptions we know they were used. The church frowned upon instruments because of their earlier role in pagan rites.

After about 1100, however, instruments were used increasingly in church. The organ was most prominent. At first, it was a primitive instrument; the keys were operated by heavy blows with the fists. It was so loud that it could be heard for miles around. Gradually it evolved into a flexible instrument that could play intricate polyphonic music. Throughout the period churchmen complained about noisy instruments that distracted the worshipers. "Whence hath the church so many Organs and Musical Instruments?" complained a twelfth-century abbot. "To what purpose, I pray you, is that terrible blowing of Bellows, expressing rather the cracks of thunder than the sweetness of a Voyce? . . . In the meantime, the common people standing by, trembling and astonished, admire the sound of Organs, the noise of the Cymballs and Musical Instruments." In the later Middle Ages instruments were a source of constant struggle between composers, who wanted to create elaborate compositions, and church authorities, who wanted music only as a discreet accompaniment to the religious service.

In the Middle Ages most of the peasantry were serfs,
bound to the soil and subject to feudal overloads
(Giraudon).

 Music in the
Middle Ages
(450–1450)

85

Architecture changed during the Middle Ages
from the Romanesque style, seen in the elev-
enth-century nave above, to the Gothic, shown in
the thirteenth-century Cathedral of Reims on the
right. Guillaume de Machaut, the leading composer of fourteenth-century France, probably
wrote the Notre Dame Mass for performance in
Reims Cathedral (Lauros—Giraudon).

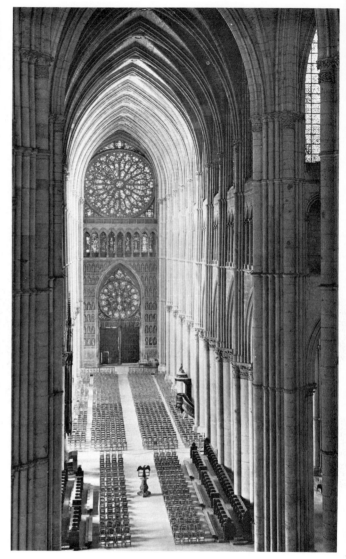

During the Middle Ages, artists were concerned more with spirituality than with lifelike representation. This early-fourteenth century *Madonna and Child Enthroned, with Five Scenes from the Passion* is by a follower of Segna di Buonaventura (The Metropolitan Museum of Art, Rogers Fund, 1918).

GREGORIAN CHANT $\|$ **2** $\|$

Gregorian Chant

For over a thousand years, the official music of the Roman Catholic Church has been **Gregorian chant,** a melody sung without accompaniment. (The chant is monophonic in texture.) Based on sacred Latin texts, the melodies of Gregorian chant were meant to enhance parts of religious services. They set the atmosphere for specific prayers and ritual actions. For centuries, composers have based original compositions on chant melodies. (Since the second Vatican Council of 1962–1965, most Roman Catholic services are celebrated in the native language of each country, and today Gregorian chant is not common.)

Gregorian chant conveys a calm, other-worldly quality; it represents the voice of the church, rather than of any single individual. Its rhythm is flexible, without meter, and has little sense of beat. The rhythm of these melodies is uncertain because precise time values were not notated. But the free-flowing rhythm gives Gregorian chant a floating, almost improvisational character. The melodies tend to move by step within a narrow range of pitches. Depending on the nature and importance of the text, they are simple or elaborate; some are little more than recitations on a single tone, while others contain complex melodic curves.

Gregorian chant is named after Pope Gregory I (The Great), who reorganized the Catholic liturgy during his reign from 590 to 604. Although medieval legend credits Pope Gregory with the creation of Gregorian chant, we know that it evolved over many centuries. Some of its practices, such as the singing of psalms, came from the Jewish synagogue of the first centuries A.D. Most of the several thousand melodies known today were created between 600 and 1300.

At first Gregorian melodies were passed along by oral tradition, but as the number of chants grew to the thousands, they were notated to ensure musical uniformity throughout the Western church. The earliest surviving chant manuscripts date from about the ninth century. The composers of Gregorian chant—like the sculptors who decorated early medieval churches—remain almost completely unknown.

The Church Modes

The "other-worldly" sound of Gregorian chant partly results from the unfamiliar scales used. These scales are called the *church modes*. Like major and minor scales, **church modes** consist of seven different tones and an eighth tone that duplicates the first an octave higher. However, their patterns of whole and half steps are different. The church modes were the basic scales of Western music during the Middle Ages and Renaissance and were used in secular music as well as sacred. Much Western folk music follows the patterns of the church modes. For example, the sea shanty "What Shall We Do with the Drunken Sailor?" is in a mode called *Dorian*, and the Civil War song "When Johnny Comes Marching Home" is in the *Aeolian* mode.

Side 1, band 1

Alleluia: Dominus dixit (before 700 A.D.)

An elaborate and jubilant Gregorian chant is the Alleluia from the First Mass for Christmas. The word *alleluia* is a Latinized form of the Hebrew *hallelujah* ("praise ye the Lord"). In this chant many notes are sung to single syllables of text. The long series of tones on *ia* is an expression of wordless joy and religious ecstasy. The monophonic texture of the chant is varied by an alternation between a soloist

Middle Ages

and a choir singing in unison. The chant is in **A B A** form; the opening Alleluia
melody is repeated after a middle section that is set to a psalm verse.

Solo voice, *Alleluia* phrase. Chorus, *Alleluia* phrase		A
repeated with long series of tones on *ia*.		
Solo voice:[1] *Domine dixit ad me*	The Lord said to me:	B
Filius meus es tu,	"You are my Son;	
ego hodie genuite.	this day I have begotten you."	
Chorus, *Alleluia* phrase with long series of tones on *ia*.		A

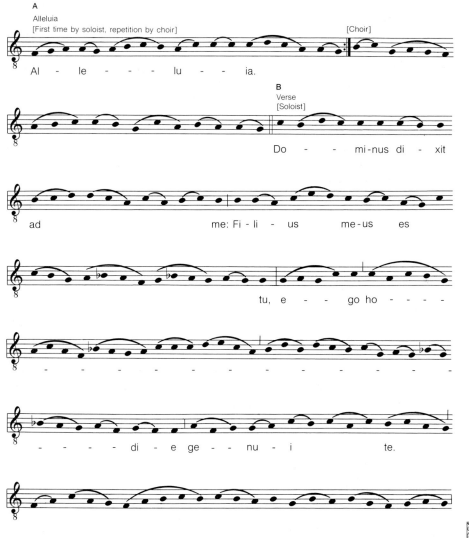

[1]In some recordings, the psalm verse is sung by the chorus.

The Church
Modes

89

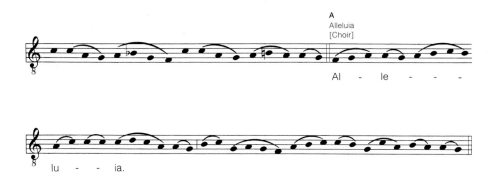

Alleluia: *Dominus dixit* is shown here in medieval chant notation:

The Nativity of Our Lord.

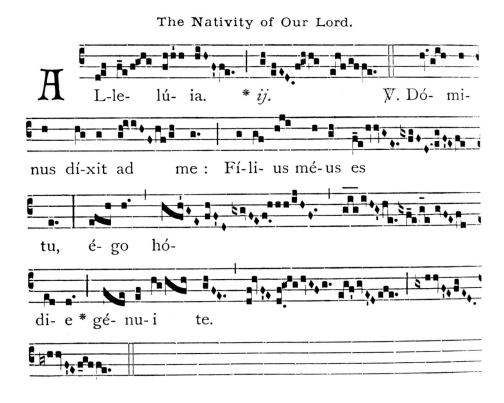

SECULAR MUSIC IN THE MIDDLE AGES

Despite the domination of Gregorian chant throughout the Middle Ages, there was much music outside the church, too. The first large body of secular songs that survives in decipherable notation was composed during the twelfth and thirteenth centuries by French noblemen called troubadours and *trouvères*. During this age of chivalry, knights gained great reputations as musical poets, as they might have done earlier by fighting bravely. Many of the love songs they sang have been preserved because nobles had clerics write them down. These songs were usually performed by court minstrels, and most of them deal with love; but there are also songs about the Crusades, dance songs, and spinning songs.

Some 1650 troubadour and trouvère melodies have been preserved. The notation does not indicate rhythm, but it's likely that many had a regular meter with a clearly defined beat. They thus differ from the free, nonmetrical rhythm of Gregorian chant.

During the Middle Ages, wandering minstrels (or *jongleurs*—"juggler" comes from this French word) performed music and acrobatic tricks in castles, taverns, and town squares. Without civil rights and on the lowest social level with prostitutes and slaves, only a few were lucky enough to find steady work in the service of the nobility. But they were an important source of information in a time with no newspapers. They usually sang songs written by others and played instrumental dances on harps, fiddles (ancestors of the violin), and lutes (plucked-string instruments).

Danse Royale (Thirteenth Century)

Side 1, band 2

One of the earliest surviving pieces of instrumental music, *Danse Royale* is a medieval dance (an *estampie*). It is monophonic in texture, and the music manuscript does not indicate which instrument plays the melodic line. In our recording, the melody is performed on a *shawm,* a double-reed ancestor of the modern oboe. During the Middle Ages, the shawm's piercingly brilliant tone was favored for outdoor music like marches and dances. A rhythmical background is provided by two medieval drums called *tabors. Danse Royale* is in triple meter and has a strong, fast beat.

Danse Royale (Thirteenth Century)

91

Most secular songs in the Middle Ages dealt with love. This illustration shows two plucked-string instruments of the period, a harp and a lute (The Bettmann Archive).

Dances in the Middle Ages were often accompanied by instrumental music (The Granger Collection).

THE DEVELOPMENT OF POLYPHONY: ORGANUM

4

For centuries Western music was basically monophonic, having a single melodic line. But sometime between 700 and 900, the first steps were taken in a revolution that eventually transformed Western music. Monks in monastery choirs began to add a second melodic line to Gregorian chant. In the beginning, this second line was improvised, not written down; it duplicated the chant melody at a different pitch. The two lines were in parallel motion, note-against-note, at the interval of a fourth or a fifth. (The interval from *do* to *fa* is a fourth; from *do* to *sol* is a fifth.)

Sit glo - ri - a Do - mi - ni in se - cu - la

Medieval music that consists of Gregorian chant and one or more additional lines is called **organum.** Between 900 and 1200 organum became truly poly-

The Development of Polyphony

93

A supreme monument of Gothic architecture, the Cathedral of Notre Dame in Paris was the center of polyphonic music around 1200 (Monkmeyer).

phonic, and the melody added to the chant became more independent. Instead of moving strictly parallel to the chant, it developed a melodic curve of its own. Sometimes this line was in contrary motion to the chant, moving up as the original melody moved down. The second line became even more independent around 1100, when the chant and the added melody no longer were restricted to a note-against-note style. Now the two lines differed rhythmically as well as melodically. The chant, on the bottom, was sung in very long notes, while the added melody, on top, moved in shorter notes. Medieval listeners must have been startled to hear religious music in which the added melody was more attractive than the chant. At times the chant tones were so slow and dronelike that the original melody was hardly recognizable. Nonetheless, the chant represented the authority of the church. And respect for the church was so great that for centuries most polyphonic music was created by placing new melodic lines against known chants.

The School of Notre Dame: Measured Rhythm

Middle Ages

After 1150, Paris—the intellectual and artistic capital of Europe—became the center of polyphonic music. The University of Paris attracted leading scholars, and the Cathedral of Notre Dame (begun in 1163) was the supreme monument of Gothic architecture. Two successive choirmasters of Notre Dame, Leonin and Perotin, are the first notable composers known by name. They and their followers are referred to as the "School of Notre Dame."

From about 1170 to 1200, Notre Dame composers developed rhythmic innovations. Earlier polyphonic music was probably performed in the free, unmeasured rhythms of Gregorian chant. But the music of Leonin and Perotin used *measured rhythm,* with definite time values and a clearly defined meter. For the first time in music history, notation indicated precise rhythms as well as pitches. At first the new notation was limited to only certain rhythmic patterns, and the beat had to be subdivided into threes, the symbol of the Trinity. Despite these limitations, much fine polyphonic music was composed during the late twelfth and thirteenth centuries.

Modern listeners sometimes find medieval polyphony hollow and thin, probably because it has relatively few triads, which in later periods became the basic consonant chords. The triad contains two intervals of a third; medieval music theorists considered this interval a dissonance. (An interval of a third separates *do* and *mi,* and *mi* and *sol.*) But as the Middle Ages advanced, triads and thirds were used more often, and polyphonic music gradually became fuller and richer by our standards. As an example of Notre Dame polyphony, we'll listen to *Alleluya Nativitas,* by Perotin.

Alleluya Nativitas (1200?), by Perotin

Perotin (late twelfth to early thirteenth century) was the first known composer to write polyphonic music with more than two voices. *Alleluya Nativitas,* an organum in three voices, is based on a Gregorian alleluia melody that Perotin placed in the lowest voice.

A chant that is used as the basis for polyphony is known as a **cantus firmus** ("fixed melody"). Above the *cantus firmus,* or preexisting melody, Perotin wrote two additional lines that move much more quickly. As many as sixty-six tones of the upper voices are sung against one long sustained tone of the chant. But only three chant tones—the first, second, and last—are treated in this dronelike way. In the middle of the piece, the chant tones are speeded up so that only about three tones are sung above each chant tone. (This speeding up was a practical necessity, since a chant sung entirely in long notes seems endless, and church services were already long enough!)

The top voices of *Alleluya Nativitas* have a clearly defined meter, which we would notate today as a fast $\frac{6}{8}$ (1–2–3–4–5–6). They relentlessly repeat rhythmic

The School of Notre Dame

95

patterns: long-short-long, long-short-long. The rhythmic contrast between bottom and top voices is typical of medieval polyphony. The narrow range of the three voices is also characteristic; they are never more than an octave apart. When sung together, the tones of the different parts produce chords that have a hollow ring. As the three voices of *Alleluya Nativitas* resounded under the vaulted ceilings of Notre Dame, they must have seemed like a cathedral of tones.

5 | FOURTEENTH-CENTURY MUSIC: THE "NEW ART" IN FRANCE AND ITALY

The fourteenth century, an age of disintegration, suffered through the Hundred Years' War (1337–1453) and the Black Death—a bubonic plague that destroyed one-fourth of Europe's population around 1350. Both the feudal system and the authority of the church had been weakened by this time. From 1378 to 1417, two rival popes claimed authority, and at one time there were three. Even devout Christians were confused. Literature of the time, such as Chaucer's *Canterbury Tales* (1387–1400) and Boccaccio's *Decameron* (after 1348), stressed graphic realism and earthy sensuality, rather than virtue and heavenly reward.

Given this atmosphere, it's not surprising that secular music became more important than sacred in the fourteenth century. Composers wrote polyphonic music that was *not* based upon Gregorian chants, including drinking songs and pieces in which bird calls, dog barks, and hunting shouts were imitated.

By the early fourteenth century, a new system of music notation had evolved, and a composer could specify almost any rhythmic pattern. Now beats could be subdivided into two as well as three. Syncopation—rarely used earlier—became an important rhythmic practice. Changes in musical style in the fourteenth century were so profound that music theorists referred to French and Italian music as the "new art" (*ars nova*, in Latin). As examples of fourteenth-century music we'll study an Italian song about hunting, and a love song and Mass by the leading French composer of the time.

Tosto che ll'alba ("As soon as the dawn"; Fourteenth Century), by Gherardello da Firenze

Tosto che ll'alba by Gherardello da Firenze (?–1363?) is a musical depiction of a deer hunt, an aristocratic pastime in fourteenth-century Italy. The text describes the hunter awakening, the calling out of the dogs, and the pursuit and capture of the deer. The music consists of a supporting part—probably for an instrument—and two lively vocal lines which sometimes suggest shouts and hunting-horn fanfares. The two voices are in strict imitation throughout as they play "follow the leader" with exactly the same melody. A composition like *Tosto che ll'alba* is appropriately called a *caccia,* which is Italian for "hunt" or "chase." We must emphasize that apart from the *caccia* (and its French counterpart, the *chace*), imitation was only rarely used in fourteenth-century music. In this piece, the imitation may be a bit difficult to spot on first hearing because it takes a while for the second voice to join the first. It's helpful to listen for exclamations like "Aiò! Aiò!" and for the vocal "horn calls" toward the end of the piece.

Tosto che ll'alba del bel giorno appare	As soon as the dawn of a fine day appears
Isveglia (gl)i cacciator.—Su, ch'egli è tempo!—	It awakens the hunters. "Get up! It is time!"
—Alletta (gl)i can!—Tè, Viola! tè, Primera!—	"Rouse the dogs!" "Up, Viola! Up, Primera!"
—Sus' alto al monte co' buon cani a mano	"Up to the mountain now, with the good dogs on their leashes,
E gli bracheti al piano,	And the hounds down on the plain,
Et nella piaggia ad ordine ciascuno!—	And on the side of the mountain every one in his place, in good order!"
—I' vegio sentir uno	"I see that one
De' nostri miglior brachi.—	Of our best hounds
—Star' avisato.—	Is on the alert.
—Bussate d'ogni lato	Watch out!
Ciascun le machie, che Quaglina suona!—	Beat the bushes on every side; The Horn is sounding!
—Aiò, aiò! a te la cerbia vene!	Hey, hey! The deer is coming your way!
Carbon l'à pres' e in bocca la tene!—	Carbon has caught it in his mouth and is holding it!"
Del monte que' che v' era su gridava:	The man who was up on the mountain called out:
—All' altra! all' altra!—e suo corno sonava.	"Now to the other deer!" And he blew his horn.

Guillaume de Machaut

The leading composer of fourteenth-century France was Guillaume de Machaut (about 1300–1377), famous as both musician and poet. Born in the French province of Champagne, he studied theology and took holy orders. Though a priest, Machaut spent most of his life as a court official for various royal families. In 1323, he became secretary to John, King of Bohemia, whom he accompanied on trips and military campaigns throughout Europe. After the king died in battle, Machaut served the royal family of France. And in later years he lived mainly in Reims as an important church official.

Guillaume de Machaut

97

Machaut traveled to many courts and presented beautifully decorated copies of his music to noble patrons. These copies make Machaut the first great composer whose works have survived. The decline of the church in the fourteenth century is reflected by Machaut's output, which consists mainly of love songs for one or two voices and instrumental accompaniment. We'll consider, first, one of his secular songs and then the Notre Dame Mass, the best-known composition of the fourteenth century.

Je puis trop bien ("I Can All Too Well"; Fourteenth Century)

Machaut wrote both the music and the poetry for this courtly love song about a hard-hearted beauty. A tender vocal melody stands out above two instrumental parts that move in longer time values. The long, subtly balanced vocal phrases sometimes contain many tones sung on one syllable. Typically, the accompanying instruments are not specified.

Je puis trop bien is a **ballade,** a French poetic and musical form that was introduced by the troubadours. It may be outlined A A′ B. The intimate, almost sentimental mood of the music re-creates the vanished world of chivalry.

Je puis trop bien ma dame comparer	I can all too well compare my lady	A
A l'ymage que fist Pymalion.	To the image which Pygmalion made.	
D'yvoire fu, tant belle et si sans per	It was of ivory, so beautiful, without peer,	A′
Que plus l'ama que Medee Jazon.	That he loved it more than Jason did Medea.	
Li folz toudis la prioit,	Out of his senses, he prayed to it unceasingly,	B
Mais l'ymage riens ne li respondoit.	But the image answered him not.	
Einssi me fait celle qui mon cuer font,	Thus does she treat me who makes my heart melt,	
Qu'ades la pri et riens ne me respont.	For I pray her ever, and she answers me not.	

The Notre Dame Mass (Mid-fourteenth Century)

One of the finest compositions known from the Middle Ages, Machaut's Notre Dame Mass is of great historical importance: It is the first polyphonic treatment of the Mass Ordinary by a known composer.

The **Mass Ordinary** consists of texts that remain the same from day to day throughout most of the church year. The five sung prayers of the Ordinary are the Kyrie, Gloria, Credo, Sanctus, and Agnus Dei. Starting in the fourteenth century, these five texts have often been set to polyphonic music and have inspired some of the greatest choral works. In each age, composers have responded to the Mass in their own particular style. This thousand-year tradition of the Mass gives invaluable insight into the long span of music and its changing styles.

The Notre Dame Mass is written for four voices, some of which were probably performed or doubled by instruments. How Machaut wanted his Mass performed and which instruments were used to support the voices are unknown. We also do not know when or why the Mass was composed. Scholars once thought it was written for the coronation of Charles V in 1364; it is now believed to have been composed for performance in the cathedral of Notre Dame at Reims, France, sometime after 1337. We'll examine the Kyrie of the Mass as an example of fourteenth-century polyphony.

Machaut's music for the Kyrie—a prayer for mercy—is solemn and elaborate. *Side 1, band 3* It is in triple meter. Complex rhythmic patterns contribute to the Kyrie's intensity. The two upper parts are rhythmically active and contain syncopation, a characteristic of fourteenth-century music. The two lower parts move in longer notes and play a supporting role.

The harmonies of the Kyrie include stark dissonances, hollow-sounding chords, and full triads. The Kyrie sounds fuller than Perotin's *Alleluya Nativitas,* which we studied as an example of earlier medieval polyphony. Here there are four parts rather than three, and the total range of pitch is wider.

The Kyrie is based on a Gregorian chant which Machaut furnished with new rhythmic patterns and placed in the tenor, one of the two lower parts. Since it is rhythmically altered and within a polyphonic web, the chant *cantus firmus* is more a musical framework than a tune to be recognized.

Like the chant melody on which it is based, the Kyrie is composed of three sections which are divided into three subsections. This division into three is thought to symbolize the Trinity. In Machaut's time, music was meant to appeal as much to the mind as to the ear. In our recording, polyphonic subsections alternate with monophonic subsections in which only the original chant melody is sung. The performance may be outlined as follows:

Kyrie (A)	Christe (B)	Kyrie (C)
a–chant–a	chant–b–chant	c–chant–c′

The monophonic texture, unmeasured rhythm, and purely vocal sound of the Gregorian chant contrast with the polyphonic texture, triple meter, and combined vocal and instrumental sound of Machaut's music.

Kyrie eleison. (three times)	Lord, have mercy upon us.
Christe eleison. (three times)	Christ, have mercy upon us.
Kyrie eleison. (three times)	Lord, have mercy upon us.

Basic Terms

Gregorian chant	cantus firmus
church modes	ballade
organum	Mass Ordinary

 Basic Terms

99

THE RENAISSANCE

1 Music in the Renaissance
  (1450–1600)

2 Sacred Music in the
  Renaissance

3 Secular Music in the
  Renaissance

During the Renaissance music was an important leisure
activity; every educated person was expected to play an
instrument and read notation. This painting shows a lute
player accompanying himself and two other singers
(National Gallery, London).

1 | MUSIC IN THE RENAISSANCE (1450–1600)

The fifteenth and sixteenth centuries in Europe have come to be known as the Renaissance. People then spoke of a "rebirth," or "renaissance," of human creativity. It was a period of exploration and adventure—consider the voyages of Christopher Columbus (1492), Vasco da Gama (1498), and Ferdinand Magellan (1519–1522). The Renaissance was an age of curiosity and individualism, too, as can be seen in the remarkable life of Leonardo da Vinci (1452–1519), great painter, sculptor, architect, engineer, scientist, and a fine musician as well.

During the Renaissance the dominant intellectual movement, called *humanism*, focused on human life and its accomplishments rather than on an afterlife in heaven or hell. Though devout Christians, the humanists were captivated by the pagan cultures of ancient Greece and Rome. They became intoxicated by the beauty of ancient languages—Greek and Latin—and by the literature of antiquity. Humanism strongly influenced art throughout the Renaissance. Sculptors and painters once again depicted the nude human body, a favorite theme of antiquity, but a subject of shame and concealment during the Middle Ages. They no longer treated the Madonna as a childlike, unearthly creature; they showed her as a beautiful young woman.

The Catholic Church was far less powerful in the Renaissance than during the Middle Ages, for the unity of Christendom was exploded by the Protestant Reformation led by Martin Luther (1483–1546). No longer did the Church monopolize learning. Aristocrats and the upper middle class now considered education a status symbol, and they hired scholars to teach their children. The invention of printing with movable type (around 1450) accelerated the spread of learning. Before 1450, books were rare and extremely expensive, because they were copied entirely by hand. But by 1500, 15 to 20 million copies of 40,000 editions had been printed in Europe.

Music and Renaissance Society

The Renaissance in music occurred between 1450 and 1600. (Some historians place the beginning of the Renaissance as early as 1400.) As with the other arts, musical horizons were expanded greatly. The invention of printing widened the circulation of music, too, and the number of composers and performers increased.

In keeping with the Renaissance ideal of the "universal man," every educated person was expected to be trained in music. "I am not pleased with the courtier if he be not also a musician," Castiglione wrote in *The Book of the Courtier* (1528). Shakespeare's stage directions call for music over three hundred times, and the plays are full of beautiful tributes to the art:

The
Renaissance

102

Renaissance sculptors and painters once again depicted the nude human body, a subject of shame and concealment during the Middle Ages. Right—Michelangelo's *David;* above—*The Birth of Venus* by Botticelli (Omikron; Alinari/ Editorial Photocolor Archives).

The man that hath no music in himself,
Nor is not mov'd with concord of sweet sounds,
Is fit for treasons, stratagems and spoils.

The Merchant of Venice

As in the past, musicians worked in churches, courts, and towns. Church choirs grew in size. (The Papal Choir in Rome increased from ten singers in 1442 to twenty-four in 1483.) Although polyphonic church music in the Middle Ages was usually sung by several soloists, during the Renaissance it was performed by an entire (male) choir. The church remained an important patron of music, but musical activity gradually shifted to the courts. Kings, princes, and dukes competed for the finest composers. The number of court musicians ranged from ten to sixty and included singers as well as instrumentalists. A court music director composed secular pieces to entertain the nobility and sacred works for the court chapel. Noblemen often brought along their musicians when traveling from one castle to another.

 Music and Renaissance Society

103

During the Renaissance the Madonna was no longer
treated as a childlike, unearthly creature. A follower of Fra
Filippo Lippi (1406–1459) painted her as a beautiful young
woman in *The Madonna and Child with Two Angels* (The
Metropolitan Museum of Art, H. O. Havemeyer Collection).

Renaissance town musicians played for civic processions, weddings, and religious services. In general, musicians enjoyed higher status and pay than ever before. Composers no longer were happy to remain unknown; like other artists, they sought credit for their work.

Many leading Renaissance composers came from the Netherlands (Flanders), an area which now includes parts of Holland, Belgium, and northern France. These Flemish composers were regarded highly and held important positions throughout Europe, but especially in Italy, which became the leading music center in the sixteenth century. Other countries with vibrant musical lives in the Renaissance were Germany, England, and Spain.

Words and Music

In the Renaissance, as in the Middle Ages, vocal music was more important than instrumental music. The humanistic interest in language influenced vocal music, creating a close relationship between words and music. Renaissance composers wrote music to enhance the meaning and emotion of the text. "When one of the words expresses weeping, pain, heartbreak, sighs, tears and other similar things, let the harmony be full of sadness," wrote Zarlino, a leading music theorist of the sixteenth century. By contrast, medieval composers had been relatively uninterested in expressing the emotions of a text.

Renaissance composers often used **word-painting,** a musical representation of specific poetic images. For example, the words *descending from heaven* might be set to a descending melodic line, and *running* might be heard with a series of rapid notes. Yet, despite this emphasis on capturing the emotion and imagery of a text, Renaissance music may seem calm and restrained to us. While there *is* a wide range of emotion in Renaissance music, it usually is expressed in a moderate, balanced way, with *no* extreme contrasts of dynamics, tone color, and rhythm.

Renaissance Texture

The texture of Renaissance music is chiefly polyphonic. A typical choral piece has four, five, or six voice parts of nearly equal melodic interest. Imitation among the voices is common: Each presents the same melodic idea in turn, as in a round. Homophonic texture, with successions of chords, is also used, especially in light music, like dances. The texture may vary within a piece to provide contrast and bring out aspects of the text as it develops.

Renaissance music sounds more full than medieval music. The bass register is used for the first time, expanding the pitch range to more than four octaves. With this new emphasis on the bass line came richer harmony. Composers began to think in terms of chords as well as of individual melodic lines. Now all the melodic lines were conceived at the same time. Earlier, during the Middle Ages, a complete melodic line was conceived, then another was added on top of it, with

 Renaissance Texture

105

relatively little attention paid to the total harmonic effect. Renaissance music sounds mild and relaxed because stable, consonant chords are favored; triads occur often, while dissonances are played down.

Renaissance choral music did not need instrumental accompaniment. For this reason, the period is sometimes called the "golden age" of *a cappella* (unaccompanied) choral music. Even so, instruments were often combined with voices. They might duplicate the vocal lines to reinforce the sound, or they might take the part of a missing singer. But parts written exclusively for instruments are rarely found in Renaissance choral music.

Renaissance Rhythm and Melody

In Renaissance music, rhythm is more a gentle flow than a sharply defined beat. This is because each melodic line has great rhythmic independence: When one singer is at the beginning of his melodic phrase, the others may already be in the middle of theirs. This technique makes singing Renaissance music both a pleasure and a challenge, for each singer must maintain an individual rhythm. But pitch patterns in Renaissance melodies are easy to sing. The melody usually moves along a scale with few large leaps.

2 | SACRED MUSIC IN THE RENAISSANCE

Two main forms of sacred Renaissance music are the *motet* and the *Mass*. They are alike in style, but the Mass is a longer composition. The Renaissance **motet** is a polyphonic choral work set to a sacred Latin text. The Renaissance **Mass** is a polyphonic choral composition made up of five sections: Kyrie, Gloria, Credo, Sanctus, and Agnus Dei.

Josquin des Prez and the Renaissance Motet

Josquin des Prez (about 1440–1521), a contemporary of Leonardo da Vinci and Christopher Columbus, was a master of Renaissance music. Like many Flemish composers, his career was international. Born in the province of Hainaut—today part of Belgium—Josquin spent much of his life in Italy, serving in dukes' private chapels and in the Papal Choir at Rome. In later years, he worked for Louis XII of France and held several church posts in his native land.

Josquin's compositions, which include Masses, motets, and secular vocal pieces, strongly influenced composers and were praised enthusiastically by music lovers. Martin Luther, for example, remarked: "God has His Gospel preached also through the medium of music; this may be seen from the compositions of Josquin, all of whose works are cheerful, gentle, mild, and lovely; they flow and move along and are neither forced nor coerced and bound by rigid and stringent rules, but, on the contrary, are like the song of the finch."

Ave Maria . . . virgo serena ("Hail, Mary"; 1520)[1]   *Side 1, band 4*

Josquin's four-voice motet *Ave Maria* is an outstanding Renaissance choral work. This Latin prayer to the Virgin is set to delicate and serene music. The opening uses polyphonic imitation, a technique typical of the period.

The short melodic phrase on *Ave Maria* is presented by the soprano voice and then imitated in turn by the alto, tenor, and bass. The next two words, *gratia plena* ("full of grace"), have a different melody which also is passed from voice to voice. Notice that each voice enters while the preceding one is in the middle of its melody. This overlapping creates a feeling of continuous flow. Josquin adapted the melody for the opening phrases from a Gregorian chant, but the rest of the motet was not based on a chant melody.

[1]Because Josquin composed other works entitled *Ave Maria*, this motet is identified by the words *virgo serena*, which come later in the text.

The
Renaissance
Motet

107

Josquin skillfully varies the texture of this motet; two, three, or four voices are heard at one time. In addition to the imitation among individual voices, there is imitation between pairs of voices: Duets between the high voices are imitated by the two lower parts. Sometimes the texture almost becomes homophonic, as at the words *Ave, vera virginitas*. Here, also, is a change from duple to triple meter, and the tempo momentarily becomes more animated. But soon the music returns to duple meter and a more peaceful mood. *Ave Maria* ends with slow chords that express Josquin's personal plea to the Virgin, "O Mother of God, remember me. Amen."

Ave Maria	Hail Mary,	Each soprano phrase imitated in turn by alto, tenor, and bass. Duple meter.
gratia plena	full of grace,	
dominus tecum,	the Lord is with thee,	
virgo serena.	serene Virgin.	
Ave, cuius conceptio,	Hail, whose conception,	High duet imitated by three lower voices
solemni plena gaudio,	full of great jubilation,	All four voices. Increased rhythmic animation reflects "new joy."
coelestia terrestria	fills Heaven and Earth	
nova replet laetitia.	with new joy.	
Ave, cuius nativitas	Hail, whose birth	High duet imitated by low duet.
nostra fuit solemnitas,	brought us joy,	
ut lucifer lux oriens	as Lucifer, the morning star,	Soprano phrase imitated by alto, tenor, and bass.
verum solem praeveniens.	went before the true sun.	
Ave, pia humilitas,	Hail, pious humility,	High duet imitated by low duet.
sine viro fecunditas,	fruitful without a man,	
cuius annuntiatio	whose Annunciation	High duet.
nostra fuit salvatio.	brought us salvation.	Low duet.
Ave, vera virginitas,	Hail, true virginity,	Triple meter.
immaculata castitas,	immaculate chastity,	
cuius purificatio	whose purification	
nostra fuit purgatio.	brought our cleansing.	
Ave, praeclara omnibus	Hail, glorious one	Duple meter, high duets imitated by lower voices.
angelicis virtutibus,	in all angelic virtues,	
cuius assumptio	whose Assumption	
nostra glorificatio.	was our glorification.	Brief pause.
O mater Dei,	O Mother of God,	Sustained chords.
memento mei. Amen.	remember me. Amen.	

Palestrina and the Renaissance Mass

During the sixteenth century, Italian composers attained the earlier excellence of such Flemish musicians as Josquin des Prez. Among the leading Italian Renaissance composers was Giovanni Pierluigi da Palestrina (about 1525–1594), who devoted himself to music for the Catholic Church. His career thus centered in Rome, where he held important Church positions, including music director for St. Peter's.

Palestrina's music includes 104 Masses and some 450 other sacred works; it is best understood against the background of the Counter-Reformation. During the early 1500s, the Catholic Church was challenged and questioned by the Protestants and, as a result, sought to correct abuses and malpractices within its structure, as well as to counter the move toward Protestantism. This need to strengthen the Church led to the founding of the Jesuit Order (1540) and the convening of the Council of Trent (1545–1563), which considered questions of dogma and organization.

During its deliberations the Council discussed Church music, which many felt had lost its purity. Years before this Council, the great scholar Desiderius Erasmus (about 1466–1536) had complained: "We have introduced an artificial and theatrical music into the church, a bawling and agitation of various voices, such as I believe had never been heard in the theaters of the Greeks and Romans. . . . Amorous and lascivious melodies are heard such as elsewhere accompany only the dances of courtesans and clowns." At the Council sessions, Church music was attacked because it used secular tunes, noisy instruments, and theatrical singing. Some complained that complicated polyphony made it impossible to understand the sacred texts; they wanted only monophonic music—Gregorian chant—for the Mass. The Council finally decreed that Church music should be composed not "to give empty pleasure to the ear," but to inspire religious contemplation.

The restraint and serenity of Palestrina's works reflect this emphasis on a more spiritual music. For centuries, Church authorities have regarded his Masses as models of church music because of their calmness and "other-wordly" quality. And even today the technical perfection of his style is a model for students of counterpoint.

Pope Marcellus Mass (1562–1563)

For a long time, the Pope Marcellus Mass was thought to have convinced the Council of Trent that polyphonic Masses should be kept in Catholic worship. While we now know that Palestrina's most famous Mass did *not* play this role, it does reflect the Council's desire for a clear projection of the sacred text. The Mass is dedicated to Pope Marcellus II, who briefly reigned in 1555 while Palestrina was a singer in the Papal Choir.

The Pope Marcellus Mass is written for an *a cappella* choir of six voice parts: soprano, alto, two tenors, and two basses. We'll focus on the first two sections of the Mass, the Kyrie and the Gloria; the Credo, Sanctus, and Agnus Dei, which follow, are similar in style.

The Kyrie has a rich polyphonic texture. Its six voice parts constantly imitate each other, yet blend beautifully. This music sounds fuller than Josquin's *Ave Maria*, in part because six voices are used rather than four. Palestrina's elegantly curved melodies summon the spirit of Gregorian chant. They flow smoothly and can be sung easily. Upward leaps are balanced at once by downward steps, as in the opening melody:

 The Renaissance Mass

Soprano

Ky - rie e - lei - - - - - son, ·

The Kyrie of the Pope Marcellus Mass is written in three sections:

1. *Kyrie eleison.*   Lord, have mercy upon us.
2. *Christe eleison.*   Christ, have mercy upon us.
3. *Kyrie eleison.*   Lord, have mercy upon us.

This text is short, and words are repeated with different melodic lines to express calm supplication. The rhythm flows continuously to the end of each section, when all voices come together on sustained chords. Each of the three sections begins in a thin texture with only some of the voices sounding, but as the other voices enter, the music becomes increasingly full and rich.

The Gloria of the Mass has a much longer text than the Kyrie, and so Palestrina does not repeat words. Here the texture is mostly homophonic, and the voices usually sing the same words at the same time. This projects the text clearly and contrasts with the imitative polyphony of the Kyrie. Palestrina brings variety to the Gloria through subtle changes in the number of parts heard at one time and through shifts between higher and lower voices. The Gloria's opening words are sung as Gregorian chant by a priest; then the choir enters with Palestrina's music. The Gloria is divided into two sections. Here is the text for the opening section:

Gloria in excelsis Deo. Et in terra pax hominibus bonae voluntatis.	Glory to God in the highest and on earth peace to men of good will.
Laudamus te, benedicimus te, adoramus te, glorificamus te.	We praise Thee; we bless Thee; we adore Thee; we glorify Thee.
Gratias agimus tibi propter magnam gloriam tuam.	We give thanks to Thee for Thy great glory.
Domine Deus, rex coelestis,	O Lord God, heavenly King,
Deus Pater omnipotens.	God the Father almighty.
Domine Fili unigenite,	O Lord the only begotten Son,
Jesu Christe, Domine Deus,	Jesus Christ, O Lord God,
Agnus Dei, Filius Patris.	Lamb of God, Son of the Father.

Renaissance

3 | SECULAR MUSIC IN THE RENAISSANCE

Vocal Music

The Renaissance

During the Renaissance, secular vocal music became increasingly popular. Throughout Europe music was set to poems in various languages, including

The development of music printing during the Renaissance helped spread secular music, and thousands of song collections became available (The Metropolitan Museum of Art, Harris Brisbane Dick Fund, 1953).

Italian, French, Spanish, German, Dutch, and English. The development of music printing helped spread secular music, and thousands of song collections became available. Music was an important leisure activity; every educated person was expected to play an instrument and read notation. The Elizabethan composer Thomas Morley (1557–1603) vividly describes the embarrassment of being unable to participate in after-dinner music making: "But supper being ended, and Musicke bookes (according to the custome) being brought to the tables, the mistresse of the house presented me with a part, earnestly requesting me to sing. But when, after many excuses, I protested unfainedly that I could not: every one began to wonder. Yea, some whispered to others, demanding how I was brought up."

Renaissance secular music was written for groups of solo voices and for solo voice with the accompaniment of one or more instruments. Word-painting—musical illustration of a text—was common. Composers delighted in imitating natural sounds such as bird calls and street cries. In a famous piece entitled *La Guerre* ("The War"), the Frenchman Clément Janequin (about 1485–1560) vividly imitated battle noises, drumbeats, and fanfares. Secular music contained more rapid shifts of mood than sacred music did. As Morley advised the composer, "You must in your music be wavering like the wind, sometimes wanton, sometimes drooping, sometimes grave and staid . . . and the more variety you show the better shall you please."

 Vocal Music

The Renaissance Madrigal

An important kind of secular vocal music during the Renaissance was the **madrigal,** a piece for several solo voices set to a short poem, usually about love. A madrigal, like a motet, combines homophonic and polyphonic textures. But it more often uses word-painting and unusual harmonies.

The Renaissance madrigal began in Italy around 1520, along with a creative explosion in Italian poetry. Madrigals were published by the thousands in sixteenth-century Italy, where they were sung by cultivated aristocrats. Among the many Italian madrigalists were Luca Marenzio (1553–1599) and Carlo Gesualdo (about 1560–1613), infamous Prince of Venosa who had his wife and her lover murdered after finding them in bed.

In 1588—the year of the Spanish Armada—a volume of translated Italian madrigals was published in London. This triggered a spurt of madrigal writing by English composers, and for about thirty years there was a steady flow of English madrigals and other secular vocal music. The time of Queen Elizabeth (1533–1603) and William Shakespeare (1564–1616) was as much a golden age in English music as it was in literature. The impetus for both arts arose in Italy. But the English madrigal became lighter and more humorous than its Italian model, and its melody and harmony were simpler.

Side 1, band 6

"As Vesta Was Descending" (1601), by Thomas Weelkes

Among the finest English madrigalists was Thomas Weelkes (about 1575–1623), an organist and church composer. Weelkes's "As Vesta Was Descending" comes from *The Triumphes of Oriana* (1601), an anthology of English madrigals written to honor Queen Elizabeth, who often was called "Oriana." The text of this six-voice madrigal pictures Vesta (Roman goddess of the hearth) coming down a hill with her attendants, "Diana's darlings." (Diana was the Roman goddess of chastity, hunting, and the moon.) At the same time, the "maiden queen," Oriana (Elizabeth), is climbing the hill with her shepherd gallants. Vesta's attendants desert her and race down the hill to join Oriana.

"As Vesta Was Descending" has the light mood typical of English madrigals. Word-painting is plentiful. For example, the word *descending* is sung to downward scales, and *ascending* to upward ones.

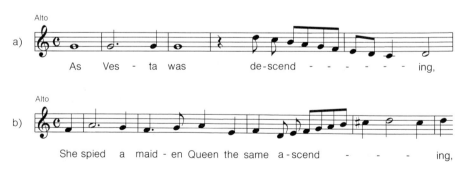

When Vesta's attendants run down the hill "first *two* by *two*, then *three* by *three* together, leaving their goddess all *alone*," we hear first *two* voices then *three* voices, and finally a *solo* voice. In the extended concluding section, "*Long* live fair Oriana," a joyous phrase is imitated among the voices. And in the bass this phrase is sung in long notes, with the longest note on the word *long*.

As Vesta was from Latmos hill descending,	Descending scales.
she spied a maiden queen the same ascending,	Ascending scales.
attended on by all the shepherds swain,	
to whom Diana's darlings	
came running down amain.	Rapid descending figures.
First two by two,	Two voices.
then three by three together,	Three voices; all voices.
leaving their goddess all alone, hasted thither,	Solo voice.
and mingling with the shepherds of her train	
with mirthful tunes her presence entertain.	
Then sang the shepherds and nymphs of Diana,	
Long live fair Oriana!	Brief joyful phrase imitated among voices; long notes in bass.

The Renaissance Lute Song

A simpler type of secular music than the madrigal was the song for solo voice and lute. The lute is a plucked-string instrument with a body shaped like half a pear. Its versatility made the lute the most popular instrument in the Renaissance home. It could play solos or accompaniments, chords, melodies, rapid scales, and even polyphonic music. In England, the lute song—called a lute "ayre"—was widely cultivated from the 1590s to about 1620. In contrast to much Renaissance music, a lute song was mostly homophonic in texture: The voice sang the melody, and the lute provided chordal support—an arrangement still practiced by folk singers today.

"It Was a Lover and His Lass" (1600), by Thomas Morley

Perhaps the most popular of all lute songs, "It Was a Lover and His Lass" was written by Thomas Morley (1557–1603), an English composer best known for madrigals. Lyrics from Shakespeare's *As You Like It* (act V, scene 3) provided the words for Morley's song. His lilting, tuneful melody evokes the delight of love and springtime that Shakespeare described in the poem. Each of the poem's four stanzas is set to the same music, which has a clear beat and the swing of an English folk song or dance. The vocal line spins out of short melodic patterns that are repeated on different pitches. Listen for the rollicking scale figures on *hey*

The Renaissance Lute Song

113

ding-a-ding-a-ding. "It Was a Lover and His Lass" was originally printed so that a singer could accompany the song on a lute; and there also was an optional part for bass viol, a bowed string instrument of the Renaissance.

It was a lover and his lass,
With a hey, with a ho, and a hey nonie no,
That o'er the green cornfields did pass
In Springtime, the only pretty ring time,
When birds do sing, hey ding-a-ding-a-ding.
Sweet lovers love the Spring.

Between the acres of the rye,
With a hey, with a ho, and hey nonie no,
These pretty country fools would lie
In Springtime, the only pretty ring time,
When birds do sing, hey ding-a-ding-a-ding.
Sweet lovers love the Spring.

This carol they began that hour,
With a hey, with a ho, and a hey nonie no,
How that a life was but a flower
In Springtime, the only pretty ring time,
When birds do sing, hey ding-a-ding-a-ding.
Sweet lovers love the Spring.

Then pretty lovers take the time,
With a hey, with a ho, and a hey nonie no,
For love is crowned with the prime
In Springtime, the only pretty ring time,
When birds do sing, hey ding-a-ding-a-ding.
Sweet lovers love the Spring.

Instrumental Music

Though subordinate to vocal music, instrumental music did become more important during the Renaissance. Traditionally instrumentalists accompanied voices or played music intended for singing. Even in the early 1500s instrumental music was largely adapted from vocal music. Instrumental groups performed polyphonic vocal pieces which were often published with the indication, "to be sung or played." Soloists used the lute, harpsichord, or organ to play simple arrangements of vocal works.

During the sixteenth century, however, instrumental music became increasingly emancipated from vocal models. More music was written specifically for instruments. Renaissance composers began to exploit the particular capacities of the lute or organ when writing instrumental solos. They developed purely instrumental forms such as theme and variations. Much of this instrumental music was intended for dancing, a popular Renaissance entertainment. Dance music was performed by instrumental groups or by soloists like harpsichordists and lutenists. A wealth of dance music published during the sixteenth century has come down to us.

The many instruments used in the Renaissance produced softer, less brilliant sounds than we hear today; most came in families of from three to eight instruments, ranging from soprano to bass. Recorders (instruments related to the flute) and viols (bowed string instruments) were among the most important Renaissance instruments. Often several members of the same instrumental family were played together, but Renaissance composers did not specify the instruments wanted. A single work might be performed by recorders, viols, or several different instruments, depending on what was available. Today's standardized orchestra did not exist. Large courts might employ, say, thirty instrumentalists of all types. And on state occasions such as a royal wedding, guests might be entertained by woodwinds, plucked and bowed strings, and keyboard instruments all playing together.

Ricercar in the Twelfth Mode (Sixteenth Century), by Andrea Gabrieli   *Side 1, band 5*

St. Mark's Cathedral in Venice became a center of instrumental music during the sixteenth century. Colorful and wealthy, it employed many instrumentalists to participate in elaborate musical performances in St. Mark's Square. The Cathedral was noted for two widely separated choir lofts, each with an organ—an architectural feature that inspired "stereophonic music" for several choruses and groups of instruments.

Andrea Gabrieli (about 1520–1586) was organist at St. Mark's from 1564 until his death. He was a leading composer of both sacred and secular vocal music, and of instrumental music. Gabrieli's Ricercar in the Twelfth Mode was written for four unspecified instruments (soprano, alto, tenor, and bass). In our recording, the Ricercar is performed by a group of recorders ranging from soprano to bass. (A **ricercar** is a polyphonic instrumental composition employing imitation. That this one is "in the Twelfth Mode" means that it is based on a scale corresponding to C major.)

This short, lively piece is composed of several contrasting sections: A B CC A. Gabrieli unifies the *Ricercar* by bringing back the opening material (A) after the two middle sections. Most of section C is in triple meter and contrasts with the duple meter of sections A and B. The work features imitation among the individual instruments and rapid echoes between the two lower and upper parts. Though relatively simple, the piece is an early step toward more elaborate instrumental music that developed in the Baroque period.

Basic Terms

word-painting   madrigal
motet   ricercar
Mass

 Basic Terms

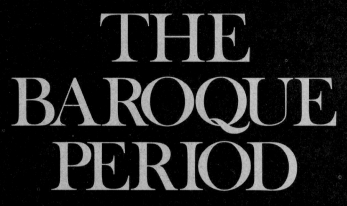

THE BAROQUE PERIOD

1 Baroque Music (1600–1750)

2 Music in Baroque Society

3 The Concerto Grosso and Ritornello Form

4 The Fugue

5 The Elements of Opera

6 Opera in the Baroque Era

7 Claudio Monteverdi

8 Henry Purcell

9 The Baroque Sonata

10 Arcangelo Corelli

11 Antonio Vivaldi

12 Johann Sebastian Bach

13 The Baroque Suite

14 The Chorale and the Church Cantata

15 The Oratorio

16 George Frideric Handel

Bernini's *Throne of St. Peter* fills space with action and movement (Anderson / Art Reference Bureau).

1 BAROQUE MUSIC (1600–1750)

Though the word *baroque* has at various times meant bizarre, flamboyant, and elaborately ornamented, modern historians use it simply to indicate a particular style in the arts. An oversimplified, but useful, characterization of Baroque style is that it fills space—canvas, stone, or sound—with action and movement. Painters, sculptors, and architects became interested in forming a total illusion, like a stage setting. Artists such as Bernini, Rubens, and Rembrandt exploited their materials to expand the potentials of color, detail, ornament, and depth; they wanted to create totally structured worlds.

Such a style was very well suited to the wishes of the Baroque aristocracy, who also thought in terms of completely integrated structures. In France, for example, Louis XIV held court in the Palace of Versailles, a magnificent setting that fused Baroque painting, sculpture, and architecture into a symbol of royal wealth and power. The Baroque style was also shaped by the needs of churches, which used the emotional and theatrical qualities of art to make worship more attractive. The middle class, too, influenced the development of the Baroque style. In Holland, for example, prosperous merchants and doctors commissioned realistic depictions of landscapes and scenes from everyday life.

It's also helpful to think of Baroque style against the backdrop of seventeenth-century scientific discovery. Galileo (1564–1642) and Newton (1642–1727) represented a new approach to science based on the union of mathematics and experiment; they discovered mathematical laws governing bodies in motion. Such scientific advances led to new inventions and the gradual improvement of medicine, mining, navigation, and industry during the Baroque era. Baroque art is a complex mixture of rationalism, sensuality, materialism, and spirituality.

In music, the Baroque style flourished during the century and a half from 1600 to 1750. The two giants of Baroque composition were George Frideric Handel and Johann Sebastian Bach. Bach's death in 1750 marks the end of the period. Other Baroque masters—Claudio Monteverdi, Henry Purcell, Arcangelo Corelli, Antonio Vivaldi—were largely forgotten until the twentieth century. But the appearance of long-playing records in the late 1940s spurred a "Baroque revival" that made these long-forgotten musicians familiar names to many music lovers.

The Baroque period has three phrases: early (1600–1640), middle (1640–1680), and late (1680–1750). Though the Baroque music best known today comes from the latest phase, the earliest period was one of the most revolutionary in music history. Monteverdi (1567–1643), for instance, strove to create unprecedented passion and dramatic contrast in his works. In Italy, especially, music was composed for texts conveying extreme emotion, and the text ruled the music. With this stress on drama and text, it is not surprising that Italian composers of the early Baroque created opera—a drama sung to orchestral accompaniment. Their melodic lines imitated the rhythms and inflections of speech.

The Baroque
Period

Peter Paul Rubens, *Henry IV Receiving the Portrait of Maria de' Medici*. Baroque artists exploited their materials to expand the potentials of color, ornament, detail, and depth (Alinari/Art Reference Bureau).

 Baroque Music (1600–1750)

The French Academy of Science by Sebastien LeClerc.
During the Baroque period, there was a new approach to
science based on the union of mathematics and experiment (Omikron).

Early Baroque composers favored homophonic texture over the polyphonic
texture typical of Renaissance music. They felt that words could be projected
more clearly by using just one main melody with a chordal accompaniment. But
note that this new emphasis on homophonic texture characterizes only the *early*
Baroque; by the *late* Baroque period, polyphonic texture returned to favor.

To depict the extreme emotions of their texts, early Baroque composers used
dissonances with a new freedom. Never before were unstable chords so prominent
and emphatic. Contrasts of sound were stressed—one or more solo singers against
a chorus, or voices against instruments. In Renaissance choral music, instruments—if used at all—duplicated a singer's melody. But in the early Baroque,
voices were accompanied with melodic lines designed for instruments.

During the middle phase of the Baroque (1640–1680), the new musical style
spread from Italy to practically every country in Europe. The medieval or church
modes—scales that had governed music for centuries—gradually gave way to
major and minor scales. By about 1680, major or minor scales were the tonal
basis of most compositions. Another feature of the middle Baroque phase was the
new importance of instrumental music. Many compositions were written for
specific instruments, the violin family being most popular.

We will focus mainly on the late Baroque period (1680–1750), which yielded
most of the Baroque music heard today. Many aspects of harmony—including

the emphasis of the dominant chord's attraction to the tonic—arose in this period. During the late Baroque, instrumental music became as important as vocal music for the first time. Early Baroque composers had emphasized homophonic texture; late Baroque composers gloried in polyphony. Let's look more closely at some features of late Baroque style. (From now on the word *Baroque* will pertain to the late Baroque phase.)

Baroque Unity of Mood

A Baroque piece usually expresses one basic mood—what begins joyfully will remain joyful throughout. Emotional states like joy, grief, and agitation were represented. (At the time, these moods were called "affections.") Composers molded a musical language to depict the affections; specific rhythms or melodic patterns were associated with specific moods. This common language gives a family resemblance to much late Baroque music.

The prime exception to this Baroque principle of unity of mood occurs in vocal music. Drastic changes of emotion in a text may inspire corresponding changes in the music. But even in such cases, one mood is maintained at some length before it yields to another.

Baroque Rhythm

Unity of mood in Baroque music is conveyed, first of all, by continuity of rhythm. Rhythmic patterns heard at the beginning of a piece are repeated throughout it. This rhythmic continuity provides a compelling drive and energy—the forward motion is rarely interrupted. The beat in Baroque music is emphasized far more than in most Renaissance music, for example.

Baroque Melody

Baroque melody also creates a feeling of continuity. An opening melody will be heard again and again in the course of a Baroque piece. And even when a melody is presented in varied form, its character tends to remain constant. There is a continuous expanding, unfolding, and unwinding of melody. This sense of directed motion is frequently the result of a melodic sequence, that is, successive repetition of a musical idea at higher or lower pitch levels. Many Baroque melodies sound elaborate and ornamental, and they are not easy to sing or remember. The Baroque melody gives the impression of dynamic expansion rather than of balance and symmetry. A short opening phrase is often followed by a longer phrase with an unbroken flow of rapid notes.

Terraced Dynamics

Paralleling continuity of rhythm and melody in Baroque music is a continuity of dynamic level: the volume tends to stay constant for a stretch of time. When the

 Terraced Dynamics

121

dynamics do shift, it's sudden, as though one had physically stepped from one level to another. This alternation between loud and soft is called **terraced dynamics.** *Gradual* changes of crescendo and descrescendo are *not* prominent features of Baroque music. However, singers and instrumentalists no doubt made some subtle dynamic inflections for expressive purposes.

The main keyboard instruments of the Baroque period were the organ and harpsichord, both well suited for continuity of dynamic level. An organist or harpsichordist could not obtain a crescendo or decrescendo by varying finger pressure, as pianists today can. A third keyboard instrument, the **clavichord,** could make gradual dynamic changes, but only within a narrow range—from about *ppp* to *mp.* Sound was produced by means of brass blades striking the strings. The clavichord usually was not used in large halls, as its tone was too weak. But for home use by amateurs it was ideal; its cost was low and its expressive sound satisfying. It had especially wide popularity in Germany.

Baroque Texture

We've noted that late Baroque music is predominantly polyphonic in texture: two or more melodic lines compete for the listener's attention. Usually, the soprano and bass lines are the most important. Imitation between the various lines or "voices" of the texture is very common. A melodic idea heard in one voice is likely to make an appearance in the other voices as well.

However, not all late Baroque music was polyphonic. A piece may shift in texture, especially in vocal music, where changes of mood in the words demand musical contrast. Also, Baroque composers differed in their treatment of musical texture. Bach inclined toward a consistently polyphonic texture, while Handel used much more contrast between polyphonic and homophonic sections.

Chords and the Basso Continuo (Figured Bass)

Chords became increasingly important during the Baroque period. In earlier times, there was more concern with the beauty of individual melodic lines than with chords formed when the lines were heard together. In a sense, chords were mere by-products of the motion of melodic lines. But in the Baroque period chords became significant in themselves. As composers wrote a melodic line, they thought of chords to mesh with it. Indeed, sometimes they composed a melody to fit a specific chord progression. This interest in chords gave new prominence to the bass part, which served as the foundation of the harmony. The whole musical structure rested on the bass part.

The new emphasis on chords and the bass part resulted in the most characteristic feature of all Baroque music, an accompaniment called the **basso continuo,** or **figured bass.** This is made up of a bass part together with numbers

(figures) which specify the chords to be played above it. The basso continuo is usually played by at least two instruments: an organ or a harpsichord and a low melodic instrument like the cello or bassoon. With the left hand, the organist or harpsichordist plays the bass part, which is also performed by the cello or bassoon. With the right hand, the keyboard player improvises chords or even a melodic line, following the indications of the numbers. These numbers specify only a basic chord, not the exact way in which the chord should be played. Thus, the performer is given a great deal of freedom. (This shorthand system is similar in principle to the chord indications found on modern song sheets, from which jazz pianists improvise.)

The basso continuo offered the advantage of emphasizing the all-important bass part as well as a steady flow of chords. Practically, the use of numbers, rather than chords with all their notes written out, saved time for busy Baroque composers. It also saved paper at a time when it was expensive.

The Baroque Orchestra

During the Baroque period the orchestra evolved into a performing group based on instruments of the violin family. By modern standards the Baroque orchestra was small, consisting of from ten to thirty or forty players. Its instrumental make-up was flexible and could vary from piece to piece. At its nucleus was the basso continuo (harpsichord plus cello, double bass, or bassoon) and upper strings (first and second violins and violas). Use of woodwind, brass, and percussion instruments was variable. To the strings and continuo could be added recorders, flutes, oboes, trumpets, horns, trombones, or timpani. One piece might use only a single flute, while another would call for two oboes, three trumpets, and timpani. Trumpets and timpani joined the orchestra mainly when the music was festive. This flexibility contrasts with the standardized orchestra of later periods, composed of four sections: string, woodwind, brass, and percussion.

The Baroque trumpet (like the early French horn) had no valves but was given rapid, complex melodic lines to play in a high register. Because the instrument was difficult to play and had a traditional association with royalty, the trumpeter was the aristocrat of the Baroque orchestra. When prisoners of war were exchanged, trumpeters were treated like military officers.

Bach, Handel, Vivaldi, and others chose their orchestral instruments with care and obtained beautiful effects from specific tone colors. They loved to experiment with different combinations of instruments. However, in the Baroque period tone color was distinctly subordinate to other musical elements—melody, rhythm, and harmony. Composers frequently rearranged their own or other composers' works for different instruments. A piece for string orchestra might become an organ solo, losing little in the process. Often, one instrument was treated like another. An oboe would play the same melody as the violins, or the flute and trumpet would imitate each other for extended sections of a piece.

The Baroque
Orchestra

123

Words and Music

Like their Renaissance predecessors, Baroque composers used music to represent the meaning of specific words. *Heaven* was set to a high tone, and *hell* to a low one. Rising scales represented upward motion, while descending scales depicted the reverse. Descending chromatic scales were associated with pain and grief. This descriptive musical language was quite standardized: A lament for a lost love might call forth the same descending chromatic scale used to depict suffering in the *Crucifixus* of the Mass.

Baroque composers emphasized words by writing many rapid notes for a single syllable of text. This also displayed a singer's virtuosity. The individual words and phrases are repeated over and over as the music continuously unfolds.

Baroque Forms

We have said that a piece of baroque music—particularly instrumental music—usually has unity of mood. Yet many Baroque compositions include a set of pieces, or movements that contrast. A **movement** is a piece that sounds fairly complete and independent but is part of a larger composition. Usually, each movement has its own themes, comes to a definite end, and is separated from the next movement by a brief pause. Thus, a Baroque composition in three movements may contain contrasts between a fast and energetic opening, a slow and solemn middle, and a conclusion that is quick, light, and humorous.

All the form types described in Elements section 9, "Musical Form," appear in Baroque music. Three-part form (A B A), two-part form (A B), and continuous or undivided form are all common. We'll consider examples of these and other forms in the following sections.

Regardless of form, Baroque music features contrasts between bodies of sound. Often there is a quite regular alternation between a small and large group of instruments, or between instruments and voices with instrumental accompaniment. This exploration of contrasting sounds was pursued with great imagination and provides a key to the understanding and enjoyment of Baroque music.

Basic Terms

terraced dynamics	basso continuo (figured bass)
clavichord	movement

MUSIC IN BAROQUE SOCIETY 2

Before 1800 most music was written to order, to meet a specific demand that came mainly from aristocratic courts and churches. Opera houses and municipalities also required a constant supply of music. In every case, the demand was for *new* music; Baroque audiences did not want to listen to pieces in an "old-fashioned" style.

The Baroque ruling class was enormously rich and powerful. While most of the population eked out a bare existence, European rulers surrounded themselves by luxury. Germany alone was subdivided into about three hundred territories governed separately. And each ruler proclaimed greatness by means of splendid palaces and magnificent court entertainments. Indeed, entertainment was necessary; most courtiers did no real work and tried to avoid boredom as much as possible.

Music was a main source of diversion. One court might employ an orchestra, a chapel choir, and opera singers—the size of the musical staff depending on the court's wealth. Bach directed about eighteen players in the orchestra of a small German court in 1717; but a large court might have more than eighty performers, including the finest opera singers of the day. The music director supervised performances and composed much of the music required, including operas, church music, dinner music, and pieces for court concerts. This overworked musician also was responsible for the discipline of other musicians, and for the upkeep of the instruments and music library.

The music director's job, like most, had good and bad features. Pay and prestige were quite high, and anything the composer wrote would be performed. But no matter how great, the composer was still a high-class servant who could neither quit nor take a trip without the patron's permission. Like everyone in Baroque society, musicians had to curry favor with the aristocracy. It is in this light that we must understand dedications like the one which Bach addressed to a nobleman along with his *Brandenburg Concertos:* "Begging Your Highness most humbly not to judge their imperfection with the rigor of the fine and delicate taste which the whole world knows Your Highness has for musical pieces; but rather to infer from them in benign Consideration the profound respect and the most humble obedience which I try to show Your Highness." Yet sometimes musicians formed personal friendships with their patrons, as did Arcangelo Corelli, who thus gained a private apartment in a palace.

Some rulers were themselves good musicians. Frederick the Great, King of Prussia during the mid-eighteenth century, was a flutist and good composer, as well as a feared general. At his nightly court concerts, Frederick played his own works and some of the hundreds of pieces supplied by his flute teacher, Johann Quantz. (Quantz was "granted the privilege" of shouting "Bravo!" after a royal performance.)

 Music in Baroque Society

125

Baroque painters, sculptors, and architects became interested in forming a total illusion, like a stage setting. Shown here is Lully's opera *Alceste* being performed at the Palace of Versailles (The Metropolitan Museum of Art, Harris Brisbane Dick Fund, 1953).

Churches also needed music, and this often was very grand. Along with an organ and choir, many Baroque churches had an orchestra to accompany the service. Indeed, church was where most ordinary citizens heard music. There were few public concerts, and the populace was rarely invited to the palace. The music director of a church, like his court counterpart, had to produce a steady flow of new music. He also was responsible for the music training of choirboys in the church school. Fine church music contributed to the prestige of cities, which often competed to attract the best musicians.

Church musicians earned lower pay and status than court musicians. Their meager income was supplemented by allotments of firewood and grain and by irregular fees for weddings and funerals. They suffered a financial pinch when "a healthy wind" blew and there were fewer funerals than usual, a situation Bach once complained about.

Large towns employed musicians to perform a variety of functions—to play in church, in processions, in concerts for visiting dignitaries, and for university

The Baroque
Period

126

Music was a main source of diversion for the Baroque ruling class, and many aristocrats were themselves good musicians. Frederick the Great, King of Prussia, is shown playing the flute, accompanied by violins and a basso continuo made up of harpsichord and cello (The Bettmann Archive).

graduations. These town musicians often played with amateurs in music clubs or university music societies, getting together at private homes, coffeehouses, and taverns.

Some Baroque musicians earned money by writing operas for commercial opera houses located mainly in Italy. In Venice, a city of 125,000 people, six opera companies performed simultaneously between 1680 and 1700. In London, Handel became music director of a commercial opera company in 1719. Backed by English nobles, this company was a corporation with shares listed on the London stock exchange. When the company went bankrupt in 1728, Handel formed his own company, for which he wrote operas and served as conductor, manager, and impresario. In filling these many roles, Handel became one of the first great "free-lance" musicians.

How did one become a musician in the Baroque period? Often the art was handed from father to son; many leading composers—Bach, Vivaldi, Purcell, Couperin, and Rameau—were sons of musicians. Or boys sometimes were apprenticed to a town musician and lived in his home. In return for instruction,

Music in
Baroque
Society

127

the boy did odd jobs, such as copying music. Many Baroque composers began their studies as choirboys, learning music in the choir school. In Italy, music schools were connected with orphanages. (Conservatory comes from the Italian for "orphans' home.") There, orphans, foundlings, and poor children were given thorough musical training, and some became the most sought-after opera singers and instrumentalists in Europe. Eminent composers such as Vivaldi were hired to teach and direct concerts in these schools.

To get a job, musicians usually had to pass a difficult examination, performing and submitting compositions. Sometimes there were nonmusical job requirements, too. An applicant might be expected to make a "voluntary contribution" to the town's treasury, or even to marry the daughter of a retiring musician. Both Bach and Handel turned down the same job because one of the conditions was marriage to the organist's spinster daughter. In general, Italian musicians held the best posts in most European courts and were frequently paid twice as much as local musicians.

Composers were an integral part of Baroque society, working for courts, churches, towns, and commercial opera houses. And even though they wrote music to fit specific needs, its quality is so high that it has become a standard element in today's concert repertory.

Baroque

3 THE CONCERTO GROSSO AND RITORNELLO FORM

We've seen that the contrast between loud and soft sounds—between large and small groups of performers—is a basic principle of Baroque music. It governs the concerto grosso, an important form of orchestral music in the late Baroque period. In the **concerto grosso,** a small group of soloists is pitted against a larger group of players called the **tutti** ("all"). Usually between two and four soloists play with anywhere from eight to twenty or more musicians for the tutti. The tutti is mainly string instruments, with a harpsichord as part of the basso continuo. A concerto grosso sounds like a competition between the tutti and the soloists, who assert their individuality and appeal for attention through brilliant and fanciful melodic lines. The soloists were the best and highest-paid members of the Baroque orchestra because their parts were more difficult than those of the other players. Concerti grossi were frequently performed by private orchestras in aristocratic palaces.

The concerto grosso consists of *several movements that contrast in tempo and character.* Most often there are three movements: (1) fast, (2) slow, (3) fast. The opening movement is usually vigorous and determined, clearly showing the contrast between tutti and soloists. The slow movement is quieter than the first, often lyrical and intimate. The last movement is lively and carefree, sometimes with a dancelike character.

The first and last movements of concerti grossi are often in **ritornello form,** an important musical procedure of the Baroque period. This form features the alternation between tutti and solo sections. In ritornello form the tutti opens with a theme called the **ritornello** ("refrain"). This ritornello, played by the tutti, returns in different keys throughout the movement. But it usually returns in fragments, not completely. Only at the end of the movement does the entire ritornello return in the home key. Although the number of times a ritornello (tutti) returns varies from piece to piece, a typical concerto grosso movement might be outlined:

1 *a.* Tutti (f), ritornello in home key.
   b. Solo.
2 *a.* Tutti (f), ritornello fragment.
   b. Solo.
3 *a.* Tutti (f), ritornello fragment.
   b. Solo.
4   Tutti (f), ritornello in home key.

In contrast to the tutti's ritornello, the solo sections offer fresh melodic ideas, softer dynamics, rapid scales, and broken chords. Soloists may also expand short melodic ideas from the tutti. The opening movement of Bach's Brandenburg Concerto No. 5 is a fine example of ritornello form in the concerto grosso.

First Movement from Brandenburg Concerto No. 5 in D Major (1721), by Johann Sebastian Bach

Side 2, band 1

With his set of six *Brandenburg Concertos,* Bach brought immortality to a German aristocrat, the Margrave of Brandenburg. Bach met the Margrave in 1718, when he was music director for another patron. The Margrave loved music and asked Bach to send him some original compositions. About three years later, Bach sent him the *Brandenburg Concertos* with the flattering dedication quoted in section 2, probably hoping for money or favors in return. (We don't know whether he got any.) These concertos had actually been composed for, and performed by, the orchestra of Bach's employer, the Prince of Cöthen. Each of the concertos is written for a different and unusual combination of instruments.

Brandenburg Concerto No. 5 uses a string orchestra and a group of soloists consisting of a flute, violin, and harpsichord. This was the first time that a harpsichord had been given the solo role in a concerto grosso. In 1719, the Prince of Cöthen bought a new harpsichord; Bach probably wanted to show off this instrument (as well as his skill as a keyboard player), and so he gave it a solo spot. The tutti is written for violins, violas, cellos, and double bass. During the tutti sections the solo violinist plays along, as does the harpsichordist, who supplies the figured bass.

The allegro movement opens with the ritornello, which is an almost continuous flow of rapid notes. After the ritornello ends very definitely, the soloists

 Brandenburg Concerto No. 5 in D

present short melodic ideas, with the flute and violin imitating each other playfully. The appearance of the soloists brings a lower dynamic level and the new tone color of the flute. After a while the tutti returns loudly with a brief fragment of the ritornello, only to give way again to the soloists. This alternation between brief, loud ritornello fragments by the tutti and longer, softer solo sections continues throughout the movement.

The soloists' music tends to be brilliant, fanciful, and personal compared with the more vigorous and straightforward tutti sections. Solo sections are also more polyphonic in texture than the tutti and stress imitation between the flute and violin. The soloists play new material of their own or varied fragments from the ritornello. These solo sections build tension and make the listener anticipate the tutti's return. Listen especially for the suspenseful solo section that begins with a new theme in minor and ends with the fluttery sound of trills in the flute and violin. (**A trill** is an ornament consisting of the rapid alternation of two tones that are a whole or half step apart.)

Only the harpsichord plays during the long final solo section. And it is spectacular! Bach builds a tense high point for the movement through irresistible rhythm and dazzling scale passages that require a virtuoso's skill. His audience must have marveled at this brilliant harpsichord solo within a concerto grosso. Audiences still do.

LISTENING OUTLINE
To be read while music is heard

Brandenburg Concerto No. 5 in D Major (1721), by Johann Sebastian Bach

First Movement: Allegro

Ritornello form, duple meter ($\frac{2}{2}$), D major

Flute, violin, harpsichord (solo group), string orchestra, continuo (tutti)

(About 11 min.)

Tutti   1   *a.* Strings, *f*, ritornello.

Solo		b. Flute, violin, harpsichord, major key.
Tutti	2	a. Strings, *f*, ritornello fragment.
Solo		b. Flute, violin, harpsichord, varied ritornello fragment.
Tutti	3	a. Strings, *f*, ritornello fragment.
Solo		b. Violin, flute, harpsichord.
Tutti	4	a. Strings, *f*, ritornello fragment, minor.
Solo		b. Harpsichord, flute, violin.
Tutti	5	a. Strings, *f*, ritornello fragment, major.
Solo		b. Flute, harpsichord, violin, varied ritornello fragment, *pp*. New theme in minor, *pp*, tossed between flute and violin, tension mounts.

Trills in flute and violin lead to

Tutti	6	a. Strings, *f*, ritornello fragment, major.
Solo		b. Violin, flute, harpsichord.
Tutti	7	a. Strings, *f*, longer ritornello fragment.
Solo		b. Violin, harpsichord, flute, varied ritornello fragment.
Tutti	8	a. Strings, *f*, ritornello fragment.
Solo		b. Violin and flute play carefree idea with rapid harpsichord scales in background.
		c. Long harpsichord solo featuring virtuoso display. Mounting tension resolved in
Tutti	9	Strings, *f*, ritornello.

Basic Terms

concerto grosso
tutti
ritornello form
ritornello
trill

Baroque

THE FUGUE ‖4‖

One cornerstone of Baroque music is the *fugue*. It is written for a group of instruments or voices, or for a single instrument like an organ or harpsichord. The **fugue** is a polyphonic composition based on one main theme, called a **subject**. Throughout a fugue, different melodic lines, or "voices," imitate the subject. The top melodic line—whether sung or played—is the soprano voice, and the bottom is the bass. A fugue's texture usually includes three, four, or five

The Fugue

131

voices. Though the fugue's subject remains fairly constant throughout, it takes on new meanings when shifted to different keys or combined with different melodic and rhythmic ideas.

The form of a fugue is extremely flexible; in fact, the only constant feature of fugues is how they begin—the subject is almost always presented in a single, unaccompanied voice. By thus highlighting the subject, the composer tells us what to remember and listen for. In getting to know a fugue, try to follow its subject through the different levels of texture. After its first presentation, the subject is imitated in turn by all the remaining voices.

The opening of a fugue in four voices may be represented as follows:

Soprano
voice   Subject _____ . . . . .etc.

Alto
voice   Subject _____ . . . . .etc.

Tenor
voice   Subject _____ . . . . .etc.

Bass
voice   Subject _____ . . . . .etc.

In this case the top voice announces the subject and then the lower voices imitate it. However, the subject may be announced by *any* voice—top, bottom, or middle—and the order in which the remaining voices imitate it is also completely flexible.

This may seem reminiscent of a round like "Row, Row, Row Your Boat," but in a fugue the game of "follow the leader" (exact imitation of the subject) does not continue indefinitely. The dotted lines in the fugue diagram show that *after a voice has presented the subject, it's free to go its own way with different melodic material.* A fugue's opening differs from a round's in another way: In a round, each voice presents the melody on the same tones. If the melody begins with the tones C–D–E, each voice will begin with these tones, whether at a higher or lower register. But in the opening of a fugue, *the subject is presented in two different scales.* First, it is based on the notes of the *tonic scale.* But when the second voice presents the subject, it is in the *dominant scale*—five scale steps higher than the tonic—and it is called the **answer.** A subject beginning with the notes C–D–E, for example, would be imitated by an answer five steps higher, on G–A–B. This alternation between the two scales of subject and answer creates variety.

In many fugues, the subject in one voice is constantly accompanied in another voice by a different melodic idea called a **countersubject.** A constant companion, the countersubject always appears with the subject, sometimes below it, sometimes above it.

After the opening of a fugue, when each voice has taken its turn at presenting the subject, a composer is free to decide how often the subject will be presented, in which voices, and in which keys. Between presentations of the subject, there are often transitional sections called **episodes,** which offer either new material or fragments of the subject or countersubject. Episodes do *not* present the subject in its entirety. They lend variety to the fugue and make reappearances of the subject sound fresh. Bach called one composer of fugues "pedantic" because he "had not shown enough fire to reanimate the theme by episodes."

Several musical procedures commonly appear in fugues. One is **stretto,** in which a subject is imitated before it is completed; one voice tries to catch the other. Another common procedure is **pedal point** (or **organ point**), in which a single tone, usually in the bass, is held while the other voices produce a series of changing harmonies against it. (The term is taken from organ music, where a low, sustained tone is produced by the organist's foot on a key of the pedal keyboard.)

A fugue subject can be varied in four principal ways:

1. It can be turned upside down, a procedure known as **inversion.** If the subject moves *upward* by leap, the inversion will move *downward* the same distance; if the subject moves *downward* by step, the inversion will move *upward* by step. In inversion, each interval in the subject is reversed in direction.

2. The subject may be presented **retrograde,** that is, by beginning with the last note of the subject and proceeding backward to the first.

3. The subject may be presented in **augmentation,** in which the original time values are lengthened.

4. The subject may appear in **diminution,** with shortened time values.

Fugues usually convey a single mood and a sense of continuous flow. They are written as independent works or as single movements within larger compositions. Very often an independent fugue is introduced by a short piece called a **prelude.**

Bach and Handel each wrote hundreds of fugues which represent the peak of that Baroque procedure. In the Baroque period, as a friend of Bach observed, "Skill in fugue was so indispensable in a composer that no one could have attained a musical post who had not worked out a given subject in all kinds of counterpoint and in a regular fugue." Fugal writing has continued into the nineteenth and twentieth centuries, but is not used as frequently as in the Baroque period. To this day musicians study how to write fugues as part of their training.

Organ Fugue in G Minor ("Little" Fugue; about 1709), by Johann Sebastian Bach

Side 3, band 3

One of Bach's best-known organ pieces is the "Little" Fugue in G minor, so called to differentiate it from another, longer fugue in G minor. The opening section of this fugue corresponds to the diagram on page 132. Each of the fugue's four voices takes its turn at presenting the tuneful subject, which is announced in the

Organ Fugue in G Minor

133

top voice and then appears in progressively lower voices, ending in the bass (played by the organist's feet on the pedal keyboard). Like many Baroque melodies, the subject gathers momentum as it goes along, beginning with relatively long time values (quarter notes) and then proceeding to shorter ones (eighth and sixteenth notes).

Starting with its second appearance, the subject is accompanied by a counter-subject that moves in short time values.

After the opening section, the subject appears five more times, each time preceded by an episode. The first episode uses both new material and a melodic idea from the countersubject.

This episode contains downward sequences, which are melodic patterns repeated in the same voice but at lower pitches.

For harmonic contrast, Bach twice presents the subject in major, rather than minor keys. The final statement of the subject—in minor—exploits the powerful bass tones of the pedal keyboard. Though the fugue is in minor, it ends with a major chord. This was a frequent practice in the Baroque period; major chords were thought more conclusive than minor.

Basic Terms

fugue	pedal point (organ point)
subject	inversion
answer	retrograde
countersubject	augmentation
episode	diminution
stretto	prelude

THE ELEMENTS OF OPERA

The Baroque era witnessed the development of a major innovation in music—**opera,** drama that is sung to orchestral accompaniment. By combining music, acting, poetry, dance, scenery, and costumes, this unique fusion of many arts creates a theatrical experience of overwhelming excitement and emotion. Since its beginnings in Italy around 1600, opera has spread to many countries, and even today it remains a powerful form of musical theater. We'll look closely at the operatic aspects of the Baroque period in the next section; but first, a general discussion of opera is in order.

An opera's characters and plot are revealed through song, rather than the speech used in ordinary drama. Once we accept this convention, opera offers great pleasure; its music both delights the ear and heightens the emotional effect of the words and story. Music makes even a complicated plot believable by depicting mood, character, and dramatic action. It's the flow of the music that carries the plot forward. In opera, the music *is* the drama.

Opera demands performers who can sing and act simultaneously. On stage are star solo singers, secondary soloists, a chorus, and sometimes dancers—all in costume. Besides the chorus of professional singers there may be "supers" (supernumeraries, or "extras"), who don't sing but who carry spears, fill out crowds, drink wine, and generally add to the opera's effect. Scenery, lighting, and stage machinery are intricate. They're called upon to create fires, floods, storms, and supernatural effects. In the orchestra pit are the instrumentalists and the conductor, whose awesome responsibility it is to hold everything together. A large

The Elements of Opera

135

opera's personnel—from conductor to stage director and assorted vocal coaches, rehearsal accompanists, technicians, and stagehands—may reach a startling total of several hundred people.

The capacity of this combined force to create spectacle and pageantry accounts for much of opera's appeal. Historically, opera has been associated with high social status. It originated in the courts of kings and princes (who could afford it) and long continued as a form of aristocratic entertainment. But as opera became more concerned with "real" people and less with royal figures, it attracted popular audiences. Today, radio and TV broadcasts and recordings have changed opera's image as an exotic and expensive diversion for the very rich. Millions of people from every economic background know opera for what it is: a powerful and pleasurable emotional experience.

The creation of an opera results from the joint efforts of a composer and a dramatist. The **libretto**, or text of the opera, is usually written by the **librettist**, or dramatist, and then set to music by the composer. But the composer often collaborates with the dramatist to ensure that the text meets his musical needs. W. H. Auden has said that a good libretto "offers as many opportunities as possible for the characters to be swept off their feet by placing them in situations which are too tragic or too fantastic for words. No good opera plot can be sensible, for people do not sing when they are feeling sensible." And it is true—opera characters are overwhelmed by love, lust, hatred, and revenge. They wear fantastic disguises and commit extraordinary acts of violence. Yet the music makes them human and real. It evokes the haughtiness of a countess or the simplicity of a peasant girl. It creates a dramatic entrance for an outraged father; depicts the tension behind sword thrusts in a duel; and portrays the bleakness of a winter dawn. A great opera composer is a master of musical timing and characterization and has a keen sense of the theater. He knows just when to have a character sing a simple phrase or a soaring melody, when to provide a stirring chorus or a graceful dance. Through his music, the composer paces the drama; he controls the speed of gestures, entrances, exits, and stage movements.

Some operas are serious, some comic, some both. They may contain spoken dialog, but most are sung entirely. (Spoken dialog is used mainly in comic opera, where stage action must be performed quickly for the most humorous effect.) Since it normally takes longer to sing words than to speak them, the text of a three-hour opera is shorter than that of a three-hour play. The librettist allows time for the composer's musical elaboration.

The range of characters found in opera is broad and varied; gods, empresses, dukes, servants, priests, prostitutes, peasants, clowns, hunchbacks, and cowboys all make an appearance. Opera soloists must create all these characters and need acting skill as well as vocal artistry. During rehearsals the stage director coaches the singers to move well, gesture meaningfully, and identify with their characters.

The basic voice ranges (soprano, alto, tenor, bass) are divided more finely in opera. Some of the **voice categories of opera** are:

The Baroque
Period

136

| Coloratura soprano | Very high range; able to execute rapid scales and trills |

Lyric soprano	Rather light voice; sings roles calling for grace and charm
Dramatic soprano	Full, powerful voice; capable of passionate intensity
Lyric tenor	Relatively light, bright voice
Dramatic tenor	Powerful voice; capable of heroic expression
Basso buffo	Takes comic roles; can sing very rapidly
Basso profundo	Very low range, powerful voice; takes roles calling for great dignity

Like plays, operas have from one to five acts subdivided into scenes. An act presents a variety of vocal and orchestral contrasts. For example, a tenor solo might be followed by a duet for soprano and bass, then a chorus, or an orchestral interlude. A section may end definitely—and provide an opportunity for applause—or be linked with the next section to form a continuous flow of music within an act.

The main attraction for many opera fans is the **aria,** a song for solo voice with orchestral accompaniment. It's an outpouring of melody that expresses an emotional state. In an aria, "I love you" may be sung ten times to accommodate the expansion of the idea. Often the action stops while the character's feelings are revealed through music. Lasting several minutes, an aria is a complete piece with a definite beginning, high point, and end. If the performance of an aria is brilliant, the audience responds with an ovation at its conclusion. Though this breaks the dramatic flow, it allows the audience to release its feelings through applause and shouts of "Bravo!"

Opera composers often lead into an aria with a **recitative,** a vocal line that imitates the rhythms and pitch fluctuations of speech. In a recitative (Italian for "recite") words are sung quickly and clearly, often on repeated tones. There's usually only one note to each syllable, as opposed to an aria, where one syllable may be stretched over many notes. Used for monologs and dialogs, the recitative connects the more melodic sections of the opera. It carries the action forward and quickly presents routine information.

Besides arias, soloists sing compositions for two or more singers: duets (two), trios (three), quartets (four), quintets (five), and sextets (six). When three or more singers are involved, the composition is called an **ensemble.** In a duet or ensemble, the performers either face the audience or move through action that develops the plot. Each character expresses his own feelings. Conflicting emotions like grief, happiness, and anger can be projected simultaneously when different melodies are combined. This special blend of feelings is the glory of opera and is possible only through music; it cannot be duplicated in spoken drama.

An opera chorus generates atmosphere and comments on the action. Its members are courtiers, sailors, peasants, prisoners, ballroom guests, and so on. Their sound creates a kind of tonal background for the soloists.

Rising just over the edge of the center stage, near the footlights, is the prompter's box. In this cramped space, invisible to the audience, is the **prompter,** who gives cues and reminds the singers of words or pitches if they momentarily

 The Elements of Opera

forget. Occasional memory lapses are inevitable with so much activity on stage.

Dance in opera is generally incidental. It provides an ornamental interlude that contrasts with and relaxes the thrust of the plot. By and large, dance occurs as part of the opera's setting—in a ballroom, at a country fair, in a pagan court—while the soloists, downstage, advance the plot's action and work out their destinies.

The nerve center for opera in performance is the orchestra pit—a sunken area directly in front of the stage. An opera orchestra has the same instruments as a full symphony orchestra, but usually it has a smaller string section. Covered lights attached to the players' music stands leave the orchestra in a deep shadow that doesn't interfere with the audience's view of the stage. The orchestra not only supports the singers but depicts mood and atmosphere and comments on the stage action. During the performance, the conductor shapes the entire work. He or she sets tempos, cues in singers, and indicates subtle dynamic gradations.

Most operas open with a purely orchestral composition called an **overture,** or **prelude.** Since the eighteenth century, the music for the overture has been drawn from material heard later in the opera. The overture is thus a short musical statement that involves the audience in the overall dramatic mood. Orchestral introductions to later acts in the opera are always called preludes. We've already discussed one of these, the Prelude to Act III of *Lohengrin,* where Wagner anticipates the wedding of the opera's hero and heroine. Because overtures and preludes, like arias, are complete compositions, they frequently appear on symphony orchestra programs.

The battle continues about translating opera. Most of the best-loved operas are in Italian, German, or French. Champions of their translation into English argue that an audience should be able to understand the plot as it develops. Why tell jokes in a comic opera if they can't be understood? On the other hand, a composer takes pains to make a special fusion of pitch and the original word. This results in a tonal color that seems absolutely right. But no matter how well a singer articulates, some words are bound to be lost, in whatever the language. For example, a sung melody can stretch one vowel over many notes; it takes a while to get to the end of a word. If the melody is placed in a soprano's highest range, the listener is really aware of the silvery vowel only and not of the word as a whole. Some operas seem to work well in translation, others don't. Much depends on the style of the opera and on the sensitivity of the translator.

Before a live opera performance in any language, it's a good idea to read the libretto or a synopsis of the plot. Even better, listen to a recording while following the libretto. This way, you're freer at the performance to appreciate the quality of production and interpretation.

Basic Terms

The Baroque Period

opera	voice categories	recitative	prompter
libretto	of opera	ensemble	overture (prelude)
librettist	aria		

OPERA IN THE BAROQUE ERA | 6 |

Opera was born in Italy. Its way was prepared by musical discussions among a small group of noblemen, poets, and composers who began to meet regularly in Florence around 1575. This group was known as the **Camerata** (Italian for "fellowship" or "society") and included the composer Vincenzo Galilei, father of the astronomer Galileo.

The Camerata members wanted to create a new vocal style modeled on the music of ancient Greek tragedy. Since no actual dramatic music had come down to them from the Greeks, they based their theories on literary accounts that had survived. It was believed that the Greek dramas were sung throughout in a style that was midway between melody and speech. The Camerata members wanted the vocal line to follow the rhythms and pitch fluctuations of speech. Because it was modeled after speech, the new vocal style became known as recitative ("recite"). It was sung by a soloist with only a simple, chordal accompaniment. The new music was therefore homophonic in texture. Polyphony was rejected by the Camerata because different words sounding simultaneously would obscure the all-important text.

Euridice by Jacopo Peri is the earliest opera that has been preserved. It was composed for the wedding of King Henri IV of France and Marie de' Medici and was performed in Florence in 1600. Seven years later Monteverdi composed *Orfeo*—the first *great* opera—for the court of the Gonzaga family in Mantua. Both these operas are based on the Greek myth of Orpheus descending into Hades to bring back his beloved Eurydice.

Much Baroque opera was composed for ceremonial occasions at court and was designed to display magnificent extravagance. The subject matter of these operas was drawn from Greek mythology and ancient history. Not only were aristocratic patrons of the Baroque fascinated by the classical civilizations of Greece and Rome, they identified with their heroes and divinities. Opera did indeed reflect the creative urge of composer and librettist, but it also was a way to flatter the aristocracy. The radiant appearance of Apollo (god of poetry, music, and the sun) might symbolize the prince's enlightened rule.

In Venice in 1637, the first public opera house opened; now anyone with the price of admission could attend an opera performance. Between 1637 and 1700 there were seventeen opera houses in Venice alone, as well as many in other Italian cities—ample evidence that opera was born in the right place at the right time. Hamburg, Leipzig, and London had public opera houses by the early 1700s, but, on the whole, public opera outside Italy took longer to develop.

Venetian opera became a great tourist attraction. An English traveler wrote in 1645 about the opera and its "variety of scenes painted and contrived with no

 Opera in the Baroque Era

139

The subject matter of Baroque opera was often drawn from ancient history, as in Handel's *Julius Caesar,* performed by the New York City Opera (Fred Fehl).

less art of perspective, and machines for flying in the air, and other wonderful motions; taken together, it is one of the most magnificent and expensive diversions the wit of man can invent." The stage machinery of Baroque opera bordered on the colossal. Stage effects were spectacular—gods descending on clouds or riding across the sky in chariots, ships tossing, boulders splitting. And set design was an art in itself. Painters turned backdrops into cities with arches and avenues that stretched into the distant horizon.

Baroque opera marked the rise of the virtuoso singer. Chief of these was the **castrato,** a male singer who had been castrated before puberty. Castrati combined the lung power of a man with the vocal range of a woman. Their agility, breath control, and unique sound (which was not like a woman's) intrigued listeners. Castrati received the highest fees of any musician. With their soprano or alto vocal ranges, they played male roles such as Caesar and Nero—Baroque audiences evidently were more interested in vocal virtuosity than dramatic realism. Some Baroque operas cannot be done today because contemporary singers aren't able to manage the fiendishly difficult castrato parts. (The castration of boy singers was common in Italy from 1600 to 1800; this was usually done with the consent of impoverished parents who hoped that their sons would become highly paid opera stars.)

During the late Baroque, operas consisted largely of arias that were linked by recitatives. All action stopped during the aria, when the singer faced the audience, expressed the feelings of the character, and displayed vocal virtuosity. The form of a typical late Baroque aria is A B A. An aria in A B A form is called a **da capo** aria: after the B section, the term *da capo* is written; this means "from the beginning" and indicates a repetition of the opening A section. However, the repetition was usually not literal because the singer was expected to embellish the returning melody with ornaments.

Combining virtuosity, nobility, and extravagance, Baroque opera perfectly expressed the spirit of a grand age.

Basic Terms

Camerata
castrato
da capo aria

CLAUDIO MONTEVERDI Baroque | **7** |

Claudio Monteverdi (1567–1643), one of the greatest composers of the early Baroque era, was born in Cremona, Italy. He served at the court of Mantua for twenty-one years, first as a singer and violist, then as music director. For this court Monteverdi created opera's earliest masterpiece, *Orfeo* ("Orpheus," 1607). Though widely recognized as a leading composer in Mantua, Monteverdi received little pay or respect: "I have never suffered greater humiliation," he wrote, "than when I had to go and beg the treasurer to obtain what was due me."

Life improved for Monteverdi in 1613, when he was appointed music director at St. Mark's in Venice, the most important church position in Italy. He stayed at St. Mark's for thirty years, until his death in 1643. There he composed not only the required sacred music but also secular vocal music for the aristocracy. He wrote operas for Venice's San Cassiano, the first public opera house in Europe. At the age of seventy-five, Monteverdi wrote his last opera, *L'incoronazione di Poppea* ("The Coronation of Poppea," 1642).

Monteverdi is a monumental figure in the history of music. His works form a musical bridge between the sixteenth and seventeenth centuries and greatly influenced composers of the time. All his music—madrigals, church music,

 Claudio Monteverdi

141

opera—is for voices, ordinarily supported by a basso continuo and other instruments.

Monteverdi wanted to create music of emotional intensity. He felt earlier music had conveyed only moderate emotion, and he wanted to extend its range to include agitation, excitement, and passion. To achieve this intensity, he used dissonances with unprecedented freedom and daring. And to evoke the angry or warlike feelings in some of his texts, he introduced new orchestral effects, including pizzicato and tremolo.

Monteverdi was the first composer of operatic masterpieces. Only three of the twelve operas he wrote are preserved, but they truly blend music and drama. His vocal lines respond marvelously to the inflections of Italian while maintaining melodic flow.

Orfeo ("Orpheus," 1607)

Fittingly enough, Monteverdi's first opera is about Orpheus, the supremely gifted musician of Greek myth. Orpheus, son of the god Apollo, is ecstatically happy after his marriage to Eurydice. But this joy is shattered when his bride is killed by a poisonous snake. Orpheus goes down to Hades hoping to bring her back to life. Because of his beautiful music, he is granted this privilege—on condition that he does not look back at Eurydice while leading her out of Hades. During a moment of anxiety, however, Orpheus does look back, and Eurydice vanishes. Nonetheless, there is a happy ending, of sorts. Apollo pities Orpheus and brings him up to heaven where he can gaze eternally at Eurydice's radiance in the sun and stars.

Orfeo was composed in 1607 for the Mantuan court, and no expenses were spared to make it a lavish production. There were star soloists, a chorus, dancers, and a large orchestra of about forty players. The aristocratic audience was wildly enthusiastic and realized the historic significance of the performance.

Monteverdi creates a variety in *Orfeo* by using many kinds of music—recitatives, arias, duets, choruses, and instrumental interludes. He uses the opera orchestra to establish atmosphere, character, and dramatic situation. With the simplest of musical means, Monteverdi makes his characters come alive. Through vocal line alone he quickly characterizes the hero's joy and despair. Monteverdi sets his text in a very flexible way, freely alternating recitatives with more melodious passages, depending on the meaning of the words.

Side 1, band 7

Act II: Recitative: *Tu se' morta* ("You are dead")

Monteverdi's mastery of the then-novel technique of recitative is shown in *Tu se' morta*, sung by Orpheus after he is told of Eurydice's death. Orpheus resolves to bring her back from Hades, and he bids an anguished farewell to the earth, sky, and sun. His vocal line is accompanied only by a basso continuo played by a small portable organ and a bass lute. (In modern performances, other instruments are sometimes substituted.) The texture is homophonic as the accompaniment simply gives harmonic support to the voice. The vocal line is rhythmically free, with little sense of beat or meter, and its phrases are irregular in length. This flexible setting of text is meant to suggest the passionate speech of an actor declaiming his lines. Monteverdi frequently uses word-painting, the musical representation of poetic images that was favored by Baroque composers. For example, words like *stars* (*stelle*) and *sun* (*sole*) are sung to climactic high tones, while *abysses* (*abissi*) and *death* (*morte*) are sung to somber low tones. Three times during the recitative the melodic line rises to a climax and then descends. Through such simple means, Monteverdi makes Orpheus's passion come alive.

Tu se' morta, se' morta, mia vita,	You are dead, you are dead, my dearest,
ed io respiro; tu se' da me partita,	And I breathe, you have left me,
se' da me partita per mai più,	You have left me forevermore,
mai più non tornare, ed io rimango—	Never to return, and I remain—
no, no, che se i versi alcuna cosa ponno,	No, no, if my verses have any power,
n'andrò sicuro a' più profondi abissi,	I will go confidently to the deepest abysses,
e, intenerito il cor del re de l'ombre,	And, having melted the heart of the king of shadows,
meco trarotti a riverder le stelle,	Will bring you back with me to see the stars again,
o se ciò negherammi empio destino,	Or, if pitiless fate denies me this,
rimarrò teco in compagnia di morte.	I will remain with you in the company of death.
Addio terra, addio cielo, e sole, addio.	Farewell earth, farewell sky, and sun, farewell.

HENRY PURCELL

Baroque

8

Henry Purcell (about 1659–1695), called the greatest of English composers, was born in London to a musician in the king's service. At about age ten, Purcell became a choirboy in the Chapel Royal, and by the late teens his extraordinary talents were winning him important music positions. In 1677, at about eighteen, he became composer to the king's string orchestra; two years later he was appointed organist of Westminster Abbey; and in 1682, he became an organist of the Chapel Royal. During the last few years of his short life, Purcell was also active composing music for plays.

Acclaimed as *the* English composer of his day, Purcell died in his thirty-sixth year and was buried beneath the organ in Westminster Abbey. He was the last native English composer of international rank until the twentieth century.

Purcell mastered all the musical forms of late seventeenth-century England. He wrote church music, secular choral music, music for small groups of instru-

Henry Purcell

143

ments, songs, and music for the stage. His only true opera is *Dido and Aeneas* (1689), which many consider the finest ever written to an English text. His other dramatic works are spoken plays with musical numbers in the form of overtures, songs, choruses, and dances.

Few composers have equaled Purcell's handling of the English language. His vocal music is faithful to English inflection and brings out the meaning of the text. Purcell developed a melodious recitative that seems to grow out of the English language. His music is filled with lively rhythms and a fresh melodic style that captures the spirit of English folk songs. He treated the chorus with great variety and was able to obtain striking effects through both simple homophonic textures and complex polyphony. His music is spiced with dissonances that seemed harsh to the generation of musicians that followed him. Some of Purcell's finest songs use a variation form found in many Baroque works—a *ground bass.*

Ground Bass

Often, in Baroque works, a musical idea in the bass is repeated over and over while the melodies above it constantly change. The repeated musical idea is called a **ground bass,** or **basso ostinato** ("obstinate" or "persistent" bass). The ground bass pattern may be as short as four notes or as long as eight measures. In this variation form, the constant repetition of the bass pattern gives unity, while the free flow of the melodic lines above it results in variety. Composers use a ground bass in both vocal and instrumental music. We'll hear a ground bass in Purcell's opera *Dido and Aeneas* as well as in Bach's B-minor Mass (section 12).

Dido and Aeneas (1689)

Dido and Aeneas, a masterpiece of Baroque opera, was written for students at a girls' boarding school. The opera lasts only an hour, is scored for strings and harpsichord continuo, and requires no elaborate stage machinery or virtuoso soloists. Most solo roles are for women. Purcell used many dances in this opera because the director of the school was a dancing master who wanted to display the students' accomplishments. The chorus plays a prominent role, both participating in the action and commenting on it.

The libretto of *Dido and Aeneas,* by Nahum Tate, was inspired by the *Aeneid,* the epic poem by the Roman poet Virgil (70–19 B.C.) The opera's main characters are Dido, queen of Carthage, and Aeneas, king of the defeated Trojans. After the destruction of his native Troy, Aeneas was ordered by the gods to seek a site for the building of a new city. He sets out on the search with twenty-one ships. Landing at Carthage, a North African seaport, Aeneas falls in love with Dido. A sorceress and two witches see this as an opportunity to plot Dido's downfall. (In

The Baroque Period

144

Purcell's time, people really believed in witches: Nineteen "witches" were hanged in Massachusetts in 1692, three years after *Dido's* first performance.) A false messenger tells Aeneas that the gods command him to leave Carthage immediately and renew his search. Aeneas agrees but is desolate at the thought of deserting Dido.

Act III: Scene between Dido and Aeneas and *Dido's Lament*

In the last act, which takes place at the harbor, Aeneas's sailors sing and dance before leaving, and the witches look on in glee. An emotional scene follows between Aeneas and Dido, who enters with her friend Belinda. Dido calls Aeneas a hypocrite and refuses his offer to stay. After he sails, Dido sings a magnificent lament and kills herself. The opera concludes with the mourning of the chorus.

Purcell uses recitative to capture the drama of the parting scene between Dido and Aeneas. After Aeneas leaves and Dido resolves to take her own life, the chorus sadly comments that "great minds against themselves conspire."

The climax of *Dido and Aeneas* is *Dido's Lament,* an aria built upon a chromatically descending ground bass that is stated eleven times. (Such chromatic ground basses were commonly used to show grief in the Baroque period.) Dido's melody moves freely above this repeated bass line, creating touching dissonances with it.

Side 1, band 8

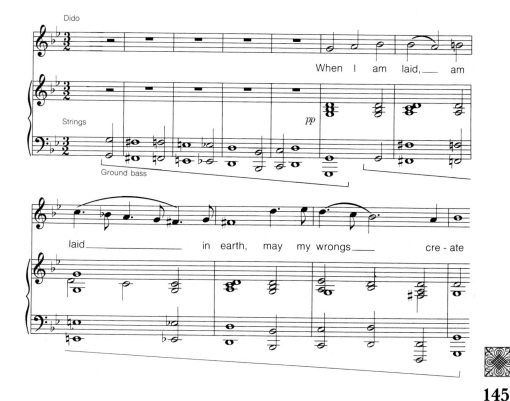

Dido and Aeneas (1689)

145

Dido's repeated "Remember me" reaches the highest note of the aria and haunts the listener.

(*Dido, Belinda, and women enter.*)
Dido:
Your counsel all is urg'd in vain,   Recitative.
To earth and heaven I will com-
    plain;
To earth and heaven why do I call?
Earth and heaven conspire my fall.
To Fate I sue, of other means be-
    reft,
The only refuge for the wretched
    left.

(*Aeneas enters*)
Belinda:
See, madam, see where the Prince
    appears!
Such sorrow in his look he bears
As would convince you still he's
    true.

Aeneas:
What shall lost Aeneas do?
How, how, royal fair, shall I impart
The gods' decree, and tell you we
    must part?

Dido:
Thus on the fatal banks of Nile
Weeps the deceitful crocodile;
Thus hypocrites that murder act
Make heav'n and gods the authors
    of the fact!

Aeneas:
By all that's good . . .
Dido:
By all that's good, no more!
All that's good you have forswore.
To your promised empire fly,
And let forsaken Dido die.

Aeneas:
In spite of Jove's commands I'll
    stay,
Offend the gods and Love obey.

Dido:
No, faithless man, thy course pursue,
I'm now resolved as well as you.
No repentance shall reclaim
The injur'd Dido's slighted flame;

For 'tis enough, what-e'er you now
 decree,
That you had once a thought of
 leaving me.
Aeneas:
Let Jove say what he please, I'll
 stay!
Dido:
Away, away! No, no, away, away!   Rapid exchanges between voices;
To Death I'll fly if longer you   then they sing together.
 delay.
Aeneas:
No, no, I'll stay, and Love obey.
(*Exit Aeneas*)
Dido:
But Death, alas! I cannot shun,   Recitative.
Death must come when he is gone.
Chorus:
Great minds against themselves con-   Chorus, begins in major, but ends
 spire,   in minor.
And shun the cure they most desire.
Dido:
Thy hand, Belinda; darkness shades   Recitative, downward melody.
 me,
On thy bosom let me rest;
More I would but Death invades
 me;
Death is now a welcome guest.
When I am laid, am laid in earth,   *Dido's Lament* (aria), melody unfolds
 may my wrongs create   over descending ground bass in
No trouble, no trouble in thy   low strings.
 breast.
Remember me! But ah! forget my
 fate.

                                      Orchestral postlude.

Chorus:
With drooping wings ye Cupids   Chorus, "drooping wings" illus-
 come,   trated by downward scale.
And scatter roses on her tomb,
Soft and gentle as her heart;
Keep here your watch and never
 part.

Basic Term

   ground bass (basso ostinato)

Basic Term

9 | THE BAROQUE SONATA

Instrumental music dramatically and rapidly gained importance during the Baroque period. A main development of instrumental music was the **sonata,** a composition in several movements for one to eight instruments. (In later periods, the term *sonata* took on a more restricted meaning.)

Composers often wrote **trio sonatas,** so called because they had three melodic lines: two high ones and a basso continuo. Yet the word *trio* is misleading, because the "trio" sonata actually involves *four* instrumentalists. There are two high instruments (commonly violins, flutes, or oboes) and two instruments for the basso continuo—a keyboard instrument (organ or harpsichord) and a low instrument (cello or bassoon).

The sonata originated in Italy but spread to Germany, England, and France during the seventeenth century. Sonatas were played in palaces, homes, and even in churches—before, during, or after the service. Sometimes composers differentiated between "church sonatas" (*sonata da chiesa*), which had a dignified character and were suitable for sacred performance, and "chamber sonatas" (*sonata da camera*), which were more dancelike in character and intended for court performance.

Basic Terms

sonata
trio sonata

10 | ARCANGELO CORELLI

Around 1700, the leading Italian violinist and composer of string music was Arcangelo Corelli (1653–1713). He studied in Bologna but spent most of his adult life in Rome. He was friend and music director to Cardinal Ottoboni, in whose palace he lived. There he mingled with the intellectual and aristocratic elite of Rome.

As a teacher, Corelli instructed some of the most eminent musicians of his time and laid the foundations of modern violin technique. He was one of the first to write double stops and chords for the violin and is unique among Italian composers in that he wrote only instrumental music: sixty sonatas and twelve concertos, all for strings.

The Baroque
Period

Though little is known about Corelli's personality, he generally is described as gentle and calm. But when he played, he seemed transformed. According to a contemporary report, "Whilst he was playing on the violin it was usual for his countenance to be distorted, his eyes to become as red as fire, and his eyeballs to roll as in an agony."

Trio Sonata in E Minor, Op. 3, No. 7 (1689)

This work is a fine example of the Baroque trio sonata. The basso continuo is for organ and cello, while upper lines are taken by two violins that play in the same high register. The violins are the center of attention; they seem to be rivals, each taking turns at the melodic ideas, intertwining, and sometimes rising above each other in pitch. Though the bass line is subordinate to the two upper voices, it is no mere accompaniment. It imitates melodic ideas presented by the violins.

The sonata consists of four short movements: (1) slow, (2) fast, (3) slow, (4) fast. All are in the same key, but they differ in meter, mood, and tempo. Each movement alone, however, has only a single mood, as is typical in Baroque instrumental music.

A solemn, dignified Grave opens the sonata in quadruple meter. The main motive is presented by the first violin and immediately imitated in turn by the other instruments before it has been completed. It's as though one instrument tries to catch the others.

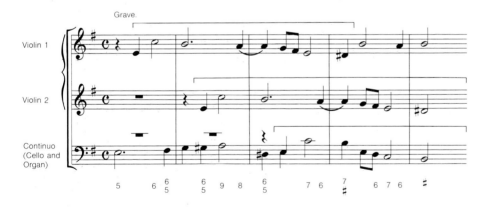

The second movement, a vigorous Allegro, is fuguelike and written in duple meter. Fugal second movements were characteristic of Baroque trio sonatas.

The third movement is songlike and soulful, an Adagio in triple meter.

The lightest movement of the sonata is the concluding Allegro, a dancelike piece in triple meter. This movement is in two-part form, and each part is repeated: A A B B. Section B is almost twice as long as A. At the end of section B, Corelli uses his only dynamic change in the sonata: The concluding phrase is repeated softly, like an echo.

Trio Sonata in E Minor, Op. 3, No. 7

149

||11|| ANTONIO VIVALDI

Antonio Vivaldi (1678–1741), a towering figure of the late Italian Baroque, was born in Venice, son of a violinist at St. Mark's Cathedral. Along with his musical training, he prepared for the priesthood and took holy orders at the age of about twenty-five. But poor health caused him to leave the ministry after a year. Because of this religious background and his red hair, Vivaldi was known as "the red priest" (*il prete rosso*).

For most of his life, Vivaldi was a violin teacher, composer, and conductor at the music school of the Pietà, an institution for orphaned or illegitimate girls in Venice. Every Sunday and holiday, about forty young women presented a concert of orchestral and vocal music in the chapel. They were placed in a gallery, "hid from any distinct view of those below by a lattice of ironwork." For this all-female group—considered one of the finest orchestras in Italy—Vivaldi composed many of his works. He also wrote for Venetian opera houses and sometimes took leave to visit foreign courts.

Vivaldi was famous and influential as a violinist and composer. Bach arranged some of his concertos. And the Emperor Charles VI, a passionate music lover, was said to have talked longer to Vivaldi "alone in fifteen days, than he talked to his ministers in two years."

But Vivaldi's popularity waned shortly before his death in 1741, and he died in poverty. Acclaimed during his lifetime, he was almost forgotten for two hundred years. The Baroque revival of the 1950s reclaimed his reputation with modern music lovers.

Although Vivaldi composed operas and fine church music, he is best known for his 450 or so concerti grossi and *solo concertos.* A solo concerto is for a *single* soloist and an orchestra. Vivaldi exploited the resources of the violin as well as other instruments. (There are concertos for solo flute, piccolo, cello, bassoon, and even mandolin.) His fast movements feature tuneful themes in vigorous rhythms, and his slow movements have impassioned, lyrical melodies that would fit an opera aria.

Concerto Grosso in A Minor, Op. 3, No. 8 (1712)

This concerto for two violins and string orchestra comes from a collection entitled "The Harmonic Whim" (*L'Estro armonico*). Like most of Vivaldi's concertos, it has three movements: (1) fast, (2) slow, (3) fast.

First Movement: Allegro

The Baroque Period

The vigorous Allegro begins with a fairly long orchestral ritornello containing several melodic ideas.

Violins

After the ritornello comes to a clear end, the dynamic level drops, and the two solo violins play a new idea which is lightly accompanied by violins and violas. But the solo section soon yields to the tutti playing the last idea of the opening ritornello. The entire movement alternates between fairly loud tutti sections presenting fragments of the ritornello theme and somewhat softer solo sections. But the solo and tutti sections contrast more in character than in loudness or tone color. The soloists seem to be improvising as they play new ideas, motives from the ritornello, or continuous successions of short notes. After a while, the solo sections offer melodies spun from a tiny ritornello motive that is repeated on different pitches.

Violin 1

A sense of hesitation is created by the rests within the melodies. While one soloist plays these melodies, the other has a continuous run of short notes.

Despite the constant shifting between solo and tutti sections, this movement has a wonderful continuity of motion and mood. Its light, homophonic texture makes it simple and direct.

Second Movement: Larghetto e spiritoso (Slow and spirited)

The tender lyricism of this slow movement breathes the spirit of an operatic love duet. Only at the beginning and end do we hear the tutti, playing a serious descending phrase in unison. These two tutti sections frame a duet between the

Concerto
Grosso in A
Minor

151

solo violins which alternate, interweave in imitative dialog, or harmoniously sing the same melody a third apart. The soloists are accompanied quietly by the orchestral violins and violas which constantly repeat the tutti theme or motives from it.

Third Movement: Allegro

Like the opening movement, the concluding Allegro features alternations between tutti and solo sections. But here Vivaldi uses contrasting thematic material in an unusual way. The first hint of something extraordinary comes with a sudden pause, followed by a series of repeated loud and soft chords, broken by rests. This dramatic break in the rhythmic motion signals an even more original stroke.

The second violin, like an opera singer addressing an audience, sings a very long legato melody accompanied softly by the rest of the orchestra. Then Vivaldi returns to the bustling motion of the tutti-solo alternation. Such contrast of thematic material was uncommon in instrumental music until the late eighteenth century. Vivaldi's use of it may well be why Bach chose to arrange this concerto grosso for organ.

Baroque

|12| JOHANN SEBASTIAN BACH

The masterpieces of Johann Sebastian Bach (1685–1750) mark the high point of Baroque music. Bach came from a long line of musicians: His father, grandfather, and great-grandfather were all church organists or town musicians in Germany. In fact, so many members of the family were musicians that their name became synonymous with "town musician." Annual family gatherings might assemble over one hundred Bachs to celebrate and make music. And Johann Sebastian Bach passed on this musical heritage—he was father to twenty children, nine of whom survived him, four to become well-known composers.

In Eisenach, his birthplace, Bach probably received his first musical training from his father, the town musician, and cousin, the church organist. But when he was nine both his parents died and Johann went to live with his oldest brother, the organist in a nearby town. At fifteen, Bach left his brother's crowded home and moved to yet another town, where he went to school and supported himself by singing in the church choir and playing the organ and violin. By this time his love of music was so great that he would walk up to thirty miles to hear a famous organist.

When he was eighteen, Bach became church organist in Arnstadt, a town not far from his birthplace. Here he came into conflict with church authorities because they felt his music was too complicated; they also questioned his meeting "a strange maiden" in the empty church to accompany her singing. Bach resolved both issues when he was twenty-three by finding a better position at Mühlhausen and by marrying "the strange maiden," his cousin Barbara. His reputation as an organist was growing steadily through his virtuoso performances, which included improvising elaborate fugues and, reportedly, playing with his feet (on the pedal keyboard) better than many performers could with their fingers.

After these two jobs as church organist, Bach obtained a more important post in 1708 as court organist in Weimar. He stayed there for nine years, becoming concertmaster of the court orchestra, but decided to leave when he was passed over for promotion. The Duke of Weimar was so annoyed at Bach's obstinacy in requesting dismissal that he put him in jail for a month! Such was the power of a minor German aristocrat. But Bach demanded his rights all his life, never fearing controversy.

Bach's most lucrative and prestigious post was as court conductor for the Prince of Cöthen. His salary equaled that of the Marshal of the Court, the second highest official. But more importantly, this was the first time in Bach's career that he was not involved with church or organ music. The prince belonged to the Reformed (Calvinistic) Church, and only simple psalm singing was permitted in the service. For the six years from 1717 to 1723, Bach directed the prince's small orchestra of about eighteen players and composed music for it. The *Brandenburg Concertos* grew out of this productive period.

In 1720 Bach's wife died, leaving him with four young children. The next year, at thirty-six, he married a twenty-one-year-old singer at the Cöthen court, and the second marriage was apparently as happy as the first.

Because he was an ardent amateur musician, the Prince of Cöthen treated Bach as a friend. However, the prince's interest began to wane when he married a young princess who did not like music, and Bach decided to look for a new job.

He found it in 1723, as Cantor (director of music) of St. Thomas Church in Leipzig, a position that involved responsibility for four main municipal churches. Bach remained here for the last twenty-seven years of his life. Though one of the most important church posts in Germany, the position carried less prestige and paid less than the one with the Prince of Cöthen. But Bach probably was interested because it was in Leipzig, a comparatively large city of 30,000, where his children could receive a good Lutheran education and go to the University. Then, too, Bach was a deeply religious man. At the beginning of each sacred composition he wrote the letters *J.J.*, for *Jesu Juva* ("Jesus help"), and at the end he put *S.D.G.*, for *Soli Deo Gloria* ("to God alone the glory").

At Leipzig, Bach rehearsed, conducted, and usually composed an extended composition for chorus, soloists, and orchestra for each Sunday and holiday of the church year. He was responsible for the musical education of some fifty-five students in the St. Thomas school. Later he became director of the Leipzig *Collegium Musicum,* a student organization that gave concerts every Friday night at a coffee house. He was also an eminent teacher of organ and composition, gave

 Johann Sebastian Bach

153

At the Church of St. Thomas, in Leipzig, Bach was cantor for the last twenty-seven years of his life (Bärenreiter Bild-Archiv).

organ recitals, and was often asked to judge the construction of organs. It's hard to imagine how he did all this while surrounded by children, relatives, and students. And he lived in the school building next to a classroom!

A year before his death in 1750, Bach was almost blind. His last composition, the organ piece, "Before Thy Throne I Step, O Lord" had to be dictated. It breaks off before the end, as though death had kept him from finishing it.

Though recognized as the most eminent organist, harpsichordist, improviser, and master of fugue, Bach was by no means considered the greatest composer of his day. He was little known outside Germany, and even his Leipzig offer came only after two other noted musicians had turned it down. By the time of Bach's maturity, the Baroque style had begun to go out of fashion, and people wanted light, uncomplicated music. Many thought his works too heavy, complex, and polyphonic.

Bach's music was largely forgotten and remained unpublished for years after his death. But a few composers of the following generations knew some of his compositions and were aware of his genius. In 1829, Felix Mendelssohn performed the *St. Matthew Passion*, and Bach's music has been the daily bread of every serious musician since then.

Bach's Music

Bach created masterpieces in every Baroque form except opera. Throughout, he fused technical mastery and emotional depth. His instrumental music includes pieces for orchestra, for small groups, and for solo organ, harpsichord, clavichord, violin, and cello. The excellence and number of these works show how prominent instrumental music became in the Baroque period. Bach's vocal music—the bulk of his output—was written mostly for the Lutheran church and often was based on hymns familiar to the congregation.

In forming his personal style, Bach drew on musical resources of three different lands. He avidly studied Italian concertos and French dance pieces, as well as the church music of his native Germany.

Bach's music is unique in its combination of polyphonic texture and rich harmony. Several melodic lines of equal importance occur at once; and so many things go on at the same time that the music conveys an awesome complexity and elaboration. Even with the great interest of individual voices, it is the progression of chords that directs the musical motion. Bach used complex and dissonant harmonies more imaginatively than his contemporaries. His works show an astounding mastery of harmony and counterpoint, and they are used as models by music students today.

Baroque music leans toward unity of mood, and this is particularly true of Bach, who liked to elaborate a single melodic idea in a piece. Such melodies can be intricate, unpredictable, and highly embellished, but unity of mood is created by an insistent rhythmic drive. Whether slow or fast, Bach's works generate perpetual motion.

By Bach's time there was little difference in style between secular and sacred music. In fact, he often created sacred music simply by rearranging instrumental pieces or works originally written for secular texts. His church music also uses operatic forms like the aria and recitative.

Bach liked to illustrate religious or pictorial ideas through musical symbolism. In an organ piece based upon the hymn tune "Old Adam's Fall" (*Durch Adams Fall*), Bach represents the serpent by twisting inner voices, and man's fall by downward leaps in the bass. And in one called *The Ten Commandments*, Bach used the theme exactly ten times.

Sometimes Bach composed music to demonstrate what he could do with a

 Bach's Music

Though recognized as the most eminent organist, harpsichordist, improviser, and master of fugue, Bach was by no means considered the great composer of his day; his music was largely forgotten and remained unpublished for years after his death (Bärenreiter Bild-Archiv).

specific musical form. His *Art of the Fugue,* for example, is a collection which displays all the resources of fugue writing. He also explored with unprecedented thoroughness a system of tuning that was being developed at the time. This system, called *equal temperament,* allowed a composer to write in any key, not just simple ones. So Bach used every major and minor key in his collection of forty-eight preludes and fugues, *The Well-Tempered Clavier* (which roughly means "The Well-tuned Keyboard Instrument"). The collection is in two volumes (1722, 1744), each with twenty-four preludes and fugues, one in each major and minor key. Today, the pieces are basic to the repertoire of keyboard players.

Brandenburg Concerto No. 5 in D Major (1721)

Second Movement: Affettuoso (Affectionately, tenderly)

We have already discussed the opening movement (Allegro) in section 3, "The Concerto Grosso and Ritornello Form." Here we'll study the two remaining movements of this concerto grosso for flute, violin, harpsichord, and orchestra.

The Affettuoso is in marked contrast to the vigorous opening movement; it's slow, in a minor key, and much quieter. It uses only the three solo instruments and a cello, which duplicates the bass line (left hand) of the harpsichordist. The harpsichord has both an accompanying and a solo role in the movement. Sometimes, as at the beginning, it serves merely as a basso continuo accompaniment to a duet between the violin and flute. In these sections, there is no notated part for the right hand; the harpsichordist is expected to improvise chords as guided by Bach's figured bass. (In modern performing editions, the editor supplies these chords for the player.) In other sections, Bach gives the harpsichordist's right hand a melody of its own, and the instrument becomes a center of attention.

The Affettuoso projects a single rather serious mood throughout and is woven entirely from two brief motives that are constantly passed among the instruments. Bach creates melodic variety by turning his motives upside down. The following example shows the two motives, marked *a* and *b,* and their inversions:

Brandenburg
Concerto
No. 5

Third Movement: Allegro

The concluding Allegro is dancelike in character. It is in A B A form; the A sections are in major, and the B section is in minor. The movement begins like a fugue, with a rollicking subject introduced by the solo violin then imitated by the flute and harpsichord.

After a while, the instruments of the tutti—not heard since the opening movement—join in playing the subject.

The middle section, in minor, begins softly with a lyrical melody for the flute.

This melody starts like the main subject but contains long notes which give it a songlike character. After the flute, the violin and harpsichord take turns playing this melody. The main subject also has a prominent role throughout the middle section and can be heard in a harpsichord solo. Bach achieves both unity and variety by combining within the middle section both the main subject and the new lyrical melody related to it.

A loud tutti signals the conclusion of the middle section. Then the solo violin, imitated by the flute, announces the return of the opening section A. The major key and lively rhythms seem even more joyful after the minor key and reflective quality of the middle section.

Mass in B Minor (begun 1733)

Over a period of years, Bach, a pious Lutheran, composed what is probably the most monumental setting of the Roman Catholic Mass. In 1733, he wrote the first two sections (Kyrie and Gloria) and sent them to a Catholic monarch with a request for the honorary title of court composer. Years later, he finished the Mass by composing new music and by fitting the Latin text to some of his earlier Lutheran church pieces. Bach probably never heard the entire work performed. Since it is far too long to be used in the Catholic service, Bach's reasons for creating it are unknown. He may simply have wanted to show what he could do with this ancient and imposing form.

Bach's B-minor Mass contrasts strikingly with the Renaissance Mass we studied. It has specific orchestral accompaniments for the voices. And each major section of the Mass—like the Kyrie or Credo—is subdivided into arias, duets, and choruses. Thus this Mass has more variety within each large section than corresponding sections of a Renaissance Mass. Each part of Bach's B-minor Mass expresses the meaning and emotion of the text.

Here are two contrasting movements from the Credo: the *Crucifixus,* a profound expression of grief at Christ's crucifixion, and *Et resurrexit,* which expresses joy at Christ's resurrection.

Crucifixus

The *Crucifixus* is scored for chorus and a small orchestra of strings, two flutes, and continuo. It is built upon a chromatically descending ground bass, or basso ostinato, the traditional symbol of grief in Baroque music (which we heard in *Dido's Lament,* by Purcell).

Over the constantly repeating ground bass, the sopranos, altos, tenors, and basses sing ever-changing melodic lines that produce dissonant harmonies. Minor key, slow tempo, and hushed dynamics—together with the generally downward-moving melodies—contribute to a feeling of infinite sorrow. One of the sublime moments in all music occurs at the very end of this movement, when there is an unexpected shift from minor to major, and the sopranos chromatically descend to their lowest tone. At this point of deepest sorrow, the major key implies hope.

Crucifixus etiam pro nobis sub Pontio Pilato, passus et sepultus est.

And was crucified also for us under Pontius Pilate. He suffered and was buried.

Et Resurrexit

The jubilant *Et resurrexit* fulfills the hope implied in the *Crucifixus.* Now Bach uses a full orchestra, including three trumpets, timpani, and two oboes. The movement is in major; a fast tempo and bright-sounding trumpets make it festive. Typically Baroque is the rising melodic line on the words *Et resurrexit* ("and He rose").

Et re-sur-re - xit, re-sur-re - xit,

Mass in B Minor (begun 1733)

Variety is achieved through repeated alternations between orchestral sections and those using voices and instruments.

Et resurrexit tertia die secundum scripturas. Et ascendit in coelum, sedet ad dexteram Dei Patris, et iterum venturus est cum gloria judicare vivos et mortuos, cujus regni non erit finis.

And the third day he rose again according to the scriptures. And ascended into Heaven. And sitteth at the right hand of God the Father. And he shall come again with glory to judge both the living and the dead; Whose kingdom shall have no end.

‖13‖ THE BAROQUE SUITE

Instrumental music has always been closely linked with dancing; much of it was written for use in palace ballrooms. During the Renaissance, dances often came in pairs—a dignified dance in quadruple meter was followed by a lively one in triple meter. In the Baroque and later periods, music was written that—while meant for listening, not dancing—was related to specific dance types in tempo, meter, and rhythm.

Baroque composers wrote **suites,** which are sets of dance-inspired movements. Whether for solo instruments, small groups, or orchestra, the movements of a Baroque suite are all written in the same key but differ in tempo, meter, and character. They also have a variety of national origins: The moderately paced *allemande* from Germany might be followed by a fast *courante* and moderate *gavotte* from France, a slow and solemn *sarabande* from Spain, and a fast *gigue* (jig) from England and Ireland. Suites were played at private homes, at court concerts, or as background music for dinner and outdoor festivities.

Dance pieces have a diverse past. Some began as folk dances, while others sprang from aristocratic ballrooms. Even the character of a dance might show dramatic evolution. The slow, solemn sarabande grew out of a sexy song and dance that a sixteenth-century moralist condemned as "so lascivious in its words, so ugly in its movements, that it is enough to inflame even very honest people." In the seventeenth century, however, the sarabande became respectable enough to be danced by a cardinal at the French court!

The movements of a suite are usually in two-part form with each section repeated: A A B B. The A section, which opens in the tonic key and modulates to the dominant, is balanced by the B section, which begins in the dominant and returns to the tonic key. Both sections use the same thematic material, and so they contrast relatively little except in key.

Suites frequently begin with a movement that is *not* dance-inspired. One common opening is the *French overture,* which is also heard at the beginning of baroque oratorios and operas. Usually written in two parts, the **French overture** first presents a slow section with dotted rhythms that is full of dignity and grandeur. The second section is quick and lighter in mood, often beginning like a fugue. Sometimes part of the opening section will return at the end of the overture.

The suite is an important instrumental form of the Baroque. Even compositions not called "suite" often have several dance-inspired movements. Music influenced by dance tends to have balanced and symmetrical phrases of the same length, because formal dancing has a set of steps in one direction symmetrically balanced by a similar motion in the opposite direction.

Bach wrote four orchestral suites called "overtures," after the French overture that begins each one. We don't know when they were composed, but it seems likely that the *collegium musicum* performed them in a Leipzig coffee house.

Suite (Overture) No. 3 in D Major, by Johann Sebastian Bach
2 oboes, 3 trumpets, timpani, strings, continuo

First Movement: Overture
The suite opens with a majestic French overture, which exploits the bright sounds of trumpets. After a slow opening section with dotted rhythms, we hear the energetic fast section. This begins like a fugue, with an upward-moving theme introduced by the first violins then imitated by the other instruments.

The fast section is like a concerto grosso in its alternation of solid tutti passages with lightly scored ones highlighting the first violins. After the fast section, the slow tempo, dotted rhythms, and majestic mood of the opening return.

Second Movement: Air

Side 2, band 3

The second movement contains one of Bach's best-loved melodies. Scored for only strings and continuo, the Air is serene and lyrical in contrast to the majestic and bustling French overture. The title suggests that the movement is written in the style of an Italian aria. Like the opening movement, the Air is not related to dance. Its A A B B form has a B section that is twice as long as the A section. The Air combines a steadily moving bass (which proceeds in upward and downward octave leaps) with a rhapsodic and rhythmically irregular melody in the violins.

Third Movement: Gavotte
After the Overture and Air, all the movements are inspired by dance, beginning with the Gavotte. Written in duple meter and in a moderate tempo, it uses the

 Suite No. 3 in D Major

161

full orchestra again. It may be outlined: Gavotte I (A A B B); Gavotte II (C C D D); Gavotte I (A B). Notice the contrast between the sections for full orchestra and those without trumpets and timpani.

Fourth Movement: Bourrée

The Bourrée is an even livelier dance, also in duple meter. Its form is A A B B, and it is the shortest movement of the suite.

Side 2, band 4

Fifth Movement: Gigue

The Suite concludes with a rollicking gigue in $\frac{6}{8}$ time, also in the form A A B B. This is Bach being simple and direct. Listen for the splendid effect when timpani and trumpets periodically join the rest of the orchestra.

Basic Terms

>   suite
>   French overture

‖14‖ THE CHORALE AND THE CHURCH CANTATA

In the Leipzig of Bach's day, the Lutheran church service on Sunday was the social event of the week: It started at seven in the morning and lasted about four hours. The sermon alone could take an hour.

Music was a significant part of the Lutheran service. While most religious services today use no more than a chorus and organ, Bach's church had a small orchestra of between fourteen and twenty-one players to accompany the twelve or so men and boys of the choir. The service was filled with music; single compositions might last half an hour.

To further direct communication that Lutheranism stressed between the believer and Christ, the rite was largely in the vernacular—German. Each service included several hymns called *chorales*. The **chorale**, or hymn tune, was sung to a German religious text. These tunes were easy to sing and remember, having only one note to a syllable and moving in steady rhythm. They had been composed in the sixteenth and seventeenth centuries, or had been adapted from folk songs and Catholic hymns. The congregation had sung these tunes since

The Baroque
Period

162

childhood, and each tune carried religious associations. Congregational singing of chorales was an important way for people to participate directly in the service. These melodies were often harmonized for church choirs. The hymn melody was sung in the top part, and the tones of the supporting harmonies were sung by the three lower parts. New church music was often based on traditional melodies written as far back as two centuries. Before the congregation began to sing a hymn, the organist might play a **chorale prelude,** a short composition based on the hymn tune that reminded the congregation of the hymn's melody. By using traditional tunes in their works, composers could involve the congregation and enhance the religious associations.

The Church Cantata

The principal musical expression in the Lutheran service, and one which employed chorales, was the church **cantata.** *Cantata* originally meant a piece that was *sung,* as distinct from the sonata, which was *played.* While many kinds of cantatas were used in Bach's day, we shall focus on the one designed for the Lutheran service in Germany in the early 1700s. Usually written for chorus, vocal soloists, organ, and a small orchestra, it had a German religious text. The text was either newly written or drawn from the Bible or familiar hymns. In the Lutheran services, there were different Gospel and Epistle readings for each Sunday and holiday, and the cantata text was related to them. In a sense, the cantata was a sermon in music which reinforced the minister's sermon, also based on the Gospel and Epistle reading. The cantata of Bach's day might last twenty-five minutes and include several different movements—choruses, recitatives, arias, and duets. We'll see that in its use of aria duet, and recitative, the cantata closely resembled the opera of the time, and it is typical of Baroque fusion of sacred and secular elements in art and music.

The cantor, or music director, had to provide church cantatas for every Sunday and holiday. Bach wrote about 295; about 195 are still in existence. In his first few years as cantor in Leipzig, he composed them at the staggering rate of almost three a month. During the remaining twenty-five years of his tenure, he was inclined to reuse cantatas, and so his output dropped.

Cantata No. 140: *Wachet auf, ruft uns die Stimme* ("Awake, a Voice Is Calling Us"; 1731)

This is Bach's best-known cantata. To fully appreciate it, we perhaps should imagine ourselves as pious Lutherans of his time. Cantata No. 140 was composed for the twenty-seventh Sunday after Trinity Sunday, when the Gospel reading was the parable of the wise and foolish virgins (Matthew, 25). The Christian believers are represented by virgins, and Christ by the Bridegroom:

 Cantata No. 140

163

Then shall the kingdom of heaven be likened unto ten virgins, which took their lamps and went forth to meet the bridegroom. And five of them were wise, and five were foolish. . . . And at midnight there was a cry made, Behold the bridegroom cometh; go ye out to meet him. Then all those virgins arose, and trimmed their lamps. And the foolish said unto the wise, Give us of your oil; for our lamps are gone out. But the wise answered, saying, Not so; lest there not be enough for us and you: but go ye rather to them that sell, and buy for yourselves. While they were away the bridegroom arrived; and those who were ready went in with him to the wedding; and the door was shut. . . . Keep awake then; for you never know the day or the hour. . . .

Bach based his cantata on the chorale tune *Wachet auf* because its text was inspired by this Sunday's Gospel. The text and melody of the chorale were written by Philipp Nicolai (1556–1608) in about 1597—over 130 years before Bach used it. This was a widely known chorale tune that had been used by other composers before Bach. The hymn has three stanzas, and each is sung to the same melody. Bach used the chorale melody and text in three of the seven movements in the cantata:

Movement	Use of Chorale	Content of Text
1 Chorus with orchestra	Chorale, stanza 1	Virgins awakened by the watchmen announcing the coming of the Bridegroom.
2 Recitative for solo tenor with continuo		The Bridegroom is coming.
3 Duet for soprano and bass with violino piccolo and continuo		Dialog between a longing Soul (soprano) and Jesus (bass).
4 Tenors of chorus sing chorale in unison; strings and continuo	Chorale, stanza 2	Zion (Christian believers) rejoices at the arrival of Lord Jesus, God's Son.
5 Recitative for bass, accompanied by strings and continuo		Jesus lovingly greets the bride.
6 Duet for soprano and bass with oboe and continuo		Joyous union between Christ (bass) and Christian (soprano).
7 Chorus doubled by orchestra	Chorale, stanza 3	Christians praise God and rejoice in union with Him.

According to a Protestant theologian and music scholar, the chorale text interprets the relationship of the Bridegroom and bride "as a picture of the union of God with his people, of Christ with the Church." The cantata's other texts, for duets and recitatives, were written by an unknown author and depict "the relationship between Jesus and the pious individual soul." They are based on the Song of Songs (Solomon) in the Bible.

Before listening to all of Cantata No. 140, it's helpful to become acquainted with the chorale tune, which the last movement presents unadorned. The melody has the form A A B.

There are nine melodic phrases, of which the first three are repeated immediately (A A). The last phrase of the A section (phrase 3) reappears at the end of the B section (phrase 9) and beautifully rounds off the chorale melody.

First Movement: Chorus and Orchestra

Side 2, band 5

2 oboes, English horn, French horn, violins 1, violins 2, violas, continuo (organ, bassoon, cello)

In the chorale text of the first movement, watchmen on the towers of Jerusalem call on the wise virgins (Christians) to awake because the Bridegroom (Christ) is coming. The movement opens with an orchestral ritornello which may have been intended to suggest a procession or march. There are dotted rhythms (long-short, long-short), a rising figure with syncopation, and a series of rising scales.

Cantata No. 140

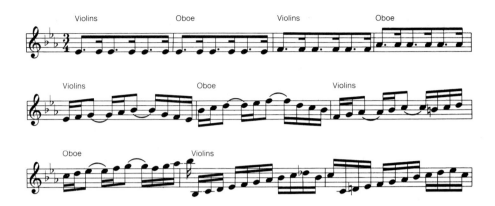

At the ritornello's closing cadence the sopranos enter and sing the chorale's first phrase in long notes. Soon the three lower voices engage in an imitative dialog based on a new motive in shorter note values. Throughout, the orchestra continues to play still shorter notes.

Thus there are three layers of sound: the chorale phrases in long notes in the soprano; the imitative dialog in shorter note values in the three lower voices; and the ever-busy orchestra playing motives from the ritornello in even shorter notes.

The chorale tune (in the soprano) is not presented as a continuous whole but rather phrase by phrase, with breaks between. After each phrase, the voices pause while the orchestra continues to play interludes of either the whole ritornello or sections from it. Sometimes the motives in the three lower voices illustrate the text, as when they have rising scale figures at the word *high* (*hoch*) and exclamations at the repeated *where* (*wo*).

Once during the movement, the three lower voices become emancipated from the soprano and jubilantly sing a melody in rapid notes on *Alleluja*. This, perhaps, is the most exciting moment in the movement.

		Orchestral ritornello.
Wachet auf,	"Awake,"	
ruft uns die Stimme	the voice of watchmen	
		Brief orchestral interlude.
der Wächter sehr	calls us from	
hoch auf der Zinne,	high on the tower,	Rising scales in lower voices depict *high* (*hoch*). Brief orchestral interlude.
wach auf,	"Awake,	
du Stadt Jerusalem!	you city of Jerusalem!"	
		Orchestral ritornello.
Mitternacht	Midnight	
heisst diese Stunde;	is this very hour;	
		Brief orchestral interlude.
sie rufen uns	they call to us	
mit hellem Munde:	with bright voices:	
		Brief orchestral interlude.
wo seid ihr	"Where are you,	
klugen Jungfrauen?	wise virgins?"	
		Long orchestral interlude.
Wohl auf,	Take cheer,	
der Bräut'gam kömmt,	the Bridegroom comes,	
		Brief orchestral interlude.
steht auf,	arise,	
die Lampen nehmt!	take up your lamps!	
Alleluja!	Hallelujah!	Altos, jubilant melody in rapid notes. Imitation by tenors, then basses.
Alleluja!	Hallelujah!	Sopranos, chorale in long notes. Orchestral interlude.
Macht euch bereit	Prepare yourselves	
		Orchestral interlude.
zu der Hochzeit	for the wedding,	
		Brief orchestral interlude.
ihr müsset ihm	you must go forth	
entgegen gehn.	to meet him.	
		Orchestral ritornello.

Cantata No. 140

167

Second Movement: Recitative for Tenor

Continuo

Third Movement: Duet for Bass (Jesus) and Soprano (Soul)

Violino piccolo, continuo

When Bach was hired as cantor by the Leipzig town council, he specifically agreed to compose church music that would *not* "make an operatic impression." These two movements, which would be appropriate for a love scene in a Baroque opera, show that Bach did not take his contract literally. The second movement, a recitative in minor, uses only a solo tenor and continuo and contrasts sharply with the brilliant opening movement in major. This is a **secco** ("dry") **recitative,** in which a speechlike melody is accompanied only by a basso continuo.

The third movement, a dialog between Jesus and a faithful Soul, conveys a sense of tender longing. This duet begins with a ritornello using the violino piccolo, a small violin tuned higher than the usual instrument. (Today a standard violin plays this part.) After a touching opening phrase, the violin's melody dissolves into a series of quick notes.

In the vocal sections, the Soul (soprano) has short questioning phrases which are answered by the reassuring Jesus (bass). Throughout, the violin's melody intertwines with the voices, while the continuo provides a steady rhythmic pulse.

Er kommt, er kommt, der Bräut'gam kommt!	He comes, he comes, the Bridegroom comes!
Ihr Töchter Zions, kommt heraus,	Daughters of Zion, come forth,
sein Ausgang eilet aus der Höhe	he is hurrying from on high
in euer Mutter Haus.	into your mother's house.
Der Bräut'gam kommt, der einem Rehe	The Bridegroom comes, who like a roe
und jungem Hirsche	and a young hart
gleich auf demen Hügeln springt	leaping upon the hills
und euch das Mahl der Hochzeit bringt.	brings you the wedding meal.

Wacht auf, ermuntert euch!	Wake up, bestir yourselves!
der Bräut'gam zu empfangen;	to receive the Bridegroom;
dort, sehet, kommt er hergegangen.	there, look, he comes along.
Wann kommst du, mein Heil?	Soul: When will you come,
	my salvation?
Ich komme, dein Teil.	Jesus: I am coming, your own.
Ich warte mit brennendem Öle:	Soul: I am waiting with burning oil.
Eröffne den Saal	Throw open the hall
zum himmlischen Mahl!	to the heavenly banquet!
Ich öffne den Saal	Jesus: I open the hall
zum himmlischen Mahl.	to the heavenly banquet.
Komm Jesu!	Soul: Come, Jesus!
komm, liebliche Seele!	Jesus: Come, lovely Soul!

Fourth Movement: Tenor Chorale   *Side 3, band 1*

Violins and violas in unison, continuo

The chorale tune returns in the fourth movement, the most popular of the cantata. Bach liked this section so much that toward the end of his life he rearranged it as a chorale prelude for organ. With miraculous ease, he sets two contrasting melodies against each other. First we hear the unison strings supported by the continuo playing a warm, flowing melody that Bach may have intended as a dancelike procession of the maidens as they "all follow to the joyful hall and share in the Lord's supper." This melody is repeated and varied throughout while the tenors sing the chorale tune against it.

The chorale tune moves in faster rhythmic values than it did in the opening movement, but here, too, it is broken into component phrases linked by the instrumental melody. It's helpful to listen several times to this movement, first

Cantata No. 140

169

focusing on the rapid rhythms of the graceful string melody; then on the sturdy, slower rhythms of the chorale tune; and finally on all lines at once.

Zion hört die Wächter singen,	Zion hears the watchmen singing,
das Herz tut ihr vor Freuden springen,	for joy her very heart is springing,
sie wachet und steht eilend auf.	she wakes and rises hastily.
Ihr Freund kommt von Himmel prächtig,	From heaven comes her friend resplendent,
von Gnaden stark, von Wahrheit mächtig,	sturdy in grace, mighty in truth,
Ihr Licht wird hell, ihr Stern geht auf.	her light shines bright, her star ascends.
Nun komm, du werte Kron,	Now come, you worthy crown,
Herr Jesu, Gottes Sohn.	Lord Jesus, God's own Son,
Hosianna!	Hosanna!
Wir folgen all'	We all follow
zum Freudensaal	to the joyful hall
und halten mit das Abendmahl.	and share the Lord's Supper.

Fifth Movement: Recitative for Bass (Jesus)
Strings, continuo

Sixth Movement: Duet for Bass (Jesus) and Soprano (Soul)
Oboe, continuo

An operatic atmosphere is again suggested in movements 5 and 6, a recitative and duet that balance movements 2 and 3. The fifth movement is called an **accompanied recitative,** because the voice is supported by strings as well as continuo. The dancelike, joyful duet (sixth movement) depicts the happy union of Christ and the Soul—but it could well suggest the bliss of any newlywed couple. A solo oboe first plays an opening ritornello and then intertwines with the voices almost throughout. Perhaps to suggest "union," the soprano and bass imitate each other and often sing together harmoniously. The movement is in A B A form.

So geh herein zu mir,	Come enter in with me,
du mir erwählte Braut!	my chosen bride!
Ich habe mich mit dir	I have pledged my troth
in Ewigkeit vertraut.	to you in eternity!
Dich will ich auf mein Herz,	I will set you as a seal upon my heart,
auf meinen Arm	and as a seal upon my arm
gleich wie ein Siegel setzen,	
und dein betrübtes Aug'ergötzen.	and restore delight to your sorrowful eye.

Vergiss, o Seele,	Forget now, o soul,
nun die Angst, den Schmerz,	the anguish, the pain
den du erdulden müssen;	which you had to suffer;
auf meiner Linken sollst du ruh'n,	on my left you shall rest,
und mein Rechte soll dich küssen.	and my right shall kiss you.
Mein Freund ist mein!	Soul: My friend is mine!
Und ich bin dein!	Jesus: and I am thine!
Die Liebe soll nichts	Both: Love shall separate
scheiden.	nothing!
Ich will mit dir in	Soul: I will feed with you
Himmels Rosen weiden,	among heaven's roses,
Du sollst mit mir in	Jesus: You shall feed with
Himmels Rosen weiden,	me among heaven's roses,
da Freunde die Fülle,	Both: There fullness of joy,
da Wonne wird sein!	there rapture shall be!

Seventh Movement: Chorale

Side 3, band 2

Chorus doubled by orchestra

Bach rounds off Cantata No. 140 by bringing back the chorale once more. For the first time since movement 1, all voices and instruments take part. Here the chorale is set in a relatively simple, homophonic texture for four voices, with the instruments simply doubling them, not playing melodies of their own. Now the chorale is heard as a continuous melody, without interludes between its phrases. The rich sound, full harmonies, and regular rhythms express praise of God, faith in Him, and joy in being in His Kingdom. No doubt the congregation joined in the singing of the final chorale, which so firmly expressed their unity and belief.

Gloria sei dir gesungen	Gloria be sung to you
mit Menschen- und englischen Zungen,	with men's and angels' tongues,
mit Harfen und mit Cymbeln schon.	with harps and beautiful cymbals.
Von zwölf Perlen sind die Pforten	Of twelve pearls are the gates
an deiner Stadt; wir sind Konsorten	at your city; we are consorts
der Engel hoch um deinen Thron.	of the angels high about your throne.
Kein Aug' hat je gespürt,	No eye has ever sensed,
kein Ohr hat je gehört	no ear has ever heard
solche Freude.	such a delight.
Des sind wir froh,	Of this we rejoice,
io, io!	io, io,
ewig in dulci jubilo.	forever in sweet joy.

Basic Terms

chorale	secco recitative
chorale prelude	accompanied recitative
cantata	

 Basic Terms

15 THE ORATORIO

With the opera and cantata, the oratorio stands as a major development in Baroque vocal music. Like opera, the **oratorio** is a large-scale composition for chorus, vocal soloists, and orchestra; it usually is set to a narrative text. Oratorio differs from opera in that it has no acting, scenery, or costumes. Most oratorios are based on biblical stories, but usually they are not intended for religious services. Today they are performed either in concert halls or churches.

An oratorio contains a succession of choruses, arias, duets, recitatives, and orchestral interludes. The chorus is especially important and serves either to comment on or to participate in the drama. A narrator's recitatives usually relate the story and connect one piece with another. Oratorios are longer than cantatas (sometimes over two hours) and have more of a story line.

Oratorios first appeared in early seventeenth-century Italy as musical dramatizations of biblical stories and were performed in prayer halls called "oratorios." During the Baroque period, the oratorio spread to other countries and assumed many forms. *Messiah* by George Frideric Handel has been for decades the best-known and most-loved oratorio.

Basic Term

oratorio

16 GEORGE FRIDERIC HANDEL

George Frideric Handel (1685–1759), master of Italian opera and English oratorio, was born in Halle, Germany, one month before J. S Bach. But Handel was not from a musical family; his father was a barber-surgeon who wanted his son to study law, not music. By nine, Handel's musical talent was so outstanding that his father relented somewhat and permitted him to study with the local organist, who also was a composer. By eleven, he was able not only to compose but also to give organ lessons. Perhaps to honor the wishes of his father, who had died when Handel was twelve, he entered Halle University to study law at seventeen. But a year later he left the university and set out for Hamburg.

Handel was drawn to Hamburg's renowned opera house. There he became a

The Baroque Period

172

violinist and harpsichordist in the orchestra, and when he was twenty, one of his operas was successfully produced.

Handel was a man of temperament and conviction. At the Hamburg opera an incident almost cost him his life. The company was performing an opera by one of Handel's friends, who insisted that he, not Handel, would play the harpsichord. Handel refused to give up his post, and their argument led to a duel. A metal button on Handel's coat broke his opponent's sword. It was a button's great contribution to posterity.

Handel's good fortune continued. At twenty-one he went to Italy for three highly productive years to establish his career. There he wrote Italian operas that were acclaimed far and wide. And he mingled with princes and leading musicians; even cardinals wrote librettos for him to set to music.

Returning to Germany in 1710, Handel took a well-paid position as music director for the Elector Georg Ludwig of Hanover. After just a month, he asked for a leave to go to London, where his opera *Rinaldo* was being produced. *Rinaldo* was a triumph, and he returned to Hanover. A year later Handel again asked the Elector for an English leave. It was granted on condition that Handel stay only a reasonable length of time in London.

This turned out to be the next half-century (1712–1759). Handel's fame in England grew as rapidly as it had in Italy. He became England's leading composer and a favorite of Queen Anne, who gave him a subsidy of two hundred pounds a year. On Queen Anne's death, a complicated arrangement made the Elector of Hanover, Georg Ludwig, King George I of England (1714). Evidently the King had not taken great offense at Handel's absence; the composers' subsidy was increased to four hundred pounds annually, and he taught music to the King's granddaughters.

Italian opera in London was an exotic entertainment for the pleasure of the aristocracy. Middle-class audiences had little desire to see works with mythological plots they considered absurd. So a few aristocrats provided the base of support for opera in London. They ran a commercial opera company called the Royal Academy of Music, and in 1719 Handel became its music director. After nine seasons the company folded because of inadequate support. But in that period Handel had composed a number of brilliant operas for outstanding prima donnas and castrati.

Handel's reputation continued to grow, and after the collapse of the Royal Academy, he decided to form a company to produce his works. (For years he had a triple career as impresario, composer, and performer.) Opera had become a political weapon. To spite him, a company called The Opera of the Nobility was formed. Its backers opposed the party in power, and Handel—friend of the King and an Establishment composer—became a scapegoat.

Both opera companies went bankrupt as a result of the competition, and Handel suffered a breakdown. He went to Germany to recuperate, and his condition moved the future King of Prussia to write, in 1737, "Handel's great days are over, his inspiration is exhausted, and his taste behind the fashion."

But the King of Prussia was mistaken. Handel recovered, returned to London,

 George Frideric Handel

and—though heavily in debt—managed again to produce operas on his own. To these he added his oratorios, and a glowing new chapter had opened.

For the English public, oratorios were a novelty. But they knew the Old Testament and liked hearing English on stage. Handel offered his oratorios during Lent, when operas were prohibited. Oratorios, unlike opera, required no expensive sets, stage machinery, or costumes, and were thus cheaper to produce. Even though Handel charged high prices, he attracted a new middle-class audience.

In 1741, the year he composed *Messiah,* Handel stopped writing operas entirely. Oratorios poured from his pen. At first, some people were scandalized that biblical words were sung in a public theater. One newspaper received a letter asserting that "the People of England were arriv'd to such a Height of *Impiety* and *Prophaneness,* that the most sacred *Things* were suffer'd to be us'd as *publick Diversions.*"

Despite sniping, the oratorio seasons were acclaimed; they had the added attraction of Handel himself performing his organ concertos between acts. But too much success can bring trouble. Some aristocrats again began to plot Handel's ruin. To them, the idea of a foreign-born musician's attaining power and prominence was too much. Concert posters were torn down, hired hoodlums robbed and assaulted concertgoers, and aristocrats made a point of giving private concerts and balls on oratorio evenings. Gradually, all this simmered down, but not before Handel had another breakdown. Again, he recovered rapidly and went on producing oratorios.

By 1753, Handel was still conducting and giving organ concerts, though he was almost blind. During his lifetime a statue of him was erected in a public park, and when he died in 1759, three thousand mourners attended his funeral in Westminster Abbey. He was stubborn, wealthy, generous, and cultivated. But above all, he was a master composer whose dramatic sense has rarely been equaled.

Handel's Music

Handel shares Bach's stature among composers of the late Baroque. Although he wrote a great deal of instrumental music—suites, organ concertos, concerti grossi—the core of his huge output consists of English oratorios and Italian operas.

Handel's English oratorios usually are based on stories from the Old Testament and have titles like *Israel in Egypt, Saul, Joshua,* and *Judas Maccabaeus.* They are *not* church music, however; they were composed to entertain paying audiences in public theaters. Most have plots and characters, even though they are performed without acting, scenery, or costumes. As we'll see, *Messiah* is an exception, in that it deals with a New Testament subject and is without a plot.

The chorus is the focus of the Handelian oratorio. Sometimes it participates in the narrative, representing the Israelites or their heathen enemies. But it also

Handel's triple career as impresario, composer, and performer brought him success and fame but led to political in-fighting and two nervous breakdowns (The Metropolitan Museum of Art, Bequest of Alexandrine Sinsheimer, 1959).

comments on the action, lamenting or exulting. Handel treats the combination of chorus and orchestra with flexibility and imagination. In his hands, a chorus can project delicacy, drama, or grandeur. Even Beethoven marveled at Handel's ability "to achieve great effects with simple means."

Handel never hesitated to reinforce an idea in his text by interrupting a polyphonic flow with a series of chords. Changes in texture are more frequent in his music than in Bach's. And he liked to present two different melodic ideas, then combine them polyphonically. Handel achieved sharp changes of mood by shifting between minor and major keys.

Handel's thirty-nine Italian operas, almost all written in London, are less well

 Handel's Music

known today than the oratorios. But after two centuries of neglect, these operas are being revived successfully by modern opera companies. Handel's operas are nearly all serious, and they are based on ancient Greek and Roman history or mythology. The heroes and heroines are royal figures like Julius Caesar and Cleopatra. Most noteworthy in Handel's opera are the arias, which are connected by long passages of recitative in which the plot develops. The arias show Handel's outstanding ability to evoke a mood or emotion. They often were written to display the virtuosity of singers, some of whom were castrati.

Messiah (1741)

Messiah lasts about $2\frac{1}{2}$ hours and was composed in just twenty-four days. Handel wrote it before going to Ireland, where a concert hall was being dedicated by performances of his works. About five months after arriving in Dublin (1742), Handel first performed *Messiah* to benefit those lingering in debtors' prisons. Rehearsals attracted wide attention: One newspaper commented that *Messiah* was thought "by the greatest Judges to be the finest Composition of Musick that ever was heard." Normally, the concert hall held 600 people; but to increase the capacity, women were asked not to wear hoopskirts, and men were asked to leave their swords at home.

Although the premiere was a success, the first London performance (1743) was poorly received, mainly because of the religious opposition to the use of a Christian text in a theater. It took *Messiah* almost a decade to find popularity in London. Not until it was performed yearly at a benefit for a London orphanage did it achieve its unique status. A contemporary wrote that *Messiah* "fed the hungry, clothed the naked, fostered the orphan."

In three parts, the oratorio starts with the prophecy of the Messiah's coming and makes celestial announcements of Christ's birth and man's redemption through His appearance. Part II is aptly described by one Handel scholar as "the accomplishment of redemption by the sacrifice of Jesus, mankind's rejection of God's offer and mankind's utter defeat when trying to oppose the power of the Almighty." Part III expresses faith in the certainty of eternal life through Christ as Redeemer.

Unlike most of Handel's oratorios, *Messiah* is meditative rather than dramatic; it lacks plot action and specific characters. *Messiah* is Handel's only English oratorio that uses the New Testament as well as the Old. Millionaire Charles Jennings, an amateur literary man, compiled the text by taking widely separated passages from the Bible—Isaiah, Psalms, and Job from the Old Testament; Luke, I Corinthians, and The Book of Revelations from the New.

Over the years, Handel rewrote some movements in *Messiah* for different performers and performances. Initially, the orchestra and chorus were smaller than we are used to: The chorus included twenty singers, all male, and the small orchestra had only strings and continuo, with trumpets and timpani used in some sections. Today we sometimes hear arranged versions (Mozart made one) played by orchestras of one hundred and choruses of several hundred.

When discussing texture (p. 67) we studied the famous *Hallelujah Chorus,* which ends part II of *Messiah.* Now we will focus on movements 1 to 4 and 12 from part I, which deals with the prophecy of the Messiah's coming. The whole oratorio has over fifty movements, and Handel ensures variety by skillfully contrasting movements and grouping them. He achieves profound effects through simple alternation of major and minor. *Side 3, band 7*

1.   Sinfonia for Orchestra (French Overture)

Grave; Allegro moderato (Moderate allegro)

Messiah opens with a French overture in minor. As is customary, a slow section featuring dotted rhythms is followed by a quite rapid section beginning like a fugue. A lively subject is passed from higher to lower instruments.

After this, the imitation mainly involves fragments of this subject. Near the end of the movement is a feature typical of Handel: In the midst of bustling motion, the orchestra, quite unexpectedly, sustains a chord, and after a brief pause, there is a closing cadence of slow chords. It's as though Handel applied a brake to bring the music to a decisive end.

The three vocal pieces following the overture form a group consisting of an accompanied recitative, an aria, and a chorus.

2. "Comfort ye, my people"   *Side 3, band 4*
Accompanied Recitative for Tenor and Orchestra

Larghetto (Slow, but less so than largo)

The second movement opens with an orchestral ritornello in major that seems "comforting" after the overture's minor key. This material returns throughout. The second movement is an arioso—the vocal line is between a recitative and an aria, more lyrical than one, less elaborate than the other. At the end, however, a heavenly voice is heard ("The voice of him that crieth in the wilderness"), and the vocal line becomes completely recitative.

The voice of him that crieth in the wilderness, Pre-

pare ye the way of the Lord, make straight in the desert a

high - way for our God.

The tenor's opening "Comfort ye" motive (long-short-long) is echoed by the strings, which repeat it reassuringly throughout.

Isaiah XL, 1-3   Comfort ye, comfort ye my people, saith your God. Speak ye comfortably to Jerusalem, and cry unto her, that her warfare is accomplish'd, that her iniquity is pardon'd. The voice of him that crieth in the wilderness, Prepare ye the way of the Lord, make straight in the desert a highway for our God.

3. "Ev'ry valley shall be exalted"
Aria for Tenor

Side 3, band 5

Andante

This aria is striking in its vivid word-painting, so characteristic of Baroque music. On a single syllable of *exalted* (raised up), forty-six rapid notes form a rising musical line.

Notice, too, the rising and falling direction of the phrase "and every mountain and hill made low."

"The crooked straight" is represented:

Plain (smooth or level), in the line "and the rough places plain," is expressed by sustained tones and a long, legato melodic line.

Isaiah XL, 4.   Ev'ry valley shall be exalted, and ev'ry mountain and hill made low, the crooked straight, and the rough places plain.

Messiah
(1741)

179

4. "And the glory of the Lord shall be revealed"
Chorus

Allegro

In quick succession Handel gives us the altos alone, the whole chorus in a chordal assertion, and then the various voices imitating each other. Four different melodic ideas are contrasted and intertwined. The solemn repeated-note idea, "For the mouth of the Lord hath spoken it," is heard against the more rhythmically active "and all flesh shall see it together."

Isaiah XL, 5   And the glory of the Lord shall be revealed, all flesh shall see it together, for the mouth of the Lord hath spoken it.

Side 3, band 6   **12. "For Unto us a Child is born"**
Chorus

This is some of Handel's most joyful music. The texture is light, often with only one or two voices singing at a time. After the sopranos announce a motive, it is imitated by the tenors, then both voices—with different rhythms—are combined.

The Baroque Period   The words "and the government shall be upon His shoulder" bring a new melodic idea in dotted rhythm.

180

Tenors

and the gov-ern-ment shall be up-on His shoul - - - - der;

Handel keeps the dynamics subdued until the magnificent chordal outburst on "Wonderful, Counsellor." This change of texture and dynamics is a master's stroke.

With such a close fusion of words and music, it may be disconcerting to learn that most of the melodic ideas in this chorus came from Handel's Italian duet for the words "No, I will not trust you, blind love, cruel Beauty! You are too treacherous, too charming a deity!" (The musical idea for *Wonderful* is new.) But remember that in Handel's time there was little difference in style between sacred and secular music. Amorous and religious joy could therefore be conveyed in the same manner.

Isaiah IX, 6   For unto us a Child is born, unto us a Son is given, and the government shall be upon His shoulder, and His Name shall be called: Wonderful, Counsellor, the Mighty God, the Everlasting Father, the Prince of Peace!

Messiah
(1741)

181

THE CLASSICAL PERIOD

1 The Classical Style (1750–1820)

2 Composer, Patron, and Public in the Classical Period

3 Sonata Form

4 Theme and Variations

5 Minuet and Trio

6 Rondo

7 The Classical Symphony

8 The Classical Concerto

9 Classical Chamber Music

10 Joseph Haydn

11 Wolfgang Amadeus Mozart

12 Ludwig van Beethoven

The six-year-old Mozart playing for Emperor Francis I and Empress Maria Theresa of Austria (The Bettmann Archive).

1 | THE CLASSICAL STYLE (1750–1820)

In looking at the Baroque era, we found that the scientific methods and discoveries of geniuses like Galileo and Newton had vastly changed man's view of the world. By the middle of the eighteenth century, faith in the power of reason was so great that it began to undermine the authority of the social and religious establishment. Philosophers and writers—especially Voltaire (1694–1778) and Denis Diderot (1713–1784)—saw their time as a great turning point in history and referred to it as the "Age of Enlightenment." They believed in progress, holding that reason, not custom or tradition, was the best guide to human conduct. Their attacks on the privileges of the aristocracy and clergy reflected the outlook of the middle class, which struggled for its rights. This new climate of opinion prepared the way for the American and French Revolutions at the end of the eighteenth century.

Revolutions in thought and action were paralleled by shifts of style in the visual arts. During the early eighteenth century, the heavy, monumental Baroque style gave way to the more intimate rococo style, with its light colors, curved lines, and graceful ornaments. Painters Antoine Watteau (1684–1721) and Jean Honoré Fragonard (1732–1806) depicted an enchanted world peopled by elegant men and women in constant pursuit of pleasure. But by the later eighteenth century there was yet another change in taste, and rococo art was thought frivolous, excessively ornamented, and lacking in ethical content. The rococo style was superseded by the neoclassical style, which attempted to recapture the "noble simplicity and calm grandeur" of ancient Greek and Roman art. Neoclassical artists emphasized firm lines, clear structures, and moralistic subject matter. The painter Jacques Louis David (1748–1825), who took part in the French Revolution, sought to inspire heroism and patriotism through his scenes of ancient Rome.

Artistic response to the decline of traditional power is evidenced further by English painter William Hogarth (1697–1764), whose socially conscious paintings satirized the manners and morals of the British aristocracy and middle class, and by the Spaniard Francisco Goya (1746–1828), whose highly personal vision lashed out against hypocrisy, oppression, and inhumanity.

In music history, the transition from the Baroque style to the full flowering of the Classical is called the "pre-Classical" period; it extends from roughly 1730 to 1770. The shift in musical taste parallels the similar, earlier trend in the visual arts. It was developing even as Bach and Handel were creating Baroque masterpieces. Among the important pioneers of this new style were Bach's sons, Carl Philipp Emanuel (1714–1788) and Johann Christian (1735–1782). Around the middle of the eighteenth century, composers concentrated on simplicity and clarity, discarding much that had enriched late Baroque music. Polyphonic texture was neglected in favor of tuneful melody and simple harmony. Carl

The Classical Period

Rococo painter Jean Honoré Fragonard depicted the game
of love in *The Meeting* (Copyright, The Frick Collection,
New York).

Neoclassical painter Jacques Louis David used moralistic subject matter in *Death of Socrates* painted in 1787 (The Metropolitan Museum of Art, Wolfe Fund, 1931).

Philipp Emanuel Bach described music with strict polyphonic imitation as "dry and despicable pieces of pedantry." Mid-eighteenth-century composers entertained their listeners with music offering contrasts of mood and theme. The term *gallant style* (*style galant*) was applied to this light, graceful music.

The term *Classical* is confusing because it has so many different meanings. It may refer to an aspect of Greek or Roman antiquity, or it may be used for any supreme accomplishment of lasting appeal (as in the expression "movie classic"). Many people take "classical music" to mean anything that is *not* rock, jazz, folk, or popular music.

Music historians have borrowed the term *Classical* from the field of art history, where it is more appropriate. Painting, sculpture, and architecture of the late eighteenth and early nineteenth centuries were often influenced by Greek and Roman models. But the music of this period shows little direct relationship to antiquity. The significant parallel between "Classical" music and "neoclassical" art is a common stress on balance and clarity of structure. These traits can be found in the fully developed Classical style in music which we will focus on. The

The Classical
Period

Monticello, Thomas Jefferson's home, shows the influence
of ancient Greek and Roman architecture (Feily/Monk-
meyer).

style flourished from about 1770 to 1820, and its master composers are Joseph
Haydn (1732–1809), Wolfgang Amadeus Mozart (1756–1791), and Ludwig van
Beethoven (1770–1827). First, we'll study some characteristics of their work.

Classical Contrast of Mood

Great variety and contrast of mood received new emphasis in Classical music.
While a late Baroque piece may convey a single emotion, a Classical composition
will fluctuate in mood. Dramatic, turbulent music may lead into a carefree dance
tune. Not only are there contrasting themes within a movement, but there also
may be striking contrasts within a single theme.

Mood in Classical music may change gradually or suddenly, expressing
conflicting surges of elation and depression. But such conflict and contrast are
under the firm control of the Classical composer. Great masters like Haydn,
Mozart, and Beethoven were able to impart unity and logic to music of wide
emotional range.

 Classical
Contrast of
Mood

Classical Rhythm

Flexibility of rhythm adds variety to Classical music. A Classical composition has a wealth of rhythmic patterns, while a Baroque piece contains a few that are reiterated throughout. Baroque works convey a sense of continuity and perpetual motion, so that after the first few bars one can predict pretty well the rhythmic character of an entire movement. But the Classical style includes unexpected pauses, syncopations, and frequent changes from long notes to shorter ones. And the change from one pattern of note-lengths to another may be either sudden or gradual.

Classical Texture

In contrast to the polyphonic texture of late Baroque music, Classical music is basically homophonic. However, texture is treated as flexibly as rhythm. Pieces shift smoothly or suddenly from one texture to another. A work may begin homophonically with a melody and simple accompaniment, but then tension and excitement are created by a change to a more complex polyphonic texture that features two simultaneous melodies or melodic fragments imitated among the various instruments.

Classical Melody

Classical melodies are among the most tuneful and easy to remember. The themes of even highly sophisticated compositions may have a folk or popular flavor. Occasionally, composers simply borrowed popular tunes. (Mozart did, in his variations on "Twinkle, Twinkle, Little Star," which he knew as the French song *Ah, vous dirai-je, maman.*) More often, they wrote original themes with a popular character.

Classical melodies often sound balanced and symmetrical because they are made up of two phrases of the same length. The second phrase may begin like the first, but it ends more conclusively. Such a melodic type, which may be diagrammed a a′, is easy to sing (it frequently is found in nursery tunes such as "Mary Had a Little Lamb"). Baroque melodies, on the contrary, tend to be less symmetrical, more elaborate, and harder to sing.

Classical Dynamics and the Piano

The Classical composers' interest in expressing shades of emotion led to widespread use of gradual dynamic change—crescendo and descrescendo. They did not restrict themselves to the terraced dynamics (abrupt shifts from loud to soft) characteristic of Baroque music. Crescendos and decrescendos were an electrifying novelty, and audiences sometimes rose excitedly from their seats.

The Classical Period

188

The Classical desire for gradual dynamic change led to the replacement of the harpsichord by the piano. By varying the finger pressure on the keys, a pianist can play more loudly or softly. Although the piano was invented in 1709, it began to replace the harpsichord only in the 1780s and 1790s. Almost all the mature keyboard compositions of Haydn, Mozart, and Beethoven were written for the piano, rather than for the harpsichord, clavichord, or organ featured in Baroque music.

The End of the Basso Continuo

The basso continuo was gradually abandoned during the Classical period. In Haydn's or Mozart's works, a harpsichordist did not need to improvise an accompaniment. The basso continuo became obsolete because more and more music was written for amateurs, who could not master the difficult art of improvising from a figured bass. Also, Classical composers wanted more control; they preferred to specify an accompaniment rather than to trust the judgment of improvisers.

The Classical Orchestra

A new orchestra evolved during the Classical period. Unlike the Baroque orchestra, it was a standard group of four sections: strings, woodwinds, brass, and percussion. In the late instrumental works of Mozart and Haydn, an orchestra might consist of the following:

Strings: violins 1, violins 2, violas, cellos, double basses
Woodwinds: 2 flutes, 2 oboes, 2 clarinets, 2 bassoons
Brass: 2 French horns, 2 trumpets
Percussion: 2 timpani

Notice that woodwind and brass instruments are paired and that clarinets are added. On the other hand, trombones were used by Haydn and Mozart only in opera and church music, not in solely instrumental works.

The number of musicians in a Classical orchestra was greater than in a Baroque group, but practice varied considerably from place to place. Haydn directed a private orchestra of only twenty-five players from 1761 to 1790. But for public concerts in London in 1795, he led a large orchestra of sixty musicians.

Classical composers exploited individual tone colors of orchestral instruments. Unlike Baroque composers, they did not treat one instrument like another. Classical composers would not let an oboe duplicate the violin melody for the entire length of a movement. A Classical piece has greater variety of tone color, and more rapid changes of color. Strings alone may begin, followed by a shift to woodwinds, and then the whole orchestra will be heard.

 The Classical Orchestra

189

Each section of the Classical orchestra had a special role. The strings were the most important section, with the first violins taking the melody most of the time, and the lower strings providing an accompaniment. The woodwinds added contrasting tone colors and were often given melodic solos. Horns and trumpets brought power to loud passages and filled out the harmony, but they did not usually play the main melody. Timpani were used for rhythmic bite and emphasis. As a whole, the Classical orchestra had developed into a flexible and colorful instrument to which composers could entrust their most powerful and dramatic musical conceptions.

Classical Form

Instrumental works of the Classical period usually consist of several movements that contrast in tempo and character. Usually four movements are arranged as follows:

1. Fast movement
2. Slow movement
3. Dance-related movement
4. Fast movement

Classical symphonies and string quartets usually follow this four-movement pattern, while Classical sonatas may consist of two, three, or four movements. A *symphony* is written for orchestra; a *string quartet* for two violins, viola, and cello; and a *sonata* for one or two instruments. (The Classical symphony, string quartet, and sonata are more fully described in sections 3 to 7 and 9.)

In writing an individual movement of a symphony, string quartet, or sonata, a Classical composer could choose from several different forms. One movement of a composition might be in A B A form, while another might be a theme and variations. The following sections will describe some forms used in Classical movements, but now we'll look at a few general characteristics of Classical form.

Classical movements often contrast themes vividly. A movement may contain two, three, or even four or more themes of different character. This use of contrasting themes distinguishes Classical from Baroque music, which often uses only one main theme. The Classical composer sometimes signals the arrival of a new theme with a brief pause.

The larger sections of a Classical movement balance each other in a satisfying and symmetrical way. Unstable sections that wander from the tonic key are balanced by stable ones that confirm it. By the end of a Classical movement, musical tensions have been resolved.

Though we speak of the Classical style, we must remember that Haydn, Mozart, and Beethoven were three individuals with dissimilar personalities. While Haydn's and Mozart's works at first may sound similar, deeper involvement reveals striking personal styles. Beethoven's music seems more powerful, violent, and emotional when compared with the apparently more restrained and elegant works of the earlier masters. But Haydn and Mozart also composed music that is passionate and dramatic. We'll see that all three composers employed similar musical procedures and forms; yet their emotional statements bear the particular stamp of each.

COMPOSER, PATRON, AND PUBLIC IN THE CLASSICAL PERIOD ‖ 2 ‖

Haydn, Mozart, Beethoven—three of the world's greatest composers—worked during a time of violent political and social upheaval. The seventy-year period from 1750 to 1820 was convulsed by the American and French Revolutions and by the Napoleonic wars. Political and economic power shifted from the aristocracy and the church to the middle class. Social mobility increased to a point where a low-born genius like Napoleon could become Emperor of France. "Subversive" new slogans like "Liberty, equality, fraternity!" sprang from the people's lips. All established ideas were being reexamined, including the existence of God.

Like everyone else, musicians were strongly affected by such changes, and in the careers of the three Classical masters we can trace the slow emancipation of the composer. First came Joseph Haydn (1732–1809), content to spend most of his life serving a wealthy aristocratic family. His contract of employment (1761) shows he was considered a skilled servant, like a gardener or gamekeeper. He had to wear a uniform and "compose such music as His Highness shall order"—and was warned to "refrain from vulgarity in eating, drinking, and conversation." Born just twenty-four years later, Wolfgang Amadeus Mozart (1756–1791) could not bear being treated as a servant; he broke from his court position and came to Vienna to try his luck as a free-lance musician. But his personality was unsuited to the struggles of such a career, and he died tragically in poverty. Ludwig van Beethoven (1770–1827) succeeded where Mozart failed. Only a few years after Mozart's death, Beethoven was able to work as an independent musician in Vienna. His success was gained through a wider middle-class market for music and a commanding personality that prompted the nobility to give him gifts and treat him as an equal.

As the eighteenth century advanced, more people made more money. Merchants, doctors, and government officials could afford larger homes, finer clothes, and better food. But the prospering middle class wanted more than material goods; it also sought aristocratic luxuries like theater, literature, and music. In fact, during the Classical period, the middle class had a great influence on

Composer, Patron, and Public

191

Spanish painter Francisco Goya lashed out at the inhumanity of war in *The Third of May, 1808,* which shows the execution of Spanish hostages by soldiers of Napoleon's army (Omikron).

music. Because palace concerts were usually closed to the townsman, he organized public concerts where, for the price of admission, he could hear the latest symphonies and concertos. Following the success of a famous concert series in Paris, the *Concert spirituel* (1725), public concerts mushroomed throughout Europe. But the merchant or lawyer was not content to hear music only in concerts. He wanted to be surrounded by music at home. He felt his own children deserved music lessons as much as did the children of aristocrats. Indeed, if his children played instruments well enough, they might be invited to palaces and eventually marry into the aristocracy. In any event, demand for printed music, instruments, and music lessons had vastly increased.

Composers in the Classical period took middle-class tastes into account. They wrote pieces that were easy for amateur musicians to play and understand. They

The old Burgtheater in Vienna, where Mozart's operas were first performed (Austrian National Library).

turned from serious to comic opera, from heroic and mythological plots dear to the nobility to middle-class subjects and folklike tunes. Their comic operas sometimes even ridiculed the aristocracy, and their minuets became less elegant and courtly, more vigorous and rustic.

Serious composition was flavored by folk and popular music. The Classical masters sometimes used familiar tunes as themes for symphonies and variations. Mozart was delighted that people danced to waltzes arranged from his opera melodies. Haydn, Mozart, and Beethoven all wrote dance music for public balls in Vienna.

Vienna

Vienna was one of the music centers of Europe during the Classical period, and Haydn, Mozart, and Beethoven were all active there. The seat of the Holy Roman Empire (which included parts of present-day Austria, Germany, Italy, Hungary, and Czechoslovakia), it was a bustling cultural and commercial center with a cosmopolitan character. Its population of almost 250,000 (1800) made Vienna the fourth largest city in Europe. All three Classical masters were born elsewhere, but they were drawn to Vienna for study and for recognition. In

Vienna

Vienna Haydn and Mozart became close friends and influenced each other's musical style. Beethoven traveled to Vienna at sixteen to play for Mozart; at twenty-two, he returned to study with Haydn.

Princes, dukes, and counts from all over the Empire spent the winter in Vienna, sometimes bringing their private orchestras. Music was an important part of court life, and a good orchestra was a symbol of prestige. Many of the nobility were excellent musicians. For instance, Empress Maria Theresa had sung in palace musicales when she was young; Emperor Joseph II was a competent cellist, and Archduke Rudolf was Beethoven's long-time student of piano and composition.

Much music was heard in private concerts, where aristocrats and wealthy commoners played alongside professional musicians. Mozart and Beethoven often earned money by performing in these intimate concerts. The nobility frequently hired servants who could double as musicians. An advertisement in the *Vienna Gazette* of 1789 reads: "Wanted, for a house of the gentry, a manservant who knows how to play the violin well."

In Vienna there was also outdoor music, light and popular in tone. Small street bands of wind and string players played at garden parties or under the windows of people likely to throw down money. A Viennese almanac reported that "on fine summer nights you may come upon serenades in the streets at all hours." Haydn and Mozart wrote many outdoor entertainment pieces, which they called *divertimentos* or *serenades.* Vienna's great love of music and its enthusiastic demand for new works made it the chosen city of Haydn, Mozart, and Beethoven.

‖3‖ SONATA FORM

An astonishing amount of great music from the Classical period to the twentieth century is composed in *sonata form* (sometimes called *sonata-allegro form*). The term **sonata form** refers to the form of a *single* movement. It should not be confused with the term sonata, which is used for a whole composition made up of *several* movements. The opening fast movement of a Classical symphony, sonata, or string quartet is usually in sonata form. This form is also used in slow movements and in fast concluding movements.

A sonata-form movement consists of three main sections: the *exposition,* where the themes are presented; the *development,* where themes are treated in new ways; and the *recapitulation,* where the themes return. These three main sections are often followed by a concluding section, the *coda* (Italian for "tail"). Remember that these sections are all within *one movement.* A sonata-form movement may be outlined as follows:

	Exposition
	First theme in tonic (home) key
	Bridge containing modulation from home key to new key
	Second theme in new key
	Closing section in key of second theme
ONE MOVEMENT	*Development*
	New treatment of themes; modulations to different keys
	Recapitulation
	First theme in tonic key
	Bridge
	Second theme in tonic key
	Closing section in tonic key
	(*Coda* in tonic key)

A movement in sonata form is sometimes preceded by a slow introduction that creates a strong feeling of expectancy.

Exposition

The **exposition** sets up a strong conflict between the tonic key and the new key, between the first theme (or group of themes) and the second theme (or group of themes). It begins with the first theme in the tonic, or home, key. There follows a **bridge,** or *transition,* leading to the second theme in a new key. Such modulation from the home key to a new key creates a feeling of harmonic tension and forward motion. The second theme often contrasts in mood with the first theme. A closing section ends the exposition in the key of the second theme. At the end of a Classical exposition there usually is a repeat sign (:‖) indicating that the whole exposition is repeated.

Development

The **development** is often the most dramatic section of the movement, keeping the listener off balance as the music moves restlessly through several different keys. Through these rapid modulations, the harmonic tension is heightened. In this section, themes are *developed,* or treated in new ways. They are broken into fragments or **motives,** which are short musical ideas developed within a composition. A motive may take on different and unexpected emotional meanings. A fragment of a comic theme, for example, may be made to sound aggressive and menacing through changes of melody, rhythm, or dynamics. Themes can be combined with new ideas or changed in texture. A complex polyphonic texture can be woven by shifting a motive rapidly among different instruments. The harmonic and thematic searching of the development builds a tension that demands resolution.

 Development

195

Recapitulation

The beginning of the **recapitulation** brings resolution as we again hear the first theme in the tonic key. In the recapitulation, the first theme, bridge, second theme, and concluding section are presented more or less as they were in the exposition, with one crucial difference: All the principal material is now in the tonic key. Earlier, in the exposition, there had been strong contrast between the first theme in the home key and the second theme and closing section in a new key; that basis for tension is resolved in the recapitulation by presenting the first theme, second theme, and closing section all in the tonic key.

Coda

An even more powerful feeling of conclusion is attained by following the recapitulation with yet another section. The **coda** rounds off a movement by repeating themes or developing them further. It always ends in the tonic key.

The amazing durability and vitality of sonata form result from its capacity for drama. The form moves from a stable situation toward conflict (the exposition), to heightened tension (the development), then back to stability and resolution of conflict (the recapitulation and coda). Here is an outline:

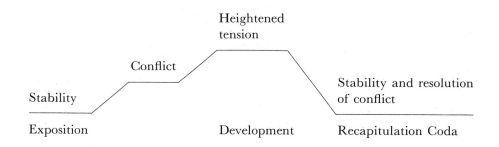

Sonata form is exceptionally flexible and subject to endless variation. It is not a rigid mold into which musical ideas are poured. Rather, it may be viewed as a set of principles that serve to shape and unify contrasts of theme and key. Haydn, Mozart, and Beethoven repeatedly used sonata form, yet each maintained individuality. Movements in sonata form may differ radically in character, length, and in the number and treatment of themes. Sonata form is so broad and useful that it's no surprise to find it spanning more than two centuries.

Side 4, band 4

Fourth Movement from Symphony No. 40 in G Minor, K. 550, by Wolfgang Amadeus Mozart

This rapid sonata-form movement from Mozart's Symphony No. 40 in G Minor conveys a feeling of controlled tension. The opening theme, in the tonic key of G minor, offers brusque contrasts of dynamics and rhythm. A soft upward arpeggio (broken chord) alternates repeatedly with a loud rushing phrase.

Excitement is maintained throughout the long bridge, which is based on the loud rushing phrase of the first theme. The bridge ends clearly with a brief pause, as do other sections in this movement.

The tender second theme is in the new key of B-flat major. A lyrical contrast to the brusque opening theme, it is softer, flows more smoothly, and uses longer notes.

Mozart weaves almost the entire development section from the upward arpeggio of the first theme. During the opening few seconds, there is an eruption of violence as the orchestra in unison plays a variation of the arpeggio and a series of jagged downward leaps. As the development continues, the texture becomes polyphonic and contrasts with the homophony of the exposition. Arpeggios press upon each other in quick imitation. Rapid shifts of key create restless intensity.

In the recapitulation, both the first and second themes are in the tonic key, G minor. This minor key now adds a touch of melancholy to the tender second theme, which was heard in major before. The passion and violence of this movement foreshadow the Romantic expression to come during the nineteenth century.

LISTENING OUTLINE
To be read while music is heard

Symphony No. 40 in G Minor, K. 550 (1788), by Wolfgang Amadeus Mozart

Fourth Movement: Allegro assai (very fast)

Sonata form, duple meter ($\frac{2}{2}$), G minor

flute, 2 oboes, 2 clarinets, 2 bassoons, 2 French horns, violins 1, violins 2, violas, cellos, double basses

(About 4½ min)

EXPOSITION
First theme   1   Upward arpeggio, *p*, explosive rushing phrase, *f*, minor key.

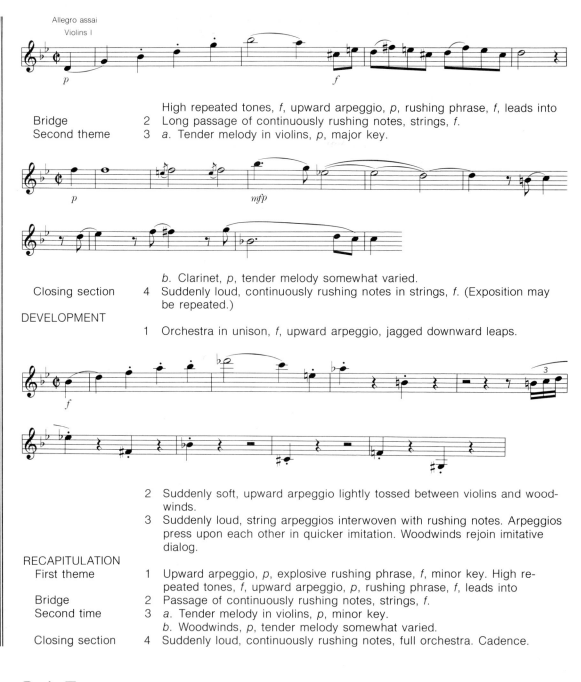

Allegro assai
Violins I

p   *f*

                High repeated tones, *f*, upward arpeggio, *p*, rushing phrase, *f*, leads into

Bridge   2   Long passage of continuously rushing notes, strings, *f*.

Second theme   3   *a.* Tender melody in violins, *p*, major key.

p   *mfp*

                b. Clarinet, *p*, tender melody somewhat varied.

Closing section   4   Suddenly loud, continuously rushing notes in strings, *f*. (Exposition may
                       be repeated.)

DEVELOPMENT

            1   Orchestra in unison, *f*, upward arpeggio, jagged downward leaps.

f

            2   Suddenly soft, upward arpeggio lightly tossed between violins and wood-
                   winds.

            3   Suddenly loud, string arpeggios interwoven with rushing notes. Arpeggios
                   press upon each other in quicker imitation. Woodwinds rejoin imitative
                   dialog.

RECAPITULATION
  First theme   1   Upward arpeggio, *p*, explosive rushing phrase, *f*, minor key. High re-
                   peated tones, *f*, upward arpeggio, *p*, rushing phrase, *f*, leads into

Bridge   2   Passage of continuously rushing notes, strings, *f*.
Second time   3   *a.* Tender melody in violins, *p*, minor key.
                  b. Woodwinds, *p*, tender melody somewhat varied.

Closing section   4   Suddenly loud, continuously rushing notes, full orchestra. Cadence.

Basic Terms

sonata form	bridge (transition)	motive	coda
exposition	development	recapitulation	

THEME AND VARIATIONS

The form called *theme and variations* is widely used in the Classical period, both as an independent piece, and as one movement of a symphony, sonata, or string quartet. In a **theme and variations,** a basic musical idea—the theme—is repeated over and over and is changed each time. This form may be outlined as Theme (A)–Variation 1 (A')–Variation 2 (A'')–Variation 3 (A'''), and so on; each prime mark indicates a variation of the basic idea.

Each variation is usually about the same length as the theme. Changes of melody, rhythm, harmony, accompaniment, dynamics, or tone color may be used to give a variation its own identity. The core melody may appear in the bass, or it may be repeated in a minor key instead of a major one. It may be heard together with a new melody. Each variation is unique and may differ in mood from the theme. The variations may be separated by pauses, or they may be connected to each other. A composer may invent an original theme or borrow someone else's. Beethoven once borrowed a little waltz tune and put it through thirty-three brilliant variations. More modest examples of theme and variations have as few as three variations.

Second Movement from Symphony No. 94 in G Major ("Surprise"), by Joseph Haydn

Side 4, band 1

The second movement (Andante) of Haydn's "Surprise" Symphony is a theme and variations. The folklike, staccato theme begins softly but is punctuated by a sudden loud chord. This is the "surprise" of the symphony. There are four variations, in which the theme is changed in tone color, dynamics, rhythm, and melody. Sometimes the original melody is accompanied by a new one called a countermelody. Such combinations of two distinctive melodies result in polyphonic texture. In one variation the theme is presented in minor instead of major. The last variation is followed by a closing section in which a gently dissonant accompaniment momentarily darkens the mood of the carefree theme.

The theme is composed of two parts, sections *a* and *b*, which are each repeated. This pattern is usually retained in the variations.

LISTENING OUTLINE
To be read while music is heard

Symphony No. 94 in G major ("Surprise"; 1791),
by Joseph Haydn (1732–1809)

Theme and Variations

199

Second Movement: Andante

Theme and variations, duple meter ($\frac{2}{4}$), C major

2 flutes, 2 oboes, 2 bassoons, 2 French horns, 2 trumpets, timpani, violins 1, violins 2, violas, cellos, double basses

(About 5½ min)

THEME

   Section *a*   Violins, *p*, staccato theme.

                     Section *a* repeated, *pp*, with pizzicato string accompaniment. Surprise chord, *ff*.

   Section *b*   Violins, *p*, continuation of theme.

                     Section *b* repeated with flute and oboe.

VARIATION 1   *a*. Theme begins *f*, higher countermelody in violins, *p*. Section *a* repeated.

                     b. Violins, *p*, continuation of theme and higher countermelody. Section *b* repeated

VARIATION 2   *a*. Theme in minor, *ff*, violin phrase in major, *p*. Section *a* repeated.

                     b. Violins, *f*, rapid downward scales, orchestra *f*. Violins alone, *p*, lead into

VARIATION 3   *a*. Oboe, *p*, theme in faster repeated notes, major key.

                     Flute and oboe, *p*, legato countermelody above staccato theme in violins, *p*.

VARIATION 4

b. Continuation of theme and countermelody. Section b repeated.
a. Theme in brasses and woodwinds, *ff*, fast notes in violins, *ff*.
Violins, *p*, legato version of theme, dotted rhythm (long-short).

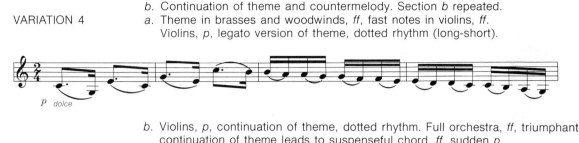

p dolce

CLOSING SECTION

b. Violins, *p*, continuation of theme, dotted rhythm. Full orchestra, *ff*, triumphant continuation of theme leads to suspenseful chord, *ff*, sudden *p*.
Theme in oboe, *p*, gently dissonant chords in strings, flute joins, *pp* conclusion.

Classical

MINUET AND TRIO | 5 |

The form known as **minuet and trio,** or **minuet,** is employed as the third movement of Classical symphonies, string quartets, and other works. Like the movements of the Baroque suite, the minuet originated as a dance. It first appeared at the French court of Louis XIV around 1650 and was danced by aristocrats throughout the eighteenth century. The minuet was a stately, dignified dance in which the couple exchanged curtsies and bows.

The minuet movement of a symphony or string quartet is written for listening, not dancing. It is in triple meter ($\frac{3}{4}$ time) and usually in a moderate tempo. The movement is in A B A form: minuet (A), trio (B), minuet (A). The trio (B) is usually quieter than the minuet (A) section and requires fewer instruments. It often contains woodwind solos. The trio section got its name during the Baroque period, when a set of two dances would be followed by a repetition of the first dance. The second dance was known as a "trio" because it usually was played by three instruments. Classical composers did not restrict themselves to three instruments in the B sections of their minuets, but the name "trio" remained.

The A (minuet) section includes smaller parts a, b, and a′ (variation of a). In the opening A (minuet) section, all the smaller parts are repeated, as follows: a (repeated) ba′ (repeated). [In the musical score, the repeat sign (:‖) indicates each repetition.] The B (trio) section is similar in form: c (repeated) dc′ (repeated). At the close of the B (trio) section, the repetition of the entire A (minuet) section is indicated by the words *da capo* ("from the beginning"). This time, however, the minuet is played straight through without the repetitions: a ba′. The whole movement can be outlined like this:

Minuet	*Trio*	*Minuet*
A	B	A
a (repeated) ba′ (repeated)	c (repeated) dc′ (repeated)	a ba′

With its A B A form and many repeated parts, the minuet is structurally the simplest movement of a symphony or string quartet.

 Minuet and Trio

201

In many of Beethoven's compositions, the third movement is not a minuet but a related form called a *scherzo*. Like a minuet, a **scherzo** is usually in A B A form and triple meter, but it moves more quickly, generating energy, rhythmic drive, and rough humor. (*Scherzo* is Italian for "joke.")

Side 4, band 5

Third Movement (Minuet) from *Eine kleine Nachtmusik*, K. 525 ("A Little Night Music"), by Wolfgang Amadeus Mozart

Mozart's *Eine kleine Nachtmusik* is a **serenade,** a work that's usually light in mood, meant for evening entertainment. It is written for a small string orchestra or for a string quartet plus a double bass. (The double bass plays the cello part an octave lower.) The third movement is a courtly minuet in A B A form. The A (minuet) section is stately, mostly loud and staccato, with a clearly marked beat. In contrast, the B (trio) section is intimate, soft, and legato. Its murmuring accompaniment contributes to the smooth flow of the music.

LISTENING OUTLINE
To be read while music is heard

Eine kleine Nachtmusik, K. 525 (1787), by Wolfgang Amadeus Mozart

Third Movement: Menuetto (Allegretto)

A B A form, triple meter ($\frac{3}{4}$), G major

violins 1, violins 2, violas, cellos, double bass

(About 2 min)

MINUET (A)   1   Stately melody, *f*, predominantly staccato. Repeated.

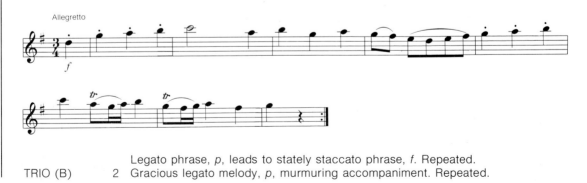

                Legato phrase, *p*, leads to stately staccato phrase, *f*. Repeated.

TRIO (B)   2   Gracious legato melody, *p*, murmuring accompaniment. Repeated.

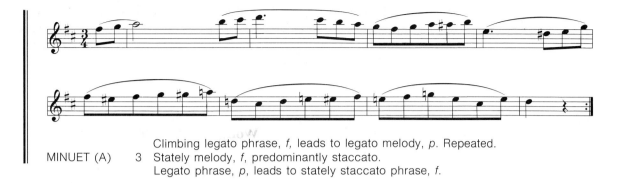

MINUET (A)   3   Climbing legato phrase, *f,* leads to legato melody, *p.* Repeated.
Stately melody, *f,* predominantly staccato.
Legato phrase, *p,* leads to stately staccato phrase, *f.*

Basic Terms

minuet and trio (minuet)
serenade
scherzo

RONDO 6

Many Classical movements are in *rondo* form. **A rondo** features a tuneful main theme (A) which returns several times in alternation with other themes. Common rondo patterns are A B A C A and A B A C A B A. The main theme is usually lively, pleasing, and simple to remember, and the listener can easily recognize its return. Because the main theme is usually stated in the tonic key, its return is all the more welcome. A rondo appears both as an independent piece and as one movement of a symphony, string quartet, or sonata. It often serves as a finale, because its liveliness, regularity, and buoyancy bring a happy sense of conclusion.

Rondo form is often combined with elements of sonata form to produce the *sonata-rondo.* The **sonata-rondo** contains a development section similar to that in sonata form and is outlined A B A–Development section–A B A.

The popularity of the rondo did not end with the Classical period. It has been used by twentieth-century composers such as Igor Stravinsky and Arnold Schoenberg.

Fourth Movement (Rondo)
from String Quartet in C Minor, Op. 18, No. 4,
by Ludwig van Beethoven

Side 5, band 5

The exciting rondo movement from Beethoven's String Quartet in C minor, Op. 18, No. 4 may be outlined A B A C A B A. Its main theme, A, is a lively gypsy

Fourth
Movement
(Rondo)

203

dance made up of two repeated parts: a a b b. An unexpected held tone in part b suggests the improvisatory playing of a gypsy fiddler. The main theme, in minor, contrasts with the other themes, which are in major. Theme B is a lyrical legato melody, while theme C is playful, with quick upward rushes. At its final return, the main theme (A) has a faster tempo, prestissimo, and leads into a frenzied concluding section.

LISTENING OUTLINE
To be read while music is heard

String Quartet in C Minor, Op. 18, No. 4 (1798–1800), by Ludwig van Beethoven

Fourth Movement: Rondo (Allegro)

Duple meter ($\frac{2}{2}$), C minor

violin 1, violin 2, viola, cello

(About $4\frac{1}{2}$ min)

A   1   Lively main theme in violin 1, minor key.

B   2   Lyrical melody, legato, major key.

A   3   Lively main theme, minor key. Theme becomes more agitated.
C   4   Upward rushes in each instrument, playful downward phrase in violin 1, major key.
A   5   Lively main theme, minor key. Crescendo to held chord, *ff*.
B   6   Lyrical melody, legato, major key. Melody repeated an octave higher. Playful phrases in violins, crescendo to *f*, sustained tones in violin 1.
A   7   Lively main theme, *ff*, faster tempo (prestissimo), minor key. Concluding section builds, downward staccato scale, high repeated tones, *p*. Upward rushes, *ff*, at end.

Basic Terms

rondo
sonata-rondo

The Classical Period

THE CLASSICAL SYMPHONY |7|

The great contribution of the Classical period to orchestral music is the symphony. Haydn wrote about one hundred and four symphonies, Mozart over forty, and Beethoven nine. Most of Haydn's symphonies were composed for his employers, who required a steady flow of works for their palace concerts. Beethoven, on the other hand, wrote a symphony only when inspired. His symphonies are longer than Haydn's or Mozart's and were conceived for performance in large concert halls.

A **symphony** is an extended, ambitious composition lasting between twenty and forty-five minutes, exploiting the expanded range of tone color and dynamics of the Classical orchestra. A Classical symphony usually consists of four movements which evoke a wide range of emotions through contrasts of tempo and mood. A typical sequence is (1) a vigorous, dramatic fast movement; (2) a lyrical slow movement; (3) a dancelike movement (minuet or scherzo); and (4) a brilliant or heroic fast movement.

The opening movement is almost always fast and in sonata form. It is usually the most dramatic movement and stresses exciting development of short motives. Sometimes a slow introduction leads to the opening fast movement and creates a feeling of anticipation.

It is in the slow second movement that we are most likely to find broad, songlike melodies. This movement, by and large, is either in sonata form, A B A form, or theme-and-variations form. Unlike the other movements in the symphony, the slow movement is generally *not* in the tonic key. For example, if the first, third, and fourth movements are in the tonic key of C major, the second movement may be in F major. The new key points up the expressive contrast of the slow movement.

In the symphonies of Haydn and Mozart, the third movement is generally a minuet and trio, which may be in a moderate or fairly quick tempo. This movement varies in character from a courtly dance to a peasant romp to a vigorous piece that is hardly dancelike. Beethoven liked fast, energetic scherzos for his third movements.

The fourth, concluding movement of a Haydn or Mozart symphony is fast, lively, and brilliant, but somewhat lighter in mood than the opening movement. (The agitated final movement of Mozart's Symphony No. 40 in G minor is not typical.) Beethoven's concluding movement tends to be more triumphant and heroic in character and sometimes is meant as the climax of the whole symphony. The final movement of a Classical symphony is most often in sonata or sonata-rondo form.

In most Classical symphonies, each movement is a self-contained composition with its own set of themes. A theme in one movement will only rarely reappear in

The Classical Symphony

205

a later movement. (Beethoven's Fifth and Ninth Symphonies are exceptions.) But a symphony is unified partly by the use of the same key in three of its movements. More important, the movements balance and complement each other both musically and emotionally.

The importance of the symphony has lasted into the middle of the twentieth century. Its great significance is reflected in such familiar terms as "symphonic music," "symphony hall," and "symphony orchestra."

Basic Term

symphony

8 | THE CLASSICAL CONCERTO

A Classical **concerto** is a three-movement work for an instrumental soloist and orchestra. It combines the soloist's virtuosity and interpretive abilities with the orchestra's wide range of tone color and dynamics. Emerging from this encounter is a contrast of ideas and sound that is dramatic and satisfying. The soloist is very much the star, and all of his or her musical talents are needed in this challenging dialog.

The Classical love of balance can be seen in the concerto, for soloist and orchestra are equally important. Together, there's an interplay of melodic lines and a spirit of give and take. One moment the soloist plays the melody while the orchestra accompanies. Then the woodwinds may unfold the main theme against rippling arpeggios (broken chords) by the soloist. Mozart and Beethoven—the greatest masters of the Classical concerto—often wrote for themselves as piano soloists, and the piano is the favored solo instrument. But other solo instruments include violin, horn, trumpet, clarinet, bassoon, and cello.

Like symphonies, concertos can last anywhere from twenty to forty-five minutes. But instead of the symphony's four movements, a concerto has three: (1) fast, (2) slow, and (3) fast. A concerto has no minuet or scherzo.

In the first movement and sometimes in the last movement, there is a special unaccompanied showpiece for the soloist, the **cadenza** (Italian for "cadence"). Near the end of the movement, the orchestra suspends forward motion by briefly sustaining a dissonant chord. This is indicated in the score by a *fermata* sign ($\frown$), meaning "pause," which is placed over the chord. The suspense announces the entry of the soloist's cadenza. For several minutes, the soloist, *without orchestra,* displays virtuosity by playing dazzling scale passages and broken chords. Themes of the movement are varied and presented in new keys. At the end of a cadenza, the soloist plays a long trill followed by a chord that meshes with the reentrance of the orchestra.

In the Classical era, the soloist, who was often the composer, generally improvised the cadenzas. In this case, the score contained only the fermata sign, indicating that a cadenza should be inserted at that point. But after the eighteenth century, the art of improvisation declined, and composers began to write cadenzas directly into the score. This gave them more control over their compositions.

Today, performers of eighteenth-century concertos may have a choice of cadenzas. For some concertos the composer may have written cadenzas for his own performance or for that of a student. And many nineteenth- and twentieth-century musicians later provided cadenzas for Classical concertos. These are best when their style matches that of the concerto. For example, the cadenzas Beethoven composed for Mozart's D-minor Piano Concerto are so strong and in the spirit of the work that pianists today still use them.

A Classical concerto begins with a movement in sonata form, but it is different—there are *two* expositions. The first is played by the orchestra, which presents several themes in the home key. This opening section sets the mood for the movement and leads us to expect the soloist's entrance. The second exposition begins with the soloist's first notes. Music for the solo entry may be powerful or quiet, but its effect is dramatic because suspense has been built. With the orchestra, the soloist explores themes from the first exposition and introduces new ones. After a modulation from the home key to a new key, the second exposition then moves to a development section, followed by the recapitulation, cadenza, and coda. The slow middle movement may take any one of several forms, but the finale is usually a quick rondo or sonata-rondo.

Basic Terms

concerto
cadenza

CLASSICAL CHAMBER MUSIC

Classical 9

Classical **chamber music** is designed for the intimate setting of a room (chamber) in a home or palace, rather than for a public concert hall. It is performed by a small group of two to nine musicians, with one player to a part. Chamber music is lighter in sound than Classical orchestral music. During the Classical period, it

Classical
Chamber
Music

was fashionable for an aristocrat or a member of the well-to-do middle class to play chamber music with friends and to hire professional musicians to entertain guests after dinner.

Chamber music is subtle and intimate, intended to please the performer as much as the listener. A chamber music group is a team. Each member is essential, and each may have a share of the important thematic material. This calls for much give and take among the instruments. Classical chamber music does not need a conductor; instead, each musician must be sensitive to what goes on and coordinate dynamics and phrasing with the other musicians. In this respect, a chamber ensemble is like a small jazz group.

The most important form of Classical chamber music is the **string quartet,** written for two violins, a viola, and a cello. Haydn, Mozart, and Beethoven wrote some of their most important music in this form. The string quartet can be compared with a conversation among four lively, sensitive, and intelligent people. And it's not surprising that the string quartet evolved when conversation was cultivated as a fine art.

Like the symphony, the string quartet usually consists of four movements: (1) fast, (2) slow, (3) minuet or scherzo, (4) fast. (Sometimes the second movement is a minuet or scherzo, and the slow movement is third.)

Other popular forms of Classical chamber music are the sonata for violin and piano, the piano trio (violin, cello, and piano), and the string quintet (two violins, two violas, and cello).

Today, as in the eighteenth century, much chamber music is performed by amateurs. By consulting the directory *Amateur Chamber Music Players,* one can find partners for chamber music almost anywhere in the United States.

Basic Terms

>   chamber music
>   string quartet

10 JOSEPH HAYDN

The first of three Classical masters, Joseph Haydn (1732–1809) was born in a tiny Austrian village called Rohrau. His father made wagon wheels, and until the age of six, Haydn's musical background consisted of folksongs his father loved to sing and the peasant dances that whirled about him on festive occasions. (This early contact with folk music later had an influence on his style.) Haydn's eager response to music was recognized, and he was sent to live with a relative who gave him basic music lessons for two years. At eight, he went to Vienna to serve as a choirboy in the Cathedral of St. Stephen. There, though his good voice

Haydn rehearsing at the Esterházy Palace (The Bettmann Archive).

was appreciated, he had no chance for composition lessons or for perfecting an instrumental technique. And when his voice changed, Haydn was dismissed from St. Stephen's and turned out on the street without a penny. "I barely managed to stay alive by giving music lessons to children for about eight years," he wrote. Throughout those years he struggled to teach himself composition and also took odd jobs, including playing violin in the popular Viennese street bands that offered evening entertainment.

Gradually, aristocratic patrons of music began to notice Haydn's talent. For a brief time he was music director at the court of a Bohemian count, but the orchestra was dissolved because of his patron's financial problems. At the age of twenty-nine, Haydn's life changed for the better, forever.

In 1761, Haydn entered the service of the Esterházys, the richest and most powerful of the noble Hungarian families. For almost thirty years, from 1761 to 1790, most of his music was composed for performance in the palaces of the family. Haydn spent much of his time at Esterház, a magnificent but isolated palace in Hungary that contained an opera house, a theater, two concert halls, and 126 guest rooms.

As a highly skilled servant, Haydn was to compose all the music requested by his patron, conduct the orchestra of about twenty-five players, coach singers, and

 Joseph Haydn

209

oversee the condition of instruments and the operation of the music library. He also was required to "appear daily in the antechamber before and after midday and inquire whether His Highness is pleased to order a performance of the orchestra." The amount of work demanded of Haydn as assistant music director and later as music director was staggering; there were usually two concerts and two opera performances weekly, as well as daily chamber music in the prince's apartment. Since Nicholas Esterházy played the baryton (a complicated stringed instrument now obsolete), Haydn wrote over 150 pieces with a baryton part.

Though today it seems degrading for a genius to be dependent on the will of a prince, in the eighteenth century patronage was taken for granted. Composers had definite advantages in that they received a steady income and their works were performed. And though Haydn felt restricted by his job from time to time, he later wisely said, "Not only did I have the encouragement of constant approval, but as conductor of an orchestra I could make experiments, observe what produced an effect and what weakened it, and was thus in a position to improve, alter, make additions or omissions, and be as bold as I pleased. I was cut off from the world; there was no one to confuse or torment me, and I was forced to become original."

Despite an unhappy marriage, Hadyn was good-humored and unselfish. He was conscientious about professional duties, and he cared about the personal interests of his musicians. Prince Nicholas loved Esterház and once stayed at the palace longer than usual. The orchestra members came to Haydn and asked to return to Vienna; they were tired of being isolated in the country, away so long from their wives and children. Haydn obliged by composing a symphony in F-sharp minor, now known as the "Farewell." At its first performance for the prince, the musicians followed the indications in the score: During the last movement, one after another stopped playing, put out his candle, and quietly left the hall. By the time that only Haydn and the first violinist remained, Nicholas took the hint; the next day he ordered the household to return to Vienna.

Haydn met the younger Mozart in the early 1780s and they became close friends. To someone finding fault with one of Mozart's operas, Haydn replied, "I cannot settle this dispute, but this I know: Mozart is the greatest composer the world possesses now."

Over a period of twenty years, word spread about the Esterházys' composer, and Haydn's music became immensely popular all over Europe. Publishers and concert organizations sent commissions for new works. After the death of Prince Nicholas Esterházy in 1790, Haydn was free to go to London where a concert series was planned around his compositions. He'd been asked by concert manager Johann Peter Salomon to write and conduct new symphonies for performance at public concerts. Six were composed for a first visit in 1791–1792 and six more for a second visit in 1794–1795. These twelve became known as the "Salomon Symphonies" or "London Symphonies."

Reports of the time say that Haydn's appearances were triumphs. By the end of the eighteenth century, London was the largest and richest city in the world. Its concert life was unusually active and attracted many foreign musicians.

Joseph Haydn (Royal College of Music).

Acclaim at Haydn's concerts was so overwhelming that some symphony movements had to be repeated. One listener noted that there was "an electrical effect on all present and such a degree of enthusiasm as almost amounted to a frenzy."

And so, a servant had become a celebrity. Haydn was wined and dined by the aristocracy, given an honorary doctorate at Oxford, and received by members of the royal family. And, as though to balance out earlier personal unhappiness, he had a love affair with a rich English widow. After thirty years of service to the Esterházys, Haydn's reception by the English moved him to write, "How sweet is some degree of liberty. The consciousness of no longer being a bond servant sweetens all my toil."

Rich and honored, Haydn returned to Vienna in 1795 and maintained good relations with Esterház. The new Prince, Nicholas II, did not have his father's wide musical interests and liked only religious music. Haydn's agreement specified that he would compose a Mass a year. There are six, and all reflect the mature, brilliant writing of the London Symphonies. In this period of his late sixties, Haydn composed two oratorios, *The Creation* (1798) and *The Seasons* (1801). They were so popular that choruses and orchestras were formed at the beginning of the nineteenth century for the sole purpose of performing them.

Haydn died in 1809, at the age of seventy-seven, while Napoleon's army occupied Vienna. A memorial service indicated the wide recognition of Haydn's

 Joseph Haydn

211

greatness: Joining the Viennese were French generals and an honor guard of French soldiers.

Haydn's Music

Haydn was a pathfinder for the Classical period, a pioneer in the development of the symphony and string quartet. Both Mozart and Beethoven were influenced by his style. Haydn's music, like his personality, is robust and direct; it radiates a healthy optimism. Haydn never forgot the peasant dances and songs of his childhood in a small village, and many of his works have a folk flavor. He quotes actual peasant tunes and composes original melodies in a folklike style. The minuets often romp and stomp rather than bow and curtsey. *The Creation* (1798) and *The Seasons* (1801), his late oratorios, reflect Haydn's love of nature. There are vivid and humorous musical descriptions of storms, hail, animals, birds, and fish.

Haydn is a master at developing themes. He splits them into small fragments that are quickly repeated by the different instruments. His skill at development made it possible for him to build a whole movement out of a single main theme. In such movements, contrast of mood results from changes in texture, key, rhythm, dynamics, and orchestration. In the "Drum Roll" Symphony (No. 103), which we'll study, Haydn takes a short dancelike tune and uses it to propel an exciting finale. The contagious joy that springs from his lively rhythms and vivid contrasts makes it clear why London went wild.

"I prefer to see the humorous side of life," Haydn once said. He produces comic effects from unexpected pauses and tempo changes and from sudden shifts in dynamics and pitch. We've heard one of his musical jokes in the second movement of the "Surprise" Symphony, where a soft theme is suddenly punctuated by a loud chord.

Haydn's enormous output revolves around the 104 symphonies, which span a period of over thirty-five years, from about 1758 to 1795. For a long time, the last twelve symphonies (Nos. 93 to 104), composed for public concerts in London during the 1790s, were the only ones regularly performed. Now, thanks to venturesome scholars and performers, the earlier symphonies composed for Esterház and other castles are heard more often. Many of Haydn's popular symphonies have nicknames, such as "Surprise" (No. 94), "Military" (No. 100), "Clock" (No. 101), and "Drum Roll" (No. 103).

Along with the symphonies, the sixty-eight string quartets are considered Haydn's most important works. Some scholars believe Haydn invented the form. He began writing string quartets for good reason—only three other musicians were on hand during the summer of 1757, when he was invited to take part in chamber music performances at a castle. The steward of the aristocratic host and the parish priest each played a violin, and there was a cellist named Albrechtsberger. Spurred by necessity, the twenty-five-year-old Haydn tried his hand at the first of the lifelong series of string quartets.

Haydn's output also includes piano sonatas, piano trios, divertimentos, operas, and Masses. The variety in his works is astounding. He was a great innovator and experimenter who hated arbitrary "rules" of composition. "What is the good of such rules? Art is free, and should be fettered by no such mechanical regulations. The educated ear is the sole authority in all these questions, and I think that I have as much right to lay down the law as anyone."

Symphony No. 103 in E-flat Major ("Drum Roll"; 1795)

Haydn composed his next-to-last symphony in 1795, during his second visit to London. It was performed at a public concert by an orchestra of sixty players, an unusually large group for the time. The London *Morning Chronicle* reported that the new symphony "had continual strokes of genius. The Introduction excited the deepest attention, the Allegro charmed, the *Andante* encored." The minuet was "playful and sweet, and the last movement was equal, if not superior to the preceding."

The nickname "Drum Roll," coined by a publisher, comes from the mysterious timpani roll at the very beginning of the symphony. No symphony had ever opened so strangely. Typical of Haydn are the musical surprises, folklike tunes, and vivid contrasts of tone color and dynamics in Symphony No. 103.

First Movement: *Side 5, band 1*
Adagio (slow introduction); Allegro con spirito (spirited allegro)

Haydn begins Symphony No. 103 with an extended slow introduction that is serious and expectant: The opening timpani roll leads to a solemn low theme played in unison by the bassoon, cellos, and basses.

Haydn integrated this material into the following Allegro in inventive and imaginative ways.

The rollicking dance tune of the Allegro contrasts delightfully with the serious introduction.

This tune is the first theme of a sonata-form movement and is followed by a long bridge section that's loud and energetic. The bridge is built mostly from fragments of the opening theme.

A lilting waltz melody serves as the second theme of the exposition.

Symphony No. 103 in E-flat Major

213

It is played softly by the first violins with an "oom-pa-pa" accompaniment in the other strings. Soon, the remaining instruments join in and bring the exposition to a rousing finish. (The exposition may be repeated.)

The development begins softly as Haydn reveals the potential of his rollicking first theme. Tiny fragments of the theme are tossed among the string instruments, and there's a crescendo to loud chords. Then, Haydn cleverly presents a quickened version of the introduction theme in the low strings.

After further development of the opening theme, the lilting waltz melody (second theme) returns and leads into the recapitulation.

For a while, all is "normal" in the recapitulation; we hear the first theme, the bridge, and the second theme. But Haydn saves his biggest surprise for the coda—he dramatically brings back the slow introduction and its mysterious timpani roll. His audience must have been astounded! But the solemn mood doesn't last long. As if in a burst of laughter, Haydn speeds up the introduction theme, and the movement rushes to a jubilant conclusion.

Second Movement:
Andante più tosto Allegretto (andante, somewhat allegretto)

Haydn's love of folk music and the countryside are reflected in the second movement. This is a set of variations based on two themes adapted from East European folk tunes. (Remember Haydn's long service in Hungary with the Esterházys.) The first theme (A), presented softly by the strings, is serious and in minor.

In contrast, the second theme (B) is festive, fuller in sound (horns and woodwinds join the strings), and in major.

Each theme is quite long and consists of repeated parts. The entire second movement may be outlined as follows:

Themes		Variations				
A	B	A^1	B^1	A^2	B^2	Coda
minor	major	minor	major	minor	major	major

Haydn embellishes tunes for variety, adding countermelodies and changing dynamics and orchestration. When he adds plaintive woodwind countermelodies in variation A^1, the theme sounds more melancholy. The melody in variation B^1 is presented in a gracefully decorated version by a solo violin, while loud brass fanfares make variation A^2 triumphant. The really rustic section is variation B^2, which features hopping bassoons and chirping flutes. An unexpected dark cloud appears in the coda, as a string tremolo and a rapid crescendo create a momentary feeling of uncertainty. But the cloud soon passes, and a lovely solo for flute and oboes leads to an exultant conclusion.

Third Movement: Menuetto

With its heavily accented downbeats, the minuet of Symphony No. 103 sounds more like a boisterous peasant romp than an elegant court dance. This movement is written in the minuet's customary A B A form:

Minuet		Trio		Minuet
A		B		A
a (repeated)	ba′ (repeated)	c (repeated)	dc′ (repeated)	a ba′

The opening melody (a) of the minuet ends comically as Haydn tosses a three-note fragment from low to high instruments.

The trio (B) section is flowing and gentle, with softer dynamics, fewer instruments, and a less strongly emphasized beat.

Symphony No. 103 in E-flat Major

Fourth Movement: Finale (Allegro con spirito)

From a single dance tune, Haydn produces the symphony's brilliant finale, in sonata-rondo form. In this movement, Haydn gets a maximum of contrast from a minimum of material.

The finale opens with two unaccompanied French horns playing a short phrase which Haydn's contemporaries associated with hunting and the outdoors. The violins present the main theme, a carefree dance tune, with the French-horn phrase serving as an accompaniment.

Instantly, Haydn plays polyphonic games as fragments of the tune are tossed from one instrument to another. These fragments can be recognized by their repeated-note beginning. With great mastery, Haydn uses polyphonic texture in this movement to convey both humor and dramatic excitement. The "Drum Roll" Symphony is an example of Haydn's genius at making rich, complex music from the simplest phrases and themes.

Classical

11 WOLFGANG AMADEUS MOZART

One of the most amazing child prodigies in history, Wolfgang Amadeus Mozart (1756–1791) was born in Salzburg, Austria, the son of a court musician. By the age of six, he could play the harpsichord and violin, improvise fugues, write minuets, and read music perfectly at first sight. At eight, he wrote a symphony; at eleven, an oratorio; and at twelve, an opera. By his early teens, Mozart had behind him many works that would have brought credit to a composer three times his age.

Mozart's father, Leopold, was understandably eager to show him off and went to great lengths to do so. Between the ages of six and fifteen, Mozart spent almost half his life on tour in Europe and England. He played for Empress Maria Theresa in Vienna, for Louis XV at Versailles, for George III in London, and for innumerable aristocrats along the way. On his trips to Italy he was able to study and master the operatic style which he later put to superb use. At fourteen, Mozart was in Rome during Holy Week, and he went to the Sistine Chapel to hear the famous choir performing a work that was its treasured property. Anyone caught copying this choral piece was to be punished by excommunication.

Wolfgang Amadeus Mozart (Courtesy of the Austrian Information Service, New York).

Wolfgang
Amadeus
Mozart

217

Mozart heard it once, wrote it out afterward almost completely, returned with his manuscript to make a few additions—and was discovered. That anyone should copy the music was a crime; that Mozart should hear and remember it accurately was incredible. He not only escaped punishment but was knighted by the Pope for his musical accomplishments.

At fifteen, Mozart returned to Salzburg, which was ruled by a new Prince-Archbishop, Hieronymus Colloredo. The Archbishop was a tyrant who did not appreciate Mozart's genius, and he refused to grant him more than a subordinate seat in the court orchestra. With his father's help, Mozart tried repeatedly over the next decade to find a suitable position, but there were never any vacancies.

The tragic irony of Mozart's life was that he won more acclaim as a boy wonder than as an adult musician. His upbringing and personality were partly to blame. As a child, his complete dependence on his father gave little opportunity to develop initiative. Even when Mozart was twenty-two, his mother tagged along when he went to Paris to seek recognition and establish himself. A Parisian observed that Mozart was "too good-natured, not active enough, too easily taken in, too little concerned with the means that may lead him to good fortune."

Unlike Haydn, Mozart began life as an international celebrity, pampered by kings. He could not tolerate being treated like a servant and eating with valets and cooks, and his relations with his patron went from bad to worse. Mozart became totally insubordinate when the Prince-Archbishop forbade him to give concerts or perform at the houses of the aristocracy. After an ugly confrontation, Mozart wrote: "He lied to my face that my salary was five hundred *gulden*, called me a scoundrel, a rascal, a vagabond. At last my blood began to boil, I could no longer contain myself, and I said, 'So Your Grace is not satisfied with me?'" He was answered with, "What, you dare to threaten me—you scoundrel? There is the door!" On his third attempt to request dismissal, Mozart was thrown out of the room by a court official and given a kick.

By 1781, when he was twenty-five, Mozart could stand it no longer. He broke free of provincial Salzburg and traveled to Vienna, intending to be a free-lance musician. To reassure his father, he wrote, "I have the best and most useful acquaintances in the world. I am liked and respected in the best houses, and all possible honors are given me, and moreover I get paid for it. I guarantee you I'll be successful."

Indeed, Mozart's first few years in Vienna were successful. His German opera *The Abduction from the Seraglio* (1782) was acclaimed. Concerts of his own music were attended by the Emperor and nobility. Pupils paid him high fees, his compositions were published, and his playing was heard in palace drawing rooms. He even went against his father's wishes by marrying Constanze Weber, who had no money and was as impractical as he. Contributing to the brightness of these years was Mozart's friendship with Haydn, who told his father, "Your son is the greatest composer that I know, either personally or by reputation; he has taste and beyond that the most consummate knowledge of the art of composition."

Then, in 1786, came his opera *The Marriage of Figaro*. Vienna loved it, and

Prague was even more enthusiastic. "They talk about nothing but *Figaro*. Nothing is played, sung, or whistled but *Figaro*," Mozart joyfully wrote. This success led a Prague opera company to commission *Don Giovanni* the following year. *Don Giovanni* was a triumph in Prague, but it pushed the Viennese too far. The Emperor Joseph II acknowledged that it was a masterwork, but not appropriate for his pleasure-loving subjects. Dark qualities and dissonance did not appeal to them.

Mozart's popularity in Vienna began to decline. It was a fickle city; one was society's darling for a few seasons, then suddenly ignored. And Mozart's music was considered complicated and hard to follow, too "highly spiced" with dissonance. A publisher warned him: "Write in a more popular style, or else I can neither print nor pay for any more of your music!" His pupils dwindled, and the elite snubbed his concerts. In desperate financial straits, he wrote to friends, "Great God, I would not wish my worst enemy to be in this position. . . . I am coming to you not with thanks but with fresh entreaties."

Many of Mozart's letters have been published. These span his life, and it is sad to move from the colorful, witty, and keenly observant notes of a prodigy on tour through his initial optimism about Vienna to the despair of "I cannot describe what I have been feeling. . . . A kind of longing that is never satisfied."

The events of Mozart's last year would have been good material for a grim opera plot. Though his health was failing in 1791, Mozart was delighted to receive a commission from a Viennese theater for a German comic opera, *The Magic Flute*. While hard at work, Mozart was visited by a stranger dressed entirely in gray who carried an anonymous letter commissioning a Requiem, a Mass for the Dead. Unknown to Mozart, the stranger was a servant of an unscrupulous nobleman who meant to claim the Requiem as his own composition. Mozart's health grew worse, and the Requiem took on ominous implications; he believed it to be for himself and rushed to finish it while on his deathbed. A final bit of happiness came to him two months before his death. *The Magic Flute* was premiered to resounding praise in Vienna. Its success probably would have brought large financial rewards, but it came too late. Mozart died shortly before his thirty-sixth birthday, and the final sections of the Requiem were not his. The work was completed from his sketches by Süssmayr, his favorite pupil.

Mozart's funeral was the poorest possible. His body was laid in a common grave assigned to paupers.

Mozart's Music

Mozart is among the most versatile of the great composers; his masterpieces represent all the musical forms of his time. The symphonies are as profound as the string quartets, the piano concertos as dramatic and lyrical as the operas. All his music sings. Even his instrumental melodies seem to grow out of the human voice. His works convey a feeling of ease, grace, and spontaneity, as well as balance, restraint, and perfect proportion. Yet mysterious harmonies bring dark

 Mozart's Music

moods that contrast with the lyricism. Mozart uniquely fuses power and elegance. However passionate and intense, his works are always sensuous and beautiful. He believed that music "must never offend the ear, but must please the hearer, or in other words, must never cease to be *music.*"

Mozart's compositions not only sound effortless, they were created with miraculous ease and rapidity. For example, he completed his last three symphonies in only six weeks! And he composed extended works completely in his mind. He could even converse while notating a score.

Mozart's more than six hundred compositions were cataloged during the nineteenth century by Ludwig von Köchel. Hence, it is customary to refer to a Mozart work by the "K" number that indicates its chronological place in his output. For example, his Piano Concerto in D minor (1785) is K.466, while his Symphony No. 40 in G minor (1788)—composed three years later—is K.550.

In Mozart's hands, the Classical concerto was raised to its highest level. Many of his greatest works take this form. Particularly important are the more than twenty piano concertos that Mozart—a brilliant virtuoso—composed mainly for his own performances. He also wrote several violin and horn concertos, two flute concertos, and a concerto each for bassoon, oboe, and clarinet. The concertos, as well as his other works, show a sensitivity to woodwind tone colors that is unmatched by earlier composers. The clarinet, especially, came into its own through Mozart. The Concerto for Clarinet, K.622 (1791), written in the last year of his life, remains the finest ever composed for that instrument.

Mozart was a master of opera, and few composers have matched his ability to coordinate music and stage action. His dramatic works reveal a keen sense of theater, an inexhaustible gift of melody, and a genius for creating characters through tone. Most of his operas are comedies, composed to librettos in German or Italian, then the international language of music. While the Italian operas are entirely sung, the German operas include spoken dialog, the custom at the time. Mozart's three masterpieces of Italian comic opera are *The Marriage of Figaro* (1786), *Don Giovanni* (1787), and *Così fan tutte* (1790); they all were composed to librettos by Lorenzo da Ponte. Mozart's finest German work is *The Magic Flute* (1791); its wide range of style embraces folk song and fugue, farcical comedy, and solemn hymns about the brotherhood of man.

The comic operas contain both humorous and serious characters who are not mere stereotypes; they are human beings who think and feel. Even when six characters sing together in a complex ensemble, the individuality of each shines through. Mozart once tried to explain how he depicted emotion in an aria: "Would you like to know how I have expressed it—and even indicated his throbbing heart? By two violins playing octaves. You feel the trembling—the faltering—you see how his throbbing breast begins to swell; this I have expressed by a crescendo. You hear the whispering and sighing—which I have indicated by the first violins with mutes and a flute playing in unison." Emotions in Mozart's arias and ensembles are not static; they continuously evolve and change. A character may feel one way at the beginning of an ensemble and a different way at its end. In a duet from *Don Giovanni*, for example, the feelings of a peasant girl change as she gradually gives in to the charm of a noble Don Juan.

Throughout his life, Mozart learned from other composers. As a boy, he was influenced by Italian operas and the graceful style of one of Bach's sons, Johann Christian Bach. The strongest influence on his later works came from Bach the father, dead and nearly forgotten, and from Haydn, the most famous composer at the time. From Bach, Mozart learned to write intricate polyphonic textures that flow smoothly. He arranged Bach's and Handel's works for performances at private concerts sponsored by Baron Gottfried van Swieten, a passionate Viennese music lover. From Haydn's works, he learned ways to develop themes. But his musical relationship with Haydn was not one-sided. Some compositions by Haydn show traces of Mozart's melodic and orchestral style.

"I am never happier," Mozart once wrote his father, "than when I have something to compose, for that, after all, is my sole delight and passion." Mozart's "delight and passion" are communicated in his works, which represent late eighteenth-century musical style at its highest level of perfection.

Don Giovanni (1787)

Don Giovanni is a unique blend of comic and serious opera, combining seduction and slapstick with violence and the supernatural. The old tale of Don Juan, the fabulous Spanish lover, had attracted many playwrights and composers before Mozart. Mozart's Don is an extremely charming but ruthless nobleman who will stop at nothing to satisfy his sexual appetite. Don Giovanni's comic servant, Leporello, is a grumbling accomplice who dreams of being in his master's place.

The Don attempts to rape a young noblewoman, Donna Anna, and her father, the Commandant, challenges him to a duel. Don Giovanni kills the old man, causing Donna Anna and her fiancé, Don Ottavio, to swear revenge. Pursued by his enemies, the Don deftly engages in new amorous adventures. During one of them, he hides in a cemetery, where he sees a marble statue of the dead Commandant. The unearthly statue utters threatening words, but Don Giovanni brazenly invites it to dinner. When the statue appears at the banquet hall, it orders the Don to repent his sins. Don Giovanni defiantly refuses and is dragged down to hell.

Overture

Mozart plunges us into a dark atmosphere at the beginning of the overture with awesome D-minor chords, anxious syncopations and sinister scale passages. There is a hair-raising effect when this slow, ominous music returns at the end of the opera for the statue's confrontation with Don Giovanni in the banquet hall. The overture continues with a fast sonata-form movement in D major, which has the

Don Giovanni (1787)

221

Don Giovanni (Sherrill Milnes) and Zerlina (Teresa Stratas)
in the duet *Là ci darem la mano* (Beth Bergman).

energy and swagger of the opera's leading character. This contrast of minor and major, mystery and brilliance, foretells the tremendous range of emotions to come.

Side 5, band 2

Act I: Introduction

The Overture leads directly into the opening scene, which is one of the most action-packed in all opera. In breathless succession we witness Leporello keeping guard, Don Giovanni struggling with Donna Anna, the Commandant dueling with the Don, and the Commandant's agonized last gasps. Mozart's music breathes life into the characters and pushes the action forward. (In the following libretto, brackets indicate that characters sing at the same time. "Etc." indicates that previous lines of text are repeated.)

Late evening outside the Commandant's palace in Seville.
Don Giovanni, concealing his identity, has stolen into Donna

Anna's room for an amorous adventure. Leporello paces back and forth.

Orchestral introduction, Molto allegro; sudden *fortes* suggest pacing and abrupt turns.

Leporello

Notte e giorno faticar,	Night and day I slave
per chi nulla sa gradir;	For one who does not appreciate it.
Piova e vento sopportar,	I put up with wind and rain,
Mangiar male e mal dormir!	Eat and sleep badly.
Voglio far il gentiluomo,	I want to be a gentleman
E non voglio più servir,	And to give up my servitude.
No, no, no, no, no, no,	No, no, no, no, no, no,
Non voglio più servir!	I want to give up my servitude.
O che caro galantuomo!	Oh, what a fine gentleman!
Voi star dentro colla bella	You stay inside with your lady
Ed io far la sentinella!	And I must play the sentinel!
Voglio far il gentiluomo, ecc.	Oh, what a fine gentleman, etc.
Ma mi par che venga gente . . .	But I think someone is coming!
Non mi voglio far sentir, ecc.	I don't want them to hear me, etc.

Leporello hides to one side. Don Giovanni and Donna Anna come down the palace stairs struggling. The Don hides his face to prevent her from recognizing him.

Orchestral crescendo.

Donna Anna

Non sperar, se non m'uccidi.	There's no hope, unless you kill me
Ch'io ti lasci fuggir mai!	That I'll ever let you go!

Don Giovanni

Donna folle, indarno gridi:	Idiot! You scream in vain.
Chi son io tu non saprai.	Who I am you'll never know!

Donna Anna

Non sperar, ecc.	There's no hope, etc.

Don Giovanni
(1787)

223

Don Giovanni

Donna folle! ecc.	Idiot! etc.

Leporello

Che tumulto! Oh ciel, che gridi!	What a racket! Heaven, what screams!
Il padron in nuovi guai.	My master in another scrape.

Donna Anna

Gente! Servi! Al traditore!	Help! Everyone! The betrayer!

Don Giovanni

Taci, e trema al mio furore!	Keep quiet! Beware my wrath!

Donna Anna

Scellerato!	Scoundrel!

Don Giovanni

Sconsigliata!	Fool!

Donna Anna

Scellerato!	Scoundrel!

Don Giovanni

Sconsigliata!	Fool!

Leporello

Sta a veder che il malandrino	We will see if this rascal
Mi farà precipitar.	Will be the ruin of me!

Donna Anna

Gente! Servi!	Help! Everyone!

Don Giovanni

Taci, e trema!	Keep quiet!

Donna Anna

Come furia disperata	Like a desperate fury
Ti saprò perseguitar! ecc.	I'll know how to pursue you! etc.
Scellerato! Gente! Servi!	Scoundrel! Help! Everyone!
Come furia disperata, ecc.	Like a desperate fury, etc.

Don Giovanni

Questa furia disperata	This desperate fury
Mi vuol far precipitar! ecc.	Is aimed at destroying me!
Sconsigliata! Taci, e trema!	Fool! Keep quiet!
Questa furia disperata, ecc.	This desperate fury, etc.

Leporello

Che tumulto! Oh ciel, che gridi!	What a racket! Heavens, what screams!
Sta a veder che il malandrino, ecc.	We will see if this rascal, etc.

Donna Anna hears the Commandant: She leaves Don Giovanni and goes into the house. The Commandant appears.

String tremolo, *ff,* shift to minor key.

Commandant

Lasciala, indegno! Battiti meco!
Leave her alone, wretch, and defend yourself.

Don Giovanni

Va, non mi degno di pugnar teco.
Go away! I disdain to fight with you.

Commandant

Così pretendi da me fuggir?
Thus you think to escape me?

Leporello

Potessi almeno di qua partir.
If I could only get out of here!

Don Giovanni

Va, non mi degno, no!
Go away! I disdain you!

Commandant

Così pretendi da me fuggir?
Thus you think to escape me!

Leporello

Potessi almeno di qua partir!
If I could only get out of here!

Commandant

Battiti!
Fight!

Don Giovanni

Misero! Attendi, se vuoi morir!
So be it, if you want to die!

They duel. The Commandant is fatally wounded.

Dueling music, upward sweeps in strings.
Death blow, suspenseful, held chord.

Commandant

Ah, soccorso! son tradito!
Help! I've been betrayed!

L'assassino m'ha ferito,
The assassin has wounded me!

E dal seno palpitante
And from my heaving breast

Sento l'anima partir.
I feel my soul escaping!

Andante, pp, pathetic minor phrases.

Don Giovanni

Ah! già cade il sciagurato!
Ah, already the wretch has fallen,

Affannosa e agonizzante
And he gasps for air.

Già dal seno palpitante
From his heaving breast I already

Veggo l'anima partir, ecc.
See his soul escaping, etc.

Leporello

Qual misfatto! Qual eccesso!
What a misdeed! What a crime!

Entro il sen dallo spavento
I can feel my heart

Palpitar il cor mi sento!
Beating hard from fright!

Don Giovanni (1787)

225

{ *Io non sò che far, che dir,* *ecc.*	I don't know what to do or say, etc.	
The Commandant dies.		

Don Giovanni

Leporello, ove sei?	Leporello, where are you?	Recitative, harpsichord accompanies.

Leporello

Son qui, per mia disgrazia. *E voi?*	I'm here, unfortunately, and you?

Don Giovanni

Son qui.	Over here.

Leporello

Chi è morto, voi, o il vec- *chio?*	Who's dead, you or the old man?

Don Giovanni

Che domanda da bestia! Il *vecchio.*	What an idiotic question! The old man.

Leporello

Bravo! Due imprese *leggiadre!*	Well done! Two mis- deeds!
Storzar la figlia, ed ammaz- *zar il padre!*	First you raped the daughter then mur- dered the father!

Don Giovanni

L'ha voluto, suo danno.	It was his own doing: too bad for him.

Leporello

Ma Donn'Anna cosa ha *voluto?*	And Donna Anna, did she ask for it too?

Don Giovanni

Taci, non mi seccar! Vien
  meco, se non vuoi qualche
  cosa ancor tu.
	Keep quiet and don't
	bother me. Now come
	along, unless you're
	anxious for something
	for yourself.

Leporello

Non vo' nulla, signor, non *parlo più.*	I have no desires, sir, and no more to say.

Side 5, band 3

Act I: Leporello's "Catalogue Aria" (*Madamina*)

Not long after the opening scene, Leporello sings his famous "Catalogue Aria" (*Madamina*) to Donna Elvira. In mocking "consolation," Leporello tells her that she is but one of many and displays a fat catalog of his master's conquests. The music bubbles with Leporello's delight as he reels off the amazing totals: "640 in Italy, 231 in Germany, 100 in France, 91 in Turkey" and "in Spain, 1003!" Mozart makes the most of comic description as Leporello proceeds to list the Don's seduction techniques for different types of women:

The Classical
Period

226

Madamina, il catalogo è questo	My dear lady, this is a list	Allegro.
Delle belle, che amò il padron mio;	Of the beauties my master has loved,	
Un catalogo egli è, che ho fatt'io	A list which I have compiled.	
Osservate, leggete con me.	Observe, read along with me.	
In Italia seicento e quaranta,	In Italy, six hundred and forty;	Staccato woodwind chuckles.
In Almagna duecento a trentuna,	In Germany, two hundred and thirty-one;	
Cento in Francia, in Turchia novantuna,	A hundred in France; in Turkey ninety-one.	
Ma in Ispagna son già mille e tre!	In Spain already one thousand and three!	Longer notes.
V'han fra queste contadine,	Among these are peasant girls	Shorter notes.
Cameriere, cittadine,	Maidservants, city girls,	
V'han contesse, baronesse,	Countesses, baronesses,	
Marchesine, principesse,	Marchionesses, princesses,	
E v'han donne d'ogni grado,	Women of every rank,	
D'ogni forma, d'orni età,	Every shape, every age.	
In Italia seicento e quaranta, ecc.	In Italy six hundred and forty, etc.	
Nella bionda egli ha l'usanza	With blondes it is his habit	Andante con moto, courtly minuet.
Di lodar la gentilezza;	To praise their kindness;	
Nella bruna, la costanza;	In brunettes, their faithfulness;	Mock heroic flourish.
Nella bianca la dolcezza	In the very blonde, their sweetness.	Suave melodic phrase.
Vuol d'inverno la grassotta,	In winter he likes fat ones,	
Vuol d'estate la magrotta;	In summer he likes thin ones.	
È la grande maestosa,	He calls the tall ones majestic.	Crescendo, melody slowly rises to high held tone.
La piccina è ognor vezzosa;	The little ones are always charming.	Spritely quick notes.
Delle vecchie fa conquista	He seduces the old ones	
Pel piacer di porle in lista.	For the pleasure of adding to the list.	
Sua passion predominante	His greatest favorite	
È la giovin principiante.	Is the young beginner.	
Non si picca se sia ricca,	It doesn't matter if she's rich,	

Don Giovanni
(1787)

227

Se sia brutta, se sia bella,	Ugly or beautiful;	
Se sia ricca, brutta, se sia bella;	If she is rich, ugly or beautiful.	
Purchè porti la gonnella,	If she wears a petticoat,	
Voi sapete quel che fa!	You know what he does.	
Purchè porti la gonnella, ecc.	If she wears a petticoat, etc.	

Side 5, band 4

Act I: Duet: *Là ci darem la mano* ("There you will give me your hand")

The Don's seduction technique is put to use in this lovely duet. Don Giovanni convinces the pretty peasant girl Zerlina to come to his palace, promising to marry her and change her life. The music magically conveys his persuasiveness and her gradual surrender, as the voices become more and more intertwined. Forgetting her fiancé, Masetto, Zerlina throws herself into the Don's arms and they sing together, "Let us go, my beloved."

Don Giovanni

Là ci darem la mano,	There you will give me your hand,	Andante, $\frac{2}{4}$, legato melody.
Là mi dirai di sì.	There you will tell me "yes."	
Vedi, non è lontano;	You see, it is not far;	
Partiam, ben mio, da qui.	Let us leave, my beloved.	

Zerlina

Vorrei e non vorrei;	I'd like to, but yet I would not.	Legato melody repeated.
Mi trema un poco il cor.	My heart trembles a little.	
Felice è ver, sarei,	It's true I would be happy,	
Ma può burlarmi ancor.	But he may just be tricking me.	

Don Giovanni

Vieni, mio bel diletto!	Come, my dearly beloved!	Quicker interchange between voices.

Zerlina

Mi fa pietà Masetto!	I'm sorry for Masetto.

Don Giovanni

Io cangierò tua sorte.	I will change your life!

Zerlina

Presto, non son più forte!	Soon I won't be able to resist.

Don Giovanni

Vieni! Vieni!	Come! Come!	
Là ci darem la mano!	There you will give me your hand.	Legato melody now shared by both voices.

	Zerlina	
Vorrei, e non vorrei!	I'd like to, but yet I would not.	
	Don Giovanni	
Là mi dirai di sì.	There you will tell me "yes."	
	Zerlina	
Mi trema un poco il cor!	My heart trembles a little.	
	Don Giovanni	
Partiam, mio ben, da qui!	Let us leave, my beloved.	
	Zerlina	
Ma può burlarmi ancor!	But he may just be tricking me.	
	Don Giovanni	
Vieni, mio bel diletto!	Come, my dearly beloved!	
	Zerlina	
Mi fa pietà Masetto!	I'm sorry for Masetto.	Voices overlap.
	Don Giovanni	
Io cangierò tua sorte.	I will change your life.	
	Zerlina	
Presto, non son più forte!	Soon I won't be able to resist.	
	Don Giovanni	
Andiam! Andiam!	Let us go!	
	Zerlina	
Andiam!	Let us go!	
	Don Giovanni and Zerlina	
Andiam, andiam, mio bene,	Let us go, let us go, my beloved,	Allegro, $\frac{6}{8}$; together they sing a new joyous tune.
A ristorar le pene	To soothe the pangs	
D'un innocente amor! ecc.	Of an innocent love, etc.	

Act II: Finale

The finale opens with Don Giovanni enjoying good food and music; it closes with a sextet celebrating his horrible punishment. Mozart's genius fuses these dissimilar events into a coherent whole. Don Giovanni dines in his banquet hall while watching Leporello's comic antics and listening to his private band play three hit tunes. The third tune is from Mozart's *Marriage of Figaro,* and Leporello comments, "This I know only too well." The frivolous mood evaporates when Donna Elvira bursts in and begs the Don to mend his ways. Terror strikes as the Commandant's marble statue enters, accompanied by the awesome music of the overture. Mozart uses this return to weld a powerful sense of unity within the opera. As the orchestra plays the dueling music from Act I, the statue commands, "Repent, change your life, it is your last moment!" Defiant to the end, Don

Don Giovanni
(1787)

229

Giovanni shouts, "No, no I do not repent!" Flames and smoke surround the Don. He cries out in agony as a chorus of demons sing of his eternal damnation. With a hideous shriek, Don Giovanni is engulfed by the flames of hell.

An epilog in a lighter mood follows this scene of terror. The other characters, learning of the Don's fate, form a sextet and jubilantly sing a moral to the audience: "This is how evil-doers end up!" This moral ending fools no one: Mozart's music has made a sinner seem very attractive.

Symphony No. 40 in G Minor, K. 550 (1788)

Symphony No. 40 in G minor is the most passionate and dramatic of Mozart's symphonies. While Classical in form and technique, the work is almost Romantic in emotional intensity. It staggers the imagination that Mozart could compose the G minor and two other great symphonies—No. 39 in E flat and No. 41 in C ("Jupiter")—during the incredibly short period of six weeks. They are his last three symphonies.

Like most Classical symphonies, the Symphony No. 40 in G minor has four movements: (1) fast, (2) slow, (3) minuet, (4) fast.

Side 4, band 2

First Movement: Molto Allegro

A quiet but agitated opening theme in the violins sets the mood for the entire first movement, which is in sonata form. A throbbing accompaniment in the violas contributes to the feeling of unrest. Dominating the violin melody is the rhythmic pattern short-short-long, first heard in the opening three-note motive.

The persistence of this rhythmic pattern gives the music a sense of urgency. Yet the melody is balanced and symmetrical. Questioning upward leaps are answered by downward scales, and the second phrase of the melody is a repetition of the first, one step lower. The exposition continues with a bridge section that presents a new staccato motive played loudly by the violins.

The lyrical second theme, in B-flat major, contrasts completely with the agitated G-minor opening. Mozart exploits the expressive resources of tone color by dividing the theme between strings and woodwinds. In the closing section of the exposition, Mozart uses a fragment from the opening theme to achieve a

The Classical
Period

230

different emotional effect. The three-note motive now sounds gentle and plaintive as it is passed between clarinet and bassoon with a sighing string background.

In the development, the movement becomes feverish. The opening theme is led into different keys and is cut into smaller and smaller pieces. The development begins mysteriously as the opening phrase ends in an unexpected way and sinks lower and lower. Then a sudden explosion of polyphonic texture increases the excitement and complexity. Mozart brusquely shifts the opening phrase between low and high strings while combining it with a furious staccato countermelody. Soon after, he demolishes the opening phrase: We hear the beginning of the theme without its upward leap.

Then the final note is lopped off.

Finally, we are left with the irreducible minimum of the original theme, the three-note motive.

The tension resolves only with the entrance of the entire opening theme in the tonic key.

In the recapitulation, exposition material is given new expressive meaning. The bridge is expanded and made more dramatic. The lyrical second theme, now in G minor, is touching and sad.

‖ LISTENING OUTLINE
To be read while music is heard

Symphony No. 40 in G Minor, K. 550 (1788), by Wolfgang Amadeus Mozart

Symphony No. 40 in G Minor, K. 550 (1788)

First Movement: Molto Allegro

Sonata form, duple meter ($\frac{2}{2}$), G minor

flute, 2 oboes, 2 clarinets, 2 bassoons, 2 French horns, violins 1, violins 2, violas, cellos, double basses

(About 7½ min)

EXPOSITION
First theme   1   *a.* Main theme in violins, *p*, throbbing accompaniment in violas, minor key.

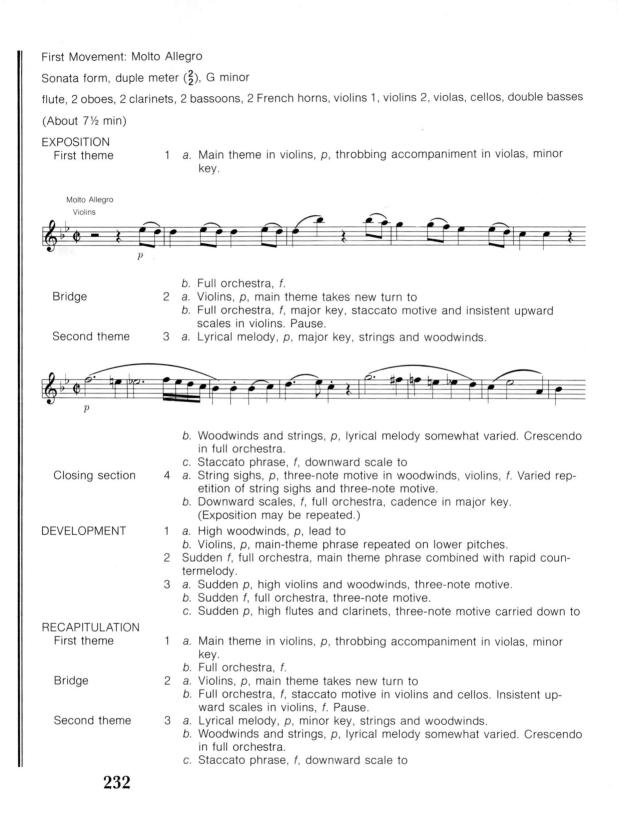

                     b. Full orchestra, *f*.

Bridge   2   *a.* Violins, *p*, main theme takes new turn to
                      b. Full orchestra, *f*, major key, staccato motive and insistent upward scales in violins. Pause.

Second theme   3   *a.* Lyrical melody, *p*, major key, strings and woodwinds.

                     b. Woodwinds and strings, *p*, lyrical melody somewhat varied. Crescendo in full orchestra.
                     c. Staccato phrase, *f*, downward scale to

Closing section   4   *a.* String sighs, *p*, three-note motive in woodwinds, violins, *f*. Varied repetition of string sighs and three-note motive.
                     b. Downward scales, *f*, full orchestra, cadence in major key.
                       (Exposition may be repeated.)

DEVELOPMENT   1   *a.* High woodwinds, *p*, lead to
                     b. Violins, *p*, main-theme phrase repeated on lower pitches.
             2   Sudden *f*, full orchestra, main theme phrase combined with rapid countermelody.
             3   *a.* Sudden *p*, high violins and woodwinds, three-note motive.
                     b. Sudden *f*, full orchestra, three-note motive.
                     c. Sudden *p*, high flutes and clarinets, three-note motive carried down to

RECAPITULATION
First theme   1   *a.* Main theme in violins, *p*, throbbing accompaniment in violas, minor key.
                     b. Full orchestra, *f*.

Bridge   2   *a.* Violins, *p*, main theme takes new turn to
                     b. Full orchestra, *f*, staccato motive in violins and cellos. Insistent upward scales in violins, *f*. Pause.

Second theme   3   *a.* Lyrical melody, *p*, minor key, strings and woodwinds.
                     b. Woodwinds and strings, *p*, lyrical melody somewhat varied. Crescendo in full orchestra.
                     c. Staccato phrase, *f*, downward scale to

Closing section	4	*a.* String sighs, *p*, three-note motive in woodwinds, violins, *f*. Varied repetition of string sighs and three-note motive.
		b. Downward scales, *f*, full orchestra.
CODA	1	*a.* Sudden *p*, main-theme motive in strings.
		b. Full orchestra, *f*, cadence in minor key.

Second Movement: Andante

The mood of the Andante hovers between gentleness and longing. Written in sonata form, the Andante is the symphony's only movement in major (E-flat). This movement develops from a series of gently pulsating notes in the opening theme.

As the theme continues, the violins introduce an airy two-note rhythmic figure which will transform almost every section of the Andante by being, at different times, graceful, insistent, and forceful.

Later, Mozart uses the airy figures as a delicate countermelody to the repeated-note idea. Floating woodwinds interwoven with strings reveal Mozart's sensitivity to tone color as an expressive resource.

Third Movement: Menuetto (Allegretto)   *Side 4, band 3*

This G-minor minuet is serious and intense; it does not sound like an aristocratic dance. The form of the minuet is A B A:

Minuet	Trio	Minuet
A	B	A
a (repeated) ba' (repeated)	c (repeated) dc' (repeated)	a ba'

Powerful syncopations give a fierce character to the A section (minuet), which is predominantly loud and in minor.

Symphony No.
40 in G Minor,
K. 550 (1788)

233

Later, Mozart increases the tension through polyphonic texture and striking dissonances. And at the end of the A section, there is a sudden drop in dynamics; the flute, supported by oboes and a bassoon, softly recalls the opening melody of the minuet.

The trio section (B) brings a shift from minor to major, from fierce energy to graceful relaxation.

This change of mood is underscored by a soft dynamic level and pastoral woodwind interludes. After the trio, a sudden *forte* announces the return of the fierce A section.

Side 4, band 4

Fourth Movement: Allegro assai

Mozart ends the symphony with the tense movement already discussed in section 3.

Piano Concerto in D Minor, K. 466 (1785)

The highly dramatic, demonic nature of the D-minor Piano Concerto made it a favorite among musicians of the Romantic period and one of the works that convinced the world of Mozart's greatness shortly after his death. Only this and one other of Mozart's more than twenty piano concertos are in a minor key. Mozart associated the particular key of D minor with moods of foreboding, conflict, and tragedy. (You'll remember that he used it for the somber opening of the Overture of *Don Giovanni* and for the appearance of the Commandant's statue at the end of the opera.)

Like all Classical concertos, this one has three movements. The middle movement is a point of repose between the tense opening movement and the finale.

Mozart composed the D-minor Piano Concerto for a concert in Vienna in 1785. At the time he was very popular, and his concerts were well attended by aristocratic music lovers eager to hear his latest works. The concerto was completed only one day before the concert, and there was not enough time for Mozart to rehearse the concluding movement with the orchestra. Nevertheless, the performance was a success. "Wolfgang played an excellent new piano concerto," wrote Father Leopold to his daughter in Salzburg. Ten years later, in 1795, Beethoven played this concerto at a benefit for Mozart's impoverished widow.

First Movement: Allegro

The Allegro does not begin with a melody, but with syncopated throbbing in the violins and violas and hushed upward rushes in the cellos and double basses. This highly original opening creates a restless atmosphere that explodes into violence with a sudden *forte* in the whole orchestra. After several orchestral themes, the piano enters, unaccompanied, with a melancholy melody that sounds almost like an improvisation. Since this melody is played only by the piano, we will call it the "solo theme." In the development section, the piano and orchestra confront each other. The piano sings its melancholy solo theme, and the orchestra responds with the restless idea heard at the opening of the movement. Toward the end of the Allegro is a cadenza, or unaccompanied showpiece for the soloist. Mozart did not notate cadenzas for this concerto, and so the pianist either supplies one or uses those written by other composers (including two that Beethoven wrote for a student).

LISTENING OUTLINE

To be read while music is heard

Piano Concerto in D Minor, K. 466 (1785), by Wolfgang Amadeus Mozart

First Movement: Allegro

Sonata form, quadruple meter ($\frac{4}{4}$), D minor

piano, flute, 2 oboes, 2 bassoons, 2 French horns, 2 trumpets, timpani, violins 1, violins 2, violas, cellos, double basses

(About 13 min)

FIRST
EXPOSITION

1   Strings, *p*, syncopated throbbing, low upward rushes, minor key.

2   *a*. Sudden *f*, full orchestra, upward rushes climb in violins.
    b. Violins, *p*, echoed by oboes.
    c. Sudden *f*, full orchestra. Brief pause.
3   Oboes, *p*, alternate with flute, dialog theme.

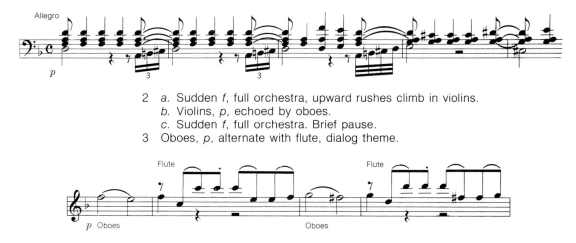

Strings, *p*, lead to

4 Sudden *f*, agitated passages in full orchestra repeatedly alternate with sighing phrase in strings, *p*. High repeated tones in violins, *f*, sudden *p* followed by

5 Tender closing theme in strings, *p*.

SECOND
EXPOSITION

1 Piano alone, solo theme in minor.

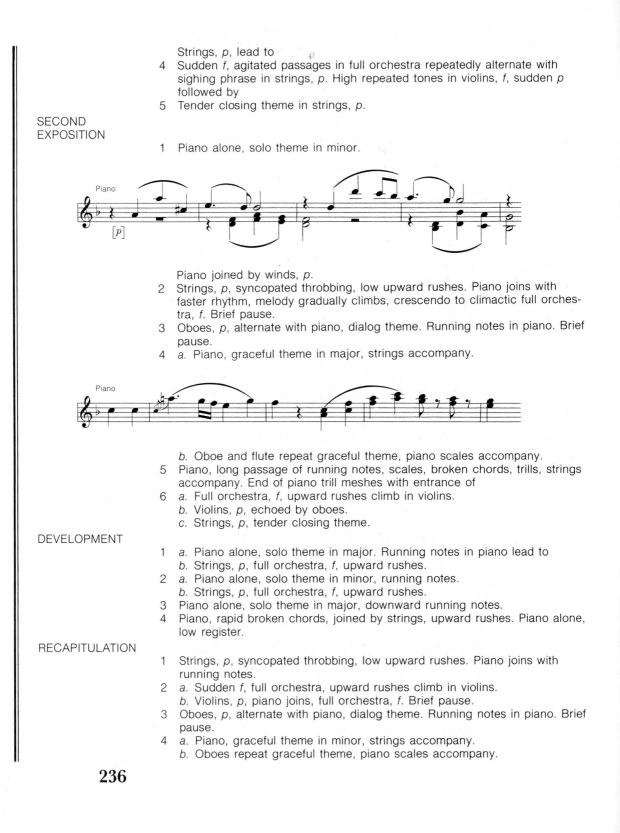

Piano joined by winds, *p*.

2 Strings, *p*, syncopated throbbing, low upward rushes. Piano joins with faster rhythm, melody gradually climbs, crescendo to climactic full orchestra, *f*. Brief pause.

3 Oboes, *p*, alternate with piano, dialog theme. Running notes in piano. Brief pause.

4 *a.* Piano, graceful theme in major, strings accompany.

b. Oboe and flute repeat graceful theme, piano scales accompany.

5 Piano, long passage of running notes, scales, broken chords, trills, strings accompany. End of piano trill meshes with entrance of

6 *a.* Full orchestra, *f*, upward rushes climb in violins.

b. Violins, *p*, echoed by oboes.

c. Strings, *p*, tender closing theme.

DEVELOPMENT

1 *a.* Piano alone, solo theme in major. Running notes in piano lead to

b. Strings, *p*, full orchestra, *f*, upward rushes.

2 *a.* Piano alone, solo theme in minor, running notes.

b. Strings, *p*, full orchestra, *f*, upward rushes.

3 Piano alone, solo theme in major, downward running notes.

4 Piano, rapid broken chords, joined by strings, upward rushes. Piano alone, low register.

RECAPITULATION

1 Strings, *p*, syncopated throbbing, low upward rushes. Piano joins with running notes.

2 *a.* Sudden *f*, full orchestra, upward rushes climb in violins.

b. Violins, *p*, piano joins, full orchestra, *f*. Brief pause.

3 Oboes, *p*, alternate with piano, dialog theme. Running notes in piano. Brief pause.

4 *a.* Piano, graceful theme in minor, strings accompany.

b. Oboes repeat graceful theme, piano scales accompany.

236

	5	Piano, long passage of running notes, scales, broken chords, trills, strings accompany. End of piano trill meshes with entrance of
	6	Full orchestra, *f*, upward rushes climb in violins. Briefly held chord.
CADENZA		
	1	Extended piano solo.
CODA		
	1	Full orchestra, *f*, agitated passage, alternates with sighing phrase in strings, *p*. High repeated tones in violins, *f*. Sudden *p* followed by
	2	Strings, *p*, tender closing theme, winds join, *p*, repeated chords at end, *pp*.

Second Movement: Romance

The Romance, in B-flat major, is a slow, lyrical movement in three-part form. The piano introduces the tender main theme, which the orchestra repeats.

We then hear an arialike melody by the piano with a discreet orchestral accompaniment. A return to the main theme rounds off the opening section of the second movement.

This movement's serene mood is shattered by a stormy middle section in G minor. Rapid rhythms and abrupt shifts from high to low pitches recall the turbulence of the first movement. After a while the agitation subsides, and the rhythm gradually slows down. This is a beautifully smooth transition to the peaceful concluding section, which begins with the tender main theme. The Romance ends as gently as it began.

Third Movement: Rondo (Allegro assai)

The last movement, in D minor, is a sonata-rondo; its fury recalls the atmosphere of the first movement. The piano announces the fiery main theme, which begins with an upward arpeggio similar to the one in the finale of Mozart's Symphony No. 40 in G minor.

After several agitated ideas in minor, Mozart lightens the mood with a carefree F-major theme that is introduced by the woodwinds and repeated by the piano. This theme returns in the D-major coda, which concludes the movement brilliantly. It's typical for late eighteenth-century music to end happily.

 Piano Concerto in D Minor, K. 466

237

LUDWIG VAN BEETHOVEN

For many people, Ludwig van Beethoven (1770–1827) represents the highest level of musical genius. His unique stature is comparable to Shakespeare's in literature and Michelangelo's in art. He opened new realms of musical expression that profoundly influenced composers throughout the nineteenth century.

Beethoven was born on December 16, 1770, in Bonn, Germany. Like Bach and Mozart before him, he came from a family of musicians. His grandfather, also named Ludwig, was music director of the court at Bonn. His father, Johann, was a tenor who held a low position in the court and who saw his talented son as a profitable prodigy like Mozart. It's told that Johann Beethoven and a musician friend would come home from the local tavern late at night, rouse young Ludwig from sleep, and make him practice at the keyboard until morning. At eleven, Beethoven served as assistant to the court organist, and by thirteen he had several piano compositions published.

Beethoven went to Vienna when he was sixteen to improvise for Mozart, who said, "Keep your eyes on him; some day he will give the world something to talk about." He then returned to Bonn because his mother was critically ill. She died shortly after, and his father, who became an alcoholic, was dismissed from the court choir. Beethoven, at eighteen, became legal guardian of two younger brothers. At court he was organist and violist, composing and practicing; suddenly, he was also head of a family.

Shortly before his twenty-second birthday, Beethoven left Bonn to study with Haydn in Vienna, where he spent the rest of his life. In 1792, Haydn was at the height of his fame, too busy composing to devote much time or energy to teaching. As a result, he overlooked errors in Beethoven's counterpoint exercises, and his pupil felt forced to go secretly to another teacher. (Haydn never learned of this.) Beethoven's drive for thoroughness and mastery—evident throughout his life—is shown by his willingness to subject himself to a strict course in counterpoint and fugue even after he had composed fine works.

Beethoven's first seven years in Vienna brought hard work, growing confidence, a strong sense of identity, and public praise. His letters of introduction from Bonn noblemen opened the doors of the social and cultural elite in this

Beethoven opened new realms of musical expression that profoundly influenced composers throughout the nineteenth century (The Granger Collection).

 Ludwig van Beethoven

239

music-loving city. He dazzled everyone with his piano virtuosity and moved them with his improvisations. "He knew how to produce such an impression on every listener," reports a contemporary, "that frequently there was not a single dry eye, while many broke out into loud sobs, for there was a certain magic in his expression." A rebel against social convention, Beethoven asserted that an artist deserved as much respect as nobles. Once, while playing in an aristocratic drawing room, he was disturbed by the loud conversation of a young count. Beethoven jumped up from the piano, exclaiming, "I will not play for such swine!" For a long time he was a guest of Prince Carl Lichnowsky, who told his personal servant that if ever he and Beethoven rang at the same time, Beethoven should be served first. The same aristocrats who had allowed Mozart to die in poverty a few years before showered Beethoven with gifts. He earned good fees from piano lessons and private concerts. Publishers were quick to buy his compositions, even though some critics complained they were "bizarre" and "excessively complicated."

Disaster struck during his twenty-ninth year: Beethoven felt the first symptoms of deafness. Doctors could do nothing to halt the course of his physical and emotional torment. In 1801 he wrote despairingly, "For two years I have avoided almost all social gatherings because it is impossible for me to say to people 'I am deaf.' If I belonged to any other profession it would be easier, but in my profession it is a dreadful state." On October 6, 1802, Beethoven was in Heiligenstadt, a village outside Vienna where he sought solitude during the summer. That day his feelings were expressed in what is now known as "The Heiligenstadt Testament," a long agonized letter addressed to his brothers. Beethoven wrote, "I would have ended my life—it was only my art that held me back. Ah, it seemed to me impossible to leave the world until I had brought forth all that I felt was within me."

Beethoven's victory over despair coincided with an important change in his musical style. Works created after his emotional crisis have a new power and heroism. From 1803 to 1804, he composed the gigantic Third Symphony, the *Eroica,* a landmark in music history. At first, he planned to name it "Bonaparte," after the First Consul of the French Republic. Beethoven saw Napoleon as the embodiment of heroism and the champion of the principles underlying the French Revolution. "Liberty, equality, fraternity" were stirring words that expressed Beethoven's democratic ideals. But when he learned that Napoleon had proclaimed himself Emperor of the French, Beethoven "flew into a rage and cried out, 'He too is nothing but an ordinary man! Now he will trample under foot all the rights of man and only indulge his ambition. He will exalt himself above all others and become a tyrant!'" Seizing his score, Beethoven tore out the title page bearing Napoleon's name and threw it on the floor. On a new title page, later, Beethoven wrote, "Heroic Symphony composed to celebrate the memory of a great man."

In 1812, Beethoven met Johann Wolfgang von Goethe, the great German poet he had long worshiped. He played for Goethe and the two artists walked and talked together. Shortly after this meeting, Goethe described Beethoven to a friend as "an utterly untamed personality." To his wife the poet wrote, "Never before have I seen an artist with more power of concentration, more energy, more inwardness." Despite such descriptions by people who knew him, Beethoven remains a mystery. He was self-educated and had read widely in Shakespeare and the ancient classics, but he was weak in elementary arithmetic. He claimed the highest moral principles, but he was often unscrupulous in dealing with publishers. Orderly and methodical when composing, Beethoven dressed sloppily and lived in incredibly messy apartments. During his thirty-five years in Vienna, he changed dwellings about forty times.

Beethoven fell in and out of love with several women, mostly of noble birth, but never was able to form a lasting relationship. To a woman referred to as "The Immortal Beloved," he wrote a passionate letter that was found in a drawer after his death. Only recently has a Beethoven scholar established her identity as the Viennese aristocrat Antonie Brentano. Beethoven took consolation for disappointments in his personal life from nature. Ideas came to him while walking through the Viennese countryside. His Sixth Symphony, the *Pastoral,* beautifully expresses his recollections of life in the country.

Beethoven was never in the service of the Viennese aristocracy. A growing musical public made it possible for him to earn a fairly good income by selling compositions to publishers. His stature was so unique that when he threatened to accept a position outside Austria in 1809, three nobles made a special arrangement to keep him in Vienna. Prince Kinsky, Prince Lobkowitz, and Archduke Rudolf—the Emperor's brother and Beethoven's pupil—obligated themselves to give Beethoven an annual income. Their only condition was that Beethoven continue to live in the Austrian capital—an unprecedented arrangement in music history.

As Beethoven's hearing weakened, so did his piano playing and conducting. By the age of forty-four, this once brilliant pianist was forced to stop playing in public. But he insisted on conducting his orchestral works long after he could do it efficiently. The players would become confused by his wild gestures on the podium, and performances were often chaotic. His sense of isolation grew with his deafness. Friends had to communicate with him through an ear trumpet, and during his last eight years he carried notebooks in which people would write questions and comments.

In 1815, his brother Caspar died, and Beethoven and the widow became coguardians of the nine-year-old son. Young Carl was the object of a savage tug-of-war. For five years, Beethoven fought legal battles for exclusive custody of his nephew; he finally won. This "victory" was a disaster for everyone. Growing up in the household of a deaf, eccentric bachelor uncle is not easy at best, and for Carl it was complicated by Beethoven's craving for love and companionship. The young man attempted suicide, a crushing event for Beethoven, whose health was already poor.

During the first three years of legal battles over Carl, Beethoven composed less, and the Viennese began to whisper that he was finished. Beethoven heard the rumor and said, "Wait a while, they'll soon learn differently!" And they did.

 Ludwig van Beethoven

241

After 1818, Beethoven's domestic problems did not prevent a creative outburst that produced some of his greatest works: the late piano sonatas, string quartets, the *Missa solemnis,* and the Ninth Symphony—out of total deafness, new realms of sound.

Beethoven's Music

"I must despise the world which does not know that music is a higher revelation than all wisdom and philosophy." For Beethoven, music was not mere entertainment, but a moral force capable of creating a vision of higher ideals. His music directly reflects his powerful, tortured personality. In both art and life, his heroic struggle resulted in victory over despair.

Beethoven's demand for perfection meant long and hard work. Unlike Mozart, he couldn't dash off three great symphonies in six weeks. Sometimes he worked years on a single symphony, writing other works at the same time. He carried music sketchbooks everywhere, jotting down new ideas, revising and refining old ones. These early notes often seem crude and uninspired when compared with their final versions, which were hammered out through great labor.

Beethoven mostly used Classical forms and techniques, but he gave them new power and intensity. The musical heir of Haydn and Mozart, he bridged the Classical and Romantic eras. Many of his innovations were used by composers who came after him.

In his works, great tension and excitement are built up through syncopations and dissonances. The range of pitch and dynamics is greater than ever before, so that contrasts of mood become more pronounced. Accents and climaxes seem titanic. Tiny rhythmic ideas are often repeated over and over to create momentum. Greater tension called for a larger musical framework, and so Beethoven expanded his forms. For example, the Third Symphony (*Eroica*) is far longer than any symphony by Haydn or Mozart and takes almost fifty minutes to perform. Beethoven was a musical architect who was unsurpassed in his ability to create large-scale structures in which every note seems inevitable. In describing Beethoven's music, it is perhaps too easy to give the impression that all of it is stormy and powerful. A lot is; but much is gentle, humorous, noble, or lyrical. His range of expression is enormous. Tempo, dynamic, and expressive indications are marked far more extensively in his scores than in those of earlier composers. For example, one direction reads, "Rather lively with the most intimate feeling." Characteristic of his explicit dynamic markings is $\texttextless\ p$, a gradual increase in loudness followed by a sudden softness.

More than his predecessors, Beethoven tried to unify the contrasting movements of a symphony, sonata, or string quartet. Musical continuity is heightened in several ways. Sometimes a movement leads directly into the next, instead of ending traditionally with a pause. In the Fifth Symphony, for example, the last two movements are linked by a suspenseful bridge section. A musical bond between different movements of the same work is also created when their themes resemble each other. In a few compositions (Fifth and Ninth Symphonies), a theme from one movement is quoted in a later movement.

Like Haydn and Mozart, Beethoven wrote many movements in sonata form. The development section is greatly expanded and becomes even more dramatic. It often contains a powerful crescendo that leads to the climactic return of the first theme (recapitulation). The coda is also expanded and serves to develop themes still further. Its length balances what came before and affirms the victory of the tonic key over the many new keys in the development section.

As the third movement of a symphony or string quartet, Beethoven most often used a scherzo rather than the traditional minuet. He transformed the courtly dance into a rapid movement with rhythmic drive. The character of this scherzo is flexible. In the Fifth Symphony it's an ominous force, while in the Sixth Symphony ("Pastoral") it depicts peasant merrymaking. Beethoven's works often have climactic, triumphant finales, toward which the previous movements seem to build. This marks an important departure from the light, relaxed ending movement favored by Haydn and Mozart.

Beethoven's most popular works are the nine symphonies, which were conceived for larger orchestras than Haydn's or Mozart's. For greater power and brilliance, Beethoven sometimes added the trombone, piccolo, and contrabassoon—instruments that were not used previously in symphonies. All the orchestral instruments have to play difficult music. For example, the French horn is assigned prominent melodies, and the timpani participate in the musical dialog, rather than merely mark the beat.

Each of Beethoven's symphonies is unique in character and style. There is a curious alternation of mood between odd-numbered symphonies (3, 5, 7, and 9), which tend to be forceful and assertive, and even-numbered ones (4, 6, 8), which are calmer and more lyrical. In the finale of the Ninth Symphony ("Choral"), Beethoven took the unprecedented step of using a chorus and four solo vocalists. They sing the text of Schiller's "Ode to Joy," a poem about human brotherhood.

A feeling for the virtuosity and improvisation that so astounded the Viennese can be gotten from Beethoven's thirty-two piano sonatas. Far more difficult than the sonatas of Haydn and Mozart, they exploit the stronger, tonally improved piano of Beethoven's time. He drew many new effects from the piano, ranging from massive chords to the hollow, mystical sounds produced when the right and left hands play far apart on the keyboard. These sonatas were experimental grounds for the compositional techniques he later expanded in the symphonies and string quartets.

Beethoven's sixteen string quartets are among the greatest music composed. Spanning the composer's entire career, they are unsurpassed in sheer invention, thematic treatment, and heart-rending expressiveness. In three of the last quartets, Beethoven again stepped beyond the conventions of classical form: He used five, six, and seven movements (Op. 132, Op. 130, Op. 131) which are connected in subtle ways. And he wrote five superb piano concertos, each remarkable in its individuality. In the fourth and fifth concertos, the opening movement begins with a brief piano solo rather than the traditional orchestral exposition.

While most of Beethoven's great works are for instruments, his sense of drama

 Beethoven's Music

243

was also expressed in vocal music. In his only opera, *Fidelio,* a wife's heroism enables justice to triumph over tyranny. Beethoven also composed two Masses. The *Missa solemnis* ("Solemn Mass," 1819–1823) is one of the most monumental and expressive settings of this sacred text.

Beethoven's total output is usually divided into three periods: early (up to 1802), middle (1803–1814), and late (1815–1827). Haydn and Mozart influence some works of the early period, while other pieces clearly show Beethoven's personal style. The compositions of the middle period are longer and heroic in tone. And the sublime works of the last period well up from the depths of a man almost totally deaf. During this period he often used the fugue to express new musical conceptions. These late works contain passages that sound surprisingly harsh and "modern." When a violinist complained that the music was very difficult to play, Beethoven reportedly replied, "Do you believe that I think of a wretched fiddle when the spirit speaks to me?"

Piano Sonata in C Minor, Op. 13 ("Pathétique"; 1798–1799)

The title "Pathétique," coined by Beethoven, suggests the tragically passionate character of this famous piano sonata. Beethoven's impetuous playing and masterful improvisational powers are mirrored in the sonata's extreme dynamic contrasts, explosive accents, and crashing chords. At age twenty-eight, during his early period, Beethoven already had created a powerful and original piano style that foreshadows nineteenth-century romanticism.

Side 7, band 1

First Movement:
Grave (solemn slow introduction);
Allegro molto e con brio (very fast and brilliant allegro)

The Pathétique begins in C minor with an intense slow introduction dominated by an opening motive in dotted rhythm: long-short-long-short-long-long.

The Classical
Period
244

This six-note idea seems to pose a series of unresolved questions as it is repeated on higher and higher pitch levels. The tragic mood is intensified by dissonant chords, sudden contrasts of dynamics and register, and pauses filled with expectancy. As in Haydn's "Drumroll" Symphony (studied in section 10), the introduction is integrated into the following Allegro in imaginative and dramatic ways.

The tension of the introduction is maintained in the Allegro con brio, a breathless fast movement in sonata form. The opening theme, in C minor, begins with a staccato idea that rapidly rises up a two-octave scale. It is accompanied by low broken octaves, the rapid alternation of two tones an octave apart.

Growing directly out of the opening theme is a bridge that is also built from a climbing staccato motive.

This bridge motive has an important role later in the movement.

Entering without a pause, the contrasting second theme is spun out of a short motive that is repeatedly shifted between low and high registers.

This restless idea begins in E-flat minor but then moves through different keys. The exposition is rounded off by several themes including a high running passage and a return of the opening staccato idea in E-flat major.

Piano Sonata
in C Minor,
Op. 13

245

(The exposition is sometimes repeated.)

The development section begins with a dramatic surprise: Beethoven brings back the opening bars of the slow introduction. This reappearance creates an enormous contrast of tempo, rhythm, and mood. After four bars of slow music, the fast tempo resumes as Beethoven combines two different ideas: the staccato bridge motive and a quickened version of the introduction motive. The introduction motive is presented in a rhythmically altered form: short-short-short-long-long.

The bridge motive is then developed in the bass, played by the pianist's left hand while the right hand has high broken octaves. After high accented notes, the brief development concludes with a running passage that leads down to the recapitulation.

For a while, the recapitulation runs its usual course as themes from the exposition are presented in the tonic key of C minor. But Beethoven has one more surprise for the coda—after a loud dissonant chord and brief pause, he again brings back the opening of the slow introduction. This time the slow music is even more moving as it is punctuated by moments of silence. Then the fast tempo resumes, and the opening staccato idea and powerful chords bring the movement to a decisive close.

Side 7, band 2

Second Movement: Adagio cantabile (lyrical adagio)

The second movement, in A-flat major, is slow, intimate, and songlike. It is in rondo form and may be outlined A B A C A Coda. The legato main theme (A), played in the piano's rich middle register, is one of Beethoven's most lyrical melodies.

This melody is immediately repeated an octave higher with fuller harmony. Section B is also legato and maintains the opening mood while introducing a new accompaniment of repeated chords. Section C is a duet between tender legato phrases in the top part and more animated staccato replies in the bass. This section brings some contrast with a shift to minor, a powerful crescendo, and a triplet rhythm in the accompaniment. On its last return, the main melody sounds more flowing because it is now accompanied by a rocking figure in triplet rhythm. The movement is rounded off by a poetic coda that descends leisurely to soft concluding chords.

Third Movement: Rondo (Allegro) *Side 7, band 3*

The last movement, in C minor, is a rapid and energetic rondo. It is outlined A B A C A B A Coda. The lively main theme (A), in minor, contrasts with the other sections, which are in major.

The B section includes several lyrical themes, while the C section is polyphonic and contains ideas that are shifted from one hand to the other. Sections B and C both end with a sustained dominant chord that creates expectancy for the return of the main theme and key. Toward the end of the stormy coda, a sustained chord is followed unexpectedly by the opening notes of the main theme in major rather than minor.

But the consolation of major is brief, as a rapid downward scale brings the movement to a powerful close in C minor.

Symphony No. 5 in C Minor, Op. 67 (1808)

The Fifth Symphony opens with one of the most famous rhythmic ideas in all music, a short-short-short-long motive. Beethoven reportedly interpreted this four-note motive as "Fate knocking at the door." It dominates the first movement and plays an important role later in the symphony, too. The entire work can be seen as an emotional progression from the conflict and struggle of the first movement, in C minor, to the exultation and victory of the final movement, in C major. The finale is the climax of the symphony; it is longer than the first

Symphony No. 5 in C Minor, Op. 67 (1808)

247

movement and more powerful in sound, employing three trombones. This was the first time that a trombone was used in a symphony.

Through several different techniques, Beethoven brilliantly welds four contrasting movements into a unified work. The basic rhythmic motive of the first movement (short-short-short-long) is used in a marchlike theme in the third movement. And this third-movement theme is later quoted dramatically within the finale. The last two movements are also connected by a bridge passage.

Beethoven worked on the Fifth Symphony off and on from 1804 to 1808, while also composing other great works.

Side 6, band 1

First Movement: Allegro con brio (Allegro with vigor)

The Allegro con brio is an enormously powerful and concentrated movement in sonata form. Its character is determined by a single rhythmic motive, short-short-short-long, from which Beethoven creates an astonishing variety of musical ideas. Tension and expectation are generated from the very beginning of the movement. Three rapid notes of the same pitch are followed by a downward leap to a held, suspenseful tone. This powerful idea is hammered out twice by all the strings in unison; the second time it is a step lower in pitch.

As the opening theme continues in C minor, Beethoven maintains excitement by quickly developing his basic idea. He crowds varied repetitions of the motive together and rapidly shifts the motive to different pitches and instruments.

The second theme, in E-flat major, dramatically combines different ideas. It begins with an unaccompanied horn call that asserts the basic motive in a varied form (short-short-short-long-long-long).

This horn-call motive announces a new legato melody which is calm and contrasts with the preceding agitation. Yet even during this lyrical moment, we are not allowed to forget the basic motive; now it is muttered in the background by cellos and double basses.

Beethoven generates tension in the development section by breaking the horn-call motive into smaller and smaller fragments until it is represented by only a single tone. Supported by a chord, this tone is echoed between woodwinds and strings in a breathtaking decrescendo. The recapitulation comes as a tremendous climax as the full orchestra thunders the basic motive. The recapitulation also brings a new expressive oboe solo at the end of the first theme. The heroic closing section of the recapitulation, in C major, moves without a break into a long and exciting coda in C minor. This coda is like a second development section in which the basic motive creates still greater power and energy.

LISTENING OUTLINE
To be read while music is heard

Symphony No. 5 in C Minor, Op. 67 (1808), by Ludwig van Beethoven

First Movement: Allegro con brio

Sonata form, duple meter ($\frac{2}{4}$), C minor

2 flutes, 2 oboes, 2 clarinets, 2 bassoons, 2 French horns, 2 trumpets, timpani, violins 1, violins 2, violas, cellos, basses

(About 6½ min)

EXPOSITION
    First theme   1   *a.* Basic motive, *ff*, repeated a step lower, strings in unison.

                                 b. Sudden *p*, strings quickly develop basic motive, minor key, powerful chords, high held tone.

Bridge   2   *a.* Basic motive, *ff*, orchestra in unison.
                                 b. Sudden *p*, strings quickly develop basic motive, crescendo, *ff*, powerful chords.
Second theme   3   *a.* Solo French horns, *ff*, horn-call motive.

                                 b. Violins, *p*, lyrical major melody. Basic motive accompanies in low strings.

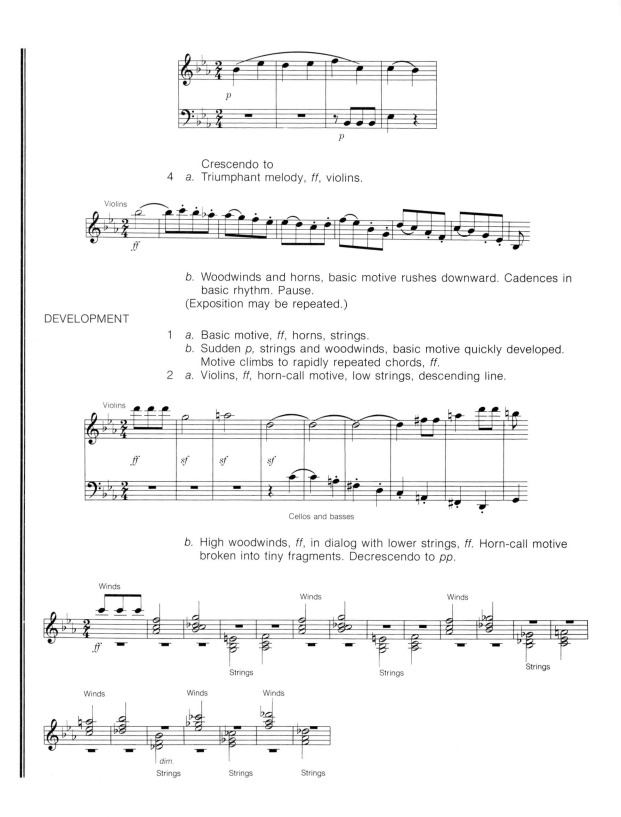

Crescendo to
4 *a.* Triumphant melody, *ff*, violins.

       b. Woodwinds and horns, basic motive rushes downward. Cadences in
          basic rhythm. Pause.
       (Exposition may be repeated.)

DEVELOPMENT

1 *a.* Basic motive, *ff*, horns, strings.
    b. Sudden *p*, strings and woodwinds, basic motive quickly developed.
       Motive climbs to rapidly repeated chords, *ff*.
2 *a.* Violins, *ff*, horn-call motive, low strings, descending line.

    b. High woodwinds, *ff*, in dialog with lower strings, *ff*. Horn-call motive
       broken into tiny fragments. Decrescendo to *pp*.

     c. Sudden *ff,* horn-call rhythm.
     d. Sudden *pp,* woodwinds echoed by strings.
     e. Sudden *ff,* repeated motive drives into

RECAPITULATION
First theme   1 *a.* Climactic basic motive, full orchestra, *ff,* repeated a step lower.
     b. Sudden *p,* strings quickly develop basic motive, minor key, chords lead to
     c. Oboe solo.
Bridge   2 Basic motive quickly developed in strings, crescendo to *ff,* full orchestra.
Second theme   3 *a.* Horn-call motive, solo bassoons, *ff* (horns sometimes added).
     b. Lyrical major melody, *p,* violins and flutes alternate. Basic motive accompanies in timpani, *p.* Crescendo to
     4 *a.* Triumphant melody, *ff,* violins.
     b. Woodwinds, basic motive rushes downward.
     Cadences in basic rhythm.

CODA

     1 *a.* Rapidly repeated chords, *ff.*
     b. Horn-call motive, lower strings, *f,* with higher violin melody, minor.

Descending violin melody, staccato, leads to
     3 *a.* New, rising theme in strings, legato and staccato.

     b. High woodwinds, *ff,* answered by lower strings in powerful interchange.
     Rapidly repeated notes lead to
     4 *a.* Basic motive, *ff,* repeated a step lower, full orchestra.
     b. Sudden *p,* basic motive quickly developed in strings and woodwinds.
     c. Sudden *ff,* powerful concluding chords.

Second Movement: Andante con moto
(moderately slow but not too slow)

Side 6, band 2

The second movement, in A-flat major, is mostly relaxed and lyrical, but it includes moments of tension and heroism. It is an extended set of variations based on two themes. The main theme (A), softly introduced by the cellos and violas, is a long legato melody of great nobility. The second theme (B) begins very gently in the clarinets but soon brings a startling contrast of mood. The full orchestra suddenly bursts in, and the clarinet melody is transformed into a

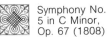

Symphony No.
5 in C Minor,
Op. 67 (1808)

251

triumphant trumpet fanfare. A hushed transitional passage then leads back to the main theme, presented now in quicker notes.

After several variations, there is a middle section in which fragments of the themes are treated in new ways. Woodwind instruments are featured, and there is a brief episode in minor. The movement concludes with a final variation of the main melody—now majestically proclaimed by the full orchestra—and a coda that poetically recalls what has come before.

LISTENING OUTLINE
To be read while music is heard

Symphony No. 5 in C Minor, Op. 67 (1808), by Ludwig van Beethoven

Second Movement: Andante con moto

Theme and variations, triple meter ($\frac{3}{8}$), A-flat major

2 flutes, 2 oboes, 2 clarinets, 2 bassoons, 2 French horns, 2 trumpets, timpani, violins 1, violins 2, violas, cellos, double basses

(About 10 min)

THEME A

1 Lyrical melody, violas and cellos, *p*.

Melody continues in higher register, violins alternate with flute.

THEME B

2 *a.* Clarinets, *p*, rising phrases.

Violins, *pp*, sudden *ff*, full orchestra.
b. Trumpets, *ff*, rising phrases.

252

VAR. A¹

Violins, *pp*, sustained notes.

3   Violas and cellos, *p*, lyrical melody in even-flowing rhythm.

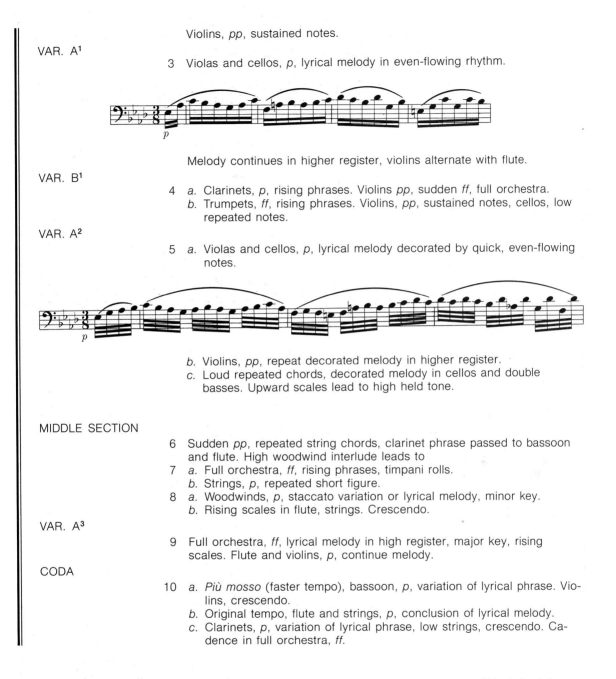

p

Melody continues in higher register, violins alternate with flute.

VAR. B¹

4   *a.* Clarinets, *p*, rising phrases. Violins *pp*, sudden *ff*, full orchestra.
    b. Trumpets, *ff*, rising phrases. Violins, *pp*, sustained notes, cellos, low
    repeated notes.

VAR. A²

5   *a.* Violas and cellos, *p*, lyrical melody decorated by quick, even-flowing
    notes.

p

   b. Violins, *pp*, repeat decorated melody in higher register.
   c. Loud repeated chords, decorated melody in cellos and double
   basses. Upward scales lead to high held tone.

MIDDLE SECTION

6   Sudden *pp*, repeated string chords, clarinet phrase passed to bassoon
    and flute. High woodwind interlude leads to
7   *a.* Full orchestra, *ff*, rising phrases, timpani rolls.
    b. Strings, *p*, repeated short figure.
8   *a.* Woodwinds, *p*, staccato variation or lyrical melody, minor key.
    b. Rising scales in flute, strings. Crescendo.

VAR. A³

9   Full orchestra, *ff*, lyrical melody in high register, major key, rising
    scales. Flute and violins, *p*, continue melody.

CODA

10 *a.* *Più mosso* (faster tempo), bassoon, *p*, variation of lyrical phrase. Vio-
    lins, crescendo.
    b. Original tempo, flute and strings, *p*, conclusion of lyrical melody.
    c. Clarinets, *p*, variation of lyrical phrase, low strings, crescendo. Ca-
    dence in full orchestra, *ff*.

Third Movement: Allegro (scherzo)   *Side 6, band 3*

The rapid third movement is a scherzo, in C minor, composed of three sections: A
(scherzo) B (trio) A′ (scherzo). The scherzo opens with a hushed, mysterious
theme played by cellos and double basses in a low register.

Soon, in sharp contrast, a bold repeated-note theme is hammered out loudly by the horns.

This theme is dominated by the rhythmic pattern short-short-short-long and recalls the basic motive of the first movement.

The B section (trio), in major, brings a gruff, hurried theme, played by cellos and double basses.

This theme is imitated, in the style of a fugue, by each of the higher strings. The bustling rhythmic motion of the B section has a feeling of energy and rough humor.

When the scherzo section (A′) returns, it is hushed and ominous throughout, sounding like a ghost of its former self. The mysterious opening theme is now played pizzicato rather than legato. The repeated-note theme is completely transformed in mood; it no longer is proclaimed by horns but is whispered by clarinets, plucked violins, and oboe.

One of the most extraordinary passages in the symphony follows the scherzo section (A′): a bridge leading from the dark, mysterious world of the scherzo to the bright sunlight of the finale. It opens with a feeling of suspended animation as the timpani softly repeat a single tone against a sustained chord in the strings. Over the timpani pulsation, the violins hesitantly play a fragment of the mysterious scherzo theme. Tension mounts as this fragment is carried higher and higher, until a sudden crescendo climaxes with the heroic opening of the finale.

Side 6, band 3 (continued) **Fourth Movement: Allegro**

The fourth movement, in sonata form, is the climax of the symphony. It brings the victory of C major over C minor, of optimism and exultation over struggle and uncertainty. For greater power and brilliance, Beethoven enlarged the orchestra to include three trombones, a piccolo, and a contrabassoon. Brass instruments are especially prominent and give a marchlike character to much of the movement.

The exposition is rich in melodic ideas; even the bridge has a theme of its own, and there is also a distinctive closing theme. The triumphant opening theme

begins with the three tones of the C-major triad, brilliantly proclaimed by the trumpets.

A bridge theme, similar in mood to the opening one, is announced by the horns and continued by the violins.

Triplets lend a joyous quality to the second theme, which contrasts loud and soft phrases.

Two powerful chords and a brief pause announce the closing theme of the exposition. Composed of descending phrases, this melody is first played by the strings and woodwinds and then forcefully repeated by the entire orchestra.

    The development focuses mainly on the second theme and its triplet rhythm. A huge climax at the end of the development is followed by one of the most marvelous surprises in all music. Beethoven dramatically quotes the whispered repeated-note theme (short-short-short-long) of the preceding scherzo movement. This ominous quotation is like a sudden recollection of past anxiety, and it creates a connection between the last two movements. Leading into a powerful recapitulation, it renews the victory over uncertainty.

    During the finale's long coda, earlier themes are heard in altered and quickened versions. Several times, the music keeps going even though the listener thinks it's coming to an end. Over and over, Beethoven affirms the tonic key and resolves the frenzied tensions built up during the symphony. Such control over tension is an essential element of Beethoven's genius.

Symphony No. 5 in C Minor, Op. 67 (1808)

THE ROMANTIC PERIOD

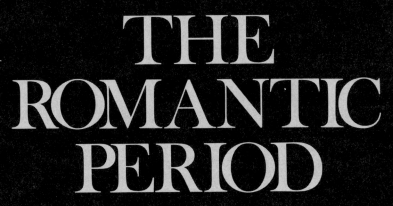

1 Romanticism in Music

2 Romantic Composers and Their Public

3 The Art Song

4 Franz Schubert

5 Robert Schumann

6 Frédéric Chopin

7 Franz Liszt

8 Felix Mendelssohn

9 Program Music

10 Hector Berlioz

11 Nationalism in Nineteenth-Century Music

12 Peter Ilyich Tchaikovsky

13 Bedřich Smetana

14 Antonin Dvořák

15 Johannes Brahms

16 Guiseppe Verdi

17 Giacomo Puccini

18 Richard Wagner

19 Gustav Mahler

John Constable, *The Cornfield* (1826). Of all the inspirations for Romantic art, none was more important than nature (The Granger Collection).

1 | ROMANTICISM IN MUSIC

The early nineteenth century brought the flowering of Romanticism, a cultural movement that stressed emotion, imagination, and individualism. In part, Romanticism was a rebellion against the neoclassicism of the eighteenth-century Age of Reason. Romantic writers broke away from time-honored conventions and emphasized freedom of expression. Painters used bolder, more brilliant colors and preferred dynamic motion to gracefully balanced poses.

But Romanticism was too diverse and complex to be defined by any single formula. It aimed to broaden all human horizons and encompass the totality of our experience. The Romantic movement was international in scope and influenced all the arts.

Emotional subjectivity was a basic quality of Romanticism in art. "All good poetry is the spontaneous overflow of powerful feelings," wrote William Wordsworth, the English Romantic poet. And "spontaneous overflow" made much Romantic literature autobiographical; authors projected their personalities in their work. Walt Whitman, the American poet, expressed this subjective attitude beautifully when he began a poem, "I celebrate myself, and sing myself."

In exploring their inner lives, the Romantics were especially drawn to the realm of fantasy: the unconscious, the irrational, the world of dreams. Romantic fiction includes tales of terror and the supernatural, such as "The Cask of Amontillado" by Edgar Allan Poe and *Frankenstein* by Mary Shelley. The writer Thomas De Quincey vividly describes his drug-induced dreams in the *Confessions of an English Opium-Eater:* "I was buried, for a thousand years, in stone coffins, with mummies and sphinxes. I was kissed, with cancerous kisses, by crocodiles." The visual arts also depict nightmarish visions. In an etching called *The Sleep of Reason Breeds Monsters,* Spanish painter Francisco Goya shows batlike monsters surrounding a sleeping figure. The realm of the unknown and the exotic also interested the French artist Eugène Delacroix, who often depicted violent scenes in far-off lands.

Romantic fascination with fantasy was paired with enthusiasm for the Middle Ages, that time of chivalry and romance. While neoclassicists had thought of the medieval period as the "dark ages," the Romantics cherished it. They were inspired by medieval folk ballads, tales of fantasy and adventure. Romantic novels set in the Middle Ages include *Ivanhoe* (1819) by Sir Walter Scott and *The Hunchback of Notre Dame* (1831) by the French writer Victor Hugo. Gothic cathedrals, which had long gone unappreciated, now seemed picturesque and mysterious. A "gothic revival" in architecture resulted in the construction of buildings such as the Houses of Parliament in London (1836–1852) and Trinity Church in New York (1839–1846).

Of all the inspirations for Romantic art, none was more important than nature. The physical world was seen as a source of consolation and a mirror of

The Romantic Period

258

Delacroix's *The Death of Sardanapalus* (1827) shows a defeated Assyrian tyrant who has his wives killed before taking his own life. This violent and sensuous painting reflects the Romantic preoccupation with the exotic (Lauros—Giraudon).

the human heart. Wordsworth, for example, thought of nature as "the nurse,/ the guide, the guardian of my heart, and soul." One of his poems begins:

> There was a time when meadow, grove, and stream,
>   The earth, and every common sight,
>   To me did seem
>   Apparelled in celestial light,
> The glory and the freshness of a dream.

 Romanticism in Music

259

The nineteenth century was the age of grand opera. Construction of the Paris Opera House was begun in 1861 (Giraudon).

John Constable captured the Romantic view of nature in
Cathedral from the Bishop's Garden (Copyright, The Frick
Collection, New York).

Romantic sensitivity to nature is revealed in landscape painting, which attained new importance. Artists like John Constable and William Turner in England were masters in conveying the movement of nature: rippling brooks, drifting clouds, stormy seas. In Turner's seascapes, the sweep of waves expresses not only the grandeur of nature, but human passion as well.

Romanticism coincided with the Industrial Revolution, thus producing an interest in the working class and the poor. The novels of Charles Dickens and the paintings of Gustave Courbet reflect this interest.

Subjectivity, fantasy, enthusiasm for nature and the Middle Ages are only a few aspects of Romanticism in literature and painting. We'll now focus on Romanticism in music.

 Romanticism in Music

The Industrial Revolution spurred an interest in the working class. *The Stone Breakers* by Gustave Courbet illustrates this trend toward a new realism in the arts (Deutsche Fotothek Dresden).

The Romantic Period in Music (1820–1900)

The Romantic period in music extended from about 1820 to 1900. Great Romantic composers include Franz Schubert, Hector Berlioz, Felix Mendelssohn, Frédéric Chopin, Robert Schumann, Franz Liszt, Richard Wagner, Giuseppe Verdi, Johannes Brahms, Peter Ilyich Tchaikovsky, and Gustav Mahler. The length of this list—even with many important composers omitted—testifies to the richness and variety of Romantic music and proves its continuing impact on today's concert and operatic repertory.

Composers of the Romantic period continued to use the musical forms of the preceding Classical era. The emotional intensity associated with Romanticism was already present in the work of Mozart and particularly in that of Beethoven, who greatly influenced composers after him. The Romantic preference for expressive, songlike melody also grew out of the Classical style. Nonetheless, there are many differences between Romantic and Classical music. Romantic works

The Romantic Period

tend to have greater ranges of tone color, dynamics, and pitch. Also, the Romantic harmonic vocabulary is broader, with more emphasis on colorful, unstable chords.

Romantic music is linked more closely to other arts, particularly to literature. New forms developed, and in all forms there was greater tension and less balance and resolution. But Romantic music is so diverse that generalizations are apt to mislead. Some Romantic composers, such as Mendelssohn and Brahms, created works that were deeply rooted in Classical tradition, while others, such as Berlioz, Liszt, and Wagner, were more revolutionary.

Individuality of Style

Romantic music puts unprecedented emphasis on self-expression and individuality of style. There is "not a bar which I have not truly felt and which is not an echo of my inner-most feelings," wrote Tchaikovsky of his Fourth Symphony. "A new world of music" was the goal of young Chopin. Many Romantics created music that sounds unique and reflects their personalities. Robert Schumann observed that "Chopin will soon be unable to write anything without people crying out at the seventh or eighth bar, 'That is indeed by him.'" And today, with some listening experience, a music lover can tell within a few minutes whether a piece is by Schumann or Chopin, Tchaikovksy or Brahms.

Expressive Aims and Subjects

The Romantics explored a universe of feeling that included flamboyance and intimacy, unpredictability and melancholy, rapture and longing. Countless songs and operas glorify romantic love. Often the lovers are unhappy and face overwhelming obstacles. Fascination with the fantastic and diabolical is expressed in music like "Dream of a Witches' Sabbath" from Berlioz's *Fantastic Symphony*. All aspects of nature attracted Romantic musicians. In this chapter we'll study music that depicts shepherds' pipes and distant thunder (Berlioz's *Fantastic Symphony*), a wild horseback ride on a stormy night (Schubert's *Erlking*), the flow of a river (Smetana's *Moldau*), and a spectacular fire and flood (Wagner's *Twilight of the Gods*). Romantic composers also dealt with subjects drawn from the Middle Ages and from Shakespeare's plays.

Nationalism and Exoticism

Nationalism was an important political movement that influenced nineteenth-century music. Musical **nationalism** was expressed when Romantic composers deliberately created music with specific national identities, using folk songs, dances, legends, and histories of their homelands. This national flavor of Romantic music—whether Polish, Russian, Bohemian, or German—contrasts with the more universal character of Classical music.

Fascination with national identity also led composers to draw on colorful

 The Romantic Period in Music

263

materials from foreign lands, a trend known as musical **exoticism.** For instance, some wrote melodies in an oriental style or used rhythms and instruments associated with distant lands. The French composer Georges Bizet wrote *Carmen,* an opera set in Spain; the Italian Giacomo Puccini evoked Japan in *Madame Butterfly;* and the Russian Rimsky-Korsakov suggested an Arabian atmosphere in his orchestral work *Scheherazade.* Musical exoticism is in keeping with the Romantics' attraction to things remote, picturesque, and mysterious.

Program Music

The nineteenth century was the great age of **program music,** instrumental music associated with a story, poem, idea, or scene. Usually the nonmusical element is specified by a title or by explanatory comments called a **program.** A programmatic instrumental piece can represent the emotions, characters, and events of a particular story, or it can evoke the sounds and motions of nature. For example, in Tchaikovsky's *Romeo and Juliet,* an orchestral work inspired by Shakespeare's play, agitated music depicts the feud between the rival families, a tender melody conveys young love, and a funeral-march rhythm suggests the lovers' tragic fate. And in *The Moldau,* an orchestral work glorifying Czechoslovakia's main river, Smetana uses musical effects that call to mind a flowing stream, a hunting scene, a peasant wedding, and the crash of waves.

While program music in some form or another has existed for centuries, it became particularly prominent in the Romantic period, when music was closely associated with literature. Composers—Berlioz, Schumann, Liszt, Wagner—were often prolific authors as well. Artists in all fields were intoxicated by the idea of a "union of the arts." Poets wanted their poetry to be musical, and musicians wanted their music to be poetic.

Expressive Tone Color

Romantic composers reveled in rich and sensuous sound, using tone color to obtain variety of mood and atmosphere. Never before had timbre been so important.

In both symphonic and operatic works, the Romantic orchestra was larger and more varied in tone color than the Classical orchestra. Toward the end of the Romantic era, an orchestra might include close to one hundred musicians. (There were twenty to sixty players in the Classical ensemble.) The constant expansion of the orchestra reflected composers' changing needs as well as the growing size of concert halls and opera houses. The brass, woodwind, and percussion sections of the orchestra took on a more active role. Romantic composers spectacularly increased the power of the brass section, calling for trombones, tubas, and more horns and trumpets. In 1824, Beethoven broke precedent by asking for nine brasses in the Ninth Symphony; and in 1894, German composer Gustav Mahler demanded twenty-five brass instruments for his Second Symphony. The addition of valves had made it easier for horns and trumpets to cope with intricate melodies.

The woodwind section took on new tone colors as the contrabassoon, bass clarinet, English horn, and piccolo became regular members of the orchestra. Improvements in the construction of instruments allowed woodwind players to perform more flexibly and accurately. Orchestral sounds became more brilliant and sensuously appealing through increased use of cymbals, the triangle, and the harp.

New sounds were drawn from all instruments of the nineteenth-century orchestra. Flutists were required to play in the breathy low register, and violinists were asked to strike the strings with the wood of their bows. These demands compelled performers to attain a higher level of technical virtuosity. New ways of blending and combining tone colors were sought to achieve the most poignant and intense sound. In 1844, Hector Berlioz's *Treatise on Modern Instrumentation and Orchestration* signaled the recognition of orchestration as an art in itself.

The piano, the favorite instrument of the Romantic age, was improved vastly during the 1820s and 1830s. A cast-iron frame held the strings under greater tension, and the hammers were covered with felt. Thus the piano's tone became more "singing," and its range was extended. With a stronger instrument, the pianist could produce more sound. And use of the damper ("loud") pedal allowed a sonorous blend of tones from all registers of the piano.

Colorful Harmony

In addition to exploiting new tone colors, the Romantics explored new chords and novel ways of using familiar chords. Seeking greater emotional intensity, composers emphasized rich, colorful, and complex harmonies. There was more prominent use of **chromatic harmony,** chords containing tones not found in the prevailing major or minor scale. Such chord tones come from the chromatic scale (which has 12 tones), rather than from the major or minor scales (which have seven different tones). Chromatic chords add color and motion to Romantic music. Dissonant, or unstable, chords were also used more freely than during the Classical era. By deliberately delaying the resolution of dissonance to a consonant, or stable, chord, Romantic composers created feelings of yearning, tension, and mystery.

A Romantic piece tends to have a wide variety of keys and rapid modulations, or changes from one key to another. Due to the nature and frequency of these key shifts, the tonic key is somewhat less clear than in Classical works. The feeling of tonal gravity tends to be less strong. By the end of the Romantic period, even more emphasis was given to harmonic instability and less to stability and resolution.

Expanded Range of Dynamics, Pitch. and Tempo

Romantic music also calls for a wide range of dynamics. It includes sharp contrasts between faint whispers and sonorities of unprecedented power. Classical dynamic extremes of *ff* and *pp* didn't meet the needs of Romantics, who some-

The Romantic Period in Music

times demanded *ffff* and *pppp*. Seeking more and more expressiveness, nineteenth-century composers used frequent crescendos and decrescendos, as well as sudden dynamic changes.

Range of pitch was expanded, too, as composers reached for extremely high or low sounds. In search of increased brilliance and depth of sound, the Romantic exploited instruments like the piccolo and contrabassoon, as well as the expanded keyboard of the piano.

Mood changes in Romantic music are often underlined by accelerandos, ritardandos, and subtle variations of pace: There are many more fluctuations in tempo than there are in Classical music. To intensify the expression of the music, Romantic performers made use of **rubato,** the slight holding back or pressing forward of tempo.

Form: Miniature and Monumental

The nineteenth century was very much an age of contradictions. Romantic composers characteristically expressed themselves both in musical miniatures and in monumental compositions. On one hand are piano pieces by Chopin and songs by Schubert that last but a few minutes. Such short forms were meant to be heard in the intimate surroundings of a home; they met the needs of the growing number of people who owned pianos. These miniatures were a perfect outlet for the Romantic genius at creating an intense mood through a melody, a few chords, or an unusual tone color. In contrast, there are gigantic works by Berlioz and Wagner that call for a huge number of performers and last for several hours. Mammoth compositions, of course, were designed for large opera houses or concert halls.

Romantic composers continued to write symphonies, sonatas, string quartets, concertos, operas, and choral works, but their individual movements tended to be longer than Haydn's and Mozart's. For example, a typical nineteenth-century symphony may last about forty-five minutes, as opposed to twenty-five minutes for an eighteenth-century symphony. And as the Romantic period drew to a close, compositions tended to become even more extended, more richly orchestrated, and more complex in harmony.

New techniques were used to unify such long works. The same theme or themes might occur in several different movements of a symphony. Here composers followed the pioneering example of Beethoven's Fifth Symphony, where a theme from the scherzo is quoted within the finale. When a melody returns in a later movement or section of a Romantic work, its character may be transformed by changes in dynamics, orchestration, or rhythm—a technique known as **thematic transformation.** A striking use of thematic transformation occurs in Liszt's Piano Concerto in E-flat major, where a lyrical, intimate melody from the slow movement becomes a jaunty march tune in the finale.

Different movements or sections of a Romantic work can also be linked through transitional passages; one movement of a symphony or concerto may lead directly into the next. Here, again, Beethoven was the pioneer. And nineteenth-century operas are unified by melodic ideas that reappear in different acts or scenes, some of which may be tied together by connecting passages.

In dealing with an age that so prized individuality, generalizations are especially difficult. The great diversity found in Romantic music can best be appreciated, perhaps, by approaching each piece as the composers did—with an open mind and heart.

Basic Terms

nationalism

exoticism

program music

program

chromatic harmony

rubato

thematic transformation

ROMANTIC COMPOSERS AND THEIR PUBLIC

The composer's role in society had changed radically during Beethoven's lifetime (1770–1827). In earlier periods, part of a musician's job was composing works for a specific occasion and audience. Thus Bach wrote cantatas for weekly church services in Leipzig, while Haydn composed symphonies for concerts in the palaces of the Esterházy family. But Beethoven, we have seen, was one of the first great composers who worked as a free-lance musician outside the system of aristocratic or church patronage.

The image of Beethoven as a "free artist" inspired Romantic musicians, who composed to fulfill an inner need rather than a nobleman's commission. Romantic composers were interested not only in pleasing contemporaries, but also in the judgment of posterity. The young Berlioz wrote to his father, "I want to leave on this earth some trace of my existence." It became common for Romantics to create extended works with no immediate prospects for performance. For example, Wagner wrote *The Rhine Gold,* a 2½-hour opera, and then had to wait fifteen years before seeing its premiere.

Sometimes the Romantic composer was a "free artist" by necessity rather than choice. Because of the French Revolution and Napoleonic Wars (from 1789 to 1814), many aristocrats could no longer afford to maintain private opera houses, orchestras, and "composers in residence." Musicians lost their jobs when many of the tiny princely states of Germany were abolished as political units and merged with neighboring territories. (In Bonn, Germany, the court and its orchestra were disbanded; Beethoven could not return to his position there even if he had wanted to.) Many composers who would have had modest but secure incomes in

Composers and Their Public

267

the past had to fight for their livelihood and sell their wares on the marketplace.

Romantic composers wrote primarily for a middle-class audience whose size and prosperity had increased because of the Industrial Revolution. During the nineteenth century, cities expanded dramatically, and a sizable number of people wanted to hear and play music.

The needs of this urban middle class led to the formation of many orchestras and opera groups during the Romantic era. While public concerts had developed during the eighteenth century, only in the nineteenth century did regular subscription concerts become common. The London Philharmonic Society was founded in 1813, the Paris *Société des Concerts du Conservatoire* in 1828, the Vienna *Philharmonische Konzerte* and the New York Philharmonic in 1842.

The middle-class public was captivated by virtuosity. Musical heros of the 1830s were the pianist Franz Liszt and the violinist Niccolò Paganini, who toured Europe and astonished audiences with their feats. Never before was instrumental virtuosity so acclaimed. After a concert by Liszt in Budapest, Hungarian nobles presented him with a jeweled sword, and a crowd of thousands formed a torchlight parade to escort the virtuoso to his dwelling. Following Liszt's example, performers began to give solo recitals in addition to their customary appearances with orchestras.

Private music making also increased during the Romantic era. The piano became a fixture in every middle-class home, and there was great demand for songs and solo piano pieces. Operas and orchestral works were transcribed, or arranged, so that they could be played on pianos in the home.

Romantic composers came from the social class that was their main audience. Berlioz was the son of a doctor; Schumann was a bookseller's son; and Mendelssohn was the son of a banker. This was a new situation. In earlier periods, music, like cabinet making, was a craft passed from one generation to another. Bach, Mozart, and Beethoven were all children of musicians. But the Romantics often had to do a great deal of persuading before their parents permitted them to undertake a musical career. Berlioz wrote to his reluctant father in 1824: "I am voluntarily driven towards a magnificent career (no other term can be applied to the career of an artist) and I am not in the least headed towards damnation. This is the way I think, the way I am, and nothing in the world will change me."

Middle-class parents had reason for concern when their children wanted to be musicians. Few Romantic composers were able to support themselves through composition alone. Only a successful opera composer like Verdi could become wealthy by selling music to opera houses and publishers. Most composers were forced to work in several areas at once. Some were touring virtuosos like Paganini and Liszt. Many taught. Chopin charged high fees for piano lessons given to rich young women in Paris. Music criticism was a source of income for Berlioz and Schumann. (And Berlioz bitterly resented having to waste time reviewing compositions of nonentities.) Some of the finest conductors of the Romantic period were composers like Mendelssohn and Mahler. Tchaikovsky and Wagner were among the few fortunates with wealthy patrons to support them while they created. And lastly, some composers, like Schubert, never really earned a livelihood, leading a Bohemian existence and dying in poverty.

THE ART SONG | **3** |

One of the most distinctive forms of Romantic music is the **art song,** a composition for solo voice and piano. The accompaniment is an integral part of the composer's conception, and it serves with the voice as an interpretive partner. Now performed in concert halls, Romantic songs were written to be sung and enjoyed at home.

Poetry and music are intimately fused in the art song. It is no accident that this form flowered with the emergence of a rich body of Romantic poetry in the early nineteenth century. Many of the finest song composers—Schubert, Schumann, Brahms—were German or Austrian and set poems in their native language. Among the poets favored by these composers were Johann Wolfgang von Goethe (1749–1832) and Heinrich Heine (1797–1856). The German word *Lied* ("song") is commonly used for a song with German text. (*Lied* is pronounced "leet"; its plural, *Lieder,* is pronounced as "leader.")

Yearning—over a lost love, toward nature, legend, other times and places—haunted the imagination of Romantic poets. Thus art songs are filled with the despair of unrequited love, the beauty of flowers, trees, and brooks, and the supernatural happenings of folk tales. There are also songs of joy, wit, and humor. But by and large, Romantic song was a reaching out of the soul.

Song composers interpreted a poem, translating its mood, atmosphere, and imagery into music. They created a vocal melody that is musically satisfying and perfectly molded to the text. Important words are emphasized by stressed tones or melodic climaxes.

The voice shares this interpretive task with the piano. Emotions and images of the text get added dimension from the keyboard commentary. Arpeggios suggest the splashing of oars or the motion of a mill-wheel. Chords in a low register depict darkness or a lover's torment. The mood is often set by a brief piano introduction and summed up at the end by a piano section called a **postlude.**

Strophic and Through-composed Form

When a poem has several stanzas, the musical setting must accommodate their total emotional impact. Composers can use **strophic form,** repeating the same music for each stanza of the poem. This makes the song easy to remember. Strophic form is used in almost all folk songs. Or composers might use **through-composed form,** writing new music for each stanza. ("Through-composed" is a translation of the German term *durchkomponiert.*) Through-composed form allows music to reflect a poem's changing moods.

The art song is not restricted to strophic or through-composed form. There are many ways that music can be molded to the structure and feeling of a poem. A

 The Art Song

269

three-stanza poem is frequently set as follows: A (stanza 1) B (stanza 2) A (stanza 3). This might be called a **modified strophic form,** since two of the three stanzas are set to the same music.

The Song Cycle

Romantic art songs are sometimes grouped in a set, or **song cycle.** A cycle may be unified by a story line that runs through the poems, or by musical ideas linking the songs. Among the great Romantic song cycles are Schubert's *Die Winterreise* ("The Winter Journey," 1827) and Schumann's *Dichterliebe* ("Poet's Love," 1840).

In the art song, Romantic composers achieved a perfect union of music and poetry. They created an intensely personal world with a tremendous variety of moods. These miniatures contain some of the most haunting melodies and harmonies in all music.

Basic Terms

art song through-composed form
postlude modified strophic form
strophic form song cycle

4 FRANZ SCHUBERT

The career of Franz Schubert (1797–1828), the earliest master of the Romantic art song, was unlike that of any great composer before him. He never held an official position as musical director or organist, and he was neither a conductor nor a virtuoso. "I have come into the world for no other purpose but to compose," he told a friend. The full measure of his genius was recognized only years after his death at the tragically early age of thirty-one.

Schubert was born in Vienna, the son of a schoolmaster. Even as a child, his musical gifts were astounding. "If I wanted to instruct him in anything new," recalled his amazed teacher, "he knew it already. Therefore I gave him no actual instructions but merely talked to him and watched him in silent astonishment." At eleven, Schubert became a choirboy in the court chapel and won a scholarship to the Imperial Seminary, an exclusive boarding school where he played first violin and occasionally conducted the orchestra. Schubert so loved music that he once sold his school books to buy a ticket for Beethoven's opera *Fidelio.*

Schubert managed to compose an extraordinary number of masterpieces in his late teens while teaching at his father's school, a job he hated. His love of poetry led him to the art song, a form that Haydn, Mozart, and Beethoven had only touched on. Inflamed by the poetry and passion of Goethe's *Faust,* seventeen-year-old Schubert composed his first great song, "Gretchen at the Spinning Wheel." The next year he composed 143 songs, including "The Erlking." At nineteen his productivity rose to a peak: He composed 179 works, including two symphonies, an opera, and a Mass.

When he was twenty-one, Schubert gave up teaching school to devote himself entirely to music. He associated with a group of Viennese poets and artists who admired his compositions. "We often wandered about town until three in the morning," recalled a friend. "One of us not seldom would sleep in the apartment of another. We were not particular about comfort in those days. Whoever happened to have money paid for us all." Schubert often lived with friends because he did not have money to rent a room of his own.

Working with incredible speed, Schubert turned out one piece after another. He worked from seven in the morning until one or two in the afternoon; then he spent his afternoon in cafes, drinking coffee, playing billiards, reading newspapers, and talking with friends. His evenings were spent at "Schubertiads," parties where only his music was played. He accompanied the songs and played his delightful waltzes while friends danced. Most of his works were composed for performance in the homes of Vienna's cultivated middle class. Unlike Beethoven, Schubert did not mingle with the aristocracy.

At twenty-five Schubert contracted venereal disease, becoming moody and prone to despair. "Think of a man," he wrote of himself, "whose health can never be restored . . . of a man whose brightest hopes have come to nothing, to whom love and friendship are but torture. . . ." Several times during his last years he applied for musical positions but never received them. Inept when it came to money, Schubert sold publishers masterpieces for next to nothing. The publication and performance of his songs brought some recognition, but he was less well known than many contemporaries who are now forgotten. His two greatest symphonies, the "Unfinished" and the "Great" C major, were not performed in public during his lifetime. Only in his last year was a public concert devoted to his works.

Schubert was thirty-one when he died of typhoid fever in 1828, a year after Beethoven's funeral. His reputation was mainly that of a fine song composer, until the "Unfinished" Symphony was performed almost forty years later. Then the world could recognize Schubert's comprehensive greatness.

Schubert's Music

It is amazing how original, varied, and numerous are the works of this composer who died at thirty-one. Along with over six hundred songs, Schubert left symphonies, string quartets, chamber music, piano sonatas, short piano pieces for two and four hands, Masses, and operatic compositions.

 Schubert's Music

Franz Schubert did not mingle with the aristocracy, preferring instead the company of other musicians, poets, and painters (Courtesy of the Austrian Information Service, New York).

The songs embrace an incredible variety of moods and types. Some are very short, others very long; their forms include strophic, modified strophic, and through-composed. Many deal with nature—the flow of a brook, the mystery of the night—or with unhappy love. These songs amply display Schubert's melodic genius. His melodies range from simple, folklike tunes to complex lines that suggest impassioned speech. And his piano accompaniments are equally rich and evocative. Many songs draw emotional power from the relentless repetition of a rhythmic idea or from a shattering climax.

Schubert's imaginative harmonies provide some of the most poetic moments in music. He uses unexpected dissonances to capture a mood, and he shifts abruptly to contrasting keys. In Schubert's hands, even the simple change from minor to major can evoke a sudden thought of love or an illusion of light breaking through clouds.

The spirit of song permeates Schubert's instrumental music, too. Many of his symphonies and chamber works have long lyrical melodies, and often Schubert writes variations on his own songs. For instance, the fourth movement of the "Trout" Quintet, for piano and strings, is a set of variations on his song "The Trout" (*Die Forelle*). And his short piano pieces such as the *Moments musicaux* ("Musical Moments") and *Impromptus* are true "songs without words."

Schubert wrote a number of symphonies and chamber works that are comparable in power and emotional intensity to those of his idol, Beethoven. The "Unfinished" Symphony (1822) and the "Great" C-major Symphony (1828) employ horns, trombones, and woodwinds with a new feeling for their poetic capacities. The "Unfinished" Symphony, Schubert's most popular orchestral work, was written six years before his death. We probably will never learn why it contains two rather than the usual four movements. The "Great" C-major Symphony was discovered ten years after Schubert's death by Robert Schumann, who was ecstatic about the work. "It is not possible to describe it to you," he wrote his fiancée. "All the instruments are human voices . . . and this length, this heavenly length. . . ." Reviewing the first public performance of this symphony, Schumann made an observation that is true of much of Schubert's music: "It bears within it the seeds of everlasting youth."

"The Erlking" (*Erlkönig;* 1815)

Side 8, band 1

Schubert's song "The Erlking" is one of the earliest and finest examples of musical Romanticism. A friend of Schubert tells how he saw the eighteen-year-old composer reading Goethe's narrative ballad of the supernatural. "He paced up and down several times with the book; suddenly he sat down, and in no time at all (just as quickly as you can write) there was the glorious ballad finished on the paper." Goethe's ballad, in dialog almost throughout, tells of a father riding on horseback through a storm with his sick child in his arms. The delirious boy has visions of the legendary Erlking, the king of the elves who symbolizes death.

 "The Erlking" (*Erlkönig;* 1815)

273

Schubert employs a through-composed setting to capture the mounting excitement of the poem. The piano part, with its rapid octaves and menacing bass motive, conveys the tension of the wild ride.

The piano's relentless triplet rhythm unifies the episodes of the song, and suggests the horse's gallop.

By imaginatively varying the music, Schubert makes one singer sound like several characters in a miniature drama. The terrified boy sings in a high register in minor. Three times during the poem he cries out, "My father, my father." Each time, the boy sings a musical outcry that is intensified through dissonant harmonies.

Mein Va - ter, mein Va - ter,

To convey mounting fear, Schubert pitches the boy's outcry higher and higher each time. The reassuring father sings in a low register that contrasts with the high-pitched outcries of his child. The Erlking, who tries to entice the boy, has coy melodies in major keys.

"Du lie - bes Kind, komm, geh mit mir! gar schö - ne Spie - le spiel' - ich mit dir;

The deeply moving climax of "The Erlking" comes when father and son arrive home and the galloping accompaniment gradually comes to a halt. In a bleak, heart-breaking recitative that allows every word to make its impact, the narrator tells us, "In his arms the child was dead!"

Piano intro-
duction,
rapid oc-
taves, *f*, bass
motive,
minor key.

Narrator

Wer reitet so spät durch Nacht und Wind?	Who rides so late through the night and the wind?	
Es ist der Vater mit seinem Kind;	It is the father with his child;	
Er hat den Knaben wohl in dem Arm,	he folds the boy close in his arms,	
Er fasst ihn sicher, er hält ihn warm.	he clasps him securely, he holds him warmly.	

Father

"Mein Sohn, was birgst du so bang dein Gesicht?"	"My son, why do you hide your face so anxiously?"	Low register.

Son

"Siehst, Vater, du den Erlkönig nicht?	"Father, don't you see the Erlking?	Higher regis-ter.
Den Erlenkönig mit Kron' und Schweif?"	The Erlking with his crown and his train?"	

Father

"Mein Sohn, es ist ein Nebel-streif."	"My son, it is a streak of mist."	Low register.

Erlking

"Du liebes Kind, komm, geh mit mir!	"Dear child, come, go with me!	Coaxing tune, *pp*, higher regis-ter, major.
Gar schöne Spiele spiel' ich mit dir,	I'll play the prettiest games with you.	
Manch bunte Blumen sind an dem Strand,	Many colored flowers grow along the shore;	
Meine Mutter hat manch gülden Gewand."	my mother has many golden garments."	

Son

"Mein Vater, mein Vater, und hörest du nicht,	"My father, my father, and don't you hear	Outcry, *f*, minor.
Was Erlenkönig mir leise ver-spricht?"	the Erlking whispering promises to me?"	

Father

"Sei ruhig, bleibe ruhig, mein Kind:	"Be quiet, stay quiet, my child;	Low register.
In dürren Blättern säuselt der Wind."	the wind is rustling in the dead leaves."	

"The Erlking"
(*Erlkönig;*
1815)

275

"Willst, feiner Knabe, du mit mir gehn?	"My handsome boy, will you come with me?	Playful tune, *pp*, major.
Meine Töchter sollen dich warten schön;	My daughters shall wait upon you;	
Meine Töchter führen den nächtlichen Reihn	my daughters lead off in the dance every night,	
Und wiegen und tanzen und singen dich ein."	and cradle and dance and sing you to sleep."	

Son

"Mein Vater, mein Vater, und siehst du nicht dort	"My father, my father, and don't you see there	Outcry, *f*, higher than before, minor.
Erlkönigs Töchter am düstern Ort?"	the Erlking's daughters in the shadows?"	

Father

"Mein Sohn, mein Sohn, ich seh' es genau:	"My son, my son, I see it clearly;	Lower register.
Es scheinen die alten Weiden so grau."	the old willows look so gray."	

Erlking

"Ich liebe dich, mich reizt deine schöne Gestalt;	"I love you, your beautiful figure delights me!	
Und bist du nicht willig, so brauch' ich Gewalt."	And if you are not willing, then I shall use force!"	

Son

"Mein Vater, mein Vater, jetzt fasst er mich an!	"My father, my father, now he is taking hold of me!	Outcry, *f*, highest yet.
Erlkönig hat mir ein Leids getan!"	The Erlking has hurt me!"	

Narrator

Dem Vater grauset's, er reitet geschwind,	The father shudders, he rides swiftly on;	
Er hält in Armen das ächzende Kind,	he holds in his arms the groaning child,	
Erreicht den Hof mit Mühe und Not;	he reaches the courtyard weary and anxious:	Piano stops.
In seinen Armen das Kind war tot.	in his arms the child was dead.	Recitative.

Side 8, band 2

Heidenröslein ("The Wild Rose"; 1815)

Like "The Erlking," the song *Heidenröslein* was composed to a poem by Goethe when Schubert was eighteen. Because of the difference in their texts, however, the songs contrast completely in form and mood. "The Erlking" is a through-composed song that generates enormous tension. *Heidenröslein* is strophic and has the simple charm of a folk song. Its text tells of a boy who picked a beautiful rosebud but paid for it with a pricked finger. The poem's three stanzas are all sung to the same melody. A delightful question and answer is formed by the melody's opening phrase and concluding third phrase. The opening phrase begins with repeated notes, descends, and then ascends to a questioning high tone:

Sah ein Knab' ein Rös - lein - stehn, Rös - lein auf der Hei - den,

In contrast, the last phrase begins with a stepwise ascent to a climactic high note, and then descends, via leaps, to the melody's lowest tone:

Rös - lein, Rös - lein, Rös - lein rot, Rös - lein auf der Hei - den.

In *Heidenröslein*, unlike "The Erlking," the piano part is distinctly subordinate to the voice. It attracts attention only in the postlude, which gracefully echoes the voice's last phrase after each stanza. The song beautifully illustrates the Romantics' attraction to nature and to folklike simplicity.

Sah ein Knab' ein Röslein stehn,
Röslein auf der Heiden,
War so jung und morgenschön,
Lief er schnell, es nah zu sehn,
Sah's mit vielen Freuden.
Röslein, Röslein, Röslein rot,
Röslein auf der Heiden.

Knabe sprach: "Ich breche dich,
Röslein auf der Heiden!"
Röslein sprach: "Ich steche dich,
Dass du ewig denkst an mich,
Und ich will's nicht leiden."
Röslein, Röslein, Röslein rot,
Röslein auf der Heiden.

Und der wilde Knabe brach
's Röslein auf der Heiden;
Röslein wehrte sich und stach
Half ihm doch kein Weh und Ach,
Musst' es eben leiden.
Röslein, Röslein, Röslein rot,
Röslein auf der Heiden.

A lad saw a rosebud,
rosebud on the heath;
it was so young in its morning beauty
that he ran to look at it more closely;
he gazed at it with great pleasure.
Rosebud red,
rosebud on the heath.

The lad said: "I'll pick you,
rosebud on the heath!"
The rosebud said: "I'll prick you,
so that you will always think of me,
and I won't regret it."
Rosebud red,
rosebud on the heath.

And the brutal lad picked
the rosebud on the heath;
the rosebud defended itself and pricked,
yet no grief and lamentation helped it:
It simply had to suffer.
Rosebud red,
rosebud on the heath.

Heidenröslein
("The Wild Rose"; 1815)

277

Fourth Movement from Piano Quintet in A Major ("Trout"; 1819)

Among the best-loved of all chamber works, the "Trout" Quintet was commissioned in 1819 by an amateur cellist who admired Schubert's song "The Trout" (*Die Forelle*) and asked the composer to write variations on it. The theme and variations is the fourth of five movements in this quintet scored for the unusual combination of piano, violin, viola, cello, and double bass. Schubert gives each a chance to present the main melodic line.

The strings alone introduce the theme, a charming D-major melody marked *Andantino* ("moderately slow"). The six variations that follow embellish the theme and combine it with countermelodies. The first three variations build in rhythmic animation and brilliance of sound, but the original melody is altered very little. Variation 4 is a dramatic climax as the key shifts to D minor and the theme is changed radically in melody, rhythm, and dynamics. Variation 5 is in the new key of B-flat major, and the theme is transformed into an intense legato melody that sounds almost new. The concluding variation brings back the original D-major melody in a faster tempo (allegretto). The music sounds fresh and sparkling as Schubert introduces a new accompaniment figure that he had used in the original song to suggest the brook trout's leaps and twists.

The theme is in two-part form: aa b. This pattern is usually retained in the variations.

LISTENING OUTLINE
To be read while music is heard

Piano Quintet in A Major ("Trout"; 1819), by Franz Schubert

Fourth Movement: Andantino

Theme and variations, duple meter ($\frac{2}{4}$), D major

Piano, violin, viola, cello, double bass

(About 8 min)

THEME   Violin, *pp*, theme, strings accompany.
(Andantino)

VARIATION 1   Piano enters, *p*, theme decorated by trills; strings accompany with broken chords, high violin trills.

VARIATION 2	Viola, *p*, theme; higher flowing countermelody in violin, *p*; piano echoes phrases of theme.
VARIATION 3	Piano *f*, rapid countermelody above bass and cello, *p*; staccato theme in low register.
VARIATION 4 (minor)	Piano and strings, *ff*, repeated chords in minor alternate with high violin phrase, *p*, in major. Trills in piano and violin, *pp*; songlike phrases in cello; viola and violin, *p*, variation ends in minor.
VARIATION 5	Cello, *p*, theme transformed into lyrical, legato melody; accompanying strings joined by piano in high register.

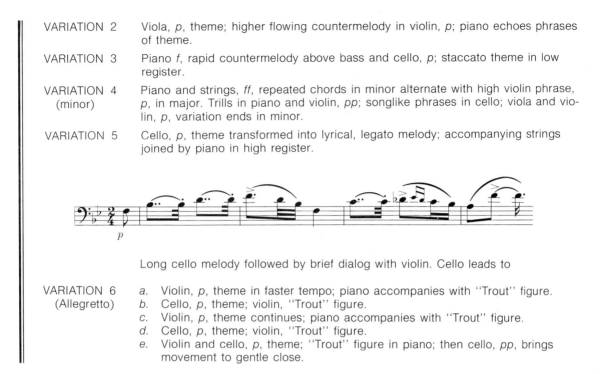

Long cello melody followed by brief dialog with violin. Cello leads to

VARIATION 6 (Allegretto)	*a.*	Violin, *p*, theme in faster tempo; piano accompanies with "Trout" figure.
	b.	Cello, *p*, theme; violin, "Trout" figure.
	c.	Violin, *p*, theme continues; piano accompanies with "Trout" figure.
	d.	Cello, *p*, theme; violin, "Trout" figure.
	e.	Violin and cello, *p*, theme; "Trout" figure in piano; then cello, *pp*, brings movement to gentle close.

ROBERT SCHUMANN | 5 |

Robert Schumann (1810–1856) in many ways embodied musical Romanticism. His works are intensely autobiographical, and they usually are linked with descriptive titles, texts, or programs. He expressed his essentially lyrical nature in startlingly original piano pieces and songs. A gifted writer and critic, he discovered and made famous some of the leading composers of his day.

Schumann was born in Zwickau, Germany. His father was a bookseller, from whom he acquired a love of literature. As a youth, Schumann wrote poetry, composed short pieces, and played the piano fairly well. To please his mother, he studied law at Leipzig University; but he rarely attended lectures and devoted his time instead to literature and music.

Schumann decided to become a piano virtuoso at the late age of twenty. To hasten his progress, he used a mechanical gadget that promoted finger independence by allowing four fingers to exercise while one was kept stiff. As a result, one finger was permanently crippled, dashing all hopes of becoming a virtuoso. "Don't be uneasy about the finger," he wrote his mother, "I can compose without it." Indeed, in his twenties he composed many poetic piano works which are a

Robert Schumann

279

basic part of the pianist's repertory even today. In Schumann's time, however, many considered his compositions too unconventional, too personal. Schumann admitted that his works were autobiographical: "I am affected by everything that goes on in the world—politics, literature, people—I think it over in my own way, and then I long to express my feelings in music."

During his twenties, too, Schumann founded and edited the *New Journal of Music* to promote musical originality and combat the commercial trash that flooded the market. In his essays, Schumann invented an imaginary "League of David" fighting against musical "Philistines," lovers of the conventional. He often signed his articles with the names "Florestan" or "Eusebius," characters who represented, respectively, the outgoing and introspective sides of his personality. The twice-weekly journal grew to be influential and contained Schumann's appreciative reviews of young "radical" composers like Chopin and Berlioz.

While studying piano, Schumann became acquainted with his teacher's daughter and prize pupil, Clara Wieck. Schumann was eighteen when they met, and Clara was a nine-year-old prodigy who was already a well-known pianist. The two were engaged when Clara was seventeen, despite bitter opposition from her father, who did not want his daughter's brilliant career to be hampered by marriage to an impoverished musician. Since Clara was not of age, the couple fought bitter court battles against Wieck before they could be married. Their marriage turned out to be a happy one that produced eight children. Clara was the ideal interpreter of her husband's piano works and introduced many of them to the public.

Apart from his gifts as a writer and editor, Schumann was temperamentally ill-suited for a regular musical position. He taught for a short time in the newly established Leipzig Conservatory of Music. He was a failure as municipal music director at Düsseldorf because of his inability to control an orchestra and chorus. During later years his mental and physical health progressively deteriorated, and in 1854 Schumann attempted suicide by throwing himself from a bridge into the Rhine. At his own request, he was committed to an asylum, where he died two years later.

Schumann's Music

Schumann's genius is most characteristically expressed in his songs and short piano pieces, which he usually organized into sets or cycles. The titles of these sets—*Carnaval, Scenes of Childhood, Night Pieces, Poet's Love, Fantasy Pieces*—provide insight into his imagination. Schumann thought of music in emotional, literary, and autobiographical terms; his work is full of extramusical references.

During the first ten years of his creative life, Schumann published only piano pieces. His basic musical style seems to grow out of piano improvisation, and these short pieces are like mosaics of vivid musical fragments. Each expresses a single mood through an intensely sensitive melody. Dance rhythms like the waltz

Clara Wieck Schumann was an ideal interpreter of husband
Robert Schumann's piano works and introduced many of
them to the public (Omikron).

are prominent, as are syncopations and dotted rhythms. Schumann's cycles of
short pieces are unified through a story or title, or by thematic connections.

In 1840, the year of his marriage, Schumann composed many art songs. The
songs, like the piano pieces, reveal Schumann's great gift for melody. Many of
the songs have piano postludes which sum up the message of the text. Schumann's song texts suit his feelings, and he often changes a poem by repeating
words, lines, and even whole stanzas.

After 1840, Schumann turned to symphonies and chamber music. This

Schumann's
Music

direction may well have resulted from Clara's influence, for she wrote in her diary, "I am infinitely delighted that Robert has at last found the sphere for which his great imagination fits him." Schumann's four symphonies are Romantic in their emphasis on lyrical second themes, their use of thematic transformation, and their connections between movements.

Side 8, band 3

Träumerei ("Dreaming") from Scenes of Childhood (*Kinderscenen*), Op. 15 (1838)

In this poetic miniature, Schumann magically weaves a spell of reverie. *Träumerei*—German for "dreaming"—is one of the Scenes of Childhood, a set of short pieces with titles like "Strange Story," "Entreating Child," and "At the Fireside." Like many other Romantics, Schumann was nostalgic for his lost childhood and attempted to recapture the past in his works.

The enchantment of this tender piece comes from the flowing legato melody, composed of phrases which arch up to high tones, linger for a moment—in wonder—then gradually drift downward.

Schumann creates a touching mood with music that is moderate in tempo and subdued in dynamics. The imaginative harmonies of the accompaniment add to the melody's haunting quality. Toward the end, there's an especially evocative moment when the melody rises to a held tone that forms a mild dissonance with the chord below it. Then the melody floats downward, and *Träumerei* ends as simply and quietly as it began.

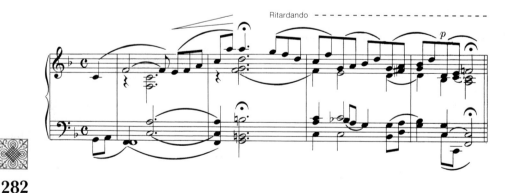

FRÉDÉRIC CHOPIN

Frédéric Chopin (1810–1849), called the poet of the piano, was the only great composer who wrote exclusively for the piano.

Chopin was brought up in Warsaw, the son of a Polish mother and a French father. At an early age his highly original style of playing and composing astonished the Polish aristocracy. After graduating from the Warsaw Conservatory, he toured Austria and Germany playing his own compositions. While he was away, the Poles revolted against the Russians. Upon learning that the Russians had conquered Warsaw, Chopin was filled with despair and guilt: "They have burnt down the town . . . and here I am—doing nothing, only heaving sighs and pouring out my grief at the piano." In 1831, the twenty-one-year-old Chopin arrived in Paris, his home for the rest of his short life.

In the 1830s Paris was a center of Romanticism and the artistic capital of Europe. Chopin met great writers like Victor Hugo, Balzac, and Heine. The painter Delacroix was a close friend, as were Liszt and Berlioz. Chopin's playing quickly gained him access to the aristocratic salons of Paris. Liszt provides a vivid description of the kind of people who attended Chopin's rare concerts: "Numerous carriages brought . . . the most elegant ladies, the most fashionable of young men, the richest financiers, the most illustrious great lords . . . an entire aristocracy of birth, fortune and beauty."

Chopin was a shy, reserved man who disliked crowds and preferred to play in salons rather than in public concert halls. It was for such intimate gatherings that he conceived short pieces like the nocturnes, preludes, and waltzes.

Chopin's frail physique made it difficult for him to draw big sounds from the piano. The fascination of his playing lay, rather, in his beautiful tone, rhythmic flexibility, atmospheric use of the pedal, and poetic subtleties of dynamics. Chopin is the only pianist in history to achieve a legendary reputation on the basis of only thirty or so public performances. He earned a good living by teaching piano to the daughters of the rich. An elegant and fashionable man of the world, Chopin lived in luxury.

Chopin's life took an increasingly productive turn after he met Madame Aurore Dudevant, the well-known novelist whose pen-name was George Sand. She was a feminist who often wore men's clothing, smoked cigars, and fought for sexual freedom. Chopin and Sand became lovers when he was twenty-eight and she thirty-four. He thrived on the care she provided, composing many of his greatest works during the nine years they lived together. After they separated, his health declined rapidly and he composed very little.

Before dying of tuberculosis at thirty-nine, Chopin asked that Mozart's *Requiem* be played at his funeral. The mourners also heard his own Funeral March from the Piano Sonata in B-flat minor.

 Frédéric Chopin

Frédéric Chopin was a shy, reserved man who disliked
crowds and preferred to play in salons rather than in public
concert halls (Cliché des Musées Nationaux, France).

Chopin's Music

By the age of eighteen, Chopin had evolved an utterly personal and original style. Compared with other great composers, he wrote relatively few works, but almost all of them remain in the pianist's repertory. Most of the pieces are short. But in these exquisite miniatures, Chopin evokes an infinite variety of moods, from melancholy to heroism. His music is always elegant and graceful. Even the virtuoso passages are melodic, not intended merely for display.

Chopin expressed his love of Poland in mazurkas and polonaises. In these stylized dances, he captured the spirit of the Polish people without actually using folk tunes. Unlike Schumann, Chopin did not attach literary programs or titles to his pieces.

No composer has made the piano sound so beautiful as Chopin. His unique melodic gift creates the illusion that the piano sings. In repeating a melody, Chopin adds delicate and graceful ornamental tones, similar to vocal decorations in the Italian opera of his time. Many of Chopin's most poetic effects come from the sensitive exploitation of the damper ("loud") pedal. He blends harmonies like washes of color. The pedal connects widely spaced tones in the left-hand accompaniment. Chopin's treatment of harmony was highly original and influenced later composers.

His compositions allow a pianist to heighten expression by slightly speeding up or slowing down the tempo, or by holding a note longer than the music actually indicates. This use of *rubato* lends a poetic and improvisatory quality to Chopin's music.

Nocturne in E-flat Major, Op. 9, No. 2 (1830–1831)

Chopin composed this popular nocturne when he was about twenty. A **nocturne,** or "night piece," is a slow, lyrical, and intimate composition for piano. Like much of Chopin's music, this nocturne is tinged with melancholy. It opens with a legato melody containing graceful upward leaps which become increasingly wide as the line unfolds.

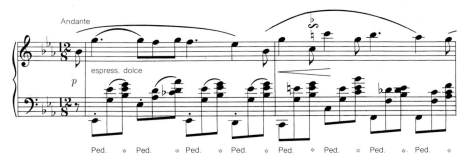

Nocturne in E-flat Major, Op. 9, No. 2

285

This melody is repeated three times during the piece. With each repetition, it is varied by ever more elaborate decorative tones and trills.

A sonorous foundation for the melody is provided by the widely spaced accompaniment notes connected by the damper ("loud") pedal.

The music is reflective in mood until near the end, when it suddenly becomes passionate. The melody rises to a high register and is played forcefully in octaves. Then, after a brilliant trill-like passage, the excitement subsides, and the nocturne ends calmly.

Étude in C Minor, Op. 10, No. 12 ("Revolutionary"; 1831?)

The Russian takeover of Warsaw in 1831 may have inspired Chopin to compose the blazing and furious "Revolutionary" étude. An **étude** is a study piece designed to help a performer master specific technical difficulties. The "Revolutionary" étude, for example, develops speed and endurance in a pianist's left hand, which must play rapid passages throughout. Chopin's études reach beyond mere exercises in technique to become masterpieces of music exciting to hear as well as master.

This étude begins with a dramatic outburst. High dissonant chords and downward rushing passages lead to the main melody, marked *appassionato* ("impassioned"), which is played in octaves by the right hand. Tension mounts because of the melody's dotted rhythms and its tempestuous accompaniment.

Toward the end of the piece, after a climax, the tension momentarily subsides. Then a torrential passage sweeps down the keyboard to come to rest in powerful closing chords.

Polonaise in A-flat Major, Op. 53 (1842)

Side 8, band 6

The **polonaise,** in triple meter, originated as a stately processional dance for the Polish nobility. Chopin's heroic polonaises evoke the ancient splendor of the Polish people.

The A-flat polonaise is majestic and powerful, with moments of lyrical contrast. It may be outlined: introduction—A B A'—coda. Its main theme makes a grand entrance.

This theme's majesty is enhanced by intervals of thirds in the right hand and by the resonant, wide-ranging accompaniment. After the main theme is repeated twice with an even richer texture, Chopin offers the contrasting middle section (B). This is a marchlike melody accompanied by relentlessly repeated rapid octaves in the left hand. This section tests a pianist's strength and endurance. Powerful crescendos bring mounting excitement. Then Chopin gradually relaxes the mood to prepare for the final return of the heroic main theme (A').

Basic Terms

nocturne   polonaise
étude

 Basic Terms

287

7 | FRANZ LISZT

During the 1840s, a handsome, long-haired, magnetic young man performed superhuman feats at the piano and overwhelmed the European musical public. Irresistible to women and an incredible showman, Franz Liszt (1811–1886) left a trail of broken hearts from Paris to Moscow. Musicians were equally impressed. Brahms said, "Whoever has not heard Liszt cannot speak of piano playing." Chopin wished he could play his own piano études the way Liszt did. Schumann wrote that Liszt "enmeshed every member of the audience with his art and did with them as he willed. Within a few seconds tenderness, boldness, exquisiteness, wildness succeed one another; the instrument glows and flashes under the master's hands."

Franz Liszt, an outstanding pacesetter in the history of music, was born in Hungary in 1811. His father was an administrator for the same Esterházy family that Haydn had served. As a boy of eleven, Liszt studied in Vienna, where he met Schubert and Beethoven.

Paris, city of Romanticism and a mecca for virtuoso performers, was Liszt's home during his teens and twenties. Already acclaimed as a brilliant pianist, nineteen-year-old Liszt was overwhelmed by the virtuosity of the great violinist Paganini. The unheard-of effects Paganini drew from his violin drove audiences into a frenzy; people half suspected he had been taught by the devil. And young Liszt was determined to become the Paganini of the piano. He withdrew from the concert stage for a few years, practiced from eight to twelve hours a day, and emerged as probably the greatest pianist of his time.

To display his incomparable piano mastery, Liszt composed the *Transcendental Études* and piano transcriptions of Paganini's violin pieces. "My piano," he wrote, "is my very self, my mother tongue, my life. . . . A man's ten fingers have the power to reproduce the harmonies which are created by hundreds of performers." Following an orchestral performance of a movement from Berlioz's *Fantastic Symphony,* Liszt played his own piano arrangement of the movement and made a more powerful effect than the entire orchestra. He toured Europe tirelessly between 1839 and 1847, playing mainly his own piano music and receiving unprecedented public adulation.

But Liszt wanted recognition as a serious composer, too. At thirty-six, he abandoned his career as traveling virtuoso to become court conductor for the Grand Duke in Weimar. He composed many orchestral pieces during the following years, and developed a new form of program music that influenced later composers. Weimar had become a center for modern music, and Liszt conducted works by such contemporaries as Berlioz, Schumann, and Wagner. One of the most unselfish and generous musicians who ever lived, Liszt provided the musical and financial support crucial to Wagner's success. Hundreds of gifted pianists flocked to Weimar, and he taught them free of charge.

Franz Liszt—handsome, long-haired, magnetic—performed
superhuman feats at the piano and overwhelmed the European musical public (Omikron).

Liszt was also an active writer about music, publishing music criticism as well as books on Chopin and gypsy music. His literary efforts were aided by two women with whom he had long-term relationships. Both were aristocrats and writers. The first, Countess Marie d'Agoult, left her husband to live with Liszt. One of their three children, Cosima, later left her own husband to marry Richard Wagner. Liszt's companion in Weimar was the Russian Princess Carolyne Sayn-Wittgenstein, a deeply religious woman who wrote a twenty-four-volume study entitled "Interior Causes of the External Weakness of the Church."

Liszt's many-sided career took another abrupt turn in 1861. Dissatisfied with conditions at Weimar, he resigned and went to Rome to pursue religious studies. In 1865 he took minor holy orders, becoming Abbé Liszt. Contemporaries were stunned by the seeming incongruity: a notorious Don Juan and diabolical virtuoso had become a churchman. In Rome, Liszt composed oratorios and Masses, feeling a mission to reform and renew church music.

During the last seventeen years of his life, Liszt traveled between Rome, Weimar, and Budapest, where he was president of the new Academy of Music. Now he began to write curious, experimental piano pieces that foreshadowed features of twentieth-century music. Though these late works went unappreciated, Liszt was a living legend. The grand duke who had once employed him said, "Liszt *was* what a prince *ought* to be."

Liszt's Music

Liszt's music is controversial. Some consider it vulgar and bombastic; others revel in its extroverted Romantic rhetoric. Yet few would deny Liszt's originality, influence, and importance as the creator of the symphonic poem.

Liszt found new ways to exploit the piano; under his hands it could give the impression of an entire orchestra. In the *Hungarian Rhapsodies,* which influenced a generation of nationalist composers, Liszt made the piano sound like a cimbalom (a Hungarian instrument in which strings are struck by hammers held in the hand) and an entire gypsy band. Liszt's piano works demand an unprecedented range of dynamics, from a whispered *ppp* to a thunderous *fff.* He requires a pianist to play rapid octaves and daring leaps. Lyrical melodies are embellished with rapid runs, and melodies in the middle register are sometimes surrounded by garlands of arpeggios which create the impression that three hands are playing, not two. Before phonograph records and frequent concerts, Liszt's transcriptions of operas and symphonies made it possible for people to play great orchestral works on their own pianos.

Liszt created the **symphonic poem,** or **tone poem,** a one-movement orchestral composition based to some extent on literary or pictorial ideas. In these and other works, Liszt unified contrasting moods through thematic transformation. A single theme recurs throughout a work but is varied so that its character is transformed. For example, in his most famous symphonic poem *Les Préludes* ("The Preludes," 1854), a basic motive is treated as a majestic melody in one section, a love theme in another, a pastoral tune in a third, and a march in the finale. Liszt's music can stand by itself without a program, as can most program music. However, he no doubt felt that particular influences from literature should be cited to make his musical process very clear. Liszt broke away from the standard four-movement symphony and from the sonata form as it was used by the Classical masters.

Among Liszt's favorite inspirations were the literary works of Goethe (the Faust Symphony, 1854) and Dante (Dante Symphony, 1856). Many of his compositions are concerned with the devil or death and bear titles like *Mephisto Waltz, Dance of Death* (*Totentanz*), or *Funérailles*. Constant changes of tempo and mood and alternations between diabolical fury and semireligious meditation contribute to a feeling of improvisation.

Liszt's music influenced many composers, including Wagner, who admitted to him: "When I compose and orchestrate, I always think only of you." As a stupendous performer, innovative composer, and charismatic personality, Liszt typified the Romantic movement.

Concerto No. 1 for Piano and Orchestra in E-flat Major (1849; revised 1853, 1856)

This blazing virtuoso concerto was first performed in 1855 with Liszt as soloist and Berlioz as conductor. Liszt composed the concerto in Weimar, after he stopped making concert tours in order to compose, conduct, and promote contemporary music. The soloist of this concerto needs enormous power and technical mastery to project massive sounds that match and sometimes triumph over the entire orchestra.

In many ways, this concerto breaks with traditional principles. Instead of three separate movements, as is customary in a concerto, there are four movements combined into one. The last three movements are played without pause, an example of the Romantic trait of linking movements of a composition. Even greater unity results from the thematic relationships among the movements. Themes from the first two movements reappear in the third movement. And the finale is based entirely on transformations of ideas heard earlier in the concerto.

Liszt was the first composer to use a triangle in a concerto. A Viennese critic was so affronted by this "lowly" instrument, which first appears in the third movement, that he contemptuously referred to the composition as "the triangle concerto." The critic's mockery was enough to keep the concerto from being heard again in Vienna for twelve years.

First Movement: Allegro maestoso (majestic allegro)

The opening movement presents the orchestra and piano as two contrasting personalities that repeatedly confront each other. While the orchestra concentrates on the decisive main theme and holds a strict tempo, the soloist has various

Concerto No. 1 for Piano and Orchestra

291

themes and a rhythmic freedom that suggests improvisation. The movement is in a very free A B A′ form. Structurally, it bears little resemblance to the first movement of a Classical concerto.

All the strings open in unison with the main theme of the entire concerto. This is a descending, staccato idea, built from a fragment of a chromatic scale and punctuated by high chords in the woodwinds and brasses.

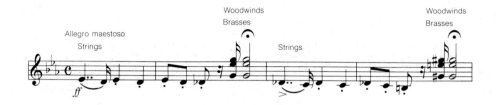

The piano immediately enters with a virtuoso passage of loud, rapid octaves that establish it as a formidable rival to the orchestra. After the unaccompanied piano briefly varies the opening theme and sweeps up to the highest register, the orchestra reenters to quietly restate the main idea. The movement alternates between orchestral restatements of the theme and cadenzalike solo passages that are brilliant, lyrical, or dramatic.

The brief middle section (B) is an intimate dialog between piano, clarinet, and violin. A new legato melody is introduced by the piano, then imitated by the clarinet.

Liszt has the soloist play with rubato, slight fluctuations of tempo that express a sense of freedom. Soon the music becomes louder and faster, building to a climactic return of the main theme in the full orchestra (A′ section). Again, the piano and orchestra alternate, followed by a quiet concluding section in which the orchestra murmurs a variation of the main theme while the soloist plays running notes.

The movement trails off into silence.

Second Movement: Quasi Adagio

The slow movement of the concerto is an intimate interlude that introduces two new melodies. This is the only movement in which neither the full orchestra nor the powerful main theme is heard. Muted strings present a lyrical theme which the piano soon extends:

THE RENAISSANCE

Plate 1—Leonardo da Vinci, *Saint Anne, the Virgin and Child,* 1506–1510 (Scala, New York/Florence).

Plate 2—Michelangelo, *Creation of Adam,* 1508–1512
(Scala/Editorial Photocolor Archives).

Symmetry, harmony, and rationalism characterized the art of the Renaissance. Unlike
artists of the previous Gothic era with its God-centered art, Renaissance artists emphasized
the power and beauty of human beings. Not only did the Renaissance in art mean the
rebirth of Greek and Roman art, it actually aimed at surpassing the ancients by combining
their innovations with Christianity and an abiding faith in the strength of man's abilities.

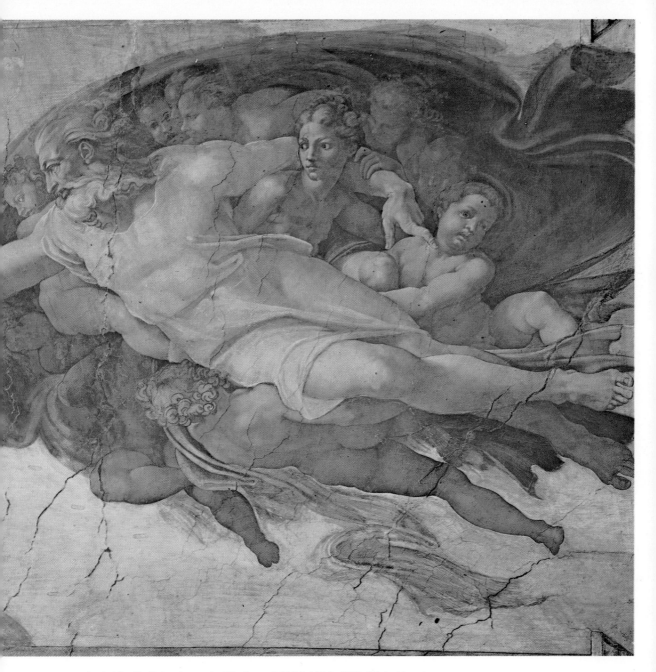

Leonardo da Vinci's *Saint Anne, the Virgin and Child,* 1506–1510 (Plate 1), set an example for many later Renaissance artists with its strongly pyramidal composition, its use of *chiaroscuro* (modeling in light and dark shadows), and its inclusion of scientifically accurate geological and botanic details.

Michelangelo's *Creation of Adam* from the Sistine Chapel ceiling (Plate 2) depicts a strong, muscular, but lethargic man about to be given life by the Divine spark from the hand of God. Adam represents the very embodiment of Renaissance man—strong, proud, and capable, but powerless without God's will.

THE BAROQUE PERIOD

Plate 3—Rembrandt van Rijn, *Night Watch*, 1642 (Rijksmuseum, Amsterdam).

Plate 4—Antoine Watteau, *Les Plaisirs du Bal,* 1719 (Dulwich College Picture Gallery, London).

The Baroque period in art laid great stress on drama, illusion, turbulence, and emotion. The calm horizontals and verticals of Renaissance art gave way to diagonals and to twisting and frenzied movement.

Rembrandt van Rijn's controversial *Night Watch,* 1642 (Plate 3), uses strong contrast, diagonal movement, and unequal emphasis of parts for a highly unconventional group portrait.

The term Rococo best characterizes eighteenth-century art, which transformed Baroque art into a frivolous, light, decorative art of the "salon." The French artist Antoine Watteau's *Les Plaisirs du Bal,* 1719 (Plate 4), typifies the airy, graceful *fêtes galantes,* showing the nobility enjoying themselves in games of flirtation. One can almost hear in the background the light, delicate mid-eighteenth-century music referred to as *style galant.*

THE CLASSICAL PERIOD

Plate 5—Jacques Louis David, *Oath of the Horatii,* 1784–1785
(Three Lions, Inc.)

Classicism in eighteenth- and early nineteenth-century art refers to Neo-Classicism, an
end to Rococo superficiality, and an emphasis on severity, strength, and heroism. Neo-
Classical artists often used Greek and Roman examples. Jacques Louis David in France, for
example, painted the *Death of Socrates,* 1787, and the *Oath of the Horatii,* 1784–1785
(Plate 5), proclaiming an end to rule by the aristocracy and a transfer of power to the
middle classes. David, known sometimes as the "Robespierre of the brush," looked to
Republican Rome as an example to the embattled people of France.

THE ROMANTIC PERIOD

Plate 6—Joseph Turner, *The Slave Ship,* 1839 (Museum of Fine Arts, Boston).

Romanticism refers more to a way of thinking and feeling than to a specific chronological period or style in art. In fact, the predominant characteristics of Romanticism such as freedom from rules, individuality, and personal emotion prohibit a formal grouping. The first half of the nineteenth century did see a golden age of Romanticism, including such giants as Eugène Delacroix in France, Joseph Turner and John Constable in England, and Francisco Goya in Spain. Turner embodied Romanticism in *The Slave Ship,* 1839 (Plate 6), in which he abstracted the forces of nature into a dynamic symbol.

THE TWENTIETH CENTURY

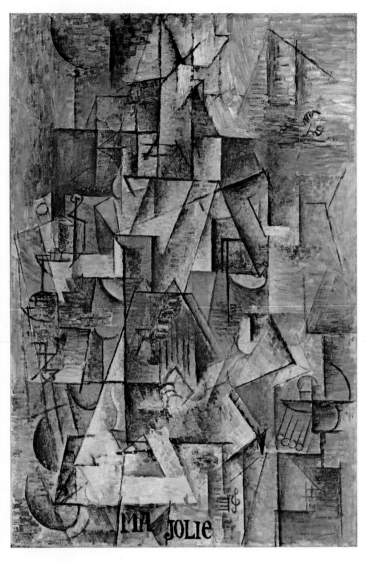

Plate 7—Pablo Picasso, *Ma Jolie,* 1911–1912 (Collection, The Museum of Modern Art, New York, acquired through the Lillie P. Bliss Bequest).

Plate 8—Hans Hofmann, *Memoria in Aeternum,* 1962 (Collection, The Museum of Modern Art, New York, gift of the artist).

At the beginning of the twentieth century painters depicted real objects in a very different way from their predecessors. The Expressionists, for example, distorted reality in order to portray the inner essence of their subject. The Expressionists were intensely emotional, whereas the Cubists stressed a more intellectual geometric approach. In *Ma Jolie,* 1911–1912 (Plate 7), Pablo Picasso distorted the reality of his subject by breaking form into geometric planes.

In the later part of the twentieth century, a variety of painting styles developed. These include such diverse approaches as the Abstract Expressionism of Hans Hofmann's *Memoria in Aeternum,* 1962 (Plate 8); the "pop art" of Andy Warhol's Campbell Soup cans; and the "op art" of Victor Vasarely's visual illusions.

J.Z.

Quasi Adagio

The dreamy mood of this legato melody is suddenly broken as the piano dramatically declaims over an accompaniment of tremolo strings. The agitation subsides as quickly as it started. A calm new woodwind melody is presented in turn by the flute, clarinet, and oboe, with a high piano trill in the background.

Flute

Dolce espressivo

Both this woodwind theme and the opening lyrical melody will be greatly transformed when they return in the finale. After a brief recollection of the lyrical theme by the clarinet, the Adagio leads without pause into the third movement, a scherzo.

Third Movement: Allegretto vivace (scherzo)

Light triangle strokes accompany the sparkling and playful scherzo theme.

Allegretto vivace

This staccato idea makes the brilliant top register of the piano ring with elfin spriteliness. After several dazzling variations of the scherzo theme, Liszt unexpectedly brings back the main theme of the first movement. This ominous recollection is played in a low register by the solo piano. Then a powerful crescendo climaxes in a proclamation of the main theme by the full orchestra. As at the beginning of the concerto, the orchestra is immediately confronted by the virtuoso piano passage of loud, rapid octaves. The woodwind theme from the slow movement is recollected, and the powerful piano passage leads directly into the finale.

Concerto No. 1 for Piano and Orchestra

293

Fourth Movement: Allegro marziale animato (martial and animated allegro)

The finale of the concerto is built entirely from variations of themes heard in earlier movements. It begins with a joyful march theme that is a complete transformation of the lyrical theme from the opening of the second movement. A melody that was originally slow, soft, and legato is now fast, loud, and staccato.

Triangle strokes heighten the orchestra's brilliance.

Soon the trombones, then the piano, loudly assert the second phrase of the lyrical theme in an altered form that sounds defiant and threatening.

The mood then lightens as the piano in a higher register presents a graceful, animated transformation of the woodwind theme from the end of the second movement.

Virtuoso running passages in the piano lead to the march theme, then to the scherzo theme with its accompanying triangle. Liszt speeds up the tempo and uses the concerto's main theme to build a triumphant conclusion.

Basic Term

symphonic poem (tone poem)

FELIX MENDELSSOHN

Felix Mendelssohn (1809–1847) was a Romantic whose music was rooted deeply in Classical tradition. Born in Hamburg, Germany, he came from a wealthy and famous family. His father was a banker, and his grandfather was the distinguished Jewish philosopher Moses Mendelssohn. He, a brother, and two sisters were raised in the Protestant faith.

Mendelssohn's talent was as phenomenal and precocious as Mozart's. By the age of nine, he was a brilliant pianist; and by thirteen, he had written symphonies, concertos, sonatas, and vocal works. And the quality of this youthful work is more astounding than its quantity. His Overture to *A Midsummer Night's Dream* (1826), composed at seventeen, is a masterpiece of startling originality. As a teenager, Mendelssohn tried out his compositions with a private orchestra in his family dining room. These Sunday musicales were attended by the intellectual and artistic elite of Berlin, where the family settled.

In 1829, at twenty, Mendelssohn conducted Bach's *St. Matthew Passion,* the first performance since the Baroque master's death. This historic concert rekindled interest in Bach's music and earned an international reputation for Mendelssohn. He often performed as pianist, organist, and conductor in Germany and in England, where his music was especially popular. When only twenty-six, Mendelssohn became conductor of the Leipzig Gewandhaus Orchestra and transformed it into one of the finest performing groups in Europe. He directed the posthumous premiere of Schubert's "Great" C-major Symphony, which his friend Schumann had discovered, as well as the first performance of two Schumann symphonies. As though all these accomplishments weren't enough, Mendelssohn founded the Leipzig Conservatory when he was thirty-three.

Besides his musical achievements, Mendelssohn was a talented painter, a fine writer, and a brilliant conversationalist in four languages. Extremely polished and charming, he was at ease in aristocratic salons. In England, he often visited the young Queen Victoria, who sang his songs while Mendelssohn accompanied her on the piano. His personal life was more conventional than that of many Romantics; he was happily married and the father of four children.

The high point of Mendelssohn's career was the triumphant premiere of his oratorio *Elijah* in Birmingham, England, in 1846. The London *Times* reported that "the last note of 'Elijah' was drowned in a long-continued unanimous volley of plaudits, vociferous and deafening." But constant travel and exhausting work had sapped Mendelssohn's strength, and the death of a beloved sister in 1847 was a violent shock. He died five months later at the age of thirty-eight.

Mendelssohn's Music

Mendelssohn's music radiates the elegance and balance of his personality. It evokes a variety of moods but avoids emotional extremes. His typical pieces

Felix
Mendelssohn

295

Besides his musical achievements, Felix Mendelssohn was
a talented painter, a fine writer, and a brilliant conversationalist in four languages (The Metropolitan Museum of Art,
The Crosby Brown Collection of Musical Instruments,
1901).

convey an elfin quality through rapid movement, lightness, and transparent orchestral texture. He was a musical landscapist who could depict a particular atmosphere in orchestral program works. For example, the *Hebrides Overture* (1830–1832; also called *Fingal's Cave*) suggests an agitated sea through swells and surges of sound. But even when Mendelssohn evokes something extramusical, his compositions have a logical form and can be enjoyed without knowing their sources of inspiration.

Mendelssohn wrote an enormous amount of music in all the forms of his day except opera. Today, few of his works are in the concert repertory, but they are extremely popular. Among his best-known compositions are the violin concerto—which we'll study—the *Midsummer Night's Dream* and *Hebrides* overtures, the Italian and Scotch symphonies (1833, 1842), the oratorio *Elijah,* and the Trio in D minor for violin, cello, and piano (1839). His collection of short piano pieces, *Songs without Words* (1829–1845), is now returning to favor after a period of neglect. They convey youthful dash and vigor as well as lyricism tinged with melancholy, basic qualities of Mendelssohn's art.

Concerto for Violin and Orchestra in E Minor, Op. 64

This concerto was inspired by Mendelssohn's friendship with the concertmaster of his orchestra, the famous violinist Ferdinand David. "I should like to make a violin concerto for you next winter," Mendelssohn wrote. "One in E minor runs in my head and its beginning gives me no rest." With David as soloist, Mendelssohn's violin concerto met great success at its premiere in 1845. Ever since, the work's unique fusion of lyricism and virtuosity has made it one of the best-loved concertos.

The concerto's three movements are played without pause, a characteristic linking technique of Romantic composers. Mendelssohn's love of balance is reflected in the cooperation and interplay between soloist and orchestra. Themes pass from one to another, producing a beautiful contrast of tone color and expression. At one moment, the violinist plays a melody while the orchestra discreetly accompanies; at another, the woodwinds present thematic fragments while the soloist has dazzling running passages.

First Movement: *Side 9, band 1*
Allegro molto appassionato (very impassioned allegro)
Though Mendelssohn usually is considered a conservative composer, a "Classical Romantic," his opening movement departs from Classical concerto form. Traditionally, the opening movement of a concerto began with an extended section for orchestra. But Mendelssohn's violin concerto begins with the soloist, who presents the main theme. This ardent, expansive melody is heard high above a murmuring string accompaniment. The orchestra then expands the violin's

 Concerto for Violin and Orchestra

theme and introduces a new, flowing melody that begins the bridge section of this sonata-form movement. Toward the end of the bridge the excitement is gradually relaxed to prepare for the second theme, a tranquil woodwind melody which the soloist accompanies with a single sustained tone. This unusual combination of instruments produces a delicate, intimate sound. Following this, the violin reclaims the spotlight and sings the tranquil theme while the woodwinds support.

The cadenza has new function in this movement. In Classical concertos, it was improvised by the soloist and played near the end of the movement. Here, the composer has written it out and placed it at the end of the development section as a transition to the recapitulation. Mendelssohn wanted the cadenza to be an integral part of the movement, not merely tacked on to display the soloist's virtuosity. Listen for the magical moment when the violinist's rapid arpeggios are joined by the orchestra softly playing the first theme of the recapitulation.

LISTENING OUTLINE
To be read while music is heard

Concerto for Violin and Orchestra in E Minor, Op. 64 (1844), by Felix Mendelssohn

First Movement: Allegro molto appassionato

Sonata form, duple meter ($\frac{2}{2}$), E minor.

solo violin, 2 flutes, 2 oboes, 2 clarinets, 2 bassoons, 2 horns, 2 trumpets, timpani, violins 1, violins 2, violas, cellos, double basses

(About 13 min)

EXPOSITION
First theme

1 *a.* Strings, *p*, introduce solo violin. Main melody in minor, high register, legato.

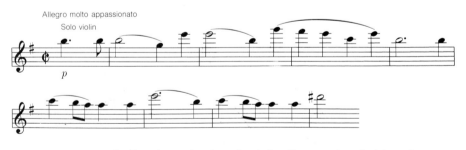

b. Running notes in solo violin. Crescendo, climbing phrases.
c. Orchestra, *ff*, main melody. Increased rhythmic motion leads to cadence.

Bridge   2 *a.* Violins, flowing bridge theme. Solo violin repeats bridge theme an oc-
              tave higher.

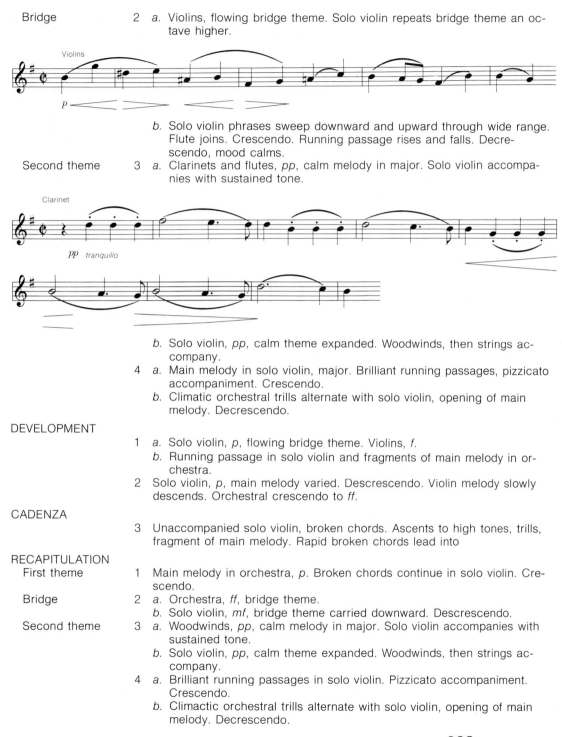

             b. Solo violin phrases sweep downward and upward through wide range.
              Flute joins. Crescendo. Running passage rises and falls. Decre-
              scendo, mood calms.

Second theme 3 *a.* Clarinets and flutes, *pp*, calm melody in major. Solo violin accompa-
              nies with sustained tone.

             b. Solo violin, *pp*, calm theme expanded. Woodwinds, then strings ac-
              company.
         4 *a.* Main melody in solo violin, major. Brilliant running passages, pizzicato
              accompaniment. Crescendo.
            b. Climatic orchestral trills alternate with solo violin, opening of main
             melody. Decrescendo.

DEVELOPMENT
         1 *a.* Solo violin, *p*, flowing bridge theme. Violins, *f*.
            b. Running passage in solo violin and fragments of main melody in or-
             chestra.
         2 Solo violin, *p*, main melody varied. Descrescendo. Violin melody slowly
            descends. Orchestral crescendo to *ff*.

CADENZA
         3 Unaccompanied solo violin, broken chords. Ascents to high tones, trills,
            fragment of main melody. Rapid broken chords lead into

RECAPITULATION
 First theme   1 Main melody in orchestra, *p*. Broken chords continue in solo violin. Cre-
            scendo.
 Bridge   2 *a.* Orchestra, *ff*, bridge theme.
            b. Solo violin, *mf*, bridge theme carried downward. Descrescendo.
 Second theme 3 *a.* Woodwinds, *pp*, calm melody in major. Solo violin accompanies with
             sustained tone.
            b. Solo violin, *pp*, calm theme expanded. Woodwinds, then strings ac-
             company.
         4 *a.* Brilliant running passages in solo violin. Pizzicato accompaniment.
             Crescendo.
            b. Climactic orchestral trills alternate with solo violin, opening of main
             melody. Decrescendo.

299

    5   Solo violin, bridge theme. Tempo becomes faster. Crescendo. Brilliant running passages. Full orchestra, *ff*. Sustained tone in bassoon connects with second movement.

Second Movement: Andante

A single bassoon tone links the brilliant opening movement with the hushed introduction to the slow second movement. The C-major Andante is a songlike, intimate piece in A B A′ form. Its opening section (A) features a warm, expansive melody in the solo violin's high register; a string accompaniment gently emphasizes the $\frac{6}{8}$ meter (1–2–3–4–5–6). The middle section (B) becomes more agitated, and the accompaniment is rhythmically more active. The orchestra plays a more important role as it engages in dialog with the soloist. Mendelssohn requires the solo violinist to play both a melody and a trembling accompaniment figure at the same time. The soloist also presents the melody in full-sounding octaves. The transition to the concluding A′ section is very smooth because the trembling accompaniment figure is maintained. The Andante ends quietly with a tender epilog for solo violin and woodwinds.

Third Movement: Allegretto non troppo (transitional section); Allegro molto vivace (very lively allegro)

A pensive transitional section for solo violin and strings connects the Andante with the concluding movement of the concerto. The very rapid finale, in sonata form, creates the lightness, joy, and brilliance so typical of Mendelssohn's art. Forceful chords in the woodwinds and upward solo figures usher in the opening theme of the exposition. Playful and mostly staccato, it is presented by the solo violin and high woodwinds.

A dazzling series of running passages and a long upward scale lead directly into the second theme, which is also a carefree one. With great effect, it combines a loud, marchlike phrase by the full orchestra with a softer motive from the opening theme.

In the development, the woodwinds softly present the marchlike phrase while the soloist plays brilliant running passages. A highlight of the development comes when the violinist presents a new legato melody which the strings lightly accompany with fragments of the opening theme.

Then there is a reversal of roles; the strings sing the lyrical melody while the soloist gracefully presents the opening theme fragment.

At the beginning of the recapitulation, the two themes are combined once again. The horn and lower strings play the warm, legato melody while the soloist brings back the sparkling first theme. After a return of the second theme, the movement builds to an exciting climax in the coda, which is fuller in sound than anything that has come before.

PROGRAM MUSIC ‖ 9 ‖

Romantic composers were particularly attracted to **program music,** or instrumental music associated with a story, poem, idea, or scene. Programmatic orchestral works such as Berlioz's *Fantastic Symphony,* Tchaikovsky's *Romeo and Juliet,* and Smetana's *The Moldau* depict emotions, characters, and events of particular stories, or the sounds and motions of nature. Such nonmusical ideas are usually specified by the title or by the composer's explanatory comments **(program)** in the concertgoer's program.

Program music draws on music's capacity to suggest and evoke. It is obvious that music can imitate certain sounds—bird songs, the rumble of thunder, bells clanging, or the howling wind. But "sound effects" are only part of music's descriptive resources. A composer can also exploit the correspondence between musical rhythm and objects in motion. A continuous flow of rapid notes, for example, can evoke a running stream or the rise and fall of waves. Most important, though, is music's capacity to create mood, emotion, and atmosphere. An agitated theme can represent a feud between rival families, just as a lyrical melody can symbolize youthful love.

Apart from the "sound effects" mentioned above, music alone makes no definite reference to ideas, emotions, and objects. Music cannot identify anything. It is the title or a verbal explanation that lets us fully grasp a composer's source of inspiration. We know that the agitated theme in Tchaikovsky's *Romeo and Juliet* is meant to suggest the feud between rival families, but in another piece, the same theme could as easily evoke a king's rage or a cavalry charge.

Program
Music

The aim of most program music is expression more than mere description. Beethoven explicitly stated this aim when he referred to his *Pastoral* Symphony (No. 6) as "an expression of feeling rather than painting." Even the most "realistic" episodes in program music can also serve a purely musical function, as in the *Pastoral's* slow movement, "By the Brook," where the songs of a nightingale, quail, and cuckoo are realistically imitated. (The names of these birds are even written in the score.) These bird calls provide a point of rest near the end of the movement and flow logically from what has come before.

Generally, one can appreciate a descriptive piece as pure music, without knowing its title or program. We can enjoy the lyrical theme of Tchaikovsky's *Romeo and Juliet,* for example, without associating it with young love. The forms used for program music are similar to those for nonprogram music, or **absolute music.** A programmatic work can be heard simply as an example of rondo, fugue, sonata form, or theme and variations. But our pleasure may be greater when we can relate music to literary or pictorial ideas. Romantic composers were well aware that verbal explanations helped listeners follow the flow of music. Occasionally, they even added titles or programs to finished works. Musicians and audiences in the Romantic period liked to read stories into all music, whether the composer so intended or not.

Clearly, the distinction between program music and absolute music is not always useful. A composition simply entitled Symphony No. 6 may have a program that its composer chooses not to reveal. Here are Tchaikovsky's comments about his Sixth Symphony ("Pathétique"): "This time a program symphony—but with a program which shall remain an enigma for everyone—let them puzzle their heads over it. This program is subjective through and through, and during my journey, while composing it in my mind, I often wept bitterly."

Most Romantic program music was written for piano or for orchestra. Schumann's *Carnaval* (1835) and Mussorgsky's *Pictures at an Exhibition* (1874)— each a set of short pieces—are well-known descriptive compositions for piano. But program music found its most varied expression in the coloristic resources of the Romantic orchestra. The main forms of orchestral program music are the *program symphony,* the *concert overture,* the *symphonic (tone) poem,* and *incidental music.*

A **program symphony** is a composition in several movements—as its name implies, a symphony with a program. Each movement usually has a descriptive title. For example, Berlioz's *Fantastic Symphony* has five movements: (1) "Reveries, Passions," (2) "A Ball," (3) "Scene in the Country," (4) "March to the Scaffold," and (5) "Dream of a Witches' Sabbath." (This work is discussed in section 10.)

A **concert overture** has one movement, usually in sonata form. The Romantic concert overture was modeled after the opera overture, a one-movement composition that establishes the mood of an opera. But the concert overture is *not* intended to usher in a stage work; it is an independent composition. Well-known concert overtures are Mendelssohn's *Hebrides* Overture and Tchaikovsky's *Overture 1812* and *Romeo and Juliet* Overture, discussed in section 12.

A **symphonic poem,** or **tone poem,** is also a one-movement composition. Symphonic poems take many traditional forms—sonata form, rondo, or theme and variations—as well as irregular forms. This flexibility of form separates the symphonic poem from the concert overture, which usually is in sonata form. Franz Liszt developed the symphonic poem in the late 1840s and 1850s, and it became the most important type of program music after 1860. Well-known tone poems include *Les Préludes* by Liszt, *Don Juan* (1888) and *Till Eulenspiegel* (1895) by Richard Strauss, and *The Sorcerer's Apprentice* (1897) by Paul Dukas. During the late nineteenth century, symphonic poems became an important expression of nationalism in music. In section 13, we'll study a nationalistic tone poem, Smetana's *The Moldau*, which depicts Czechoslovakia's main river as it winds through the countryside.

Incidental music is intended to be performed before or during a play. It is "incidental" to the staged drama, but it sets the mood for certain scenes. Interludes, background music, marches, and dances are all incidental music (as are today's movie scores). Mendelssohn's incidental music for *A Midsummer Night's Dream* includes his famous *Wedding March*.

Basic Terms

program music
program
absolute music
program symphony

concert overture
symphonic poem (tone poem)
incidental music

HECTOR BERLIOZ

10

Hector Berlioz (1803–1869), the first French Romantic composer and a daring creator of new orchestral sounds, was born in a small town near Grenoble. Berlioz was twenty before he could devote himself to music. His father, a physician, sent him to Paris to study medicine, but Berlioz was "filled with horror" by the dissecting room. He shocked his parents by abandoning his medical studies to pursue a career in music.

It did not take long for Berlioz to fill the gaps in his musical knowledge. He studied at the Paris Conservatory, analyzed musical scores, haunted the opera house, and composed. He memorized many operas and became furious if a conductor tampered with the orchestration. This fiery young fanatic would stand during a performance and shout, "Not two flutes, you scoundrels! Two piccolos! Two piccolos!"

At twenty-three, Berlioz was overwhelmed by Shakespeare. He also fell madly in love with Harriet Smithson, a Shakespearean actress whose portrayals of

 Hector Berlioz

303

Ophelia and Juliet had captivated the Parisian public. Berlioz wrote Harriet letters that were so wild and impassioned that she thought he was a lunatic and refused to see him. He grieved: "If she could for one moment conceive all the poetry, all the infinity of such a love, she would fly into my arms." Instead, Harriet Smithson left Paris without meeting Berlioz. That came later.

To depict his "endless and unquenchable passion," Berlioz wrote the *Fantastic Symphony* in 1830. Parisians were startled by the sensationally autobiographical program for the symphony, its amazingly novel orchestration, and its vivid depiction of the weird and diabolical. At twenty-six, Berlioz had become the musical counterpart of revolutionary French Romantics like Victor Hugo and Delacroix.

In 1830, too, Berlioz won the Prix de Rome (Rome prize), the highest award of the Paris Conservatory. It subsidized two years' study in the Eternal City. When he returned to Paris, Berlioz presented a concert featuring his *Fantastic Symphony*. In the audience was Harriet Smithson. When she realized that Berlioz's music depicted her, "she felt the room reel about her; she heard no more but sat in a dream." The next day they met, and a year later they were married. Alas, the fantasy was more successful than reality—they separated after only a few years.

Berlioz's unconventional music irritated the directors of the main Paris opera house and concert society. To get a hearing for his work, Berlioz arranged concerts at his own expense. This involved hiring a hall, rounding up hundreds of musicians, writing publicity, getting the music copied, and countless other petty chores; it drained Berlioz financially, physically, and emotionally. "The main reason for the long war against me," he wrote at fifty-four, "lies in the antagonism existing between my musical feeling and that of the great mass of the Parisian public." He complained that "all music off the beaten track . . . seemed to these people the music of madness." But Berlioz was not completely unappreciated in Paris. He had a following of about 1,200 who faithfully bought tickets to his concerts. Nevertheless, this was not enough support for a composer of difficult and monumental works requiring much rehearsal time and hundreds of performers. To support his family, Berlioz turned to musical journalism. He was one of the most brilliant and witty music critics who ever lived. He made it his mission to convince the Parisian public that music was not merely a form of entertainment but a dramatic emotional expression.

Outside France, Berlioz's stock was higher. Liszt directed a German orchestra in several "Berlioz weeks," performing nothing but his works. After 1840, he was in demand throughout Europe, conducting his own music and that of others. As one of the first great orchestral conductors, he influenced a whole generation of musicians. In 1860, Wagner wrote to Liszt, saying that the three greatest composers of the time were Wagner, Liszt, and Berlioz.

Berlioz's later years were bitter. He was repeatedly passed over for important conducting positions and academic honors. He composed very little during the six years before his death at sixty-five.

Berlioz's Music

"The prevailing qualities of my music," wrote Berlioz, "are passionate expressiveness, inner fire, rhythmic drive, and unexpectedness." Above all, Berlioz's music sounds unique. It includes abrupt contrasts between high woodwinds and low strings, snarling brass, and rumbling percussion. The dynamics fluctuate constantly, and the tempo changes many times.

Berlioz was extraordinarily imaginative in treating the orchestra, creating tone colors never before heard. At a time when the average orchestra contained about sixty players, Berlioz often assembled hundreds of musicians to achieve an enormous range of power and instrumental timbre. More than any earlier composer, he made tone color a basic part of his musical language. A list of orchestral effects in the *Fantastic Symphony* alone would include four kettle drums combining to play a chord, bells combined with brasses, and violinists striking the strings with the bow-stick.

Berlioz's compositions are full of long melodies that take unexpected turns and are irregular and asymmetrical in construction. To critics who complained that his works lacked melodies, Berlioz replied, "To deny their existence is unfair and absurd. But as they are often on a large scale, an immature or unappreciative mind cannot appreciate their forms."

Most of Berlioz's works are for orchestra, or for orchestra with chorus and vocal soloists. All his major works are dramatic in nature and relate either to a literary program or to a text. He invented new forms: His "dramatic symphony" *Romeo and Juliet* (1839) is for orchestra, chorus, and vocal soloists, and his "dramatic legend" *The Damnation of Faust* (1846) combines opera and oratorio. Berlioz wrote three operas, *Benvenuto Cellini* (1838), *The Trojans* (1856–1858), and *Beatrice and Benedict* (1860–1862). Some of his works are grandiose and monumental, such as his *Requiem* (1837). He knew he was a pioneer in this territory: "In the *Requiem*, for example, I employ four distinct brass orchestras, answering each other at certain distances around the main orchestra and chorus. The result of this immensity of form is that either one entirely misses the drift of the music or is crushed by a tremendous emotion. . . . I have seen one man listening in terror, shaken to the depths of his soul, while his next neighbor could not catch an idea, though trying with all his might to do so."

Fantastic Symphony (Symphonie fantastique; 1830)

This astonishing program symphony by the twenty-six-year-old Berlioz is a Romantic manifesto. Both the symphony and Berlioz's program reflect the young composer's unrequited passion for the actress Harriet Smithson:

A young musician of extraordinary sensibility and abundant imagination, in the depths of despair because of hopeless love, has poisoned himself with opium. The drug is too feeble to kill him but plunges him into a heavy sleep accompanied by weird

Fantastic Symphony (1830)

305

visions. His sensations, emotions, and memories, as they pass through his affected mind, are transformed into musical images and ideas. The beloved one herself becomes to him a melody, a recurrent theme (*idée fixe*) which haunts him continually.

A single melody which Berlioz called the *idée fixe*, or "fixed idea," is used to represent the beloved. It appears in all five movements and unifies the contrasting episodes of the symphony. This recurrence of the same theme in every movement of a symphony was a striking novelty in Berlioz's day. The theme changes in character during the work, sounding, in turn, exultant, waltzlike, and vulgar.

Another innovation of the symphony is its requirement of a very large and colorful orchestra: piccolo, 2 flutes, 2 oboes, English horn, 2 clarinets, 4 bassoons, 4 horns, 2 cornets, 2 trumpets, 3 trombones, 2 tubas, 4 timpani, bass drum, snare drum, cymbals, bells, 2 harps, and strings. Beethoven had not used the English horn, tuba, bells, cornet, or harp in his symphonies. Berlioz saves the heaviest orchestration for the last two movements, where he depicts the fantastic and diabolical. Though the macabre and supernatural had long been dealt with in opera (in Mozart's *Don Giovanni*, for example), this is its first expression in an important symphony.

First Movement: Reveries, Passions. Largo (slow introduction); Allegro agitato e appassionato assai (agitated and very impassioned allegro)

First he remembers that weariness of the soul, that indefinable longing, that somber melancholia and those objectless joys which he experienced before meeting his beloved. Then, the volcanic love with which she suddenly inspired him, his delirious suffering, his return to tenderness, his religious consolations.

The symphony opens with an extended slow introduction—almost a movement in itself—in which fluctuations of tempo and mood help create a dreamlike atmosphere. A long muted violin melody expresses, in Berlioz's words, "the overpowering sadness of a young heart first caught in the toils of a hopeless love."

The allegro movement following the introduction is written in a modified sonata form. Its first theme, played by the violins and flutes, is the *idée fixe* ("fixed idea"). Berlioz described this expansive, upward-groping melody as "passionate but at the same time noble and shy."

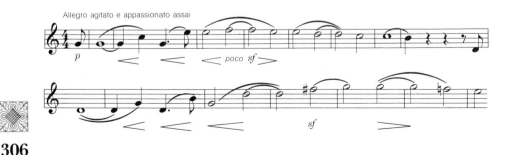

In the development, Berlioz uses a fragment of the *idée fixe* and builds tension through rising and falling chromatic scales played by staccato strings. A shattering climax is followed by a pregnant moment of silence. Yet another climax occurs toward the end of the movement when the full orchestra plays the *idée fixe* in a hysterically jubilant transformation. The movement concludes with slow chords that evoke the "religious consolations" mentioned in the program.

Second Movement: A Ball. Allegro non troppo

He finds his beloved again at a ball in the midst of the tumult of a brilliant party.

The second movement is a waltz, the most popular dance of the Romantic era. Its form may be outlined: Introduction–A B A'–Coda. A shimmering atmosphere is created in the introduction by string tremolos and delicate harp arpeggios. The lilting waltz theme is introduced by the violins (A section).

The B section brings a return of the *idée fixe,* now transformed into a waltz played by woodwinds.

The *idée fixe* is soon joined by an oom-pah-pah accompaniment and intertwined with fragments of the lilting waltz theme.

In the coda, Berlioz builds to a climax that is suddenly interrupted by yet another reminiscence of the *idée fixe*—this time played soulfully by a solo clarinet. The movement concludes brilliantly.

Third Movement: Scene in the Country. Adagio

On a summer evening in the country, he hears two herders calling each other with their shepherd melodies. The pastoral duet in such surroundings, the gentle rustle of the trees softly swayed by the wind, some reasons for hope which had come to his knowledge recently—all unite to fill his heart with a rare tranquility and lend brighter colors to his ideas. But his beloved appears anew, spasms contract his heart, and he is filled with dark premonitions. What if she were deceiving him? One of the shepherds resumes his rustic tune, the other does not reply. The sun sets. Far away there is rumbling thunder—solitude—silence.

Fantastic Symphony (1830)

Like the preceding waltz movement, the Adagio has the form: Introduction–A B A'–Coda. In the introduction, Berlioz evokes a mood of loneliness in the midst of nature: A solo English horn is echoed by an oboe an octave higher. No previous symphonic movement had ever begun with a duet between these two instruments. The A section opens with an extended melody for flute and violins—"delightful reverie."

The *idée fixe* returns in the B section. Played by the oboe and flute, it is now set against an agitated low countermelody in the cellos and basses. This combination of contrasting melodies in widely separated registers and different tone colors is a typically brilliant stroke. At the end of the coda, we again hear the English horn solo, but this time the oboe does not answer. Instead, four timpani suggest "the rumbling of distant thunder." Berlioz explains that his aim is not merely to imitate thunder, "but rather to make silence more perceptible, and thus to increase the impression of uneasy sadness and painful isolation."

Side 9, band 2

Fourth Movement: March to the Scaffold. Allegretto non troppo

> He dreams that he murdered his beloved, that he has been condemned to death and is being led to execution. A march that is alternately somber and wild, brilliant and solemn, accompanies the procession. . . . The tumultuous outbursts are followed without transition by the muffled sound of heavy steps. At the end, the fixed idea returns for a moment, like a last thought of love interrupted by the death blow.

"The March to the Scaffold is fifty times more frightening than I expected," Berlioz gleefully observed after the first rehearsals of the *Fantastic Symphony.* It is not until this fiendish fourth movement that all the brass and percussion instruments enter the action. Berlioz creates a menacing atmosphere with the opening orchestral sound, a unique combination of muted horns, timpani tuned a third apart, and basses playing pizzicato chords. The first theme, stated by the cellos and basses, moves steadily downward for two octaves.

This idea is repeated several times with countermelodies in the bassoons. Then we hear a syncopated march tune blared by the brasses and woodwinds.

f

At the end of the march a solo clarinet begins to play the *idée fixe* but is savagely interrupted by a very loud chord representing the fall of the guillotine's blade.

Fifth Movement: Dream of a Witches' Sabbath. Larghetto; Allegro

> He sees himself at a witches' sabbath in the midst of a hideous crowd of ghouls, sorcerers, and monsters of every description, united for his funeral. Strange noises, groans, shrieks of laughter, distant cries, which other cries seem to answer. The melody of the loved one is heard, but it has lost its character of nobleness and timidity; it is no more than a dance tune, ignoble, trivial, and grotesque. It is she who comes to the sabbath! . . . A howl of joy greets her arrival. . . . She participates in the diabolical orgy . . . the funeral knell, burlesque of the *Dies irae*. Witches' dance. The dance and the *Dies irae* combined.

The "Dream of a Witches' Sabbath" is the most "fantastic" movement of the symphony; it depicts a series of grotesque events. Its slow, hushed introduction (Larghetto) immediately draws the listener into the realm of the macabre and supernatural, evoking "strange noises, groans, shrieks of laughter" and "distant cries." Eerie tremolos in high muted strings and menacing low tones of cellos and basses begin a succession of fragmentary ideas in starkly contrasting tone colors, registers, and dynamics. In the exploratory spirit of his Romantic age, Berlioz dared to create sounds that are weird rather than conventionally pleasing.

In the Allegro section, the beloved is revealed to be a witch. Her theme, the once "noble and timid" *idée fixe,* is transformed into a dance tune that is "trivial and grotesque." Played shrilly by a high-pitched clarinet, the tune moves in quick notes decorated by trills.

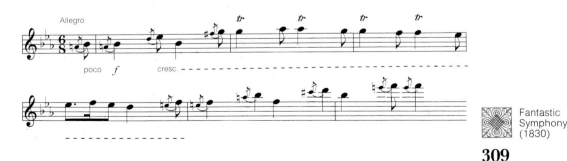

Fantastic Symphony (1830)

309

A "funeral knell" of sonorous bells lends an awesome atmosphere to the next part of the movement. Tubas and bassoons intone a solemn low melody in long even notes.

This melody is the medieval chant *Dies irae* ("Day of Wrath"), traditionally sung in the Mass for the Dead. Berlioz quotes it here as a symbol of eternal damnation. Soon the chant melody is shifted up to a high register and played by woodwinds and pizzicato strings in a quick dancelike rhythm.

Thus Berlioz dared to parody a sacred chant by transforming it into a trivial tune, as he did earlier with the *idée fixe.*

Berlioz conveys the frenzy of a witches' dance in a fuguelike section. The fugue subject (witches' dance) is introduced by the lower strings and then imitated by other instruments.

A crescendo builds to a powerful climax in which the rapid witches' dance is set against the slower-moving *Dies irae* proclaimed by the brasses and woodwinds. This musical nightmare ends in an orgy of orchestral power.

NATIONALISM IN NINETEENTH-CENTURY MUSIC

During the nineteenth century all Europeans felt their homelands merited loyalty and self-sacrifice. These nationalistic feelings were awakened during the upheavals of the French Revolution and Napoleonic Wars (1789–1814), when French armies invaded much of Europe. In many countries, military resistance to Napoleon aroused the citizens' sense of national identity. Common bonds of language, culture, and history were strengthened, since now battles were fought by soldiers drawn from the general population, not by mercenaries, as in the past. Patriotic feeling was intensified, too, by Romanticism, which glorified love for one's national heritage.

As a revolutionary political movement, nationalism led to the unification of lands—like Germany and Italy—that had previously been divided into tiny states. It spurred revolts in countries under foreign rule, such as Poland and Bohemia (now part of Czechoslovakia).

Nationalism was a potent cultural movement, as well, particularly regarding language. In lands dominated by foreign powers, the national language was used increasingly in textbooks, newspapers, and official documents. For example, in Bohemia there was a revival of the Czech language, which before 1800 had lost ground to the German spoken by Austrian rulers. By the 1830s and 1840s, important textbooks on astronomy and chemistry were written in Czech, and there were many collections of Czech folk poetry. In every land, the "national spirit" was felt to reside in the "folk," the peasantry. The national past became a subject of intense historical investigation, and there was new enthusiasm for folk songs, dances, legends, and fairy tales.

Nationalism influenced Romantic music, as composers deliberately gave their works a distinctive national identity. They used folk songs and dances and created original melodies with a folk flavor. Nationalist composers wrote operas and program music inspired by the history, legends, and landscapes of their native lands. Their works bear titles like *Russian Easter Overture* (Rimsky-Korsakov), *Finlandia* (Sibelius), and *Slavonic Dances* (Dvořák). But a genuine feeling of national style does not come merely through the use of folk songs or patriotic subjects. A piece of music will *sound* French, Russian, or Italian when its rhythm, tone color, texture, and melody spring from national tradition. There had been regional traits in music before the Romantic period, but never had differences of national style been emphasized so strongly or consciously.

In these revolutionary times, musical compositions symbolized nationalist yearnings and sometimes stirred audiences to violent political demonstrations. The Italian opera composer Giuseppe Verdi deliberately chose librettos that

 Nationalism in Nineteenth-Century Music

311

fanned public hatred for Austrian overlords. And censors constantly pressured him to change scenes that might be interpreted as anti-Austrian or antimonarchical. In the twentieth century, the Nazis banned performances of Smetana's *The Moldau* in Prague, the composer's home city.

Nationalism's strongest impact was felt in lands whose own musical heritage had been dominated by the music of Italy, France, Germany, or Austria. During the Romantic period, Poland, Russia, Bohemia, and the Scandinavian countries produced important composers whose music had a national flavor. Early in the nineteenth century, Chopin transformed his native Polish dances into great art. After about 1860, groups or "schools" of composers consciously delcared their musical independence and established national styles. Among the leading musical nationalists were Mussorgsky, Rimsky-Korsakov, and Borodin from Russia; Smetana and Dvořák from Bohemia; Grieg from Norway; and Sibelius from Finland. We will focus on the most important of the national schools, the Russian.

"The Russian Five"

The most distinctive national music arose in Russia, where folk songs pervaded daily life. "Every muzhik, carpenter, bricklayer, doorkeeper, cabman; every peasant woman, laundry-maid and cook, every nurse and wet-nurse—all bring the folk songs of their villages with them to Petersburg, Moscow, to each and every city, and we hear them the whole year round," wrote a Russian music critic of the nineteenth century. The folk music of Russia sounds different from that of Western Europe. It is often based on ancient church modes, rather than on major or minor scales. (Like major and minor scales, church modes consist of eight tones within an octave, but they have different patterns of whole and half steps.) Russian folk tunes also tend to be irregular in meter. A measure may contain five beats ($\frac{5}{4}$ time), instead of the customary two, three, four, or six. And the meter may change within a song so that two bars in $\frac{3}{4}$ time will be followed by one in $\frac{5}{4}$. Russian nationalist composers thus were able to draw on folk music that was both distinctive and highly varied.

Before 1800 there had been no important Russian composers of art music. Tsars imported Italian and German composers to provide court music. But in the early 1800s a composer emerged who is considered the father of Russian music—Mikhail Glinka (1804–1857). His opera *A Life for the Tsar* (1836) incorporated peasant and folk tunes in a convincing way and laid the groundwork for the development of a national style.

But it was only in the 1860s that a true "school" of national music came into being. (This decade saw the appearance of the great Russian novels *Crime and Punishment* by Dostoevsky and *War and Peace* by Tolstoy.) Five young men, now known as "The Russian Five," met together in St. Petersburg with the aim of creating a truly Russian music. They criticized each other's works and asserted the necessity of breaking from some of the traditional techniques of German,

Italian, and French composers. Remarkably, all but one began as amateurs; most had nonmusical jobs and could compose only in their spare time. At first, the only professional musician was Mily Balakirev (1837–1910). The other members were César Cui (1835–1918), an army engineer; Alexander Borodin (1833–1887), a chemist; Nikolai Rimsky-Korsakov (1844–1908), a naval officer; and Modest Mussorgsky (1839–1881), a civil servant. Mussorgsky was most original and probably the greatest of the "Russian Five." We'll focus on his opera *Boris Godunov,* a masterpiece of musical nationalism.

Boris Godunov (1874), by Modest Mussorgsky

The son of a wealthy landowner, Modest Mussorgsky (1839–1881) was educated in a military academy, becoming an army officer at seventeen. After two years he left the army to devote himself to music. But the emancipation of the Russian serfs in 1861 caused financial hardship to his family, and Mussorgsky had to find a job. He became a government clerk in St. Petersburg and remained in that position for most of his life.

Though a competent pianist, Mussorgsky had little training in composition. He taught himself, except for occasional advice from Balakirev—one of the Russian Five. Mussorgsky was plagued by severe psychological problems and eventually became an alcoholic. When he died at forty-two, he left relatively few compositions: These include *Boris Godunov,* some songs, the symphonic poem *Night on Bald Mountain,* and the piano piece *Pictures at an Exhibition,* which Maurice Ravel later arranged for orchestra.

Mussorgsky's highly original music is imbued with the spirit of Russian folk music. His melodies reflect the rhythms, accents, and pitch fluctuations of everyday Russian speech. "I should like to make my characters speak on the stage exactly as they do in real life," he wrote. Contemporaries condemned Mussorgsky's unconventional chord progressions as "crude" and "incorrect." Today, we can appreciate their color, strength, and originality.

Mussorgsky adapted the libretto of *Boris Godunov* (1874) from a drama by Alexander Pushkin, the Russian Romantic poet. The opera deals with a violent chapter in Russian history and centers around the powerful personality of Tsar Boris, who reigned from 1598 to 1605. Boris gained the throne by causing the murder of its rightful heir, the child Dimitri. In a series of episodes, Mussorgsky vividly depicts Boris's coronation, his anguished feelings of guilt, his political enemies, his love of family and country, and his tragic death.

While the opera's central character is Tsar Boris, the Russian people emerge as its real "hero." In 1873 Mussorgsky wrote, "It is the people I want to depict. When I sleep I see them, when I eat I think of them, when I drink—I can visualize them, integral, big, untainted, and without any tinsel." Through massive choruses and vocal solos, he offers realistic portraits of the Russian peasant, nobleman, nursemaid, soldier, policeman, vagabond monk, and village idiot. In this "musical folk-drama" (as *Boris* is subtitled), Mussorgsky's aim was

Boris Godunov
by Modest
Mussorgsky

313

not merely to create a work of art, but to reveal the depth and variety of the Russian character.

Boris was acclaimed by the Russian public during Mussorgsky's lifetime, but it was dropped from the repertory not long after his death in 1881. In 1896 and again in 1908, the score was revised by Rimsky-Korsakov, who edited and published Mussorgsky's works. Rimsky changed many passages and made the orchestration more brilliant. Though scholars debate the merits of Rimsky's revision, it is the one usually performed today. We'll focus on the spectacular "Coronation Scene" from the Prologue to Act I.

Side 8, band 7

Prologue to Act I: "Coronation Scene"

Set in the courtyard of the Kremlin in Moscow, this dazzling scene calls up the splendor, pageantry, and religious fervor of ancient Russia. The Cathedral of the Archangels, burial place of tsars, is on one side of the stage; on the other side is the Cathedral of the Assumption, where tsars are crowned. The courtyard is filled with a mass of common people, kneeling, who are watched by police.

In a brilliant and highly original orchestral introduction, Mussorgsky depicts the tolling of all the great bells of the Kremlin. Bells were a characteristic feature of ancient Russia and were linked with events that marked the passing of time—births, deaths, weddings, and coronations. The orchestral introduction is built entirely from the repeated alternation of just two dissonant chords:

This particular succession of chords was highly unusual in Mussorgsky's day, and no other composer has repeated it to create such a special atmosphere. Mussorgsky's technique of repetition was to have profound influence on twentieth-century composers such as Igor Stravinsky.

A solemn procession of nobles moves toward the cathedral for the coronation of Boris. From the porch of the cathedral, Prince Shuisky, Boris's adviser, exclaims, "Long live Tsar Boris." Then the chorus sings an exultant hymn of praise which Mussorgsky based on a Russian folk song.

To the sun in all splen - dor ris - en be glo - ry, glo - ry!

As the tsar's procession emerges from the cathedral, the music builds to a climax. When Boris appears, the mood changes dramatically. Clad in magnificent royal garb and followed by his two children, Boris at first voices "dark foreboding" about his fate and prays for God's blessing. Then he invites everyone present—nobles and lowly poor—to a feast, and his melody becomes powerful and determined. The bell-chords and choral hymn of praise recur as Boris's proces-

The Romantic Period

sion continues to the Cathedral of the Archangels to pay homage before the tombs of Russia's tsars.

Prince Shuisky

Da zdrávstvuyet Tsar Borís Feódorovich!   Long life Tsar Boris Feodorovich!

Chorus

Zhiví i zdrávstvui, Tsar násh bátyushka!   Long live the Tsar, our little father!

Prince Shuisky

Slávte!   Glory to you!

Chorus

Uzh kák na nébe sólntsu krásnomu,   Even as glory to the radiant sun in the
Sláva!   sky, so glory to Tsar Boris in Russia!
Uzh i sláva no Rusí Tsaryú Borísu!
Sláva!

(An imperial procession from the Cathedral. Police officers keep the people in line on both sides of the procession.)

Zhivi i zdrávstvui!   Long live the Tsar! Rejoice and make
Ráduisya, veselísya pravoslávnyi lyud!   merry, all ye faithful of the Russian
Velichái Tsaryá Borísa i sláv!   church, and glory to the great Tsar Boris.

(from the porch)

Nobles

Da zdrávstvuyet Tsar Borís Feódorovich!   All hail to Tsar Boris Feodorovich!

Chorus

Da zdrávstvuyet!   All hail!

(Boris now appears and crosses the stage.)

Uzh, kák na Rusí Tsaryú Borísu!   Glory to Tsar Boris in all Russia! Glory,
Sláva, sláva Tsaryú!   glory to the Tsar! Glory, glory, glory!
Sláva, sláva, sláva!

Boris

Skorbit dushá!   My soul is torn with anguish! Involuntary
Kakói-to strákh nevólnyi   fears and sinister forebodings clutch my
Zlovéschim predchúvstviyem   heart. Oh, righteous and sovereign Father,
Skovál mne sérdtse.   look down from heaven and behold the
O právednik, o mói otéts derzhávnyi!   tears of these your faithful servants!
Vozzrí s nebés na slyózy vérnykh slug   Bestow Thy sacred blessings upon me and
I nisposhlí ty mné svyaschénnoye na vlást   my dominion! Help me to be kind and
Blagoslovénye.   just like Thyself, and rule over my people
Da búdu blag i práveden kak tý,   in glory! And now let us bow in homage
Dá v sláve právlyu svói naród.   to the great departed rulers of Russia.
Tepér poklónimsya pochíyuschim   Then let us summon the people, from the
Vlastítelyam Rusíyi.   noble to the blind begger, to a feast. All
A tám szyvát naród na pir,   are free to come and be my dear and
Vsekh, ot boyár do nischevo sleptsá,   welcome guests.
Vsem vólnyi vkhod, vse gósti dorogíye.

(Bells are rung on stage as the procession continues to the Archangels Cathedral.)

 Boris Godunov
by Modest
Mussorgsky

Chorus

Zhiví zdrávstvui Tsár nash bátyushka.   Long live the Tsar, our little father!

(Police officers try to restore order, but the people break away and dash towards the Archangels Cathedral.)

Uzh kák na nébe sólntsu krásnomu,
Sláva, sláva!
Uzh, kák na Rusí Tsaryú Borísu,
Sláva, sláva i mnógaya léta!

Even as glory to the radiant sun in the sky, so glory to Tsar Boris in Russia! Glory, glory and a long life!

(Great commotion. The police officers struggle with the people. Boris *emerges from the Archangels Cathedral and proceeds to his chambers.)*

Basic Term

nationalism

Romantic

|12| PETER ILYICH TCHAIKOVSKY

Peter Ilyich Tchaikovsky (1840–1893), the most famous Russian composer, came from the small town of Votkinsk, where his father was a mining inspector. At ten, he and his family moved to St. Petersburg (Leningrad), where he studied at the School of Jurisprudence. Graduating at nineteen, Tchaikovsky became a government clerk. He began to study music theory at the relatively late age of twenty-one. While keeping his government position, he entered the newly established St. Petersburg Conservatory, the first college-level music school in Russia. Two days after the opening of the conservatory, he wrote to his sister: "Sooner or later I shall abandon my present job for music. . . . Of course, I won't resign from my present job till I'm certain that I'm no longer a clerk, but a musician." The next year he did just that. So rapid was his progress in music that after graduating he became professor of harmony at the new Moscow Conservatory, a position he held for twelve years. As though to make up for his late start, Tchaikovsky composed furiously; a symphony, an opera, and a tone poem flowed from his pen, and by the age of thirty, he had composed his first great orchestral work, *Romeo and Juliet.*

The year 1877 was bitterly dramatic. He took the disastrous step of marrying a twenty-eight-year-old conservatory student who adored him and his music. Tchaikovsky seems to have married only to conceal his homosexuality. A few days after the wedding, he was writing of "ghastly spiritual torture." Two weeks

Peter Ilyich Tchaikovsky, the first Russian composer to gain fame internationally (The Granger Collection).

 Peter Ilyich Tchaikovsky

317

later he waded into the icy Moscow River, intending to commit suicide by getting pneumonia. But a strong constitution saved him, and he fled to St. Petersburg, where a nervous collapse resulted in a coma for two days. He separated from his wife, never seeing her again.

In 1877 Tchaikovsky also acquired a benefactress, Nedezhda von Meck. A very rich widow of forty-six with eleven children, she passionately loved Tchaikovsky's music. Madame von Meck gave him an annuity that allowed him to quit his conservatory position and devote himself to composition. For fourteen years they corresponded, but they agreed never to meet. "I prefer to think of you from afar," she wrote, "to hear you speak in your music and to share your feelings through it." After so many years of this curious but intimate friendship, Tchaikovsky was deeply hurt when she abruptly cut off the annuity and stopped corresponding. "This situation lowers me in my own eyes," he wrote her son-in-law, "it makes the memory of the money I accepted from her almost unbearable. . . ."

During these years, Tchaikovsky more and more conducted his own works, achieving success throughout Europe. Yet success did not bring spiritual peace. His brother observed, "The weariness and suffering which sprang up in Tchaikovsky's soul . . . reached their greatest intensity at the moment of his greatest triumphs." In 1891 he was invited to the United States, where he participated in four concerts inaugurating Carnegie Hall in New York and two concerts of his music in Baltimore and Philadelphia.

On October 28, 1893, Tchaikovsky conducted the premiere of his last great work, the Symphony No. 6 ("Pathétique"), which ends unconventionally with a slow, despairing finale. An epidemic of cholera was then rampant in St. Petersburg, and people were cautioned against drinking unboiled water. Tchaikovsky disregarded the warning, caught the infection, and died at fifty-three.

Tchaikovsky's Music

"I grew up in the backwoods, filling myself from earliest childhood with the inexplicable beauty of the characteristic traits of Russian folk music. . . . I passionately love the Russian element in all its manifestations." Tchaikovsky thought of himself as "*Russian* in the fullest sense of the word." But Russian folk song was only one influence on his art. His style also contains elements of French, Italian, and German music.

Tchaikovsky's works are much more in the Western tradition than are the compositions of his contemporaries, the "Russian Five." He fused national and international elements to produce intensely subjective and passionate music. "At the moment of composing," Tchaikovsky wrote, "when I am aglow with emotion, it flashes across my mind that all who will hear my music will experience some reflection of what I am feeling myself." And indeed, the brooding melancholy that plagued Tchaikovsky is a prominent feature in much of his music.

Tchaikovsky was a prolific composer of both instrumental and vocal works.

Among his most popular orchestral compositions are the Fourth, Fifth, and Sixth ("Pathétique") Symphonies (1877, 1888, 1893), the Piano Concerto No. 1 in B-flat minor (1875), the Violin Concerto (1878), and the overture-fantasy *Romeo and Juliet* (1869), which we'll study. Tchaikovsky wrote some of his best music for ballet: *Swan Lake* (1876), *Sleeping Beauty* (1889), and *The Nutcracker* (1892). He reworked these ballet scores into concert suites, of which *The Nutcracker* is best known. The spirit of ballet permeates much of Tchaikovsky's music. Of his eight operas, *Eugene Onegin* (1877–1878) and *Pique Dame* (*The Queen of Spades;* 1890) are performed with some frequency. There also are the orchestral showpieces *Marche slave* and *Overture 1812*.

All of Tchaikovsky's music contains beautiful melodies that stretch and leap widely, like dancers. He repeats melodies over and over, sometimes transforming an intimate, lyrical utterance into an intense outcry by means of louder dynamics and fuller orchestration. His treatment of the orchestra is extremely colorful, marked by striking contrasts and alternations of strings, woodwinds, and brasses. The emotional quality of his music results from sharp contrasts of tempo, dynamics, and thematic material, as well as from ever more powerful climaxes.

Romeo and Juliet, Overture-Fantasy

Side 10, band 1

Romantic composers felt an artistic kinship to Shakespeare because of his passionate poetry, dramatic contrast, and profound knowledge of the human heart. Shakespeare's plays inspired many of the finest nineteenth-century compositions. Among these were *Macbeth* and *Othello,* set as operas by Verdi, and *A Midsummer Night's Dream,* depicted in incidental music by Mendelssohn. *Romeo and Juliet* inspired both a "dramatic symphony" by Berlioz and a concert overture by Tchaikovsky.

Tchaikovsky composed *Romeo and Juliet* at twenty-nine, near the beginning of his musical career. Now one of the best-loved orchestral works, *Romeo and Juliet* was a dismal failure at its premiere in 1870. "After the concert we dined. . . . No one said a single word to me about the overture the whole evening. And yet I yearned so for appreciation and kindness." Tchaikovsky decided to revise the overture. He composed a new theme to represent Friar Laurence, adopting the suggestion of his friend Balakirev. Despite this, the work remained unappreciated. Only about twenty years later, after further revisions, did *Romeo and Juliet* achieve worldwide popularity.

Like Shakespeare's play, Tchaikovsky's *Romeo and Juliet* glorifies a romantic love powerful enough to triumph over death. He captures the essential emotions of Shakespeare's play without defining each character or the exact course of events. Highly contrasted themes are used to express the conflict between family hatred and youthful love. Tchaikovsky also depicts the gentle and philosophical Friar Laurence, intermediary between the lovers and the harsh outside world.

Romeo and Juliet is a concert overture consisting of a slow introduction and a fast movement in sonata form. (Tchaikovsky's title, "Overture-Fantasy," implies

Romeo and Juliet

319

that he treated the musical material in a free and imaginative way.) We can enjoy *Romeo and Juliet* as an exciting orchestral piece without knowing the play. However, a new dimension is added to our listening experience when we associate the music with the drama.

Tchaikovsky opens the overture with the Friar Laurence theme, a solemn hymnlike melody. As the slow introduction unfolds, brooding strings set an atmosphere of impending tragedy. The clash of swords and the anger of the feud between the Montagues and the Capulets is suggested by the violent first theme of the Allegro. Syncopations, rushing strings, and massive sounds create enormous excitement. The second theme of the exposition, a tender love theme, is expressively scored for English horn and muted violas. When the love theme returns in the recapitulation, it has a new exultant character, as Tchaikovsky envelops the listener in waves of opulent orchestral sound. There are long crescendos as the melody is led higher and higher to ever more passionate climaxes.

In the coda, Tchaikovsky transforms the love theme into a song of mourning, while timpani softly beat the rhythm of a funeral march. Then, a new hymn and a tender reminiscence of the love theme suggest that Romeo and Juliet are reunited in death.

LISTENING OUTLINE
To be read while music is heard

Romeo and Juliet, Overture-Fantasy (1869), by Peter Ilyich Tchaikovsky

Andante non tanto quasi Moderato (andante, almost a moderate tempo, slow introduction); Allegro giusto (moderate allegro)

Sonata form, quadruple meter ($\frac{4}{4}$), B minor

piccolo, 2 flutes, 2 oboes, English horn, 2 clarinets, 2 bassoons, 4 horns, 2 trumpets, 3 trombones, tuba, timpani, cymbals, bass drum, harp, violins 1, violins 2, violas, cellos, basses.

(About 18½ min)

Andante non tanto
quasi moderato
(slow introduction)   1   *a.* Low clarinets and bassoons, *p*, hymnlike Friar Laurence theme.

        b. Strings and horns, *p*, sustained tones. Basses.
        c. Woodwinds and strings, crescendo. Harp, *mf*, flutes, *p*.

2 a. Pizzicato strings accompany high woodwinds, *p*, Friar Laurence theme.
   b. Strings and horns, *p*, sustained tones. Basses.
   c. Strings and woodwinds, crescendo. Harp, *mf*, violins, *p*.
3 a. Strings answered by high woodwinds, *mf*. Crescendo to *ff*, full orchestra, accelerando. Timpani roll, decrescendo, much slower tempo.
   b. Strings, *p*, answered by woodwind chords, *pp*. Crescendo and accelerando to

Allegro giusto
EXPOSITION
  First theme   1 a. Orchestra, *f*, feud theme, minor.

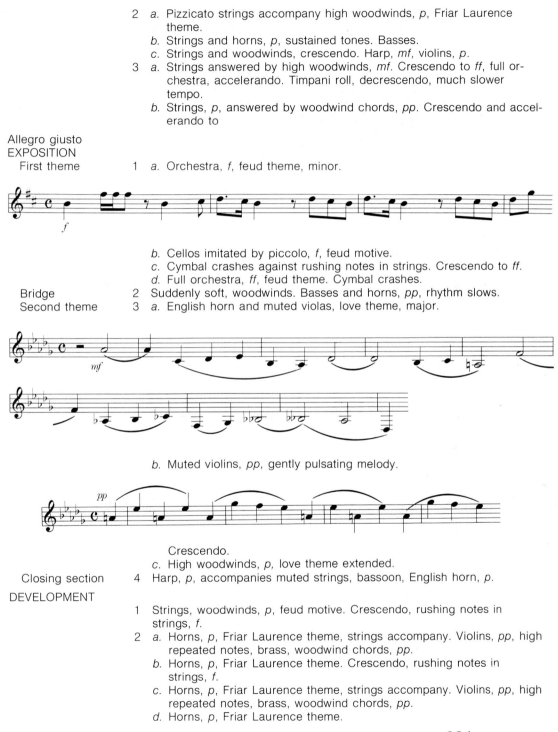

   b. Cellos imitated by piccolo, *f*, feud motive.
   c. Cymbal crashes against rushing notes in strings. Crescendo to *ff*.
   d. Full orchestra, *ff*, feud theme. Cymbal crashes.
Bridge   2 Suddenly soft, woodwinds. Basses and horns, *pp*, rhythm slows.
Second theme   3 a. English horn and muted violas, love theme, major.

   b. Muted violins, *pp*, gently pulsating melody.

   Crescendo.
   c. High woodwinds, *p*, love theme extended.
Closing section   4 Harp, *p*, accompanies muted strings, bassoon, English horn, *p*.
DEVELOPMENT
                             1 Strings, woodwinds, *p*, feud motive. Crescendo, rushing notes in strings, *f*.
                             2 a. Horns, *p*, Friar Laurence theme, strings accompany. Violins, *pp*, high repeated notes, brass, woodwind chords, *pp*.
                                b. Horns, *p*, Friar Laurence theme. Crescendo, rushing notes in strings, *f*.
                                c. Horns, *p*, Friar Laurence theme, strings accompany. Violins, *pp*, high repeated notes, brass, woodwind chords, *pp*.
                                d. Horns, *p*, Friar Laurence theme.

321

3 Low strings, *f*, answered by woodwinds, *f*, feud motive. Crescendo to *ff*, cymbal crashes.
4 *a.* Trumpets, *ff*, Friar Laurence theme.
  b. Strings, *ff*, rushing notes, cymbal crashes.

RECAPITULATION
First theme

1 Full orchestra, *ff*, feud theme, minor, cymbal crashes. Downward rushing notes in strings.

Second theme

2 Oboes, *p*, gently pulsating melody, major. Violins accompany *pp*. Crescendo.
3 *a.* Strings, *f*, love theme extended. Crescendo to *ff*. Love theme repeated. Decrescendo.
  b. Cellos, woodwinds, *mf*, love-theme phrases. Horn. Crescendo.
  c. Strings, *ff*, love theme. Feud motive cymbal crashes.
4 *a.* Full orchestra, *ff*, feud theme, cymbal crashes.
  b. Brasses, *ff*, Friar Laurence theme.
  c. Full orchestra, *ff*, feud theme, cymbal crashes.
  d. Brasses, *ff*, Friar Laurence theme.
  e. Full orchestra, *ff*, cymbal crashes. Cellos and basses, timpani roll, decrescendo to *p*.

Coda

1 Timpani, *p*, funeral-march rhythm. Strings, *mf*, love theme transformed into song of mourning. Very moderate tempo.

2 Woodwinds, *pp*, hymnlike melody. Harp.
3 Violins, *mf*, love theme varied. Timpani roll, crescendo.
4 Full orchestra, *ff*, repeated chords.

Romantic

13 | BEDŘICH SMETANA

Bedřich Smetana (1824–1884) is the founder of Czech national music. His works are steeped in the folk songs, dances, and legends of his native Bohemia (now part of Czechoslovakia). Smetana grew up when Bohemia was under Austrian domination, and the official language in Prague schools and government bureaus was German, not Czech. Young Smetana's feelings of national identity were inflamed during the revolutions of 1848, when Czech radicals fought for political freedom and the abolition of serfdom. As a member of the armed Citizen Corps, he probably manned the barricades when the Austrians bombarded Prague. The insurrection was a failure and resulted in a harsh reaction from Austria; censorship was increased and patriots were imprisoned.

In this repressive atmosphere, Smetana's musical nationalism could make little headway. Though he was recognized as a pianist, his compositions were scorned by those opposed to nationalism or "modernity" of any variety. In 1856, Smetana emigrated to Sweden, where he taught, conducted, and composed symphonic poems in the style of Franz Liszt. He returned to Prague only in 1862, when Austria's military defeats had resulted in some liberal concessions. Political prisoners were released, Czech-language newspapers were established, and there were Czech theaters for drama and opera. For one of these theaters Smetana wrote *The Bartered Bride,* his most famous opera, based on Bohemian legend and folk material. Smetana was active in Prague not only as a composer, but as a pianist, conductor, teacher, and tireless propagandist for Czech musical nationalism.

At the age of fifty, Smetana suffered the same fate as Beethoven—he became completely deaf. Yet some of his finest works followed, including *My Country (Má Vlast;* 1874–1879), a cycle of six symphonic poems glorifying Bohemian history and legend, the fertile Czech countryside, and peasant songs and dances. Smetana's last ten years passed in acute physical and mental torment caused by syphilis. He died in an insane asylum at the age of sixty.

The Moldau (Vltava)

Side 9, band 3

"Today I took an excursion to the St. John Rapids where I sailed in a boat through huge waves. . . . The view of the landscape was both beautiful and grand." Smetana's trip inspired his famous symphonic poem, *The Moldau (Vltava),* which depicts Bohemia's main river as it flows through the countryside. This orchestral work, part of the cycle *My Country,* is both a Romantic representation of nature and a display of Czech nationalism. It was written in three weeks shortly after Smetana became deaf. *The Moldau*'s fresh, optimistic mood gives no hint of the composer's anguish and despair. Smetana wrote the following program to preface his score:

> The composition depicts the course of the river, beginning from its two small sources, one cold the other warm, the joining of both streams into one, then the flow of the Vltava (Moldau) through forests and across meadows, through the countryside where merry feasts are celebrated; water nymphs dance in the moonlight; on nearby rocks can be seen the outline of ruined castles, proudly soaring into the sky. Vltava swirls through the St. John Rapids and flows in a broad stream toward Prague. It passes Vyšehrad [where an ancient royal castle once stood] and finally the river disappears in the distance as it flows majestically into the Elbe.

The Moldau falls into contrasting musical sections that represent different scenes and episodes described in the program. Hunting at the river bank is suggested by horn fanfares, a peasant wedding by a rustic polka—the Bohemian dance; and a moonlit night is represented by shimmering woodwinds and a

The Moldau
(Vltava)

323

serene melody in high muted strings. An expansive folklike theme that recurs several times symbolizes the river. Smetana unifies the symphonic poem by running notes evoking the movement of water, sometimes rippling, sometimes turbulent.

LISTENING OUTLINE

To be read while music is heard

The Moldau (*Vltava;* 1874), by Bedřich Smetana

Allegro commodo non agitato (unhurried allegro, not agitated), sextuple meter ($\frac{6}{8}$), E minor

piccolo, 2 flutes, 2 oboes, 2 clarinets, 2 bassoons, 4 horns, 2 trumpets, 3 trombones, tuba, timpani, bass drum, triangle, cymbals, harp, violins 1, violins 2, violas, cellos, basses

(About 11½ min)

Two springs   1   *a.* Flutes, *p*, running notes. Harp, pizzicato violins.

         Clarinets, *p*, join, running notes.
         b. Lower strings, *p*, running notes lead to

The river   2   Violins, songlike river theme, minor key. Running-note accompaniment in strings.

         River theme extended.

Forest hunt   3   *a.* Horns and trumpets, *f*, hunting calls. Strings, running notes. Crescendo to *ff*.
         b. Decrescendo to *ppp*.

Peasant wedding   4   *a.* Strings, *p*, polka.

         Crescendo to *f*, triangle strokes.
         b. Decrescendo to *ppp*, melody descends.

Moonlight dance of water nymphs	5	*a.* Woodwinds, *pp*, sustained tones. Flutes, *p*, running notes lead to *b.* High muted violins, *pp*, serene legato melody. Harp, *p*. *c.* Brasses, *pp*. Staccato chords join accompaniment to violin melody. *d.* Crescendo. Woodwinds, running notes lead to
The river	6	Violins, river theme. Running-note accompaniment in strings.
The rapids	7	*a.* Full orchestra, *ff*. Brasses, timpani roll, piccolo, cymbal crashes. *b.* Strings, *pp*. Quick crescendo.
The river at its widest point	8	Full orchestra, *ff*, river theme in major key. Faster tempo.
Vyšehrad, the ancient castle	9	*a.* Brasses and woodwinds, *ff*, hymnlike melody. Cymbal crashes. *b.* Decrescendo. Violins, *ppp*. Full orchestra, *ff*, closing chords.

ANTONIN DVOŘÁK

Romantic

14

Antonin Dvořák (1841–1904) followed Smetana as the leader of Czech national music. He infused his symphonies and chamber music with the spirit of Bohemian folk song and dance.

Dvořák's father was a poor innkeeper and butcher in a small town near Prague. After working in his father's butcher shop, the sixteen-year-old Dvořák left home to study music in Prague. For years he earned a meager living by playing in an opera orchestra under Smetana's direction. He was little known as a composer until his works came to the attention of Brahms. The German master recommended Dvořák to his own publisher: "I took much pleasure in the works of Dvořák of Prague. If you play them through, you will enjoy them as much as I have done. Decidedly he is a very talented man."

From this time on—Dvořák was about thirty-six—his fame spread rapidly. He was invited several times to England, where the melodiousness of his symphonies, chamber music, Slavonic dances, and choral works appealed to the English love for folk music and the countryside. Although Dvořák rarely quoted actual folk tunes, his works breathe a folk quality and express a cheerful and direct personality.

In 1892, Dvořák went to New York to spend almost three years as the Director of the National Conservatory of Music. He received a salary of $15,000, about twenty times what he was earning as a professor at the Prague Conservatory. Dvořák encouraged American composers to write nationalistic music. Besides his urban impressions, Dvořák learned about the American heartland by spending a summer in Spillville, Iowa, where there was a colony of Czechs.

Dvořák soon became interested in American Indian melodies and Negro spirituals, which he learned about from his student Henry T. Burleigh, a black

Antonin Dvořák

325

composer and baritone. "In the Negro songs," Dvořák told a reporter from the New York *Herald,* "I have found a secure basis for a new national musical school. America can have her own music, a fine music growing up from her own soil and having its own character—the natural voice of a free and great nation." In 1895 Dvořák returned to his homeland and rejoined the faculty of the Prague Conservatory, becoming its director six years later.

Symphony No. 9 in E Minor, "From the New World"

The *New World Symphony* was written during Dvořák's first year in the United States. One of the best known of all symphonies, it glorifies the folk spirit of both America and Czechoslovakia. Its popular character grows out of Dvořák's use of syncopations, pentatonic (five-note) scales, and modal scales often found in folk music. Colorful orchestration and melodious thematic material add to the *New World Symphony*'s attractiveness. The symphony's four contrasting movements are unified through quotation of thematic material: Themes from the first movement are recalled in the second and third, and the finale brings back themes from all three preceding movements.

First Movement: Adagio (slow introduction); Allegro molto

The slow introduction builds great tension and contains an ominous bass motive that foreshadows the opening theme of the energetic Allegro that follows. In the exposition of this sonata-form movement, there are three distinctive themes. The first begins in minor with a syncopated arpeggio motive that dominates the entire symphony. Also in minor, the dancelike second theme is gentler than the first and narrower in range. Dvořák shifts to a major key for the third theme, a gracious melody which resembles the spiritual, "Swing Low, Sweet Chariot." (In the Listening Outline this is called the "Swing Low theme," without implying that Dvořák meant it to recall the spiritual.) Between these themes come beautiful bridge passages that rise to a climax and then calm down to usher in new melodic material. In his development, Dvořák concentrates on the first and third themes, which he varies and combines. The recapitulation of all three themes is followed by a coda, which brings the movement to a climactic close.

LISTENING OUTLINE
To be read while music is heard

Symphony No. 9 in E Minor,
"From the New World" (1893), by Antonin Dvořák

First Movement Adagio (slow introduction); Allegro molto

Sonata form, duple meter ($\frac{2}{4}$), E minor

piccolo, 2 flutes, 2 oboes, 2 clarinets, 2 bassoons, 4 horns, 2 trumpets, 3 trombones, timpani, violins 1, violins 2, violas, cellos, basses

(About 11 min)

Adagio
(slow introduction)   1   *a.* Cellos, *pp*, downward phrases. Horns.

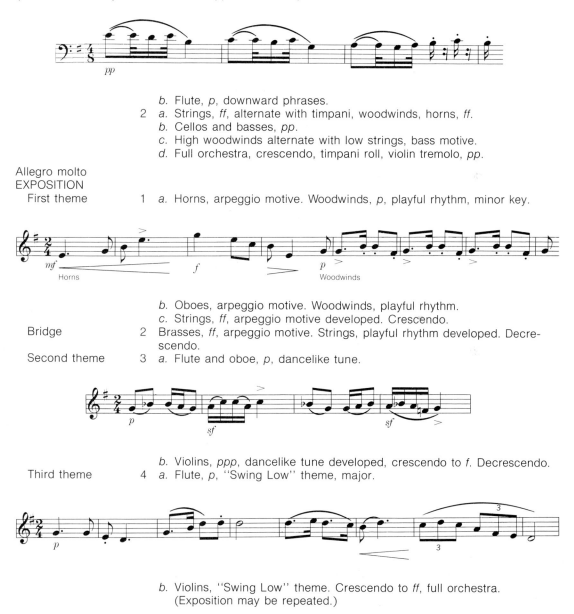

                           b. Flute, *p*, downward phrases.
          2   *a.* Strings, *ff*, alternate with timpani, woodwinds, horns, *ff*.
               b. Cellos and basses, *pp*.
               c. High woodwinds alternate with low strings, bass motive.
               d. Full orchestra, crescendo, timpani roll, violin tremolo, *pp*.

Allegro molto
EXPOSITION
   First theme   1   *a.* Horns, arpeggio motive. Woodwinds, *p*, playful rhythm, minor key.

                           b. Oboes, arpeggio motive. Woodwinds, playful rhythm.
                           c. Strings, *ff*, arpeggio motive developed. Crescendo.
   Bridge   2   Brasses, *ff*, arpeggio motive. Strings, playful rhythm developed. Decrescendo.
   Second theme   3   *a.* Flute and oboe, *p*, dancelike tune.

                           b. Violins, *ppp*, dancelike tune developed, crescendo to *f*. Decrescendo.
   Third theme   4   *a.* Flute, *p*, "Swing Low" theme, major.

                           b. Violins, "Swing Low" theme. Crescendo to *ff*, full orchestra.
                           (Exposition may be repeated.)

327

DEVELOPMENT

1   Strings, decrescendo.
2   *a.* Horn, *p*, "Swing Low" motive, piccolo. Crescendo.
     b. Trumpets, *f*, "Swing Low" motive. Trombones, *f*, arpeggio motive. Horns, *ff*. Strings, *ff*.
     c. Trombones, *ff*, arpeggio motive. High violins, *ff*. Rhythm quickens.
3   Oboes, *p*, arpeggio motive, flute. Crescendo.

RECAPITULATION

First theme
1   *a.* Horns, *mf*, arpeggio motive. Woodwinds, *p*, playful rhythm, minor.
     b. Oboes, arpeggio motive. Woodwinds, *p*, playful rhythm.
     c. Strings, *ff*, arpeggio motive developed. Decrescendo.

Second theme
2   *a.* Flute, *p*, dancelike tune.
     b. Woodwinds, *p*, dancelike tune. Strings, dancelike tune developed, crescendo to *ff*. Decrescendo.

Third theme
3   *a.* Flute, *p*, "Swing Low" theme, major.
     b. Violins, "Swing Low" theme. Crescendo.

CODA
1   *a.* Full orchestra, *fff*. "Swing Low" and arpeggio motives, minor.
     b. Repeated chords, *ff*, at end.

Second Movement: Largo

After introductory chords, we hear the famous Largo melody, which has a nostalgic quality heightened by the timbre of the English horn. Dvořák uses tone color expressively throughout the second movement, frequently passing musical ideas among different instruments. The Largo is in the form A B–Bridge–A'. Its gentle mood is broken only in the bridge, which contains a climactic quotation of motives from the first movement.

LISTENING OUTLINE

To be read while music is heard

Symphony No. 9 in E Minor, "From the New World" (1893), by Antonin Dvořák

Second Movement: Largo

A B–bridge–A' form, quadruple meter ($\frac{4}{4}$), D-flat major

2 flutes, 2 oboes, English horn, 2 clarinets, 2 bassoons, 4 horns, 2 trumpets, 3 trombones, tuba, timpani, violins 1, violins 2, violas, cellos, basses

(About 14½ min)

Introduction
1   Brasses and woodwinds, *pp*, solemn chords. Crescendo and decrescendo.
2   Muted strings, *ppp*.

A
1   *a.* English horn, *p*, main melody, major key.

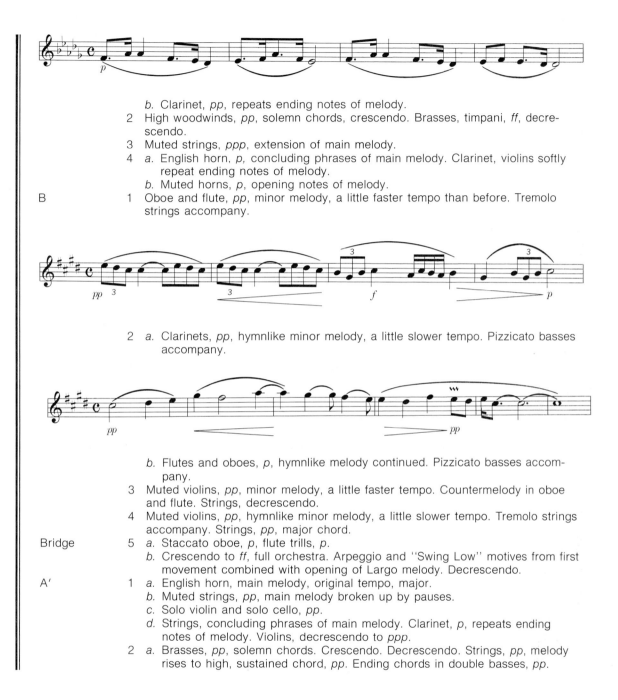

b. Clarinet, *pp*, repeats ending notes of melody.

2 High woodwinds, *pp*, solemn chords, crescendo. Brasses, timpani, *ff*, decrescendo.

3 Muted strings, *ppp*, extension of main melody.

4 a. English horn, *p,* concluding phrases of main melody. Clarinet, violins softly repeat ending notes of melody.

   b. Muted horns, *p*, opening notes of melody.

B 1 Oboe and flute, *pp*, minor melody, a little faster tempo than before. Tremolo strings accompany.

2 a. Clarinets, *pp*, hymnlike minor melody, a little slower tempo. Pizzicato basses accompany.

   b. Flutes and oboes, *p*, hymnlike melody continued. Pizzicato basses accompany.

3 Muted violins, *pp*, minor melody, a little faster tempo. Countermelody in oboe and flute. Strings, decrescendo.

4 Muted violins, *pp*, hymnlike minor melody, a little slower tempo. Tremolo strings accompany. Strings, *pp*, major chord.

Bridge 5 a. Staccato oboe, *p*, flute trills, *p*.

   b. Crescendo to *ff*, full orchestra. Arpeggio and "Swing Low" motives from first movement combined with opening of Largo melody. Decrescendo.

A' 1 a. English horn, main melody, original tempo, major.

   b. Muted strings, *pp*, main melody broken up by pauses.

   c. Solo violin and solo cello, *pp*.

   d. Strings, concluding phrases of main melody. Clarinet, *p*, repeats ending notes of melody. Violins, decrescendo to *ppp*.

2 a. Brasses, *pp*, solemn chords. Crescendo. Decrescendo. Strings, *pp*, melody rises to high, sustained chord, *pp*. Ending chords in double basses, *pp*.

Third Movement: Scherzo (Molto vivace)

The exciting Scherzo breathes the spirit of dancing. Its form is outlined: A (scherzo)–Bridge–B (trio)–Bridge–A (scherzo)–Coda. Motives from the first

Symphony No. 9 in E Minor

329

movement are recalled in the bridge to the trio and in the coda. The opening part of the scherzo (A) section, in minor, has great rhythmic drive and features a short motive which chases itself in close imitation.

Dvořák then relaxes the tension with a lilting legato melody in a major key; the charm is heightened by delicate strokes of the triangle.

In the bridge to the trio (B), the cellos recall the arpeggio motive from the first movement.

The trio (B) section, in major, features two staccato dance tunes that might be performed by a town band. The first is softly played by the woodwinds with the triangle accompanying.

The second tune, graced by delightful trills, alternates between violins and woodwinds.

The scherzo section (A) is played again, and then we hear a dramatic string tremolo that ushers in the coda. Horns vigorously recalling the arpeggio motive are whimsically answered by *p* woodwinds playing the scherzo motive. The movement fades into silence before ending with a powerful chord for full orchestra.

Fourth Movement: Allegro con fuoco (allegro with fire)

The *New World Symphony* ends with a sonata-form finale of great power and splendor. Dvořák skillfully combines finale themes with motives from the earlier three movements.

After a brief string introduction, the horns and trumpets proclaim the first theme, which sounds like a proud march song.

A solo clarinet presents the yearning second theme, accompanied by a cello countermelody in faster time values.

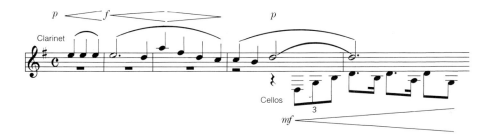

The third theme, jubilant and folklike, ends with a three-tone descending figure that resembles "Three Blind Mice."

Dvořák plays with the three-tone figure, shifting it from low to high instruments and embellishing it with humorous variations.

In the develoment, motives from preceding movements are quoted and varied. Flutes and clarinets softly recall the Largo melody, which is combined with the marchlike finale theme and reminiscences of the Scherzo. A crescendo builds to the opening of the recapitulation, as brasses proclaim the marchlike theme. The remainder of the recapitulation is subdued in dynamics, and from it the coda emerges as a passionate and triumphant summary of the whole symphony.

Symphony No. 9 in E Minor

15 | JOHANNES BRAHMS

Johannes Brahms (1833–1897) was a Romantic who poured new life into Classical forms. He was born in Hamburg, Germany, where his father made a precarious living as a string bass player. At thirteen, Brahms led a double life: During the day he studied piano, music theory, and composition; at night he played dance music for prostitutes and their clients in waterfront bars. Brahms's first concert tour when he was twenty gave him a chance to meet two of the greatest living composers, Liszt and Schumann. The contact with Liszt was not helpful. Brahms, a product of conservative musical education, was repelled by what he considered the bombast and lack of form in Liszt's music.

Schumann, on the other hand, was to shape the course of Brahms's artistic and personal life. Moments after presenting himself at Schumann's home, Brahms began to play one of his own piano sonatas. At the end of the first movement, Schumann called his wife Clara, the famous piano virtuoso, and they listened enthusiastically to Brahms's music for hours. Four weeks later, Schumann published a magazine article hailing young Brahms as a musical Messiah "called to give ideal expression to his time." Brahms was both overjoyed and apprehensive about his overnight fame. "The open praise which you gave me," he wrote Schumann, "has probably excited the expectations of the public to such a degree that I don't know how I can come anywhere near fulfilling them."

As Brahms was preparing new works for an eager publisher, Schumann had a recurrence of his nervous illness and tried to drown himself. He was committed to an asylum, leaving Clara Schumann with seven children to support. Brahms rushed to her aid and helped care for the children while she went on concert tours to earn money. For two years Brahms lived in the Schumann home, becoming increasingly involved with Clara, who was fourteen years older. The conflict between his loyalty to Robert and his passion for Clara may well have accounted for the stormy music he wrote at the time. Robert Schumann's death left Brahms and Clara Schumann free to marry, yet they did not. Since they destroyed many of their letters, we'll never know what passed between them. A few months later they separated, remaining lifelong intimate friends. Brahms never married; for him, Clara Schumann was "the most beautiful experience of my life."

Brahms desperately wanted to become conductor of the Philharmonic Orchestra in Hamburg, his birthplace. When he was passed over for the post in 1862, the disappointment was overwhelming. "For me this was much sadder even than you can possibly imagine," he wrote Clara Schumann, "perhaps even sadder than you can understand." He left his native city to settle in Vienna, where he spent the last thirty-five years of his life. For several years he conducted a Viennese musical society and introduced many forgotten masterpieces by Bach, Handel, and Mozart to the public. Brahms had a wide knowledge of older music; he edited Baroque and Classical compositions, and he was an ardent collector of music manuscripts.

Schumann published a magazine article hailing young Johannes Brahms as a musical Messiah "called to give ideal expression to his time" (Omikron).

His intimate knowledge of past masterpieces made Brahms extremely critical of his own work. Once, after a violinist played a Bach piece, he threw his own music to the floor, exclaiming, "After that, how could anyone play such stuff as this!" Brahms was obsessed by Beethoven. "You have no idea," he told a friend, "how the likes of us feel when we hear the tramp of a giant like him behind us." He worked at his First Symphony on and off for twenty years and completed it only when he was forty-three. Brahms endlessly revised compositions and sent them to friends for advice and criticism. He sent some songs to Clara Schumann with the request, "Write me if possible one short word about each . . . such as: Op. 10, No. 5, bad, No. 6, shameful, No. 7 ridiculous."

In 1879 an honorary doctoral degree from Breslau University calling Brahms "the first among today's masters" provoked a venomous attack from Richard

 Johannes Brahms

Wagner, who sneered, "Compose, compose, even if you don't have the slightest of ideas!" Music critics of the time pitted Brahms's fondness for traditional forms against Wagner's innovative music dramas. Actually, their musical paths hardly ever crossed; Brahms never wrote opera, Wagner's special territory.

Brahms always lived frugally, even though he earned a good income from publishers and from playing and conducting his works. He hid a shy, sensitive nature behind a mask of sarcasm and rudeness. On leaving a party, he reportedly announced, "If there is anyone here I have not insulted, I apologize!" Yet this gruff bear could be extremely generous to talented young musicians. He helped Dvořák find a publisher, and the grateful Czech composer wrote: "I am so overcome by his kindness that I cannot help but love him! What a warm heart and great spirit there is in that man!"

When Brahms's beloved Clara Schumann lay dying in 1896, his grief found expression in the haunting *Four Serious Songs,* set to biblical texts. Not long after, it was discovered that he had cancer; on March 7, 1897, he dragged himself to hear a performance of his Fourth Symphony. The audience and orchestra gave him a tremendous ovation. Less than a month later, at the age of sixty-four, he died.

Brahm's Music

Brahms created masterpieces in all the traditional forms except opera. His varied output includes four symphonies, two concertos for piano and one for violin, short piano pieces, over two hundred songs, and magnificent choral music such as the *German Requiem* (1868). Some of Brahms's finest music may be found in the two dozen chamber works written for many different instrumental combinations, including duo sonatas for cello and piano (Op. 38 and Op. 99), a trio for violin, horn, and piano (Op. 40), and a quintet for clarinet and strings (Op. 115).

Brahms's works, though very personal in style, are rooted deeply in the music of Haydn, Mozart, and Beethoven. They reinterpret Classical forms while using the harmonic and instrumental resources of Brahms's own time. Brahms was the greatest master of theme-and-variations form since Beethoven. He wrote variations which sound completely different from their thematic source, while retaining the theme's basic structure. We'll study this aspect of Brahms's art in the *Variations on a Theme by Haydn* for orchestra (Op. 56a).

While Brahms's music embraces a range of moods, it particularly has an autumnal or world-weary feeling and a sense of lyrical warmth. Lyricism pervades even the rich polyphonic textures he was so fond of. One Brahms scholar has aptly observed, "It is possible to sing every Brahms movement from beginning to end as though it were a single, uninterrupted melody. Through all its polyphonic intricacies, the clear flow of invention always remains distinctly recognizable."

Among Romantics, Brahms is outstanding in his ability to make intricate polyphonic texture sound natural and spontaneous. In his twenties, he and a violinist friend gave each other difficult contrapuntal exercises to correct. "Why shouldn't we two serious and intelligent people," Brahms wrote, "be able to teach each other better than some professor could?"

All of Brahms's music is rhythmically exciting. Contrasting rhythmic patterns are set against one another; one instrument plays two even notes to the beat, while another plays three. The use of "two against three," as this rhythmic technique is called, is one of Brahms's trademarks. He also delights in all sorts of syncopations and in phrases of irregular length that push against the prevailing meter.

The quality of sound in Brahms's music is very special. He liked rich, dark tone colors. In his orchestral music, he usually blended the different instrumental choirs, favoring mellow instruments like the viola, clarinet, and French horn. (It's characteristic of Brahms's feeling for tradition that he preferred the old-fashioned hunting-type horn to the modern horn with valves.) The rich sound often results from his practice of doubling melodies in thirds and sixths; the same melody is duplicated at the interval of a third or sixth.

All of Brahms's music radiates the security and solidity of a complete master. He justified Schumann's prediction of greatness for the "young eagle."

Variations on a Theme by Haydn for Orchestra, Op. 56a (1873) *Side 11, band 1*

These Variations have an unusual history. One of Brahms's friends, an eminent music historian, showed him a score for wind instruments thought to be by Haydn. Brahms was fascinated by the second movement, entitled "Chorale St. Antoni," probably a traditional Austrian pilgrim song. He copied the Chorale into his notebook and three years later, in 1873, used it as the theme for a set of variations. Today scholars doubt that the Chorale really is by Haydn, but Brahms's composition is still called by its original title. Brahms wrote the Variations in two versions: one for orchestra, which we'll consider, and one for two pianos (Op. 56b).

The work consists of a theme, eight variations, and an extended finale. The theme is like a processional, with moderate tempo (Andante) and clear duple meter. Brahms based his orchestration on the original scoring for wind band. He uses woodwinds and brasses, with no strings except pizzicato cellos and double basses to reinforce the lowest line. The form of the theme may be outlined as: a (repeated) ba′ (repeated). The opening phrases are each five measures, rather than the usual four.

Variations on a Theme by Haydn

335

Each variation is unique and differs in mood from the simple theme. Together, they vary in tempo, meter, rhythm, and orchestration. Two are in minor, though the theme is in major. Most astonishing is how Brahms disguises the original melody. Many variations sound completely new, though some original tones are retained. Brahms's delight in disguising a theme was noted by contemporaries. When he grew a beard one summer, a friend joked that Brahms's face was now as hard to recognize under the beard as the theme in his variations.

The variations maintain the basic form, harmonies, and phrase structure of the theme. Some concentrate on particular features of the theme, such as the dotted rhythm (long-short) of the opening notes, or the repeated chords of the closing bar. Though separated by brief pauses, each variation seems to arise naturally from what precedes, either through contrast or continuation of mood.

Variation 1: Poco più animato (a little more animated)

The woodwinds and brasses intone the series of repeated notes that rounded off the theme. In the strings, there is an interweaving of flowing melodic lines.

Variation 2: Più vivace

Variation 2 is based on the dotted rhythm (long-short) heard at the beginning of the theme. Patterns like long-short-long-short are heard throughout. A loud, abrupt idea is repeatedly followed by softer phrases that are dancelike or lyrical.

Variation 3: Con moto

Now the original theme is transformed into a legato, even-flowing melody introduced by the oboe and repeated by the violins.

The second part of the variation features a beautiful interplay among the horn, woodwinds, and strings.

Variation 4: Andante con moto

The mood darkens in Variation 4, which presents a new melody in a minor key. Throughout, a more quick-flowing countermelody accompanies the main melody, either below or above it.

Variation 5: Vivace

This joking, rhythmically animated music, in major, provides emotional release from the melancholy of Variation 4. It contains much syncopation and is brightened by the sound of high, staccato woodwinds.

Variation 6: Vivace

The original theme is more easily recognized in this variation, which is festive like the preceding one. It opens with a horn phrase that is answered by the woodwinds. In the second part of this variation, the full orchestra is heard for the first time, producing a vibrant, heroic sound.

Variation 7: Grazioso (gracefully)

A relaxed feeling pervades this variation, which has a rocking sextuple meter ($\frac{6}{8}$; 1–2–3–4–5–6); it is subdued in dynamics. The graceful new melody played by strings and flute has a rhythm traditionally associated with pastoral scenes.

Variation 8: Presto non troppo

Hushed, mysterious, and in a minor key, this variation moves so quickly that it is over almost before we know it. Scurrying figures alternate between muted strings and high woodwinds.

Finale (ground bass, or passacaglia): Andante

In the extended Finale, Brahms uses the Baroque ground bass form (also called passacaglia) that we've heard in works by Purcell and Bach. (Brahms also used a ground bass to stunning effect in the Finale of his Fourth Symphony.) A five-bar musical idea derived from the theme is presented seventeen times in a row, mostly in the bass.

Variations on a Theme by Haydn

337

Over this repeated idea, Brahms weaves imaginative variations that flow smoothly into one another. Like the Baroque masters he revered, Brahms focuses the listener's attention on the ever-changing melodic lines, rather than on the repeated ground bass.

The finale begins in a calm, hymnlike mood and soon builds to a climax through a rise in pitch and dynamic level. After the climax, there is a relaxed, lyrical interlude in which a syncopated oboe solo is followed by a winding, legato melody in the flute. Then a shift from major to minor brings a momentary darkening of mood. The five-bar idea is transferred from the bass to a high register, where it is played in turn by the oboe and violins. The dark minor soon gives way to a bright major, as the main theme, the "Chorale St. Antoni," triumphantly returns in the full orchestra. Now embellished by triangle strokes and high woodwind scales, the theme brings the Finale to a brilliant and joyous conclusion.

Romantic

16 ‖ GIUSEPPE VERDI

The most popular of all opera composers, Giuseppe Verdi (1813–1901) was born in a tiny Italian village. His father was a poor tavern keeper who could neither read nor write. At the age of ten, Verdi went to live in a nearby town, Busseto, to study music and go to school. Every Sunday for nine years, he walked three miles barefoot to serve as church organist in his own village, carrying his shoes to preserve them. A wealthy music patron took Verdi into his home and later supported his studies in Milan. Finishing his music education at twenty-two, Verdi returned to Busseto and became municipal music director. Thus assured of a regular income, he was able to marry his patron's daughter, a young woman he had known and loved since childhood.

But the small town couldn't fulfill Verdi's needs for long. After three years he returned to Milan with the score of his first opera, *Oberto* (1839). With the help of an influential friend, the young provincial's work was produced at La Scala, Italy's most important opera house. Though response to *Oberto* was only modest, it was enough to win Verdi a contract for three more operas. Just when Verdi's future seemed bright, disaster struck. While he was working on his next opera—a comedy—his wife fell ill and died. This tragedy completed the destruction of his family, since two infant children had died within the previous two years. Verdi managed to complete the opera, but it understandably lacked inspiration and was greeted by boos and hisses. In despair, he vowed to compose no more.

He changed his mind after reading a libretto about the ancient Jews exiled from their homeland. Verdi was an ardent nationalist who yearned to see the Italian people free from Austrian domination and unified into one nation. For

The Romantic
Period

338

Giuseppe Verdi was one of the greatest opera composers and an ardent Italian nationalist (Brown Brothers).

him, the ancient Jews symbolized the enslaved Italians. He quickly composed *Nabucco* (Nebuchadnezzar, King of Babylon), which was an enormous success. One melody, "Oh my country so beautiful and lost!" became a national liberation hymn sung by all Italian patriots. From that time on, Verdi and his operas symbolized a free and united Italy. A poet wrote that "the very soul of Italy . . . has today its voice in the name of Giuseppe Verdi." As Italy approached war with Austria, the cry "Viva Verdi" stood also for the patriotic slogan, *Vittorio Emmanuele Re D'Italia* (Victor Emmanuel, King of Italy).

In his late thirties, Verdi composed *Rigoletto* (1851), *Il Trovatore* (1853), and *La Traviata* (1853), the first of his operas which are now universally known. While the

Giuseppe Verdi

339

public loved these works, critics were often scandalized by their subject matter. *Rigoletto* seemed to condone rape and suicide, while *La Traviata* glorified free love and made a heroine out of a kept woman. But Verdi was a fiercely independent man, who himself lived openly with his second wife for ten years before marrying her.

Now wealthy, Verdi bought an estate at Busseto. He was elected deputy to the first Italian parliament in 1861 after Italy had become a nation. Verdi was Italy's most famous native son when he wrote *Aïda* (1871), an opera written to commemorate the completion of the Suez Canal. In 1887, the seventy-three-year-old Verdi had a triumphant success with *Otello,* one of his greatest operas. Even this masterpiece did not still his creative urge. At the incredible age of seventy-nine, Verdi completed *Falstaff* (1893), his first comedy since the failure of his second opera fifty years earlier.

Verdi's Music

"In the theater," Verdi once wrote, "lengthy is synonymous with boring, and of all styles the boring style is the worst." He composed not for the musical elite, but for a mass public whose main entertainment was opera. Verdi wanted subjects that were "original, interesting . . . and passionate; passions above all!" An aria "needs the greatest variety of mood; irony, contempt, rage, all thrown into sharp profile." Almost all of Verdi's mature works are serious and end unhappily. The operas move fast and involve characters who are plunged quickly into extremes of hatred, love, jealousy, and fear. His powerful music summons up heroes and villains and vividly underlines dramatic situations.

Expressive vocal melody is the soul of a Verdi opera. No matter how elaborate or atmospheric the orchestral part, the musical center lies in the voice. There are many duets, trios, and quartets, in which each character is given melodies superbly tailored to the emotions depicted. Choruses—of gypsies, Egyptian priests, conspirators, and monks, for example—play an important role in his operas.

In the course of a long life, Verdi's style became less conventional, more subtle and flexible. His later works have greater musical continuity. He used fewer pauses between sections and lessened the difference between aria and recitative. His orchestration became more imaginative and the accompaniments richer.

Verdi's last three operas are perhaps his greatest. *Aïda* is a true "grand opera" with spectacular pageants, ballets, and choruses. Yet for all its spectacle, there are many scenes of tender and intimate beauty. *Otello* and *Falstaff,* the operas of Verdi's old age, have marvelous librettos based on the plays by Shakespeare. The librettist was Arrigo Boito, himself a gifted opera composer. For *Otello,* the seventy-three-year-old Verdi wrote sensuous, overpowering music that completely fuses with the poetry and action. The opera rivals Shakespeare's play in its dramatic force and lyricism. Verdi's last opera, *Falstaff,* is incomparably witty, imaginative, and sparkling. The aged composer ended this comic masterwork with a carefree fugue to the words, "All the world's a joke!"

Rigoletto (1851)

Verdi dared to create an operatic hero out of a hunchback, a court jester named Rigoletto, whose only redeeming quality is an intense love for his daughter Gilda. Rigoletto's master, the licentious Duke of Mantua, has won Gilda's love while posing as a poor student. He seduces the innocent girl, causing Rigoletto to plot his death. Gilda loves the Duke even after learning about his dissolute character, and she ultimately sacrifices her own life to save his. Vice triumphs in this powerful drama.

Act III: *La donna è mobile* and Quartet

Act III of *Rigoletto* contains two of the most popular pieces in opera, the Duke's aria *La donna è mobile* and the Quartet. The scene is a run-down inn where the Duke has come to meet Maddalena, voluptuous sister of the cutthroat Sparafucile.

The carefree and tuneful *La donna è mobile* ("Woman is fickle") perfectly expresses the Duke's pleasure-loving personality. Even before *Rigoletto*'s premiere in Venice, Verdi knew that *La donna è mobile* would be a hit. Afraid that his catchy tune would leak out during rehearsals and be sung by every Venetian gondolier, he waited until the last possible moment before giving it to the tenor.

The Quartet is sung as Rigoletto and Gilda peer through a crack in the wall of the inn, observing the Duke flirting with Maddalena. Verdi projects four conflicting emotions at one time, characterizing each singer with an appropriate melodic line. The Duke attempts to seduce Maddalena with a suave and ardent legato melody. Maddalena coquettishly repels his advances with quick, staccato laughs. Outside the inn, Gilda laments her fate with anguished sobs punctuated by rests, while Rigoletto curses and mutters threats of vengeance in repeated notes. Verdi lets us hear each voice separately before combining them in a glorious ensemble.

Aria. Orchestra
introduces
Duke's
melody.

Duke

La donna è mobile	Woman is fickle
Qual piuma al vento,	Like a feather in the wind,
Muta d'accento	She changes her words
E di pensiero.	And her thoughts.

Rigoletto
(1851)

Sempre un amabile	Always a lovable	
Leggiadro viso,	And lovely face,	
In pianto o in riso,	Weeping or laughing,	
È menzognero.	Is lying.	
La donna è mobil, ecc.	Woman is fickle, etc.	
		Orchestra.
È sempre misero	The man's always	Duke's
	wretched	melody
Chi a lei s'affida,	Who believes in her,	repeated with
Chi le confida	Who recklessly entrusts	different
Mal cauto il core!	His heart to her!	words.
Pur mai non sentesi	And yet one who never	
Felice appieno	Drinks love on that breast	
Chi su quel seno	Never feels	
Non liba amore!	Entirely happy!	
La donna è mobil, ecc.	Woman is fickle, etc.	

Sparafucile comes back in with a bottle of wine and two glasses, which he sets on the table; then he strikes the ceiling twice with the hilt of his long sword. At this signal, a laughing young girl, in a gypsy dress, leaps down the stairs: the Duke runs to embrace her, but she escapes him. Meanwhile Sparafucile has gone out into the road, where he says softly to Rigoletto: — Duke's melody in orchestra, decrescendo.

Sparafucile

È là vostr'uomo . . .	Your man is there . . .
Viver dee o morire?	Must he live or die?

Rigoletto

Più tardi tornerò l'opra a compire	I'll return later to complete the deed.

Sparafucile goes off behind the house toward the river. Gilda and Rigoletto remain in the street, the Duke and Maddalena on the ground floor. — Brief pause.

Duke

Un dì, se ben rammentomi,	One day, if I remember right,
O bella, t'incontrai . . .	I met you, O beauty . . .
Mi piacque di te chiedere,	I was pleased to ask about you,
E intesi che qui stai.	And I learned that you live here.
Or sappi, che d'allora	Know then, that since that time
Sol te quest'alma adora!	My soul adores only you!

Allegro.

Gilda

Iniquo!	Villain!

Maddalena

Ah, ah! . . . e vent'altre appresso	Ha, ha! . . . And does it now perhaps

Le scorda forse adesso?	Forget twenty others?	
Ha un'aria il signorino	The young gentleman looks like	
Da vero libertino . . .	A true libertine . . .	

Duke (*starting to embrace her*)

Si . . . un mostro son . . .	Yes . . . I'm a monster . . .	

Gilda

Ah padre mio!	Ah, Father!	

Maddalena

Lasciatemi, stordito.	Let me go, foolish man!	

Duke

Ih, che fracasso!	Ah, what a fuss!	

Maddalena

Stia saggio.	Be good.	

Duke

E tu sii docile,	And you, be yielding,	
Non fare tanto chiasso.	Don't make so much noise.	
Ogni saggezza chiudesi	All wisdom concludes	Rhythm slows.
Nel gaudio e nell'amore.	In pleasure and in love.	

(*He takes her hand.*)
La bella mano candida!	What a lovely, white hand!	Quick rhythm resumes.

Maddalena

Scherzate voi, signore.	You're joking, sir.	

Duke

No, no.	No, no.	

Maddalena

Son brutta.	I'm ugly.	

Duke

Abbracciami.	Embrace me.	

Gilda

Iniquo!	Villain!	

Maddalena

Ebro!	You're drunk!	

Duke

D'amor ardente	With ardent love!	

Maddalena

Signor l'indifferente,	My indifferent sir,	
Vi piace canzonar?	Do you enjoy teasing?	

Duke

No, no, ti vo'sposar.	No, no, I want to marry you.	

Maddalena

Ne voglio la parola.	I want your word.	

 Rigoletto (1851)

343

	Duke (*ironic*)	
Amabile figliuola!	Lovable maiden!	

Rigoletto

(*To Gilda, who has seen and heard all*)

E non ti basta ancor?	Isn't that enough for you yet?	

Gilda

Iniquo traditor!	Villainous betrayer!	Characters sing simultaneously.

Maddalena

Ne voglio la parola.	I want your word.	

Duke

Amabile figliuola!	Lovable maiden!	

Rigoletto

E non ti basta ancor?	Isn't that enough for you yet?	Short pause.

Duke

Bella figlia dell'amore,	Beautiful daughter of love,	Quartet, Andante.

Schiavo son de' vezzi tuoi;	I am the slave of your charms;
Con un detto sol tu puoi	With a single word you can
Le mie pene consolar.	Console my sufferings.

Vieni, e senti del mio core	Come, and feel the quick beating
Il frequente palpitar . . .	Of my heart . . .
Con un detto sol tu puoi	With a single word you can
Le mie pene consolar.	Console my sufferings.

Maddalena

Ah! ah! rido ben di core,	Ha! Ha! I laugh heartily,
Chè tai baie costan poco.	For such tales cost little.

Maddalena

Ah! ah! ri - do ben di co - re, chè tai ba - ie cos-tan po-co;

Gilda

Ah! così parlar d'amore . . . — Ah! To speak thus of love . . .

Gilda

Ah!_____ co - sì_____ par-lar_____ d'a-mo-re!

Maddalena

Quanto valga il vostro gioco,	Believe me, I can judge
Mel credete, so apprezzar.	How much your game is worth.

Gilda

. . . a me pur l'infame ho udito!	. . . I too have heard the villain so!

Rigoletto (*to Gilda*)

Taci, il piangere non vale. — Hush, weeping is of no avail.

Rigoletto

Ta - ci, il pian-ge- re non va - le;

Gilda

Infelice cor tradito,	Unhappy, betrayed heart.	Characters sing simultaneously.
Per angoscia non scoppiar.	Do not burst with anguish.	
Ah, no!	Ah, no!	

Maddalena

Son avvezza, bel signore,	I'm accustomed, handsome sir,
Ad un simile scherzare.	To similar joking.
Mio bel signor!	My handsome sir!

Duke

Bella figlia dell'amore, ecc.	Beautiful daughter of love, etc.
Vieni!	Come!

Rigoletto

Ch'ei mentiva sei sicura.	You are sure that he was lying.
Taci, e mia sarà la cura	Hush, and I will take care
La vendetta d'affrettar.	To hasten vengeance.

Rigoletto
(1851)

345

Sì, pronto fia, sarà fatale,	Yes, it will be swift and fatal,
Io saprollo fulminar.	I will know how to strike him down.
Taci, taci . . .	Hush, hush . . .

17 | GIACOMO PUCCINI

Some of the best-loved operas were created by Giacomo Puccini (1858–1924), who succeeded Verdi as the leading Italian opera composer of his time. Puccini came from a long line of composers and church organists. During his student years at the Milan Conservatory (1880–1883), he lived a hand-to-mouth existence, usually eating on credit at a restaurant fittingly named Aïda. The success of his first opera, written shortly after graduation, brought him to the attention of Italy's leading music publisher, who commissioned new works and gave him an annual income.

In 1893 Puccini became well known throughout Italy because of *Manon Lescaut,* and after 1896, he was wealthy and world-famous from the enormous success of *La Bohème,* which presents a "Bohemian" life similar to Puccini's as an impoverished music student. *La Bohème,* along with two other very popular operas, *Tosca* (1900) and *Madame Butterfly* (1904), was writen in collaboration with the librettists Luigi Illica and Giuseppe Giacosa. Puccini was very concerned with the literary and dramatic qualities of his librettos, often demanding endless changes from his collaborators. He spent as much time polishing the librettos as he did composing the music. His last opera, *Turandot,* was based on a Chinese fairy tale. He died before finishing it; the work was completed from Puccini's sketches by a friend, Franco Alfano.

Puccini's marvelous sense of theater has given his operas lasting appeal. He knew just when to introduce new musical material or a moment of silence, and he was able to provide smooth transitions from one scene or mood to another. His melodies have short easy-to-remember phrases and are intensely emotional. He uses the orchestra to reinforce the vocal melody and to suggest atmosphere, landscape, and mood. As Verdi did in his late works, Puccini minimized the difference between aria and recitative, thus creating a continuous flow of music. He got unity and continuity also by using the same material in various acts, particularly when characters reflect on past events or emotions.

Some of Puccini's operas—notably *Tosca*—reflect an artistic trend of the 1890s known as *verismo,* "realism" or the quality of being "true to life." Operas related to this realistic movement deal with ordinary people rather than kings, gods, or great heroes, and often contain many shockingly violent scenes with music of raw emotional power. *Cavalleria rusticana* ("Rustic Chivalry," 1890) by Pietro Mas-

Giacomo Puccini became wealthy and world-famous from the enormous success of *La Bohème*, which presents a "Bohemian" life similar to his own as an impoverished music student (Brown Brothers).

cagni and *I Pagliacci* ("The Clowns," 1892) by Ruggiero Leoncavallo are other famous examples of *verismo*. Puccini's operas also feature exoticism. Not only is *Madame Butterfly* set in Japan and *Turandot* in China, but Puccini used melodic and rhythmic elements derived from Oriental music. His melodies cast a Romantic glow over any subject matter, whether realistic or exotic.

La Bohème (1896)

La Bohème ("Bohemian life") takes place in the Latin Quarter of Paris around 1830. Its hero is Rodolfo, a young poet who shares a garret with Marcello, a painter, Colline, a philosopher, and Schaunard, a musician. Mimi, the heroine, is a poor tubercular seamstress who lives in the same building. The simple, touching plot has been aptly summarized as "boy meets girl, boy loses girl, boy and girl are reunited as girl dies of consumption in boy's arms and curtain falls." Everyone can relate to the characters and emotions of this enchanting opera. Though there are many realistic touches in this picture of "Bohemian" life, it is seen through a Romantic haze.

Side 12, band 1

Act I: Scene between Rodolfo and Mimi

Toward the end of Act I, Mimi and Rodolfo meet and fall in love. Her candle has blown out, and she knocks on his door asking for a light. After a short musical conversation, Mimi realizes she has lost her key, and they both search for it in the dark. When their hands touch, Rodolfo sings the aria, *Che gelida manina* ("What a cold little hand"). He sings about himself, his dreams and his fantasies. Mimi responds with a poetic description of her simple life in the aria, *Mi chiamano Mimi* ("They call me Mimi"). Under the spell of their new-found love, they join in a duet which closes the act.

Puccini's sensuous melody casts a glow over the entire scene. His music has an improvisatory quality due to many fluctuations of tempo. When Mimi enters, the orchestra murmurs a touching phrase, the Mimi theme, which suggests her fragility and tenderness. Each aria begins simply, almost in conversation. Then the melody grows warmer until it reaches a climax in a broad, passionate phrase. The climactic phrase of Rodolfo's aria, sung to the word's, *Talor dal mio forziere* ("My hoard of treasure is robbed by two thieves: a pair of beautiful eyes"), is the love theme of the whole opera. Mimi's emotional high point is reached when she dreams about the end of winter (*ma quando vien la sgelo*), when "the first kiss of April" is hers. Returning to reality at the end of her aria, she sings in conversational repeated tones. The tension breaks momentarily as Rodolfo has a brief exchange with his friends in the courtyard—an example of Puccini's great theatrical timing, for he provides a moment of relaxation before the lovers join in the closing duet. First, Rodolfo sings alone, then both voices beautifully unite in a declaration of love.

Rodolfo closes the door, sets his light on the table, and tries to write. But he tears up the paper and throws the pen down.

Flute melody.

Rodolfo

Non sono in vena. — I'm not in the mood.

A timid knock at the door.

Chi è la? — Who's there?

Speechlike.

Mimi

Scusi. — Excuse me . . .

Rodolfo

Una donna! — A woman!

Mimi

Di grazia, mi si è spento Il lume. — I'm sorry . . . my light Has gone out.

Mimi theme, *pp,* in orchestra.

Rodolfo

Ecco. — (*opens*) Here.

Mimi

(in the doorway, with a candle-stick and a key)

Vorrebbe . . .? — Would you . . .?

Rodolfo

S'accomodi un momento. — Come in for a moment.

Mimi

Non occorre. — There's no need.

Rodolfo

La prego, entri. — Please . . . come in.

Mimi enters, has a fit of coughing.

Faster, agitated.

Rodolfo

Si sente male? — You're not well?

Mimi

No . . . nulla. — No . . . it's nothing.

Rodolfo

Impallidisce! — You're pale!

Mimi

È il respir . . . quelle scale . . . — I'm out of breath . . . the stairs . . .

She faints, and Rodolfo is just in time to support her and help her to a chair. The key and the candlestick fall from her hands.

Oboe.

Rodolfo

Ed ora come faccio? — Now what shall I do?

He gets some water and sprinkles her face.

Così. — So.

Che viso d'ammalata! — How ill she looks!

La Bohème (1896)

349

Mimi comes to.

<table>
<tr><td>*Si sente meglio?*</td><td>Are you better now?</td><td>Staccato muted
strings.</td></tr>
</table>

Mimi

Sì. | Yes.

Rodolfo

Qui c'è tanto freddo. It's so cold here.
Segga vicino al fuoco. Come and sit by the fire.

He helps her to a chair by the stove.

Aspetti . . . un po' di vino. Wait . . . some wine.

Mimi

Grazie. Thank you.

Rodolfo

A lei. Here.

Mimi

Poco, poco. Just a little.

Rodolfo

Così. There.

Mimi

Grazie. Thank you.

Rodolfo

Che bella bambina! What a lovely creature!

Mimi

Ora permetta Now, please,
Che accenda il lume. Relight my candle.
È tutto passato. I'm better now.

Rodolfo

Tanta fretta. Such a hurry.

Mimi

Sì. Yes.

Rodolfo lights her candle for her.

Mimi

Grazie. Buona sera. Thank you. Good evening.

Rodolfo

Buono sera. Good evening.

Mimi goes out, then reappears at the door.

Mimi

Oh! sventata, sventata, Oh! foolish me! . . .

A little faster.
Tuneful vocal
melody.

La chiave della stanza Where have I left
Dove l'ho lasciata? The key to my room?

Rodolfo

Non stia sull'uscio:	Don't stand in the door:
Il lume vacilla al vento.	The wind makes your light flicker.

Her candle goes out.

Mimi

Oh Dio! Torni ad accenderlo.	Heavens! Will you relight it?

    Rodolfo rushes to her with his light, but when he reaches the door, his candle goes out, too. The room is dark.

Rodolfo

Oh Dio! Anche il mio s'è spento.	There . . . Now mine's out, too.

Mimi

Ah! E la chiave ove sarà?	Ah! And where can my key be?

Rodolfo

Buio pesto!	Pitch dark!

Mimi

Disgraziata!	Unlucky me!

Rodolfo

Ove sarà?	Where can it be?

Mimi

Importuna è la vicina . . .	You've a bothersome neighbor . . .

Rodolfo

Ma le pare!	Not at all.

Mimi

Importuna è la vicina . . .	You've a bothersome neighbor . . .

Rodolfo

Cosa dice, ma le pare!	What do you mean? Not at all.

Mimi

Cerchi.	Search.

Rodolfo

Cerco.	I'm searching.

    They both grope on the floor for the key.

Mimi

Ove sarà?	Where can it be?

Rodolfo

Ah!	Ah! (*finds the key, pockets it*)

La Bohème
(1896)

351

	Mimi	
L'ha trovata?	Did you find it?	
	Rodolfo	
No.	No.	
	Mimi	
Mi parve . . .	I thought . . .	
	Rodolfo	
In verità!	Truthfully!	
	Mimi	
Cerca?	Are you hunting?	
	Rodolfo	
Cerco.	I'm hunting for it.	

Guided by her voice, Rodolfo pretends to search as he draws closer to her. Then his hand meets hers, and he holds it.

Orchestra alone, tempo slows.

	Mimi
Ah!	(*surprised*) Ah!

They rise. Rodolfo continues to hold Mimi's hand.

	Rodolfo	
Che gelida manina,	What a cold little hand,	Rodolfo's aria.
Se la lasci riscaldar.	Let me warm it.	

		Harp.
Cercar che giova? Al buio	What's the use of searching?	
Non si trova. Ma per fortuna	We'll never find it now.	
È una notte di luna,	But luckily there's a moon,	
E qui la luna l'abbiamo vicina.	And she's our neighbor here.	
Aspetti, signorina,	Just wait, my dear young lady,	
Le dirò con due parole chi son,	And meanwhile I'll tell you	
Chi son, e che faccio, come vivo.	In a word who and what I am.	
Vuole?	Shall I?	

Mimi is silent.

Chi son? Chi son? Son un poeta.	Who am I? I'm a poet.
Che cosa faccio? Scrivo.	My business? Writing.
E come vivo? Vivo.	How do I live? I live.
In povertà mia lieta	In my happy poverty
Scialo da gran signore	I squander like a prince
Rima ed inni d'amore.	My poems and songs of love.
Per sogni e per chimere	In hopes and dreams

E per castelli in aria	And castles in air,	
L'anima ho milionaria.	I'm a millionaire in spirit.	
Talor dal mio forziere	My hoard of treasure	Love theme.
Ruban tutti i gioielli	Is robbed by two thieves:	
Due ladri: gli occhi belli.	A pair of beautiful eyes.	

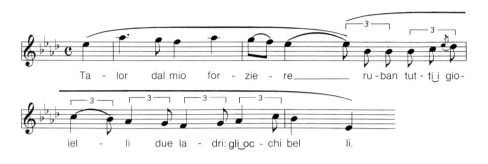

Ta - lor dal mio for - zie - re___ ru-ban tut - ti i gio-

iel - li due la - dri: gli oc - chi bel li.

V'entrar con voi pur ora	They came in now with you
Ed i miei sogni usati,	And all my lovely dreams,
Ed i bei sogni miei	My dreams of the past,
Tosto si dileguar!	Were soon stolen away.
Ma il furto non m'accora	But the theft doesn't upset me,
Poichè, poichè v'ha preso stanza	Since the empty place was filled
La speranza.	With hope.
Or che mi conoscete	Now that you know me,
Parlate voi. Deh parlate.	It's your turn to speak.
Chi siete? Vi piaccia dir?	Tell me, please, who are you?

Mimi

Sì.	Yes.	
Mi chiamano Mimì,	They call me Mimi,	Mimi's aria.
Ma il mio nome è Lucia.	But my real name is Lucia.	

Andante lento

Mi chia - ma - no Mi - mì, ma il mio no - me è Lu - ci - a___

La storia mia è breve.	My story is brief.
A tela o a seta	I embroider silk and satin
Ricamo in casa e fuori.	At home or outside.
Son tranquilla e lieta,	I'm tranquil and happy,
Ed è mio svago	And my pastime
Far gigli e rose.	Is making lilies and roses.
Mi piaccion quelle cose	I love all things

La Bohème
(1896)

353

Che han si dolce malia,	That have a gentle magic,
Che parlano d'amor, di prima- *vere,*	That talk of love, of spring,
Che parlano di sogni e di *chimere,*	That talk of dreams and fan- cies—
Quelle cose che han nome *poesia . . .*	The things called poetry . . .
Lei m'intende?	Do you understand me?

Rodolfo

Sì.	Yes.

Mimì

Mi chiamano Mimì.	They call me Mimi—
Il perchè non so.	I don't know why.
Sola, mi fo il pranzo	I live all by myself
Da me stessa.	And I eat all alone.
Non vado sempre a messa,	I don't often go to church,
Ma prego assai il Signor.	But I like to pray.
Vivo sola, soletta,	I stay all alone
Là in una bianca cameretta;	In my tiny white room,
Guardo sui tetti e in cielo.	I look at the roofs and the sky.
Ma quando vien lo sgelo	But when the thaw comes
Il primo sole è mio,	The first sunshine is mine,
Il primo bacio	The first kiss
Dell'aprile è mio!	Of April is mine!
Il primo sole è mio!	The first sunshine is mine!
Germoglia in un vaso una rosa,	A rose blossoms in my vase,
Foglia a foglia l'aspiro.	I breathe in its perfume,
Così gentil è il profumo d'un *fior.*	Petal by petal. So lovely,
Ma i fior ch'io faccio, ahimè,	So sweet is the flower's per- fume.
I fior ch'io faccio,	But the flowers I make,
Ahimè non hanno odore.	Alas, have no scent.
Altro di me non le saprei nar- *rare.*	What else can I say?
Sono la sua vicina	I'm your neighbor,
Che la vien fuori d'ora a impor- *tunare.*	Disturbing you at this impos- sible hour.

Schaunard

Eh! Rodolfo!	(*from below*) Hey! Rodolfo!

Colline

Rodolfo!	Rodolfo!

Marcello

Olà! Non senti?	Hey! Can't you hear?
Lumaca!	You snail!

Colline

Poetucolo!	You fake!

Schaunard

Accidenti al pigro!	To hell with that lazy one!

Rodolfo, impatient, goes to the window to answer. When the window is opened, the moonlight comes in, lighting up the room.

Rodolfo

Scrivo ancora tre righe a volo.	I've a few more words to write.

Mimi

Chi son?	Who are they?

Rodolfo

Amici.	Friends.

Schaunard

Sentirai le tue.	You'll hear about this.

Marcello

Che te ne fai lì solo?	What are you doing there alone?

Rodolfo

Non son solo. Siamo in due.	I'm not alone. There're two of us.
Andate da Momus, tenete il posto.	Go to Momus and get a table.
Ci saremo tosto.	We'll be there soon.

Marcello, Schaunard, Colline

Momus, Momus, Momus,	Momus, Momus, Momus.
Zitti e discreti andiamocene via.	Quietly, discreetly, we're off.
Momus, Momus, Momus.	Momus, Momus, Momus.
Trovò poesia.	He's found his poem at last.

Turning, Rodolfo sees Mimi wrapped in a halo of moonlight. He contemplates her, in ecstasy.

Rodolfo

O soave fanciulla, o dolce viso	Oh! lovely girl, oh! sweet face	Duet.
Di mite circonfuso alba lunar,	Bathed in the soft moonlight.	
In te, ravviso il sogno	I see in you the dream	
Ch'io vorrei sempre sognar!	I'd dream forever!	
Fremon già nell'anima	Already I taste in spirit	Voices unite, love theme.
Le dolcezze estreme,	The heights of tenderness!	
Amor nel bacio freme!	Love trembles in our kiss!	

Mimi

Ah, tu sol comandi, amore. . . .	Ah! Love, you rule alone. . . .
Oh! come dolci scendono	How sweet his praises
Le sue lusinghe al core. . . .	Enter my heart. . . .
Tu sol comandi, amore!	Love, yout alone rule!

Rodolfo kisses her.

La Bohème
(1896)

355

	Mimi	
No, per pietà!	No, please!	
	Rodolfo	
Sei mia!	You're mine!	
	Mimi	
V'aspettan gli amici. . . .	Your friends are waiting.	
	Rodolfo	
Già mi mandi via?	You send me away already?	
	Mimi	
Vorrei dir . . . ma non oso.	I daren't say what I'd like. . . .	
	Rodolfo	
Di'.	Tell me.	
	Mimi	
Se venissi con voi?	If I came with you?	
	Rodolfo	
Che? Mimì!	What? Mimi!	
Sarebbe così dolce restar qui.	It would be so fine to stay here.	
C'è freddo fuori.	Outside it's cold.	
	Mimi	
Vi starò vicina!	I'd be near you!	
	Rodolfo	
E al ritorno?	And when we come back?	
	Mimi	
Curioso!	Who knows?	
	Rodolfo	
Dammi il braccio, o mia piccina . . .	Give me your arm, my dear . . .	Melody from Rodolfo's aria.
	Mimi	
Obbedisco, signor!	Your servant, sir . . .	
	Rodolfo	
Che m'ami . . .di' . . .	Tell me you love me!	
	Mimi	
Io t'amo.	I love you.	
	Rodolfo	
Amor!	My love!	
	Mimi	
Amor!	My love!	
	Rodolfo and Mimi	
Amor!	Beloved!	

RICHARD WAGNER 18

Few composers have had so powerful an impact on their time as Richard Wagner (1813–1883). During the last decades of the nineteenth century, his operas and artistic philosophy influenced not only musicians, but poets, painters, and playwrights, too. Such was his preeminence that an opera house of his own design was built in Bayreuth, Germany, solely for performances of his music dramas.

Born in Leipzig, Wagner grew up in a theatrical atmosphere. Both his stepfather and two sisters were actors, and another sister was an opera singer. His boyhood dream was to be a poet and playwright. But at fifteen he was overwhelmed by the power of Beethoven's music, and he decided to become a composer. The young Wagner taught himself by studying scores. He never tried to master an instrument and had only six months of formal training in music theory.

When he was seventeen, Wagner enrolled in Leipzig University, where he was more interested in riotous student club life than in academic studies. His family thought him good for nothing because of his dueling, drinking, and gambling. The pattern continued throughout his life; Wagner shamelessly lived off other people and accumulated enormous debts that he never repaid.

During his early twenties, Wagner conducted in small German theaters, wrote several operas, and married Minna Planer, a beautiful and well-known actress. In 1839 he decided to try his luck in Paris, then the center of grand opera. Unpaid debts prevented his getting a passport, and so he and Minna illegally crossed the frontier. Their two years in Paris were miserable. Unable to get an opera performed, Wagner was reduced to musical hack work. He ran up such bills that he was briefly confined to a debtors' prison.

Wagner returned to Germany in 1842 to supervise the production of *Rienzi* at the Dresden opera. The work was immensely successful, and Wagner was appointed conductor of the Dresden opera, a lifetime position with a good salary. He spent six years there, becoming famous both as an opera composer and as a great conductor. Wagner demanded that his orchestra play with enormous dynamic subtlety and rhythmic freedom. "When he conducts," a musician observed, "he is almost beside himself with excitement. . . . Every sinew in his body speaks. His whole appearance is of arrogance and despotism personified."

The revolutions of 1848 swept across Europe like a forest fire and marked an important turning point in Wagner's career. His life in Dresden had become increasingly difficult because of debts he had again accumulated (he owed more than ten times his annual salary). Hoping that a new society would wipe out his debts and produce conditions favorable to his art, Wagner participated in the Dresden insurrection. He ordered hand grenades and tried to incite disobedience among the king's soldiers. When a warrant was issued for his arrest, Wagner fled to Switzerland.

Richard
Wagner

357

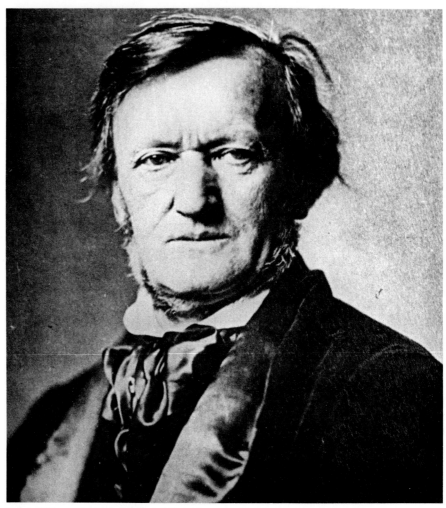
Richard Wagner's operas and artistic philosophy had a powerful impact on his time (The Bettmann Archive).

For several years Wagner did no composing; instead he worked out theories of art in essays such as *Art and Revolution* (1849), *The Art Work of the Future* (1850), and *Opera and Drama* (1851). More important, he completed the librettos to *The Ring of the Nibelung*, a set of four operas based on Nordic mythology. *The Ring* was to occupy Wagner for a quarter of a century. He began the text in 1848 and finished the music in 1874. Wagner's amazing self-confidence and belief in his greatness enabled him to compose one gigantic opera after another, with no prospects for their performance. He composed the first opera of the *Ring* cycle, *The Rhine Gold* (1853–1854), then the second, *The Valkyrie* (1854–1856), and the first two acts of the third, *Siegfried* (1856–1857). Then he interrupted his work to compose *Tristan and Isolde* (1857–1859), which he hoped would have a better chance for performance. In this opera, sexual passion is musically presented with unprecedented power and vividness.

Wagner had several bad years after finishing *Tristan*. His opera *Tannhäuser* was a failure at the Paris Opera, and *Tristan* was abandoned by the Vienna Opera after many rehearsals. Creditors banged on his door, demanding payment for the silks, satins, laces, and perfumes he "needed" for his lifestyle.

In 1864 Wagner was rescued from his desperate situation by King Ludwig of Bavaria, an eighteen-year-old fanatical Wagnerite who was determined to help Wagner produce his operas and complete *The Ring*. All the resources of the Munich Opera were put at Wagner's disposal. *Tristan* and *The Mastersingers of Nuremberg* (1862–1867) were lavishly produced in Munich. Wagner completed *Siegfried* (1869–1870) and composed the final opera of *The Ring*, *The Twilight of the Gods* (1869–1874).

During this period, Wagner fell in love with Cosima von Bülow. She was Liszt's daughter and the wife of Hans von Bülow, Wagner's close friend and favorite conductor. Cosima gave birth to two of Wagner's children while still married to von Bülow. Shortly after Wagner's first wife died, he married Cosima.

In Richard Wagner, towering musical genius was allied with utter selfishness, ruthlessness, and an absolute conviction about his place in history. A rabid German nationalist, he wrote in his diary, "I am the most German of beings. I am the German spirit." He bent people to his will. Indeed, he forged an audience for his complex music dramas from a public accustomed to conventional opera.

Wagner designed a theater to suit performances of *The Ring*. With the help of King Ludwig and contributions from Wagner clubs which had been formed all over Germany, Wagner's festival theater was constructed in Bayreuth, a small Bavarian town. The premiere of the *Ring* cycle in 1876 was perhaps the single most important musical event of the century. Sixty newspaper correspondents from all over the world attended, including two from the United States. Though some critics still found his music too dissonant, heavily orchestrated, and long-winded, Wagner was generally acclaimed the greatest composer of his time. A year after completing *Parsifal* (1877–1882), his last opera, Wagner visited Venice, where he died at the age of sixty-nine.

Wagner's Music

For Wagner, an opera house was a temple in which the spectator was to be overwhelmed by music and drama. He wrote his own librettos, based on medieval Germanic legends and myths. His characters are usually larger than life—heroes, gods, demigods.

Wagner called his works "music dramas" rather than operas, to emphasize the close relationship between music and drama. He envisioned music drama as a "universal art work" (*Gesamtkunstwerk*) in which all the arts—music, drama, dance, painting—are fused. Today, however, many find Wagner's music more

Wagner's Music

exciting than his rather static drama. For long stretches of time his characters exult, lament, or relate what has happened to them.

Within each act, there is a continuous musical flow which Wagner described as "unending melody." The music is not broken into traditional arias, recitatives, and duets. He achieves musical and dramatic continuity by smoothly connecting each section to the next. There are no breaks where applause can disturb the listener's concentration. Wagner conceived his vocal line as a "speech song" combining the speechlike quality of a recitative with the lyricism of an aria. The vocal line is inspired by rhythms and pitch fluctuations in the German text.

Wagner revolutionized opera by shifting the musical center of gravity from the voice toward the orchestra. His expanded and colorful orchestration brilliantly expresses the drama and reveals characters' thoughts and feelings. He treats the orchestra symphonically, constantly developing, transforming, and intertwining musical ideas. Many long orchestral interludes graphically depict scenic effects like floods, sunrises, and flames.

Wagner loved to exploit the rich power of the brasses. *The Ring* calls for eight horns and new brass instruments (called "Wagner tubas") that he designed. The orchestral sound is so full that only singers with unusually powerful voices, such as a "Wagnerian soprano" or a "heroic tenor," can cut through it.

Wagner spins an orchestral web out of recurrent musical ideas called *leitmotifs* or *leading motives*. A **leitmotif** is a short musical idea associated with a person, object, or thought in the drama. When the text refers to Siegfried, his leitmotif is usually heard in the orchestra. These motives are sometimes in the vocal parts, too. They are varied and transformed to convey the evolving dramatic situation and changes of character. When Siegfried is murdered, his leitmotif is set against strident dissonant harmonies. As Wagner develops his leitmotifs, he sets one against another to suggest the clash of two persons or ideas. Such leitmotifs unify Wagner's greatly extended music dramas.

The emotional tension of Wagner's music is heightened by chromatic and dissonant harmonies. He creates motion and color through rapid shifts from one key to another and through many chromatic chords in each key. The listener often expects a resolution to a stable chord only to hear yet another dissonance. Wagner's chromatic harmony ultimately led to the breakdown of tonality and to the new musical language of the twentieth century.

The Twilight of the Gods (*Götterdämmerung,* 1874)

The Twilight of the Gods is the fourth and concluding music drama in Wagner's gigantic cycle, *The Ring of the Nibelung*. With all its gods, giants, dwarfs, and magic fire, *The Ring* is really about Wagner's view of nineteenth-century society. He uses Nordic mythology to warn that society destroys itself through lust for money and power. It is fitting that Wagner first sketched the plot of *The Ring* in 1848, a year that brought Marx's *Communist Manifesto* and revolutions throughout Europe.

Act III: Immolation Scene

Wagner builds an overwhelming climax at the end of *The Ring* as men and gods are punished for their crimes by a spectacular fire and flood. To grasp this scene fully, it's helpful to know what has taken place in the three preceding music dramas.

A Nibelung dwarf has stolen gold belonging to the Rhinemaidens, mermaids in the Rhine river. From this gold, the dwarf fashions a ring that can bestow world power on anyone who wears it and is willing to renounce love. The dwarf, in turn, is robbed of his prize by Wotan, king of the gods. (Wednesday comes from "Wotan's day.") Furious, the dwarf casts a curse on the ring and anyone who wears it. Soon Wotan is forced to give up the ring; he lives in fear that someone will use it to destroy him. Hoping to protect himself, he surrounds his castle, Valhalla, with a bodyguard of heroes. His daughters, goddesses called Valkyries, swoop over battlefields on horseback bearing away the dead bodies of the bravest warriors.

Brünnhilde, one of the Valkyries, is Wotan's favorite daughter. Thinking she is following Wotan's inner feelings, Brünnhilde disobeys her father by saving Siegmund, a hero fated to die. She is punished by being turned into a mortal. Cast into a deep sleep by Wotan, she lies on a mountain surrounded by magic fire. The hero Siegfried, son of Siegmund, penetrates the fire, awakens Brünnhilde, and becomes her husband.

In the course of his adventures, Siegfried has gained possession of the ring, but he is unaware of its power. Shortly before the Immolation Scene, Siegfried is murdered through the treachery of Hagen, who wants the ring.

The Immolation Scene occurs in front of a castle on the Rhine. Brünnhilde sings an exalted farewell before sacrificing herself to join Siegfried in death. At her command, warriors build a huge funeral pyre of logs. As Siegfried's body is lifted onto the pyre, Brünnhilde takes the magic ring from him and puts it on, bequeathing it to the Rhinemaidens. The following excerpt begins as Brünnhilde addresses a pair of ravens, Wotan's messengers.

In this glorious conclusion to *The Twilight of the Gods,* Brünnhilde's soaring vocal line is matched by the powerful orchestra. Various leitmotifs are heard, sometimes together. After Brünnhilde rides into the funeral pyre, the orchestra magnificently depicts the flames and the overflowing of the Rhine. The opera ends as Valhalla, the castle of the gods, is engulfed in flames accompanied by the leitmotif "Redemption by love." Wagner seems to be expressing the feeling that despite the destruction of men and gods, a new world will be reborn through love. (In the following libretto, words in quotation marks—like "Law" and "Magic fire"—refer to specific leitmotifs. These leitmotifs are indicated where they can be most clearly heard.)

Brünnhilde has put the Ring on her finger and now takes a firebrand from one of the men.	Trumpets and trombones, *f,* "Law."

The Twilight of the Gods

361

"Law"

Brünnhilde

Fliegt heim, ihr Raben!	Fly home, ye ravens!
raunt es eurem Herren,	Tell your lord
was hier am Rhein ihr gehört!	what you heard here on the Rhine!

Full orchestra, *f*,
"Magic fire,"
"Loge, god of
fire."

An Brünnhildes Felsen	Fly past Brünnhilde's rock,
fliegt vorbei:	where Loge is still flaming,
der dort noch lodert,	and bid him go
weiset Loge nach Walhall!	to Valhalla!
Denn der Götter Ende	For the end of the gods
dämmert nun auf:	is now dawning.
so—werf' ich den Brand	See—I throw the firebrand
in Walhalls prangende Burg.	into Valhalla's glorious citadel!

Cymbal crash.

*She hurls the torch onto the pyre. Two ravens fly up and disappear
in the background. She turns to her horse.*

Strings surge
upward as
pyre bursts
into flames.

Grane, mein Ross.	Grane, my steed,
sei mir gegrüsst!	greetings to you!

Horns, "Ride of
the Valky-
ries."

"Ride of the Valkyries"

Weisst du auch, mein Freund,	My friend, do you know
wohin ich dich führe?	where I lead you?
Im Feuer leuchtend	In the bright fire

Flute and voice,
"Redemption
by love."

Flute

"Redemption by love"

liegt dort dein Herr,	there lies your master,	
Siegfried, mein seliger Held.	Siegfried, my blessed hero.	
Dem Freunde zu folgen,	Are you neighing,	
wieherst du freudig?	eager to follow your friend?	
Lockt dich zu ihm	Do the laughing flames	
die lachende Lohe?	allure you?	
Fühl' meine Brust auch,	Feel my breast, too,	
wie sie entbrennt;	how it is burning;	
helles Feuer	bright flames	
das Herz mir erfasst.	seize on my heart.	
Ihn zu umschlingen,	To clasp him to me,	
umschlossen, von ihm,	to be held fast in his arms,	
in mächtigster Minne	to be united with him	
vermählt ihm zu sein!	by the power of love!	Trumpet, "Siegfried."
Hei-a-ja-ho! Grane!	Hei-a-ya-ho! Grane!	
Grüss deinen Herren!	Greet your lord!	
Siegfried! Siegfried! Sieh!	Siegfried! Siegfried! See!	
selig grüsst dich dein Weib!	Your wife greets you joyfully!	

She swings herself onto the horse and makes it leap into the burning pyre.

Brasses, "Ride of the Valkyries."

Flames fill the whole space in front of the castle, which itself catches fire. Men and women press to the front of the stage in terror.

Full orchestra, *ff*, "Magic Fire."

"Magic Fire"

When all seems wrapped in flames, the glow is suddenly extinguished, so that only a cloud of smoke is seen.

Decrescendo, descending chromatic scale, "Magic sleep."

At the same time the Rhine upswells mightily and pours its waters over the pyre. The three Rhinemaidens ride the waves and appear by the pyre. At their appearance Hagen—Siegfried's murderer—is seized with alarm. He flings away his spear, shield, and helmet, and madly plunges into the flood, crying:

Strings, upward running-notes. Crescendo.

Hagen

Zurück vom Ring!   Away from the Ring!

The Twilight of
the Gods

Two Rhinemaidens grab Hagen around the neck and drag him down into the water. A Rhinemaiden exultantly holds up the recovered Ring.

Downward strings and decrescendo depict drowning. Oboes, and clarinets, lilting "Rhinemaidens."

cresc. -

"Rhinemaidens"

Through the bank of clouds which lie on the horizon, a red glow breaks forth with increasing brightness.

Brasses, solemn "Valhalla."

"Valhalla"

In its light, the Rhine is observed to have returned to its bed, and the Rhinemaidens are circling and playing with the Ring in the calm water.

Interweaving of leitmotifs: Oboes and clarinets, "Rhinemaidens"; violins, "Redemption by love"; brasses, "Valhalla."

From the ruins of the half-burned castle, the men and women perceive the red glow in the heavens, in which appears the castle of Valhalla, where the gods and heroes are sitting together.

Crescendo. Trumpets and trombones, *f*, "Siegfried."

"Siegfried"

Bright flames seize Valhalla. The curtain falls as the gods become entirely hidden by the flames.

Violins, *p*, "Redemption by love."

Basic Term

leitmotif

GUSTAV MAHLER ‖**19**‖

Gustav Mahler (1860–1911) was the last great Austrian Romantic composer. He opened new realms of orchestral sound that influenced composers of the early twentieth century, but his works were fully appreciated only a half-century after his death.

Mahler was born in Bohemia and grew up in a small town where his father was a tavern keeper. His musical environment included Bohemian peasant songs and dances and marches played by a local military band. (This early contact with folk music and marches later had an influence on his style.) As a boy, he studied piano and composed constantly. At fifteen he entered the Vienna Conservatory, where he studied for three years. He also took courses in history, Greek art, and ancient literature at the University of Vienna. At twenty he began his conducting career, directing musical comedies at a summer resort. In the years that followed, Mahler steadily gained in professional status, working as opera conductor in theaters of increasing importance. By twenty-eight, he was director of the Budapest Opera. Brahms heard one of his performances there and declared that to hear "the true *Don Giovanni*" you had to go to Budapest. Mahler's ambition as a performer was to direct the famed Vienna Opera, but there was one obstacle: He was Jewish. However, in 1897 he converted to Roman Catholicism and at thirty-seven became director of the Vienna Opera, a position he held for ten years. Mahler brought the Vienna Opera to new heights of excellence, supervising every aspect of its performances: music, acting, costumes, and scenery. He was uncompromising in artistic matters, with the result that many performers regarded him as a tyrant.

While Mahler quickly won fame as a conductor, he had to struggle for recognition as a composer. Performances of his symphonies often met with a mixed reception. Critics would acknowledge his talent but complain about harsh dissonances, overelaborate orchestration, and confusing shifts of mood. Mahler composed much of his music during summer vacations, since he was preoccupied by his feverish activity as a conductor during most of the year. In addition to his directorship of the Vienna Opera, he also conducted the Vienna Philharmonic orchestra.

 Gustave Mahler

At the age of forty-two, Mahler married the beautiful and musically talented Alma Schindler, who was nineteen years his junior. Two daughters were born to the couple within the first two years of their marriage. Tragically, Maria ("Puzi"), the older daughter, died of scarlet fever at age four, leaving Mahler a broken man.

In 1908, Mahler traveled to the United States to become principal conductor of the Metropolitan Opera in New York. The next year he was elected director of the New York Philharmonic orchestra. Mahler's experiences in New York were not happy. His own works were received cooly; he aroused the dislike of many of his players; and he was unable to get along with the socialites who supported the orchestra. In 1911 he became seriously ill and returned to Europe. He died in Vienna at the age of fifty.

A passionately intense man, Mahler was full of conflicts and contradictions. He was an active leader and administrator, but he often craved solitude. His moods frequently shifted from exaltation to despair. He could be cruel to his players and yet gave generous support to young musicians like Bruno Walter and Arnold Schoenberg.

Mahler's Music

Mahler's music is often programmatic and reflects his constant search for life's meaning. His output consists basically of nine symphonies (plus an unfinished Tenth Symphony that is also performed) and several song cycles for voice and orchestra, including *The Boy's Magic Horn* (*Des Knaben Wunderhorn*, 1888) and his monumental masterpiece, *The Song of the Earth* (*Das Lied von der Erde*, 1908). "The symphony is the world!" Mahler once explained. "The symphony must embrace everything." Following the example of Beethoven's Ninth Symphony, Mahler used voices in four of his symphonies. And his symphonies are often monumental in length and in their performing forces. His Eighth Symphony ("Symphony of a Thousand," 1907), for example, lasts about an hour and a half and calls for eight vocal soloists, a boys' choir, two choruses, and a gigantic orchestra. Yet Mahler often uses his gigantic orchestra to achieve delicate chamber music effects in which only a few instruments are heard at a time. He created polyphonic textures in which several themes are presented simultaneously in contrasting tone colors. His use of unconventional instruments like cowbells, celesta, guitar, and mandolin influenced twentieth-century Viennese composers such as Arnold Schoenberg, Anton Webern, and Alban Berg. As with Schubert—whose music was a source of inspiration—the spirit of song permeates Mahler's instrumental music. Many of his symphonic movements are based on themes from his songs. He loved to use folklike tunes and march music, perhaps remembering his childhood in a small Bohemian town. But sometimes he parodies a tune by giving it an unusual twist or grotesque glissando, and there are many sudden and extreme shifts of mood in his music—an intensely emotional section may be interrupted by something light and frivolous.

A source of inspiration for the funeral-march movement of Mahler's First Symphony was *The Hunter's Funeral Procession* by the German Romantic artist Moritz von Schwind (Courtesy of the New York Public Library; Astor, Lenox and Tilden Foundations).

Symphony No. 1 in D Major: Third Movement (Funeral March)

Mahler's popular First Symphony, composed between 1885 and 1888, shows most features of his mature style. The first and third of the symphony's four movements (in an early version there were five) use themes from songs Mahler had composed earlier. The first movement, in sonata form, beautifully evokes the sounds of nature through distant trumpet fanfares and bird calls. The second movement is a folklike scherzo. The last movement, also in sonata form, is by far the most extended; it thematically transforms material from the opening movement.

The third movement, a funeral march, is the most strikingly original of the symphony. Mahler wrote that it was inspired by a satirical engraving "The Hunter's Funeral Procession," well known to all Austrian children from an old book of fairy tales. (See the illustration shown above.) "The forest animals accompany the dead hunter's coffin to the grave. Hares carry the banner, before them march a band of Bohemian musicians, accompanied by singing cats, toads, crows, etc. Stags, deer, foxes, and other four-legged and feathered animals accompany the funeral procession in all kinds of farcical postures. The music is intended to express alternating moods of ironical gaiety and uncanny gloom."

The funeral march is in three sections (A B A′) that contain extraordinary contrasts of sound and theme. The weird procession is depicted by a distorted, minor-key version of the round *Frère Jacques* ("Are You Sleeping, Brother John?"). The tune is introduced by a solo, muted double bass straining in its top register, and then it is imitated by other instruments.

A relentless funeral-march beat in the timpani accompanies sounds that are, in Mahler's words, "dull and muffled, as if shadows were passing by." The *Frère*

Symphony No. 1 in D Major

367

Jacques round is soon joined by a staccato oboe countermelody that seems like a mocking commentary. A feeling of even greater mockery comes with the appearance to two deliberately banal tunes—one minor and the other major—scored to sound like a Bohemian village band (complete with bass drum and cymbals).

The middle section (B) brings a shift to a lyrical, dreamlike mood as Mahler quotes part of the last song in his cycle "Songs of a Wayfarer." Its major key, muted strings and harp, and expansive legato melody offer a striking contrast to the minor keys, brass band sounds, and staccato phrases heard earlier.

The third section (A′) is a condensed and varied return of the opening. The *Frère Jacques* round is now in a somewhat faster tempo, beginning with woodwinds instead of a solo double bass. After the return of a "village band" theme, there is a moment of agitation as the tempo quickens and several contrasting themes are presented simultaneously. The processional mood and tempo soon return, and the funeral march gradually fades into silence.

LISTENING OUTLINE
To be read while music is heard

Symphony No. 1 in D Major (1885–1888), by Gustav Mahler

Third Movement: Moderate and solemn, not too slow

Quadruple meter ($\frac{4}{4}$), D minor

4 flutes, 2 oboes, English horn, 4 clarinets, bass clarinet, 2 bassoons, 7 French horns, 2 trumpets, 3 trombones, tuba, timpani, bass drum, gong, cymbals, harp, violins 1, violins 2, violas, cellos, basses

(About 10 min)

A   1   *a.* Muted timpani, *pp*, funeral-march beat. Solo muted double bass in high register, *Frère Jacques* in minor. *Frère Jacques* imitated as a round by bassoon, cellos, tuba, *pp*.

         b. Oboe, *p*, staccato countermelody enters as *Frère Jacques* round continues.

         c. Oboe and clarinet, *p*, repeat staccato countermelody. *Frère Jacques* round fades away, tempo slows.

    2   *a.* Oboes, *p*, legato minor tune in dotted rhythm; pizzicato strings accompany, *p*.

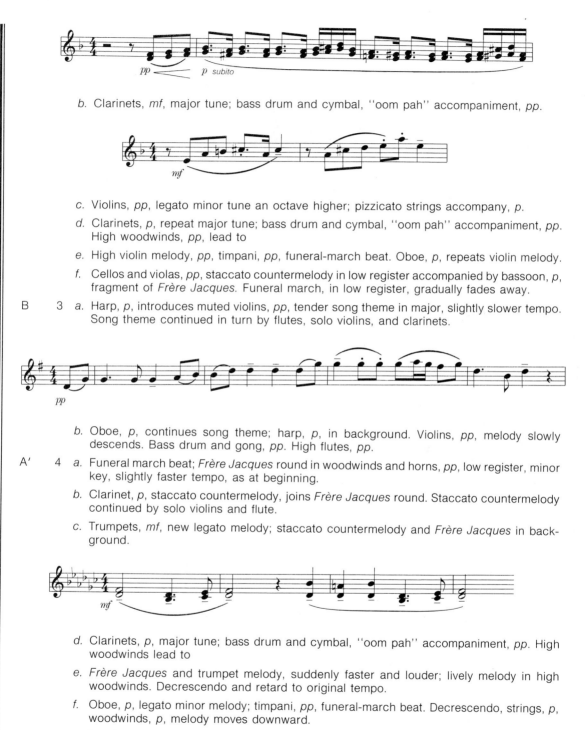

pp ———— *p subito*

    b. Clarinets, *mf*, major tune; bass drum and cymbal, "oom pah" accompaniment, *pp*.

mf

    c. Violins, *pp*, legato minor tune an octave higher; pizzicato strings accompany, *p*.

    d. Clarinets, *p*, repeat major tune; bass drum and cymbal, "oom pah" accompaniment, *pp*. High woodwinds, *pp*, lead to

    e. High violin melody, *pp*, timpani, *pp*, funeral-march beat. Oboe, *p*, repeats violin melody.

    f. Cellos and violas, *pp*, staccato countermelody in low register accompanied by bassoon, *p*, fragment of *Frère Jacques*. Funeral march, in low register, gradually fades away.

B   3 *a.* Harp, *p*, introduces muted violins, *pp*, tender song theme in major, slightly slower tempo. Song theme continued in turn by flutes, solo violins, and clarinets.

pp

    b. Oboe, *p*, continues song theme; harp, *p*, in background. Violins, *pp*, melody slowly descends. Bass drum and gong, *pp*. High flutes, *pp*.

A′   4 *a.* Funeral march beat; *Frère Jacques* round in woodwinds and horns, *pp*, low register, minor key, slightly faster tempo, as at beginning.

    b. Clarinet, *p*, staccato countermelody, joins *Frère Jacques* round. Staccato countermelody continued by solo violins and flute.

    c. Trumpets, *mf*, new legato melody; staccato countermelody and *Frère Jacques* in background.

mf

    d. Clarinets, *p*, major tune; bass drum and cymbal, "oom pah" accompaniment, *pp*. High woodwinds lead to

    e. *Frère Jacques* and trumpet melody, suddenly faster and louder; lively melody in high woodwinds. Decrescendo and retard to original tempo.

    f. Oboe, *p*, legato minor melody; timpani, *pp*, funeral-march beat. Decrescendo, strings, *p*, woodwinds, *p*, melody moves downward.

    g. Low bassoon, *p*, staccato countermelody; timpani, *pp*, funeral-march beat. Funeral march fades away with faint sounds from gong and bass drum.

THE TWENTIETH CENTURY

1 Musical Styles: 1900–1950

2 Music and Musicians in Society

3 Impressionism and Symbolism

4 Claude Debussy

5 Neoclassicism

6 Igor Stravinsky

7 Expressionism

8 Arnold Schoenberg

9 Alban Berg

10 Anton Webern

11 Béla Bartók

12 Charles Ives

13 Aaron Copland

14 Musical Styles Since 1950

15 Music Since 1950: Six Representative Pieces

Pablo Picasso, *Violin and Grapes* (1912). The years following 1900 brought radical new developments in the arts (Collection, The Museum of Modern Art, New York, Mrs. David M. Levy Bequest).

1 MUSICAL STYLES: 1900-1950

The years 1900 to 1913 brought radical new developments in science and art. During the period preceding World War I, discoveries were made that overturned long-held beliefs. Sigmund Freud explored the unconscious and developed psychoanalysis, and Albert Einstein revolutionized the view of the universe with his "Special Theory of Relativity." Pablo Picasso's painting and sculpture distorted human figures and objects with unprecedented daring, showing them from several angles at one time; Wassily Kandinsky's abstract paintings no longer tried to represent the visual world.

In music, too, the early twentieth century was a time of revolt. The years following 1900 saw more fundamental changes in the language of music than any time since the beginning of the Baroque era. There were entirely new approaches to the organization of pitch and rhythm and a vast expansion in the vocabulary of sounds used, especially percussive sounds. Some compositions so broke with tradition that they were met with violent hostility. The most famous riot in music history occurred in Paris on May 29, 1913, at the premiere of Igor Stravinsky's ballet *The Rite of Spring* (*Le Sacre du printemps*). Police had to be called in as hecklers booed, laughed, made animal noises, and actually fought with those in the audience who wanted to hear Stravinsky's evocation of primitive rites. One music critic complained that *The Rite of Spring* produced the "sensation of acute and almost cruel dissonance" and that "from the first measure to the last, whatever note one expects is never the one that comes. . . ." Another wrote, "To say that much of it is hideous in sound is a mild description. . . . It has no relation to music at all as most of us understand the word."

Today, we are amused by the initial failure of some music critics to understand this composition, now recognized to be a masterpiece. Chords, rhythms, and percussive sounds that were baffling in 1913 are now commonly heard in jazz, rock, and music for movies and television. But the hostile critics of the early 1900s were right in seeing that a great transformation in musical language was taking place.

From the late 1600s to about 1900, musical structure was governed by certain general principles. As different as the works of Bach, Beethoven, and Brahms may be, they share fundamental techniques of organizing pitches around a central tone. After 1900, however, no single system governs the organization of pitch in all musical compositions. Each piece is more likely to have a system of pitch relationships unique to that particular piece.

In the past, composers depended on the listener's awareness—conscious or unconscious—of general principles underlying the interrelationship of tones and chords. For example, they relied on the listener's expectation that a dominant chord would normally be followed by a tonic chord. By substituting another chord for the expected one, the composer could create a feeling of suspense, drama, or surprise. Twentieth-century music relies less on preestablished relationships and expectations. Listeners are guided by musical cues contained only within an individual composition. This new approach to the organization of sound makes twentieth-century music fascinating. When we listen openly, with no assumptions about how tones "should" relate, modern music is an adventure.

1900–1950: An Age of Musical Diversity

The range of musical styles during the first half of our century was vast. The stylistic diversity in the works of Claude Debussy, Igor Stravinsky, Arnold Schoenberg, Alban Berg, Anton Webern, Béla Bartók, Charles Ives, and Aaron Copland—to name only composers studied here—is a continuation and intensification of the diversity we've seen in Romantic music. During the twentieth century, differences among styles are so great that it seems as though composers use different musical languages, not merely different dialects of the same musical language. Radical changes of style occur even within the works of individual composers.

Such great variety of musical styles reflected the diversity of life during the early twentieth century. More people were free to choose where to live, how to earn a living, and how to spend their time. The automobile, airplane, telephone, phonograph, movies, and radio all made the world seem smaller and expanded the range of experiences.

Through the work of scholars and performers, a wider range of music became available. Composers drew inspiration from an enormous variety of sources, including folk and popular music from all over the world, the music of Asia and Africa, and European art music from the Middle Ages through the nineteenth century.

Elements of folk and popular music were often incorporated within personal styles. Composers were attracted especially to unconventional rhythms, sounds, and melodic patterns that deviated from the common practice of Western music. Folk music was studied more systematically than ever before, and scholars now could record the actual sounds of peasant songs. One of the greatest twentieth-century composers, Béla Bartók, was also a leading scholar of the peasant music of his native Hungary and other parts of Eastern Europe. "Studies of folk music in the countryside," he wrote, "are as necessary to me as fresh air is to other people." Bartók's imagination was fired by Hungarian, Bulgarian, and Rumanian folk songs, and he believed that peasant music provided "the ideal starting point for a musical renaissance." Other composers stimulated by folklore were Stravinsky, who drew upon the folk songs of his native Russia, and Charles Ives, who used American revival hymns, ragtime, and patriotic songs.

During the early twentieth century, non-European music had a deep influence on the music of the West. Composers and painters were more receptive and

 An Age of Musical Diversity

Marcel Duchamp in *Nude Descending the Staircase No. 2*
(1912) (left) and Picasso in *Girl before a Mirror* (1932)
(above) distorted human figures with unprecedented daring
(Philadelphia Museum of Art, The Louise and Walter Arens-
berg Collection; Collection, The Museum of Modern Art,
New York, Gift of Mrs. Simon Guggenheim).

An Age of
Musical
Diversity

375

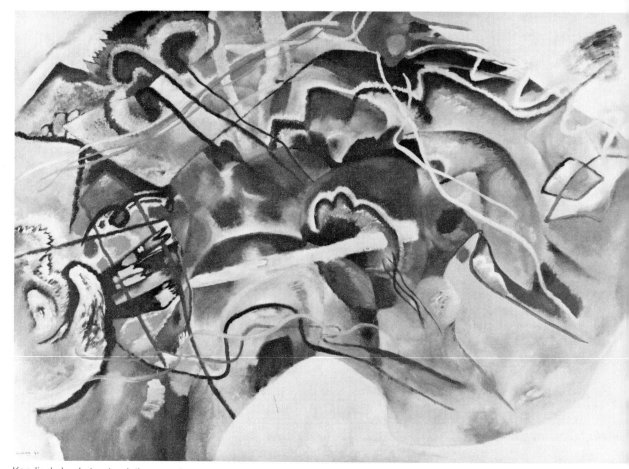

Kandinsky's abstract paintings, such as *Picture with White Border, No. 173* (1913), no longer tried to represent the visual world (Collection, The Solomon R. Guggenheim Museum, New York).

sympathetic to Asian and African cultures than they had been earlier. For example, in 1862, Hector Berlioz could say that "the Chinese sing like dogs howling, like a cat screeching when it has swallowed a toad." But in 1889, Debussy was delighted by the Javanese music he heard at the Paris International Exhibition. "If we listen without European prejudice to the charm of their percussion," he wrote later, "we must confess that our percussion is like primitive noises at a country fair." Echoes of the gamelan (Indonesian orchestra) can be heard in the bell-like sounds and five-tone melodic patterns of Debussy's piano piece *Pagodes* (*Pagodas*, 1903). Another composer influenced by Asian culture is the Frenchman Olivier Messiaen (b. 1908), whose novel rhythmic procedures grew out of his study of Indian music.

American jazz is another non-European influence on twentieth-century composers. Musicians were fascinated by its syncopated rhythms and improvisational quality, as well as by the unique tone colors of jazz bands. Unlike a string-dominated symphony orchestra, a jazz band emphasizes woodwinds, brasses, and percussion.

Jazz elements were used in works as early as Debussy's "Golliwog's Cake Walk" (from the suite *Children's Corner,* 1908) and Stravinsky's "Ragtime" (from *The Soldier's Tale,* 1918). But the peak of jazz influence came during the "Jazz Age" of the 1920s, with works such as the ballet *The Creation of the World (La Création du monde,* 1923) by the Frenchman Darius Milhaud and *Piano Concerto* (1926) by the American Aaron Copland. For Americans, jazz idioms represented a kind of musical nationalism, a search for an "American sound." For European composers, it was a kind of musical exoticism. During the 1920s and 1930s, popular composers such as George Gershwin (1898–1937) used jazz and popular elements within "classical" forms. His *Rhapsody in Blue* (1924) and the opera *Porgy and Bess* (1934–1935) are well known.

Modern composers can also draw inspiration from a wider historical range of music. During the twentieth century, music from remote times has been unearthed by scholars and then published, performed, and recorded. There has been a rediscovery of earlier masters like Perotin and Machaut from the medieval period, Josquin des Prez and Gesualdo from the Renaissance, and Purcell and Vivaldi from the Baroque. Some leading modern composers have been music historians, like Anton Webern, or experts in the performance of "old" music, like Paul Hindemith.

Music from the past is a fruitful source of forms, rhythms, tone colors, textures, and compositional techniques. Baroque dances like the gavotte and gigue and forms like the passacaglia and concerto grosso are being used again. The long-forgotten harpsichord has been put to new use in compositions such as Elliott Carter's Sonata for Flute, Cello, Oboe and Harpsichord (1952), which we'll study. In the *Classical Symphony* (1917) by the Russian composer Sergei Prokofiev (1891–1953), a Classical orchestra is used, and the texture is light and transparent like much late eighteenth-century music. Occasionally a twentieth-century composer uses themes of earlier composers, as Benjamin Britten did in *A Young Person's Guide to the Orchestra,* which is based on a theme by Henry Purcell (about 1659–1695).

While modern compositions may be inspired by older music, they do not simply imitate past styles. Instead, a traditional form might be used with harmonies, rhythms, melodies, and tone colors that would have been inconceivable before the twentieth century.

Modern composers were also influenced by the music of the immediate past. Nineteenth-century composers such as Wagner, Brahms, Mahler, Richard Strauss, and Mussorgsky were musical points of departure for composers of the early twentieth century. Wagner's music, in particular, was as potent an influence as Beethoven's was for Romantic musicians. Composers took Wagner's style as a departure point or violently reacted against all he stood for.

 An Age of Musical Diversity

Having reviewed some sources of inspiration for twentieth-century music, let's now examine some of its musical characteristics.

Tone Color

During the twentieth century tone color has become a more important element of music than ever before. Its role is often major, creating variety, continuity, and mood. In Webern's *Orchestral Piece,* Op. 10, No. 3 (1913), for example, the use of eerie, bell-like sounds at the beginning and end is vital to the form. If this composition were altered in tone color by being played on a piano, it would lose much. An orchestral work from an earlier period, say Beethoven's Fifth Symphony, suffers less in a piano arrangement.

In modern music, noiselike and percussive sounds are often used, and instruments are played at the very top or bottom of their ranges. Uncommon playing techniques have become normal. For example, the **glissando,** a rapid slide up or down a scale, is more widely used. Woodwind and brass players are often asked to produce a fluttery sound by rapidly rolling their tongues while they play. And string players frequently strike the strings with the stick, rather than with the hair of the bow.

Percussion instruments have become prominent and numerous, reflecting twentieth-century interest in unusual rhythms and tone colors. Instruments that have become standard during the 1900s include the xylophone, celesta, and wood block, to name a few. Composers occasionally call for noisemakers—typewriters, sirens, and automobile brake drums. A piano is often used to add a percussive edge to the sound of an orchestra. Modern composers often draw hard, drumlike sounds from the piano, in contrast to the Romantics, who wanted the instrument to "sing." Besides expanding the percussion section of the orchestra, early twentieth-century composers wrote works for unconventional performing groups in which percussion plays a major role. Well-known examples are Stravinsky's *The Wedding (Les Noces,* 1914–1923) for vocal soloists, chorus, four pianos, and percussion, Bartók's *Music for Strings, Percussion and Celesta* (1936), and Varèse's *Ionisation* (1931), one of the first works for percussion ensemble.

Modern orchestral and chamber works often sound transparent; individual tone colors are heard clearly. To bring out the individuality of different melodic lines that are played simultaneously, a composer will often assign each line to a different timbre. In general, there is less emphasis on blended sound than during the Romantic period. Many twentieth-century works are written for nonstandard chamber groups made up of instruments with sharply contrasting tone colors. Stravinsky's *The Soldier's Tale (L'Histoire du soldat,* 1918), for example, is scored for violin, double bass, clarinet, bassoon, cornet, trombone, and percussion. Even orchestral works often sound as though they are scored for a group of soloists.

Harmony

Consonance and Dissonance

The twentieth century brought fundamental changes in the way chords are treated. Up to about 1900, chords were divided into two opposing types: consonant and dissonant. A consonant chord was stable; it functioned as a point of rest or arrival. A dissonant chord was unstable; its tension demanded onward motion, or resolution to a stable, consonant chord. Traditionally, only the triad, a three-tone chord, could be consonant. All others were considered dissonant. In the nineteenth century, composers came to use ever more dissonant chords, and they treated dissonances with increasing freedom. By the early twentieth century, the traditional distinction between consonance and dissonance was abandoned in much music. A combination of tones that earlier would have been used to generate instability and expectation might now be treated as a stable chord, a point of arrival. In Stravinsky's words, dissonance "is no longer tied down to its former function. Having become an entity in itself, it frequently happens that dissonance neither prepares nor anticipates anything. Dissonance is thus no more an agent of disorder than consonance is a guarantee of security."

This "emancipation of the dissonance" does not prevent composers from differentiating between chords of greater or lesser tension. Relatively mild-sounding chords may be goals of motion, while harsher chords are used for transitional sounds. But no longer is there a general principle that determines whether a chord is stable or not. It is now entirely up to the composer's discretion. "We find ourself confronted with a new logic of music that would have appeared unthinkable to the masters of the past," wrote Stravinsky. "This new logic has opened our eyes to riches whose existence we never suspected."

New Chord Structures

Before 1900, there were general principles governing chord construction: Certain combinations of tones were considered chords, while others were not. At the core of traditional harmony is the triad. A triad might be made up of alternate tones of a major scale, such as the first (*do*), third (*mi*), and fifth (*sol*). Within a triad, there are two intervals of a third.

While the triad often appears in twentieth-century music, it no longer is so fundamental.

Some twentieth-century composers create fresh harmonies by placing one traditional chord against another. Such a combination of two chords heard at the same time is called a **polychord**.

 Harmony

379

Copland, *Appalachian Spring*

A polychord can be heard either as a single block of sound or as two distinct layers, depending on whether the two combined chords contrast in tone color and register.

Another development of twentieth-century music is the use of chordal structures *not* based on triads. One used commonly is the **fourth chord,** in which the tones are a fourth apart, instead of a third. (From *do* to *fa*, or from *re* to *sol*, is an interval of a fourth.)

Ives, *The Cage*

Harmonic resources have been extended also through the **tone cluster,** a chord made up of tones only a half step or a whole step apart. A tone cluster can be produced on a piano by striking a group of adjacent keys with the fist or forearm.

Ives, *The Majority*

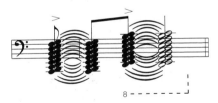

Alternatives to the Traditional Tonal System

In addition to creating new chord structures, twentieth-century composers explored alternatives to the traditional tonal system. Known as tonality or key, this system of tonal gravity governed the organization of pitch from the 1600s to about 1900. By the late nineteenth century, the gravitational pull of a central tonality had been weakened by rapid and frequent key shifts. After 1900, some composers continued to use the traditional system, but others modified it greatly. Still others discarded it entirely.

Before looking at new approaches to pitch organization, recall the basic principles of the traditional tonal system. As we saw in the Elements section, *tonality,* or *key,* refers to the use of a central tone, scale, and chord within a composition. The central tone, called the *tonic* or *keynote* (*do*), is the composition's resting point. The tonic major or minor scale and the tonic triad are built on this tone. Since the tonic triad is stable and restful, compositions almost always ended with it. Next in importance to the tonic triad is the *dominant chord,* which is built on the fifth (*sol*) tone of the tonic scale. There is a special gravitational pull from the dominant chord toward the tonic chord, and the motion from dominant to tonic is the essential chord progression of the tonal system. This cadence provides a strong sense of conclusion, and traditionally it was used to round off melodies, sections, and entire pieces. In summary, the tonal system is based on a central tone, a major or minor scale, and a triad; and there is a special relationship between the tonic and dominant chords.

After 1900, this system was modified in many different ways. The new techniques of pitch organization are so varied as to resist easy generalization. Some compositions have a central tone, but other traditional elements are missing, such as the tonic triad, the central major or minor scale, or the dominant-tonic relationship. This approach is reflected even in the titles of compositions, which are less likely to include the terms *major* or *minor.* For example, one Stravinsky piano piece is entitled *Serenade in A* to show that it revolves around the tone A but is not in a major or minor key.

To create fresh sounds, composers used scales other than major or minor. For example, they breathed new life into the ancient church modes, scales that had been used widely before 1600, as well as in folk songs of every period. Other scales were borrowed from the musical traditions of lands outside Western Europe, and still others were invented by composers.

Twentieth-century compositions are often organized around a central chord other than the triad. Thus, the basic chord may well be one that was considered a dissonance earlier. In some works, the traditional relationship between dominant and tonic triads is replaced by other chord relationships. Melodies, sections, or entire pieces are rounded off not by the usual dominant-tonic cadence, but by other chord progressions.

Another twentieth-century approach to pitch organization is **polytonality,** the use of two or more keys at one time. When only two different keys are used at once—as is most common—the technique is called **bitonality.** A famous bitonal passage occurs in Stravinsky's ballet *Petrushka,* when one clarinet plays in C major and another plays in F-sharp major:

Alternatives to
the Traditional
Tonal System

381

In general, the greater the contrast of tone color, register, and rhythm between the different layers of sound, the more we can hear the different keys.

A further departure from tradition is **atonality,** the absence of tonality or key. Atonality was foreshadowed in nineteenth-century works such as Wagner's *Tristan and Isolde,* where the pull of a central key is weakened by frequent modulations and by liberal use of all twelve tones in the chromatic scale. Arnold Schoenberg wrote the first significant atonal pieces around 1908. He avoided traditional chord progressions in these works and used all twelve tones without regard to their traditional relationship to major or minor scales. But atonality is not a specific technique of composition; each atonal work is structured according to its needs. (Though the word *atonality* is imprecise and negative, no other term has yet come into general use.)

Before long Schoenberg felt the need for a more systematic approach to atonal composition, and during the early 1920s he developed the *twelve-tone system,* a new technique of pitch organization. This system gives equal prominence to each of the twelve chromatic tones, rather than singling out one pitch, as the tonal system does. For about twenty years, only Schoenberg and a few disciples used the twelve-tone system, but during the 1950s it came to be used by composers all over the world.

Rhythm

The new techniques of pitch organization were accompanied by new ways to organize rhythm. Music's rhythmic vocabulary was expanded, with increased emphasis on irregularity and unpredictability. Rhythm is one of the most striking elements of twentieth-century music; it is used to generate power, drive, and excitement.

In the twentieth century, new rhythmic procedures are drawn from many sources, including folk music from all over the world, jazz, and European art music from the Middle Ages through the nineteenth century. Béla Bartók used the "free and varied rhythmic structures" of East European peasant music. The syncopations and complex rhythmic combinations of jazz fired the imagination of Stravinsky and Copland. And irregular phrase structures in Brahms's music inspired rhythmic innovations in Schoenberg's works.

Rapidly changing meters are characteristic of twentieth-century music, while Baroque, Classical, and Romantic music maintains a single meter throughout a movement or section. Before the twentieth century, beats were organized into regularly recurring groups; the accented beat came at equal time intervals. Rhythmic irregularities such as syncopations or accents on weak beats were heard against a pervasive meter. But in many twentieth-century compositions, beats are grouped irregularly, and the accented beat comes at unequal time intervals. In some modern music the meter changes with almost every bar, so that we might count *1–2–3, 1–2–3–4–5, 1–2–3–4–5, 1–2–3, 1–2–3–4, 1–2–3–4–5, 1–2–3–4–5–6, 1–2–3–4–5, 1–2, 1–2–3–4–5–6.*

Stravinsky, "Ritual of Abduction" from *The Rite of Spring*

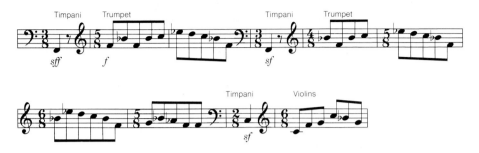

Count this again quickly and experience some of the rhythmic excitement of twentieth-century music, which often has a rapid and vigorous beat with jolting accents at unexpected times.

The rhythmic resources of twentieth-century music have also been expanded through the use of unconventional meters. Along with traditional meters such as duple and triple, modern composers use meters with five or seven beats to the measure. The pulses within a measure of any length may be grouped in irregular, asymmetrical ways. For example, eight quick pulses within a measure may be subdivided 3 + 3 + 2, or 1–2–3–4–5–6–7–8, 1–2–3–4–5–6–7–8. This meter, common in East European folk music, is used by Bartók in one of his *Six Dances in Bulgarian Rhythm.*

Twentieth-century music often uses two or more contrasting and independent rhythms at the same time, a procedure called **polyrhythm.** Each part of the musical texture goes its own rhythmic way, often creating accents that are out of phase with accents in the other parts. Different meters are used at the same time. For example, one instrument may play in duple meter (*1–2, 1–2*), while another plays in triple meter (*1–2–3, 1–2–3*). While polyrhythm occasionally occurs in Classical and Romantic music, it became both more common and more complex after 1900. The polyrhythms of jazz strongly influenced composers in the 1920s and 1930s.

Rhythmic repetition of a group of pitches is a widely used unifying technique in twentieth-century music. Many modern compositions contain an **ostinato,** a

Rhythm

383

motive or phrase that is repeated persistently at the same pitch throughout a section. The ostinato may occur in the melody or in the accompaniment. (The accompaniment for the last music example has an eight-note ostinato: 1–2–3–4–5–6–7–8.) Ostinatos can be found in music from various periods and cultures. In twentieth-century music, they usually serve to stabilize particular groups of pitches.

Melody

The new techniques of pitch and rhythmic organization that we've surveyed had a strong impact on twentieth-century melody. Melody no longer is necessarily tied to traditional chords or major and minor keys. It may be based on a wide variety of scales or freely use all twelve chromatic tones and not have a tonal center. Melody today often contains wide leaps that are difficult to sing. Rhythmic irregularity and changing meters tend to make twentieth-century melodies unpredictable. They often consist of a series of phrases that are irregular in length. In general, twentieth-century music relies less than Classical and Romantic music on melodies that are easy to sing and remember. Melody is as rich and varied as twentieth-century music itself; neither can be classified easily.

Basic Terms

polychord	tone cluster	bitonality	atonality	ostinato
fourth chord	polytonality	polyrhythm	glissando	

|2| MUSIC AND MUSICIANS IN SOCIETY

The twentieth century has seen dramatic changes in how music reaches its listeners. The living room has become the new "concert hall" through phonograph records, tape recordings, radio, and television. These technological advances have brought music to a larger audience than ever before, as well as vastly increasing the range of music available. Today's repertory of recorded music includes not only familiar classics but also Renaissance, early Baroque, non-Western, and unconventional twentieth-century works—music not often played in concert. Recordings of such lesser-known music multiplied with the appearance of long-playing discs in 1948. But as early as 1904, composers' interpretations of their own works were recorded, giving composers an unprecedented opportunity to communicate precisely their intentions about phrasing, dynamics, and tempo.

Radio broadcasts of live or recorded music began to reach a large audience during the 1920s. In the thirties, radio networks in several countries formed orchestras specifically to broadcast live music. The best-known American ensemble of this kind was the NBC Symphony Orchestra, directed by Arturo Toscanini. In addition to such radio-sponsored groups, regular broadcasts of the Metropolitan Opera's Saturday matinee performances have made opera available to millions of people.

With television, broadcast music performances can be seen as well as heard. Christmas Eve 1951 brought the premiere of the first opera created for television, *Amahl and the Night Visitors* by Italian-American composer Gian Carlo Menotti. Other television highlights included the appearances of Leonard Bernstein conducting the New York Philharmonic Orchestra. But apart from such notable exceptions, commercial television has devoted little time to opera and symphonic music. Public television, however, has brought a wide range of music to home viewers.

In the first half of this century, the concert and operatic repertory was dominated by music from earlier periods rather than by contemporary works. This was a new situation in music history. In Mozart's time, audiences demanded and got the latest music, not operas by Handel or cantatas by Bach. Even during the Romantic period, when interest in past music was high, concert programs consisted mainly of recent works.

After 1900, however, listeners and performers were often baffled by the dissonances, percussive sounds, and irregular rhythms in some of the new music. (Remember the riot at the first performance of Stravinsky's *Rite of Spring*.) To avoid alienating audiences, many conductors chose not to perform "difficult" contemporary works, favoring those that were relatively accessible in style. One result was that some of the most innovative twentieth-century composers—Ives, Webern, and Varèse, for example—were neglected.

After World War I, organizations were formed for the specific purpose of giving the public a greater opportunity to hear new music. The International Society for Contemporary Music was the most influential, with branches in many countries.

During the 1950s and 1960s, major orchestras and opera companies began to program more twentieth-century music. Long-playing recordings gave access to works that had seemed incomprehensible; they could now be played repeatedly until they were understood and enjoyed. Musicians themselves grew more accustomed to intricate modern rhythms and thus were better able to perform them.

Many modern compositions were commissioned by ballet and opera companies, foundations, orchestras, performers, film studios, and wealthy music lovers. Developments in the dance had an especially strong impact on twentieth-century music. A single company, Sergei Diaghilev's Russian Ballet, provided the

 Music and Musicians in Society

385

impetus for masterpieces such as Stravinsky's *Petrushka* (1911), Ravel's *Daphnis et Chloé* (1912), and Debussy's *Jeux* (1913). Films provided a new stimulus for music, too. Though most film scores were merely background music, some, like Prokofiev's *Lieutenant Kije* (1934), were enjoyed apart from the movie. Philanthropic foundations have become significant music patrons in our time. One, most active in the field of chamber music, was established by Mrs. Elizabeth Sprague Coolidge in 1925 at the Library of Congress in Washington. Mrs. Coolidge's generosity spurred the creation of many fine compositions, including Bartók's *Fifth String Quartet* (1934) and Schoenberg's *Fourth String Quartet* (1936). Yet, however important commissions have been in our century, few serious musicians can live on them alone. Most modern composers are also teachers, conductors, or performers.

Like all people, musicians have been affected by the political, economic, and social upheavals of the twentieth century. Hitler's rise to power in Germany in 1933 had an especially dramatic impact on their lives and careers. Avant-garde, socialist, and Jewish musicians were abruptly ousted from their jobs, and their works were no longer performed. Dictatorship, persecution, and the onset of World War II (1939–1945) led to the largest migration of artists and intellectuals in history. Many leading composers, including Stravinsky, Bartók, Schoenberg, and Hindemith, left Europe for the United States. Such distinguished refugees made enormous contributions to America's musical culture. Schoenberg and Hindemith, for example, taught in universities and helped train some of America's finest composers.

During this century, the United States became a potent force in music. American jazz and popular music swept the world. With more first-rank symphony orchestras than any other country, after 1920 America produced a large group of composers representing a wide spectrum of contemporary styles.

American colleges and universities have played an unusually vital role in our musical culture. They have trained and employed many of our leading composers, performers, and scholars. Music courses have expanded the horizons and interests of countless students. And since midcentury, many universities have sponsored performing groups specializing in twentieth-century music. In addition, they housed most of the electronic music studios. Thus, American colleges and universities have indirectly become patrons of music, as the church and nobility were in earlier times.

IMPRESSIONISM AND SYMBOLISM $\|3\|$

Many different musical styles coexisted around the turn of the century. Among the most important was impressionism, best represented by the music of French composer Claude Debussy (1862–1918). We'll look closely at musical impressionism in section 4; first, two related, but slightly earlier artistic movements in France demand our attention: impressionist painting and symbolist poetry.

French Impressionist Painting

In 1874, a group of French painters including Claude Monet (1840–1926), Auguste Renoir (1841–1919), and Camille Pissarro (1830–1903) had an exhibition in Paris. One Monet painting entitled *Impression: Sunrise*—a misty scene of boats in port—particularly annoyed an art critic, who wrote, "Wallpaper in its embryonic state is more finished than that seascape." Using Monet's title, the critic mockingly called the entire show "the exhibition of the impressionists." The term *impressionist* stuck, but it eventually lost its derisive implication.

Today most of us appreciate impressionist paintings, which colorfully depict the joys of life and the beauties of nature. But during the 1870s, they were seen as formless collections of tiny colored patches—which they are, when viewed closely. But from a distance, the brush strokes blend and merge into recognizable forms and shimmering colors. Impressionist painters were concerned primarily with effects of light, color, and atmosphere—with impermanence, change, and fluidity. Monet created a series of twenty paintings (1892–1894) showing Rouen Cathedral at different times of the day, from dawn to dusk. In this series, the cathedral's stone facade is desolidified and looks like colored mist. (In section 4, we'll study Debussy's piano piece *The Sunken Cathedral* (1910), which is a musical analogy to Monet's cathedral paintings.) Many impressionist painters preferred to work in the open air, rather than in a studio. They were fascinated by outdoor scenes from contemporary life, picnics in the woods, and crowds on Parisian boulevards. But most of all, the impressionists were obsessed by water. Using light, pastel colors, they depicted the ripples and waves of the ocean and sailboats on the river Seine.

French Symbolist Poetry

As impressionist painters broke from traditional depictions of reality, writers called *symbolists* rebelled against the conventions of French poetry. Like the painters, poets such as Stéphane Mallarmé (1842–1898), Paul Verlaine (1844– French Symbolist Poetry

387

Impressionist painters were concerned primarily with effects of light, color, and atmosphere. In Claude Monet's *Rouen Cathedral,* the cathedral's stone facade is desolidified and looks like colored mist (The Metropolitan Museum of Art, The Theodore M. Davis Collection, 1915).

1896), and Arthur Rimbaud (1854–1891) emphasized fluidity and suggestion. "To *name* an object," insisted Mallarmé, "is to suppress three-quarters of the enjoyment of a poem, which is made up of gradually guessing; the dream is to *suggest* it." Symbolist writers emphasized the purely musical, or sonorous, effects of words.

Claude Debussy was a close friend of many symbolist poets, especially Mallarmé, whose poem *L'Après-midi d'un faune* (*The Afternoon of a Faun*) inspired Debussy's most famous orchestral work. Many poems by Verlaine became texts for Debussy's songs. (And, more personally, Verlaine's mother-in-law was his first piano teacher.) Both impressionist painting and symbolist poetry were catalysts for many developments during the twentieth century. The next section describes their effect on music.

CLAUDE DEBUSSY ‖ 4 ‖

French impressionist composer Claude Debussy (1862–1918) linked the Romantic era with the twentieth century. He was born in St. Germain-en-Laye, a small town near Paris. At the early age of ten, he entered the Paris Conservatory, where he studied until he was twenty-two. Debussy's teachers regarded him as a talented rebel who improvised unorthodox chord progressions of dissonances that did not resolve. (While Debussy was at the Conservatory, the impressionists exhibited their paintings in Paris.)

In his late teens, Debussy worked summers as pianist for Mme. von Meck, the Russian patroness of Tchaikovsky. During these stays in Russia, Debussy's lifelong interest in Russian music took root. In 1884, he won France's highest award for composers, the Prix de Rome, which subsidized three years of study in the Eternal City. But he left Italy after only two years because he lacked musical inspiration away from his beloved Paris.

When Debussy returned to Paris in 1887, the music and ideas of Richard Wagner had a profound influence on French composers and writers. Many of Debussy's friends wrote articles for *The Wagnerian Review* (*La Revue Wagnérienne*), a periodical devoted to the German master. During the summers of 1888 and 1889, Debussy traveled to Bayreuth, Germany, to hear Wagner's music dramas. They were memorable events for the young Frenchman, who was both attracted and repelled by Wagner's music.

Oriental music performed at the Paris International Exhibition of 1889 also had a strong impact on Debussy. "Do you not remember the Javanese music," he wrote a friend, "able to express every shade of meaning . . . and which makes our tonic and dominant seem like ghosts."

Claude
Debussy

389

For years Debussy led an unsettled life, earning a small income by teaching piano. His friends were mostly writers, such as Stéphane Mallarmé, whose literary gatherings he attended regularly. In cafes and cabarets he mingled with jockeys and entertainers like those immortalized in the paintings of Toulouse-Lautrec. Until the age of thirty-one, he was little known to the musical public and not completely sure of himself. "There are still things that I am not able to do—create masterpieces for example," he wrote in 1893. But that same year Debussy did complete a masterpiece, the *String Quartet*. And in 1894 he created another, the tone poem *Prelude to "The Afternoon of a Faun,"* which has become his most popular orchestral work.

A dramatic turning point in Debussy's career came in 1902, with his opera *Pelléas et Mélisande*. Critics were sharply divided. Some complained about the absence of melody and the harmonies that broke traditional rules; others were delighted by the poetic atmosphere and subtle tone colors. The opera soon caught on, and Debussy was recognized as France's leading composer. Musicians all over the world imitated his style.

This artistic triumph was surrounded by a personal life filled with financial and emotional crises. Debussy constantly borrowed money for luxuries he craved: fine food, beautiful clothes, and art works. The attempted suicides of two women in his life were major scandals in Paris. His longtime mistress shot herself when he left her for Rosalie Texier, a milliner who became his first wife. Then Rosalie Texier, in turn, shot herself when Debussy left *her* for Emma Bardac, an intelligent, talented, and rich society woman.

Debussy's marriage to Emma Bardac caused him to undertake concert tours to maintain their high standard of living. Though he was not gifted as a conductor and hated appearing in public, he presented his music throughout Europe. At fifty he developed cancer. The onset of World War I in 1914 heightened his sense of nationalism, and he began to sign his works "Claude Debussy, French musician." He died in Paris on March 25, 1918, while the city was being shelled by German artillery.

Debussy's Music

Like the French impressionist painters and symbolist poets, Debussy was a master at evoking a fleeting mood and misty atmosphere. His interest in the effects of fluidity, intangibility, and impermanence is mirrored even in his titles: *Reflections in the Water* (*Reflets dans l'eau*), *Clouds* (*Nuages*), and *The Sounds and the Perfumes Swirl in the Evening Air* (*Les sons et les parfums tournent dans l'air du soir*). Literary and pictorial ideas often inspired Debussy, and most of his compositions have descriptive titles. His music sounds free and spontaneous, almost improvised. He once wrote, "I am more and more convinced that music is not, in essence, a thing which can be cast into a traditional and fixed form. It is made up of colors and rhythms." This stress on tone color, atmosphere, and fluidity is characteristic of **impressionism** in music.

Tone color truly gets unprecedented attention in Debussy's works. His subtle changes of timbre are as crucial to his music as thematic contrasts are in earlier music. The sensuous, beautiful sound he sought is never harsh. The entire orchestra seldom plays together to produce massive sound. Instead, there are brief but frequent instrumental solos. The woodwinds are especially prominent and are used in unusual registers. (The velvety low register of the flute is featured in the *Prelude to "The Afternoon of a Faun."*) Strings and brasses are often muted; their sound seems to come from far off. Atmosphere is created through the shimmer of a string tremolo or the splash of a harp.

Debussy wrote some of his finest music for piano, again creating new sonorities. Frequent use of the damper pedal, which allows a pianist to sustain tones after the keys are released, results in hazy sounds. Chords are often blended together, and the pianist is directed to let the sounds vibrate. The rich variety of bell and gong sounds in Debussy's piano works may reflect the influence of Asian music he heard at the Paris International Exposition in 1889.

Debussy's treatment of harmony was a revolutionary aspect of musical impressionism. He tends to use a chord more for its special color and sensuous quality than for its function in a standard harmonic progression. He uses successions of dissonant chords that do not resolve. (When young, Debussy was asked which harmonic rules he followed; he replied, simply, "My pleasure.") He freely shifts a dissonant chord up or down the scale, and such parallel chords characterize his style.

Debussy, *The Sunken Cathedral*[1]

Debussy's harmonic vocabulary is large. Along with traditional three- and four-note chords, he uses five-note chords with a lush, rich sound. Chord progressions that were highly unorthodox when Debussy wrote them soon came to seem mild and natural.

"One must drown the sense of tonality," Debussy wrote. While he never actually abandoned tonality, Debussy weakened it by deliberately avoiding chord progressions that strongly affirm the key. The traditional dominant-tonic cadence is relatively rare in his music. He also "drowns" tonality by using scales in which the main tone is less emphasized than in major or minor scales. He turned to the medieval church modes, which he knew from Gregorian chant. He also used the pentatonic, or five-tone, scales heard in Javanese music. These

Debussy's
Music

391

pentatonic scales lend an Oriental atmosphere to some of Debussy's music. (A pentatonic scale is produced by five successive black keys of the piano: F♯–G♯–A♯–C♯–D♯.)

Debussy's most unusual and tonally vague scale is the **whole-tone scale,** made up of six different notes each a whole step away from the next (C–D–E–F♯–G♯–A♯–C). Unlike major and minor, the whole-tone scale has no special pull from *ti* to *do*, since its tones are all the same distance apart. And because no single tone stands out, the scale creates a blurred, indistinct effect.

Debussy, *Voiles* (Sails)[2]

The pulse in Debussy's music is sometimes as vague as tonality. "Rhythms cannot be contained within bars," he wrote. He avoids recurring strong accents that coincide with the bar line. His rhythmic flexibility reflects the fluid, unaccented quality of the French language. In fact, few composers have set French to music so sensitively as Debussy. He composed fifty-nine art songs, many of which are set to symbolist poems by Charles Baudelaire, Paul Verlaine, and Stéphane Mallarmé. His only opera, *Pelléas et Mélisande,* is an almost word-for-word setting of a symbolist play by the Belgian poet Maurice Maeterlinck. This great and highly original opera is the essence of musical impressionism. Its vague, mysterious plot includes characters who barely communicate with each other. There are no arias, and the melodic line is almost entirely speechlike. The play's dreamlike atmosphere is magically evoked by an orchestral accompaniment that is discreet and understated; it's as though Debussy consciously sought to avoid the powerful sound of Wagner's orchestral parts.

While not large, Debussy's output is remarkably varied. Along with his opera, he contributed masterpieces to the literature of the piano, orchestra, chamber ensemble, and art song. We have said that Debussy's music is tonally vague and has an improvisational, floating quality. It's not surprising, then, that he avoided sonata form, which traditionally calls for a clear contrast of keys and systematic development of themes. One section of Debussy's music melts into the next; melodic lines tend to be brief and fragmentary.

Echoes of Debussy's music can be heard in the works of many composers during the first two decades of the twentieth century. However, no other leading musician can so fairly be described as an impressionist. Even the composer most similar to Debussy, his younger French contemporary Maurice Ravel (1875–1937), wrote music with greater clarity of form. Debussy's impressionist style was both a final expression of Romanticism and the beginning of a new era. His use of tone color as a vital element of form and his novel harmonic techniques made

him the immediate forerunner of later twentieth-century musicians. Igor Stravinsky was perceptive when he remarked, "I and the members of my generation owe most to Debussy."

Prelude to "The Afternoon of a Faun" (*Prélude à "L'Après-midi d'un faune"*)

Side 12, band 2

"The music of this Prelude," wrote Debussy, "is a very free illustration of the beautiful poem by Stéphane Mallarmé, *The Afternoon of a Faun*." This poem evokes the dreams and erotic fantasies of a pagan forest creature who is half man, half goat. While playing "a long solo" on his flute, the intoxicated faun tries to recall whether he actually carried off two beautiful nymphs or only dreamed of doing so. Exhausted by the effort, he falls back to sleep in the warm sunshine.

Debussy intended his music to suggest "the successive scenes through which pass the desires and dreams of the faun in the heat of this afternoon." The subtle, sensuous timbres of this miniature tone poem were new in Debussy's day. Woodwind solos, muted horn calls, and harp glissandos create a rich variety of delicate sounds. The dynamics are usually subdued, and the entire orchestra—from which trombones, trumpets, and timpani are excluded—rarely plays at one time. The music often swells sensuously, only to subside in voluptuous exhaustion.

The Prelude begins with an unaccompanied flute melody; its vague pulse and tonality make it dreamlike and improvisatory. This flute melody is heard again and again, faster, slower, and against a variety of lush chords. Though the form of the Prelude may be thought of as A B A', one section blends with the next. It has a continuous ebb and flow. The fluidity and weightlessness typical of impressionism are found in this music. We are never tempted to beat time to its subtle rhythms. The Prelude ends magically with the main melody, played by muted horns, seeming to come from far off. The bell-like tones of antique cymbals finally evaporate into silence. With all its new sounds and musical techniques, the piece has aptly been described as a "quiet revolution" in the history of music.

‖ LISTENING OUTLINE
To be read while music is heard

Prelude to "The Afternoon of a Faun" (*Prélude à "L'Après-midi d'un faune"*; 1894), by Claude Debussy

At a very moderate tempo, A B A' form, E major

3 flutes, 2 oboes, 1 English horn, 2 clarinets, 2 bassoons, 4 horns, 2 harps, antique cymbals, violins 1, violins 2, violas, cellos, double basses

393

(About 10 min)

A   1   *a.* Solo flute, *p*, main melody.

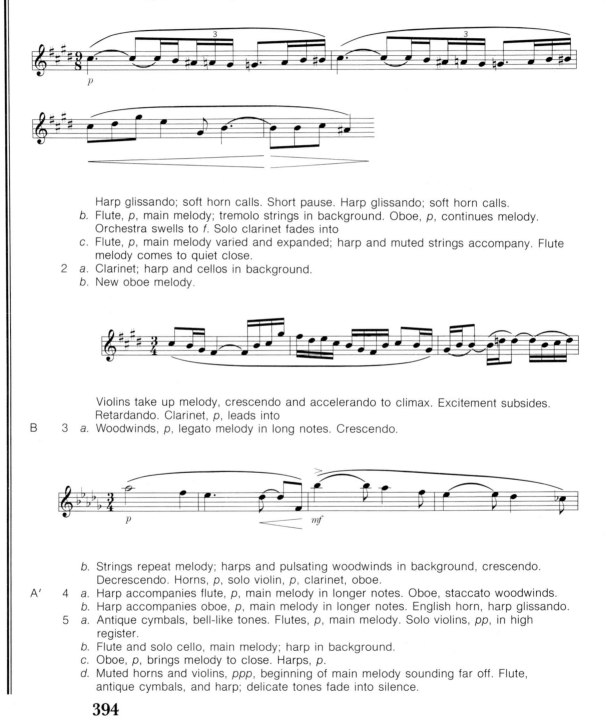

Harp glissando; soft horn calls. Short pause. Harp glissando; soft horn calls.
    b. Flute, *p*, main melody; tremolo strings in background. Oboe, *p*, continues melody. Orchestra swells to *f*. Solo clarinet fades into
    c. Flute, *p*, main melody varied and expanded; harp and muted strings accompany. Flute melody comes to quiet close.
  2   *a.* Clarinet; harp and cellos in background.
    b. New oboe melody.

Violins take up melody, crescendo and accelerando to climax. Excitement subsides. Retardando. Clarinet, *p*, leads into

B   3   *a.* Woodwinds, *p*, legato melody in long notes. Crescendo.

    b. Strings repeat melody; harps and pulsating woodwinds in background, crescendo. Decrescendo. Horns, *p*, solo violin, *p*, clarinet, oboe.

A′ 4   *a.* Harp accompanies flute, *p*, main melody in longer notes. Oboe, staccato woodwinds.
    b. Harp accompanies oboe, *p*, main melody in longer notes. English horn, harp glissando.
  5   *a.* Antique cymbals, bell-like tones. Flutes, *p*, main melody. Solo violins, *pp*, in high register.
    b. Flute and solo cello, main melody; harp in background.
    c. Oboe, *p*, brings melody to close. Harps, *p*.
    d. Muted horns and violins, *ppp*, beginning of main melody sounding far off. Flute, antique cymbals, and harp; delicate tones fade into silence.

394

The Sunken Cathedral (*La Cathédrale engloutie*), from *Preludes* for piano (Book I, 1910)

This piano piece was inspired by a French legend about the Cathedral of Ys, which had sunk beneath the sea. According to legend, the cathedral sometimes rises, its bells tolling and its priests chanting a hymn. Then it slowly sinks back beneath the waves.

Debussy uses the piano's damper pedal to create lingering vibrations that suggest different effects, including waves, mist, the murmur of the sea, and a variety of bells. The opening is "profoundly calm, in a softly sonorous mist." Mysterious bell-tolls merge with legato, upward-moving chords that have a hollow sound.

The music "gradually comes out of the mist," as low rumbling sounds depict waves. With a crescendo the bell sounds grow richer and more sonorous. Then the cathedral is suggested by a majestic, hymnlike melody accompanied by deep, repeated bell-tolls in the bass.

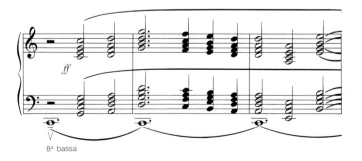

The Sunken Cathedral

In this hymnlike passage, the chords move in parallel motion; that is, the same chord structure is shifted to different pitch levels. This technique is characteristic of impressionist style.

Debussy suggests the cathedral's return to the ocean depths by a faint echo of the hymnlike melody. Now it is muffled, in a lower register, and accompanied by a murmuring repeated figure in the bass. The piece ends "in the sonority of the beginning" with legato upward-moving chords (now slightly dissonant) and quiet bell sounds.

Basic Terms

impressionism
whole-tone scale

5 NEOCLASSICISM

From about 1920 to 1950 the music of many composers, including Igor Stravinsky and Paul Hindemith, reflected an artistic movement known as **neoclassicism.** Neoclassicism is marked by emotional restraint, balance, and clarity; neoclassical compositions use musical forms and stylistic features of earlier periods, particularly of the eighteenth century. Stravinsky summed it up: "I attempted to build a new music on eighteenth-century classicism." Neoclassical music is not merely a revival of old forms and styles; it uses earlier techniques to organize twentieth-century harmonies and rhythms.

"Back to Bach" was the slogan of this movement that reacted against Romanticism and impressionism. (Since many neoclassical compositions were modeled after Bach's music, the term *neobaroque* might have been more appropriate.) Neoclassical composers turned away from program music and the gigantic orchestras favored at the turn of the century. They preferred absolute (nonprogrammatic) music for chamber groups. This preference for smaller performing groups partly reflected economic necessity: During the post-World War I period, economic conditions were so bad in parts of Europe that there was little money to hire large orchestras. Favoring clear polyphonic textures, composers wrote fugues, concerti grossi, and Baroque dance suites. Most neoclassical music was tonal and used major and minor scales. Still, neoclassicism was more an attitude than a style. Schoenberg wrote minuets and gigues using his twelve-tone system. And though neoclassical composers referred to many past styles, their works sound completely modern. They play on the delightful tension between our expectations about old forms and styles and the novel harmonies and rhythms. In section 6, we'll study a neoclassical work by Stravinsky, the *Symphony of Psalms* (1930).

Neoclassicism was an important trend in other arts, too. Poet T. S. Eliot often quoted and alluded to earlier writers. Picasso, who designed sets for Stravinsky's first neoclassical work, *Pulcinella* (1920), went through a phase where he created paintings that show the influence of ancient Greek art. Picasso described the neoclassical attitude by saying that artists "must pick out what is good for us where we find it. When I am shown a portfolio of old drawings, for instance, I have no qualms about taking anything I want from them."

Basic Term

neoclassicism

IGOR STRAVINSKY ‖ 6 ‖

Even before his death in 1971 at the age of eighty-eight, Igor Stravinsky (1882–1971) was a legendary figure regarded as the world's greatest composer. His once revolutionary works were modern classics; he was a restless innovator who influenced three generations of composers and inspired many painters, writers, and choreographers. Cultural giants like Picasso and T. S. Eliot were his friends; President John F. Kennedy honored him at a White House dinner in his eightieth year.

Born in a small town near St. Petersburg (Leningrad), Russia, Stravinsky grew up in a musical atmosphere. His father was a leading singer at the St. Petersburg opera. Despite Stravinsky's obvious talent, his parents insisted that he study law at the University of St. Petersburg. Soon he began to neglect his studies and devote himself to composition. At twenty-one, he became a private student of Nikolai Rimsky-Korsakov.

 Igor Stravinsky

397

Igor Stravinsky in a sketch by Picasso (Omikron).

Stravinsky's life took a sudden turn in 1909, when the great impresario Sergei Diaghilev heard his music at a concert in St. Petersburg. Diaghilev was director of the Russian Ballet. Based in Paris, this troupe had a powerful impact on both Stravinsky and the entire cultural scene in Europe from 1909 to 1929. It employed great masters in all arts. Its dancers included Vaslav Nijinsky, and choreographers Mikhail Fokine and George Balanchine created works for the troupe. It commissioned stage designs from great painters like Picasso and ballet music from outstanding musicians like Stravinsky, Debussy, Ravel, and Proko-fiev. Diaghilev asked twenty-six-year-old Stravinsky to orchestrate piano pieces by Chopin as ballet music for the first season of the Russian Ballet in 1909. In 1910, Stravinsky was commissioned to compose an original ballet, *The Firebird*. Based on a Russian fairy tale, this ballet's immense success immediately estab-lished Stravinsky as a leading young composer. His second ballet, *Petrushka*

(1911), was performed a year later, and at twenty-nine Stravinsky was hailed as a modern master. His incisive rhythms, witty musical satire, and brilliant orchestral colors delighted sophisticated Parisians.

A now-legendary riot erupted in the audience when Stravinsky's third ballet, *The Rite of Spring,* was performed in Paris in 1913. Spectators hissed and booed at the music's "primitive" evocation of pagan fertility rites, at its harshly insistent dissonance, at its percussiveness and pounding rhythms. One audience member reported that someone excitedly "began to beat rhythmically on top of my head with his fists. My emotion was so great that I did not feel the blows." Soon after, however, the ballet was recognized as a masterpiece; it influenced composers all over the world.

The outbreak of World War I in 1914 forced Stravinsky to seek refuge in neutral Switzerland, where he lived for six years with his wife and children. Since the Russian Revolution of 1917 ended his private income, he met financial difficulties for the first time in his life. To "escape from this alarming situation," Stravinsky wrote *The Soldier's Tale* (1918), a theatrical work that required few performers and was easy to present under wartime conditions.

After the armistice in 1918, Stravinsky moved to France, his home until the onset of World War II. Now Stravinsky was an international figure, constantly touring Europe and the United States to play and conduct his music. His voluntary exile from Russia coincided with his turning away from Russian folk music as a source of inspiration. Stravinsky's works in the twenties and thirties seemed excessively cool and objective to some music lovers, who preferred the early Russian-flavored ballets.

Unlike his great contemporaries Schoenberg and Bartók, Stravinsky got well-paying commissions for his work and was an astute businessman. He described himself as composing "every day, regularly, like a man with banking hours." Stravinsky's love of order and discipline was reflected in his studio, which had, in the words of a friend, "all the instruments needed for writing, copying, drawing, pasting, cutting, clipping, filing, sharpening, and gluing that the combined effects of a stationery and hardware store can furnish."

World War II caused Stravinsky to settle in yet another country, the United States. He lived outside Los Angeles not far from Arnold Schoenberg, but the two never visited. Their different musical philosophies created an unbridgeable gulf, and each had his group of loyal disciples. In 1948, Stravinsky engaged Robert Craft, a twenty-four-year-old conductor, as his musical assistant. Craft encouraged Stravinsky to become more familiar with the works of Schoenberg, Berg, and Webern. By the 1950s, all three composers were dead, and Stravinsky astonished his followers by adopting Schoenberg's twelve-tone system. And in his seventies and eighties, despite physical pain, this incredible man toured the world from Chile to Tahiti conducting his rich and intense late works. He also, for the first time in fifty years, returned to Russia and bared his soul to a group of Soviet composers: "The smell of the Russian earth is different. . . . A man has one birthplace, one fatherland, one country."

 Igor Stravinsky

399

Stravinsky's Music

Stravinsky had an enormous influence on twentieth-century music. His innovations in rhythm, harmony, and tone color inspired musicians throughout the world. No contemporary contributed so many masterpieces to the international repertory. Stravinsky's extensive output includes music of almost every kind, for both voices and instruments. His many works for the stage include thirteen ballet scores.

Like his friend Picasso, Stravinsky's development shows dramatic changes of style. His three early ballets—*The Firebird* (1910), *Petrushka* (1911), and *The Rite of Spring* (1913)—call for very large orchestras and draw upon Russian folklore and folk tunes. During World War I, Stravinsky abandoned the large orchestra and wrote for small chamber groups with unconventional combinations of instruments. Ragtime rhythms and popular dances (for example, the tango) were used in such works as *The Soldier's Tale* (1918). During the period from about 1920 to 1951 (discussed earlier as the era of neoclassicism) he gradually turned from Russian folklore and drew inspiration largely from eighteenth-century music. First came the ballet *Pulcinella* (1920), based on the music of Giovanni Battista Pergolesi, an Italian composer of the early eighteenth century; the period ended with his opera *The Rake's Progress* (1951), modeled after Mozart's operas. Emphasizing emotional restraint, balance, and wit, Stravinsky's work at this time was far removed from the violence and "primitivism" of *The Rite*. Many pieces feature woodwind and brass instruments, which Stravinsky felt to be less "romantic" in sound than strings. Some works are based on subjects from antiquity, like the opera-oratorio *Oedipus Rex* (1927); others were inspired by sacred texts, like the *Symphony of Psalms* (1930).

Whatever Stravinsky's current style, he had always written music with a clear tonal center. So the musical world was startled when he shifted from tonality to the twelve-tone system. This dramatic change of approach came during the 1950s, when Stravinsky was in his seventies. Taking inspiration from the music of Anton Webern (1883–1945), Stravinsky now wrote brief works in which melodic lines were "atomized" into brief fragments in constantly changing tone colors and registers.

Despite such style changes, all of his music has an unmistakable "Stravinsky sound." His tone colors tend to be dry and clear, while the beat is strong and regular.

Stravinsky's rhythmic imagination was one of the most fertile in our century. His music abounds in changing and irregular meters; sometimes several meters are heard at once. Ostinatos, or repeated rhythmic patterns, frequently unify sections of a piece. They also accompany melodies with highly irregular phrase structures.

Stravinsky's treatment of musical form is also unique. Rather than connecting themes with bridge passages, he shifts abruptly from one section to the next. One idea is repeated and varied for a while, only to be broken off by something new. "Here, you see, I cut off the fugue with a pair of scissors," he remarked of a fugue that is repeatedly punctuated by contrasting material. But despite all the sudden changes, Stravinsky's music sounds unified and continuous.

Tone color is an integral part of his work. The effectiveness of his rhythms, chords, and melodies depends largely on how they are orchestrated. Much of his music is scored for unconventional groups of instruments. Highly contrasting tone colors are often combined: A violin is set against a trumpet, or a piano against a trombone. Instruments play in unusual registers, too. For example, *The Rite of Spring* opens with the highest tones of a solo bassoon. Stravinsky uses percussion instruments imaginatively, often giving them solo roles. (He even acquired percussion instruments so that he could personally try out his drum parts.) The writer with whom he collaborated on *The Soldier's Tale* reported that he and Stravinsky met almost daily "in the blue room . . . surrounded by side drums, kettle drums, bass drums, and every kind of percussion instrument."

Stravinsky's music has rich, novel harmonies, such as the famous "Petrushka chord," a bitonal combination of a C-major triad with an F♯-major triad. He makes even conventional chords sound unique through spacing, doubling, and the orchestration of their tones. The spirit of this composer's approach is seen in his exclamation about one such novel-sounding harmony: "How happy I was when I discovered this chord!"

Stravinsky often used known material to create original music. He drew on a vast range of styles, from Russian folk songs to Baroque melodies, from Renaissance madrigals to tango rhythms. Sometimes he gave another composer's melody new harmonies and orchestration. But more often, the music is entirely Stravinsky's, while vaguely suggesting a past style. Stravinsky spoke of a "lifelong need for outside nourishment." He believed that tradition is "a living force that animates and informs the present. . . . It appears as an heirloom, a heritage that one receives on condition of making it bear fruit before passing it on to one's descendants."

Petrushka (1911)

Petrushka was Stravinsky's second ballet score for the Russian Ballet in Paris. It is a fantasy that unfolds against the backdrop of a Russian street fair during the St. Petersburg Carnival in the 1830s. Its main characters are three life-sized puppets—Petrushka, the Moor, and the Ballerina—who are brought to life by an old magician. In Stravinsky's words, Petrushka is "the immortal and unhappy hero of every fair in all countries." In a way, he's the Russian counterpart of the puppet Pinocchio. Petrushka competes with the Moor for the affection of the Ballerina. In the fourth and last scene of the ballet, the Moor strikes Petrushka with a sword and kills him, to the crowd's astonishment.

Petrushka (1911)

401

Petrushka's music is, by turns, brilliant, grotesque, and humorous. It perfectly matches the story line. Stravinsky uses Russian folk songs as well as popular songs and dances to capture the atmosphere of the Russian street fair. The sheer color and imagination of the score make *Petrushka* as popular in the concert hall as it is in the theater. We'll now focus on the ballet's opening scene, which is divided into three sections: (1) The Crowds, (2) The Magic Trick, and (3) The Russian Dance.

Opening Scene

The curtain rises on a street fair with booths, a puppet theater, and a milling crowd. Soon an organ grinder and a street dancer compete with a music-box player and another dancer for the crowd's attention. The music is marvelously descriptive; trills and running notes match the lively activity on stage. The general confusion of a crowd is suggested through polyrhythm—the double basses play in one meter, while piccolos play in another. Woodwinds perfectly imitate the sound of a barrel organ.

The most important borrowed melody in the first section is an Easter song from the Smolensk region of Russia. The tune begins with a tone that is repeated several times. After its introduction by the double basses, the melody is played by the full orchestra as a group of drunken merrymakers dance across stage. There are two different barrel-organ tunes. The second was originally a French music-hall favorite, "She had a wooden leg," which Stravinsky actually heard outside his window while he was composing this scene.

The opening section of *Petrushka* is in three-part form: A (crowd) B (soloists: barrel organ and music box) A′ (crowd). The two outer sections are more complex musically, with the many abrupt changes characteristic of Stravinsky—rapidly changing meters, irregular rhythms, and twentieth-century chord structures. In the contrasting middle section (B), the harmonies and rhythms are conventional, in keeping with the humble folk instruments shown playing them on stage.

The second and third sections of this scene—The Magic Trick and The Russian Dance—are much shorter than the first. An old magician appears at the puppet theater and brings the three puppets to life by playing a magic flute. The puppets then do a frantic Russian dance, first dangling on their strings in the theater and then out in the street among the amazed crowd.

Stravinsky uses a descending figure in the bassoon to represent the old magician. Strange chromatic harmonies and wisps of sound from the celesta and harp create a mysterious atmosphere.

The Russian Dance suggests the puppets' jerky movements by a rapid, powerful beat and bright, percussive tone colors. Piano, xylophone, and woodwinds often have solo parts. The main theme has a narrow range and is spun out of a small group of tones; these are repeated again and again with slight rhythmic variations. Repeated rhythmic figures occur in the accompaniment, too.

LISTENING OUTLINE
To be read while music is heard

Opening scene from *Petrushka* (original 1911 version), by Igor Stravinsky

2 piccolos, 2 flutes, 4 oboes, English horn, 4 clarinets, bass clarinet, 4 bassoons, contrabassoon, 4 horns, 2 cornets, 2 trumpets, 3 trombones, tuba, timpani, bass drum, cymbals, gong, triangle, tambourine, snare drum, xylophone, glockenspiel, 2 harps, piano, celesta, violins 1, violins 2, violas, cellos, double bases

(About 10 min)

Section I: Crowds (Vivace)
Bustling crowd. 1 *a.* High flute, crowd theme; accompanying trills in clarinets and horns.

b. Low basses, opening of Russian tune.

c. High flute, crowd theme; accompanying trills in clarinets and horns.
d. Low basses, Russian tune. High piccolos join Russian tune in faster notes. Crescendo, trumpets.

A group of drunken merry- 2 *a.* Full orchestra, *fff*, Russian tune; powerful beat, cymbals.
makers pass by, dancing.

b. Suddenly softer, Russian tune in woodwinds and violins, pizzicato. Brass chord crescendo.

The old showman of the fair 3 *a.* Timpani; staccato repeated notes in strings; irregular accents. Staccato brasses, *f*.
entertains the crowd from
the height of his booth.

b. High piccolos, crowd theme.

An organ-grinder with a *c.* Timpani. Clarinets, opening of first barrel-organ tune.
street dancer appears in *d.* Timpani; staccato repeated notes in strings. Staccato
the crowd. brasses, *ff*.
e. High violins, crowd theme.

403

Organ-grinder begins to play   4   *a.* Clarinets, first barrel-organ tune; slow "oom-pah-pah" accompaniment.

The street dancer dances, beating time on the triangle.

     b. Triangle accompanies second barrel-organ tune in flutes and clarinets.

The organ-grinder, continuing to turn the crank with one hand, plays the cornet with the other.
On the other side of the stage a music box begins to play. Another street dancer dances around it.
The barrel-organ and the music box stop playing. The old showman again entertains the crowd.

Trumpet joins. Violins, crowd theme bursts in.

     c. Glockenspiel (bells), music-box tune; clarinets, first barrel-organ tune. Triangle accompanies second barrel-organ tune in flutes and clarinets. High violins, crowd theme bursts in.
     d. Timpani; staccato repeated notes in strings; irregular accents.

The drunken merrymakers return.

5   High crowd theme with bustling accompaniment. Piccolos and trumpets join, crescendo.
6   *a.* Russian tune, orchestra, *fff*, powerful beat; cymbals.
     b. Suddenly softer, Russian tune in woodwinds and violins, pizzicato. Brass chord crescendo.
7   *a.* Timpani; staccato repeated notes in strings, irregular accents. Staccato brasses, *f*.
     b. High piccolo, crowd theme.
     c. Timpani; staccato repeated notes in strings, irregular accents. Staccato brasses, *f*.
     d. High piccolo, crowd theme. Trumpets join, crescendo to *fff* climax.
     e. Drum rolls.

Two drummers standing in front of the little theater attract the attention of the crowd by their drum rolls.

Section II: The Magic Trick (Lento)

Out of the little theater steps the old magician.
The magician plays the flute.

1   Solo bassoon, *p*, low descending figure. High, mysterious sounds in celesta, harp, and violins. Chord in strings.
2   Solo flute, *p*, upward and downward arpeggios.

The curtain of the little theater opens, and the crowd sees three puppets: Petrushka, the Moor, and the Ballerina.	3 Violins, *pp*, high descending figure. Mysterious sounds in celesta, harps, and woodwinds.
The magician animates them by touching them with his flute.	Solo flute, piccolo (two tones for each puppet).

Section III: The Russian Dance (Allegro, in strict time)

Petrushka, the Moor, and the Ballerina begin to dance together, to the great surprise of all.	1 *a.* Main theme, *f*. Upward glissando to

  b. Brief solos by cornet, clarinet, and oboe. Other instruments join on melody, crescendo.
2 *a.* Main theme, *ff*, full orchestra.
  b. Oboe solo punctuated by loud percussive sounds.
3 *a.* Piano solo, second theme. Solo violin takes second theme. Xylophone, main theme.
  b. Clarinet and English horn, *p*, main theme in slower tempo.
4 Solo piano, *f*, main theme in fast tempo. Other instruments join. Running notes punctuated by loud chords. Abrupt concluding cadence.

The Rite of Spring (*Le Sacre du printemps;* 1913)

Few compositions have had so powerful an impact on twentieth-century music as *The Rite of Spring,* Stravinsky's third ballet score for the Russian Ballet. Its harsh dissonances, percussive orchestration, rapidly changing meters, violent off-beat accents, and ostinatos fired the imaginations of many composers. The idea for *The Rite* came to Stravinsky as "a fleeting vision," while he was completing *The Firebird* in St. Petersburg in 1910. "I saw in imagination a solemn pagan rite: wise elders, seated in a circle, watching a young girl dance herself to death. They were sacrificing her to propitiate the god of spring." Later in life, Stravinsky revealed that "the most wonderful event" of every year of his childhood was "the violent Russian spring that seemed to begin in an hour and was like the whole earth crackling."

Stravinsky's interest in a so-called "primitive" or nonliterate culture was shared by many artists and scholars in the early 1900s. In 1907, Picasso's violent and path-breaking painting *Les Demoiselles d'Avignon* reflected the influence of

The Rite of Spring

In 1907, Picasso's painting *Les Demoiselles d'Avignon* reflected the influence of African sculpture (Collection, The Museum of Modern Art, New York. Acquired through the Lillie P. Bliss Bequest).

African sculpture. In 1913—the same year as *The Rite of Spring*—Freud published *Totem and Taboo,* a study of the "resemblances between the psychic lives of savages and neurotics." But **primitivism**—the deliberate evocation of primitive power through insistent rhythms and percussive sounds—did not have a lasting impact on early twentieth-century music. Stravinsky never again wrote anything like *The Rite;* and with the exception of works like *Allegro barbaro* (1911), a piano piece by Bartók, few primitivistic compositions have entered the repertory.

The Rite of Spring consists of two large parts which are subdivided into sections with varying speeds. These subsections follow each other without pause. The titles of the dances suggest their primitive subject matter: Part I, The Adoration of the Earth: (1) Introduction; (2) Omens of Spring: Dances of the Youths and Maidens; (3) Ritual of Abduction; (4) Spring Rounds; (5) Games of the Rival Tribes; (6) Procession of the Wise Elder; (7) Adoration of the Earth; (8) Dance of the Earth. Part II, The Sacrifice: (1) Introduction; (2) Mysterious Circles of the Young Girls; (3) Glorification of the Chosen Maiden; (4) Evocation of the Ancestors; (5) Ritual of the Ancestors; (6) Sacrificial Dance. Each of the two large parts begins with a slow introduction and ends with a frenzied, climactic dance.

The Rite of Spring is written for an enormous orchestra including eight horns, four tubas, and a very important percussion section made up of five timpani, bass drum, tambourine, tam-tam, triangle, antique cymbals, and a guiro (a notched gourd scraped with a stick). Though *The Rite* contains only one folk song, its melodies are folklike. They have narrow ranges like ancient Russian folk tunes and are made up of fragments that are repeated with slight changes in rhythm and pitch. Many individual chords are repeated, and each change of harmony produces a great impact. This melodic and harmonic repetition gives the music a ritualistic, hypnotic quality. Rhythm is a vital form-building element in *The Rite;* it has a life of its own, almost independent of melody and harmony. Today, *The Rite of Spring* is rarely presented as a ballet and is usually heard in the concert hall.

We shall now take a closer look at four sections of *The Rite:* the Introduction, Dances of the Youths and Maidens, and Ritual of Abduction, which open Part I; and the Sacrificial Dance, which concludes Part II.

Part I: Introduction

Side 13, band 1

For Stravinsky, the Introduction to Part I represented "the awakening of nature, the scratching, gnawing, wiggling of birds and beasts." It begins with the strangely penetrating sound of a solo bassoon straining at the top of its register. As though improvising, the bassoon repeats a fragment of a Lithuanian folk tune in irregular ways.

The Rite of Spring

407

Soon other woodwind instruments join the bassoon with repeated fragments of their own. The impression of improvisation is strengthened by the absence of a clearly defined pulse or meter. Dissonant, unconventional chord structures are used. Toward the end of the Introduction, different layers of sounds—mostly from woodwinds and brasses—are piled on top of each other, and the music builds to a piercing climax. But suddenly, all sound is cut off; only the solo bassoon forlornly repeats its opening melody. Then the violins, playing pizzicato, introduce a repeated four-note figure.

This figure later serves as an ostinato in the Dances of the Youths and Maidens, which immediately follows the Introduction.

Side 13, band 1 (continued)

Omens of Spring: Dances of the Youths and Maidens

Sounding almost like drums, the strings pound out a dissonant chord. There are unexpected and irregular accents whose violence is heightened by jabbing sounds from eight horns. This is the way the passage might be counted (with a rapid pulse): 1–2–3-4, 1–2–3-4, 1–2–**3**-4, 1–2–3-4, 1–**2**–3-4, 1–2–3-4, 1–**2**–3-4, 1–2–3-4. The unchanging dissonant harmony is a polychord that combines two different traditional chords.

A succession of melodic fragments soon join the pounding chord and other repeated figures. Played by brass and woodwind instruments, the melodic fragments are narrow in range and are repeated over and over with slight variations.

c) Trumpets

mp

The rhythmic activity is constant and exciting, and gradually more and more instruments are added.

It's interesting to contrast Stravinsky's musical techniques in Dances of the Youths and Maidens with those of a Classical movement in sonata form. A Classical movement grows out of conflicts between different keys; this section of *The Rite of Spring* is based almost entirely on the repetition of a few chords. The themes in a Classical movement are developed through different keys, varied and broken into fragments that take on new emotional meanings. In Dances of the Youths and Maidens, Stravinsky simply repeats melodic fragments with relatively slight variation. His novel techniques grew out of the Russian musical tradition of the nineteenth century. The Coronation Scene from *Boris Godunov* (1874), by Mussorgsky, also uses just a few chords that are repeated throughout a section. Like some of his Russian forebears, Stravinsky relies on variations of rhythm and tone color to create movement and growth.

Ritual of Abduction

Side 13, band 1 (continued)

The frenzied Ritual of Abduction grows out of the preceding section and is marked by violent strokes on the timpani and bass drum. Enormous tension is generated by powerful accents and rapid changes of meter (see the music example on page 383). This section of *The Rite of Spring* closes with high trills in the strings and flutes.

Part II: Sacrificial Dance

The Sacrificial Dance is the overwhelming climax of the whole work. It consists of sections that can be outlined: A B A' C A'' (very brief) C A'''. In the opening section (A), explosive, percussive chords fight brutal blows on the timpani. The time signature changes with almost every bar: $\frac{3}{16} \frac{2}{16} \frac{3}{16} \frac{2}{8} \frac{2}{16} \frac{3}{16}$. The rapid pulse and irregular, jolting accents create intense excitement. The second section (B) begins with a sudden drop in dynamic level as a single chord is repeated obsessively. Brief silences between these repeated chords urge the listener to supply accents. Section C features brasses and percussive sounds from five timpani, a tam-tam (gong), and a bass drum. The Sacrificial Dance glorifies the power of rhythm, as does the entire *Rite of Spring*.

Symphony of Psalms (1930)

A masterpiece from Stravinsky's "neoclassical period," the *Symphony of Psalms* was written for the fiftieth anniversary of the Boston Symphony Orchestra in 1930. It

Symphony of Psalms (1930)

409

has three movements and is scored for chorus and orchestra. The Latin text is taken from three psalms in the Vulgate Bible. Stravinsky chose the Latin version to evoke the feeling of an ancient and solemn ritual. An austere, archaic quality is also communicated through chantlike melodies that sometimes are restricted to one or two tones.

The neoclassical features of the *Symphony of Psalms* include its use of tonality, major and minor triads, fugue, and the deliberate evocation of the past. Yet the music sounds completely of this century. As in many works by Stravinsky, the orchestra is highly unconventional. There are no violins, violas, or clarinets; the sounds of woodwinds, brasses, and two pianos predominate. Stravinsky intended the voices and instruments to "be on an equal footing, neither of them outweighing the other." He uses the term "symphony" not in its usual sense, but simply to indicate a work in several movements that calls for an orchestra. The three movements are related motivically and are performed without interruption. We'll focus on the first and second movements.

Side 13, band 2 **First Movement: Psalm 38 (Vulgate), verses 13–14[1]**

Based on a psalm beginning "Hear my prayer, O Lord," the brief opening movement is a prelude to the successively longer movements that follow. First, a staccato orchestral chord repeatedly punctuates woodwind solos. Though a standard E-minor triad, this chord sounds unique because its tones are spaced and orchestrated in a novel way. After this orchestral introduction, the alto voices of the chorus sing a chantlike melody composed of just two notes that alternate.

This chantlike theme is supported by ostinatos in the woodwinds.

[1]Psalm 38 in the Vulgate is Psalm 39 in the King James version.

The first part of the movement is marked by abrupt contrasts between the staccato chord, woodwind interludes, and brief passages for chorus and orchestra. The second part of the movement is more continuous as the chorus and orchestra are always heard together. The movement ends in triumph, with a sustained G-major triad that has a great impact because it is the movement's only *major* triad; it vividly contrasts with the staccato minor triads heard earlier.

		Orchestral introduction; loud staccato chord punctuates solos by oboe, bassoon. Piano. High cello.
Exaudi orationem meam, Domine.	Hear my prayer, O Lord,	Altos, chantlike theme.
et deprecationem meam;	and my supplication;	Full chorus. Oboe.
auribus percipe lacrymas meas.	give ear to my tears.	Altos, chantlike theme.
		Staccato chord.
Ne sileas,	Be not silent:	Tenors and altos, *f*; staccato chord.
quoniam advena ego sum apud te,	for I am a stranger with thee,	Altos, basses. Other voices join.
et peregrinus sicut omnes patres mei.	and a sojourner as all my fathers were.	Crescendo to *ff*.
Remitte mihi, (remitte mini,)	O forgive me, (O forgive me,)	Suddenly softer, chant-like theme in tenors, sopranos.
ut refrigerer priusquam abeam et amplius non ero.	that I may be refreshed, before I go hence, and be no more.	Major chord, *ff*.

Second Movement: Psalm 39 (Vulgate), verses 2–4[2]

Stravinsky based the second movement on a psalm which he described as "a prayer that a new canticle (song) may be put into our mouths." The movement is a fugue with two different subjects, or themes. One is played by instruments only, while the other is entirely vocal. A solo oboe introduces the instrumental subject, a jagged melody with upward and downward leaps.

[2] Psalm 39 in the Vulgate is Psalm 40 in the King James version.

Symphony of Psalms (1930)

411

This subject is imitated in turn by a flute, second flute, and second oboe. This use of only woodwind instruments in a high register is an unusual feature of the opening fugue. This music does follow certain traditions of fugue technique, but it has a twentieth-century sound due to its unconventional harmonies.

After the extended section for woodwinds, the sopranos of the chorus announce the vocal subject, which begins with a downward leap.

Ex - pec____ tans ex - pec - ta_____ vi DO - MI - NUM,

The vocal subject is imitated by the other chorus parts, while fragments of the instrumental subject appear in the background. Refreshing changes of tone color occur as a beautiful passage for unaccompanied chorus is followed by one for instruments alone. The words "And he put a new canticle into my mouth" bring the first fortissimo in the movement, and the chorus and orchestra are reunited. The movement ends calmly as the chorus sings a repeated tone while instruments recall the opening fugue subject.

		Solo oboe, instrumental fugue subject; imitation by flute, 2nd flute, 2nd oboe.
Expectans, expectavi Dominum,	With expectation I have waited for the Lord:	Sopranos, vocal fugue subject; imitation by altos, tenors, basses; instrumental fugue subject in background.
et intendit mihi.	and he was attentive to me.	
Et exaudivit preces meas, et eduxit me de lacu miseriae	And he heard my prayers, and brought me out of the pit of misery	
et de luto faecis.	and the mire of dregs.	
Et statuit super petram pedes meos,	And he set my feet upon a rock,	Chorus alone, *p.*
et direxit gressus meos.	and directed my steps.	
		Orchestra alone, *p*, fragment of instrumental fugue subject imitated. Brief pause.

Et immisit in os meum	And he put a new	Sudden *ff*, chorus
canticum novum,	canticle into my mouth,	and orchestra;
carmen Deo nostro.	a song to our God.	dotted rhythms.
Videbunt multi,	Many shall see	Parts of both
et timebunt,	and shall fear:	fugue subjects.
et sperabunt in Domino.	and they shall hope	Sudden *p*; chorus
	in the Lord.	sings repeated
		tone while in-
		struments recall
		opening fugue
		subject

Basic Term

primitivism

EXPRESSIONISM 7

Much twentieth century music reflects an artistic movement called **expression-ism,** which stressed intense, subjective emotion. It was largely centered in Germany and Austria from 1905 to 1925. Painters, writers, and composers explored inner feelings rather than depicting outward appearances. They used deliberate distortions to assault and shock their audience, to communicate the tensions and anguish of the human psyche. Expressionism grew out of the same intellectual climate as Freud's studies of hysteria and the unconscious. The German expressionist painters were reacting against French impressionism, with its pleasant subjects, delicate pastel colors, and shimmering surfaces.

The expressionists rejected conventional prettiness. Their works may seem "ugly" in their preoccupation with madness and death. Expressionist painters such as Ernst Ludwig Kirchner, Emil Nolde, and Oskar Kokoschka often use jarring colors and grotesquely distorted shapes. Expressionist art is fragmentary; the scenes of an expressionist play may be episodic and discontinuous. Expressionism is an art concerned with social protest. It movingly conveyed the anguish felt by the poor and oppressed. Many expressionists opposed World War I and used art to depict their horror of bloodshed.

There was close communication between expressionist writers, painters, and musicians. Many were creative in several different areas. Painter Wassily Kandinsky wrote essays, poetry, and plays, while the composer Schoenberg painted and even participated in the shows of expressionist artists.

Twentieth-century musical expressionism grows out of the emotional turbulence in the works of late Romantics like Wagner, Richard Strauss, and Gustav Mahler. In the following sections, we'll study four expressionistic compositions:

 Expressionism

413

Ernst Ludwig Kirchner, *Street, Dresden* (1908). German expressionist painters reacted against French impressionism; they often used jarring colors and grotesquely distorted shapes to explore the subconscious (Collection, The Museum of Modern Art, New York).

Five Pieces for Orchestra, Op. 16 (1909), and *A Survivor from Warsaw*, Op. 46 (1947), by Schoenberg; the opera *Wozzeck* (1917–1922) by Alban Berg; and *Five Pieces for Orchestra*, Op. 10 (1911–1913), by Anton Webern. They share a stress on harsh dissonance, fragmentation, an exploitation of extreme registers, and unusual instrumental effects. All four pieces avoid tonality and traditional chord progressions. Both *A Survivor from Warsaw* and *Wozzeck* depict a nightmarish world and express a profound empathy with the poor and tormented.

The Twentieth
Century

Basic Term

expressionism

ARNOLD SCHOENBERG │ **8** │

Arnold Schoenberg (1874–1951) was born in Vienna, the city of Mozart, Beethoven, and Brahms. Unlike such earlier masters, he was an almost entirely self-taught musician. "I began studying the violin at eight and almost immediately started composing," he later recalled. Schoenberg acquired his profound knowledge of music by studying scores, by playing in amateur chamber groups, and by going to concerts. His first musical hero was Brahms, then the greatest living German composer. He soon became "an equally confirmed addict" of Wagner; he saw each of Wagner's operas from twenty to thirty times.

When Schoenberg was sixteen, his father died and he had to work for several years as a bank clerk. When he lost this job at twenty-one, he decided to devote himself to music. He earned a poor living by conducting a choir of metal workers in an industrial center outside Vienna. He also orchestrated operettas written by popular composers of the time. Performances of his own early works met with hostility from the conservative Viennese public. One music critic suggested that Schoenberg be put in an insane asylum without music paper.

Schoenberg began to teach music theory and composition in Vienna in 1904. His personality inspired love and loyalty among his students. Two of his disciples, Alban Berg and Anton Webern, themselves became leading composers.

Around 1908 Schoenberg took the revolutionary step of abandoning the traditional tonal system. "I already feel the opposition that I shall have to overcome," he wrote in a program note for his first atonal works. Schoenberg was a man possessed. "I have a mission. I have a task. . . . I am but the loudspeaker of an idea." His productivity between 1908 and 1915 was incredible. Besides creating many dazzlingly original works at lightning speed, he published a harmony textbook, wrote his own librettos, and entered his paintings in exhibitions of the German expressionists.

Following this fertile period came a span of eight years encompassing World War I and the difficult postwar period when Schoenberg published nothing. He searched for a way to organize the new musical resources he had discovered. Finally, in the summer of 1921, he told a student, "I have made a discovery which will insure the supremacy of German music for the next hundred years." From 1923 to 1925 Schoenberg published compositions using his newly developed twelve-tone system. While his music did not find a large audience, leading musicians respected it. At fifty-one, Schoenberg received an important academic post: director of the master class in musical composition at the Prussian Academy of Arts in Berlin.

This period of official recognition was cut short in 1933, when the Nazis seized power in Germany. Schoenberg was dismissed from the faculty of the Prussian Academy. This shattering experience caused him to return to Judaism. (He had converted to Protestantism when he was eighteen.) The same year he and his family left Germany for the United States, where he soon joined the music

Arnold
Schoenberg

415

Arnold Schoenberg (Omikron).

faculty at the University of California in Los Angeles. But Schoenberg felt neglected in his adopted country. His music was rarely performed, and he was refused a grant from the Guggenheim Foundation. At the age of seventy he was forced to retire from UCLA with a pension of less than forty dollars a month. "I am quite conscious," he wrote in 1947, "that a full understanding of my work cannot be expected before some decades . . . and I know that—success or not—it is my historic duty to write what my destiny orders me to write." But appreciation came earlier than Schoenberg anticipated. Since his death in 1951, the twelve-tone system has been used increasingly by composers throughout the world.

Schoenberg's Music

"I claim the distinction of having written a truly new music which, based upon tradition as it is, is destined to become tradition." This proud assertion by Schoenberg contains a great deal of truth. His musical language was indeed new, yet rooted in the past and the result of a gradual stylistic evolution. And his musical system *was* eventually adopted by many other composers.

Schoenberg's point of departure was the music of Wagner, Brahms, and Mahler. His early works, like the string sextet *Verklärte Nacht* ("Transfigured Night," 1899), show many features of the late Romantic style. The music is emotionally intense and often has a literary program. Some early compositions use the gigantic orchestras favored by late nineteenth-century composers. For example, the immense cantata *Gurre-Lieder* ("Songs of Gurre," 1901; orchestration, 1911) calls for five vocal soloists, a speaker-narrator, four choruses, and a greatly expanded orchestra including about fifty woodwind and brass players. A feeling of subjectivity is generated through dissonances that resolve in unexpected ways and through angular melodies that have wide ranges and big leaps. There is prominent use of chromatic harmony, or chords with tones that do not belong to the prevailing major or minor scale. The pull of a central tonality is weakened because the music rapidly moves through keys remote from the main one.

During the years 1903 to 1907, Schoenberg moved farther from the harmonic language of the late Romantics. In compositions such as the *Chamber Symphony, Op. 9* (1906), for fifteen solo instruments, he uses whole-tone scales and fourth chords.

Atonality

Around 1908, Schoenberg finally began to write atonal music. Though a revolutionary development, **atonality**—the absence of key—evolved from Schoenberg's earlier emphasis on chromatic harmony and liberal use of all twelve tones in the chromatic scale. But in his atonal works, all twelve tones are used without regard for their traditional relationship to major or minor scales. Dissonances are "emancipated" from the necessity of resolving to consonances. Schoenberg explained atonality as a style based on the "emancipation of the dissonance"; it "treats dissonances like consonances and renounces a tonal center. By avoiding the establishment of a key, modulation is excluded, since modulation means leaving an established tonality and establishing another tonality." In Schoenberg's atonal music from 1908 to 1914, triads and the traditional vocabulary of chord progressions are deliberately avoided, as are major and minor scales. But "atonality" does not imply a single system of composition. Each atonal composition has its own means of achieving unity. A piece usually grows out of a few short motives that are transformed in many different ways.

Among the best-known of Schoenberg's atonal compositions are the *Five Pieces for Orchestra*, Op. 16 (1909) and *Pierrot lunaire*, Op. 21 ("Moonstruck Pierrot,"

1912), a setting of twenty-one poems. The jagged melodies, novel instrumental effects, and extreme contrasts of dynamics and register in Schoenberg's music are like the distorted figures and shocking colors in expressionist paintings. The texture is polyphonic and very complex. Phrases are of irregular length, and melodic repetition is avoided. *Pierrot lunaire* and other Schoenberg works call for an unusual style of vocal performance halfway between speaking and singing. This is called **Sprechstimme,** which literally means "speech-voice" in German. The vocal part is written in music notation, but small *x*'s on the note stems indicate that the pitches are only approximate.

Schoenberg's atonal language was soon adopted by his students Berg and Webern. Their early atonal works, like Schoenberg's, tended to be extremely emotional and very short. Without a musical system like tonality, the three composers could create extended compositions only when they had a long text to serve as an organizing force.

The Twelve-tone System

During the years 1914 to 1920, Schoenberg finished very few works as he tried to develop a more systematic method of organizing atonal music. In the early 1920s, he finally developed what he called the "method of composing with twelve tones." He partly applied this new technique in the *Five Piano Pieces,* Op. 23, and the *Serenade,* Op. 24, and then fully elaborated it in the *Suite* for piano, Op. 25. All were composed from 1920 to 1923. These and some other works of the 1920s are less subjective and expressionistic than Schoenberg's earlier and later music. They use traditional forms (sonata form) and eighteenth-century dance types (the minuet and trio, gavotte, and gigue).

The twelve-tone system enabled Schoenberg to write more extended compositions than he had when using free atonality. In 1928 he composed the monumental *Variations for Orchestra,* and in the years 1930 to 1932 he wrote the opera *Moses und Aron,* which is based entirely on a single tone row. Though he never finished the third act of this great masterpiece, the opera has an overwhelming impact. From the time of his arrival in the United States in 1933 to his death in 1951, Schoenberg used the twelve-tone system in many rich and varied works, including the *Violin Concerto,* Op. 36 (1936), the *Fourth String Quartet,* Op. 37 (1936), the *Piano Concerto,* Op. 42 (1942), and the cantata *A Survivor from Warsaw,* Op. 46 (1947).

The **twelve-tone system** offers the composer a new way of organizing pitch in a composition. It is a twentieth-century alternative to tonality. The twelve-tone system gives equal importance to each of the twelve chromatic tones, rather than emphasizing one central tone as the tonal system does. The twelve-tone method is a systematized form of atonality. It grew out of Schoenberg's desire to structure his music "*consciously* on a unifying idea."

In a twelve-tone composition, all pitches are derived from a special ordering of the twelve chromatic tones. This ordering or unifying idea is called a **tone row, set,** or **series.**[3] The composer creates a unique tone row for each specific piece. The

---

[3] Because of the systematic use of a *series* of tones, the twelve-tone method is also refered to as "serial technique."

choice of rows is practically limitless, since there are 479,001,600 possible arrangements of the twelve chromatic tones. The tone row must be constructed with great care because it vitally affects the total sound and is the source of every melody and chord in a piece. Here is an example of a row, the one used by Schoenberg in his *Suite* for piano, Op. 25:

E	F	G	Db	Gb	Eb	Ab	D	B	C	A	Bb
1	2	3	4	5	6	7	8	9	10	11	12

Notice that no pitch occurs more than once within a row. This prevents any single tone from receiving too much emphasis. An entire composition is built by manipulating a single twelve-tone row. The row may be presented in four basic forms: forward (original form), backward (retrograde), upside down (inversion), and backward and upside down (retrograde inversion). The retrograde (backward) form simply presents the original tone row in reverse.

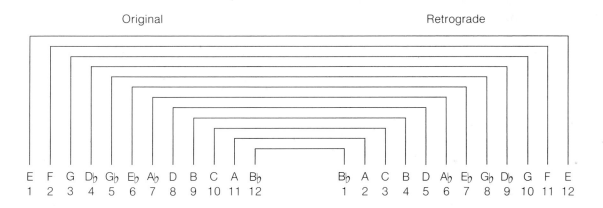

The inverted (upside down) form keeps the original sequence of intervals between tones, but the intervals move in the opposite direction. For example, the original row begins by moving *up* a half step from E to F. The inversion begins by moving *down* a half step from E to Eb.

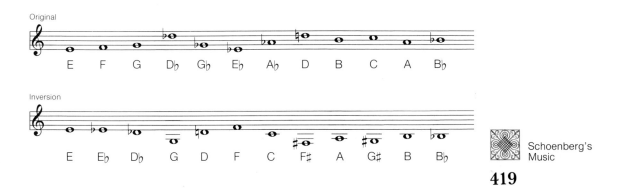

The retrograde inversion (backward and upside down) presents the tones of the inversion in reverse:

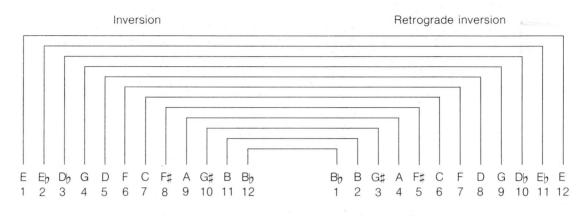

Inversion   Retrograde inversion

| E | E♭ | D♭ | G | D | F | C | F♯ | A | G♯ | B | B♭ |
| 1 | 2 | 3 | 4 | 5 | 6 | 7 | 8 | 9 | 10 | 11 | 12 |

| B♭ | B | G♯ | A | F♯ | C | F | D | G | D♭ | E♭ | E |
| 1 | 2 | 3 | 4 | 5 | 6 | 7 | 8 | 9 | 10 | 11 | 12 |

A tone row may be shifted to any pitch level. That is, it may begin on any of the twelve chromatic tones while keeping the original pattern of intervals. This applies to all four forms of the row: original, retrograde, inversion, and retrograde inversion. Since a row may begin on any one of twelve pitches and exist in four forms, there are forty-eight (twelve times four) possible versions of a row. This gives the composer a great deal of flexibility.

Each tone of a row may also be placed in any register, allowing an infinite variety of melodic shapes to be drawn from a single row. For example, given a row that begins with tones E–F–G, a composer could have the tones move upward by step, or he could have the E leap up to a high F and the F leap down to a low G.

This further increases the flexibility of the system and may partially explain why so many twelve-tone melodies have unusually wide leaps. The tones of a row may be presented one after another, to form a melodic line, or at the same time, to form chords. Here is the same row treated in two different ways.

a) Prelude   E F G   D♭ G♭ E♭ A♭ D   B   C A B♭

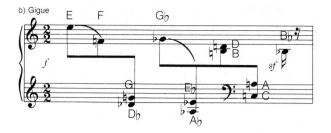
b) Gigue

We'll now study two works by Schoenberg: the "freely" atonal *Five Pieces for Orchestra*, Op. 16 (1909), and the twelve-tone cantata, *A Survivor from Warsaw*, Op. 46 (1947), composed almost forty years later.

Five Pieces for Orchestra, Op. 16 (1909)

"I can promise you something really colossal, especially in sound and mood," wrote Schoenberg to composer and conductor Richard Strauss after completing *Five Pieces for Orchestra*, Op. 16, in 1909. These revolutionary pieces were the first atonal works for full orchestra. Though Schoenberg calls for an especially large orchestra, he treats it as a group of soloists. (In 1949, Schoenberg rearranged the *Five Pieces* for a conventional orchestra.) Many novel orchestral effects are exploited, and instruments are often used at the top or bottom of their ranges. The pieces, especially the third, embody Schoenberg's concept of a **tone-color melody** (*Klangfarbenmelodie* in German), a succession of varying tone colors used as a musical idea in a composition. The third piece, *Summer Morning by a Lake: Colors* (also called *The Changing Chord*), is based on subtly shifting tone colors of a gradually changing chord. Schoenberg wrote in the score that "the change of harmonies should occur gently, without emphasis on instrumental entries, so that only a difference in tone color is perceived."

Schoenberg added descriptive titles after he composed the music. Each piece is quite brief; at the time, Schoenberg unconsciously felt the need to "counterbalance extreme emotionality with extraordinary shortness." The first two pieces, *Premonitions* and *Yesteryears*, show contrasting sides of Schoenberg's musical personality.

Premonitions (Vorgefühle)

Side 13, band 3

An amazing amount of musical activity takes place in the two-minute span of *Premonitions*. It is "just an uninterrupted change of colors, rhythms, and moods," according to Schoenberg. The constant intensity and desperate energy of *Premonitions* are typically expressionistic.

The piece consists of two connected sections: an introductory part lasting about half a minute, and a main part three times as long. The introduction sounds fragmentary and has a bewildering succession of musical ideas in dif-

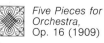
Five Pieces for Orchestra, Op. 16 (1909)

421

ferent tempos, tone colors, dynamics, and registers. As though holding his full resources in reserve, Schoenberg uses only a few instruments at any one time. First, muted cellos introduce an abrupt upward motive (short-long-long, short-long-long):

The entire piece is built from rhythmic and melodic transformations of this idea.

The second part of *Premonitions* is rhythmically more continuous; it becomes increasingly complex in both texture and sound.

The cellos begin with a steady succession of rapid notes. They have a three-note figure that is repeated as a background ostinato throughout the piece.

The sound becomes increasingly loud and dense as more and more melodic fragments are piled on top of one another. After an ear-splitting climax, the texture thins, and the volume decreases. *Premonitions* ends with a snarling chord played by trombones and tuba. (The effect results from flutter-tonguing; each brass player rapidly rolls the tongue as if pronouncing *d-r-r-r.*) This chord is sustained in the background throughout most of *Premonitions,* and it unifies the flow of free associations in the piece.

Yesteryears (Vergangenes)

This slow, lyrical piece evokes a feeling of brooding over the past. As its title might suggest, *Yesteryears* is somewhat more traditional in harmony and form than the other pieces. It has a great variety of delicate and beautiful tone colors. Its dynamics are subdued; instruments are often muted. Except for a brief moment at the climax, the entire orchestra never plays simultaneously. Instead, groups of soloists engage in complex polyphonic conversations. Ostinatos play an important role in *Yesteryears*. Several different repeated figures are piled on top of one other to form different layers of sound. You'll easily recognize the ostinato played by the celesta because of its distinctive bell-like sound.

Yesteryears has three parts: an opening, an extended middle section, and a brief conclusion. The piece becomes increasingly complex in texture; it begins in relatively simply homophony, but becomes more and more polyphonic. The texture is most dense at the end of the middle section, which has the greatest variety of tone colors and the most intricate polyrhythms. The conclusion of *Yesteryears* is truly a "remembrance of things past": all the earlier motives are recalled softly.

LISTENING OUTLINE
To be read while music is heard

Yesteryears (*Vergangenes*) from *Five Pieces for Orchestra,* Op. 16 (1909), by Arnold Schoenberg

2 piccolos, 2 flutes, 2 oboes, English horn, 2 clarinets, bass clarinet, 2 bassoons, contrabassoon, 4 horns, 2 trumpets, 4 trombones, tuba, xylophone, cymbals, triangle, harp, celesta, violins 1, violins 2, violas, cellos, double basses

Moderate tempo

(About 5½ min)

1　*a.* Legato melody, *p*, solo muted cello; clarinet and English horn continue melody; brief pause.

　　b. Celesta, *p*, accompanies soft woodwinds and muted trumpet, which share interwoven melodic lines.
　　c. English horn, *p*, opening of legato melody; low trombone phrase, *pp*; briefly held chord.
2　*a.* Solo muted viola, *pp*, presents new motive which is softly imitated by other solo instruments; complex polyphonic texture; celesta, *pp*, high violins.

　　b. Celesta, *pp*, flutes, then staccato bassoons simultaneously play different repeated motives (ostinatos); soft, short solos in harp and muted violin.
　　c. Muted viola melody returns; polyphonic texture becomes more complex; crescendo to climax, *f*, entire orchestra. Decrescendo, tempo slows down; sustained string harmonics.
3　Oboe, *p*, opening legato melody; flute and celesta ostinatos; soft recollection of previous motives by solo instruments; sustained orchestral chord, *pp*.

423

A Survivor from Warsaw, Op. 46 (1947)

A dramatic cantata for narrator, male chorus, and orchestra, *A Survivor from Warsaw* deals with a single episode in the murder of six million Jews by the Nazis during World War II. Schoenberg wrote the text himself, partly basing it on a direct report by one of the few survivors of the Warsaw ghetto. Over 400,000 Jews from this ghetto died in extermination camps or of starvation, while many others perished during a heroic revolt against the Nazis in 1943. The narrator's text is spoken in English, except for some terrifying Nazi commands which are shouted in German. The narrator's part is a kind of *Sprechstimme,* the novel speech-singing developed by Schoenberg. The rhythms of the spoken words are precisely notated, but their pitch fluctuations are indicated only approximately.

I cannot remember ev'rything,   I must have been un-conscious most of the time;

Besides English and German, the text includes Hebrew. These were the three languages of Schoenberg's life: German, his native tongue; English, his adopted language in America; and Hebrew, the language of the faith to which he returned. The six-minute cantata builds to an overwhelming conclusion when the male chorus sings in unison the Hebrew words of the prayer *Shema Yisroel* ("Hear, O Israel"). For centuries this has been the prayer of Jewish martyrs in their last agonized moments.

A Survivor from Warsaw is a twelve-tone composition written in 1947 when Schoenberg was seventy-two. Its tense, expressionistic style recalls the composer's orchestral piece *Premonitions,* written almost forty years earlier. The music vividly sets off every detail in the text.

A Survivor from Warsaw opens with a brief orchestral introduction that captures the nightmarish atmosphere as Nazi soldiers awakened the Warsaw Jews for transport to death camps. We hear a weirdly shrill reveille in the trumpet and fragmentary sounds in the military drum and high xylophone.

During the narrator's opening lines, Schoenberg already prepares for the concluding Hebrew prayer. As the narrator speaks of "the old prayer they had neglected for so many years," a French horn softly intones the beginning of the melody that is later proclaimed by the chorus.

French horn
pp

An especially vivid musical description comes when the narrator describes how the Nazis counted their victims: "They began again, first slowly: One, two, three, four, became faster and faster. . . ." The music itself becomes faster and louder, building to the powerful entrance of the chorus. The sung Hebrew contrasts dramatically with the spoken English and German that came before, and it is the first extended melody in the work.

I cannot remember everything. I must have been unconscious most of the time; I remember only the grandiose moment when they all started to sing, as if prearranged, the old prayer they had neglected for so many years—the forgotten creed!

But I have no recollection how I got underground to live in the sewers of Warsaw so long a time.

The day began as usual. Reveille when it still was dark—get out whether you slept or whether worries kept you awake the whole night: you had been separated from your children, from your wife, from your parents, you don't know what happened to them; how could you sleep?

They shouted again: "Get out! The sergeant will be furious!" They came out; some very slow, the old ones, the sick men, some with nervous agility. They fear the sergeant. They hurry as much as they can. In vain! Much too much noise, much too much commotion and not fast enough!

The Feldwebel shouts: *"Achtung! Still gestanden! Na wird's mal, oder soll ich mit dem Gewehrkolben nachhelfen? Na jut; wenn Ihr's durchaus haben wollt!"* ("Attention! Stand still! How about it, or should I help you along with the butt of my rifle? All right, Jew, if you really want to have it!")

The sergeant and his subordinates hit everyone: young or old, strong or sick, guilty or innocent—it was painful to hear the groaning and moaning.

I heard it though I had been hit very hard, so hard that I could not help falling down. We all on the ground who could not stand up were then beaten over the head.

I must have been unconscious. The next thing I knew was a soldier saying, "They are all dead!" Whereupon the sergeant ordered to do away with us.

There I lay aside half conscious. It had become very still—fear and pain—Then I heard the sergeant shouting: *"Abzählen!"* ("Count Off!")

They started slowly, and irregularly: One, two, three, four, *"Achtung."* The sergeant shouted again: *"Rascher! Nochmals von vorn anfangen! In einer Minute will ich wissen wieviele ich zur Gaskammer abliefere! Abzählen!"* ("Faster! Once more, start from the beginning! In a minute I will know how many I am going to send off to the gas chamber! Count off!")

They began again, first slowly: one, two, three, four, became faster and faster, so fast that it finally sounded like a stampede of wild horses, and all of a sudden, in the middle of it, they began singing the *Shema Yisroel.*

Shema Yisroel Adonoy elohenoo Adonoy eḥod. Veohavto es Adonoy eloheḥo beḥol levoveḥo ooveḥol nafsheḥo oovehol meodeḥo. Vehoyoo haddevoreem hoelleh asher onoḥee metsavveḥo hayyom al levoveḥo. Veshinnantom levoneḥo vedibbarto bom beshivteḥo beveteḥo oovelehteḥo baddereḥ ooveshohḥeḥo oovekoomeḥo. ("Hear, O Israel, the Lord our God the Lord is One! And thou shalt love the Lord thy God with all thy heart, and with all thy soul, and with all thy might. And these words, which I command thee this day, shall be in thy heart. And thou shalt teach them diligently unto thy children, and speak of them when thou sittest in thy house, and when thou goest on the way, and when thou liest down, and when thou risest up.")

 A Survivor from Warsaw, Op. 46 (1947)

425

Technical Postscript

A Survivor from Warsaw is built from the following twelve-tone row: F♯–G–C–A♭–E–D♯–B♭–D♭–A–D–F–B. The opening of the choral melody uses two different transformations of the row: The original form shifted four half-steps higher (B♭–B♮–E–C–A♭–G–D–F–D♭–F♯–A–E♭) and the inverted form shifted nine half-steps higher (E♭–D–A–C♯–E♯–F♯–B–G♯–C–G♮–E♮–B♭).

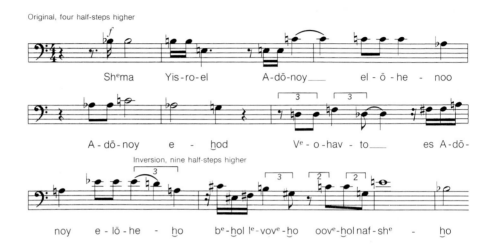

Original, four half-steps higher

Sh⁰ma   Yis-ro-el   A-dō-noy____   el - ō - he - noo

A - dō - noy   e - hod   V⁰ - o-hav - to____   es A-dō-

Inversion, nine half-steps higher

noy   e - lō - he - ho   b⁰-hol l⁰-vov⁰-ho oov⁰-hol naf-sh⁰ - ho

At the opening of the work, Schoenberg uses the first six notes of the original form in the first trumpet and violins, and the first six notes of the inversion shifted five half-steps higher in the second trumpet and contrabasses (C♭–B♭–F–A–C♯–D).

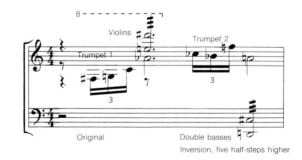

Original   Double basses

Inversion, five half-steps higher

Basic Terms

atonality
Sprechstimme
twelve-tone system
tone row (set, series)
tone-color melody

ALBAN BERG || 9 ||

Alban Berg (1885–1935), a student of Schoenberg, wrote music that is a unique synthesis of traditional and twentieth-century elements. He combines Romantic sounds and time-honored forms with the techniques of free atonality and the twelve-tone system. A wide audience has been attracted by the lyrical warmth, vivid tone colors, and theatrical qualities of Berg's compositions.

Like his teacher, Berg was born in Vienna. At nineteen, he began studying privately with Schoenberg and continued working with him from 1904 to 1911. After serving in the Austrian army during World War I, he became codirector (with Schoenberg) of the Society for Private Musical Performances in Vienna. The goal of the society, which lasted from 1918 to 1921, was to "give artists and music-lovers a real and exact knowledge of modern music" through repeated and well-rehearsed performances.

Berg first attracted international attention in 1925, when his opera *Wozzeck* premiered in Berlin. Though the opera's atonality baffled many critics, *Wozzeck* made such a powerful impression on the public that it was soon performed throughout Europe and in the United States.

Perhaps because of chronic ill-health, Berg did not perform or conduct and composed relatively few works. From the time he finished *Wozzeck* (1922) until his death at the age of fifty, his works include the *Chamber Concerto* for piano, violin, and thirteen winds (1925), the *Lyric Suite* for string quartet (1926), the opera *Lulu* (1929–1935, orchestration not completed), and the *Violin Concerto* (1935).

Wozzeck (1917–1922)

Wozzeck is the tragic story of a soldier who is driven to murder and madness by a hostile society. An antihero obsessed by strange visions, Wozzeck is persecuted by his sadistic captain, used as a guinea pig by a half-demented doctor, and betrayed by his mistress Marie. Wozzeck stabs Marie to death and drowns while trying to wash her blood from his hands.

Berg's musical imagination was fired in 1914 when he saw *Woyzeck,* a play by the German dramatist and revolutionary Georg Büchner (1813–1837). Though written in the early 1830s, the play is amazingly modern in its starkly realistic dialog and disconnected scenes. Berg adapted the play into an opera while in the Austrian army in World War I. His traumatic army experiences may well have deepened his sympathy for Wozzeck.

The opera's nightmarish atmosphere makes it a musical counterpart of expressionist painting and literature. Berg conveys the tensions and torments of the unconscious through harsh dissonances and grotesque distortions. The music's range of emotions and styles is tremendous. Though most of *Wozzeck* is freely atonal—it does not use the twelve-tone system—major and minor

Wozzeck
(1917–1922)

427

keys occasionally add contrast. The vocal line includes speaking, shrieking, *Sprechstimme,* distorted folk songs, and melodies with wide leaps that are difficult to sing. The gigantic orchestra closely parallels the dialog and stage action. Descriptive effects include vivid orchestral depiction of the moon rising, frogs croaking, and water engulfing the drowning Wozzeck. Berg's music rapidly shifts between very high and very low registers, between *ffff* and *pppp*.

Wozzeck has three acts, each with five scenes. Connecting the scenes are short orchestral interludes that comment on the preceding action and serve as preparation for what is to come. As in the music dramas of Wagner, there is a continuous musical flow within each act, and characters are associated with specific musical ideas. A novel feature of *Wozzeck* is that music for each scene is a self-contained composition with a particular form (passacaglia, sonata form, etc.) or of a definite type (military march, lullaby). The five scenes of the last act—which we'll study—are organized as (1) variations on a theme, (2) variations on a single tone, (3) variations on a rhythmic pattern, (4) variations on a chord, and (5) variations on continuous running notes. But Berg did not intend for the listener to concentrate on or even be aware of these unifying techniques. He wanted the audience to be caught up in the opera's dramatic flow. Before Act III, Wozzeck has been driven to desperation by his mistress's infidelity and by a savage-beating from the man who slept with her.

Act III

Scene 1: Marie's room

In the touching first scene of Act III, Wozzeck's unfaithful mistress Marie reads the story of Mary Magdalene from the Bible and laments her own weakness. Berg dramatically highlights Marie's anguish by having her alternate between speech and song. When Marie reads or tells a story to her child, we hear *Sprechstimme;* when she expresses her anguish, we hear jagged, hysterical phrases that are sung.

Berg also contrasts tonality and atonality for dramatic effect. When Marie relates a fairy tale to her son ("And once there was a poor wee child"), Berg uses Romantic harmonies in the clearly defined key of F minor. For Berg, this key symbolized "the vanished world of the fairy tale."

Scene 2: A path near a pond

Wozzeck stabs Marie to death while walking along a forest path near a pond. In an almost impressionistic way the orchestra depicts the eerie night-time sounds in a forest. Wozzeck's obsession with Marie's murder is symbolized by the note B, which appears throughout the scene in different registers and in various instruments. Most of the time the tone is barely audible. But when Wozzeck pulls out his knife and kills Marie, the B is forced into the listener's consciousness through relentless timpani strokes. The obsessive B becomes overpowering during the orchestral interlude following the murder, when there are two ear-splitting crescendos on this note. Between the crescendos, drums hammer out a rhythmic pattern that will be repeated and developed in the next scene.

(This rhythm can be represented as long-long, short-long, long, short-short-long.)

Scene 3: A tavern
At a tavern, Wozzeck, almost insane, desperately struggles to forget his crime. Dissonant and distorted dance music is heard from a tiny on-stage piano that is supposed to sound out-of-tune. Marie's friend Margret sings a weirdly distorted folk tune for Wozzeck. When she notices his bloody hands, Wozzeck flees in terror.

Scene 4: A path near a pond
Wozzeck returns to the scene of the crime to dispose of his knife. Berg's orchestra vividly evokes the dark forest scene as a background to Wozzeck's anguished shrieks. Rising harp tones suggest the blood-red moon coming up through the clouds. Wozzeck goes mad and drowns in the pond while trying to wash the blood from his hands. Soft chromatic slides depict the engulfing water as the Captain and the Doctor, Wozzeck's tormentors, indifferently comment that someone is drowning. As Wozzeck drowns, the slides become slower and narrower in range.

The long orchestral interlude that follows is a deeply moving expression of grief for Wozzeck's tragic fate. It recalls the musical themes associated with his life. Berg described it as "a confession of the author stepping outside the dramatic events of the theater and appealing to the public as representing mankind." For this outpouring of compassion, Berg returns to tonality (the interlude is in D minor) and the musical language of late Romanticism.

Scene 5: A street before Marie's door
Children are playing in front of Marie's house; bright sunshine brings glaring contrast to the darkness of the preceding scenes. One of the children cruelly tells Wozzeck's son: "Hey! Your mother is dead." The boy rides off on his hobby horse with the other children to see the body. The orchestra is reduced in size to produce delicate sounds that match the children's high voices, and a continuous rhythm symbolizes their utter indifference. The opera does not end with a conclusive chord. It simply breaks off as though to suggest that the tragedy could begin again.

Side 13, band 6

Side 13, band 6 (continued)

Wozzeck (1917–1922)

429

Scene 1

(Marie's room. It is night. Candlelight. Marie, alone with her child, is sitting at the table, turning the pages of the Bible and reading.)

Marie

		Viola, *p.* imitated by cello.
"Und ist kein Betrug in seinem Munde erfunden worden . . ."	"And out of His mouth there came forth neither deceit nor falsehood . . ."	Spoken (*Sprechstimme*).
Herr-Gott! Herr-Gott! Sieh' mich nicht an!	Lord God! Lord God! Look not at me! *(She turns the pages.)*	Sung, *f.*
		Brief pause. High violin, *pp,* imitated by high cello.
"Aber die Pharisäer brachten ein Weib zu ihm, so im Ehebruch lebte. Jesus aber sprach: 'So verdamme ich dich auch nicht, geh' hin, und sündige hinfort nicht mehr.'"	"Wherefore the Pharisees had taken and brought to Him an adulterous woman. Jesus said to her: 'Thus condemned shall you not be. Go forth, go forth in peace, and sin no more.'"	Spoken, *p.*
Herr-Gott!	Lord God! *(She covers her face with her hands. The child presses up to Marie.)*	Sung, *f.*
Der Bub' gibt mir einen Stich in's Herz. Fort!	The boy looks at me and stabs my heart. Be off! *(Pushes the child away.)*	
Das brüst' sich in der Sonne!	Go proudly in the sunlight! *(Suddenly, more gently.)*	
Nein, komm, komm, her! Komm zu mir!	Ah, no! Come here! *(Draws him closer.)* Come to me.	
"Es war einmal ein armes Kind und hatt' keinen Vater und keine Mutter . . . war Alles tot und war Niemand auf der Welt, und es hat gehungert und geweint Tag und Nacht. Und weil es Niemand mehr hatt' auf der Welt . . ."	"And once there was a poor wee child and he had no father, nor any mother . . . for all were dead, there was no one in the world, therefore he did hunger and did weep day and night. Since he had no one else left in the world . . ."	Spoken. Romantic harmonies.
Der Franz ist nit kommen, gestern nit, heut' nit . . . Wie steht es geschrieben von der Magdalena? . . .	But Franz had not come yet, yesterday, this day . . . *(She hastily turns the pages of the Bible.)* What is written here of Mary Magdalene? . . .	Sung.

<table>
<tr>
<td>

"Und kniete hin zu seinen Füssen and weinte und küsste seine Füsse und netzte sie mit Tränen und salbte sie mit Salben!"

</td>
<td>

"And falling on her knees before Him and weeping, she kissed His feet and washed them, and washed them with her tears, annointing them with ointment!"(*Beats her breast.*)

</td>
<td>

Voice alone. Solo strings, *pp*, join.

</td>
</tr>
<tr>
<td>

Heiland! Ich möchte Dir die Füsse salben! Heiland! Du hast Dich ihrer erbarmt, erbarme Dich auch meiner!

</td>
<td>

Savior! Could I anoint Thy feet with ointment! Savior! As Thou hadst mercy on her, have mercy now on me, Lord!

</td>
<td>

Crescendo.

Orchestral interlude, trombones, *ff*. Decrescendo.

</td>
</tr>
</table>

Scene 2

(Forest path by a pond. Dusk is falling. Marie enters with Wozzeck, from the right.)

Low tone, B, in background, *p*.

Marie

Dort links geht's in die Stadt, 's ist noch weit. Komm schneller!

The town lies over there. It's still far. Let's hurry!

Wozzeck

Du sollst dableiben, Marie. Komm, setz' Dich.

You must stay awhile, Marie. Come, sit here.

Marie

Aber ich muss fort.

But it's getting late.

Wozzeck

Komm. Bist weit gegangen, Marie. Sollst Dir die Füsse nicht mehr wund laufen. 's ist still hier! Und so dunkel— Weisst noch, Marie, wie lang' es jetzt ist, dass wir uns kennen?

Come! (*They sit down.*) So far you've wandered, Marie. You must not make your feet so sore, walking. It's still, here in the darkness—Tell me, Marie, how long has it been since our first meeting?

Marie

Zu Pfingsten drei Jahre.

At Whitsun, three years.

Wozzeck

Und was meinst, wie lang' es noch dauern wird?

And how long, how long will it still go on?

Marie

Ich muss fort.

(*Jumping up.*) I must go!

Wozzeck
(1917–1922)

431

Wozzeck

Fürchst Dich, Marie? Und bist doch fromm? Und gut! Und treu!	Trembling, Marie? But you are good (*laughing*) and kind and true! (*He pulls her down again on the seat; he bends over her, in deadly earnest.*) Ah! How your lips are sweet to touch, Marie! (*Kisses her.*) All heaven I would give, and eternal bliss, if I still could sometimes kiss you so! But yet I dare not! You shiver?	Upward harp glissando, *pp*.
Was Du für süsse Lippen hast, Marie! Den Himmel gäb ich drum und die Seligkeit, wenn ich		
Dich noch oft so küssen dürft! Aber ich darf nicht! Was zitterst?		Xylophone taps, *pp*.

Marie

Der Nachttau fällt.	The night dew falls.	

Wozzeck

Wer kalt ist, den friert nicht mehr! Dich wird beim Morgentau nicht frieren.	(*Whispering to himself.*) Who cold is, you who shiver, will freeze no more in cold morning dew.	

Marie

Was sagst Du da?	What are you saying?	

Wozzeck

Nix.	Nothing. (*A long silence. The moon rises.*)	Brasses, *pp*, rising tones.

Marie

Wie der Mond rot aufgeht!	How the moon rises red!	

Wozzeck

Wie ein blutig Eisen!	Like a blood-red iron! (*He draws a knife.*)	Obsessive timpani strokes. Crescendo.

Marie

Was zitterst? Was willst?	You shiver? (*She jumps up.*) What now?	

Wozzeck

Ich nicht, Marie! Und kein Andrer auch nicht!	No one, Marie! If not me then no one! (*He seizes her and plunges the knife into her throat.*)	

Marie

Hilfe!	Help! (*She sinks down. Wozzeck bends over her. She dies.*)	Decrescendo.

<table>
<tr><td></td><td>Wozzeck</td></tr>
<tr><td>Tot!</td><td>Dead! (He rises to his feet anxiously, and then rushes silently away.)</td></tr>
</table>

		Orchestral inter- lude, crescendo on tone B. Drums beat ob- sessive rhythm. Second orches- tral crescendo on B.

Scene 3

(A tavern. Night. Badly lit. Girls, among them Margret, and ap-prentices are dancing a wild and rapid polka. Wozzeck is seated at one of the tables.)   "Out-of-tune" piano.

Wozzeck

Tanzt Alle; tanzt nur zu, springt, schwitzt und stinkt, es holt Euch doch noch einmal der Teufel!	Dance, all you, dance away! Leap, sweat and reek. For some day soon he'll fetch you, the Devil! (*Dashes down his glass; then, shouting down the pianist.*)
Es ritten drei Reiter wohl an den Rhein,	Three riders came riding up to the Rhine,
Bei einer Frau Wirtin da kehrten sie ein.	And went to my hostess to taste of her wine.
Mein Wein ist gut, mein Bier ist klar,	My wine is good, my beer is clear,
Mein Töchterlein liegt auf der . . .	My daughter dear lies on her . . .
Verdammt! Komm, Margret! Komm, setz Dich her, Margret! Margret, Du bist so heiss. Wart nur, wirst auch kalt werden! Kannst nicht singen?	Be damned! (*jumps up.*) Come, Margret. (*Dances a few steps with her, then suddenly stops.*) Come, let's sit down, Margret. (*Leads Margret to his table, and pulls her onto his lap.*) Margret, you're hot as fire. (*Presses her to him; lets her go.*) But wait till you're cold also! Can't you sing, girl?

Wozzeck
(1917–1922)

433

Margret

In's Schwabenland, da mag ich nit,

To Swabia I will not go,

Distorted folklike melody accompanied by "out-of-tune" piano.

Und lange Kleider trag ich nit,
Denn lange Kleider, spitze Schuh,
Die kommen keiner Dienstmagd zu.

And your long dresses I'll not wear,
For trailing dresses, pointed shoes,
Do not belong to servant girls.

Wozzeck

Nein! keine Schuh, man kann auch blossfüssig in die Höll' geh'n! Ich möcht heut raufen, raufen . . .

(*Flaming up.*) No! Wear no shoes! For one can bare footed go to hell-fire. I want to wrestle, wrestle . . .

Margret

Aber was hast Du an der Hand?

But what is that there on your hand?

Wozzeck

Ich? Ich?

Mine? Mine?

Margret

Rot! Blut!

Red! Blood!

Wozzeck

Blut? Blut?

Blood? Blood!

(*People gather round Margret and Wozzeck*)

Margret

Freilich . . . Blut!

Surely . . . blood!

Wozzeck

Ich glaub', ich hab' mich geschnitten da an der rechten Hand . . .

I think, I must have, I've cut it sometime, on my right hand . . .

Gradual crescendo. Voices together.

Margret

Wie kommt's denn zum Ellenbogen?

How comes it then on your elbow?

Wozzeck

Ich hab's daran abgewischt.

I've wiped my hand on it there.

Apprentices

Mit der rechten Hand am rechten Arm?

His right elbow wiped with his right hand?

The Twentieth Century

434

	Wozzeck	
Was wollt Ihr? Was geht's Euch an?	What do you mean? That's my affair.	
	Margret	
Puh! Puh! Da stinkt's nach Menschenblut!	Pooh! Pooh! It smells of human blood!	
	Wozzeck	
Bin ich ein Mörder?	Am I a murderer?	
	Apprentices	
Blut, Blut, Blut, Blut!	Blood, blood, blood, blood!	
	Girls	
Freilich, da stinkt's nach Menschenblut!	Surely, it smells of human blood!	
	Wozzeck	
Platz! oder es geht wer zum Teufel!	Off! Or else someone pays the Devil! (*Rushes out.*)	
		Orchestral interlude, *ff.* Snaredrum roll.

Scene 4

(*Forest path by the pond. Moonlit night as before. Wozzeck staggers on hastily, and then stops as he searches for something.*)

	Wozzeck	
		Winds, *p,* repeated chord.
Das Messer? Wo ist das Messer? Ich hab's dagelassen . . . Näher, noch näher. Mir graut's! Da regt sich was.	Where is it? Where has the knife gone? Somewhere here I left it . . . Somewhere here, somewhere. Oh! Horror! There something moved!	Spoken.
Still! Alles still und tot . . . Mörder! Mörder! Ha! Da ruft's. Nein, ich selbst. Marie! Marie! Was hast Du für eine rote Schnur um den Hals? Hast Dir das rote Halsband verdient, wie die Ohrringlein, mit Deiner Sünde! Was hängen Dir die schwarzen Haare so wild? Mörder! Mörder! Sie werden nach mir suchen . . . Das Messer verrät mich! Da, da	Still! All is still and dead! . . . Murder! Murder! Ah, who cried? No, 'twas me. (*Still searching, he staggers forward a few more steps, and comes on the corpse.*) Marie! Marie! What is that so like a crimson cord round your neck? And was that crimson necklace well earned, like the gold earrings: the price of sinning! Why	Shouted.

Wozzeck
(1917–1922)

435

ist's. So! Da hinunter. Es tauch ins dunkle Wasser wie ein Stein.

hangs your fine black hair so wild on your head? Murder! Murder! For me they'll soon be searching . . . That knife will betray me! (*Seeks it feverishly.*) Ah! It's here! (*At the pond.*) Down to the bottom! (*Throws the knife in.*) It sinks through deep dark water like a stone.

(The moon comes up blood-red through the clouds.)

Rising harp tones, *pp.*

Aber der Mond verrät mich . . . der Mond ist blutig. Will denn die ganze Welt es ausplaudern?!—Das Messer, es liegt zu weit vorn, sie finden's beim Baden oder wenn sie nach Muscheln tauchen. Ich find's nicht . . . Aber ich muss mich waschen. Ich bin blutig. Da ein Fleck . . . und noch einer. Weh! Weh! Ich wasche mich mit Blut! Das Wasser ist Blut . . . Blut . . .

See how the moon betrays me . . . the moon is bloody! Must then the whole wide world be blabbing it?—The knife there, too near to the shore! They'll find it when bathing, maybe when they are mussel-gathering. (*He wades into the pond.*) It's gone now. I ought to wash my body. I am bloody. Here's a spot . . . and here . . . something. Woe! Woe! I wash myself with blood! The water is blood . . . blood . . . (*He drowns.*)

Water music. Upward orchestral slides, *pp.* Rhythm gradually slows.

(After a short time the Doctor enters, followed by the Captain.)

Captain

Halt!

Stop!

Spoken.

Doctor

Hören Sie? Dort!

(*Stands still.*) Do you hear? There!

Captain

Jesus! Das war ein Ton.

Heavens! There was a sound. (*Stands still.*)

Doctor

Ja, dort!

(*Pointing to the pond.*) Yes, there!

Es ist das Wasser im Teich. Das Wasser ruft. Es ist schon lange Niemand ertrunken. Kommen Sie, Doktor! Es ist nicht gut zu hören.

It is the water in the pond. The water calls. It is a long time since anyone was drowned. Come, Doctor, this is not good to hear. (*He tries to drag off the Doctor.*)

Doctor

Das stöhnt . . . als stürbe ein Mensch. Da ertrinkt Jemand!

(*Stands still and listens.*) It groans . . . like a dying man. There's someone drowning!

Captain

Unheimlich! Der Mond rot und die Nebel grau. Hören Sie? . . . Jetzt wieder das Ächzen.

It's uncanny! The moon is red, and the mist is grey. Do you hear? . . . That groaning again.

Celesta.

Doctor

Stiller, . . . jetzt gans still.

It's getting softer . . . and now quite gone.

Captain

Kommen Sie! Kommen Sie schnell.

Come away! Quick! (*Drags the Doctor off with him.*)

Extended orchestral interlude.

Scene 5

(*Street before Marie's door. Bright morning. Sunshine. Children are playing and shouting. Marie's child is riding a hobby-horse.*)

Children

Ringel, Ringel, Rosenkranz, Ringelreih'n!

Ring-a-ring-a-roses, all fall down!

Ringel, Ringel, Rosenkranz, Rin . . .

Ring-a-ring-a-roses, all . . .

(*They stop, and other children come rushing on.*)

One of them

Du Käthe! . . . Die Marie . . .

Katie! . . . Marie . . .

Second Child

Was is?

What is it?

First Child

Weisst' es nit? Sie sind schon Alle 'naus.

Don't you know? They've all gone out there.

Wozzeck
(1917–1922)

437

	Third child
Du! Dein Mutter ist tot!	(*To Marie's child.*) Hey! Your mother is dead.

	Marie's Child
Hopp, hopp! Hopp, hopp! Hopp, hopp!	(*Still riding his horse.*) Hop, hop! Hop, hop! Hop hop!

	Second Child
Wo is sie denn?	Where is she now?

	First Child
Draus' liegt sie, am Weg, neben dem Teich.	Out there, on the path by the pond.

	Third Child
Kommt, anschaun!	Let's go and look! (*All the children run off.*)

	Marie's Child
Hopp, hopp! Hopp, hopp! Hopp, hopp!	(*Continues to ride.*) Hop, hop! Hop, hop! Hop, hop! (*He hesitates a moment, and then rides off after the other children.*)

Music breaks off.

‖10‖ ANTON WEBERN

Neglected during his lifetime, Anton Webern (1883–1945) did not live to see his music influence composers throughout the world during the 1950s and 1960s.

He was born in Vienna, the son of a mining engineer. As a young man, he composed constantly and studied piano, cello, and music theory. At eighteen, he entered the University of Vienna and later earned a doctorate in music history. While at the university, he studied composition privately with Arnold Schoenberg.

After finishing his studies with Schoenberg, Webern earned a modest living conducting various orchestras and choruses. His career was solid but unspectacular. His most important position was as director of the Vienna Workers' Symphony Concerts, where traditional and contemporary compositions were performed for a working-class audience. Rare performances of his own works were usually met with ridicule.

Webern was a shy man, devoted to his wife and children. A Christian mystic, he loved to commune with nature while mountain climbing in the Austrian Alps. "It is not the beautiful landscape, the beautiful flowers in the usual romantic sense, that move me," he wrote to his friend Alban Berg. "My object is the deep, bottomless, inexhaustible meaning in all. I love all nature, but most of all that which is found in the mountains."

With the rise of Nazism in Austria in 1934, Webern's orchestra and chorus—sponsored by the Social Democratic party—were dissolved. In 1938, when Nazi Germany annexed Austria, Webern lost his job with the government radio, and his music was banned. He was forced to eke out a living by proofreading for his Viennese publisher.

While Webern's life seems ordinary enough, his death was a bizarre tragedy. Toward the end of World War II, he took refuge from the bombing of Vienna in the small Austrian town of Mittersill. His daughter lived there with her husband and three children. In 1945, victorious American soldiers occupied the town; on the night of September 15 they arrested Webern's son-in-law, who was suspected of dealing in the black market. During the questioning, Webern and his wife—who were unaware of their son-in-law's activities—went into the bedroom where their grandchildren were sleeping. Later, Webern stepped outside the house to smoke a cigar without disturbing the children. Minutes later, an American soldier left the house and bumped into Webern in the darkness. Nervous and in a hostile foreign country, the soldier mistakenly thought he was being attacked. He fired three shots, and Webern was dead.

Webern's Music

Poetic lyricism pervades Webern's music, which is amazingly original in its brevity, quietness, and concentration. Webern distills a musical universe into miniatures lasting only two or three minutes; every single tone is of such crucial importance that the listener experiences time with a new intensity. Schoenberg aptly observed that Webern "expressed a novel in a single gesture, a joy in a breath."

Rarely has a composer achieved such worldwide influence on the basis of so little music; virtually all of Webern's mature music is on only four long-playing records. Choral works and songs make up about half of his output. The rest is music written for chamber orchestra or small chamber groups (as in the *Quartet* for clarinet, tenor saxophone, violin, and piano, Op. 22; 1930). Webern's first atonal works date from 1908 to 1909, around the same time as Schoenberg's. He adopted the twelve-tone system in the late 1920s, not long after his teacher developed it.

Webern exploited Schoenberg's idea of a "melody built of tone colors." His melodic lines are "atomized" into two- or three-note fragments which are presented in constantly changing tone colors and registers. He forces us to focus on the tone color, dynamic level, and register of each note. At first his music may

 Webern's Music

seem like isolated wisps of sound, but repeated hearings reveal that the fragments add up to a unified whole.

The texture of Webern's music is delicate and transparent; usually not more than a few solo instruments play at once. In his twelve-tone works, there is often strict polyphonic imitation among the lines of the texture. This technique may well reflect Webern's profound knowledge of Renaissance choral music, in which polyphonic imitation is so important. Texture, tone color, and dynamics play a crucial role in creating form in Webern's music.

Composers in the 1950s and 1960s used Webern's special way of manipulating a tone row as a musical point of departure. They were fascinated by his use of texture, tone color, dynamics, and register as unifying elements, and they often imitated the deceptively "cool" sound of his later music. Works that appealed to very few during Webern's lifetime have become a source of inspiration after his death.

Five Pieces for Orchestra, Op. 10 (1911–1913)

Webern's unique style is fully revealed in these early atonal works, composed before he adopted the twelve-tone system. These five "expressions of musical lyricism," as Webern called them, are among the shortest orchestral compositions ever written. The fourth piece is only $6\frac{1}{3}$ measures long and lasts less than thirty seconds. Webern's chamber orchestra of eighteen soloists includes unconventional instruments like the mandolin, guitar, cowbells, and harmonium (a small organ with metal reeds). Each piece is scored for a different number and combination of instruments.

Melodic fragments are whispered by ever-changing solo instruments and framed by poetic silences. Tone-color melodies replace "tunes" in this music. There are few notes, but each is crucial. The tempo constantly fluctuates. Brasses and strings are usually muted.

1. Very calm and tender

Changes of texture help create the form of this quiet miniature, which lasts only about thirty seconds. It opens with a single melodic line, then becomes more complex as several lines are presented at once. Then the original monophonic texture returns. The opening melodic line is a clear example of a tone-color melody; the first seven pitches are assigned a variety of timbres:

Pitch 1:	harp, muted trumpet
Pitch 2:	celesta, harp harmonic, viola harmonic
Pitch 3:	harp, flute flutter-tongue
Pitches 4–6:	glockenspiel
Pitch 7:	celesta trill

2. Lively and tenderly animated

Lasting less than a half a minute, this piece quickly moves from a soft beginning to a climactic *ff* ending that features high woodwinds, horn, trumpet, and glockenspiel (a set of metal bars struck by two hammers).

3. Very slow and extremely calm

Side 13, band 5

With its bell sounds coming as though from far off, this piece has a feeling of solitude and eerie stillness. The dynamics never rise above *pp*. The sustained bell-like sounds—produced by mandolin, celesta, guitar, harp, glockenspiel, cowbells, chimes, and harmonium—are heard both at the beginning and at the ending. This creates a vague A B A' effect. Melodic fragments in ever-changing solo instruments are set apart from one another by brief moments of near silence.

‖ LISTENING OUTLINE
To be read while music is heard

Third Piece (1913) from *Five Pieces for Orchestra,* Op. 10 (1911–1913), by Anton Webern

clarinet, muted horn, muted trombone, harmonium, mandolin, guitar, celesta, harp, bass drum, snare drum, chimes, cowbells, violin, muted viola, muted cello

Very slow and extremely calm

(About 1½ min)

1   *a.* Pulsating bell-like sounds, *ppp.*
    b. Violin, *pp*, pulsating bell-like sounds, *ppp.*
    c. Muted horn, *pp*, chimes, *ppp.*
2   Quicker notes in clarinet. Muted viola.
3   *a.* Pulsating bell-like sounds, *ppp.*
    b. Muted trombone, *ppp*; pulsating bell-like sounds, *ppp.* Snaredrum roll, extremely soft.

4. Flowing, extremely tender

The shortest piece in the orchestral repertory, this touching miniature demands the utmost concentration. Its few notes are all soft and in a fairly high register. The pulse and meter are barely perceptible. The piece is scored for clarinet, mandolin, celesta, harp, and snare drum, as well as the following muted instruments: trumpet, trombone, violin, and viola. While most of the instruments have sustained or repeated tones, tiny melodic fragments are played by the mandolin, trumpet, trombone, and violin.

Five Pieces for Orchestra, Op. 10 (1911–1913)

441

5. Very flowing

This is scored for twenty instruments, more than any other piece of the set. Webern begins with a few rarefied sounds but moves to a piercing climax at the exact center of the piece. The dynamics quickly return to *pp*, and the piece ends with an "extremely tender" note on the viola and a faint tap on the celesta.

‖11‖ BÉLA BARTÓK

Béla Bartók (1881–1945), whose music is infused with the spirit of East European folk song, was born in the Hungarian town of Nagyszentmiklós. When Bartók was seven, his father died and his mother was forced to move with her son from town to town while she earned a living as a schoolteacher. She gave him his first lessons on the piano, an instrument which played an important role in his career. For twenty-seven years (1907–1934), Bartók taught piano at his alma mater, the Budapest Academy of Music, and gave recitals throughout Europe.

During the early 1900s, Bartók was influenced by the nationalist movement that swept Hungary. He came to love the music of Hungarian peasants, and he spent most of his free time in tiny villages recording folk songs on a cylinder phonograph. Bartók became a leading authority on the peasant music of the Magyars, Rumanians, Slovaks, Turks, and the Arabs of North Africa. Soon his own music was profoundly affected by the folk music he knew so well.

Though Bartók was recognized early as an important composer abroad, he was neglected in Hungary. For a time after 1911, he even refused to play in Hungary because of "the indifference and animosity" of his countrymen. It was only after the successful Budapest premiere of his ballet *The Wooden Prince* in 1917 that Bartók's music gained acceptance in his homeland. During a tour of the United States in 1927 to 1928 one newspaper headline warned readers: "Hungarian Modernist Advances upon Los Angeles to Convince Scoffers." By 1939 he was able to gleefully report to his son that "Since 1934, I have worked almost exclusively upon commissions!"

Hitler's rise posed a serious problem for Bartók, who was violently anti-Nazi. After Germany's annexation of Austria in 1938, he wrote a friend: "There is the imminent danger that Hungary will also surrender to this system of robbery and murder. How I could then continue to live or—which amounts to the same thing—work in such a country is quite inconceivable." Bartók did not allow his music to be performed in Germany or on any radio station that could be heard in Germany or Italy.

In 1940, Bartók finally emigrated to the United States, where he spent the last five years of his life. This was a bleak period for him; he had little money, was in poor health, and felt isolated and neglected. "My career as a composer is as much

Caught up in the nationalist movement that swept Hungary, Bartók spent most of his free time in tiny villages recording folk songs on a cylinder phonograph (© G. D. Hackett, New York).

as finished," he wrote in 1942. "The quasi-boycott of my works by the leading orchestras continues. . . ." For three years he stopped composing. He held a position as a research scholar in folk music at Columbia University, but the grant ended before he could finish his work. In 1943, his health declined alarmingly. After his weight fell to eighty-seven pounds, he entered a New York hospital, where he unexpectedly received a commission for the *Concerto for Orchestra*, his best-known work. The success of its first performance in 1944 resulted in a series of commissions for the once-ignored composer. Tragically, Bartók had only a year to live and could write just two more compositions, the *Sonata* for solo violin (1944) and the *Third Piano Concerto* (1945).

Soon after his death in New York in 1945, Bartók became one of the most popular twentieth-century composers.

 Béla Bartók

443

Bartók's Music

"I do not reject any influence," wrote Bartók, "whether its source be Slovak, Rumanian, Arab, or some other; provided this source be pure, fresh and healthy." But he emphasized that the "Hungarian influence is the strongest." Bartók evolved a completely individual style that fused folk elements, classical forms, and twentieth-century sounds. He believed that peasant music helped liberate him from the "exclusive rule of the major or minor system." Most folk melodies, he observed, "adhere to the old church modes or the ancient Greek modes and certain still older modes (especially pentatonic), and moreover display extremely free and varied rhythmic structures and changes of meter. . . ." Bartók arranged many Hungarian and Rumanian folk tunes, often giving them highly dissonant accompaniments. In most of his works, however, Bartók does not quote folk melodies; he uses original themes that have a folk flavor. His aim was to "assimilate the idiom of peasant music so completely" that he could "forget all about it and use it as his mother tongue."

Bartók's genius found its most characteristic expression in instrumental music. He wrote many works for piano solo, six string quartets, other chamber music, three concertos for piano, one for violin, and several compositions for orchestra. Embracing a wide range of emotions, Bartók's music is deeply expressive. Fast movements can convey a primitive brutality or the vitality and swing of a peasant dance. Slow movements often suggest feelings of bleakness and profound pessimism. They frequently contain atmospheric, almost impressionistic music suggesting nocturnal insect noises and the chirping of birds. Such mysterious passages are known as Bartók's "night music."

Bartók revitalized and reinterpreted traditional forms such as the rondo, fugue, and sonata form. He unifies the contrasting movements of a composition by bringing back a theme in transformed versions. He also creates formal unity by beginning and ending a movement in the same way. For example, the second movement of the *Concerto for Orchestra* (1943) opens and closes with a solo on the side drum. Polyphonic imitation and motivic development often generate tension and excitement.

Bartók always organized his works around a tonal center. But within this tonal framework, he often used harsh dissonances, polychords, and tone clusters. In some of his late works, however, he returned to a more traditional and less dissonant vocabulary. Bartók's music is rhythmically characterized by a powerful beat, unexpected accents, and changing meters. The irregular meters and asymmetrical rhythmic patterns of East European folk music are used imaginatively. (See Bartók's *Six Dances in Bulgarian Rhythm* in section 1.)

Bartók was also imaginative in his use of tone colors, particularly of percussion instruments. In works such as *Music for Strings, Percussion and Celesta* (1936), and the *Sonata for Two Pianos and Percussion* (1937), he drew unusual sounds from the xylophone and timpani. Bartók was especially fond of glissandos on the timpani (this sliding effect is produced by a pedal mechanism). Like many twentieth-century composers, Bartók drew percussive, drumlike sounds from the piano as well.

Bartók's six string quartets are widely thought to be the finest since those of Beethoven. The works abound in exciting glissandos and pizzicatos that produce a "snap" when the string rebounds against the fingerboard. But Bartók's string quartets are more than a collection of novel sounds; they reflect the composer's profundity and nobility of spirit.

Concerto for Orchestra (1943)

The commission which led to the *Concerto for Orchestra* was offered to Bartók in 1943, while he was hospitalized in New York City. Serge Koussevitsky, the conductor of the Boston Symphony Orchestra, offered him a thousand-dollar commission for a new work. While recuperating at Saranac Lake, New York, Bartók was able to work "practically day and night" on his new composition. He finished it in six weeks. The *Concerto for Orchestra* was an enormous success at its premiere in Boston in 1944 and has since become Bartók's most popular work.

"The general mood of the work," wrote Bartók, "represents, apart from the jesting second movement, a gradual transition from the sternness of the first movement and the lugubrious death-song of the third, to the life-assertion of the last one." Bartók explained that the unusual title "Concerto for Orchestra" reflects the work's "tendency to treat the single orchestral instruments in a *concertant* or soloistic manner."

Written for an orchestra of virtuosos, this dazzling showpiece is Romantic in spirit because of its emotional intensity, memorable themes, and vivid contrasts of mood. Though its melodies were original with Bartók, they have a distinct folk flavor. The concerto is an example of Bartók's mellow "late" style, which is characterized by more frequent use of traditional chords. In all five movements, time-honored procedures like A B A, sonata form, and fugue are fused with twentieth-century rhythms and tone colors.

First Movement: *Introduction* (Andante non troppo); Allegro vivace

Side 14, band 1

The concerto begins with an extended slow Introduction based on two melodic ideas that grow in intensity as they are varied. Low cellos and double basses mysteriously introduce the first idea, a short phrase that climbs and then falls. The cello phrase returns twice, each time ascending higher before it descends. The flute then softly introduces the second thematic idea, an exotic-sounding figure that circles around a single tone. This theme also returns twice. First it is varied and expanded by the trumpets playing very softly, and then it is transformed into a passionate outcry by the strings.

The Allegro vivace is a type of sonata form. Themes are broken into fragments that are shifted among different instruments. In this movement there are frequent alternations between fast, powerful sections featuring strings and brasses and slower, calmer sections in which woodwinds are most prominent.

Concerto for Orchestra (1943)

445

The assertive opening theme of the exposition is marked by the rapidly changing meter so typical of twentieth-century music.

Its descending second phrase is an inversion, or upside-down form, of the ascending first phrase.

Before the contrasting second theme enters, the trombone plays a somber phrase. This has an important role later in the movement. The atmosphere of the Middle East is evoked by the plaintive second theme, which is first played by the oboe. It features an alternation between two tones, and it has a static, dronelike accompaniment that is common in folk music.

In the development section, the trombone motive from the exposition grows into an exciting brass fanfare. It is polyphonically imitated among the trombones, trumpets, French horns, and tuba. The recapitulation of the movement is unusual because the second theme comes before—rather than after—the first theme. The Allegro vivace ends decisively with the trombone motive, played in unison by all the brasses.

LISTENING OUTLINE
To be read while music is heard

Concerto for Orchestra (1943), by Béla Bartók

First Movement: *Introduction* (Andante non troppo); Allegro vivace

Sonata form

piccolo, 3 flutes, 3 oboes, English horn, 3 clarinets, bass clarinet, 3 bassoons, 4 horns, 3 trumpets, 3 trombones, tuba, timpani, cymbals, 2 harps, violins 1, violins 2, violas, cellos, basses

(About 9 min)

Andante non troppo   1   *a.* Low strings, *p*, ascending and descending phrase. High string
INTRODUCTION   tremolo, *pp*, flutes.

          b. Low strings, *p*, phrase ascends higher, then descends. High string
             tremolo, *pp*, flutes.

                c. Low strings, phrase ascends stilll higher, then descends.

2   *a.* Flute, *p*, new phrase. Strings, *p*.

        b. Trumpets, *pp*, new phrase varied and extended. Strings in background.

        c. Violins, *f*, new phrase transformed into forceful melody.

        d. Crescendo, bass motive repeated faster and faster, leading into

Allegro vivace
EXPOSITION
  First theme   1   *a.* Violins, *f*, main theme. Fast tempo. Violin melody becomes slightly softer. Crescendo to *f*.

        b. Trombone motive, *mf*. Flute, *p*, descending melody.

Second theme   2   *a.* Oboe, *p*, folklike melody, slower tempo. Strings and harp accompany.

        b. Folklike melody repeated and extended by clarinets, flutes, *p*. Strings and harp accompany.

DEVELOPMENT

        1 Orchestra, *f*, fragments of main theme in imitation. Allegro vivace. Crescendo to *ff*.

        2 Clarinet, *p*, new legato melody, slower tempo. Melody extended by English horn, flute, *p*.

        3 Strings, *ff*. Brasses, trombone motive in imitation. Allegro vivace. Orchestra, *fff*, high sustained tone.

RECAPITULATION
  Second theme   1   *a.* Clarinet, *p*, folklike melody, slower tempo. Strings and harp accompany.

                                b. Folklike melody repeated and extended by flutes, oboe, *p*. Strings
    and harp accompany.

    c. Low strings alternate with higher woodwinds. Crescendo and
    accelerando to

First theme   2   Orchestra, *ff*, main theme. Allegro vivace. Brasses, *ff*, trombone motive
ends movement.

Second Movement: *Game of Pairs* (Allegretto scherzando)

In A B A′ form, the jesting second movement is a "game" involving different "pairs" of woodwind and brass instruments. The instruments of each pair move in parallel motion and are separated by a distinctive pitch interval. In the opening section (A), a chain of five melodies is played consecutively by pairs of bassoons, oboes, clarinets, flutes, and muted trumpets. The contrasting middle section (B) is a hymnlike melody softly played by brass instruments. When the opening section returns (A′), it has a more active accompaniment. The incisive sound of a side drum (without snares) is prominent throughout the movement. It plays syncopated solos at both the beginning and the end, as well as in the hymnlike middle section.

LISTENING OUTLINE
To be read while music is heard

Concerto for Orchestra (1943), by Béla Bartók

Second Movement: *Game of Pairs* (Allegretto scherzando)

A B A′ form, duple meter ($\frac{2}{4}$)

2 flutes, 2 oboes, 2 clarinets, 3 bassoons, 4 horns, 2 trumpets, 2 trombones, tuba, timpani, side drum, 2 harps, violins 1, violins 2, violas, cellos, basses

(About 6½ min)

A   1   Solo side drum (without snares), *mf*.

      2   Two bassoons, *p*, accompanied by pizzicato strings.

      3   *a.* Two oboes, *p*, in higher register. Pizzicato strings accompany.

            b. Low strings, pizzicato, while oboes sustain tones.

      4   *a.* Two clarinets.

            b. Low strings, accented notes.

      5   *a.* Two flutes, *mf*, in higher register.

            b. Low strings, pizzicato, while flutes sustain tones.

      6   Two muted trumpets, *p*. Muted string tremolos, *pp*, in background.

B   1   *a.* Brasses, *mf*, hymnlike legato melody. Side drum accompanies.

            b. Horns, *p*, conclude hymnlike melody and sustain chord.

      2   Oboe, flute, and clarinet, *p*, lead to

A′   1   Two bassoons, *p*, opening melody. Staccato bassoon in background.

      2   *a.* Two oboes, *p*, in higher register. Clarinets and strings in background.

     b. Low strings, pizzicato, while oboes sustain tones.
3 *a.* Two clarinets. Flutes and strings in background.
     b. Low strings, accented notes.
4 *a.* Two flutes, *mf*, in higher register. Woodwinds and strings in background.
     b. Low strings, pizzicato, while flutes sustain tones.
5 Two muted trumpets, *mf*. Harp glissandos and muted string tremolos in background.
6 Woodwinds, *p*, repeated chord; solo side drum, decrescendo, ends *Game of Pairs.*

Third Movement: *Elegy* (Andante, non troppo)

Bartók thought of this deeply moving music as a "death song." The Elegy is based largely on themes from the slow Introduction to the first movement. Mysterious opening bars—similar to those of the Introduction—lead into a section of "night music." A misty, nocturnal atmosphere is evoked by soft harp glissandos, splashes of woodwind sound, chirps from the piccolo, and a mournful oboe line.

The central section of the Elegy is louder and more melodic than the rest. High violins proclaim a theme that was played softly by trumpets in the Introduction to the first movement. A folklike melody is then introduced by violas and repeated, at a higher pitch, by woodwinds. The Elegy ends as it began, with misty "night music" and faint chirps from a piccolo.

Fourth Movement: *Interrupted Intermezzo* (Allegretto)

There is an amusing story behind the title of this movement. While working on his *Concerto for Orchestra*, Bartók heard a radio broadcast of the Seventh Symphony by Soviet composer Dimitri Shostakovich. Bartók found one of its themes to be so silly that he decided to parody it. In the middle of the movement, which is outlined A B A–Interruption–B A, we hear this tune in the clarinet mocked by vulgar and noisy "interruptions" from the entire orchestra.

The Interrupted Intermezzo begins with a wistful folklike melody (A) played by the oboe.

Constant alternation between $\frac{2}{4}$ and $\frac{5}{8}$ meter makes the tune delightfully irregular. The strings play an ardent, expansive melody (B). After the "interruption," there is a return of both melodies in reverse order, and the movement ends abruptly and humorously.

Concerto for
Orchestra (1943)

449

Fifth Movement: *Finale* (Presto)

The Finale, in sonata form, sounds like a frenzied dance. An opening horn motive introduces a fiery "perpetual motion" theme in the violins. Tension drops when Bartók introduces a quiet woodwind episode, and the tempo slows. But the dancelike mood and rapid tempo are soon resumed when a trumpet introduces a fanfare theme with staccato repeated notes.

The fanfare theme is immediately imitated by a second trumpet, but in inverted, or upside-down, form. After a gentle harp passage, the fanfare theme is further developed in a fuguelike section, first by the strings, then by the whole orchestra. The shortened recapitulation ends with brasses proclaiming a slowed-down form of the fanfare theme.

|12| CHARLES IVES

American composer Charles Ives (1874–1954) wrote startlingly original music that was far ahead of its time. He was born in Danbury, Connecticut, the son of a bandmaster who loved to experiment with unusual sounds. "Pa taught me what I know," Ives later recalled. He learned to play many instruments and to follow the "rules" of harmony and counterpoint. But his father also encouraged independence of mind and ear by instructing ten-year-old Charles to sing a tune in one key while being accompanied in another. At thirteen, Ives held a regular job as church organist, and his compositions were performed publicly. Still he was prouder of his ability as a baseball player than of his musical skill. When asked what he played, he gruffly replied "Shortstop!"

When he was twenty, Ives entered Yale University to study musical composition. His conservative teacher, Horatio Parker, frowned on his musical experimentation. Faced with choosing a profession on graduating, Ives decided that he could keep his music "stronger, cleaner, bigger, and freer" if he did not try to make a living out of it. He knew that his unconventional music would not be popular, and he did not want to raise a family that might "starve on his

Charles Ives knew that his unconventional music would not
be popular, and he did not want to raise a family that might
"starve on his dissonances" (Omikron).

dissonances." Ives therefore went into the insurance business, starting out as a
clerk in a New York firm. Eventually he founded a successful insurance agency
and became very wealthy. A creative businessman, Ives invented the concept of
"estate planning" and wrote a textbook widely used by insurance agents.

Ives composed furiously each day after business until two or three in the
morning and on weekends and holidays. During the years he composed, he was
isolated from the music world; none of his major works was publicly performed.
Musicians for whom he occasionally played his compositions commented: "It is
not music," "It makes no sense," or "How can you like horrible sounds like that?"
They urged him to write more conventionally. His wife—a clergyman's daughter

Charles Ives

451

appropriately named Harmony—believed in his genius and supported his refusal to compromise. Completely unknown, his scores accumulated in the barn of his Connecticut farm.

America's participation in World War I from 1917 to 1918 dampened Ives's creative urge. "I did practically nothing in music. I did not seem to feel like it," he recalled. "We were very busy at the office at this time with the extra Red Cross and Liberty Loan drives, and all the problems that the War brought on." Then, in October 1918, shortly before the end of the war, the forty-four-year-old Ives had a heart attack from which he never completely recovered. He composed almost nothing after 1921. Instead, he began to make his compositions known to the public.

From 1920 to 1922, Ives privately printed his monumental *Concord Sonata* for piano, his explanatory *Essays before a Sonata,* and a collection of *114 Songs* and sent them to musicians, critics, and libraries. At first, the volumes aroused little more than ridicule. ("It was the fate of many of them," wrote Henry Cowell, Ives's biographer, "to be used to adjust the height of the piano bench in the studios of more than one" well-known musician.) Gradually a few young composers and performers recognized that Ives was enormously original. In 1939, when Ives was sixty-four, his *Concord Sonata* (1909–1915) aroused an ovation at its first complete New York performance. By the 1940s, many thought Ives to be America's first great composer. In 1947 he won a Pulitzer Prize for his Third Symphony (1904–1911), written some forty years earlier. Newspapers and magazines all over the country took up the story of the businessman who had lived a secret life as a composer. Ives's typically gruff reaction to the Pulitzer Prize was, "Prizes are for boys. I'm grown up."

A few years before his death, Ives received a letter from Arnold Schoenberg's widow, who had found the following note among her husband's papers: "There is a great Man living in this Country—a composer. He has solved the problem how to preserve one's self and to learn. He responds to negligence by contempt. He is not forced to accept praise or blame. His name is Ives."

Ives's Music

Though experimental and far ahead of their time, Ives's compositions are rooted deeply in the folk and popular music he knew as a boy: revival hymns and ragtime, village bands and church choirs, patriotic songs and barn dances. Ives was inspired by the "unconventional" features of the American tradition: the village fiddler playing slightly out of tune, the cornetist a fraction ahead of the rest of the band, the church organist accidentally holding one chord while the choir sings another. While earlier American composers made folk material conform to academic "rules," Ives reveled in its irregular rhythms and asymmetrical melodies. His polyrhythms, polytonality, and tone clusters grew out of the music he knew.

To evoke nostalgic memories, Ives often quotes snatches of familiar tunes—"Yankee Doodle," "Columbia, the Gem of the Ocean," "America"—along with revival hymns and college songs. These snatches are not merely quoted but are developed and integrated within his music. Even the titles of his works evoke Ives's New England heritage: the Second Piano Sonata is subtitled "Concord, Mass. 1840–60"; its movements are "Emerson," "Hawthorne," "The Alcotts," and "Thoreau." We'll study one movement from a set of orchestral pieces entitled *Three Places in New England.* His large and varied output includes five symphonies and other orchestral music; music for piano, chorus, and chamber ensembles; and over two hundred songs. Many of his instrumental works have philosophical or descriptive programs.

A boyhood incident seems to have had an important influence on Ives. Two bands playing different music passed each other as they marched by him in different directions. Their dissonant clash fascinated the young boy. In later works Ives simultaneously presents musical events that seem unrelated: Two bands play in different keys, consonant chords are set against dissonant chords; conflicting meters and rhythmic patterns are intertwined.

Ive's music shows a wide range of emotions, styles, and musical techniques. It includes mild-sounding consonant chords and ear-splitting dissonances that caused his contemporaries to think of him as a crank. Ives scorned those who couldn't take dissonance. "Beauty in music," he wrote, "is too often confused with something that lets the ears lie back in an easy chair." Once, when dissonant music of his friend Carl Ruggles was hissed at a concert, Ives jumped up and shouted, "You goddamn sissy. . . . When you hear strong masculine music like this, get up and use your ears like a man!" Interested only in satisfying his inner ear, Ives created music that is extraordinarily difficult to perform. "The impossibilities of today are the possibilities of tomorrow," he wrote.

The Unanswered Question for Chamber Orchestra (1906)

Side 14, band 2

The Unanswered Question depicts the search for life's meaning. This brief but highly original work for chamber orchestra has a philosophical program. The music represents a "Cosmic Landscape" in which eternal silence is broken by vain attempts to answer the "Perennial Question of Existence." To convey this idea, Ives calls for an unconventional performing group composed of a trumpet, four flutes, and muted strings which are placed off stage or away from the other instruments. Each tone color is assigned a completely different kind of music, so that there are three separate layers of sound and rhythm functioning simultaneously. The strings have soft, slow, hymnlike music that represents silence. Mostly consonant, the string chords move serenely and are unaffected by what is played by the trumpet and flutes. Seven times during the piece, the trumpet intones the same short phrase that represents "the Question":

The Unanswered Question

453

This questioning phrase is indefinite in key and does not harmonize with the string chords. To the trumpet phrase, the flutes reply six times with harsh dissonances as they "hunt for the invisible answer." Each flute reply is louder and faster in tempo than the one before, growing from *p* and *adagio* to *ffff* and *presto*. The last response is the longest and shrillest as the flutes "seem to realize a futility and begin to mock 'the Question.'" At the end, the flutes make no further attempt to answer the trumpet's question, and the strings fade into silence.

Putnam's Camp, Redding, Connecticut (1903–1911), from *Three Places in New England* (1903–1914)

Three Places in New England is a set of three movements for orchestra that evokes American history, life, and landscape. Completed in 1914, it was not performed until 1930, when it was booed and hissed in Boston. Today, it is one of Ives's most popular works and a landmark in American music.

The daring and brilliant second movement, *Putnam's Camp, Redding, Connecticut,* is a child's impression of a Fourth of July picnic. Ives recaptures his boyhood memory of two marching bands clashing dissonantly as they play different tunes. He quotes many fragments from once well-known marches by John Philip Sousa (1854–1932), the American composer nicknamed the "March King." Snatches of patriotic songs and folklike tunes written by Ives contribute to the piece's popular flavor.

In his preface to this score, Ives wrote, "Near Redding Center, Conn., is a small park preserved as a Revolutionary Memorial; for here General Israel Putnam's soldiers had their winter quarters in 1778–1779." One Fourth of July, "a child went there on a picnic held under the auspices of the First Church and the Village Cornet Band." The child wanders "away from the rest of the children past the camp ground into the woods. As he rests on the hillside of laurel and hickories, the tunes of the band and the songs of the children grow fainter. . . ." He falls asleep and dreams of the discouraged American soldiers breaking camp, marching out "with fife and drum to a popular tune of the day. Suddenly a new national note is heard. Putnam is coming over the hills from the center,—the soldiers turn back and cheer. The little boy awakes, he hears the children's songs and runs down past the monument to 'listen to the band' and join in the games and dances."

Putnam's Camp is in three sections (A B A') that parallel the descriptive program. The first, marked "quick step time," captures the gaiety and confusion of a Fourth of July picnic in a nineteenth-century town. After a raucous, highly dissonant introduction, the strings play the main theme, a vigorous march that begins with conventional harmonies.

Such abrupt shifts between harsh dissonances and mild-sounding consonances are typical of Ives and are heard throughout *Putnam's Camp*. The piano, woodwinds, and brasses begin to compete for the listener's attention, and soon it sounds as though two bands are playing against each other. The mood becomes even more comic when a parody of the opening phrase of "Yankee Doodle" is quickly played by the trumpet, flute, and violins.

After more orchestral confusion, the music gradually becomes softer and slows to a halt, depicting the child falling asleep.

A mysterious high chord in the strings ushers in the middle section, which depicts the child's dream. Repeated piano and drum beats that seem out of phase with the rest of the orchestra begin one of the boldest parts of the score. Ives creates the impression of two bands playing at different tempos. (One band employs strings and woodwinds; the other has piano, drums, and trumpet.) Here the conductor must beat four bars with one hand against three bars in the other. The bands merge, and we hear a flute playing "The British Grenadiers," a favorite tune of the Revolutionary army.

The riotous concluding section creates deliberate melodic and rhythmic confusion as the main march theme is combined with "The British Grenadiers" and other fragments. *Putnam's Camp* ends with an ear-splitting dissonant chord. (In some recordings, the raucous sounds at the end drown out Ives's quotation from "The Star-Spangled Banner" in the last two bars.)

*Three
Places in New
England*

455

‖**13**‖ AARON COPLAND

Aaron Copland (b. 1900), a leading American composer, was born in Brooklyn in 1900 of Russian-Jewish immigrant parents. "No one ever talked music to me or took me to a concert," he recalled of his boyhood. "Music as an art was a discovery I made all by myself." At fifteen he decided to become a composer. He studied with a competent but conservative teacher who discouraged contact with "modern" music. This only made the forbidden fruit more attractive. Copland showed only his academic exercises to his teacher, keeping his more original efforts to himself.

In 1921 Copland went to France, where he was the first American to study composition with Nadia Boulanger. This extraordinary Frenchwoman was sympathetic to modern musical trends and became the teacher of several generations of American composers. Both Mlle. Boulanger's teaching and the stimulating atmosphere of Paris—where expatriates like Picasso, Stravinsky, and Ernest Hemingway felt at home—were to have a lasting influence on Copland's music.

When he returned to New York after three years in Paris, Copland was "anxious to write a work that would immediately be recognized as American in character." For Copland in 1925 "American" meant jazz. In his *Music for the Theater* (1925), a work for small orchestra, elements of the blues and ragtime are combined with an approach to rhythm and harmony that is like Stravinsky's. Copland's "jazz period" lasted only a few years. During the early 1930s he composed serious, highly dissonant works that were accessible only to sophisticated listeners. Compositions like the extraordinary *Piano Variations* (1930) convey starkness, power, percussiveness, and intense concentration.

In the late 1930s, Copland modified his style again, writing more accessible works for a larger audience. To understand this shift, recall that the 1930s brought the Great Depression; artists throughout the world were appalled by the economic misery surrounding them. To many composers, it seemed futile to write merely for a sophisticated elite, and they simplified their music to reach a wider audience. "I began to feel an increasing dissatisfaction with the relations of the music-loving public and the living composer," Copland later explained. Most concertgoers, he felt, could not grasp complex, highly dissonant music and wanted to hear only familiar music by Beethoven and Brahms. "It made no sense to ignore them and to continue writing as if they did not exist. I felt that it was worth the effort to see if I couldn't say what I had to say in the simplest possible terms." Copland drew on American folklore for his ballets *Billy the Kid* (1938), *Rodeo* (1942), and *Appalachian Spring* (1944). The use of jazz, revival hymns, cowboy songs, and other folk tunes helped make Copland's name synonymous with American music. His scores for films such as *Of Mice and Men* (1939) and *Our Town* (1940) brought his music before a mass public, as did patriotic works such as *A Lincoln Portrait* (1942).

Aaron Copland (Omikron).

Copland accomplished the difficult feat of writing simple, yet highly professional music. The texture of his music is clear and transparent. There are slow-moving, almost motionless harmonies that seem to evoke the openness of the American landscape. While strongly tonal, his works embody twentieth-century techniques such as polychords, polyrhythm, changing meters, and percussive orchestration. Since 1950, Copland has used serial technique—the

Aaron Copland

457

manipulation of a tone row or series—in such works as *Connotations* for orchestra (1962). This composition recalls the austere, uncompromising style of Copland's music during the early 1930s. Like Stravinsky, who also turned to serial technique during the 1950s, Copland used a tone row to create music that is completely personal in style.

Aside from his extraordinary compositions, Copland made other valuable contributions to music in America. He directed composers' groups, organized concerts of American music, lectured around the country, wrote books and magazine articles. At the request of the U. S. State Department, he was a musical ambassador to South America, where he talked with many composers and listened to their works. For twenty-five years, he taught young composers every summer at the Berkshire Music Center in Tanglewood. And at fifty, Copland began yet another career, that of conductor. He has conducted over fifty orchestras—primarily in his own music—throughout the world.

Appalachian Spring (1943–1944)

Appalachian Spring originated as a ballet score for Martha Graham, the great modern dancer and choreographer. It took Copland about a year to finish the music. At the time he thought, "How foolhardy it is to be spending all this time writing a thirty-five-minute score for a modern-dance company, knowing how short-lived most ballets *and* their scores are." But Copland arranged parts of the ballet as a Suite for full orchestra (originally the ballet used only thirteen instrumentalists) that won important prizes and brought his name to a large public. Today, *Appalachian Spring* is widely performed both as a ballet and as a concert piece.

The ballet concerns a "pioneer celebration in spring around a newly built farmhouse in the Pennsylvania hills" in the early 1800s. The rhythms and melodies are American-sounding and suggest barn dances, fiddle tunes, and revival hymns. But Copland uses only one actual folk tune in the score—a Shaker melody entitled, "Simple Gifts." (The Shakers were a religious sect established in America around the time of the Revolution. They expressed religious fervor through shaking, leaping, dancing, and singing.) *Appalachian Spring* is bright and transparent, has a clear tonality, and is basically tender and calm in mood. The score's rhythmic excitement comes from delightful syncopations and rapid changes of meter. As in many twentieth-century works, the orchestra contains a piano and a large percussion section, including xylophone, snare drum, wood block, and glockenspiel. The eight sections of the suite follow each other without pause and are described in Copland's synopsis of the score.

Section 1: "Very slowly. Introduction of the characters (bride, groom, a neighbor, revivalist preacher and his flock), one by one, in a suffused light." The peaceful open countryside is evoked by quiet dynamics, sustained harmonies, and evenly flowing rhythms.

Copland composed the music for Martha Graham's ballet
Appalachian Spring (Arnold Eagle).

Section 2: "Fast." Strings and piano in unison suddenly begin a joyful dance tune that is American in flavor.

"A sentiment both elated and religious" grows as the dance tune is combined with a solemn hymnlike melody in the *ff* winds. The section ends calmly; strings softly sing the hymnlike melody, while the flute recalls the dance tune.

 Appalachian Spring (1943–1944)

Section 3: "Moderate. Duo for the Bride and her Intended—scene of tenderness and passion." Gentle woodwind solos frame an intense dissonant passage for muted strings.

Section 4: "Quite fast. The Revivalist and his flock. Folksy feeling—suggestions of square dances and country fiddlers." Off-beat accents produce a delightfully humorous effect. After a brief pause, a slow transition begins with an "eloquent" *ff* passage and leads to

Section 5: "Still faster. Solo dance of the Bride—presentiment of motherhood. Extremes of joy and fear and wonder." Breathless motion and rapid syncopations create excitement.

Section 6: "Very slowly (as at first)." A high solo violin begins this "Transition scene to music reminiscent of the Introduction." Again, the peaceful countryside is evoked.

Side 14, band 3

Section 7: "Calm and flowing. Scenes of daily activity for the Bride and her Farmer-husband." There are five variations on the Shaker melody, "Simple Gifts." The theme is introduced by a clarinet.

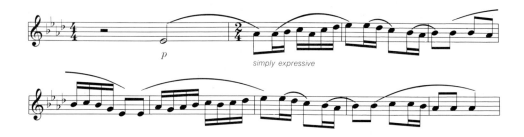

Variation 1: An oboe presents the theme "a trifle faster" and in a higher register.

Variation 2: Against high sounds in the piano and harp, the violas play the theme at half its previous speed. Then the violins and cellos in turn imitate the theme, creating a polyphonic texture. A brief transition leads to

Variation 3: Trumpets and trombones proclaim the theme at twice the previous speed, against rapid notes in the strings.

Variation 4: Woodwinds quietly play the second part of the theme at "a trifle slower" tempo than the preceding variation.

Variation 5: The first part of the theme is majestically played *fff* by the full orchestra.

Section 8: Moderate. "The Bride takes her place among her neighbors." After a hushed passage for muted strings marked "like a prayer," there is a quiet recollection of the hymnlike melody. The neighbors leave and the bride and groom are left "quiet and strong in their new house."

MUSICAL STYLES
SINCE 1950 ‖**14**‖

Since World War II, we have lived with instant communication—television, computers, and space satellites provide access to a virtually unlimited flow of information. We have been bombarded by an incredible variety of stimuli. And there is a constant demand for novelty. New styles in fashion and the visual arts rapidly spread and then disappear.

In music as well, emphasis has been on novelty and change. Musical innovations since 1950 have been even more far-reaching than those of the earlier 1900s. There have been many new directions, and the range of musical styles and systems is wider than ever. As American composer Hugo Weisgall has observed, "Many composers today change their musical points of view with astonishing rapidity, composing this way and that, moving easily from complete traditionalism into the 'avant' *avant garde.*"

Accurately describing the recent past is a difficult task. Yet any overview of music since 1950 must include the following major developments:

1. An increased use of the twelve-tone system.
2. The composition of music in which tone color, texture, dynamics, and rhythm are as important as pitch.
3. The spread of *chance music,* in which a composer chooses pitches, tone colors, and rhythms by random methods, or allows a performer to choose much of the musical material.
4. The development of electronic music.
5. A greater exploitation of noiselike sounds.

Since 1950, long-playing records and audiotape have spread new musical ideas far and wide.

Increased Use of the Twelve-tone System

A striking development after World War II (1945) was the gradual abandonment of tonality in favor of the twelve-tone system. From the early 1920s—when Schoenberg invented the system—to about 1950, most composers still wrote music with a tonal center. Few were attracted to the new method because it was associated with Schoenberg's expressionist style, which went out of fashion. During the 1950s, however, the twelve-tone system was adopted by many composers, including Stravinsky, who had been the leading composer of tonal music.

What contributed to this dramatic shift? In Europe, the end of the war brought a strong desire for new musical beginnings. During the Nazi years,

 Increased Use
of the Twelve-
tone System

461

Robert Motherwell, *In Black and White No. 2* (1975). Since 1950, there have been many new styles in the visual arts (Collection Norman Breman, Miami).

composers had been denied access to the twelve-tone works of Schoenberg and Webern; when peace came, they were eager to explore unfamiliar musical territory. In the United States, twelve-tone music was now available on long-playing records, and complex scores became easier to study.

But the most important reasons for the shift to the twelve-tone system were the resources of the system itself. Composers discovered that it was a compositional technique rather than a special musical style. Musicians as different as Bach, Mozart, and Chopin had all used the tonal system, and a comparable diversity of style was possible within the twelve-tone system. The new method also had the advantage of stimulating unconventional approaches to melody, harmony, and form. As Aaron Copland expressed it recently, "I began to hear chords that I wouldn't have heard otherwise. Heretofore I had been thinking tonally, but this was a new way of moving tones about. It freshened up one's technique and one's approach."

Many composers of the 1950s and 1960s chose to write music that was stylistically reminiscent of Anton Webern, Schoenberg's disciple. They created "pointillist" music in which melodic lines are "atomized" into tiny fragments that are heard in widely separated registers and framed by moments of silence. Webern's style answered the needs of the post-World War II generation. His music had a lean, "modern" sound, while Schoenberg's was considered too "Romantic" and traditional in form. The French composer Pierre Boulez (b. 1925) spoke for many of his generation in 1952 when he unfavorably compared Schoenberg's alliance with "the decadence of the great German Romantic tradition" with Webern's reaction "against all inherited rhetoric."

Extensions of the Twelve-tone System: Serialism

During the late 1940s and early 1950s, the techniques of the twelve-tone system came to be used to organize dimensions of music other than pitch, such as rhythm, dynamics, and tone color. Recall that in early twelve-tone music the system was used primarily to order *pitch* relationships. All the pitches of a twelve-tone composition would be derived from a single tone row, or series. After 1950, a series of durations (rhythmic values), dynamic levels, or tone colors also could serve as a unifying idea. A rhythmic or dynamic series might be manipulated like the series of twelve tones. The use of a series, or ordered group of musical elements, to organize several dimensions of a composition is called **serialism.** The leading proponents of serialism include Milton Babbitt (b. 1916) of America, Karlheinz Stockhausen (b. 1928) of Germany, and Olivier Messiaen and Pierre Boulez of France. While their methods led to a totally controlled and organized music, the actual sound—in certain cases—could seem random and chaotic. The music's complex relationships are often difficult to perceive.

Chance Music

The 1950s witnessed not only serialism but an opposite approach known as *chance,* or *aleatory,* music (from the Latin *alea,* or "game of chance"). In **chance music,** composers choose pitches, tone colors, and rhythms by random methods such as throwing coins. They may also ask performers to choose the ordering of the musical material, or even to choose much of the material itself. For example, a composer might write out brief passages of a composition but ask the performer to play them in any desired order. Or a composer might indicate a group of pitches but direct the performer to invent rhythmic patterns.

The most famous and influential creator of chance music is the American John Cage. At the very beginning of this book we mentioned his silent "composition" entitled *4'33"* (1952), which requires the performer *not* to make a sound for four minutes and thirty-three seconds. The "music" is made up of the unintentional sounds that an audience might produce in this time span. "I try to arrange my composing means," explains Cage, "so that I won't have any knowledge of what might happen. . . . My purpose is to eliminate purpose." For Cage, "The purpose of this purposeless music would be achieved if people learned to listen. Then when they listened they might discover that they preferred the sounds of everyday life to the ones they would presently hear in the musical program. . . . That was all right as far as I was concerned." Cage's approach is also illustrated by his *Imaginary Landscape No. 4* (1951), for twelve radios. The score gives precise directions to the performers—two at each radio—for manipulating the dials affecting wavelength and volume. Yet all the indications in the score were chosen by chance means. They show no regard for local station wavelengths or the time of performance. "At the actual performance of *Imaginary Landscape,*" reported one member of the audience, "the hour was later than anticipated before the work's

  Chance Music

463

turn came on the program, so that the instruments were unable to capture programs diversified enough to present a really interesting result." This is not surprising, since Cage chose the wavelengths and dynamics by throwing dice.

With Cage's work as an example, serial composers such as Pierre Boulez and Karlheinz Stockhausen introduced elements of chance into their compositions during the mid-1950s. Stockhausen's *Piano Piece No. 11* (1956) has nineteen short segments of music printed on a large roll of paper that measures 37 by 21 inches. The segments can be played in any order, and the performer is instructed to begin with the fragment that first catches the eye. The piece is likely to be different each time it is played.

Chance music makes a complete break from traditional values in music. It asserts, in effect, that one sound or ordering of sounds is as meaningful as another. To most listeners, a piece of chance music is more often significant as an idea than as a collection of actual sounds. Some composers may be attracted by the sheer novelty of chance music, by its ability to shock and attract attention. Others are influenced by Oriental philosophies such as Zen Buddhism, which is not structured according to Western concepts of logic. Finally, some composers may want to give performers a major part in the creative process.

Electronic Music

Since the development of tape studios, synthesizers, and computers in the 1950s and 1960s, composers now have potentially unlimited resources for the production and control of sound. Electronic music is as diverse as nonelectronic music. Its spectrum includes rock, chance music, and serial compositions.

Electronic instruments let composers control tone color, duration, dynamics, and pitch with unprecedented precision. Composers are no longer limited by human performers. For the first time, they can work *directly* in their own medium—sound. There is no more need for intermediaries, the performers. The audiotape of a composition *is* the composition. Thus, a composer alone is now responsible for putting into music the subtle variations of rhythm, tone color, and dynamics that once rested with the performer.

Many composers have felt a need to "humanize" their electronic music by combining it with live performers. This can be done in several ways. Some pieces use live performer(s) and taped sounds. The taped sounds may be electronic pitches or noises, or they may be previously recorded sounds of live performers. In some cases, performers may be involved in a duet with themselves, or with electronically manipulated versions of their own performances. In combining live performers with taped sounds, composers face the problem of synchronizing sounds that change from performance to performance—those of live musicians—and the taped sounds, which don't vary.

There are also works for traditional instruments and electronic synthesizers that are performed "live." Traditional instruments are also "electrified" through amplification. Composers use "electric" pianos and violins.

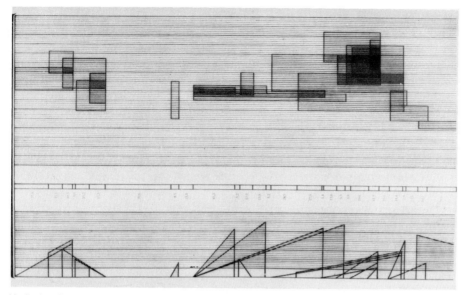

Karlheinz Stockhausen's *Etude II* was the first published electronic score (Universal Edition, London).

Electronic music is important not only in itself, but in its influence on musical thought in general. Electronic instruments have suggested new sounds and new forms of rhythmic organization. "These limitless electronic media," said Milton Babbitt, "have shown us new boundaries and new limits that are not yet understood—the very mysterious limits, for example, of the human capacity to hear, to conceptualize, and to perceive. Very often we will specify something and discover that the ear can't take in what we have specified. . . . The human organism simply cannot respond quickly enough, cannot perceive and differentiate as rapidly and precisely as the synthesizer can produce it and as the loudspeaker can reproduce it."

"The Liberation of Sound"

Composers today use a wider variety of sounds than ever, including many that were once considered undesirable noises. Composers have achieved what Edgard Varèse called "the liberation of sound . . . the right to make music with any and all sounds. . . ." Electronic music may include environmental sounds like thunder or electronically generated hisses and blips. But composers also may draw novel sounds from voices and nonelectronic instruments. Singers are asked to scream, whisper, laugh, groan, sneeze, cough, whistle, and click their tongues. They may sing phonetic sounds rather than words. Composers may treat their vocal text merely as a collection of sounds and not attempt to make the meaning of the words clear to the audience.

"The Liberation of Sound"

465

Wind and string players tap, scrape, and rub the bodies of their instruments. A brass or woodwind player may hum while playing, thus creating two pitches at once. A flutist may click the keys of the instrument without producing a tone; a pianist may reach inside the piano to pluck a string and then run a chisel along it, creating a sliding sound. To communicate their intentions to performers, composers may devise new systems of music notation, because standard notation makes no provision for many noiselike sounds. Recent music scores contain graphlike diagrams, new note shapes and symbols, and novel ways of arranging notation on the page. But composers are not the only ones to invent unusual sounds. Often the players themselves discover new possibilities for their instruments. Many modern works have been inspired by the discoveries of inventive performers.

The greatest expansion and experimentation have involved percussion instruments. In many recent compositions, percussion instruments outnumber strings, woodwinds, and brasses. Traditional percussion instruments are struck with new types of beaters made of glass, metal, wood, and cloth. Unconventional instruments now widely used include tom-toms, bongos, slapstick, maracas, guiro, and vibraphone.

In the search for novel sounds, increased use has been made of **microtones,** intervals smaller than the half step. Small intervals like quarter tones have long been used in non-Western music, but they have only recently become an important resource for Western composers. Electronic instruments have stimulated this development, since they are not restricted to conventional scales and do not force players to unlearn performance habits.

Composers such as Krzysztof Penderecki (b. 1933) create sounds bordering on electronic noise through tone clusters, groups of closely spaced tones played together. Clusters are unlike traditional chords in that one usually does not hear individual tones but a mass, block, or band of sound. Composers may achieve a sense of growth or change by widening or narrowing such a band, or by making it more or less dense.

The directional aspect of sounds—how they are projected in space—has taken on new importance. Loudspeakers or groups of instruments may be placed at opposite ends of the stage, in the balcony, or at the back and sides of the auditorium. In electronic compositions like Edgard Varèse's *Poème électronique* (1958) and nonelectronic works like Elliott Carter's *Double Concerto* for harpsichord and piano with two chamber orchestras (1961), sounds are made to travel gradually in space, passing from one loudspeaker or player to another.

Mixed Media

Electronic music often has visual counterparts such as slide projections, films, light shows, gestures, and theatrical actions. One such mixed-media presentation was Varèse's *Poème électronique,* which combined electronic sounds with images projected on walls. But multimedia works are not confined to electronic music.

Chance music and other types of recent music sometimes require performers to function as actors as well as sound producers, as in *Ancient Voices of Children* (1970), by George Crumb. Mixed-media presentations generally are intended to break down the ritual surrounding traditional concerts and to increase communication between a composer and the audience.

Rhythm and Form

Rhythm and form have undergone some of the most striking changes in music since 1950. Earlier in the century composers often changed meters or used unconventional ones such as $\frac{7}{8}$ and $\frac{5}{8}$. Today, some composers abandon the concepts of beat and meter altogether. This is a natural outcome of electronic music, which needs no beat to keep performers together. In nonelectronic music, too, the composer may specify duration in absolute units like seconds rather than relative units like beats. In some recent music, there may be several different speeds at the same time.

More than ever, each piece of music follows its own laws, and its form grows out of its material. Many composers no longer write music in traditional forms like A B A, sonata form, or rondo. Indeed, form may unfold with little or no obvious repetition of material.

Basic Terms

serialism
chance music (aleatory music)
microtone

Twentieth
Century

MUSIC SINCE 1950: SIX REPRESENTATIVE PIECES ‖15‖

Sonata for Flute, Oboe, Cello, and Harpsichord (1952), by Elliott Carter

Elliott Carter (b. 1908) is an American composer recognized as a major figure in contemporary music. He first attracted international attention when his *String Quartet* No. 1 (1951) won first prize at a composition contest held by the city of

Sonata for Flute, Oboe, Cello, and Harpsichord

467

Liège in Belgium in 1953. Since then, he has produced an imposing series of instrumental works, including two other string quartets (1959, 1972), the *Variations for Orchestra* (1955), the *Double Concerto* (1961), the *Piano Concerto* (1966), and the *Concerto for Orchestra* (1969). Carter does not belong to any compositional "school" but has evolved a personal style that we'll study in his *Sonata for Flute, Oboe, Cello, and Harpsichord* (1952).

"The *Sonata*," explains Carter, "was commissioned by the Harpsichord Quartet of New York. My idea was to stress as much as possible the vast and wonderful array of tone-colors available on the modern harpsichord. . . . This aim of using the wide variety of the harpsichord involved many tone colors which can only be produced very softly and therefore conditioned very drastically the type and range of musical expression, all the details of shape, phrasing, rhythm, texture, as well as the large form." Carter has said that at the time of composition in 1952, "it seemed very important to have the harpsichord speak in a new voice, expressing characters unfamiliar to its extensive Baroque repertory."

Each of the four instrumental parts has a separate, highly individual identity, like a character in a drama. As Carter put it, "I regard my scores as scenarios, auditory scenarios, for performers to act out with their instruments, dramatizing the players as individuals and participants in the ensemble. . . ."

The texture of Carter's sonata is complex and polyphonic; several different, apparently unrelated things go on at once. Each of the simultaneous instrumental parts has individualized rhythms and melodic gestures. The music has many tempo changes that are precisely regulated. Carter developed a technique called **metrical modulation,** which has been defined as "a means of going smoothly, but with complete accuracy, from one absolute metronomic speed to another, by lengthening or shortening the value of the basic note unit." The three movements of the sonata are not in traditional forms; they have a feeling of purposeful improvisation.

Side 14, band 4

First Movement: *Risoluto* (Determined)

"The music starts, *Risoluto*," writes Carter, "with a splashing dramatic gesture whose subsiding ripples form the rest of the movement." After the opening, the harpsichord often plays a succession of even notes while the other instruments comment with short phrases or single tones. This brief movement ends calmly with a high tone from the harpsichord.

Second Movement: *Lento*

Carter described the second movement of his sonata as "an expressive dialogue between the harpsichord and the others with an undercurrent of fast music that bursts out briefly near the end." The *Lento* opens with a one-note theme: The tone G is played softly in turn by the flute, oboe, cello, and harpsichord. Soon, other tones grow out of the G, and longer phrases unfold. A long section follows, in which the harpsichord repeatedly alternates with the three other instruments playing together. At first the harpsichord's assertive phrases are answered timidly by the other instruments, but soon the other instruments also begin to sound determined. A change from Lento to a very fast tempo brings the first extended passage for all four performers at once. Toward the end of this seven-minute movement, the slow tempo returns, along with some of the opening thematic material. The *Lento* concludes on the same tone it began with, but now the G is played loudly, rather than softly.

Third Movement: *Allegro*

The last movement uses the rhythmic pattern of the *forlana*, a Baroque dance associated with the gondoliers of Venice. It is a carefree dance in $\frac{6}{8}$ meter with dotted rhythms. Carter writes that he "draws out of the characteristic rhythmic cell of that dance all sorts of rhythmic changes." The movement has many different dance rhythms, and often one fades into another.

Threnody for the Victims of Hiroshima, by Krzysztof Penderecki

During the late 1950s a group of avant-garde composers unexpectedly emerged in Poland. For years all artistic experimentation had been actively discouraged by the Soviet government and by other regimes of Eastern Europe. However, after the revolt against Stalinism in 1955–1956, the new Polish government encouraged cultural independence and free artistic expression in films, painting, theater, and music. Composers had at their disposal well-trained performing groups and electronic music studios. The best-known younger Polish composer is Krzysztof Penderecki (b. 1933).

Penderecki was a young boy when the Nazis occupied Poland and massacred most of its Jewish population. Although not threatened personally, Penderecki felt great compassion for the victims. "That great war crime," he wrote, "has undoubtedly been in my subconscious mind since the war, when, as a child, I saw the destruction of the ghetto in my small native town of Debica." His compassion for human suffering has been expressed in works like the *Dies irae* (1967), to the memory of the victims of Auschwitz, and the *Threnody for the Victims of Hiroshima*. In these works, and in his well-known *St. Luke Passion* (1963–1965), Penderecki draws spectacular and novel sounds from voices and conventional instruments. He often calls for tone clusters, glissandos, noiselike and percussive effects, and choral hissing, laughing, shouting, and whistling.

Penderecki's Threnody, or song of mourning, is an almost unbearably intense work; its sounds are not intended to be "pleasant." Fifty-two string instruments—violins, violas, cellos, and double basses—produce a wide variety of noiselike sounds that often seem to come from electronic generators. Many of these sounds are tone clusters. At the beginning of this nine-minute work, shrill clusters are produced by ten groups of instruments playing "the highest note of

Threnody for the Victims of Hiroshima

the instrument (no definite pitch)." At the end of the piece, a huge cluster that sounds like the roar of a jet engine is produced by all fifty-two strings playing pitches a quarter-tone apart. Penderecki often uses slides or glissandos to make the clusters expand and contract. Noiselike sounds are also produced by tapping on the body of the instrument and bowing on the tailpiece.

There is no feeling of beat in this music. The duration of its various musical events is indicated in seconds at the bottom of the score. The Threnody is divided into six sections. Some feature sustained sounds, while others contain a variety of rapid percussive attacks. Noiselike sounds are so predominant that a definite pitch at the beginning of section two is very striking. An overall sense of coherence is produced by the general similarity of the first and last sections, as well as by the climactic character of section four.

LISTENING OUTLINE
To be read while music is heard

Threnody for the Victims of Hiroshima for 52 strings (1960), by Krzysztof Penderecki

24 violins, 10 violas, 10 cellos, 8 double basses

(About 9½ min)

1   *a.* Shrill, sustained clusters, one entering after the other.
    b. Suddenly soft.
    c. Pizzicatos. Soft, rapid squeaks. Increased rhythmic activity.
    d. Clusters fade out, squeaks and pizzicatos remain.
2   *a.* Single sustained tone surrounded by squeaks.
    b. Only sustained tone remains. Tone moves down a half step.
    c. Upward and downward glissandos (slides). Single, sustained tones expand into clusters, clusters contract into single tones.
    d. High sustained tone.
3   *a.* Low, sustained cluster, *p.* Higher sustained cluster, *f.* Other clusters join.
    b. Glassy sounds slide upward. Decrescendo into silence.
4   *a.* Quick attacks of single tones build to very wide and loud cluster.
    b. Low, roaring cluster. Slides. Low cluster narrows to single sustained cello tone. Decrescendo into 5-sec pause.
5   Disconnected pizzicatos, tremolos, blips, scratches at various dynamics and registers. Percussive sounds lead to
6   *a.* High sustained clusters, crescendo. Low clusters with high squeaks. Suddenly soft.
    b. Sustained cluster like jet roar. Sound gradually fades into silence.

Side 14, band 5   ### *Poème électronique* ("Electronic Poem"), by Edgard Varèse

Edgard Varèse (1883–1965), one of the great innovators of twentieth-century music, was born in France but spent most of his life in the United States. As early

Edgard Varèse, composer of *Poème électronique,* using a
tape recorder (The Bettmann Archive).

as 1916, he dreamed of freeing music from the limitations of traditional instruments and expanding the vocabulary of sounds used. During the 1920s and 1930s, Varèse pioneered in the exploration of percussive and noiselike sounds, and he wrote the first important work for percussion ensemble (*Ionisation;* 1931).

But it was the new electronic developments of the 1950s that enabled Varèse to realize his vision of the "liberation of sound." In 1958, at the age of seventy-five, he composed *Poème électronique,* one of the earliest masterpieces of electronic music created in a tape studio. The eight-minute work was designed to be heard within the pavilion of the Philips Radio Corporation at the 1958 Brussels World Fair. Varèse obtained unique spatial effects by projecting sound from 425 loudspeakers placed all over the interior surfaces of the pavilion. The composer worked in collaboration with the architect Le Corbusier, who selected the series of images—photographs, paintings, and writing—that were projected on the walls as the music was heard. But there was no attempt to synchronize the sounds with the images, which included "birds and beasts, fish and reptiles . . . masks and skeletons, idols, girls clad and unclad, cities in normal appearance and then suddenly askew," as well as atomic mushroom clouds.

Varèse's raw sound material—tones and noises—came from a wide variety of sources, including electronic generators, church bells, sirens, organs, human

 Poème électronique
("Electronic Poem")
by Edgard Varèse

471

voices, and machines. The sounds are often electronically processed in such a way that they cannot be precisely identified. In the listening outline, the effect of such sounds is conveyed by words placed in quotation marks, like "woodblocks" or "animal noises." Varèse organized his sounds into an electronic poem that seems weird, yet is amazingly logical and compelling.

Poème électronique is subdivided into two main sections, the first lasting two minutes thirty-six seconds and the second five minutes twenty-nine seconds. Each section begins with low bell-tolls and ends with sirens. Heard several times during the *Poème* is a distinctive group of three rising tones. Human voices and recognizable organ tones appear only during the second section. Varèse once remarked about the female voice heard toward the end of the *Poème:* "I wanted it to express tragedy—and inquisition."

Created in a tape studio, *Poème électronique* exists in only a single "performance" whose duration is fixed on audiotape. Thus the listening outline can indicate the precise moment at which a sound occurs.

LISTENING OUTLINE
To be read while music is heard

Poème électronique ("Electronic Poem"; 1958), by Edgard Varèse (1883–1965)

Tape studio

(8 min 5 sec)

0 sec	1	a.	Low bell-tolls. "Woodblocks." Sirens. Fast taps lead into high piercing sounds. 2-sec pause.
43 sec		b.	"Bongo" tones and higher grating noises. Short "squawks." Three-tone group stated three times.
1 min 11 sec		c.	Low sustained tones with grating noises. Sirens. Short "squawks." Three-tone group. 2-sec pause.
1 min 40 sec		d.	Short "squawks." High "chirps." Variety of "shots," "honks," "machine noises." Sirens. Taps lead to
2 min 36 sec	2	a.	Low bell-tolls. Sustained electronic tones. Repeated "bongo" tones. High and sustained electronic tones. Low tone, crescendo. Rhythmic noises lead to
3 min 41 sec		b.	Voice, "Oh-gah." 4-sec pause. Voice continues softly.
4 min 17 sec		c.	Suddenly loud. Rhythmic percussive sounds joined by voice. Low "animal noises," scraping, shuffling, hollow vocal sounds. Decrescendo into 7-sec pause.
5 min 47 sec		d.	Sustained electronic tones, crescendo and decrescendo. Rhythmic percussive sounds. Higher sustained electronic tones, crescendo. "Airplane rumble," "chimes," jangling.
6 min 47 sec		e.	Female voice. Male chorus. Electronic noises, organ. High taps. Swooping organ sound. Three-note group stated twice. Rumble, sirens, crescendo (8 min 5 sec).

Composition for Synthesizer (1960–1961), by Milton Babbitt

American Milton Babbitt (b. 1916) is a leading composer and theorist of twelve-tone music and a major figure in the development of electronic music. A brilliant teacher who is now Conant Professor of Music at Princeton University, Babbitt has profoundly influenced many young composers. He was the first composer to extend serial principles of organization to all musical dimensions—rhythm, dynamics, and tone color, as well as pitch. Not only are all the pitches in a Babbitt work derived from a tone row, but all the rhythms are drawn from a "durational row," a series of rhythmic values. His earliest works to use such techniques of serialism date from the late 1940s: *Three Compositions for Piano* (1947), *Composition for Four Instruments* (1947–1948), and *Composition for Twelve Instruments* (1948).

Babbitt's desire to control every aspect of his music attracted him to the possibilities of electronic music. Since 1959 he has made extensive use of the RCA Mark II synthesizer, an enormous machine that fills an entire wall at the Columbia-Princeton Electronic Music Center in New York City. "If you know how to specify it, any sound that can be passed by a loudspeaker can be created by this machine," Babbitt has explained. "I could synthesize the equivalent of a recorded violin sound if I knew exactly what the relevant dimensions of such a violin sound are." Through the RCA synthesizer, composers can precisely control the pitch, duration, tone color, and dynamic level of sounds. Using a mechanism like a typewriter, composers punch their musical specifications into a wide roll of paper that is fed into the synthesizer. The sounds produced may then be recorded on audiotape. The RCA synthesizer is very complex, and few composers other than Babbitt have used it. (He is a trained mathematician as well.) The synthesizer is not "played" as one plays an organ or a piano, and composers may spend many hours with the machine to produce a few minutes of music. Babbitt has used the RCA synthesizer to produce works such as *Vision and Prayer* for soprano and synthesized accompaniment (1961); *Philomel* for soprano, recorded soprano, and synthesized tape (1964); *Ensembles for Synthesizer* (1962–1964); and *Composition for Synthesizer* (1960–1961), which we'll now study.

In *Composition for Synthesizer* both pitch and rhythm are governed by serial organization. Here is the basic twelve-tone row: G–E–A♭–E♭–B–C–D–A–B♭–D♭–F–G♭. Babbitt has written that the *Composition* is less concerned with "new sounds and timbres" than with the control and specification of rhythm made possible by the RCA synthesizer. Electronic music, he explains, provides "a means of controlling rhythm in all its aspects, including speed and flexibility of pitch succession and time rate of change of dynamics, something that was never afforded a composer before." Though some noiselike sounds are heard in *Composition for Synthesizer,* most of the sounds have definite pitches.

The opening 45 seconds of *Composition* clearly show Babbitt's skillful use of contrasting textures and registers. There is a regular alternation between gonglike chords and melodic fragments, which are shifted to different registers, changed in speed, and presented in backward (retrograde) and upside-down (inverted) form.

Composition for Synthesizer, by Milton Babbitt

473

The texture becomes more and more complex as the number of melodic lines increases from one to four. This increasing complexity can be seen in the following outline:

1 a. Gonglike sustained chord stated twice.
   b. One staccato melody.
2 a. Sustained chord stated twice.
   b. Two staccato melodies.
3 a. Sustained chord.
   b. Low legato melody joined by two higher staccato melodies.
4 a. Sustained chord.
   b. Two very low melodies joined by two higher staccato melodies.

Many trill-like figures are heard in the section that follows. Their speed and evenness could be achieved only through electronic means.

Questions on Nature (1964), by Miriam Gideon

American composer Miriam Gideon (b. 1906) is well known for works in which a solo voice is combined with a small instrumental group. *Questions on Nature* is a cycle of seven songs for voice, oboe, piano, glockenspiel, and tam-tam (gong). Gideon has described the work as "a setting of questions propounded by the English philosopher Adelard of Bath in the early 12th century." Adelard poses such questions as "How the Earth moves," "Why we hear echoes," and "Why men universally die." The composer explains that "the instrumental sonorities as well as the character of the vocal line are intended to convey the mystery and the childlike directness of the topics contemplated." We'll study the first two songs of the cycle, which contrast in rhythm, dynamics, and mood.

Side 15, band 1

In the opening song, Gideon creates an atmosphere of mystery and wonderment with music that is moderate in tempo and subdued in dynamics. The oboe's questioning legato phrases, the tam-tam's low rumbles, and the vocal melody's sustained tones all contribute to the song's haunting quality.

How the Earth moves.
How or why the globe of the earth is held up in the middle of the air.
If the sphere of the earth were perforated, where a stone thrown into it would fall.

Side 15, band 1
(continued)

The second song is faster, louder, and more animated than the first. Phrases of staccato running notes are repeatedly tossed between the piano and oboe, perhaps reflecting the text's image of revolving planets. The bright sound of the glockenspiel is more prominent in this song, and the vocal melody uses quicker rhythms. The music is lively until near the end, when the tempo slows and the mood becomes mysterious and questioning, as in the opening song.

Why the planets and especially the sun do not keep their courses without revolution
  through the middle of the aplanon (the outermost and the immovable sphere of
  heaven)
Whether the aplanon should be called an animate body, or God.

Ancient Voices of Children (1970), by George Crumb

During the late 1960s, American composer George Crumb (b. 1929) became
prominent with a series of works that were acclaimed highly by both audiences
and critics. His music is personal and emotionally intense; it is distinguished by
an imaginative use of novel and delicate tone colors. Currently Crumb teaches
composition at the University of Pennsylvania.

Like much of his recent music, Crumb's *Ancient Voices of Children* is set to poetry
by Federico Garcia Lorca, the great Spanish writer who was murdered in 1936
during his country's civil war. "I have sought musical images," wrote Crumb,
"that enhance and reinforce the powerful, yet strangely haunting imagery of
Lorca's poetry. I feel that the essential meaning of this poetry is concerned with
the most primary things: life, death, love, the smell of the earth, the sounds of the
wind and the sea."

Ancient Voices of Children is a cycle of five songs with two instrumental interludes. The work is written for mezzo-soprano, boy soprano, oboe, mandolin,
harp, percussion, and "electric piano." (A normal grand piano is amplified by
means of contact microphones attached to its sounding board.) Three percussionists command a wide variety of instruments, including such unconventional
ones as tuned tom-toms, Tibetan prayer stones, and Japanese temple bells. The
pianist also plays a toy piano (in the fourth song); the oboist, a harmonica
(fourth song); and the mandolinist, a "musical saw" (an ordinary saw played
with a double-bass bow).

"Perhaps the most characteristic vocal effect in *Ancient Voices*," writes Crumb,
"is produced by the mezzo-soprano singing a kind of fantastic vocalise (on purely
phonetic sounds) into an amplified piano, thereby producing a shimmering aura
of echoes." (A *vocalise* is an extended melody sung without a text, only on vowels.)
Gradually fading sounds are produced by gongs, harp, vibraphone, and marim-
bas—among other instruments—and contribute to the vaguely Oriental atmosphere. The composer wants us to savor individual tone colors; in many passages,
only a single instrument or voice is heard.

Ancient Voices is theatrical in character and has already been used as ballet
music by several companies. A boy soprano singing off stage heightens the
drama. Even the instrumentalists play a dramatic role, occasionally being
required to sing, shout, or whisper. "In composing *Ancient Voices of Children*,"
Crumb explains, "I was conscious of an urge to fuse various unrelated stylistic
elements . . . a suggestion of Flamenco with a Baroque quotation . . . or a
reminiscence of Mahler with a breath of the Orient." We'll focus on the third and
fourth songs of the cycle.

 Ancient Voices
of Children

"From where do you come, my love, my child?"
("Dance of the Sacred Life-Cycle")

The most spectacular part of *Ancient Voices*, this central song uses the characteristic rhythm of a bolero, a Spanish dance in triple meter. The song opens with a soprano solo on phonetic sounds, sung into the amplified piano. During this solo, the singer is required to trill the tongue and make laughing sounds. Then the percussionists begin an ostinato in bolero rhythm that continues throughout the piece. They make a gradual crescendo and descrescendo, and progress from whispering to shouting, then back to whispering. Each of the poem's three stanzas has a half-sung question and answer by the two vocalists, a decorative oboe phrase, and an exuberant soprano melody.

¿De dónde vienes, amor, mi niño?	From where do you come, my love, my child?
De la cresta del duro frío.	From the ridge of hard frost.
¿Qué necesitas, amor, mi niño?	What do you need, my love, my child?
La tibia tela de tu vestido.	The warm cloth of your dress.
¡Que se agiten las ramas al sol	Let the branches ruffle in the sun
y salten las fuentes alrededor!	and the fountains leap all around!
En el patio ladra el perro,	In the courtyard a dog barks,
en los árboles canta el viento.	in the trees the wind sings.
Los bueyes mugen al boyero	The oxen low to the ox-herd
y la luna me riza los cabellos.	and the moon curls my hair.
¿Qué pides, niño, desde tan lejos?	What do you ask for, my child, from so far away?
Los blancos montes que hay en tu pecho.	The white mountains of your breast.
¡Que se agiten las ramas al sol	Let the branches ruffle in the sun
y salten las fuentes alrededor!	and the fountains leap all around!
Te diré, niño mío, que sí,	I'll tell you, my child, yes,
tronchada y rota soy para ti.	I am torn and broken for you.
¡Cómo me duele esta cintura	How painful is this waist
donde tendrás primera cuna!	where you will have your first cradle!
¿Cuándo mi niño, vas a venir?	When, my child, will you come?
Cuando tu carne huela a jazmín.	When your flesh smells of jasmine flowers.
¡Que se agiten las ramas al sol	Let the branches ruffle in the sun
y salten las fuentes alrededor!	and the fountains leap all around![1]

"Each afternoon in Granada, a child dies each afternoon"

This is the shortest song of the cycle; it is marked, "Hushed, intimate; with a sense of suspended time." In the background is a sustained chord produced very, very softly by the marimba, by percussionists who hum and sing, and by the harmonica. Just three simple phrases are sung by the soprano. Then the toy piano plays a brief quotation from a song by Bach. The song was originally

476

[1]J. L. Gili, *Lorca.* Copyright © J. L. Gili, 1960. Reprinted by permission of New Directions.

meant for Bach's wife, Anna Magdalena, and its original text began with the words "Be thou but near, and I contented will go to Death, which is my rest." The toy piano gradually slows down, "like the clockwork of a toy running down," and stops just before the cadence. This poetic use of a musical quotation symbolizes a child's death.

Todas las tardes en Granada,	Each afternoon in Granada,
todas las tardes se muere un niño.	a child dies each afternoon.[2]

[2] Federico Garcia Lorca, *Selected Poems.* Translated by Edwin Honig. Copyright 1955 by New Directions Publishing Corporation. Reprinted by permission of New Directions.

 Ancient Voices of Children

JAZZ

1 Jazz Styles: 1900–1950

2 Ragtime

3 The Blues

4 New Orleans Style

5 Swing

6 Bebop

7 Jazz Styles since 1950

Jazz can be described generally as music rooted in improvisation and characterized by syncopated rhythm, a steady beat, and distinctive tone colors and techniques of performance. Louis Armstrong, Billie Holiday, and Barney Bigard are shown here in 1947 (Photo Files).

1 ‖ JAZZ STYLES: 1900-1950

About the time Schoenberg and Stravinsky were changing the language of music in Europe, a new musical style called *jazz* was being developed in America.[1] It was created by musicians—predominantly black Americans—performing in the streets, bars, bawdy houses, and dance halls of New Orleans and other Southern cities. **Jazz** can be described generally as music rooted in improvisation and characterized by syncopated rhythm, a steady beat, and distinctive tone colors and techniques of performance. While the term "jazz" became current around 1915, the music itself was probably heard as early as 1900. We do not know exactly when early jazz started or how it sounded, because this new music was mostly improvised; it existed in performance, not musical notation. Moreover, very little jazz was captured on recordings before 1923, and none at all before the Original Dixieland Band recorded in 1917.

Since its beginnings, jazz has developed a rich variety of substyles such as New Orleans style (or Dixieland), swing, bebop, cool, and free jazz. It has produced such outstanding figures as Louis Armstrong, Duke Ellington, Benny Goodman, Charlie Parker, and John Coltrane. Its impact has been enormous and world-wide, affecting not only many kinds of popular music, but the music of such composers as Maurice Ravel, Darius Milhaud, and Aaron Copland.

The Roots of Jazz

Early jazz blended elements from many musical cultures, including West African, black and white American, and European. Most American slaves originally came from West Africa, an area that today includes Ghana and Nigeria as well as many other countries. West African elements that influenced jazz include the emphasis on improvisation, drumming, percussive sounds, and complex rhythms and syncopations. Another element of jazz that was probably derived from West Africa is known as *call-and-response.* In much West African vocal music, a soloist's phrases are repeatedly answered by a chorus. In jazz, **call-and-response** occurs when a voice is answered by an instrument, or when one instrument (or group of instruments) is answered by another instrument (or group). The call-and-response pattern of jazz was also derived from American church services in which the congregation vocally responds to the preacher's "call." In America, blacks developed a rich body of music that became a vital source of jazz. This music included work songs, spirituals, gospel hymns, and dances like the cakewalk. Much of this music was never written down and is now lost to us. But it was probably performed in a way that created sounds and rhythms similar to those of early jazz.

[1]An excellent recorded anthology of jazz is *The Smithsonian Collection of Classic Jazz* (distributed by W. W. Norton, Inc.).

One major source of jazz was the American band tradition
(New Orleans Jazz Club Collections of the Louisiana State
Museum).

Black music influenced and was influenced by the music of white America, which included hymns, popular songs, folk tunes, dances, marches, and piano pieces. In origin, this repertory was partly American and partly written or influenced by European composers. Nineteenth-century American and European musical traditions provided melodies, harmonies, and forms that became elements in the background of jazz.

One major source of jazz was the American band tradition. Bands—both black and white—played an important role in American life during the late nineteenth and early twentieth centuries. Virtually every village had its band and bandstand; bands performed at picnics, parades, political rallies, dances, and carnivals. Many of the instruments used in marching bands—the trumpet,

 The Roots of Jazz

cornet, trombone, tuba, clarinet, and drums—were also used in early jazz bands. And band music also influenced the forms and rhythms of early jazz.

Along with band music, the immediate sources of jazz were ragtime and the blues. Ragtime is a style of syncopated piano music that was popular from the 1890s to about 1915. The term "blues" refers, among other things, to a style of black vocal music involving "bent" notes and slides of pitch. Ragtime and the blues will be discussed more fully in sections 2 and 3.

Jazz in Society

The world of jazz has witnessed many changes since its beginnings at the turn of our century. Geographically, its center has shifted from New Orleans to Chicago, Kansas City, and New York. Today, it is hard to speak of *a* jazz center since good jazz is heard worldwide, from Paris to Tokyo. Jazz has changed in function, too. For a long time, it was basically music for dancing; but since the 1950s, many newer jazz styles are intended for listening. Now we are as likely to hear jazz in a concert hall or college classroom as in a bar or nightclub. The image of jazz has also changed. Originally condemned for its emphasis on sexuality, jazz has long since become respectable. Since the 1960s and the liturgical reforms of the Second Vatican Council, jazz even can be heard in American houses of worship.

The Elements of Jazz

Like other music of the twentieth century, jazz is too diverse and complex to be defined by any single formula. We'll now consider some elements of jazz created before 1950. Jazz after 1950 is discussed in section 7.

Tone Color

Jazz is generally played by a small group (or *combo*) containing from three to eight players, or by a "big band" with ten to fifteen musicians. The backbone of a jazz ensemble is its rhythm section, which is comparable to the basso continuo in Baroque music. Usually made up of piano, plucked double bass (bass), percussion, and—sometimes—guitar, the **rhythm section** maintains the beat, adds rhythmic interest, and provides supporting harmonies. Modern percussionists produce a variety of sounds from several drums and cymbals, using sticks, mallets, wire brushes, and bare hands.

The main solo instruments of jazz are the trumpet, saxophone (soprano, alto, tenor, baritone), piano, clarinet, vibraphone, and trombone. Jazz emphasizes brasses, woodwinds, and percussion rather than the bowed strings that dominate symphonic music. Brass players produce a wide variety of tone colors by using different mutes and muting techniques. A jazz performance usually involves both solo and ensemble sections. For example, a full ensemble might be followed

Jazz

The drummer and bass player are part of a jazz ensemble's rhythm section (Margot Granitsas/Photo Researchers).

 The Elements of Jazz

483

by a trumpet solo then by a clarinet solo or a duet for saxophone and trumpet.

Compared with "classical" musicians, jazz performers aim for more individuality of sound and tone color. For example, it is usually easier to distinguish between two jazz saxophone players than between two "classical" flutists. While jazz is basically instrumental music, its players try to match the personal quality of singing. In all, the distinctive sounds of jazz are easy to recognize but hard to describe. A jazz sound results from the particular way tones are attacked, "bent," and released; from the type of vibrato employed; and from a variety of pitch inflections that might be described as "smears," "scoops," "fall-offs," and "shakes."

Improvisation

At the heart of jazz lies improvisation. Jazz musicians create a special electricity as they simultaneously create and perform, making decisions at lightning speed. The fertility of great improvisers is staggering. Their recorded performances represent only a tiny fraction of the music they create almost nightly. Of course, not all jazz is improvised, and most contains both improvised and composed sections. Yet it is improvisation that contributes most to the freshness and spontaneity of jazz. The reputations of jazz performers rest mainly on the originality of their improvisations.

A jazz improvisation is usually in theme-and-variations form. The theme is often a popular song melody made up of thirty-two **bars,** or measures. The improviser varies this original melody by adding embellishments and changing its pitches and rhythms. Some improvised variations are similar to the original theme, but others are so different that the tune may be difficult to recognize. Often, jazz improvisations are based not on a melody but on a set of chords. The set of chords will be repeated over and over while the improviser creates melodies above it. In jazz, each statement of the basic harmonic pattern or melody is called a **chorus.** For example, a jazz performance that is based on a thirty-two-bar melody might be outlined as follows:

Chorus 1 (32 bars)	Theme
Chorus 2 (32 bars)	Variation 1
Chorus 3 (32 bars)	Variation 2
Chorus 4 (32 bars)	Variation 3

A jazz performance usually includes improvised solos by various members of the ensemble. In addition, there may be sections of *collective* improvisation, during which several musicians make up different melodies simultaneously. Their music is held together by the underlying chords. Until the introduction of long-playing records in 1948, most recorded jazz performances were about three minutes in length, the duration of a 78 RPM record.

Rhythm, Melody, and Harmony

Syncopation and rhythmic swing are two of the most distinctive features of jazz. We say jazz performers "swing" when they combine a steady beat with a feeling of lilt, precision, and relaxed vitality. In most jazz styles, the beat is provided by the percussionist (on drums or cymbals) and by the bass player. There are usually four beats to the bar. Accents often come on the weak beats: 1–2–3–4. Many kinds of syncopated rhythms result when accented notes come *between* the beats. Jazz musicians also create a swing feeling by playing a series of notes slightly unevenly. For example, the second note of a pair will be shorter yet more accented than the first:

But the rhythms of jazz are so irregular that it is difficult to notate them accurately. A performer must deviate from the notated rhythms to get a true jazz feeling. And as jazz has evolved, rhythms have become ever more irregular and complex.

Jazz melodies are as flexible in pitch as in rhythm. They employ a major scale in which the third, fifth, and seventh notes are often lowered or flatted. These "bent" or "blue" notes came into jazz through the vocal blues, as we'll see in section 3. Jazz uses chord progressions like those of the traditional tonal system. But over the years, the harmonic vocabulary of jazz—like its rhythm—has become increasingly complex and sophisticated.

Basic Terms

jazz	bar
call-and-response	chorus
rhythm section	

RAGTIME

Jazz
2

Ragtime is a style of composed piano music that flourished from the 1890s to about 1915. It was developed primarily by black pianists who traveled in the Midwest and South playing in saloons and dance halls. Not long after it originated, ragtime became a nationally popular style that reached millions of people—both black and white—through sheet music, player-pianos, ragtime songs, and arrangements for dance and marching bands.

 Ragtime

Scott Joplin was the leading ragtime composer (Omikron).

Ragtime piano music is generally in duple meter ($\frac{2}{4}$) and is performed at a moderate march tempo. The pianist's right hand plays a highly syncopated melody, while the left hand steadily maintains the beat with an "oom-pah" accompaniment. A ragtime piece usually consists of several melodies that are similar in character. It takes such forms as AA BB A CC DD or Introduction–AA BB CC DD EE. While the forms derive from European marches and dances, the rhythms of ragtime are rooted in black folk music.

Early jazz musicians often used ragtime melodies as a springboard for their improvisations. The syncopations, steady beat, and piano style of ragtime were an important legacy for jazz.

Scott Joplin

The acknowledged "King of Ragtime" was Scott Joplin (1868–1917), a composer and pianist whose father had been a slave. Joplin was trained in "classical" music and wrote a ballet and two operas as well as many piano rags. His most famous piano piece was *Maple Leaf Rag*, named after the saloon in Sedalia, Missouri, where Joplin worked as a pianist. Published in 1899, *Maple Leaf Rag* sold hundreds of thousands of copies. This success allowed Joplin to quit his saloon job and move to St. Louis, where he taught and composed.

In 1909, Joplin settled in New York City, where he spent the last years of his life. This was a bleak period for him: His health was poor, and he was unsuccessful in his desperate attempts to get a professional production of his opera *Treemonisha* (1911). Finally, in 1915, he mounted the opera himself in Harlem—without scenery, costumes, or orchestra. The failure of this endeavor led Joplin to a physical and mental breakdown. He was confined to a hospital in 1916 and died the following year. Only recently has *Treemonisha* been revived, and with great success.

Maple Leaf Rag (1899)   *Side 15, band 3*

A classic example of ragtime, *Maple Leaf Rag* lasts about three minutes and has the standard ragtime form AA BB A CC DD. Each section is exactly sixteen bars in length. The opening melody (A), marked *Tempo di Marcia* ("march tempo"), features the right-hand syncopations so typical of the style:

Tempo di Marcia

Section C modulates to a new key and has the "oom-pah" accompaniment characteristic of ragtime. Played by the left hand, the accompaniment includes low octaves followed by higher chords:

The final section (D) returns to the home key and ends with a decisive cadence.

Basic Term

    ragtime

|3| THE BLUES

Among the most important sources of jazz is music known as the **blues.** The term refers to a form of vocal and instrumental music and to a style of performance. The blues grew out of such black folk music as work songs, spirituals, and the field hollers of slaves. It is uncertain exactly when the blues originated, but by around the 1890s they were sung in rural areas of the South. Usually performed with a guitar accompaniment, these "country blues" were unstandardized in form or style.

The poetic and musical form of the blues crystallized around 1910 and gained popularity through the publication of "Memphis Blues" (1912) and "St. Louis Blues" (1914) by William Christopher Handy. By the 1920s, the blues had become a national craze. Records by leading blues singers like Bessie Smith sold in the millions. The 1920s also saw the blues become a musical form widely used by jazz instrumentalists as well as blues singers. Since then, jazz and the blues have been intertwined. The continuing impact of the blues is apparent in such popular styles as rhythm-and-blues, rock 'n' roll, and soul.

Vocal blues are intensely personal; they often contain sexual references and deal with the pain of betrayal, desertion, and unrequited love. The lyrics consist of several three-line stanzas, each in the same poetic and musical form. The first line is sung and then repeated to roughly the same melodic phrase (a a′); the third line has a different melodic phrase (b):

a   I'm going to leave baby, ain't going to say goodbye.
a′ I'm going to leave baby, ain't going to say goodbye.
b   But I'll write you and tell you the reason why.

A blue stanza is set to a chord progression that is usually twelve bars in length. Known as the **twelve-bar blues**, this chord progression involves only three basic chords: the tonic (I), the *subdominant* (IV), and the dominant (V). (The **subdominant** is the triad based on the fourth note—*fa*—of the scale.) The specific ordering of these chords can be outlined as: tonic (four bars)–subdominant (two bars)–tonic (two bars)–dominant (two bars)–tonic (two bars). Here is how the three-line stanza is set to this chord progression:

	Line 1 (a)				Line 2 (a′)				Line 3 (b)			
Bars	1	2	3	4	5	6	7	8	9	10	11	12
Chords	I				IV		I		V		I	

Each stanza of the text is sung to the same chord progression, although other chords may be inserted between the basic ones of the twelve-bar blues. Singers either repeat the same basic melody for each stanza or improvise new melodies to reflect the changing moods of the lyrics. The music is in quadruple meter ($\frac{4}{4}$), and so each bar contains four beats.

The twelve-bar blues is divided into three phrases that are four bars long. The soloist takes only about two bars to sing a line. This leaves the remainder of the four-bar phrase to be filled in by the supporting instrument(s). In blues recordings of the 1920s and 1930s, instrumental responses to the singer's lines were often improvised by leading jazz musicians like trumpeter Louis Armstrong. The following example shows how the vocal lines and instrumental responses fit into the twelve-bar blues pattern (some pitches and rhythms are approximate):

Bessie Smith, "Lost Your Head Blues," fourth stanza

Instrumental response (cornet)

I'm going to leave   ba - by, ain't going to say good-bye,   I'm

Tonic _____

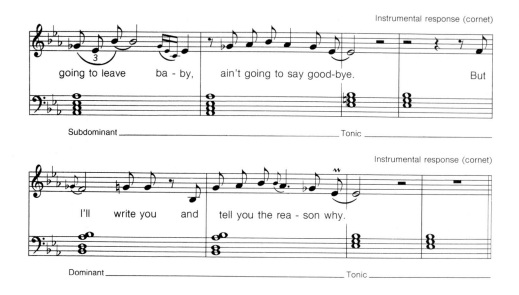

Instrumental response (cornet)

going to leave   ba - by,   ain't going to say good-bye.   But

Subdominant _____ Tonic _____

Instrumental response (cornet)

I'll   write you   and   tell you the rea - son why.

Dominant _____ Tonic _____

Blues singers have a special style of performance involving "bent" notes, microtonal shadings, and vocal scoops and slides. Their melodies contain many "blue" notes, which are produced by slightly lowering or flatting the third, fifth, and seventh tones of a major scale. Blues rhythm is also very flexible. Performers often sing "around" the beat, accenting notes either just before or after it.

Jazz instrumentalists imitate the performing style of blues singers and use the chord progression of the twelve-bar blues as a basis for improvisation. This twelve-bar pattern is repeated over and over while new melodies are improvised above it. As with the Baroque ground bass, the repeated chord progression provides unity while the free flow of improvised melodic lines contributes variety. Music in this twelve-bar form can be happy or sad, fast or slow, and in a wide range of styles. Later sections will consider two instrumental blues: *Dippermouth Blues,* an example of New Orleans jazz, and Charlie Parker's *Perhaps,* a piece in bebop style. Now we'll study a vocal blues by Bessie Smith.

Side 15, band 4

"Lost Your Head Blues" (1926), by Bessie Smith

Bessie Smith (1894–1937), known as the "Empress of the Blues," was the most famous blues singer of the 1920s. Her "Lost Your Head Blues" is a fine example of blues form and performance style. The lyrics express the feelings of a woman who plans to leave her man because she's "been treated wrong." Each of the poem's five stanzas is set to the twelve-bar blues pattern. Typically, a cornet response follows each line that is sung (see the example on pp. 489–490).

"Lost Your Head Blues" begins with a four-bar introduction by the accompanying cornet (Joe Smith) and piano (Fletcher Henderson). Bessie Smith then

Jazz

490

Bessie Smith, one of the most influential blues singers
(CBS Records).

sings a melody that she'll repeat—with extensive variations of pitch and rhythm—in each stanza. Her "blue" notes, microtonal shadings, and slides between pitches are essential to the effect of the song. Notice the eloquent slides up to *I* in her singing of "I was with you baby," as well as the ornamental quiver when she sings the words "your good gal *down.*" There are many syncopated rhythms as words often are sung just before or after the beat. Bessie Smith's vocal melody is highly sensitive to the words. For example, the long, high notes at the beginning of the last stanza ("*Days* are lonesome, *nights* are long") produce a wonderful climax. Throughout the song, Bessie Smith's vocal inflections are perfectly matched by the cornet's improvised responses and echoes.

I was with you baby when you did not have a dime.
I was with you baby when you did not have a dime.
Now since you got plenty money you have throw'd your good gal down.

Once ain't for always, two ain't for twice.
Once ain't for always, two ain't for twice.
When you get a good gal you better treat her nice.

When you were lonesome I tried to treat you kind
When you were lonesome I tried to treat you kind.
But since you've got money, it's done changed your mind.

I'm going to leave baby, ain't going to say goodbye.
I'm going to leave baby, ain't going to say goodbye.
But I'll write you and tell you the reason why.

Days are lonesome, nights are long.
Days are lonesome, nights are so long.
I'm a good old gal, but I've just been treated wrong.

Basic Terms

blues
twelve-bar blues
subdominant

NEW ORLEANS STYLE

From about 1900 to 1917, jazz developed in a number of American cities, but the major center was New Orleans. The Crescent City was the home of such important jazz musicians as Ferdinand "Jelly Roll" Morton, Joseph "King" Oliver, and Louis Armstrong.

Around the turn of the century New Orleans was a major port and a thriving cultural and commercial center with a cosmopolitan character. Its diverse population included people of African, French, Spanish, Portugese, English, Italian, and Cuban ancestry. A special group in New Orleans were those of mixed African, French, and Spanish descent. This diversity of population was mirrored in the rich musical life of New Orleans. It included opera and chamber music as well as folk, popular, dance, and sacred music of all kinds. The tradition of marching and dance bands was particularly strong. There were frequent competitions between bands to see which could play more loudly or more brilliantly. Some band musicians were trained in classical music and could read notation, while others played by ear and relied on improvisation. Many were only part-time performers who worked full time at trades like bricklaying, carpentry, and cigar making.

Band music—including early jazz—was heard at picnics, parades, political meetings, and dance halls. Black bands often played jazz during funeral processions. In the words of one New Orleans musician: "You'd march to the graveyard playing very solemn and very slow, then on the way back all hell would break loose! . . . We didn't know what a sheet of music was. Just six or seven pieces, half a dozen men pounding it out all together, each in his own way and yet somehow fitting in all right with the others."

But the main home of early jazz was Storyville, a red-light district of whorehouses, gambling joints, saloons, and dance halls. These establishments often employed a piano player or small band. Storyville provided not only employment but an atmosphere in which musicians felt free to improvise. When Storyville was closed down in 1917 on orders of the Navy Department, many jazz musicians left New Orleans. The center of jazz soon shifted from the Crescent City to Chicago, Kansas City, and New York.

New Orleans style (or **Dixieland**) was typically played by a small group of from five to eight performers. The melodic instruments, or **front line,** included the cornet (or trumpet), clarinet, and trombone. The front-line players would improvise several contrasting melodic lines at once, producing a kind of polyphonic texture. This collective improvisation was the most distinctive feature of New Orleans jazz. Each instrument had a special role. The cornet was the leader, playing variations of the main melody. Above the cornet, the clarinet wove a countermelody, usually in a faster rhythm. The trombone played a bass line that

New Orleans Style

493

New Orleans style (or Dixieland) typically was played by a small group of from five to eight performers. King Oliver (standing on left rear) is shown here with his Creole Jazz Band in 1923, including Louis Armstrong (seated in the center) and Lil Hardin Armstrong, at piano (Photo Files).

was simpler than the upper ones, but melodically interesting nevertheless. The syncopations and rhythmic independence of the melodic instruments created a marvelous sense of excitement.

The front-line instruments were supported by a rhythm section that clearly marked the beat and provided a background of chords. This section usually included drums, chordal instruments (banjo, guitar, piano), and a single-note low instrument (plucked bass or tuba).

New Orleans jazz was usually based on a march or church melody, a ragtime piece, a popular song, or the twelve-bar blues. Well-known tunes associated with this style are "When the Saints Go Marching In" and "Didn't He Ramble?" One or more choruses of collective improvisation generally occurred at the beginning and end of the piece. In between, individual players were featured in improvised solos, accompanied by the rhythm section or by the whole band. Sometimes there were brief unaccompanied solos called *breaks*. The band's performance might begin with an introduction and end with a brief coda, or *tag*.

As the New Orleans style evolved during the 1920s—mainly in Chicago—solo playing came to be emphasized more than collective improvisation. Soloists began to base their improvisations less on the original melody than on its harmonies. In addition, the trumpet gradually replaced the cornet, and the saxophone became a member of the band.

Dippermouth Blues (1923), by King Oliver's Creole Jazz Band *Side 15, band 5*

Performed in 1923 by King Oliver's Creole Jazz Band, *Dippermouth Blues* is a fine example of the New Orleans style. It is based on the chord progression of the twelve-bar blues. Nine choruses of twelve-bar blues are preceded by an introduction and followed by a brief tag (coda). Choruses 1, 2, 5, and 9 are for full ensemble and illustrate a style of collective improvisation that is typical of New Orleans jazz. Choruses 3 and 4 feature a clarinet solo with an accompaniment in repeated rhythm. The climax of *Dippermouth Blues* is King Oliver's muted cornet solo (in choruses 6 to 8), which is heard against a background of improvisation by the other instruments. Oliver's solo, with its "blue" notes and swinging syncopations, was widely imitated by other jazz musicians.

LISTENING OUTLINE
To be read while music is heard

Dippermouth Blues (1923), by King Oliver's Creole Jazz Band

2 cornets (King Oliver, Louis Armstrong), clarinet (Johnny Dodds), trombone (Honoré Dutrey), piano (Lil Hardin), banjo and voice (Bud Scott), drums (Baby Dodds)

Fast tempo, quadruple meter ($\frac{4}{4}$)

Introduction–nine choruses of twelve-bar blues–tag.

(About 2½ min)

Introduction (4 bars)	1	*a.* Cornets introduce
Choruses 1–2 (12 + 12 bars)		*b.* All instruments.
Choruses 3–4 (12 + 12 bars)	2	High clarinet melody, chordal accompaniment in repeated rhythm. Clarinet melody repeated.
Chorus 5 (12 bars)	3	All instruments.

495

Choruses 6–8 (12 + 12 + 12 bars)	4	Muted cornet melody with "blue" notes; other instruments in background. Voice: "Oh play that thing."
Chorus 9 (12 bars + 2-bar tag)	5	All instruments.

Louis Armstrong

As both a trumpeter and singer, Louis "Satchmo" Armstrong (1900–1971) had a worldwide impact on jazz. He was born on the Fourth of July in a poor, black section of New Orleans, and he learned to play the cornet in a reformatory (where he was sent at thirteen for shooting a gun into the air during a New Year's celebration). Released a year later, Armstrong soon played in honky-tonks at night and drove a coal wagon during the day. His musical ambitions were encouraged by cornetist King Oliver, who took a fatherly interest in the young boy and gave him some lessons. When Oliver left for Chicago in 1918—after Storyville was closed down—Armstrong took his place in the famous Kid Ory Band. Four years later, Armstrong himself went to Chicago to be second cornetist in King Oliver's Creole Jazz Band.

In 1925, he started to make a series of extraordinary recordings with bands known as Louis Armstrong's Hot Five and Hot Seven. The Hot Five included three New Orleans musicians—Johnny Dodds (clarinet), Kid Ory (trombone), and Johnny St. Cyr (banjo)—along with Lil Hardin (piano), whom Armstrong had married a year earlier. These recordings established his reputation as the leading jazz trumpeter. After 1930 he appeared with a wide variety of groups, made many tours, and was featured in many films. During the 1950s and 1960s Armstrong served as a "goodwill ambassador" for the United States. And at the age of sixty-four, he had his greatest popular success, the hit recording of "Hello, Dolly!"

Armstrong was one of the greatest jazz improvisers, able to invent extraordinary solos and to transform even ordinary tunes into swinging melodies through changes of rhythms and pitch. He revealed new dimensions of the trumpet, showing that it could be played in a higher register than was thought possible. His playing style featured "rips" up to high pitches, along with a tone that was both beautiful and alive. One jazz expert has singled out the "subtly varied repertory of vibratos and shakes with which Armstrong colors and embellishes individual notes." Armstrong also introduced *scat singing*, the vocalization of a melodic line with nonsense syllables. His gravel-throated voice was not "beautiful" in a conventional sense, but it conveyed the same jazz feeling as his trumpet playing did.

Side 15, band 6   "Hotter Than That," by Louis Armstrong and His Hot Five, was discussed in Part I, section 1. It shows how the New Orleans style developed in Chicago during the 1920s (see the listening outline on p. 9). The emphasis is on improvisatory solos. Collective improvisation—so important in earlier New Orleans style—is restricted to the introduction and closing chorus (items 1 and 6b in the listening outline). Listen for the exciting vocal and instrumental breaks (items 2, 3, 4, and 6a), the syncopations of Armstrong's vocal melody (item 4), and the dissonant guitar chord that provides "Hotter Than That" with an unusual and inconclusive ending.

Basic Terms

New Orleans style (Dixieland)
front line

SWING ‖5‖

A new jazz style called *swing* developed in the late 1920s and flourished from 1935 to 1945, a decade nicknamed the "swing era." (In this section, the term "swing" refers to a specific style rather than to the rhythmic vitality characteristic of all jazz.)

Swing was played mainly by big bands, whose powerful sound could fill the large dance halls and ballrooms that mushroomed across the country, particularly after the repeal of prohibition in 1933. There were hundreds of "name" bands—both black and white—like those of Duke Ellington, Count Basie, Glen Miller, Tommy Dorsey, and Benny Goodman (the "King of Swing"). Some bands contained such leading musicians as saxophonists Coleman Hawkins and Lester Young and featured singers like Billie Holiday, Ella Fitzgerald, and Frank Sinatra. During the 1930s and 1940s, the big band was as important as the rock group has been since the 1950s. Jazz became a truly popular music reaching millions of people. Benny Goodman's band, for example, was heard coast to coast on a weekly radio show called "Let's Dance." The kind of music once associated with honky-tonks and whorehouses had achieved a new respectability, symbolized by Benny Goodman's historic jazz concert at Carnegie Hall in 1938.

In section 4 we noted that New Orleans jazz was performed by small groups of from five to eight musicians and featured collective improvisation by several soloists. The typical **swing band** included about fourteen or fifteen musicians grouped into three sections: saxophones (three to five players, some doubling on clarinet); brasses (three or four each of trumpet and trombone); and rhythm (piano, percussion, guitar, and bass). Such big bands needed music that was composed and *arranged,* or notated in written-out parts from which the musicians could read. With swing, the arranger became an important figure in jazz.

 Swing

497

Typically, a swing band included about fourteen or fifteen musicians. The Benny Goodman Band was one of the leading swing ensembles (Culver).

Usually, the swing band's ensemble playing was arranged rather than improvised. Melodies were often performed by entire sections either in unison or in harmony. Solo improvisations tended to be restricted in length. The main melody was frequently accompanied by saxophones playing sustained chords, or by saxophones and brasses playing short, repeated phrases called **riffs.** Arrangers often used a rapid alternation of brass and sax riffs to create tension and excitement. Each band took pride in the distinctiveness of its sound.

Not only was the swing band larger and more dependent on arrangements than the New Orleans style band, it had other distinctive features as well. For example, the saxophone became one of the most important solo instruments during the swing era. In addition, percussionists—such as Gene Krupa—had a more prominent role, often taking spectacular solos. They also kept the beat in a new way. While they continued to maintain the pulse on the bass drum, percussionists now used the cymbals to stress the second and fourth beats of the bar:

Jazz

498

The harmonic vocabulary of swing was richer and more varied than that of earlier jazz, but its forms were essentially the same. As before, jazz performances were usually based on the twelve-bar blues or on a thirty-two-bar popular song melody. Such melodies usually can be outlined as A A B A. An eight-bar phrase is stated and then repeated (A A); a contrasting eight-bar phrase (B) follows; and then there's a return to the opening phrase (A). The song "Blue Skies," by Irving Berlin, is in A A B A form. We'll now see how it was performed by the Benny Goodman Band, one of the leading swing ensembles.

"Blue Skies," by Irving Berlin; as performed by the Benny Goodman Band (1938)

Side 15, band 7

One very popular recording of the swing era is "Blue Skies," as performed by the Benny Goodman Band and arranged by Fletcher Henderson. The version on the record set is a "live" performance from the historic Benny Goodman jazz concert at Carnegie Hall in 1938. The band's playing is smooth and polished—and swinging. The piece consists of an eight-bar introduction and four choruses in A A B A form (thirty-two bars each). The following outline will clarify the form of each chorus:

Introduction	(band)
Chorus 1	A A (band)–B (saxes, trombone solo)–A (saxes)
Chorus 2	A A (trumpets)–B A (tenor sax solo)
Chorus 3	A A (trumpet solo)–B A (band)
Chorus 4	A A (clarinet solo and band)–B (saxes)–A (band)

Only the soloists have an opportunity to improvise. Typically, their solos are quite short, lasting less than a full chorus. Some soloists stay close to the original melody, while others depart from it almost completely, following only the original harmonies. Listen for the great variety of tone color as the melody is played by the full band, by sections, or by soloists. Often the melody is accompanied by chords or riffs in the saxophone section. Benny Goodman's clarinet solos are followed by responses from the band. This is the typical jazz pattern of call-and-response.

Duke Ellington

Edward Kennedy "Duke" Ellington (1899–1974) was perhaps the most important swing-band composer, arranger, and conductor; he certainly ranks among the leading figures in the history of jazz. Spanning half a century, Ellington's

 Duke Ellington

499

Duke Ellington and his orchestra, 1943. Ellington was perhaps the most important swing-band composer, arranger, and conductor (United Press International).

works include hundreds of three-minute band pieces as well as music for film, television, ballet, theater, and church. He was among the first jazz composers to break the three-minute "sound barrier" imposed by the 78 RPM record, creating extended jazz compositions like *Black, Brown, and Beige.* Ellington accomplished all this while playing piano, touring the world, and writing such hit songs as "Satin Doll," "Sophisticated Lady," and "In a Sentimental Mood."

Ellington's music—sometimes created in collaboration with arranger Billy Strayhorn—is the product of constant experimentation and improvisation. "There is no set system," he once observed. "Most times I write it and arrange it. Sometimes I write it and the band and I collaborate on the arrangement. . . . When we're all working together, a guy may have an idea and he plays it on his horn. Another guy may add to it and make something out of it. Someone may play a riff and ask, 'How do you like this?'"

"My band is my instrument," Ellington once remarked. His arrangements are outstanding for their rich variety of sensuous tone colors and for their exploitation of the distinctive sounds of individual musicians. "You've got to write with certain men in mind," he once explained. "I know what Tricky Sam can play on a trombone and I know what Lawrence Brown can play on the trombone, and it is not the same." Ellington's compositions include miniature "concertos" built around individual performers. (We'll study his *Concerto for Cootie,* written for trumpeter Cootie Williams.) With his respect for their talents, it's no wonder that many of Ellington's musicians remained in the band for long periods of time.

Ellington's works are richer in harmony and more varied in form than those of his contemporaries. Their variety of mood may be sampled in such works as *Ko-ko, Harlem Air Shaft, In a Mellotone,* and *Blue Serge* (all included in *The Smithsonian Collection of Classic Jazz*).

Concerto for Cootie (1940)   *Side 15, band 8*

Concerto for Cootie is designed to display the great variety of tone colors that trumpeter Cootie Williams can draw from his instrument. While the trumpet is the star of this piece, the band accompaniment adds much by discreetly responding to the soloist's phrases and by linking one section to the next. Several years after writing the *Concerto,* Ellington adapted it into the hit song "Do Nothin' Till You Hear from Me."

Concerto for Cootie consists of an introduction and three main sections. The opening section has the standard A A B A form of popular songs, but its phrases are irregular in length. (The A phrases are ten bars long instead of eight.) The main melody (A) consists of a repeated idea that is narrow in range, winding around a single tone. This is always played with a mute, but the soloist uses a variety of vibratos and muting techniques so that the melody sounds different each time. Listen for the subtlety of Ellington's orchestration: The bass, which provides much of the *Concerto's* relaxed swing, enters only after the soloist is well into the melody. The middle section (C) is a striking contrast to the opening because now the trumpeter plays an expansive new melody in a higher register and without a mute. The *Concerto* is rounded off by a brief third section in which a shortened and varied return of A is followed by a coda.

LISTENING OUTLINE
To be read while music is heard

Concerto for Cootie (1940), by Duke Ellington

trumpet solo (Cootie Williams), piano (Duke Ellington), trumpet (Wallace Jones), cornet (Rex Stewart), 2 trombones (Joe Nanton, Lawrence Brown), valve trombone (Juan Tizol), clarinet, tenor saxophone (Barney Bigard), 2 alto saxophones (Otto Hardwicke, Johnny Hodges), tenor saxophone (Ben Webster), baritone saxophone (Harry Carney), guitar (Fred Guy), bass (Jimmy Blanton), percussion (Sonny Greer)

Moderate tempo, quadruple meter ($\frac{4}{4}$), F major

(About 3 min)

| Introduction | 1 | *a.* Solo muted trumpet, *p*, main motive; saxophones respond, *p*; brasses join, cresc. |

A

b. Trumpet, *p*, main melody, "shake" on held tones;

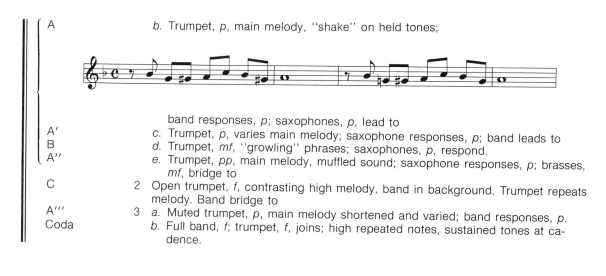

band responses, *p*; saxophones, *p*, lead to

A'
B
A''

c. Trumpet, *p*, varies main melody; saxophone responses, *p*; band leads to
d. Trumpet, *mf*, "growling" phrases; saxophones, *p*, respond.
e. Trumpet, *pp*, main melody, muffled sound; saxophone responses, *p*; brasses, *mf*, bridge to

C

2 Open trumpet, *f*, contrasting high melody, band in background. Trumpet repeats melody. Band bridge to

A'''
Coda

3 *a.* Muted trumpet, *p*, main melody shortened and varied; band responses, *p*.
b. Full band, *f*; trumpet, *f*, joins; high repeated notes, sustained tones at cadence.

Basic Terms

swing band
riff

Jazz

|6| BEBOP

The early 1940s saw the development of **bebop** (or **bop**), a complex style of music for small jazz groups including three to six players. In part, bebop was a rebellion by creative improvisers against the commercialism and written arrangements of the 1930s swing bands. The new music was meant for attentive listening, not dancing, and its sophisticated harmonies and unpredictable rhythms bewildered many listeners. Bop performers were a special "in" group who sometimes drove other jazz musicians from the bandstand by using unusual chord progressions. "We knew that they couldn't make those chord changes," one bop drummer recalled. "We kept the riff-raff out and built our clique on new chords."

Bebop performers also differentiated themselves from other musicians by their goatees, berets, and special "hip" language. The bebop center in the early 1940s was a Harlem club called Minton's Playhouse, where young innovators like alto saxophonist Charlie Parker, trumpeter Dizzy Gillespie, and pianist Thelonious Monk came to participate in jam sessions.

Jazz

Bebop Style

A typical bebop group might include a saxophone and trumpet supported by a rhythm section of piano, bass, and percussion. The role of bebop rhythm instruments was different from that in earlier jazz. For example, the bass drum no longer marked the beat but was reserved for occasional irregular accents called "bombs." Similarly, the pianist's left hand no longer emphasized the basic pulse but supplied chords at irregular intervals. The beat, then, was marked mainly by the pizzicato bass.

The rhythms in bop melodies were more varied and unpredictable than in earlier jazz. In an improvised solo by Charlie Parker, for example, accented notes might come on weak or strong beats, or at varying points within the beat. Bop melodies often contained a stream of short notes with accents on the off-beats.

The new style may well have gotten its name from a vocalization of the two fast notes ("be-bop") that often end phrases. The melodic phrases themselves were often varied and irregular in length. A two- or three-note fragment would be followed by a melodic unit lasting several bars. And the harmonies of bop were as complex as its rhythms. Performers often built melodies on chords containing six or seven notes rather than on the four- or five-note chords used in earlier jazz.

A bop performance generally began and ended with a statement of the main theme by one soloist, or by two soloists in unison. The remainder of the piece was made up of solo improvisations based on the melody or harmonic structure. As in earlier jazz, bebop musicians used popular song melodies and the twelve-bar blues as a springboard for improvisation. Often, however, they composed *new* tunes to fit the basic harmonies of familiar melodies. As an "in" joke, a bop musician would give a tune a new title so that only sophisticated listeners could guess its origin. (Charlie Parker's *KoKo*, for example, is based on the harmonies of the popular song "Cherokee.")

Charlie "Bird" Parker

Charlie Parker (1920–1955), alto saxophonist, was a towering figure among bebop musicians and one of the greatest of all jazz improvisers. His enormous influence was felt not only by other alto saxophonists but by performers of many other instruments.

Parker was born in Kansas City, Kansas, and grew up in Kansas City, Missouri. As a youngster, he roamed the streets listening outside nightclub doors to the jazz of Lester Young and the Count Basie Band. He was a professional musician by the age of fifteen, having dropped out of school. In his twenties, Parker lived in New York and participated in Harlem jam sessions. He made his first bebop recordings in 1944, and by the late 1940s he was a featured soloist in jazz clubs.

Parker became a leading musician despite severe personal problems including

Charlie "Bird" Parker

503

Bebop musician Charlie Parker, far right, is shown with performers representing other jazz styles. From left to right
are Max Kaminsky, Lester Young, and "Hot Lips" Page
(United Press International).

drug addiction, alcoholism, ulcers, and emotional illness. But after 1950, his playing declined along with his physical and emotional health. He died in 1955 at the age of thirty-four.

All the style characteristics of bebop were embodied in Parker's improvisations. He was able to control a rich flow of ideas at either slow or very rapid tempos. His amazing technique enabled him to create lightning-fast melodies that sound jagged and angular because of frequent changes of direction. Unlike earlier saxophonists, whose tone was lush and sweet, Parker produced a sound that was rather hard and dry. It perfectly matched the nervous intensity of his melodic lines.

Side 16, band 1   Bebop style and Parker's improvisatory genius are both illustrated in *Perhaps*, which is performed by a group of five outstanding musicians (see the listening outline). The main theme is a Parker melody that follows the harmonic outline of the twelve-bar blues.

LISTENING OUTLINE
To be read while music is heard

Perhaps (1948), by Charlie Parker

alto saxophone (Charlie Parker), trumpet (Miles Davis), piano (John Lewis), bass (Curly Russell), percussion (Max Roach)

Introduction + ten choruses of twelve-bar blues

Very fast tempo, quadruple meter ($\frac{4}{4}$), C major

(About 2½ min)

Introduction (4 bars)	1	*a.* Piano, bass, cymbal.
Chorus 1 (12 bars)		*b.* Alto saxophone and trumpet in unison, main theme; rhythm section accompanies.
Choruses 2–4 (12 + 12 + 12 bars)	2	Alto saxophone, improvised solo; rhythm section accompanies.
Choruses 5–7 (12 + 12 + 12 bars)	3	Trumpet, improvised solo; rhythm section accompanies.
Choruses 8–9 (12 + 12 bars)	4	Piano, improvised solo; bass and cymbal accompany.
Chorus 10 (12 bars)	5	Alto saxophone and trumpet in unison, main theme; rhythm section accompanies.

Basic Term

Bebop (bop)

JAZZ STYLES SINCE 1950

Since 1950, there have been many innovations and new directions in jazz. The range of styles is wider than ever. But as new styles proliferate, older jazz—from Dixieland to bebop—remains very much alive.

The introduction of long-playing records in 1948 inspired more extended jazz compositions and improvisations. Typically, a recorded jazz performance might last from five to fifteen minutes, compared with the three minutes permitted by 78 RPM records before 1948. Also, more jazz now was meant for listening than for dancing. It was often heard at concerts on college campuses. Increasingly, jazz musicians studied at colleges and music schools and became familiar with much music other than jazz.

Since 1950 there has been an expansion in the musical resources used in jazz. New meters, rhythms, harmonies, forms, and tone colors have been explored. Orchestral instruments like the flute, French horn, and cello have become a part of jazz. Since the 1960s, synthesizers and the electric piano and bass have come to be used more and more. Also, some musicians of the 1960s created *free jazz*, which discarded many of the forms and basic chord patterns of earlier jazz. Performers drew inspiration from a great variety of sources, including Bach, rock, and the

Jazz Styles since 1950

505

music of Africa and Asia. The interaction between jazz and rock has led to a style known as *jazz rock.* Some musicians, such as Gunther Schuller (b. 1925), created a *third stream* style that is not quite jazz or "classical" but a blend of both. Among all these recent developments in jazz, we will consider two of the most important influences: cool jazz and free jazz.

Cool Jazz

During the early 1950s, a jazz style emerged that was related to bop but was far more calm and relaxed in character. It was called **cool jazz** (in contrast to the "hot" jazz of an earlier era). The leaders of cool jazz were Stan Getz (b. 1927), tenor saxophonist; Lennie Tristano (1919–1978), pianist; and Miles Davis (b. 1926), a trumpeter and bandleader who was also an important figure in jazz during the 1960s and 1970s. Performers of cool jazz played in a relatively subdued manner, with a gentle attack and little vibrato. Cool jazz pieces tended to be longer than bebop works and relied more heavily on arrangements. They sometimes used instruments that were new to jazz, including the French horn, flute, and cello.

One of the finest works in cool jazz style is *Boblicity* (1949), by Miles Davis and arranger Gil Evans (*Smithsonian Collection of Classic Jazz,* side 9, band 1). It is scored for an unusual ensemble of nine different instruments: trumpet, trombone, French horn, tuba, alto and baritone saxophones, piano, bass, and drums. The smooth, mellow, and blended sound of this ensemble is typical of cool jazz.

Some cool jazz groups, such as the Modern Jazz Quartet, were influenced by the works of Bach and favored polyphonic textures and imitation. Another prominent group that was influenced by "classical" music was the Dave Brubeck Quartet. It pioneered in the use of meters that had been considered unusual in jazz, such as $\frac{3}{4}$, $\frac{5}{4}$ (in *Take Five*), and $\frac{7}{4}$ (in *Unsquare Dance,* studied in Part I section 3).

Free Jazz: Ornette Coleman and John Coltrane

Until about 1960, jazz improvisations tended to be quite regular in form. That is, improvised variations kept the original theme's length and chord structure, even if they abandoned the original melody. During the 1960s, some musicians broke from this tradition and created **free jazz,** a style that was not based on regular forms and established chord patterns. "If I'm going to follow a preset chord sequence, I may as well write out my solo," commented Ornette Coleman (b. 1930), alto saxophonist and a major composer of free jazz. In 1960 Coleman assembled eight musicians in a recording studio to improvise individually and collectively with almost no guidelines of melody, form, or harmony. The result was *Free Jazz,* a performance whose apparent randomness can be compared with the chance music created during the same period by John Cage and his followers.

Jazz

506

John Coltrane, one of the leaders of free jazz (United
Press International).

Free Jazz:
Ornette Coleman;
John Coltrane

(An excerpt from *Free Jazz* is included in *The Smithsonian Collection of Classic Jazz,* side 12, band 3.) "I don't tell the members of my group what to do," Coleman has explained. "I let everyone express himself just as he wants to." Nevertheless, many performances by Coleman are structured more highly than *Free Jazz,* since they begin and end with a composed theme. (One example is *Lonely Woman,* included in *The Smithsonian Collection of Classic Jazz,* side 12, band 1.) Like other free-jazz improvisers, Coleman develops melodic and rhythmic ideas from the theme. In many of his performances, a steady beat and tempo are emphasized much less than in earlier jazz, and his bass and percussion players are given more melodic and rhythmic freedom.

Another musician who searched for rhythmic and harmonic freedom during the 1960s was John Coltrane (1926–1967), extremely influential as an improviser, tenor and soprano saxophonist, and composer. Coltrane's tone was large, intense, and equally powerful in all registers—an unusual trait. He could play higher than the normal top range of his instrument, and his arpeggios were flung at such lightning speed that they became "sheets of sound." The fury and passion of his improvisations sometimes led to sounds that might be described as "cries," "wails," and "shrieks."

Coltrane's style evolved steadily from the late 1950s, when he worked with Miles Davis, to his untimely death at the age of forty in 1967. His early performances—like the pathbreaking *Giant Steps* of 1959—feature many complex chords that change very rapidly. Later works, on the other hand, often are based on a background of only two or three chords, each sustained in the accompaniment for many bars. Coltrane's pianist, McCoy Tyner, often sustained a single tone in the bass as a drone, or pedal point, while Coltrane improvised on modes, or scales, other than the conventional major or minor. Coltrane's growing use of drones and unusual scales may well have been influenced by his deep interest in Indian and Arabic music.

A drone accompaniment is used in Coltrane's meditative work *Alabama* (1963), for tenor saxophone, piano, bass, and drums (*Smithsonian Collection of Classic Jazz,* side 12, band 4). This short piece is in A B A' form. In the opening section, the saxophone melody is accompanied only by a sustained low broken chord in the piano. The contemplative melody conveys little sense of beat or meter. It is only in the middle section that a definite beat is heard. When the opening section returns (A'), there is a more active accompaniment as the bass and drums have complex rhythms.

The free jazz developed by Coleman and Coltrane was only one of the substyles that could be heard during the 1970s. Every kind of jazz we've studied—New Orleans, swing, bebop, cool jazz, and free jazz—had its fans and devoted performers. Rock music also became a potent influence on jazz during the 1970s, as jazz musicians turned to rock rhythms, tunes, and instruments. For example, Ornette Coleman recently played free jazz with a group that included two electric guitars and an electric bass along with two drummers and a conventional bass. As they have since the early days, jazz musicians continue to explore new resources to further the development of their art.

Basic Terms

cool jazz
free jazz

ROCK

1 Rock Styles

2 Rock Music in American Society

3 The Beatles

The Bee Gees made a successful transition from 1960s
rock to 1970s disco (Michael Putland/Retna).

1 | ROCK STYLES

The mid-1950s saw the growth of a new kind of popular music that was first called "rock 'n' roll" and then, simply, "rock." Though diverse in style, **rock** tends to be vocal music with a hard, driving beat often featuring electric guitar accompaniment and heavily amplified sound. Early rock grew mainly out of *rhythm and blues,* a dance music of American blacks that fused blues, jazz, and gospel styles. Rock also drew upon *country and western,* a folklike, guitar-based style associated with rural white Americans and the Nashville Grand Ole Opry. In little more than a decade, rock evolved from a simple, dance-oriented style to a music that was highly varied in its tone colors, lyrics, and electronic technology.

Starting in the late 1940s, rhythm and blues was the dominant style in America's black community. Rhythm and blues of the 1950s differed from earlier blues in its more powerful beat and its use of the saxophone and electric guitar. Among the leading performers were Little Richard, Chuck Berry, and such vocal groups as the Platters. During the 1950s many rhythm-and-blues hits were issued by white performers in versions with less sexually explicit lyrics. The impact of rhythm and blues on rock styles was tremendous.

The earliest of the leading rock 'n' roll groups was Bill Haley and His Comets, whose "Rock Around the Clock" was the first big hit of the new style. Significantly, it was a film about youthful rebellion, *Blackboard Jungle* (1955), that popularized "Rock Around the Clock." To many people at the time, the new music itself seemed rebellious in its loudness, pounding beat, and sexual directness. The image of a youthful rebel was also projected by Elvis Presley, who reigned as "king" of rock 'n' roll for almost a decade.

During the 1960s, much music by black performers was called *soul,* a term that emphasized the style's emotionality, gospel roots, and relationship to the black community. Leading soul musicians included James Brown, Ray Charles, and Aretha Franklin. A type of soul music that blended rhythm and blues with popular music was known as "Motown," after the name of a record company based in Detroit. Motown has been described aptly as a combination of "gospel rhythms, modern harmonies, soft melodies, and bright lyrics." Among the Motown stars were Diana Ross and the Supremes, and Stevie Wonder, whose first big hit came in 1963, when he was only thirteen.

A new era in rock history began in 1964 with the American tour of the Beatles, an English group. Along with their countrymen, the Rolling Stones, the Beatles came to dominate the popular music scene in America. Under their influence, rock musicians of the middle and late 1960s explored a wider range of sources for sounds and musical ideas. They experimented with electronic effects, with "classical" and non-Western instruments, and with unconventional chord progressions.

Rock of the 1960s also absorbed elements of folk music and employed lyrics dealing with such contemporary issues as war and racial injustice. This develop-

Rock

512

During the 1950s, Chuck Berry was a leading performer of
rhythm and blues (J. Stevens/Photo Trends).

ment was spurred by the success of songwriter-singer Bob Dylan, whose "Blowin'
in the Wind"—a song against racial bigotry—articulated the feelings of many
young people.

During the late 1960s, the popular music scene was enormously varied. The
diversity of rock styles is reflected in the many terms that arose: "folk rock," "jazz
rock," "hard rock," "psychedelic rock," "acid rock," "Baroque rock," "classical
rock," and "raga rock." This period saw the first rock musical—*Hair*, by Galt
MacDermot—and the first rock opera—*Tommy*, written by Peter Townshend and
featuring The Who, an English group.

In 1970 and 1971 rock music suffered major losses: The Beatles announced
their dissolution, and, more tragically, three leading performers died—Jimi
Hendrix and Janis Joplin of heroin overdose and Jim Morrison of a heart attack. Rock Styles

513

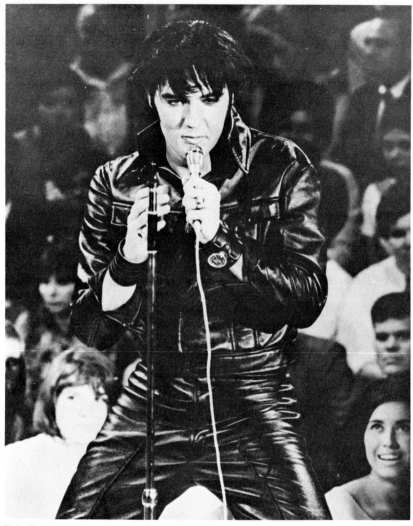

Elvis Presley was the "king" of rock 'n' roll for almost a decade (United Press International).

Yet, during the 1970s rock was as popular as ever. This decade saw the continuation of many 1960s styles, the revival of early rock 'n' roll, and the rise of a dance music called *disco*. Veteran performers of the 1960s—such as Bob Dylan, Stevie Wonder, and the Rolling Stones—continued to be active; but new stars also emerged, such as Linda Ronstadt, Billy Joel, Bruce Springsteen, and "disco queen" Donna Summer. Some groups, including Emerson, Lake, and Palmer, performed "classical rock," consisting of rock arrangements of such compositions as *Pictures at an Exhibition* by the nineteenth-century Russian composer Modeste

Rock

Partly because of the influence of Bob Dylan, rock of the 1960s absorbed elements of folk music and used lyrics dealing with contemporary issues. During the 1970s, Dylan continued as a leading rock performer (Peter L. Gould/Keystone Press).

Mussorgsky. And during the 1970s, jazz rock reached a wider audience than ever before through groups like Chicago and Blood, Sweat, and Tears.

Having briefly outlined the development of rock, we'll now consider its musical elements.

Rock Tone Color

The electric-guitar sound of rock is very different from the brass-reed sound of the "big band" heard in earlier popular music. Rock music is amplified powerfully, and the guitar is often manipulated electronically to produce a wide range of tone colors. Along with singers (who also play instruments), a rock group typically includes two electric guitars (lead and rhythm), electric bass, percussion, and such keyboard instruments as piano, electric piano, and synthesizer. Some groups also include one or more trumpets, trombones, or saxophones.

As rock evolved during the 1960s, a wide range of instruments—from harpsi-

 Rock Tone Color

515

Linda Ronstadt, a leading singer of the 1970s (David Redfern/Retna).

chord to Indian sitar—was occasionally added to the basic rock group, particularly for recording sessions. Rock recordings use such diverse sounds as electronic blips, crowd noises, or a fifty-piece orchestra.

The singing style of rock is drawn largely from black, folk, and country-and-western music. While rock singing styles vary, they all are different from the crooning sound cultivated by earlier popular vocalists. Rock singers shout, cry, wail, growl, and use gutteral sounds as well as *falsetto,* a method of singing used by males to reach notes higher than their normal range. Nonsense syllables and repeated chants (like "Yeah! Yeah! Yeah!") are also featured.

Rock Rhythm

Rock is based on a very powerful beat in quadruple ($\frac{4}{4}$) meter with strong accents on the second and fourth beats of the bar. The rhythmic excitement is heightened because each beat is subdivided into two equal notes. This produces eight faster pulses, which are superimposed on the four basic beats. To get the effect, count

Rock

516

out the following: 1-and-**2**-and-3-and-**4**-and. Rock of the 1960s and 1970s often combined more complex rhythms with this basic pattern; for example, the bass player may emphasize the off-beats—the *and*s.

Rock Form, Melody, and Harmony

Rock music is usually in twelve-bar blues form (see "Jazz," section 3); in thirty-two-bar A A B A form (see "Jazz," section 5); or in variants of these forms. While earlier popular songs usually consisted of four- or eight-bar phrases, rock melodies sometimes contain phrases that are irregular in length. A famous example is the seven-bar opening of "Yesterday" (see "Elements," section 5). Rock songs tend to have short melodic patterns that are repeated several times. They occasionally are built on modes, rather than on traditional major or minor scales.

The harmonic progressions of rock are usually quite simple, often consisting of just three or four basic chords. Sometimes, the harmony can be restricted deliberately to only two chords, as in "Eleanor Rigby," by John Lennon and Paul McCartney. Rock often uses chord progressions that are rare in earlier popular music, such as this one:

Basic Term

rock

ROCK MUSIC IN AMERICAN SOCIETY

2

"Hey! that's our music, that was written for us!" shouted fourteen-year-old Bob Dylan when he first heard Bill Haley's "Rock Around the Clock" in 1955. Like Dylan, millions of young people felt that rock music belonged to them and expressed their search for identity and independence. Many leading rock performers and songwriters were themselves in their teens or early twenties. In

Rock Music in American Society

517

The Woodstock rock festival in August 1969 attracted
over 300,000 people (Shelly Rusten).

contrast to rock, popular music before the 1950s appealed about equally to people of all ages.

As a result of the "baby boom" after World War II, there were more American young people in the 1950s and 1960s than ever before. And they had more money to spend, because of a generally rising economy. American industry quickly responded to this vast youth market, and rock music became a big business. Sales of electric guitars, phonographs, records, and transistor radios increased dramatically. Rock superstars struck it rich through record royalties, movie contracts, and astronomical concert fees. Rock performances took place everywhere: in auditoriums, gymnasiums, sports arenas, and baseball stadiums. A single concert by a leading group could gross several hundred thousand dollars and be seen by an audience of up to seventy-five thousand people. There even were rock festivals, like the three-day Woodstock Music and Art Fair in August 1969. At that event, over three hundred thousand people listened in the open fields to the Music of Joan Baez, Janis Joplin, Jimi Hendrix, and the Jefferson Airplane, among others. Documenting this gathering was *Woodstock*, one of the most important of many rock films.

Rock

518

The theatricality of 1970s rock is shown by three members of the group Kiss (Michael Putland/Retna).

Often, rock performances were as much theatrical as musical events. From the earliest days of rock 'n' roll, costumes and staging were essential to the show. For example, Elvis Presley's appeal was heightened by tight-fitting sequined pants, a leather jacket, and gyrations that made him known as "Elvis the Pelvis." In the late 1960s, Jimi Hendrix smashed and burned his guitar on stage. The impact of "psychedelic rock" was heightened by flashing strobe lights that simulated the effects of a drug experience. Rock performances of the 1970s became even more theatrical. Alice Cooper—a male—appeared on stage with a boa constrictor and performed acts of simulated violence. The members of a group called Kiss wore macho glitter costumes and makeup influenced by the Kabuki theater of Japan. Their act involved flames, smoke, and explosions. David Bowie, who wore women's clothing and dyed his hair bright orange, often said that his records were only "half there," because the visual aspect was missing. The theatrics and music of rock performers often generated hysterical excitement: Fans screamed, moaned, and rushed the stage.

Rock songs often reflected major trends in American life, such as the increased sexual openness. Lyrics tended to be more sexually explicit than in the senti-

 Rock Music in American Society

mental ("moon-June-spoon") love songs of the 1930s and 1940s. (In fact, the term *rock 'n' roll* originally had sexual connotations.) During the 1960s, rock performers often sang about the Vietnam war, the experiences associated with drugs, and the struggle for civil rights. And performers often wrote their own songs. For many young people of the time, rock music was part of a lifestyle that seemed less inhibited and less materialistic than that of their parents. They quickly adopted the longer hairstyles and casual dress popularized by rock stars. Within a short time, many older people also cultivated a casual appearance.

During the 1970s, rock became integrated into the mainstream of American popular music. While rock concerts still appealed primarily to the young, a wide variety of rock records were purchased by people of all ages. And rock songs of the 1970s were less likely to deal with social and political issues.

Rock Music and Recordings

Unlike earlier popular music, rock spread more through radio and recordings than through live performances. There was a growing number of radio stations, and many broadcast only rock music. Disk jockeys like Alan Freed—who popularized the term *rock 'n' roll*—became important personalities who strongly influenced musical tastes. Most early rock 'n' roll records were produced by small, specialized companies. But the tremendous financial success of rock soon led major companies to enter the field as well. By the 1960s and 1970s, major companies produced most rock recordings.

During the 1960s, the sound of rock recordings became quite different from what was heard at a live performance. Increasingly, rock groups took advantage of multitrack recording. "With a small group," wrote one record producer, "every instrument can be recorded on a different track. Each track has a separate volume control and a tone control to adjust to the desired treble or bass. Several kinds of echoes can be added to each instrument." Recording sessions were often a "layer-cake" operation, with each sound layer being produced separately and then combined later. The Beatles, for example, would first record the instrumental accompaniment to a song, a process that might take a whole day. Another day would be devoted to recording the voice parts. Then, various instrumental and electronic sounds might be added before the recording was complete. With such a complex process, it's no wonder that a record like their *Sgt. Pepper and His Lonely Hearts Club Band* took as long as four months to be produced.

Rock Music and Dancing

Since its beginning, rock music has accompanied a dizzying succession of dances with names like the Twist, the Frug, the Monkey, the Shake, and the Mashed Potato. In most rock dances of the 1960s, partners did not hold each other, as in earlier dances, but moved individually to the music's powerful beat. Most rock

Disco became the dominant dance music of the 1970s
(Eric Kroll/Taurus Photos; Charles Gatewood/Magnum).

dances were improvisational and did not require dancers to learn a series
of complicated steps. Among the best-known rock dances was the Twist, associated with a New York nightclub called the Peppermint Lounge and popularized
in 1961 through a television performance by singer Chubby Checker. By the
1960s, many adults became influenced by the youth culture and danced to rock
music at nightclubs called "discotheques."

During the 1970s thousands of discotheques—mostly featuring recorded
music—mushroomed around the country. *Disco* became the dominant dance
music. While many dances of the 1960s had been formless and improvisational,
dances of the 1970s—such as the Hustle and its variants—often required intricate steps and turns. Moreover, the dances frequently required partners
once again to touch each other. Also popular again were line dances, in
which many dancers performed the same movements. During the late 1970s, the
movie *Saturday Night Fever* conveyed the excitement of this disco scene to millions
of people.

 Rock Music and
Dancing

3 | THE BEATLES

The Beatles—singer-guitarists Paul McCartney, John Lennon, and George Harrison, along with drummer Ringo Starr—were the most influential performing group in the history of rock. Their music, hairstyle, dress, and lifestyle were imitated all over the world, resulting in a phenomenon known as "Beatle-mania."

All four Beatles were born during the early 1940s in Liverpool, England, and dropped out of school in their teens to devote themselves to rock. Lennon and McCartney, the main songwriters of the group, began working together in 1956 and were joined by Harrison about two years later. In 1962 Ringo Starr became their new drummer. The group gained experience by performing in Hamburg, Germany, and in Liverpool, a port to which sailors brought the latest American rock, rhythm-and-blues, and country-and-western records. In 1961 the group made its first record, and by 1963 the Beatles were England's top rock group. In 1964, they triumphed in the United States, breaking attendance records everywhere and dominating the record market. Audiences often became hysterical, and the police had to protect the Beatles from their fans. Beatle dolls, wigs, sweatshirts, and jackets flooded the market. Along with a steady flow of successful records, the Beatles made such hit movies as *A Hard Day's Night, Help!* and *Yellow Submarine.*

The Beatles stopped touring in 1966, possibly because some of their most imaginative effects were achieved in the recording studio and could not be duplicated in live performance. For several years they devoted themselves to recording, producing such long-playing albums as *Sgt. Pepper's Lonely Hearts Club Band* (1967), *Magical Mystery Tour* (1967), *The Beatles* (1968; a double record set nicknamed the "White Album"), and *Abbey Road* (1969). In 1970 the Beatles disbanded to pursue individual careers.

The Beatles' highly original style derived from a variety of sources, including traditional blues, the rhythm and blues of Chuck Berry, the rock 'n' roll of Elvis Presley, English folk songs, and the lyrics of Bob Dylan. The impact of Indian religions led Harrison to use the sitar. And the Beatles' brief period of experimentation with hallucinogenic drugs was reflected in some of their songs of 1967. In their early days, the Beatles strove for originality so strongly that they consciously eliminated clichés of melody and harmony from their songs. Their style evolved continuously, growing in sophistication with each new album.

The Beatles' vocal delivery sounded carefree and spontaneous, and the Lennon-McCartney lyrics were unusually inventive. Their songs were often based on modes—rather than major or minor scales—and their harmonic vocabulary was richer than that of most rock music. Sometimes, their songs contained changes of meter and phrases of irregular length. Most striking was the Beatles' use of many electronic and instrumental sounds not previously associated with rock. Many of these novel features can be heard on the long-playing record *Sgt. Pepper's Lonely Hearts Club Band.*

Rock

The Beatles were the most influential performing group in
the history of rock (Keystone Press).

Sgt. Pepper's Lonely Hearts Club Band (1967)

This long-playing record is among the Beatles' finest achievements and a
landmark in the history of rock music. It was one of the first rock recordings to
be presented as a unified song cycle with lyrics important enough to be printed
on the record jacket. The cycle's thirteen songs are unified by the illusion of a
music hall show in which the audience is entertained by a dazzling variety of
acts. The opening two songs are addressed to the audience, and we hear the
sounds of crowd noises, instruments being tried out, applause, and the brasses of
Sgt. Pepper's band. The closing song of the first record side ("Being for the
Benefit of Mr. Kite") tells the audience about an evening performance. After
"Within You Without You," which opens side 2, we hear the laughter of the
audience. Contributing to the record's musical continuity is the reprise of the
opening "Sgt. Pepper's Lonely Hearts Club Band" as the next-to-last song, as
well as the lack of pauses between the first two songs and the final three songs.

*Sgt. Pepper's
Lonely Hearts
Club Band* (1967)

523

The impact of this record comes largely from its tremendous range of sounds and electronic effects. Audience noises, barnyard sounds, and weird orchestral tone clusters are heard, along with such instruments as harpsichord, harp, and sitar. The record also has a wide range of musical styles. Along with traditional rock 'n' roll, it includes a parody of a 1920s music-hall tune ("When I'm Sixty-four"), an old-fashioned melodramatic ballad using harpsichord and strings but no guitars or percussion ("She's Leaving Home"), and a song featuring the exotic sounds of Indian music ("Within You Without You"). We'll now focus on two of the record's most original songs, "Lucy in the Sky with Diamonds" and "A Day in the Life."

"Lucy in the Sky with Diamonds"

"Lucy in the Sky with Diamonds," the third song of the cycle, evokes a world of daydream and fantasy. But the dreamlike mood is shattered by a brusque refrain. Apart from its introduction, the song is made up of three sections that are repeated: A, B, and C. Sections A and B are relatively soft, gently pulsating, and in triple meter. In contrast, section C (the refrain "Lucy in the sky") is loud, heavily accented, and in quadruple meter. Here is an outline:

Introduction	Unaccompanied melody; synthesized sound suggests electric harpsichord.
A	Soft, triple meter; stepwise vocal melody repeats three-note idea in narrow range. Introductory melody, electric bass, and lightly stroked cymbals in background.
B ("Cellophane flowers")	Moderately soft, triple meter; repeated-note melody. Voice doubled by guitar and electronically manipulated to sound slightly "unreal." Fuller accompaniment, electric bass more active, marks beat.
C (Refrain)	Loud, quadruple meter; single phrase sung three times (during some repetitions, phrase doubled at higher pitch). Higher range than in sections A and B. Driving rhythm; drummer accents second and fourth beats of each bar.
A	Soft, triple meter.
B ("Newspaper taxis")	Moderately soft, triple meter.
C (Refrain)	Loud, quadruple meter.
A	Soft, triple meter.
CC (Refrain)	Loud, quadruple meter; fade-out at end.

"A Day in the Life"

"A Day in the Life," the concluding song of the cycle, uses electronic effects with an inventiveness that was unprecedented in rock. Here, fantasy blends with harsh and humdrum reality. The song is outlined: Introduction–A A' A"–First interlude–B–Second interlude–A"–Postlude. In sections A, A', and A", John Lennon

Rock

sounds "unreal" as he sings of violence and war in a curiously detached way. Section A′ begins with "He blew his mind out" and ends with a high note on "House of Lords." Section A″ opens with "I saw a film today" and concludes with a fade-out on a trill-like setting of "turn you on." These words generate the hallucinatory first interlude, in which a gigantic block of electronic and orchestral sound—superimposed over a percussive beat—gradually gets louder and higher.

Suddenly, the massive sound is cut off, giving way to insistent pulsations and the soft ringing of an alarm clock. As though awakened from a bad dream, Paul McCartney describes ordinary events in his daily life (section B). Section B contrasts with the opening sections because of its more powerful beat, livelier rhythms, and more natural vocal sound. "I went into a dream" ushers in the second interlude, in which far-off voices sing "ah" and the orchestral sound gradually becomes melodically prominent.

After the return of A″ ("I read the news") and the final words ("turn you on") comes a postlude similar to the first interlude but with an even more powerful buildup of electronic and orchestral sound. The postlude ends with a low E-major chord that takes more than half a minute to fade away. It is as though the slow fade-out attempts to resolve the tremendous tensions of the song cycle.

Sgt. Pepper's Lonely Hearts Club Band (1967)

NON-WESTERN MUSIC

1 Music in Non-Western Cultures

2 Music in Sub-Saharan Africa

3 The Classical Music of India

4 Koto Music of Japan

All over the world, music is an indispensable accompaniment to daily activities, magic rites, and ceremonies marking important phases of life. In this funeral ceremony of the Onitsha Ibo people of Nigeria, the chief blows an elephant-tusk trumpet, an instrument symbolizing royalty (Peter Buckley/Photo Researchers).

1 | MUSIC IN NON-WESTERN CULTURES

Non-Western music reflects the diversity of the world's languages, religions, geographical conditions, and social and economic systems.[1] The varied peoples of the world have music that seems to express their distinctive values, beliefs, and ways of life. The many different musical cultures each exhibit characteristic instruments, performance practices, tonal systems, and melodic and rhythmic patterns. Non-Western societies differ in their range of musical styles as well. Some peoples, for example, have only folk music, or music that is commonly performed by almost anyone in a village. Other cultures also have popular music, or music that is learned largely through recordings, films, and radio broadcasts. In addition to folk and popular music, some cultures also have classical music of a complexity that requires highly trained performers.

Non-Western music offers a wide range of fresh listening experiences and can provide insights into cultures very different from our own. The enormous musical resources of non-Western traditions have been an important source of inspiration for twentieth-century Western music. The influence of Asian and African music has been felt by musicians as diverse as French composer Claude Debussy, British rock star George Harrison, and Afro-American jazz artist John Coltrane.

Music of the non-Western world is too varied to allow easy generalizations. Yet some features are common to most musical traditions. All over the world, music is closely linked with literature, religion, dance, and drama. Used in a wide variety of situations, music is both a form of entertainment and an indispensable accompaniment to daily activities, magic rites, and ceremonies marking important phases of life. In addition, music is often employed to communicate messages and to relate the traditions of a people.

Oral Tradition

Non-Western music is most often transmitted orally from parent to child or from teacher to student. Compositions and performance techniques are learned by rote and imitation. Music notation is far less important in non-Western than in Western culture. Many musical cultures—such as those of Central Asia and sub-Saharan Africa—do not have notation. Even where notation exists, as in China and India, written music traditionally serves only as a record and is rarely used in teaching or performance.

[1]Discographies of non-Western music may be found in several of the books listed in Appendix II.

Improvisation

Improvisation is basic to many non-Western musical cultures. Performers usually base their improvisations on traditional melodic phrases and rhythmic patterns. In some parts of the world, including India and the Middle East, improvisation is a highly disciplined art that requires years of training. Indian and Islamic musicians create within a framework of melody types, each associated with a specific mood, set of tones, and characteristic phrases. There are many melody types, and within each the improviser can create a practically limitless variety of music.

Most musical cultures have a repertory of traditional songs or instrumental pieces. In some cultures, these pieces are relatively fixed and are performed similarly from generation to generation. This is the case in Japan, a country where improvisation in classical music is practically nonexistent. In other traditions, however, pieces are treated with great flexibility. In Iran (Persia) and sub-Saharan Africa, for example, performers freely vary melodies and add sections.

Voices

Singing is the most important way of making music in the vast majority of non-Western cultures. Preferred vocal timbres vary widely from one musical tradition to another. In the Middle East and North Africa, for example, singers cultivate a nasal, intense, and strained tone. A more relaxed and open-throated sound is generally preferred by singers in sub-Saharan Africa. The vast range of vocal techniques includes shouting, crying, whispering, sighing, humming, yodeling, and singing through the teeth. A most amazing vocal technique is employed among the Tuvins, a Siberian people located northwest of Mongolia. A male singer can produce two sounds at the same time: a low sustained tone together with a high, eerie melody.

Instruments

Non-Western instruments produce a tremendous wealth of sounds and come in a wide variety of sizes, shapes, and materials. Scholars usually group these instruments into the following basic categories, based on what actually generates the sound:

1. **Chordophones** are instruments—such as harps and lutes—whose sound generator is a stretched string.
2. **Aerophones** are instruments—such as flutes and trumpets—whose sound generator is a column of air.

 Instruments

529

3. **Membranophones** are instruments—basically, drums—whose sound generator is a stretched skin or other membrane.
4. **Idiophones** are instruments—such as bells, gongs, scrapers, rattles, and xylophones—whose own material is the sound generator (no tension is applied).

The musical style of a culture is among the important factors influencing its choice of instruments. For example, chordophones (strings) are prominent in Islamic and Indian classical music, whose highly ornamented melodies require instruments with great flexibility of pitch. Idiophones and membranophones (such as bells, rattles, and drums) are featured in sub-Saharan Africa, where rhythm is strongly emphasized and music is closely linked with dancing.

A culture's use of instruments is also influenced by its geography and raw materials. Bronze idiophones are especially prominent in Southeast Asia, where metallurgy developed around five thousand years ago. Indonesian orchestras (gamelans) contain up to eighty instruments, including many bronze gongs, chimes, and xylophones. Instruments made of animal skins and horns are common in parts of sub-Saharan Africa, where these materials are easily found. Among the Aniocha Ibos of Nigeria, for example, drums are made of animal skins, and aerophones (winds) made from elephant tusks are used by members of the royal family and some chiefs. Where raw material is scarce, as in the deserts of Australia, instruments may be few in number.

Along with musical style and geography, religious beliefs may influence the choice of materials. In Tibet, for example, trumpets and drums are made from the bones and skulls of criminals in order to appease demons. Instruments often have symbolic associations and are linked with specific gods and goddesses. They may be shaped like birds, animals, or fish.

Melody, Rhythm, and Texture

Most music of Asia, the Near East, and North Africa emphasizes melody and rhythm, rather than harmony or polyphony. In the music of these cultures, the texture is often monophonic, consisting of an unaccompanied melody or a melody supported by percussion. In India and the Near East, the melodic line is frequently supported by a drone, one or more tones sustained throughout the performance. In many parts of the world—such as North Africa, the Middle East, Southeast Asia, and the Far East—music often has a texture in which all parts perform the same basic melody, but in versions that differ in ornamentation or rhythm. (This texture, called *heterophony,* is considered in section 4.) Homophonic and polyphonic textures tend to be somewhat more common in sub-Saharan Africa than in most parts of Asia.

A wide variety of scales are employed in non-Western music. Most often, they contain five, six, or seven tones. Non-Western melodies commonly employ intervals smaller or larger than those standard in the West. Microtones—intervals smaller than the Western half step—are frequent in the music of India and the Near East. And much non-Western music employs very complex rhythms.

Non-Western
Music

530

A bowed-string instrument from India, the *mayuri* is shaped like a peacock (The Metropolitan Museum of Art, Gift of Alice E. Getty, 1946).

Because of the complexity of rhythms used, drummers in India and sub-Saharan Africa spend years learning their sophisticated art.

Interaction between Non-Western and Western Music

During the twentieth century, non-Western music has felt the impact of America and Europe. This influence has been spurred by increased urbanization, adoption of Western technology, and access to radios, films, recordings, and Western instruments. Western elements are often found in the popular music heard in the large cities of Africa, Asia, and the Near East. One example of such popular music is the *highlife* of West Africa, which combines European instruments with the steady rhythm characteristic of Africa. Some composers in the non-Western world combine traditional elements with Western forms and styles. And in many areas, Western and traditional music exist side by side. Yet there are vast areas of the world where traditional music is dominant. Many governments subsidize traditional performing groups to preserve their rich national heritage.

In the following sections the traditional music of three areas—sub-Saharan Africa, India, and Japan—will be studied as a tiny sample of the vast wealth of non-Western music.

Basic Terms

chordophone   aerophone
membranophone   idiophone

Basic Terms

531

2 | MUSIC IN SUB-SAHARAN AFRICA

More than three times the size of the United States, the African continent can be subdivided into two large geographical areas: North Africa includes such countries as Morocco, Algeria, Tunisia, and Egypt; and sub-Saharan Africa (south of the Sahara Desert) includes Ghana, Nigeria, Mozambique, and Angola, among many other countries. The population of North Africa is predominantly Moslem and Arabic-speaking, and its music is closely related to that of the Middle East. This section focuses on the music of sub-Saharan Africa, sometimes called "black Africa."[2] Environmentally and culturally diverse, sub-Saharan Africa includes several thousand peoples with different religions, social customs, and ways of life. They speak over seven hundred different languages (more than on any other continent). Though urban growth and industrialization are transforming sub-Saharan Africa today, many Africans still hold to traditional ways of life. Most peoples have polytheistic religions, live in villages, and devote themselves to such traditional occupations as agriculture and cattle raising.

The music of sub-Saharan Africa is as diverse as its people. Even so, most music features complex rhythms and polyrhythms, percussive sounds, and a wide variety of instrumental ensembles. Vocal music is often performed by a soloist and a responding chorus. Of course, the different cultures of Africa have mutually influenced each other. For example, in parts of sub-Saharan Africa, such as Ghana and northern Nigeria, musical styles have been influenced by Arabic culture. Generally, in this section the word *Africa* will pertain to sub-Saharan Africa.

Music in Society

Music permeates virtually every aspect of African life. It is used to entertain; to accompany dances, plays, religious ceremonies, and magic rites; and to mark such events as birth, puberty, marriage, and death. Healers use specific songs and dances to treat the ill. There are work songs to accompany digging, grinding, chopping, and harvesting. Litigation songs are sung when people are in court arguing about property ownership. There are songs praising leaders, criticizing authority, and recounting history. Singing and playing instruments are so interwoven into the fabric of life that the abstract word "music"—as it is understood in the West—is not used by most African peoples. (However, there *are* words for "song," "dance," and "poetry.")

[2]A useful recorded anthology is *Africa South of the Sahara* (Ethnic Folkways Library FE 4506).

An extraordinarily large number of songs are meant for particular occasions. For example, among the Fon—a people in Dohomey (West Africa)—children sing a special song when they lose their first tooth. The Akan of Ghana have a ritual song to cure bed-wetters. The Tutsi of Rwanda—a small country in east central Africa that depends on cattle raising—have many different songs to praise cows and to accompany their care and feeding.

Music is essential to many African ceremonies. Scholar Alan P. Merriam reports that among the Basongye of the Congo, the funeral of an important person requires the services of a professional musician who announces the death and praises the deceased. The musician clowns to cheer up the people at the funeral, allowing them to vent emotion.

African music is closely associated with dancing; both arts are basic to many ceremonies, rituals, and celebrations. While moving, a dancer often sings or plays rattles or other idiophones that are held or tied to the body.

African music is also intimately linked with language. Most languages are "tone languages," in which the meaning of a word is determined by the relative pitch at which it is spoken. The same word can have four different meanings, depending on its pitch. Tone languages permit the use of music for communication. Drummers, trumpeters, and other musicians convey messages and tell stories by imitating the rhythms and pitch fluctuations of words. "Talking drums"—capable of two or more different pitches—are often used to send musical messages. A musician can even describe an event with the aid of a talking drum.

In Africa, music making is a social activity in which almost everyone participates. As a result, music is usually performed outdoors—in streets, courtyards, or village squares. There is spontaneous music making as well as performances by social and music groups at ceremonies and feasts. As in other cultures, the level of musical skill and training varies from one individual to another. Some highly trained musicians are employed at royal courts to entertain the king. Others are hired to sing songs of praise. Musicians may receive money or goods in return for their services. Musical tradition is orally transmitted, as is folklore and history. There is no musical notation, since the cultures of sub-Saharan Africa do not emphasize literacy.

Rhythm and Percussion

Rhythm and percussive sounds are highly emphasized in African music. This rhythmic and percussive emphasis reflects the close link between music and dance in African culture. The rhythmic organization of African music tends to be complex. Usually, several different rhythmic patterns are played simultaneously and repeated over and over. Each instrument goes its own rhythmic way, producing accents that appear to be out of phase with those of the other parts. Dancers may choose any of several rhythmic patterns to dance to. For example,

 Rhythm and Percussion

533

African music is closely associated with dancing. While moving, a dancer often sings or plays an instrument (John Moss/Black Star).

while one dancer follows a bell's pattern, another may dance to the rattle, while yet another follows the drum.

Percussion ensembles consisting mainly of drums, xylophones, or rattles are widely employed. The instruments of percussion ensembles are carefully chosen to provide contrasts of tone color and pitch. The human body itself is often used as a percussion instrument. Handclaps, foot stamps, and thigh or chest slaps are common sounds in African music.

Vocal Music

African singers use a wide variety of vocal sounds. Even within a single performance a singer may shift from an open, relaxed tone to one that is more tight and constricted. Singers sometimes whisper, hum, grunt, shout, and imitate animal noises. Yodeling—the quick movement from a chest voice to a falsetto—is practiced by the Pygmies, among others.

Much African vocal music is characterized by a performance style known as **call-and-response,** in which the phrases of a soloist are repeatedly answered by those of a chorus. An exciting overlap of sound often results when the leader resumes singing before the chorus has completed its response. Singers are often accompanied by ostinatos (repeated rhythmic patterns) played by percussion. Typically, African vocal music has short phrases that are repeated over and over to different words.

Texture

Unlike many other non-Western cultures, African societies often have music that is homophonic or polyphonic in texture. Several voice parts may sing the same melody at different pitch levels, occasionally producing a series of parallel chords. Some African peoples also perform polyphonic music in which the different melodic lines are quite independent.

African Instruments

A great variety of instruments and instrumental ensembles are found in Africa. Ensembles include from two to twenty or more players. According to Ghanian scholar J. H. Kwabena Nketia, performing groups often combine instruments of different types (chordophones, aerophones, membranophones, and idiophones). They range from ensembles of instruments of indefinite pitch (bells, rattles, log drums) to those containing instruments of definite pitch (flutes, trumpets, xylophones, plucked lutes). There are also groups that combine instruments of both definite and indefinite pitch (flutes, drums, bells).

Idiophones

The most common instruments in Africa are idiophones, such as bells, rattles, scrapers, xylophones, and log drums. Most of these instruments are struck or shaken, but others are scraped, rubbed, plucked, or stamped against the ground. Many—like rattles, bells, and stone clappers—are instruments of indefinite pitch. A few—like the xylophone and *mbira*, or "thumb piano"—are tuned instruments.

Xylophones are particularly important in Africa; they are played solo, in small groups, and in orchestras of from ten to more than thirty members. The Chopi, a people of Southeast Africa, are noted for large xylophone ensembles including

African Instruments

535

A xylophone ensemble of the Chopi people of Mozambique
(International Library of African Music).

instruments of different sizes ranging from soprano to double bass. In some parts of Africa, a single large xylophone is played by several performers simultaneously. Xylophones have from about ten to over twenty slats, sometimes with gourd resonators attached. Spider webs are often placed over small holes in the resonators to create the buzzing sound favored by African musicians.

Native to Africa, the *mbira* (*sansa, kalimba,* or "thumb piano") is a melodic idiophone capable of producing elaborate melodies. From eight to over thirty tongues made of metal or bamboo are attached to a sounding board or box. The tongues are plucked with the thumbs and forefingers. The *mbira*'s gentle sweet tone is often enriched by the jingle of shells or metal pieces attached to the resonator. Vocalists often use the *mbira* to accompany themselves.

Another important idiophone is the slit drum, a hollowed-out log with a long slit on top. Some are small enough to be held in the hand, while others are tree trunks over twenty feet long. Variations in the width of the slit allow two and sometimes four different tones to be produced when the slit is struck. The slit drum is used both as a "talking drum" for signaling and as a musical instrument, often together with membranophone drums.

Membranophones

Non-Western Music

536

Drums are extremely important in African culture. They are essential to many religious and political ceremonies, and they are used for dancing and regulating

A musician can play elaborate melodies on a *mbira*, or
''thumb piano'' (© Jacques Jangoux/Peter Arnold,
Inc.).

African
Instruments

537

Two musicians play a slit drum while three others play membranophones (© Jacques Jangoux/Peter Arnold, Inc.).

the pace of work. "Talking drums" are employed to send messages over long distances. Drums are often considered sacred or magical; some Africans believe that drums contain the spirits of ancestral drummers. The manufacture of drums is usually accompanied by special rites, and drums sometimes are housed in special shrines and are given food and offered sacrifices. Drums are often regarded as the property of the group, rather than that of an individual. And they frequently symbolize power and royalty. Some African chiefs are accompanied by official drummers when they move from place to place.

Drums are usually played in groups of two to four. However, in parts of East Africa—Berundi, Uganda, Rwanda—ensembles of up to fifteen drums are played by four to six performers. The drums are often tuned to different pitches and are used to perform melodic music similar to that of xylophone ensembles.

African drummers are among the most sophisticated in the world. They can produce not only complicated rhythms but a wide range of tone colors and pitches as well. Within an ensemble, drummers have specific roles. It is usually the chief drummer who has the freedom to improvise as much as he wishes

The pressure drum can produce a variety of pitches during
a performance. Bells are attached to embellish the basic
sound (Hubertus Kanus/Rapho/Photo Researchers).

African
Instruments

539

The musical bow is a widely used chordophone. One type of musical bow is the mouth bow, which uses the player's mouth as the resonator (International Library of African Music).

(within the traditional framework). Other drummers repeat certain rhythmic patterns over and over.

Drums come in a wide variety of sizes, shapes, and forms. There are drums shaped like cones, cylinders, kettles, barrels, goblets, and hourglasses. They are made from logs, gourds, and clay. They may have one or two drum heads made from skins of such animals as snakes, lizards, goats, and monkeys. While some drums produce just a single sound, others—like the hourglass-shaped *pressure drum*—can produce a variety of pitches during a performance. The two heads of this drum are connected by thongs; by varying the arm pressure on the thongs, a player can control the tension of the heads and so change the pitch. The pitches of the pressure drum often imitate the "tone language" spoken by the people.

Aerophones and Chordophones

The most common aerophones (winds) are flutes, whistles, horns, and trumpets. Reed instruments are less widespread. Flutes are usually made of bamboo, cane, or wood, while horns and trumpets are made from animal horns, elephant tusks, wood, bamboo, and gourds.

Chordophones (strings) are used throughout Africa and come in many different types and sizes. Most are plucked or struck, perhaps reflecting the African musician's preference for percussive sounds. One of the most widely used chordophones is the musical bow, which looks like a hunting bow. The string is plucked or struck with a stick. Some musical bows have a gourd resonator attached, while with others the player's mouth is used as the resonator.

We'll now study three examples of music from sub-Saharan Africa.

Song from Angola

Side 16, band 4

A call-and-response pattern dominates this song from Angola. The performance involves (a) brief solos for male voice, (b) even shorter choral responses, and (c) longer phrases for chorus alone or for chorus together with the soloist. The song consists of four statements of the pattern ababc:

1. Solo (a)–chorus (b)–solo (a)–chorus (b)–longer choral phrases (c)
2. Solo (a)–chorus (b)–solo (a)–chorus (b)–longer choral phrases with single note interjected by soloist (c)
3. Solo (a)–chorus (b)–solo (a)–chorus (b)–longer choral phrases together with soloist (c)
4. Solo (a)–soloist with chorus (b)–solo (a)–soloist with chorus (b)–longer choral phrases together with soloist (c)

Notice how the soloist's voice—somewhat tense and nasal in quality—becomes increasingly intertwined with the chorus. In the background, several drummers perform different rhythms simultaneously.

 Song from Angola

541

Side 16, band 5 **Mitamba Yalagala Kumchuzi**

Percussive sounds and complex polyrhythms are featured in this dance song of the Zaramo people in Tanganyika. First we hear percussion instruments—five tuned goblet drums, four tuned cylindrical drums, and tin rattles—producing a variety of rhythms, pitches, and tone colors. After about half a minute, the percussion instruments are joined by a group of voices singing a dance melody.

Side 16, band 6 **Hinganyengisa masingita**

A xylophone orchestra of the Chopi people of Mozambique plays one movement from a dance. A complete orchestral dance may contain as many as fifteen movements, most having their own lyrics sung by the dancers. In this movement, the xylophone orchestra first is heard alone and then is joined by voices. Several times, a solo male voice is followed by a male chorus singing in unison. Excited high-pitched yodeling can also be heard. The singing dancers are inspired by the xylophone orchestra, which creates enormous drive through its ostinatos.

Basic Term

call-and-response

Non-Western

3 | THE CLASSICAL MUSIC OF INDIA

Dating back over three thousand years, India's musical traditions are among the oldest in the world.[3] Around the thirteenth century, Indian classical music began dividing into two main branches: *Karnatak music* of South India and *Hindustani music* of North India (an area that now includes Pakistan). The centers of North Indian music were the princely courts, while South Indian music was performed in temples. In North India, music absorbed many Persian elements because many rulers came from Persia and were Moslems. The music of South India developed more along its own lines.

When India came under British rule—during the nineteenth century—North Indian classical music was still performed mainly for small elite audiences at

Non-Western Music

542

[3] A useful recorded anthology is *The Anthology of Indian Music* (World Pacific Records WDM-6200 WDS-26200).

princely courts. But aristocratic patronage declined during the twentieth century as India made the transition from British rule to independence. Many musicians lost their jobs around 1947—the date of India's independence—when almost six hundred princely states of India were abolished as political units and merged with neighboring territories. Indian performers turned to the general public for support, just as European musicians did during the eighteenth and nineteenth centuries. Today, Indian musicians broadcast on the radio, make recordings, and compose music for films. Some teach in colleges or give concerts for large audiences. Many Indian artists now travel and give concerts throughout the world.

Indian Performers

Indian performers consider their music to be spiritual in character. "We view music as a kind of spiritual discipline that raises one's inner being to divine peacefulness and bliss," writes Ravi Shankar (b. 1920), one of India's leading musicians. "The highest aim of our music is to reveal the essence of the universe it reflects . . . through music, one can reach God." This spiritual emphasis is reflected in the texts of South Indian songs, which have religious associations. Indian musicians venerate their guru (master-teacher) as representative of the divine. A special initiation ceremony usually occurs when the guru accepts a disciple. The student then is expected to surrender his or her personality to the guru.

Musical traditions are orally transmitted from master to disciple, who learns by imitation, not by studying textbooks or written music. For example, Indian music students imitate their teacher phrase by phrase at lessons and sing or play along at concerts. Although India has various systems of musical notation, they give only the basic melodic and rhythmic elements. The development of these elements—the essential ornaments and musical elaborations—cannot be notated and must be learned from a teacher.

Improvisation

Improvisation plays an important role in Indian music, especially in North India. In few other cultures is improvisation as highly developed and sophisticated. The improviser is guided by complex melodic and rhythmic systems that govern the choice of tones, ornaments, and rhythms. Before being allowed to improvise, young musicians must study for years and practice many hours a day mastering the basic rules and techniques. Improvisations are generally performed by a soloist and a drummer. They last anywhere from a few minutes to several hours, depending on the occasion and the mood of the performer and the audience. Both vocalists and instrumentalists improvise.

 Improvisation

543

Elements of Indian Classical Music

Indian music is based on the human voice—so much so, that the pitch range of all Indian music is restricted to less than four octaves. Instrumentalists often imitate a vocal style of performance. Composed pieces are songs that are performed by the singer or instrumentalist, with the instrumentalist imitating vocal styles. And songs are used as a springboard for improvisation.

There have been many composers in South India, producing thousands of songs. The greatest composers were Tyagaraja (1767–1847), Muthuswamy Dikshitar (1775–1835), and Shyama Sastri (1762–1827). These three musicians were born in the same village and were contemporaries of Haydn, Mozart, and Beethoven; they are referred to as the "musical trinity."

Highly embellished melody—both vocal and instrumental—is characteristic of Indian music. Melodies often move by microtones (intervals smaller than a half step). Melodic lines are subtly embellished by microtonal ornaments, tiny pitch fluctuations around notes. Slides of pitch provide graceful transitions from one note to another.

Indian melodies are almost always accompanied by a drone instrument that plays the tonic and dominant (or subdominant) notes throughout the performance. The basic texture of Indian music, therefore, consists of a single melody performed over an unchanging background. Rather than the harmonic progression and polyphonic texture of Western music, there is melodic and rhythmic tension and relaxation. The main drone instrument is the **tambura,** a long-necked lute with four metal strings that are plucked in succession continuously. The constant sound of the drone vitally contributes to the atmosphere of the music. Besides the soloist and the tambura players, there is a drummer who maintains the rhythmic structure and may also perform rhythmic improvisations.

Melodic Structure: Raga

In Indian classical music, melody is created within a melodic framework called *raga.* A **raga** is a pattern of notes. A particular raga is defined partly by the number of its tones and the pattern of its intervals. Each raga has an ascending and descending form with characteristic melodic phrases and tonal emphases. Particular ornaments and slides from one note to another give each raga its individuality. Two ragas are shown here:

Raga Malkauns

Raga Yaman Kalyan

The term *raga* comes from a word meaning "color" or "atmosphere," and an ancient saying describes raga as "that which colors the mind." Ragas have many extramusical associations. Each raga is linked with a particular mood, such as tranquility, love, or heroism. Ragas are also associated with specific gods, seasons, festivals, and times of day or night. They involve so many dimensions that Indian musicians spend a long period of time learning each one. Some distinguished musicians restrict themselves to performing only about a dozen ragas. Within the framework of a raga, great artists can create and improvise a limitless variety of music.

Rhythmic Structure: Tala

Rhythm is organized into cycles called *tala*. A **tala** consists of a repeated cycle of beats. Although beat cycles range from three to more than one hundred beats in length, the most common cycles include from six to sixteen beats. A cycle is divided into groups of beats. For example, the ten-beat tala called *Jhaptal* is divided 2–3–2–3, while the ten-beat tala called *Shultal* is divided 4–2–4:

Jhaptal | 1   2 | 3   4   5 | 6   7 | 8   9   10 |

Shultal | 1   2   3   4 | 5   6 | 7   8   9   10 |

Each beat may be divided into smaller time values, just as a quarter note in Western music may be divided into eighth or sixteenth notes. The most important beat is the first beat of the tala cycle. The soloist usually plays an important note of the raga on the first beat. Apart from the main beat, other beats receive secondary accents at the beginning of each group division. Singers and members of the audience often keep time with hand and finger movements on accented beats and hand waving on less important ones. Talas are performed in a variety of tempos ranging from slow to very fast.

The rhythm of Indian music is remarkably complex and sophisticated. Young drummers spend years with a master drummer memorizing hundreds of talas and their variations. Drummers and instrumental soloists sometimes have exciting "dialogs" in which rhythmically intricate phrases are rapidly tossed back and forth.

Elements of Indian Classical Music

The sitar (*top*) and vina (*bottom*) are two popular lute-type
instruments of India (Omikron; The Metropolitan Museum
of Art, Gift of Alice E. Getty, 1946).

Instruments

While the most important performing medium in India is the voice, there is a dazzling variety of instruments of all kinds. In North Indian classical music, instruments have become about as popular as the voice. Many instruments are associated with specific gods and goddesses. For example, the flute is associated with the Hindu god Krishna, and the *vina*—a plucked string instrument—is linked with Sarasvati, the Hindu goddess of wisdom. We will describe only a few of the best-known instruments.

The **sitar** is the most popular chordophone of North India. It is a long-necked lute with nineteen to twenty-three movable frets. There are seven strings, which are plucked: Five are used for melodies, and two supply drone and rhythmic effects. The sitar also has nine to thirteen sympathetically vibrating strings that give the instrument its characteristic sound. These strings lie under the frets, almost parallel to the plucked strings. The most famous sitarist today is Ravi Shankar.

The *vina* is the most ancient plucked string instrument of South India. It has four strings for playing melodies, and three strings at the side of the fingerboard can be used for drone and rhythmic effects.

The *sarod* is a North Indian string instrument plucked with a plectrum of ivory or coconut shell. It has six main strings: four for melodies and two for drones and rhythm. Eleven to sixteen other strings vibrate sympathetically.

The *mridangam* is a two-headed barrel drum popular in South India. It is played with the open hands and fingers. The right drum head is tuned to the tonic, and the left head functions as a bass.

The North Indian counterpart of the *mridangam* is the **tabla,** a pair of single-headed drums played by one performer. The right-hand drum is generally tuned to the tonic note, and the left-hand drum functions as a bass drum. Played with the hands and fingers, these drums can produce a wide variety of pitches and tone colors. The tabla is vital to North Indian concerts and is used for solos as well as accompaniments.

Maru-Bihag, by Ravi Shankar

Side 16, band 7

This performance is an improvisation by sitarist Ravi Shankar on the evening raga *Maru-Bihag.* As usual, the sitar is accompanied by a pair of drums (tabla) with the *tambura* (a drone instrument) in the background. In his spoken introduction to the recorded performance, Ravi Shankar illustrates the raga pattern and the tala (beat cycle) used as a basis for this performance. The ascending and descending melodic forms of raga *Maru-Bihag* are:

Raga Maru-Bihag

547

Sitarist Ravi Shankar is accompanied by the tabla—a pair of single-headed drums—and the tambura, a drone instrument (Loomis Dean, Life Magazine © 1958 Time Inc.).

The tala, played by the tabla, consists of ten beats divided 2–3–2–3. In the illustration as well as the performance, it is not easy to perceive the beats. Each one is often subdivided into shorter drum strokes, and accents often come off the beat.

The performance opens with the *alap,* a rhapsodic introductory section in which the sitar is accompanied only by the tambura playing the tonic and fifth notes of the raga pattern. The sitarist plays in free rhythm, without regular beat or meter. Ravi Shankar conveys the basic mood and character of the raga by gradually unfolding its melodic pattern, characteristic phrases, and important tones. There are many long notes, microtonal ornaments, and slides from tone to tone. After opening with a downward glissando (glide) across the sympathetic strings, Ravi Shankar first explores the lowest notes of the melody and then plays slightly higher ones. In this performance the introductory section (alap) is two minutes in length. (In other performances, however, the alap can last as long as an hour.)

The entrance of the tabla playing the tala (beat cycle) marks the second phase of the performance. Ravi Shankar presents the *gat,* a short composed phrase that recurs many times. Between these recurrences, there are longer sections of improvisation. As the improvisation progresses, Ravi Shankar generates excitement by using increasingly rapid notes and by moving through the low and high registers of the sitar. This performance is a spectacular display of virtuosity and musical imagination.

Basic Terms

raga	sitar
tala	tabla
tambura	

KOTO MUSIC OF JAPAN ‖ 4 ‖

The rich musical culture of Japan embraces both folk music and a tradition of classical music that goes back over a thousand years. Traditional Japanese classical music includes sacred and secular works, theater music, vocal and instrumental music, and works for orchestra, chamber ensemble, and soloists. A wide variety of styles, forms, instruments, and musical techniques are employed. We shall explore some characteristic features of this music by focusing on the *koto*, a plucked-string instrument whose importance in Japanese music is comparable to that of the piano in Western music.[4]

The Koto

The **koto** has thirteen strings—of silk or nylon—that are stretched over a hollow sound board about six feet long (see the next page). Each string has a movable bridge. The player tunes the thirteen strings by adjusting the placement of their individual bridges. The two most common koto tunings—called *hira-joshi* and *kumoi-joshi*—both employ only five different pitches:

Hira-joshi Tuning

E A B C E F A B C E F A B

Koto strings: 1 2 3 4 5 6 7 8 9 10 11 12 13

---

[4]Some recordings of Japanese koto music are *Koto: 18th Century Traditional Music of Japan* (Everest 3306); *Classical Japanese Koto Music* (Everest 3206); and *Japanese Koto Classics: Shinichi Yuize Koto Master* (Nonesuch Explorer Series H-72008).

 The Koto

549

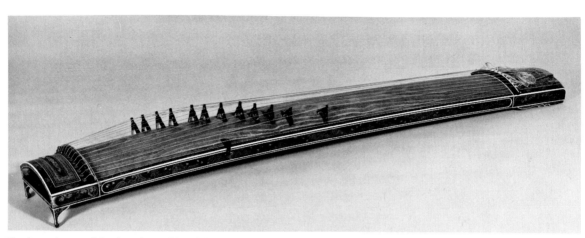

The importance of the koto in traditional Japanese music is comparable to that of the piano in Western music (Asian Art Museum of San Francisco).

Kumoi-joshi Tuning

E   A   B♭   D   E   F   A   B♭   D   E   F   A   B♭

Koto strings: 1   2   3   4   5   6   7   8   9   10   11   12   13

The koto strings are plucked with ivory plectra worn on the thumb, index, and middle fingers of the right hand. The strings may also be struck and scraped with the plectra to produce a variety of tone colors and musical effects. The glissando (a slide across the strings) and the tremolo (a rapid shaking of a string) are two common right-hand playing techniques.

The koto is not limited to the pitches produced by plucking an open string. The player may raise the pitch of a string—usually by a half or a whole step—by using the left hand to press down the string on the left side of the movable bridge. Left-hand pressure is also used to obtain ornamental pitch slides and "bent" tones.

Historical Background

Like Buddhism, woodblock printing, and much else in Japanese culture, the koto came to Japan from China. It was imported sometime between 650 and 750, along with Chinese and Korean musicians who came to play in the Japanese

Fusako Yoshida, a master of the koto (Fusako Yoshida).

court orchestra. The koto was used in Japanese court music (*gagaku*), which is among the world's oldest surviving orchestral music. By the tenth century, the koto was also used as a solo instrument by the court aristocracy. The earliest surviving solo koto music dates from the sixteenth century. Ceremonial in character and heard mostly in temples, this music was performed only by Buddhist priests, Confucian scholars, and noblemen.

Most masterpieces of traditional koto music were composed during the Edo period (1615–1868), when the capital of Japan was moved to Edo (now Tokyo). During this period, Japan isolated itself from contacts with foreign cultures. An

 Historical Background

551

increasingly wealthy merchant class stimulated new developments in the arts such as color woodblock prints and the kabuki theater, a form of drama that combines acting with brilliant music and dance.

The early Edo period saw the rise of koto music intended for entertainment, rather than for religious rites. It was composed by blind professional musicians, not by scholars or priests. These blind musicians belonged to a special guild that protected their professional and economic interests. The guild also bestowed ranks, of which the highest was *kengyō,* or master of koto. Koto masters earned their living by teaching young women from well-to-do families. The blind musician Yatsuhashi Kengyō (1614–1685) is known as the founder of modern koto music.

Koto Music

The koto is used for solos and duets, for vocal accompaniments, and in combination with one or more other instruments (with or without voice). An important chamber ensemble consists of koto and voice together with the *shakuhachi* (an end-blown bamboo flute with five holes) and the *shamisen* (an instrument with three strings that are plucked).

The most important type of music for solo koto is a theme-and-variation form known as *danmono.* The theme is presented in the first section (*dan*) and then is varied in subsequent sections, which have increasingly faster tempos. New melodic material is also placed between phrases of the original theme. Each section consists of 104 beats in duple meter (except the first section, which has 108). Danmono pieces were composed during the seventeenth and eighteenth centuries. The most famous piece of this type is *Rokudan* (six sections), attributed to Yatsuhashi Kengyō. Since the nineteenth century, these solo pieces have often been arranged for two koto or for other instruments such as shamisen and shakuhachi.

Another basic form of koto music is *tegotomono,* a song cycle with extended instrumental interludes. The simplest type of song cycle consists of three parts: Song–Instrumental interlude–Song. Tegotomono developed during the eighteenth century. Today song cycles are performed by an ensemble consisting of voice, koto, shamisen, and shakuhachi.

The Japanese koto repertory is made up of traditional pieces that are passed down from teacher to student and learned by rote. Rote learning was a necessity, since many koto masters were blind. Though a system of musical notation had long existed, musical scores were not used in teaching or performance until after World War II.

Most koto music is based on pentatonic (five-tone) scales that correspond to A–B–C–E–F or E–F–A–B–C on the piano. In this music, the precise quality of each individual tone is of great importance. The performer strives to give each tone the proper dynamic level, tone color, pitch inflection, and ornamentation. When the koto is used as part of a chamber ensemble, no instrument (or voice) is allowed to outshine the others. They blend together without losing their individual qualities. Music for koto and other instruments or for koto and voice is usually *heterophonic* in texture. **Heterophonic texture** occurs when all parts perform the same basic melody, but in versions that differ in ornamentation or rhythm. However, the parts sometimes become so independent that the texture becomes polyphonic.

"Song of the Plovers (*Chidori No Kyoku;* 1855), by Yoshizawa Kengyō

Side 16, band 8

"Song of the Plovers" is a song cycle for voice, two koto, and shakuhachi (bamboo flute) by Yoshizawa Kengyō (1800–1872), a leading composer of the nineteenth century.[5] Like most Japanese chamber music, the opening song is in heterophonic texture. (Part of this song is included in the record set.) In the instrumental introduction, the shakuhachi and koto play the same basic melody, but the shakuhachi's version is slightly more decorated. When the voice enters, there is greater melodic and rhythmic differentiation among the parts, even though they continue to perform the same basic melody. The vocal line is highly embellished, often with several notes to a single syllable. The singer projects the emotion of the text through a vocal sound that is extremely intense. The text of "The Song of the Plover" was written in praise of the emperor. (The plover is a type of sea gull.)

Shio no yama	Plovers themselves that nestle on Mount Shio
Sashide no iso	And Sashide-on-Sea, as thou must know—
Sumuchidori . . .	[They sing a wish thy reign may attain thousands of years.]

Godan-Ginuta (Nineteenth Century), by Mitsuzaki Kengyō

Side 16, band 9

Godan-Ginuta by Mitsuzaki Kengyō (?–1853) is one of the earliest and most brilliant pieces conceived as a duet for two koto. As its title indicates, *Godan-Ginuta* is composed of five sections (*godan* means "five sections") and evokes the sound of cloth beating against a wooden block called a *kinuta* (*ginuta*). Japanese women once used the kinuta to clean and soften cloth in autumn, and so the music of *Godan-Ginuta* is associated with that season.

In this duet, the koto are tuned to different scales, and one instrument is pitched five steps higher than the other. The two koto are of about equal importance and often engage in a lively dialog with rapid give-and-take. Variety is created through changes among monophonic, heterophonic, and polyphonic textures. Typical of koto music are the many tones which are "bent" upwards or downwards. Also characteristic is the duple meter and the flexible tempo, which is often held back or pressed forward. *Godan-Ginuta*'s rhythm is particularly exciting and features much syncopation. We'll now

---

[5]The second koto part in this cycle was added during the twentieth century.

 Koto Music

553

focus on the opening section of the piece, which is included in the record set.

Godan-Ginuta opens with the two koto playing long notes in unison. These tones represent the sound of the kinuta (wooden block for beating cloth). As the section unfolds, the tempo quickens and the rhythm becomes increasingly animated. Toward the middle of the piece we hear two characteristic koto sounds: a downward glissando and rapid scrapes of the plectrum along the top of the string. This section of *Godan-Ginuta* ends with a point of repose when a long note is played in unison by the two koto.

Basic Terms

koto
heterophonic
   texture

APPENDIXES

I Chronology

II Reading List

III Tone Color and the
Harmonic Series

IV Key Signatures

I CHRONOLOGY

MIDDLE AGES (450–1450)

Musicians	Artists and Writers	Historical and Cultural Events
		Sack of Rome by Vandals (455)
		Reign of Pope Gregory I (590–604)
		First Crusade (1096–99)
Perotin (late 12th century)		Beginning of Notre Dame cathedral in Paris (1163)
		King John signs Magna Carta (1215)
	Dante (1265–1321)	
	Giotto (1266–1337)	
Guillaume de Machaut (c. 1300–1377)		
	Boccaccio (1313–1375)	
	Chaucer (c. 1343–1400)	Hundred Years' War (1337–1453)
		The Black Death (1348–1350)

RENAISSANCE (1450–1600)

Musicians	Artists and Writers	Historical and Cultural Events
Guillaume Dufay (c. 1400–1474)		Fall of Constantinople (1453)
Josquin des Prez (c. 1440–1521)	Leonardo da Vinci (1452–1519)	Gutenberg Bible (1456)
		Columbus discovers America (1492)
	Michelangelo (1475–1564)	
	Raphael (1483–1520)	Martin Luther's ninety-five theses (1517)
	Titian (c. 1477–1576)	
	François Rabelais (c. 1494–c. 1553)	
Andrea Gabrelli (c. 1520–1586)		
Giovanni Pierluigi da Palestrina (c. 1525–1594)		Council of Trent (1545–1563)
Roland de Lassus (1532–1594)	Michel de Montaigne (1533–1592)	

556

Musicians	Artists and Writers	Historical and Cultural Events
William Byrd (1543–1623)		
Thomas Morley (1557–1603)	Cervantes (1547–1616)	Elizabeth I, Queen of England (1558–1603)
	William Shakespeare (1564–1616)	
		Spanish Armada defeated (1588)
Thomas Weelkes (1575–1623)		

BAROQUE (1600–1750)

		Jamestown founded (1607)
Claudio Monteverdi (1567–1643)		
	Peter Paul Rubens (1577–1640)	
Heinrich Schütz (1585–1672)		Thirty Years' War (1618–1648)
	Gian Lorenzo Bernini (1598–1680)	
	Rembrandt (1606–1669)	
	John Milton (1608–1674)	
Jean-Baptiste Lully (1632–1687)	Molière (1622–1673)	Louis XIV reigns in France (1643–1715)
	Baruch Spinoza (1632–1677)	
Arcangelo Corelli (1653–1713)		
Henry Purcell (c. 1659–1695)	Jonathan Swift (1667–1745)	Newton, *Principia Mathematica* (1687)
François Couperin (1668–1733)		
Antonio Vivaldi (1678–1741)		Louis XV reigns in France (1715–1774)
Johann Sebastian Bach (1685–1750)	Jean Antoine Watteau (1684–1721)	
George Frideric Handel (1685–1759)		

CLASSICAL (1750–1820)

	Voltaire (1694–1778)	Maria Theresa reigns in Austria (1740–1780)
		Frederic the Great reigns in Prussia (1740–1786)
	Benjamin Franklin (1706–1790)	Publication of the French *Encyclopedia* begins (1751)

Musicians	Artists and Writers	Historical and Cultural Events
Christoph Gluck (1714–1787)	Jean Jacques Rousseau (1712–1778)	
		Seven Years' War (1756–1763)
Carl Philipp Emanuel Bach (1714–1788)		Winckelmann's *History of the Art of Antiquity* (1764)
	Immanuel Kant (1724–1804)	
Joseph Haydn (1732–1809)		
	Goya (1746–1828)	
	Jacques Louis David (1748–1825)	
	Johann Wolfgang von Goethe (1749–1832)	Louis XVI reigns in France (1774–1792)
Wolfgang Amadeus Mozart (1756–1791)		American Declaration of Independence (1776)
Ludwig van Beethoven (1770–1827)		French Revolution begins (1789)
		Eli Whitney invents cotton gin (1792)
		Napoleon becomes First Consul of France (1799)
		Battle of Waterloo (1815)

ROMANTIC (1820–1900)

Musicians	Artists and Writers	Historical and Cultural Events
	William Wordsworth (1770–1850)	
	J. M. W. Turner (1775–1851)	
Carl Maria von Weber (1786–1826)		
Gioacchino Rossini (1792–1868)		
Franz Schubert (1797–1828)	Heinrich Heine (1797–1856)	
	Eugène Delacroix (1798–1863)	
	Honoré de Balzac (1799–1850)	Revolutions in France, Belgium, Poland (1830)
Hector Berlioz (1803–1869)	Victor Hugo (1802–1885)	
	George Sand (1804–1876)	First Reform Bill in Britain (1832)
Felix Mendelssohn (1809–1847)	Edgar Allan Poe (1809–1849)	
Frédéric Chopin (1810–1849)		Revolutions of 1848; Marx and Engels, *The Communist Manifesto* (1848)
Robert Schumann (1810–1856)		
		Darwin's *Origin of Species* (1859)

558

Musicians	Artists and Writers	Historical and Cultural Events
Franz Liszt (1811–1886)		American Civil War (1861–1865)
	Charles Dickens (1812–1870)	
Richard Wagner (1813–1883)		Franco-Prussian War (1870)
Giuseppe Verdi (1813–1901)		
César Franck (1822–1890)	Fëdor Dostoevsky (1821–1881)	
Anton Bruckner (1824–1896)		
Bedřich Smetana (1824–1884)	Leo Tolstoy (1828–1910)	
	Emily Dickinson (1830–1886)	
Johannes Brahms (1833–1897)	Edouard Manet (1832–1883)	
Georges Bizet (1838–1875)	Paul Cézanne (1839–1906)	
Modest Mussorgsky (1839–1881)		
Peter Ilyich Tchaikovsky (1840–1893)	Claude Monet (1840–1926)	First group exhibition of Impressionists in Paris (1874)
Antonin Dvořák (1841–1904)	Stéphane Mallarmé (1842–1898)	
Giacomo Puccini (1858–1924)	Friedrich Nietzsche (1844–1900)	Bell invents telephone (1876)
Gustav Mahler (1860–1911)		
	Vincent Van Gogh (1853–1890)	
Richard Strauss (1864–1949)		Spanish-American War (1898)

TWENTIETH CENTURY

Musicians	Artists and Writers	Historical and Cultural Events
		Freud, *The Psychopathology of Everyday Life* (1904)
Claude Debussy (1862–1918)	Wassily Kandinsky (1866–1944)	Einstein, "Special Theory of Relativity" (1905)
Scott Joplin (1868–1917)		
	Henri Matisse (1869–1954)	
	Marcel Proust (1871–1922)	
Arnold Schoenberg (1874–1951)	Gertrude Stein (1874–1946)	
		World War I (1914–1918)
Charles Ives (1874–1954)		Russian Revolution begins (1917)
Maurice Ravel (1875–1937)		
Béla Bartók (1881–1945)	Pablo Picasso (1881–1973)	
	James Joyce (1882–1941)	Beginning of Great Depression (1929)
	Virginia Woolf (1882–1945)	
Igor Stravinsky (1882–1971)		
	Franz Kafka (1883–1924)	Franklin D. Roosevelt inaugurated (1933)

559

Musicians	Artists and Writers	Historical and Cultural Events
Anton Webern (1883–1945)		Hitler Chancellor of Germany (1933)
Edgard Varèse (1883–1965)		
Alban Berg (1885–1935)		
	T. S. Eliot (1888–1965)	World War II (1939–1945)
Sergei Prokofiev (1891–1953)		
Bessie Smith (1894–1937)		
Paul Hindemith (1895–1963)		
Roger Sessions (b. 1896)		
George Gershwin (1898–1937)	William Faulkner (1897–1962)	
E. K. ("Duke") Ellington (1899–1974)	Henry Moore (b. 1898)	
	Ernest Hemingway (1899–1961)	
Louis Armstrong (1900–1971)		
Aaron Copland (b. 1900)	Isaac Bashevis Singer (b. 1904)	
Ruth Crawford (1901–1953)		
Miriam Gideon (b. 1906)	Willem de Kooning (b. 1904)	
Dmitri Shostakovich (1906–1975)	Jean Paul Sartre (b. 1905)	
Elliott Carter (b. 1908)	David Smith (1906–1965)	
Olivier Messiaen (b. 1908)		Atomic bomb destroys Hiroshima (1945)
John Cage (b. 1912)		
Hugo Weisgall (b. 1912)		Korean war begins (1950)
Benjamin Britten (1913–1976)	Jackson Pollock (1912–1956)	
Billie Holiday (1915–1959)	Albert Camus (1913–1960)	
	Saul Bellow (b. 1915)	
Milton Babbitt (b. 1916)	Andrew Wyeth (b. 1917)	
Charlie Parker (1920–1955)	Alexander Solzhenitsyn (b. 1918)	
Pierre Boulez (b. 1925)	Roy Lichtenstein (b. 1923)	
John Coltrane (1926–1967)	Norman Mailer (b. 1923)	
Karlheinz Stockhausen (b. 1928)	James Baldwin (b. 1924)	American involvement in Vietnam increases dramatically (1965)
	John Hollander (b. 1928)	
George Crumb (b. 1929)		
Krzysztof Penderecki (b. 1933)		American astronauts land on moon (1969)
Mario Davidovsky (b. 1934)		

560

Charles Wuorinen (b. 1938)

Resignation of President Nixon (1974)

End of American involvement in Vietnam (1975)

United States and China establish diplomatic relations (1979)

Revolution in Iran (1979)

READING LIST | Appendix II

GENERAL

Apel, Willi. *Harvard Dictionary of Music,* 2d ed. rev. Cambridge, Mass.: Harvard, 1973.

Apel, Willi, and R. T. Daniel. *The Harvard Brief Dictionary of Music.* Cambridge, Mass.: Harvard, 1970.

Baker's Biographical Dictionary of Musicians, 6th ed. (ed. Nicolas Slonimsky), New York: Schirmer, 1978.

Downes, Edward. *The New York Philharmonic Guide to the Symphony.* New York: Walker, 1976.

Grout, Donald Jay. *A History of Western Music,* rev. ed. New York: Norton, 1973.

Hughes, David G. *A History of European Music.* New York: McGraw-Hill, 1974.

Kamien, Roger (ed.). *The Norton Scores: An Anthology for Listening,* 2 vols. New York: Norton, 1977.

Lang, Paul Henry. *Music in Western Civilization.* New York: Norton, 1941.

The New Grove Dictionary of Music and Musicians (ed. Stanley Sadie), 20 vols. Washington, D.C.: Grove's Dictionaries of Music, 1980.

Raynor, Henry. *A Social History of Music: From the Middle Ages to Beethoven.* New York: Schocken, 1972.

Tovey, Donald Francis. *The Forms of Music.* Cleveland, Ohio: Meridian, 1963.

I. ELEMENTS

Aldwell, Edward, and Carl Schachter. *Harmony and Voice Leading,* vol. 1. New York: Harcourt, Brace, Jovanovich, 1978.

Backus, John. *The Acoustical Foundations of Music.* New York: Norton, 1969.

Carse, Adam. *The History of Orchestration.* New York: Dover, 1964.

Cooper, Grosvenor W., and Leonard Meyer. *The Rhythmic Structure of Music.* Chicago: University of Chicago, 1960.

Donington, Robert. *The Interpretation of Early Music.* New York: St. Martin's, 1963.

Harrison, Frank, and Joan Rimmer. *European Musical Instruments.* New York: Norton, 1964.

Manoff, Tom. *The Music Kit.* New York: Norton, 1976.

Marcuse, Sybil. *Musical Instruments: A Comprehensive Dictionary.* New York: Norton, 1975.

Meyer, Leonard B. *Emotion and Meaning in Music.* Chicago: University of Chicago, 1956.

Sachs, Curt. *The History of Musical Instruments.* New York: Norton, 1940.

Schwarz, Elliott. *Electronic Music: A Listener's Guide.* New York: Praeger, 1973.

Shapiro, Meyer. "Style," in *Aesthetics Today,* ed. Morris Philipson, New York: Meridian, 1961.

II. MIDDLE AGES

Hoppin, Richard H. *Medieval Music.* New York: Norton, 1978.

Munrow, David. *Instruments of the Middle Ages and Renaissance.* London: Oxford, 1976.

Reese, Gustave. *Music in the Middle Ages.* New York: Norton, 1940.

Sachs, Curt. *The Rise of Music in the Ancient World.* New York: Norton, 1943.

Seay, Albert. *Music in the Medieval World,* 2d ed., Englewood Cliffs, N.J.: Prentice-Hall, 1975.

Strunk, Oliver (ed.). *Source Readings in Music History: Antiquity and the Middle Ages.* New York: Norton, 1965.

III. THE RENAISSANCE

Brown, Howard Mayer. *Music in the Renaissance.* Englewood Cliffs, N.J.: Prentice-Hall, 1976.

Lowinsky, Edward E. "Music in the Culture of the Renaissance," in *Renaissance Essays,* ed. Paul Oskar Kristeller and Philip P. Wiener. New York: Harper & Row, 1968.

Reese, Gustave. *Music in the Renaissance,* rev. ed. New York: Norton, 1959.

Strunk, Oliver (ed.). *Source Readings in Music History: The Renaissance.* New York: Norton, 1965.

IV. THE BAROQUE PERIOD

General

Bukofzer, Manfred F. *Music in the Baroque Era.* New York: Norton, 1947.

Palisca, Claude V. *Baroque Music.* Englewood Cliffs, N.J.: Prentice-Hall, 1968.

Strunk, Oliver (ed.). *Source Readings in Music History: The Baroque Era.* New York: Norton, 1965.

Specific Topics

Grout, Donald. *A Short History of Opera,* 2d ed. New York: Columbia, 1965.

Kerman, Joseph. *Opera as Drama.* New York: Vintage, 1956.

Kobbé's Complete Opera Book, rev. ed. (ed. Earl of Harewood). New York: Putnam, 1972.

Newman, Ernest. *Great Operas: The Definitive Treatment of Their History, Stories, and Music,* 2 vols. New York: Vintage, 1958.

Newman, William S. *The Sonata in the Baroque Era.* New York: Norton, 1972.
Smither, Howard E. *A History of the Oratorio,* vols. I–II. Chapel Hill, N.C.: University of North Carolina, 1977.
Weisstein, Ulrich (ed.). *The Essence of Opera.* New York: Norton, 1969.

Individual Composers

Bach
David, Hans T., and Arthur Mendel (eds.). *The Bach Reader,* rev. ed. New York: Norton, 1966.
Geiringer, Karl, with Irene Geiringer. *Johann Sebastian Bach: The Culmination of an Era,* New York: Oxford, 1966.

Corelli
Pincherle, Marc. *Corelli: His Life, His Work.* New York: Norton, 1956.

Handel
Lang, Paul Henry. *George Frideric Handel.* New York: Norton, 1966.
Larsen, Jens Peter. *Handel's Messiah: Origins, Composition, Sources.* New York: Norton, 1972.

Monteverdi
Schrade, Leo. *Monteverdi, Creator of Modern Music.* New York: Norton, 1969.

Purcell
Westrup, Jack A. *Purcell.* New York: Octagon, 1975.

Vivaldi
Pincherle, Marc. *Vivaldi: Genius of the Baroque.* New York: Norton, 1962.

V. THE CLASSICAL PERIOD

General
Blume, Friedrich. *Classic and Romantic Music.* New York: Norton, 1970.
Pauly, Reinhard. *Music in the Classic Period,* 2d ed. Englewood Cliffs, N.J.: Prentice-Hall, 1973.
Rosen, Charles. *The Classical Style: Haydn, Mozart, Beethoven.* New York: Norton, 1972.
Wellesz, Egon and Frederick Sternfeld (eds.). *The Age of Enlightenment: 1745–1790* (vol. 7 of the *New Oxford History of Music*). London: Oxford, 1973.

Specific Topics
Newman, William S. *The Sonata in the Classic Era.* New York: Norton, 1972.
Ulrich, Homer. *Chamber Music,* 2d ed. New York: Columbia, 1966.

Individual Composers

Beethoven
Anderson, Emily (ed. & tr.). *The Letters of Beethoven,* rev. ed. New York: St. Martin's, 1964.
Arnold, Denis, and Nigel Fortune (eds.). *The Beethoven Reader.* New York: Norton, 1971.
Kerman, Joseph. *The Beethoven Quartets.* New York: Knopf, 1967.
Solomon, Maynard. *Beethoven.* New York: Schirmer, 1977.
Thayer, Alexander W. *Life of Beethoven,* rev. ed. (ed. Elliot Forbes). Princeton, N.J.: Princeton, 1973.
Tovey, Donald F. *Beethoven.* London: Oxford, 1963.

Haydn

Geiringer, Karl. *Haydn, a Creative Life in Music,* rev. ed. Berkeley, Calif.: University of California, 1968.

Landon, H. C. Robbins: *The Symphonies of Joseph Haydn.* London: Rockcliff and Universal Edition, 1955; supplement, 1961.

Mozart

Anderson, Emily (ed.). *Letters of Mozart and His Family,* 2 vols., 2d ed. (eds. A. Hyatt King and Monica Carolan). New York: St. Martin's, 1966.

Dent, Edward. *Mozart's Operas: A Critical Study,* 2d ed. London: Oxford, 1960.

Einstein, Alfred. *Mozart: His Character, His Work.* New York: Oxford, 1945.

VI. THE ROMANTIC PERIOD

General

Abraham, Gerald. *A Hundred Years of Music,* 3d ed. Chicago: Aldine, 1964.

Blume, Friedrich. *Classic and Romantic Music.* New York: Norton, 1970.

Einstein, Alfred. *Music in the Romantic Era.* New York: Norton, 1947.

Longyear, Rey M. *Nineteenth-century Romanticism in Music,* 2d ed. Englewood Cliffs, N.J.: Prentice-Hall, 1973.

Strunk, Oliver: *Source Readings in Music History: The Romantic Era.* New York: Norton, 1965.

Specific Topics

Loesser, Arthur. *Men, Women, and Pianos: A Social History.* New York: Simon & Schuster, 1954.

Newman, William S. *The Sonata Since Beethoven.* New York: Norton, 1972.

Stevens, Denis (ed.) *A History of Song.* New York: Norton, 1961.

Individual Composers

Berlioz

Barzun, Jacques. *Berlioz and the Romantic Century,* 2 vols., 3d ed. New York: Columbia, 1969.

Berlioz, Hector. *Memoirs* (ed. and tr. David Cairns). New York: Knopf, 1969.

Brahms

Gal, Hans. *Johannes Brahms: His Work and Personality.* London: Weidenfeld & Nicolson, 1963.

Geiringer, Karl. *Brahms: His Life and Works,* 2d ed. New York: Oxford, 1947.

Chopin

Hedley, Arthur. *Chopin.* London: Dent, 1947.

Dvořák

Clapham, John. *Antonin Dvořák: Musician and Craftsman.* New York: St. Martin's, 1966.

Liszt

Searle, Humphrey. *The Music of Liszt.* New York: Dover, 1966.

Perényi, Eleanor. *Liszt: The Artist as Romantic Hero.* Toronto and Boston: Atlantic; Little, Brown, 1974.

Mahler

Blaukopf, Kurt. *Mahler.* New York: Praeger, 1973.

Cardus, Neville. *Gustav Mahler: His Mind and His Music.* New York: St. Martin's, 1965.
de La Grange, Henry-Louis. *Mahler,* vol. 1. Garden City, N.Y.: Doubleday, 1973.

Mendelssohn
Werner, Eric. *Felix Mendelssohn: A New Image of the Composer and His Age.* New York: Free Press, 1963.

Mussorgsky
Calvocoressi, Michael D. *Modest Mussorgsky: His Life and Works.* Fair Lawn, N.J.: Essential Books, 1956.

Puccini
Hughes, Patrick Cairns. *Famous Puccini Operas,* 2d rev. ed. New York: Dover, 1972.

Schubert
Brown, Maurice J. E. *Schubert: A Critical Biography.* New York: St. Martin's, 1958.
Brown, Maurice J. E. *Schubert Songs.* Seattle, Wash.: University of Washington, 1969.

Schumann
Brion, Marcel. *Schumann and the Romantic Age.* New York: Macmillan, 1956.
Schumann, Robert. *On Music and Musicians.* New York: Norton, 1969.

Smetana
Large, Brian. *Smetana.* New York: Praeger, 1970.

Tchaikovsky
Abraham, Gerald. *The Music of Tchaikovsky.* New York: Norton, 1974.
Weinstock, Herbert. *Tchaikovsky.* New York: Knopf, 1973.

Verdi
Toye, Francis. *Giuseppe Verdi: His Life and Works.* New York: Vienna House, 1972.

Wagner
Goldman, Albert and Evert Sprinchorn (eds.). *Wagner on Music and Drama: A Compendium of Richard Wagner's Prose Works.* New York: Dutton, 1964.
Newman, Ernest. *The Life of Richard Wagner,* 4 vols. New York: Knopf, 1933–1946.
Newman, Ernest. *The Wagner Operas.* New York: Knopf, 1949.
White, Chappell. *An Introduction to the Life and Works of Richard Wagner.* Englewood Cliffs, N.J.: Prentice-Hall, 1967.

VII. THE TWENTIETH CENTURY

General
Austin, William, *Music in the Twentieth Century.* New York: Norton, 1966.
Machlis, Joseph. *Introduction to Contemporary Music,* 2d ed. New York: Norton, 1979.
Salzman, Eric. *Twentieth-century Music. An Introduction,* 2d ed. Englewood Cliffs, N.J.: Prentice-Hall, 1974.
Slonimsky, Nicolas. *Music Since 1900,* 4th ed. New York: Scribner, 1971.
Stuckenschmidt, H. H. *Twentieth Century Music.* New York: McGraw-Hill, 1970.
Vinton, John (ed.). *Dictionary of Contemporary Music.* New York: Dutton, 1974.

Specific Topics
Chase, Gilbert. *America's Music,* rev. 2d ed. New York: McGraw-Hill, 1966.

 Appendix II

565

Cope, David. *New Directions in Music.* Dubuque, Iowa: Brown, 1973.
Hitchcock, H. Wiley. *Music in the United States: A Historical Introduction,* 2d ed. Englewood Cliffs, N.J.: Prentice-Hall, 1974.
Meyer, Leonard B. *Music, the Arts, and Ideas.* Chicago: University of Chicago, 1969.
Music Educators Journal. November 1968 (issue devoted to electronic music).
Schwarz, Boris. *Music and Musical Life in Soviet Russia, 1917–1970.* New York: Norton, 1972.
Schwarz, Elliott. *Electronic Music: A Listener's Guide.* New York: Praeger, 1973.

Individual Composers

Babbitt
Babbitt, Milton, "Who Cares If You Listen?" *High Fidelity,* VII, 2 (February 1958).

Bartók
Stevens, Halsey. *The Life and Music of Béla Bartók,* rev. ed. New York: Oxford, 1967.

Berg
Carner, Mosco. *Alban Berg: The Man and the Work.* New York: Holmes & Meier, 1977.

Cage
Cage, John. *Silence.* Cambridge, Mass.: M.I.T., 1971.

Carter
Edwards, Allen. *Flawed Words and Stubborn Sounds: A Conversation with Elliott Carter.* New York: Norton, 1972.

Copland
Berger, Arthur. *Aaron Copland.* New York: Oxford, 1953.
Copland, Aaron. *Copland on Music.* New York: Norton, 1963.

Debussy
Lockspeiser, Edward. *Debussy: His Life and Mind,* 2 vols. London, Cassel, 1962, 1965.

Ives
Cowell, Henry and Sidney Cowell. *Charles Ives and His Music.* New York: Oxford, 1969.
Hitchcock, H. Wiley. *Ives.* New York: Oxford, 1977.
Ives, Charles. *Essays Before a Sonata and Other Writings* (ed. Howard Boatwright). New York: Norton, 1962.
Kirkpatrick, John (ed.). *Charles E. Ives: Memos.* New York: Norton, 1972.

Ravel
Orenstein, Arbie. *Ravel: Man and Musician.* New York: Columbia, 1975.

Schoenberg
Rosen, Charles. *Arnold Schoenberg.* New York: Viking, 1975.
Schoenberg, Arnold. *Letters* (ed. E. Stein). New York: St. Martin's, 1965.
Schoenberg, Arnold. *Style and Idea* (ed. Leonard Stein). New York: St. Martin's, 1975.
Stuckenschmidt, H. H. *Arnold Schoenberg: His Life, World, and Work.* London: Calder, 1977.

Stravinsky
Craft, Robert. *Stravinsky: Chronicle of a Friendship: 1948–1971.* New York: Vintage, 1973.
Stravinsky, Igor. *An Autobiography.* New York: Norton, 1962.
Stravinsky, Igor. *Poetics of Music.* New York: Vintage, 1956.

Stravinsky, Igor and Robert Craft. *Conversations with Igor Stravinsky.* New York: Doubleday, 1959.

Stravinsky, Igor and Robert Craft. *Retrospectives and Conclusions.* New York: Knopf, 1969.

White, Eric Walter. *Stravinsky: The Composer and His Works.* Berkeley, Calif.: University of California, 1966.

Varèse

Ouellete, Fernard. *Edgard Varèse.* London: Calder & Boyars, 1973.

Webern

Kolneder, Walter. *Anton Webern: An Introduction to His Works.* Berkeley, Calif.: University of California, 1968.

VIII. JAZZ

General

Feather, Leonard. *The Encyclopedia of Jazz,* rev. ed. New York: Horizon, 1960.

Gridley, Mark C. *Jazz Styles.* Englewood Cliffs, N.J.: Prentice-Hall, 1978.

Schuller, Gunther. *Early Jazz: Its Roots and Musical Development.* New York: Oxford, 1968.

Southern, Eileen. *The Music of Black Americans: A History.* New York: Norton, 1971.

Tirro, Frank. *Jazz: A History.* New York: Norton, 1977.

Williams, Martin. *Where's the Melody? A Listener's Introduction to Jazz,* rev. ed. New York: Pantheon, 1968.

Specific Topics

Blesh, Rudi and Harriet Janis. *They All Played Ragtime,* 4th ed. New York: Oak Publications, 1971.

Charters, Samuel B. *The Country Blues.* New York: Rinehart, 1959.

Keil, Charles. *Urban Blues.* Chicago: University of Chicago, 1966.

Williams, Martin. *Jazz Masters in Transition, 1957–1969.* New York: Macmillan, 1970.

IX. ROCK

Davies, Hunter. *The Beatles,* rev. ed. New York: McGraw-Hill, 1978.

Gillett, Charles. *The Sound of the City,* 2d ed. New York: Dell, 1972.

Miller, Jim (ed.). *The Rolling Stone Illustrated History of Rock & Roll.* New York: Random House, 1976.

Roxon, Lillian. *Rock Encyclopedia.* New York: Grosset & Dunlap, 1974.

Stambler, Irwin. *Encyclopedia of Pop, Rock & Soul.* New York: St. Martin's, 1977.

X. NON-WESTERN MUSIC

General

Hood, Mantle. *The Ethnomusicologist.* New York: McGraw-Hill, 1971.

Malm, William P. *Music Cultures of the Pacific, the Near East, and Asia,* 2d ed., Englewood Cliffs, N.J.: Prentice-Hall, 1977.

Merriam, Alan P. *The Anthropology of Music.* Evanston, Ill.: Northwestern, 1964.

Music Educators Journal. October 1972 (issue devoted to non-Western music).

Nettl, Bruno. *Folk and Traditional Music of the Western Continents,* 2d ed. Englewood Cliffs, N.J.: Prentice-Hall, 1973.

Reck, David. *Music of the Whole Earth.* New York: Scribner, 1977.

Sachs, Curt. *The Rise of Music in the Ancient World.* New York: Norton, 1943.

Specific Topics

Adriaansz, Willem. *The Kumiuta and Danmono Traditions of Japanese Koto Music.* Berkeley, Calif.: University of California, 1973.

Barnett, B. Elise. *A Discography of the Art Music of India.* Ann Arbor, Mich.: Society for Ethnomusicology, 1975.

Brown, Robert E. "India's Music," *Readings in Ethnomusicology* (ed. David P. McAllester). New York and London: Johnson Reprint, 1971.

Holroyde, Peggy. *The Music of India.* New York: Praeger, 1972.

Jones, A. M. *Studies in African Music.* London: Oxford, 1959.

Malm, William P. *Japanese Music and Musical Instruments.* Rutland, Vt.: Tuttle, 1959.

Merriam, Alan P. "African Music," *Continuity and Change in African Cultures* (ed. William R. Bascom and Melville J. Hershkovits). Chicago: University of Chicago, 1959.

Merriam, Alan P. *African Music on LP: An Annotated Discography.* Evanston, Ill.: Northwestern, 1970.

Nketia, J. H. Kwabena. *The Music of Africa.* New York: Norton, 1974.

Shankar, Ravi. *My Music, My Life.* New York: Simon & Schuster, 1968.

Wade, Bonnie. *Tegotomono: Music for the Japanese Koto.* Westport, Conn.: Greenwood, 1976.

III TONE COLOR AND THE HARMONIC SERIES

What we perceive as a single musical tone is actually a mixture of a number of different tones heard at the same time. The pitches making up a single musical tone are called *harmonics* (or *partials*). To understand what harmonics are, recall that a musical tone is produced by a vibrating body, such as a string or air column.

A string vibrates not only in its entirety but also in segments such as halves, thirds, fourths, fifths, and so on. These vibrating segments produce faint tones that are higher in pitch than the *fundamental tone* (or first harmonic), produced by the string vibrating as a whole. The halves produce a tone twice the frequency of the fundamental tone, the thirds produce a tone three times the frequency of the fundamental tone, and so forth. The entire group of component pitches is called the *harmonic series*. Here are the first sixteen harmonics of the tone C.

1 2 3 4   5 6 7 8 9 10 11 12 13 14 15 16

(The 7th, 11th, 13th, and 14th harmonics—indicated by black notes—are markedly out of tune with the scales used in Western music.)

A tone's color or timbre is determined by the number and relative intensity of its harmonics. For example, an oboe tone has almost all the harmonics, but a clarinet tone lacks the even-numbered harmonics.

String players can produce audible harmonics—high, whistlelike tones—by lightly touching the string at certain points. A light touch half-way along a string's length produces the second harmonic, which is an octave higher than the fundamental tone.

KEY SIGNATURES

Appendix IV

569

ACKNOWLEDGMENTS

Alleluia: dominus dixit from *Liber Usualis,* Desclée éditeurs, Tournai, 1961, p. 394.

Gherardello da Firenze, *Tosto che ll'alba* from Instituto Italiano di Cultura, New York, N.Y.

Josquin des Prez, *Ave Maria . . . virgo serena* from *Josquin des Prez, Motets, 1490–1520* (Telefunken Decca, SAWT 9480, Hamburg, Germany).

Machaut, *Je puis trop bien* from Archibald Davidson and Willi Apel, eds., *Historical Anthology of Music,* Harvard University Press © 1946, 1949 by the President and Fellows of Harvard College; © 1974, 1977 by Alice D. Humez and Willie Apel.

Bach, *Cantata No. 140* from Gerhard Herz, trans., R. Kamien, ed., *The Norton Scores* (New York: W.W. Norton, 1970), pp. 173–175.

Mozart, *Don Giovanni,* William Murray translation, copyright © 1961 Capitol Records, Inc. Reprinted by kind permission of Angel Records.

Schubert, "The Erlking" and "Heidenröslein" (pp. 28–29) from *The Ring of Words* edited by Philip L. Miller. Reprinted by permission of Doubleday & Company, Inc. and Philip L. Miller.

Berlioz, *Fantastic Symphony.* English translation from *Symphonie Fantastique* (New York: Edition Eulenburg), p. III.

Mussorgsky, Petrovich, *Boris Godunov,* Coronation Scene, from Louis Biancolli, trans., *Boris Godunov* (RCA Victor, LM 6403, 1952).

Smetana, *The Moldau* from Brian Large, *Smetana* (New York: Praeger; London: Duckworth & Co., Ltd. 1970), p. 273. John Clapham, *Smetana* (London: Dent & Sons Ltd., 1972), p. 77.

Verdi, *Rigoletto,* Act III, from *Verdi Librettos,* translated by William Weaver. Copyright © 1963 by William Weaver. Reprinted by permission of Doubleday & Company, Inc.

Puccini, *La Bohème,* William Weaver translation, copyright © 1952 Capitol Records, Inc. Reprinted by kind permission of Angel Records.

Wagner, *The Twilight of the Gods,* Act III, from G.M. Holland, trans., *The Twilight of the Gods* (Copyright © 1965, The Decca Record Company Limited, London. Exclusive U.S. Agents, London Records, Inc., New York, N.Y. Used by Permission.)

Debussy, Claude, *The Sunken Cathedral* and *Voiles.* Copyright 1910 Durand et Cie. Used by permission of the Publisher Elkan-Vogel, Inc. Sole representative, U.S.A.

Stravinsky, *Symphony of Psalms.* Copyright 1931 by Russischer Musikverlag. Renewed 1958. Copyright and renewal assigned 1947 to Boosey & Hawkes, Inc. Revised version copyright 1948 by Boosey & Hawkes, Inc. Renewed 1975. Reprinted by permission.

Schoenberg, Arnold, *A Survivor from Warsaw.* Copyright 1949 by Boelke-Bomart, Inc., Hillsdale, NY. Used by permission of Associated Music Publishers, Inc.

Schoenberg, Arnold, *Five Pieces for Orchestra.* Copyright 1952 by Henmar Press, Inc., New York. Reprint permission granted by the publisher.

Schoenberg, Arnold, *Suite for Piano.* Used by permission of Belmont Music Publishers, Los Angeles, California 90049.

Berg, *Wozzeck,* Act III. English translation from Eric Blackall and Vida Harford, *Wozzeck.* Copyright 1923, 1931, by Universal Edition, A.G., Wien. English translation copyright 1952 by Alfred A. Kalmus. Used by permission of European American Music Distributors Corp., sole U.S. agent.

✣ INDEX

The symbol (LO) following page numbers indicates that there is a Listening Outline within the given pages.

A A B form, example of, 165
A B (binary) form:
  in Baroque music, 124
  described, 71
  examples of, 7(LO), 71–72(LO), 149
  in suite movements, 161, 162
A B A (ternary) form:
  in Baroque music, 124, 141
  in Bartók concerto, 445, 448–450(LO)
  in *da capo* aria, 141
  described, 70
  examples of, 6(LO), 70–71(LO), 89,
    158, 170, 215, 233, 393–394(LO),
    448(LO)
  free, example of, 292
  impressionistic, example of, 393–
    394(LO)
  minuet and trio as, 201
Abbey Road (Beatles), 522
Abduction from the Seraglio, The (Mozart),
  218
Absolute music:
  described, 396–397
  program music and, defined, 302
A cappella, defined, 106, 109
Accelerando, defined, 39
Accent(s):
  defined, 38
  irregular, 408, 503
  syncopation and, 38–39
  unexpected, in Bartók, 444
Accompanied recitative, defined, 170
Accordian as keyboard instrument, 28, 30
Acid rock, 513
  (*See also* Rock music)
Adagio, defined, 39
Adagio cantabile, defined, 246
Adelard of Bath, 474
Aeneid (Virgil), 144
Aeolian mode, 88
  (*See also* Church modes)
Aerophones:
  chordophones and, 541
  defined, 529
Affettuoso, described, 157
Africa South of the Sahara, 532n.
African art, influence of, 405–407
African music (sub-Saharan), 532–542
  and American jazz origins, 480
  dancing and, 533–534

influences in Western music, 528
instruments for, 530, 535–541
language and, 533
rhythm and percussion in, 533, 534
social functions of, 532–533
song examples, 541–542
texture in, 535
vocal, 535
"Afternoon of a Faun, The" (Debussy) (see
  Prelude to "The Afternoon of a Faun")
*Afternoon of a Faun, The (L'Après-midi d'un
  faune)* (Mallarmé), 389
Age of Enlightenment, 184
  (*See also* Classical style)
Age of reason, Romanticism as rebellion
  against, 258
  (*See also* Classical music)
Aïda (Verdi), 340
Air (melody), example of, 161
Akan (of Ghana), 533
Alabama (Coltrane), 508
Alap, described, 548
Albrechtsberger, Johann Georg, 212
Alceste (Lully), 126
Aleatory music (*see* Chance music)
Alfano, Franco, 346
Allegretto, defined, 39
Allegretto non troppo, defined, 300
Allegretto scherzando, 448
Allegro, defined, 39
Allegro agitato e appassionato assai, de-
  fined, 306
Allegro assai, defined, 197
Allegro barbaro (Bartók), 407
Allegro commodo non agitato, defined,
  324
Allegro con brio, defined, 248
Allegro con fuoco, defined, 331
Allegro con spirito, defined, 213
Allegro giusto, defined, 323
Allegro maestoso, defined, 291
Allegro marziale animato, defined, 294
Allegro moderato, defined, 177
Allegro molto, defined, 39
Allegro molto appassionato, defined, 297
Allegro molto e con brio, defined, 244
Allegro molto vivace, defined, 300
Allegro non troppo, defined, 39
Alleluia: Dominus dixit, 88–90
Alleluya Nativitas (Perotin)), 95–96

Allemande, 160
Alto (voice), 10
  operatic categories of, 136–137
Amahl and the Night Visitors (Menotti), 385
Amateur Chamber Music Players directory,
  208
"America" *(My country 'tis of thee)*, 36–37
American folklore (*see* American themes)
American music, jazz and popular: influ-
  ence of, 373, 386
  (*See also* Jazz; *specific composers*)
American Revolution, 191, 455
American themes:
  in Copland works, 456–460
  in Dvořák works, 325–331
  in Ives works, 373, 452–455
  (*See also* Black music; Jazz)
Ancient Voices of Children (Crumb), 467,
  475–477
  "From where do you come, my love, my
    child?" ("Dance of the Sacred Life-
    Cycle"), 476
Andante, defined, 39
Andante con moto, defined, 251
Andante non tanto quasi Moderato, de-
  fined, 323
Andante più tosto Allegretto, defined, 214
Anne, Queen, Handel and, 173
Answer (fugue), described, 132
Appalachian Spring (Copland), 380, 456,
  458–460
  polychords in, 380
Architecture, gothic, revival of, 258
Aria:
  Baroque, 141
  da capo, defined, 141
  described, 137, 178
  examples of, 145, 147, 179, 220, 226–
    228, 341, 352, 353
Arioso, defined, 178
Aristocracy as patrons:
  in Baroque period, 125–129, 139, 153
  in Classical period, 191–194, 209–211,
    216, 240, 241
  during Renaissance, 103
Armstrong, Lillian Hardin, 8, 496
  pictured with Louis and His Hot Five,
    494
Armstrong, Louis "Satchmo," 480, 489,
    493, 496–497

Armstrong, Louis "Satchmo,":
  and His Hot Five, 8–9(LO), 496
  "Hotter Than That," 8–9(LO), 496
  impact on jazz, 496
  pictured, 478, 494
Arpeggio (broken chord), defined, 55
Art and Revolution (Wagner), 358
Art of the Fugue (Bach), 157
Art song, 269–270
  Brahms and, 332–334
  Debussy and, 392
  non-Western, 541–542
  Schubert and, 270–277
  Schumann and, 279–282
  subjects and form of, 269–270
Art Work of the Future, The (Wagner), 358
"As Vesta Was Descending" (Weelkes),
  112–113
As You Like It (Shakespeare), 113–114
Asian music:
  Chinese, 550
  Indian (*see* Indian classical music)
  influences of, in Western music, 376,
    389, 391, 528
  Japanese, 549–554
  Javanese, 376, 389, 391
  Korean, 550
Atonality, 417–418
  defined, 382
  examples of, 417–418, 421–423(LO),
    440–442(LO)
  Schoenberg and, 382, 417–421
  twelve-tone system as systemized form
    of, 417–418
  Wagner as precursor of, 377, 382
Auden, W. H., 136
Augmentation (fugue), defined, 133
Avant-garde, described, 461
Ave Maria (Josquin des Prez), 107–108

Babbitt, Milton:
  Composition for Four Instruments, 473
  Composition for Synthesizer, 473–474
  Composition for Twelve Instruments, 473
  electronic music and, 32, 465
  Ensembles for Synthesizer, 473
  Philomel for soprano, recorded soprano,
    and synthesized tape, 473
  serialism of, 32, 463
  Three Compositions for Piano, 473
  Vision and Prayer for soprano and syn-
    thesized accompaniment, 473
Bach, Carl Philipp Emanuel, 184, 186
Bach, Johann Christian, 184
  Mozart influenced by, 221
Bach, Johann Sebastian, 73, 118, 127, 128,
    152–171
  Art of the Fugue, 157
  "Before Thy Throne I Step, O Lord,"
    154

biographical sketch of, 152–155
Brahms influenced by, 332
Brandenburg Concerti, 125, 129, 153,
  157–158
Brandenburg Concerto No. 5 in D Major,
  129–131(LO), 157–158
Cantata No. 140: *Wachet auf, ruft uns die
  Stimme,* 163–167
compositions, style, and techniques of,
  155–156
cool jazz and, 506
criticism of, 155
Mass in B Minor, 158–160
"Old Adam's Fall" (*Durch Adams Fall*),
  155
Organ Fugue in G Minor ("Little"
  Fugue), 133–135
portrait of, 156
Prelude in C Minor from *The Well-
  Tempered Clavier,* Book 2, 71–
  72(LO)
St. Matthew Passion, 155, 295
Suite (Overture) No. 3 in D major,
  161–163
Ten Commandments, The, 155
Vivaldi and, 150, 152
Well-Tempered Clavier, The, 71–72(LO),
  157
Baez, Joan, 53, 518
Balakirev, Mily, 313, 319
  (*See also* "Russian Five, The")
Balanchine, George, 398
Ballade, example of, 98
Ballet music:
  of Copland, 456, 458–460
  of Stravinsky, 398–409
  of Tchaikovsky, 319
  (*See also* Russian Ballet)
Balzac, Honoré de, 283
Bardac, Emma (Emma Bardac Debussy),
  390
Baritone (voice), 10
  operatic categories of, 136–137
Baritone horn, 24
Baroque, defined, 118
Baroque music, 118–181
  Bach and, 71–72(LO), 133–135, 152–
    171
  chorale and church cantata, 162–171
  Classical and, compared, 184, 187–191
  composers of, 125–128
  concerto grosso and ritornello form,
    128–131(LO), 157–158
  Corelli and, 125, 148–149
  dance forms, 160–162, 377, 397, 469
  forms, 124
  fugue as cornerstone of, 131–135
  Handel and, 172–181
  instrumental, 121, 123–124, 128–
    131(LO), 133–135, 148–152,
    157–162

instruments central in, 122–123
melody, 121
Monteverdi and, 118, 141–143
music directors, tasks of, 125–126
opera, 118, 135–147, 173, 175–176
oratorio, 172, 174–181
orchestra, 123
patronage, 125–129, 139, 153, 173–174
phases of, 118, 120–121
Purcell and, 118, 143–147
"revival" of, 118, 150, 377
rhythm in, 121
sociocultural background to, 125–128
sonata, 148
stylistic features of, 121–124
suite, 160–162, 397
texture, 122
twentieth-century rediscovery of, 377,
  397
unity of mood in, 121
Vivaldi and, 150–152
vocal, 135–147, 162–181
word-music relationships, 124
Baroque opera, 118, 139–141
  elements of, 135–141
  Monteverdi, 139, 141–143
  Purcell, 143–147
  stage machinery of, 140
  (*See also* Opera)
Baroque period:
  defined, 79
  socioeconomics of, 125–128
  three phases of, 118, 120–121
"Baroque revival" in 1940s, 118, 150, 377
Baroque rock, 513
  (*See also* Rock music)
Baroque style:
  in art, 118–120
  defined, 118
  sociocultural aspects of, 118, 125–128
Bars (measures) in jazz, described, 484
Bartered Bride, The (Smetana), 323
Bartók, Béla, 373, 442–450
  Allegro barbaro, 407
  biographical sketch, 442–443
  compositions, styles, forms, and
    techniques of, 444–450
  Concerto for Orchestra, 443–450(LO)
  Fifth String Quartet, 386
  and folk music, 373, 442–446
  multicultural influences on, 442–444
  Music for Strings, Percussion and Celesta,
    378, 444
  "night music" of, 444
  as refugee, 386
  rhythmic innovations by, 382, 444
  Six Dances in Bulgarian Rhythm, 383
  Sonata for solo violin, 443
  Sonata for Two Pianos and Percussion, 444
  Third Piano Concerto, 443
  The Wooden Prince, 442

574

Baryton, 210
Basie, Count, swing and, 497
Basongye (of the Congo), 533
Bass (voice), 10
  operatic categories of, 137
Bass, electric, in jazz, 505
Bass clarinet, 18, 20
  in Romantic music, 265
Bass clef, defined, 42
Bass drum, described, 24–25
"Bass fiddle" (double bass), 3, 14–15, 17
Basso buffo, defined, 137
Basso continuo (figured bass):
  of Bach, 157
  defined, described, 122–123
  end of use in Classical music, 189
  example of, 168–170
  jazz rhythm section and, compared, 482
Basso ostinato (see Ground bass)
Basso profundo (voice), defined, 137
Bassoon, 18, 20
Baton, described, 75
Baudelaire, Charles, 392
Beat, defined, 36–37
"Beatlemania," 522
Beatles, The, 522–525
  elements and techniques of, 522
  movies by, 522
  pictured, 523
  recording procedure of, 520
  rock music and, 512, 513, 522–525
  Sgt. Pepper's Lonely Hearts Club Band,
    522–525
  style, sources of, 522
  "Yesterday," 51
Beatles, The ("White Album") (Beatles), 522
Beatrice and Benedict (Berlioz), 305
Bebop (bop), 502–505
Beethoven, Carl, 241
Beethoven, Caspar, 241
Beethoven, Johann, 238
Beethoven, Ludwig van, 73, 187, 238–255
  biographical sketch of, 238–242
  Brahms influenced by, 333
  as Classical composer, 187, 189–191,
    193–194, 199, 203–208
  composition form, style, and techniques
    of, 242–255
  Fidelio, 244
  as free-lance musician, 267
  Goethe and, 240
  Haydn and, 212, 238, 243, 244
  Missa solemnis, 242, 244
  Mozart and, 242–244
  musical continuity techniques of, 242–
    243
  musical style, change in, 240
  Piano Sonata in C Minor, Op. 13
    (Pathétique), 244–247
  piano sonatas by, 243
  portrait of, 239

String Quartet in C Minor, Op. 18, No.
    4, 203–204(LO)
  string quartets by, 243
  Symphony No. 3 (Eroica), 240, 242
  Symphony No. 5 in C Minor, Op. 67,
    242, 247–255(LO)
  Symphony No. 6 (Pastoral), 241,
    243, 302
  Symphony No. 9 (Choral), 242
  Wagner influenced by, 357
"Before Thy Throne I Step, O Lord"
    (Bach), 154
Benny Goodman Band, 499
Benvenuto Cellini (Berlioz), 305
Berg, Alban, 373, 427–438
  biographical sketch of, 427
  Chamber Concerto, 427
  influenced by Mahler, 366
  Lulu, 427
  Lyric Suite, 427
  as Schoenberg disciple, 415
  Violin Concerto, 427
  Wozzeck, 414, 427–438
Berkshire Music Center in Tanglewood,
    Copland and, 458
Berlin, Irving, 499
Berlioz, Harriet Smithson, 303–304
Berlioz, Hector, 262, 267, 303–309
  Beatrice and Benedict, 305
  Benvenuto Cellini, 305
  biographical sketch, 303–304
  on career choice, 268
  compositions, style, forms and
    techniques of, 305–310
  as critic, 268, 304
  The Damnation of Faust, 305
  "dramatic" form innovations, 305–306
  Fantastic Symphony (Symphonie fantas-
    tique), 263, 288, 301, 302, 304–310
  idée fixe, 306–310
  Requiem, 305
  Romeo and Juliet, 305
  Treatise on Modern Instrumentation and Or-
    chestration, 265
  The Trojans, 305
Bernini, Giovanni Lorenzo, 116, 118
Bernstein, Leonard, as conductor of New
    York Philharmonic Orchestra, 385
Berry, Chuck, 512, 513
Big bands (see Swing)
Bigard, Barney, 478
Bill Haley and His Comets, 512, 517
Billy Joel, 514
Billy the Kid (Copland), 456
Binary form (see A B form)
Birth of Venus, The (Botticelli), 103
Bitonality:
  defined, example of, 381
  "Petrushka chord" defined, 401
Bizet, Georges:
  Carmen, 264

Farandole from L'Arlésienne Suite No. 2,
    65–67(LO)
Black, Brown, and Beige (Ellington), 500
Black music (American), 480–509
  African roots of, 480
  blues (see Blues)
  Dvořák and, 325–326
  jazz, 480–509
    (See also Jazz)
  New Orleans and [see New Orleans
    (Dixieland) style]
  ragtime (see Ragtime)
  slavery and, 488
  soul, 512
  spirituals, 325–326, 488
  swing (see Swing)
  work song, 488
Blackboard Jungle (film), effects of, 512
Blood, Sweat, and Tears, jazz rock and, 515
"Blowin' in the Wind" (Dylan), 513
"Blue Skies" (Berlin), 499
Blue stanza, described, 489
Blues, 482, 484–485, 488–492
  defined, 488
  elements of, in Copland, 456
  lyrics and elements of, 488–489
  rhythm, 490
  twelve-bar form (see Twelve-bar blues)
Boblicity (Davis), 506
Boccaccio, Giovanni, 96
Body of violin, described, 14–15
Bohéme, La (Puccini), 346, 348–356
  Che gelida manina ("What a cold little
    hand"), 348, 352–353
  Mi chiamano Mimi ("They call me Mimi"),
    348, 353–354
Boito, Arrigo, 340
"Bombs" in bebop, defined, 503
Book of the Courtier, The (Castiglione), 102
Boris Godunov (Mussorgsky):
  Coronation Scene, 314–316, 409
  from Pushkin story, 313–316
Borodin, Alexander, 313
  (See also "Russian Five, The")
Boston Symphony Orchestra, 410, 445
Botticelli, Sandro, 103
Boulanger, Nadia, 456
Boulez, Pierre:
  as composer, 462
  serialism and, 463, 464
Bourée, example of, 162
Bow:
  illustration, 15
  use of, 14–18
Bowie, David, 519
Boy's Magic Horn, The (Des Knaben Wun-
    derhorn) (Mahler), 366
Brahms, Johannes, 262, 332–338
  biographical sketch of, 332–334
  compositions, subjects, style and forms
    of, 334–338

575

Brahms, Johannes:
  Dvořák and, 325, 334
  Four Serious Songs, 334
  German Requiem, 334
  influence of Beethoven, 333
  influence on Schoenberg, 415
  Liszt and, 332
  portrait of, 333
  Schumanns and, 332–334
  songs of, 269, 332–334
  Variations on a Theme by Haydn, 334–338
  Wagner and, 333–334
Brandenburg Concerti (Bach), 125, 129, 153
  Concerto No. 5 in D Major, 130–131(LO), 157–158
Brass instruments, 11, 13, 22–24
  in Classical orchestra, 190
  distribution of, in orchestra, 13
  in jazz, 482, 484
  in Romantic music, 264
  in twentieth-century neoclassical music, 400–413
  (*See also specific instrument*)
Breaks in jazz, defined, 495
Brentano, Antonie, Beethoven and, 241
Bridge (transition):
  defined, 195
  examples of, 242, 245, 246, 248, 249, 251, 255, 299, 321(LO)
  (*See also* Sonata form)
Bridge (violin), described, 14–15
"British Grenadiers, The" in Ives, 455
Britten, Benjamin, *A Young Person's Guide to the Orchestra,* Op. 32, 33–34, 377
Broken chord (arpeggio), defined, 55
Brown, James, 512
Brubeck, Dave, 506
  Unsquare Dance, 40
  (*See also* Dave Brubeck Quartet)
Brussels World Fair of 1958, 471
Büchner, Georg, 427
Budapest Opera, Mahler as director of, 365
Bülow, Cosima von (Cosima Liszt von Bülow Wagner), 290, 359
Burleigh, Henry T., 325

Caccia, described, 97
Cadence:
  defined, 48, 55
  dominant-tonic, twentieth-century alternatives to, 381
  [*See also* Chord(s): Tonal system]
Cadenza:
  in Classical concerti, 206–207
  example of, 237(LO)
  piano, example of, 299
  in Romantic music, 297
Cage, John:
  chance music and, 463–464
  4'33", 2, 464

fourth chords in, 380
  Imaginary Landscape No. 4, 463
Caldwell, Sarah, 75
Call-and-response:
  in African vocal music, 535, 541
  example of, 499
  in jazz, defined, 480
Camerata, defined, 139
Cantata, 162–171
  church, defined, 163
Cantata No. 140: *Wachet auf, ruft uns die Stimme* (Bach), 163–167
Canterbury Tales (Chaucer), 96
Cantus firmus, defined, 95
Cardinal Ottoboni, 148
Carmen (Bizet), 264
Carnaval (Schumann), 280
  as program music, 302
Carter, Elliott, 467–469
  Concerto for Orchestra, 468
  Double Concerto, 466, 468
  Piano Concerto, 468
  Sonata for Flute, Cello, Oboe, and Harpsichord, 377, 467–469
  String Quartet No. 1, 467
  Variations for Orchestra, 468
"Cask of Amontillado, The" (Poe), 258
Castiglione, Baldassare, 102
Castrato in Baroque opera, 140
"Catalogue Aria" (*Madamina*) from *Don Giovanni* (Mozart), 226–228
Cathedral from the Bishop's Garden (Constable), 261
Cavalleria rusticana (Mascagni), 346
Celesta, described, 24, 26
Cello (violoncello), 14, 16
  in jazz, 505, 506
Chamber Concerto (Berg), 427
Chamber music:
  Classical, 207–208
  of Haydn, 212
  twentieth-century tone color in, 378
  (*See also* String quartet)
Chamber sonatas (*sonata da camera*), 148
Chamber Symphony, Op. 9 (Schoenberg), 417
Chance music (aleatory music):
  Cage and, 463–464
  defined, proponents of, 461, 463–464
  electronic music and, 464
  free jazz and, compared, 506
Charles VI, Emperor, 150
Charles, Ray, 512
Chaucer, Geoffrey, 96
Chicago (group), jazz rock and, 515
Chimes, described, 24, 26
Chinese music, Japanese koto music and, 500
Chopin, Frédéric, 8, 262, 283–287
  Berlioz and, 283
  biographical sketch of, 283

composition styles, forms and techniques of, 285–287
  Étude in C Minor, Op. 10, No. 12 (*Revolutionary*), 286–287
  individuality of, 263
  Liszt comments on, 283
  Nocturne in E-flat Major, Op. 9, No. 2, 285–286
  Piano Sonata in B-flat Minor, 283
  Polonaise in A-flat Major, Op. 53, 287
  portrait of, 284
  Prelude in C Minor for Piano, Op. 28, No. 20, 7(LO)
  Prelude in E Minor for Piano, Op. 28, No. 4, 55–56
Choral music:
  in Middle Ages, 87–90
  in Renaissance, 103, 106–110
  (*See also* Gregorian chant; *specific titles*)
Chorale, 162–171
  and church cantata, 162–171
  defined, 162
Chorale prelude, defined, 163
Chord(s), 52–56
  Baroque emphasis on, 122–123
  in bebop, 503
  central, 381
  consonant and dissonant, 53–54, 379
  defined, 52
  dissonant, examples of, 391, 395–396
  dominant, 54, 381
  fourth, use of, 417
  parallel, example of, 391, 535
  subdominant, in blues stanza, 489
  tonic, 54
  triad (*see* Triad)
  twentieth-century treatment of, 379–382, 391–392, 395–396
Chord progression, 52–55
  in bebop, 502
  defined, 52
  of dissonances, by Debussy, 389
  in jazz, 485, 502
  traditional and twentieth-century, compared, 381–382
  twelve-bar blues, 489–490, 495
  unorthodox, examples of, 391, 395–396
Chordophones:
  and aerophones, 541
  defined, 529
  use of, 530
Chorus:
  in Handelian oratorio, 174–175, 180–181
  in jazz, described, 484
Chromatic harmony:
  defined, 265
  in *Petrushka,* 402
  in Romantic music, 265
  Schoenberg use of, 417
Chromatic scale, described, 60–61

Chronology in relation to style, 556–561
Chubby Checker, the Twist and, 521
Church modes, described, 88–90
Church music:
    Baroque, 126, 162–181
    cantata, 162–171
    Council of Trent and, 109
    Gregorian chant (see Gregorian chant)
    medieval, 84, 87–90, 93–96, 98–99
    oratorio, 172–181
    Palestrina and, 108–110
    Renaissance, 103, 105, 106–110
Church sonatas (sonata da chiesa), 148
Cimbalom, described, 290
Civil rights, rock music reflecting issues of,
    520
Clarinet, 18, 20
    in jazz, 482
Classical music, 79, 184–255
    Baroque and, compared, 184, 187–191
    Beethoven and, 187, 189–191, 193–
        194, 199, 203–208, 238–255
    chamber music, 207–208
    characteristics of, 187–191
    concerto, 206–207, 220, 234–238(LO)
    defined, 186
    dynamics and piano in, 188–189
    form, 190
    Haydn and (see Haydn, Joseph, as Clas-
        sical composer)
    instrumental, 189–191, 194–198(LO),
        199–201(LO), 201–203(LO),
        203–204(LO), 205–208, 212–216,
        230–234(LO), 234–238(LO),
        242–255(LO)
    major composers of, 184
    melody, 188
    minuet and trio form, 201–203(LO),
        215, 233–234(LO)
    moods in, 187
    Mozart and (see Mozart, Wolfgang
        Amadeus, as Classical composer)
    orchestra, 189–190
    patronage, 191–194, 209–212, 216,
        218, 240, 241
    "pre-Classical" and, 184
    rhythm, 188
    Romantic and, compared, 258, 262–
        267
    rondo form, 203–204(LO)
    sociocultural background to, 184–187,
        191–194
    sonata form, 194–198(LO)
    style characteristics, 187–191
    symphony as major contribution of,
        205–206, 230–234
    texture, 188
    theme-and-variation form, 199–
        201(LO)
Classical rock, 513, 514
    (See also Rock music)

Classical style:
    in art, 184–187
    described, 184–191
Classical Symphony (Prokofiev), 377
Clavichord in Baroque period, 122
Clef, defined, 42
Cliburn, Van, 29
Climax of melody, defined, 49
"Clock" Symphony No. 101 (Haydn), 212
Clouds (Nuages) (Debussy), 390
Coda:
    examples of, 233(LO), 237(LO),
        251(LO), 300, 322(LO), 328(LO)
    in sonata form, 196
Coleman, Ornette, free jazz and, 508–509
Collective improvisation in jazz, 494–497
    (See also Improvisation)
Collegium Musicum, 153, 161
Coloratura soprano, defined, 136
Coltrane, John, 480, 528
    Alabama, 508
    free jazz and, 506, 508–509
    Giant Steps, 508
    pictured, 507
Columbia-Princeton Electronic Music
    Center (New York City), 32, 473
Columbia University, Bartók at, 443
"Comfort ye, my people" from Messiah
    (Handel), 177–179
Comic opera (opera buffo):
    Classical, 192–193
    Don Giovanni (Mozart), 219–230
    by Mozart, 218–221
Composition for Four Instruments (Babbitt),
    473
Composition for Synthesizer (Babbitt), 473–474
Composition for Twelve Instruments (Babbitt),
    473
Compound meters, notation of, 47
Computers:
    as composing tool, 33
    and post-1950 music, 461, 464–467
    (See also Electronic music)
Concert overture, defined, 302
Concert spirituel, 192
Concertmaster, functions of, described, 77
Concerto:
    Classical, described, 206–207, 220,
        234–238(LO)
    solo, 150
Concerto for Cootie (Ellington), 500–502(LO)
Concerto for Orchestra (Bartók), 443–
    450(LO)
Concerto for Orchestra (Carter), 468
Concerto for Violin and Orchestra in E
    Minor, Op. 64 (Mendelssohn), 297–
    301(LO)
Concerto grosso:
    described, 128
    examples of, 129–131(LO), 157–158
    twentieth-century rediscovery of, 397

Concerto Grosso in A Minor, Op. 3, No. 8
    (Vivaldi), 150–152
Concerto No. 1 for Piano and Orchestra in
    E-flat Major (Liszt), 291–294
Concord Sonata (Ives), 452
Conductor(s):
    functions of, 75, 77
    of Romantic period, 268
    See also specific names
Confessions of an English Opium-Eater
    (DeQuincey), 258
Connotation (Copland), 458
Consonance:
    defined, 53
    dissonance and, 53–54, 417–418
    in twentieth-century music, 379, 417–
        418
Constable, John, 261
Contrabassoon:
    described, 18, 21
    in Romantic music, 265, 266
Contralto (alto), 10
    operatic categories of, 136–137
Contrapuntal texture (see Polyphonic tex-
    ture)
Contrast as form technique, 69
Cool jazz:
    described, 506
    leaders of, 506
Coolidge, Elizabeth Sprague, 386
Cooper, Alice, 519
Copland, Aaron, 373, 456–460
    Appalachian Spring, 380, 456, 458–460
    ballet scores, 458–460
    Billy the Kid, 456
    biographical sketch, 456–458
    connotations, 458
    jazz and, 480
    A Lincoln Portrait, 457
    Of Mice and Men, 456
    Music for the Theatre, 456
    Our Town, 456–457
    Piano Concerto, 377
    Piano Variations, 456
    portrait of, 457
    rhythmic innovations of, 382, 456–460
    Rodeo, 456
    and serial techniques, use of, 458
    "Simple Gifts," 458, 460
    twelve-tone system and, 462
Corelli, Arcangelo, 118, 125, 148–149
    Trio Sonata in E Minor, Op. 3, No. 7, 149
Cornet:
    described, 24
    in New Orleans jazz, 493
Coronation of Poppea, The (L'incoronazione di
    Poppea) (Monteverdi), 141
"Coronation Scene" from Boris Godunov
    (Mussorgsky), 314–316, 409
Così fan tutte (Mozart), 220
Cöthen, Prince of, 153

577

Council of Trent, effect on church music, 109
Count Basie Band, 503
Counterpoint, defined, 63
Counter-Reformation, 109
Countersubject in fugue, 132, 134
Country and Western music, rock and, 512
Couperin, François, 127
Courante, described, 160
Courbet, Gustave, 261
Cowell, Henry, biographer of Ives, 452
Craft, Robert, Stravinsky and, 399
Creation, The (Haydn), 211, 212
Creation of the World, The (La Création du monde) (Milhaud), 377
Creole Jazz Band, 494–496
   Dippermouth Blues, 495–496(LO)
Crescendo *(cresc.),* defined, 5
Crime and Punishment (Dostoevsky), 312
Critic, music: Berlioz as, 304
      Liszt as, 290
      Schoenberg as, 415
      Schumann as, 268
Crumb, George, 467, 475–477
Cui, César, 313
   (*See also* "Russian Five, The")
Cymbals:
   described, 24, 27
   in Romantic music, 265

Da capo aria, defined, 141
d'Agoult, Countess Marie, Liszt and, 290
Damnation of Faust, The (Berlioz), 305
Damper pedal (piano), 28, 395
Dance:
   African music for, 533–534
   ballet and twentieth-century music for, 385–386, 398–409
   (*See also* Ballet music)
   forms, Baroque, 160–162, 377, 397, 469
   in opera, 138
   Renaissance music for, 114–115
   rock music and, 520–521
Dance of Death (Totentanz) (Liszt), 291
"Dance of the Reed Pipes" from the *Nutcracker Suite* (Tchaikovsky), 70–71(LO)
Dance-related music, 114–115, 160–162, 190, 193, 201–204, 212–214, 287, 322–324, 377, 458–460
   Baroque dance forms, 160–162, 377, 397, 469
   Baroque suite, 160–162, 397
   Chopin and, 287
   minuet and trio, 201–204(LO)
   (*See also* Minuet and trio)
   polka, 323, 324
   waltz, 38, 307
   (*See also* Ballet music)
Dance suite, Baroque, 160–162, 397

Danmono, defined, 552
Danse Royale (estampie), 91
Dante Alighieri, influence on Liszt, 291
Dante Symphony (Liszt), 291
Daphnis et Chloé (Ravel), 386
Dave Brubeck Quartet, 506
David (Michelangelo), 103
David, Ferdinand, 297
David, Jacques Louis, 184, 186
Davis, Miles:
   and Coltrane, 508
   cool jazz and, 506
"Day in the Life, A" (Beatles), 524–525
Death of Sardanapalus, The (Delacroix), 258
Death of Socrates (David), 186
Debussy, Claude, 373, 389–396
   biographical sketch of, 389
   chords used by, 391–392, 395–396
   Clouds (Nuages), 390
   composition style, form and techniques, 373, 376–377, 386, 390–396
   as conductor, 390
   "Golliwog's Cake Walk" from *Children's Corner,* 377
   as Impressionist, 387, 389–393
   Javanese music and, 376, 389, 391
   Jeux, 386
   non-Western musical influences on, 376, 389, 391, 528
   Pagodes, 376
   Pelléas et Mélisande, 390, 392
   Prelude to "The Afternoon of a Faun" (Prélude à "L'Après-midi d'un faune"), 390–391, 393–394(LO)
   Reflections in the Water (Reflets dans l'eau), 390
   rhythmic flexibility of, 392
   Russian Ballet and, 398
   The Sounds and the Perfumes Swirl in the Evening Air (Les sons et les parfums tournent dans l'air du soir), 360
   String Quartet, 390
   The Sunken Cathedral (La Cathédrale engloutie), 387, 391, 395–396
   and symbolist poets, 387, 389, 392
   Voiles (Sails), 392
Debussy, Emma Bardac, 390
Decameron (Boccaccio), 96
Decrescendo *(decresc.),* defined, 5
Delacroix, Eugène, 258, 259
Demoiselles d'Avignon, Les (Picasso), 405–407
De Quincey, Thomas, 258
Development:
   defined, 194–195
   examples of, 198, 232(LO), 236(LO), 246, 250(LO), 299, 321–322(LO), 328(LO), 447
Diaghilev, Sergei:
   ballet company (Russian Ballet), 385–386, 398
   Stravinsky and, 398

Dichterliebe ("Poet's Love") (Schumann), 270, 280
Dickens, Charles, 261
Diderot, Denis, 184
Dido and Aeneas (Purcell), 144–147
   Dido's Lament, 145–146
   story of, 144–145
Dies irae (Penderecki), 469
Dikshitar, Muthuswamy, 544
   (*See also* Indian classical music)
Diminuendo *(dim.),* defined, 5
Diminution in fugue, defined, 133
Dippermouth Blues (Oliver/Creole Jazz Band), 490, 495–496(LO)
Disco dancing, 514, 521
Dissonance:
   of Beethoven, 242, 244
   consonance and, in atonality, 53–54, 417–418
   defined, 53
   in expressionistic music, 414
   of Ives, 453–455
   in twentieth-century music, 379
   (*See also* Atonality; Twelve-tone system)
Dixieland (*see* New Orleans style)
"Do Nothin' Till You Hear from Me" (Ellington), 501
Dodds, Johnny, 496
Dominant chord, defined, 54–55
Don Giovanni (Mozart), 219–230
   story of, 221
Don Juan (Strauss), as tone poem, 303
"Donna è mobile, La" from *Rigoletto* (Verdi), 341
Dorian mode, 88
   (*See also* Church modes)
Dorsey, Tommy, swing and, 497
Dostoevsky, Fëdor, 312
Dotted note, defined, 45
Dotted rhythm, defined, 45–46
Double bass ("bass fiddle"), 3, 14–15, 17
Double Concerto for harpsichord and piano with two chamber orchestras (Carter), 466, 468
Double-reed woodwinds, examples of, 22
Double stop, defined, 15
Downbeat, defined, 38
Dramatic legend, example of, 305
Dramatic soprano, defined, 137
Dramatic symphony, example of, 305
Dramatic tenor, defined, 137
"Dream of a Witches' Sabbath" from *Fantastic Symphony* (Berlioz), 263, 309–310
Dresden opera, Wagner and, 357
Drugs, rock music and, 520
"Drum Roll" Symphony No. 103 in E-flat Major (Haydn), 212–216, 245
Drums, 12, 24–25, 530
   African, 4, 12, 530, 534, 536, 538–541
   in bebop, 503
   Indian, 545, 547, 548

in jazz, 483, 485
pictured, 25, 534, 539, 548
pressure (African), 541
religious uses for, 12, 532–534
(*See also* Membranophones)
Dubbing, described, 77
Duchamp, Marcel, 375
Dudevant, Madame Aurore (George Sand), 283
Dukas, Paul, 303
Duple meter:
defined, 37
notation of, 47
Piano Quintet in A Major (*"Trout"*) (Schubert), Fourth Movement as example, 235–238
Durations (rhythmic values) in serialism, 463
Dvořák, Antonin, 312, 325–331
biographical sketch of, 325–326
Brahms and, 334
Slavonic Dances, 311
Symphony No. 9 in E Minor "From the New World" (*New World Symphony*), 326–331(LO)
Dylan, Bob:
pictured, 515
rock music and, 513, 514, 517
Dynamic accent, defined, 4
Dynamics:
Baroque, 121–122
Classical, and piano, 188–189
defined and described, 2, 4–5
examples of, 6–9(LO)
indications for, 5
in Romantic music, range of, 265–266
terraced, 121–122
Webern and, 439–440

Edo period in koto music, 551–552
Eine kleine Nachtmusik, K. 525 ("A Little Night Music") (Mozart), minuet from, 202–203(LO)
Einstein, Albert, influences of, 372
Electric guitar, use of, in rock, 515, 518
Electric piano, 464, 475, 476, 515
in jazz, 505
Electronic instruments, 31–33, 464–465
Electronic music:
Babbitt and, 473–474
described, 464–465
instruments used for, described, 31–33, 464–465
mixed media and, 466–467
rhythm and form in, 467
Electronic score, example of, 465
Elements of music, 1–80
dynamics, 2, 4–5
form, 68–72(LO)
harmony, 52–56

key, 56–62
media (instruments and voices), 9–35
melody, 47–52
notation, 41–47
performance, 73–78
pitch, 2–4, 24
rhythm, 35–40
sound properties, 2–9
style, 79–80
texture, 62–68
tone color, 2, 5–6
Elijah (Mendelssohn), 295
Eliot, T. S., as neoclassicist, 397
Elizabeth, Queen, 112
Elizabethan music, 111–114
(*See also* Renaissance music)
Ellington, Edward Kennedy "Duke":
Black, Brown, and Beige, 500
Concerto for Cootie, 500–502(LO)
and his orchestra, 500
"In a Sentimental Mood," 500
"Satin Doll," 500
"Sophisticated Lady," 500
swing and, 480, 497, 499–502
variety of works by, 501
"Elvis the Pelvis" (Elvis Presley), 512, 514, 519
Embellishments, defined, 73
Emerson, Lake, and Palmer (group), classical rock and, 514
"Empress of the Blues" (Bessie Smith), 488, 490–492
English horn:
described, 18, 19
in Romantic music, 265, 306
Ensemble in opera, defined, 137
(*See also* Chamber music)
Ensembles for Synthesizer (Babbitt), 473
Episodes (fugal), defined, 133
Equal temperament, defined, 157
Erasmus, Desiderius, 109
"Erlking, The" (*Erlkönig*) (Goethe-Schubert), 271, 273–276
"Eroica" Symphony No. 3 (Beethoven), 240, 242
Espressivo, defined, 55
Essays before a Sonata (Ives), 452
Esterházy, Prince Nicholas, 210
Esterházy family, patronage by, 209–211
Étude, defined, 286
Étude in C Minor, Op. 10, No. 12 (*Revolutionary*) (Chopin), 286–287
Etude II (Stockhausen), electronic score of, 465
Eugene Onegin (Tchaikovsky), 319
Euridice (Peri), 139
Evans, Gil, 506
"Ev'ry valley shall be exalted" from *Messiah* (Handel), 179
Exoticism in Romantic music, 263–264

Exposition:
defined, 195
examples of, 197, 232(LO), 235–236(LO), 246, 249(LO), 298, 321(LO), 327(LO), 447
Expressionism, 413–414
defined, 413
Schoenberg and, 415
Expressionist painters, influence of, 413–414

Falsetto in rock music, described, 516
Falstaff (Verdi), 340
Fantastic Symphony (Symphonie fantastique) (Berlioz), 263
inspiration for, 304
Liszt piano arrangements of, 288
orchestral effects in, 305
as programmatic music, 301, 302, 305–310
Fantasy in Romanticism, 258
Fantasy Pieces (Schumann), 280
Farandole from *L'Arlésienne Suite No. 2* (Bizet), 65–67(LO)
"Farewell" Symphony in F-sharp Minor (Haydn), 210
Faust (Goethe), 271
Faust Symphony (Liszt), 291
Fermata sign, 206
Fiddle in Middle Ages, 91
Fidelio (Beethoven), 244
Fifth String Quartet (Bartok), 386
Figured bass (*see* Basso continuo)
Fingal's Cave (*Hebrides* Overture) (Mendelssohn), 297, 302
Fingerboard of violin, described, 14–15
Finlandia (Sibelius), 311
Firebird, The (Stravinsky), 8, 398
Firebird Suite, 7–8(LO)
Firenze, Gherardello da, 96–97
Fitzgerald, Ella, swing and, 497
Five Piano Pieces, Op. 23, (Schoenberg), 418
Five Pieces for Orchestra, Op. 16 (Schoenberg), 414, 417, 421–423(LO)
Premonitions (Vorgefühle), 421–422
Summer Morning by a Lake: Colors (The Changing Chord), 421
Yesteryears (Vergangenes), 422–423(LO)
Five Pieces for Orchestra, Op. 10 (Webern), 414, 440–442(LO)
Third Piece, 441–442(LO)
Five-tone melodic pattern by Debussy, 376
(*See also* Pentatonic scale)
Fixed idea (*idée fixe*):
described, 306
examples of, 307–310
Flat sign, 44
Flute:
described, 18, 19

Flute:
  in jazz, 505, 506
  in *Prelude to "The Afternoon of a Faun,"*
    391, 394
Fokine, Mikhail, 398
Folk music:
  American, 325–331, 373, 452, 453, 456
  Bartók and, 373, 442–446
  in Classical music, 193
  Copland and, 456–460
  Dvořák and, 325–331
  English, 144
  influence on composers, 52, 162, 193, 208,
    212, 215, 220, 263, 311–314, 318, 323,
    325–326, 365–368, 373, 382, 400–401
  Ives and, 373, 452–455
  nationalism and, 263, 312–313, 318,
    322–324, 444–446
  popular and, in twentieth-century
    music, 373, 386
  (*See also* Black music; Jazz)
  Russian, 312–316, 318
Folk rock, 513
Fon (of Dohomey), 533
"For unto us a child is born" from *Messiah*
  (Handel), 180–181
Forelle, Die ("The Trout") (Schubert),
  278–279(LO)
Forlana, defined, 469
Form(s):
  in Baroque music, 124
  Classical, 190
  creating, techniques for, 68–69
  defined, 68
  in post-1950 music, 467, 505
  of rock music, 517
  in Romantic music, 266–267
  strophic, defined, 269
  through-composed, defined, 269–270
  types of, 69–72
  used by Beethoven, 242–244
  used by Stravinsky, 400–401
Forte (*f*), defined, 5
Fortissimo (*ff*), defined, 5
4'33" (Cage), 2, 463
Four Serious Songs (Brahms), 334
Fourteenth-century music, examples of, 96–99
  (*See also* Medieval music)
Fourth chord(s):
  defined, example of, 380
  Schoenberg use of, 417
Fourth String Quartet, Op. 37 (Schoenberg),
  386, 418
Fragmentation in expressionistic music, 414
Fragonard, Jean Honoré, 184, 185
Frankenstein (Shelley), 258
Frederick the Great, King of Prussia, 125, 127
Free jazz:
  Coleman and Coltrane as composers of,
    506–509
  described, 505–506

Free Jazz (Coleman), 506, 508
Freed, Alan, disc jockey, 520
French Academy of Science, The (Le Clerc),
  120
French horn:
  Beethoven use of, 243, 249, 252
  described, 22
  in jazz, 505, 506
  in orchestra, 23–24
  in Romantic music, 262, 368
French overture, 161
French Revolution, effects on music and
  musicians, 191, 311
Frequency tone, 3
  (*See also* Pitch)
Frère Jacques as round, 367–369
Freud, Sigmund:
  influence of, 372, 413
  Totem and Taboo, 407
Frog of bow, described, 15
"From where do you come, my love, my
  child?" ("Dance of the Sacred Life-
  Cycle") from *Ancient Voices of Children*
  (Crumb), 476
Front line, New Orleans jazz ensemble,
  493–494
Frug, the (rock dance), 520
Fugue, 131–135
  in Bartók concerto, 445–450
  defined, 131
  form, 132
  reinterpreted by Bartók, 444
  twentieth-century rediscovery of, 397
  variation techniques of, 133
Funérailles (Liszt), 291

Gabrieli, Andrea, 115
Galilei, Galileo, 118, 184
Galilei, Vincenzo, 139
Gallant style (*style galant*), 186
Game of Pairs from *Concerto for Orchestra*
  (Bartók), 448–449(LO)
Gamelan (Indonesian orchestra), 376
  described, 530
Gat, defined, 548
Gavotte, 161–162, 377
Georg Ludwig, Elector of Hanover, 173
George I, King, 173
George III, King, 216
German Requiem (Brahms), 334
Gershwin, George:
  Porgy and Bess, 377
  Rhapsody in Blue, 377
Gesamtkunstwerk, defined, 359
Gesualdo, Carlo:
  as madrigalist, 112
  rediscovery of, 377
Getz, Stan, 506
Gherardello da Firenze, 96–97
Giacosa, Giuseppe, 346

Giant Steps (Coltrane), 508
Gideon, Miriam, 474–475
Gigue:
  defined, 160
  example of, 162, 377
  in twelve-tone system, 397
Gillespie, Dizzy, 502
Girl Before a Mirror (Picasso), 375
Glinka, Mikhail, 312
Glissando:
  Bartók use of, 444–445
  defined, 378
  in Penderecki works, 469, 470
  on timpani, 444
Glockenspiel, 24, 26, 440
Godan-Ginuta (Mitsuzaki Kengyo), 553–
  554
Goethe, Johann Wolfgang von, 240
  Beethoven and, 240
  "The Erlking" (*Erlkönig*), 273–276
  Faust, 271
  Heidenröslein ("The Wild Rose"), 276–
    277
  Liszt influenced by, 291
  as poet for art songs, 269, 273, 276
"Golliwog's Cake Walk" from *Children's
  Corner* (Debussy), 377
Gong (tam-tam), described, 24, 27
Goodman, Benny, 20, 480
  swing and, 497
Gothic architecture, example of, 94
Gothic revival in Romantic era, 258
Götterdämmerung (Twilight of the Gods, The)
  (Wagner), 359–365
Goya, Francisco, 184, 192, 258
Graham, Martha, 458, 459
Grand opera, age of, 260, 338–365
Grand staff, defined, 42–43
Grave, defined, 39, 244
Grazioso, defined, 337
"Great" C Major Symphony (Schubert),
  273, 295
Great Depression, effects on composers,
  456
Gregorian chant, 87–90, 109, 391
  described, 87
  examples of, 89, 90
  and Jewish liturgical music, 88
  and organum, 93–96
  in Pope Marcellus Mass (Palestrina), 110
  and Renaissance motet, compared, 107
Gregory I, Pope, 88
"Gretchen at the Spinning Wheel"
  (*Gretchen am Spinnrade*) (Schubert),
  271
Grieg, Edvard, 312
Ground bass (basso ostinato or passacaglia):
  in Baroque music and blues, compared,
    490
  defined, 144
  examples of, 144–147, 337

Guerre, La (Janequin), 111
Guggenheim Foundation, 416
Guiraud, Ernest, 66*n.*
Guitar:
  in blues, 488
  described, 11, 18, 52
  in jazz, 482
  pictured, 17
  in rock, 513, 515, 518, 519, 523
Gurre-Lieder ("Songs of Gurre") (Schoenberg), 417

Hair (MacDermot), 513
Haley, Bill, and His Comets, 512, 517
Half step, defined, 57
"Hallelujah Chorus" from *Messiah* (Handel), 67–68(LO), 177
Handel, George Frederick, 118, 127, 128, 172–181
  biographical sketch, 172–174
  Brahms and, 332
  composition style and techniques, 174–181
  "Hallelujah Chorus" from *Messiah,* 67–68(LO)
  Israel in Egypt, 174
  Joshua, 174
  Judas Maccabaeus, 174
  Julius Caesar, 140
  Messiah, 172, 174, 176–181
  operas by, 173–176
  oratorios by, 174–181
  portrait of, 175
  Rinaldo, 173
  Saul, 174
Handy, William Christopher, 488
Hard Day's Night, A (movie), 522
Hard rock, 513
  (*See also* Rock music)
Hardin, Lillian (Armstrong, Lillian Hardin), 8, 494, 496
Harmonic minor, 59*n.*
Harmonic series, 568–569
"Harmonic Whim, The" (*L'Estro armonico*) (Vivaldi), 150
Harmonics:
  defined, 18
  and tone color, 568–569
Harmony:
  in African music, 535
  in Baroque music, 120–121
  in bebop, 502, 503
  in blues, 490
  chromatic, defined, 265
  and counterpoint, Bach and, 155, 159
  Debussy techniques, 389, 391–393
  defined, 52
  elements and examples of, 52–56
  in Indian classical music, 544
  in jazz, 485

in koto music, 552–553
in post-1950 jazz, 505
in Renaissance madrigal, 112
in rock music, 517
in Romantic music, 265
Stravinsky innovations in, 379, 400–401, 408, 410
twentieth-century developments in, 379–380, 400–401, 408, 410
[*See also* Chord(s); Twelve-tone system]
Harp:
  described and pictured, 17–18
  increased use of, in Romantic music, 265
  in Middle Ages, 91–92
Harpsichord:
  in Baroque period, 122, 129–131
  in Classical period, piano replacement of, 189
  continuo, example of, 144–145
  described, 28–30
  resurgent use of, 12
  as solo instrument, 129, 130–131(LO)
  twentieth-century use of, 12, 377, 468–469
Harpsichord Quartet of New York, 468
Harrison, George, 522
  non-Western musical influences on, 528
Hawkins, Coleman, 497
Haydn, Joseph:
  and Beethoven, 212, 238, 243, 244
  biographical sketch, 208–212
  Brahms and, 335
  as Classical composer, 187, 189–191, 199–201, 205, 208–216, 218, 221, 238, 242, 244, 245, 267
  composition styles and techniques of, 212–216
  The Creation, 211, 212
  "London (Salomon) Symphonies," 210–212
  and Mozart, 196, 210, 212, 218, 221
  popular symphonies of, 212
  portrait of, 211
  The Seasons, 211
  Symphony in F-sharp Minor *(Farewell),* 210
  Symphony No. 94 in G Major *(Surprise),* 199–201(LO), 212
  Symphony No. 103 in E-flat Major, *(Drum Roll),* 212–216, 245
Hebrides Overture *(Fingal's Cave)* (Mendelssohn), 297, 302
Heidenröslein ("The Wild Rose") (Goethe-Schubert), 276–277
"Heiligenstadt Testament, The," 240
Heine, Heinrich, 269, 283
"Hello Dolly!," 496
Hendrix, Jimi, 513, 518, 519
Henry IV, King of France, 139
Henry IV Receiving the Portrait of Maria de'Medici (Rubens), 119

Heroic ("helden") tenor, 360
Heterophonic texture in koto music, 553
Heterophony in non-Western music, 530, 553
Hieronymus Colleredo, Prince-Archbishop, 218
Highlife of West Africa, 531
Hindemith, Paul:
  as musicologist, 377
  as neoclassicist, 396
  as refugee, 386
Hindustani music (*see* Indian classical music)
Hinganyengisa masingita, 542
Hira-joshi koto tuning, 549
Hitler, Adolf, effects on musicians, 386, 442
  (*See also* Nazism)
Hogarth, William, 184
Holiday, Billie, 478, 497
Home key (tonic key), defined, 62
Homophonic texture:
  defined, 64–65
  in early Baroque, 121
  examples of, 66–68
  in lute song, 113
"Hotter Than That" (Armstrong), 8–9(LO), 496
Hugo, Victor, 258, 283, 304
Humanism, defined, 102
Hunchback of Notre Dame, The (Hugo), 258
Hungarian Rhapsodies (Liszt), 290
Hunting song, medieval, 96–97
Hustle, the (rock dance), 521

Idée fixe (fixed idea):
  described, 306
  examples of, 307–310
Idiophones:
  of Africa, 535–536
  defined, 530
  use of, 530
Illicà, Luigi, 346
Imaginary Landscape No. 4 (Cage), 463
Imitation:
  in Baroque music, 122
  described, 63
  in fourteenth-century music, 97
  in fugue, 131–135
  in Renaissance music, 105, 107, 110, 113, 115, 440
  in ricercar, 115
  in round, 64
  in Webern works, 440
Impression: Sunrise (Monet), 387
Impressionism:
  in art, 387
  characteristics of, 390
  expressionism as reaction against, 413
  in literature (symbolism), 387, 389

581

Impressionism:
  musical, 387–396
    Debussy as representative of, 389–396(LO)
    described, 390
    rhythm and, 392
Impressionist, defined, 387
Impromptus (Schubert), 273
Improvisation:
  Armstrong and, 496–497
  in Baroque music, 123, 157
  in bebop, 503–504
  of cadenza, 206, 297
  collective, 493–498
  Coltrane and, 507–509
  defined, 73
  in Indian classical music, 543
  in jazz (*see* Jazz, improvisation in)
  in non-Western music, 73, 529, 543
"In a Sentimental Mood" (Ellington), 500
Incidental music, described, 303
Indian classical music, 542–547
  composers, "musical trinity," 544
  elements of, 544–545
  improvisation in, 543
  influence of, on Western music, 376, 389, 391
  instruments, 546–547
  melodic structure (raga), 544–545
  performers, 543
  religious aspects of, 543
  rhythmic structure (tala), 545
  two branches of, 542
Indian Music, The Anthology of, 542n.
Industrial Revolution, Romanticism and, 261, 268
Instrumental music (*see specific periods and composers*)
Instruments:
  African, 530, 535–541
  brass, 22–24
  categories and descriptions of, 11–35
  classifications, 11
  defined, 11
  "electrified," 464
  electronic, 31–33, 464–465
  front-line, in New Orleans jazz, 493–494
  functions of, 12–14
  keyboard, 28–30
  non-Western, 529–530, 535–541, 546–547, 549–550
  orchestra (*see* Orchestra)
  percussion, 24–28
    (*See also* Percussion instruments)
  plucked-string, pictured, 92
  Renaissance, 115
  in rock music, 515–516
  string, 14–18
  unconventional, in modern works, 378, 440, 441, 465–466, 475, 476
  woodwind, 11, 13, 18–23
  (*See also specific instruments*)

International Society for Contemporary Music, 385
Interrupted Intermezzo from *Concerto for Orchestra* (Bartók), 449
Intervals:
  defined, 3
  in Indian raga, 544–545, 547
  on koto, 550, 552
  microtones, 466, 530
  quarter tones, 466
  steps, half and whole, 57–60
  steps and leaps, melodic, 48
Inversion:
  example of, 473
  in fugue, defined, 133
  in twelve-tone composition, 419–420
Ionisation (Varèse), 28, 378, 471
Israel in Egypt (Handel), 174
"It Was a Lover and His Lass" (Morley), 113–114
Italian Symphony (Mendelssohn), 297
Ivanhoe (Scott), 258
Ives, Charles, 373, 450–455
  biographical sketch of, 450–452
  The Cage, 380
  compositions, styles, forms and techniques of, 452–455
  Concord Sonata for piano, 452
  Essays before a Sonata, 452
  The Majority, 380
  114 Songs, 452
  portrait of, 451
  Schoenberg comments on, 452
  Second Piano Sonata ("Concord, Mass. 1840–60"), 452
  Third Symphony, Pulitzer Prize for, 452
  Three Places in New England, 453
    Putnam's Camp, Redding, Connecticut, 454–455
  The Unanswered Question for Chamber Orchestra, 453–454

Jam sessions in bebop, 502, 503
Janequin, Clément, 111
Japanese music for koto (*see* Koto music)
Japanese temple bells, 475
Javanese music, Debussy and, 376, 389, 391
Jazz, 52, 53, 480–509
  African elements in, 480
  as "American" art form, 377, 480–482
  Armstrong and, 8–9(LO), 496–497
  bands (*see* Jazz bands)
  bebop, 502–505
  blues, 482, 484–485, 488–492
  "breaks," 495
  Coltrane and, 506–509
  in Copland works, 456
  described, 480

elements of, 482–485
Ellington and (*see* Ellington, Edward Kennedy)
ensemble, rhythm section in, 482
forms (*see* Jazz forms)
free, described, 505–509
improvisation in, 9(LO), 52, 73, 480, 484, 493–498(LO), 503–504(LO), 506–509
influence of, 377
innovations in, since 1950, 505–509
instruments new to, 506
jam sessions, 502, 503
Joplin and, 487–488
musicians (*see specific musicians*)
New Orleans (Dixieland) style (*see* New Orleans style)
orchestral instruments in, 505
Parker and, 503–505(LO)
polyrhythms in, 383
post-1950 forms of, 505
ragtime (*see* Ragtime)
rhythm and blues, 512
rhythm section for, 482, 494, 503
rhythms of, in twentieth-century music, 377, 382, 400, 480
riffs, defined, 498
rock and, 506, 508
roots of, 480–482
Schuller and, 506
in society, 482
solo instruments used in, 482
in Stravinsky works, 377, 400
substyles of, 480
swing (*see* Swing)
syncopation as part of, 39, 382, 480, 482, 485, 487
"tag" defined, 495
third stream, 506
"Jazz Age," defined, 377
Jazz bands:
  Armstrong and His Hot Five, 8–9(LO), 496–497
  cool, 506
  elements of, 482–485
  influence of, 377
  New Orleans, 493–495(LO), 496–497
  sources of, 481
  swing, 497–502(LO)
Jazz forms:
  A A B A (thirty-two bar), 484, 499
  after 1950, 505–507
  call-and-response, 480
  improvisation as basis, 484
  in ragtime, 487
  theme-and-variation, 484
  twelve-bar blues, 489–490, 492, 495, 504–505(LO)
Jazz rock, 506, 513
  groups and performers of, 515
  (*See also* Jazz)

Je puis trop bien (Machaut), 98
Jefferson Airplane, 518
Jesu Juva (Bach), 153
Jeux (Debussy), 386
Jewish liturgical music, Gregorian chant and, 88
Jewish musicians, migration of, 386
   (*See also* Nazism)
Jhaptal, defined, 545
Johnson, Lonnie, 8
Jongleurs, functions of, 91
Joplin, Janis, 513, 518
Joplin, Scott, 487–488
   Maple Leaf Rag, 487–488
   pictured, 486
   Treemonisha, 487
Joshua (Handel), 174
Josquin des Prez:
   rediscovery of, 377
   Renaissance music and, 106–108
Judas Maccabaeus (Handel), 174
Julius Caesar (Handel), 140
"Jupiter" Symphony No. 41 in C (Mozart), 230

Kabuki theatre of Japan, 519
Kalimba (*see* Mbira)
Kandinsky, Wassily:
   expressionism and, 413
   influence of, 372, 376
Karnatak music (*see* Indian classical music)
Kengyō (master of koto), 552
Kengyō, Mitsuzaki, 553–554
Kengyō, Yatsuhashi, 552
Kengyō, Yoshizawa, 553
Kennedy, John F., 397
Kettledrums (*see* Timpani)
Key (tonality), 56–62
   in atonality, 417
   Debussy comments on, 391
   defined, 57
   equal temperament and, 157
   modulation, 61, 265
   principles of, 56–62, 381
   tonic (home, keynote), 62, 381
   twentieth-century alternatives to, 380–382, 417, 418
   (*See also* Atonality; Tonal system; Twelve-tone system)
Key changes (modulation) in Romantic music, 265
Key signature(s):
   defined, 60
   major and minor scale, 569
Keyboard instruments:
   in Baroque period, 122
   categories and descriptions of, 28–30
   (*See also specific instruments*)
Keynote (tonic), defined, 57
Kid Ory Band, 496
"King" Oliver (*see* Oliver, Joseph "King")

"King of Ragtime" (*see* Joplin, Scott)
"King of Swing" (*see* Goodman, Benny)
Kinsky, Prince of Austria, 241
Kirchner, Ernst Ludwig, 413, 414
   (*See also* Expressionism)
Kiss (rock group), 519
Klangfarbenmelodie, defined, 421
Knaben Wunderhorn, Des (The Boy's Magic Horn) (Mahler), 366
Köchel, Ludwig von, 220
KoKo (Parker), 503
Kokoschka, Oskar, 413
   (*See also* Expressionism)
Korean music, Japanese koto music and, 550
Koto, 549–552
   described, 549–550
   historical background of, 550–552
   pictured, 550
   tuning systems, 549–550
Koto music, 549–554
   elements of, 552–554
   forms of, 552
   historical background of, 551–552
   recordings of, listed, 549*n.*
   song cycles in, 552
   theme-and-variation form (*danmono*), 552
Koussevitsky, Serge, 445
Krupa, Gene, 498
Kumoi-joshi koto tuning, 550

Là ci darem la mano ("There you will give me your hand") from *Don Giovanni* (Mozart), 228–229
Language, African music and, 533
L'Après-midi d'un faune (The Afternoon of a Faun) (Mallarmé), 389
Larghetto, defined, 178
Larghetto e spiritoso, defined, 151
Largo, defined, 39
L'Arlésienne Suites No. 1 and *No. 2* (Bizet), 65–67(LO)
Leap (interval), defined, 48
LeClerc, Sebastien, 120
Le Corbusier, 471
Ledger lines, 42
Legato, defined, 48
Leipzig Conservatory, Mendelssohn as founder, 295
Leipzig Gewandhaus Orchestra, Mendelssohn as conductor, 295
Leitmotif (leading motive):
   described, 360
   examples of, 361, 364
Lennon, John, 522
   "Yesterday," 51(LO)
Leoncavallo, Ruggiero, 348
"Let's Dance" radio show, 497
"Liberation of sound, the," in post-1950 music, 465–466

Librettist:
   defined, 136
   for Puccini, 346
Libretto(s):
   defined, 136
   by Wagner, 358
Lichnowsky, Prince Carl, 240
Lied, lieder, 269
   (*See also* Art song)
Lied von der Erde, Das (The Song of the Earth) (Mahler), 366
Lieutenant Kije (Prokofiev), 386
Life for the Tsar, A (Glinka), 312
Lincoln Portrait, A (Copland), 457
L'incoronazione di Poppea (Monteverdi), 141
Line (melodic curve), defined, 48
Listening Outlines (LO):
   Brandenburg Concerto No. 5 in D Major (Bach), First Movement, 130–131
   Concerto for Cootie (Ellington), 501–502
   Concerto for Orchestra (Bartók):
     First Movement, 446–448
     Second Movement, 448–450
   Concerto for Violin and Orchestra in E Minor, Op. 64 (Mendelssohn), First Movement, 298–301
   "Dance of the Reed Pipes" from *Nutcracker Suite* (Tchaikovsky), 70–71
   Dippermouth Blues (Creole Jazz Band), 495–496
   Eine kleine Nachtmusik, K. 525 (Mozart), Third Movement, 202–203
   Farandole from *L'Arlésienne Suite No. 2* (Bizet), 65–67
   Firebird Suite (Stravinsky), Finale, 7–8
   "Hallelujah Chorus" from *Messiah* (Handel), 67–68
   "Hotter Than That" (Armstrong and His Hot Five), 8–9
   Lohengrin, Prelude to Act III (Wagner), 6–7
   "Lucy in the Sky with Diamonds" (Beatles), 524
   The Moldau (Vltava) (Smetana), 324–325
   Perhaps (Parker), 504–505
   Petrushka (Stravinsky), Opening scene, 403–405
   Piano Concerto in D Minor, K. 466 (Mozart), First Movement, 235–238
   Piano Quintet in A Major (*"Trout"*) (Schubert), Fourth Movement, 278–279
   Poème électronique ("Electronic Poem") (Varèse), 472
   Prelude in C Minor for Piano, Op. 28, No. 20 (Chopin), 7
   Prelude in C Minor from *The Well-Tempered Clavier*, Book 2 (Bach), 71–72
   Prelude to "The Afternoon of a Faun" (Debussy), 393–394

583

Listening Outlines (LO):
Romeo and Juliet, Overture-Fantasy (Tchaikovsky), 320–322
String Quartet in C Minor, Op. 18, No. 4 (Beethoven), Fourth Movement, 204
Symphony No. 1 in D Major (Mahler), Third Movement, 367–369
Symphony No. 5 in C Minor, Op. 67 (Beethoven):
    First Movement, 249–252
    Second Movement, 252–255
Symphony No. 9 in E Minor, "From the New World" (Dvořák):
    First movement, 326–328
    Second Movement, 328–331
Symphony No. 40 in G Minor, K. 550 (Mozart):
    First Movement, 231–233
    Fourth Movement, 196–198
Symphony No. 94 in G Major *(Surprise)* (Haydn), Second Movement, 199–201
Third Piece from *Five Pieces for Orchestra,* Op. 10 (Webern), 441–442
Threnody for the Victims of Hiroshima for 52 strings (Penderecki), 470
Yesteryears (Vergangenes) from *Five Pieces for Orchestra,* Op. 16 (Schoenberg), 423
Liszt, Franz, 262, 288–294
    biographical sketch of, 288–290
    Brahms and, 288, 332
    composition style, form and technique, 290–294
    Concerto No. 1 for Piano and Orchestra in E-flat Major, 266, 291–294
    as conductor, 288
    Dance of Death (Totentanz), 291
    Dante Symphony, 291
    Faust Symphony, 291
    Funérailles, 291
    Hungarian Rhapsodies, 290
    literary efforts of, 289
    Mephisto Waltz, 291
    Paganini transcriptions for piano, 288
    portrait of, 289
    Les Préludes, 290–291, 303
    Transcendental Études, 288
    Schumann on, 288
    Smetana and, 323
    as virtuoso, 268
Little Richard, 512
Lobkowitz, Prince of Austria, 241
Lohengrin, Prelude to Act III (Wagner), 6–7(LO), 138
London, eighteenth-century music in, 210
London Philharmonic Society, 268
"London Symphonies" (Haydn), 210–212
Lorca, Federico Garcia, 475
"Lost Your Head Blues" (Smith), 489–492

Loudness, defined, 4
    (*See also* Dynamics)
Louis XIV, King, Baroque music and, 118
Louis XV, King, Classical music and, 216
"Lucy in the Sky with Diamonds" (Beatles), 524(LO)
Ludwig, Georg, Elector of Hanover, 173
Ludwig, King of Bavaria, 359
Lully, Jean Baptist, 126
Lulu (Berg), 427
Lute:
    in Middle Ages, 91, 92
    non-Western versions of, 529, 546, 547, 549–550
    in Renaissance, 113, 114
Lute song (ayre), described, 113–114
Luther, Martin, 102, 107
Lutheran church service, music in, 162–163
Lyric soprano, defined, 137
Lyric Suite (Berg), 427
Lyric tenor, defined, 137

Má Vlast (My Country) (Smetana), 323
Macbeth (Verdi), 319
McCartney, Paul, 522
    "Yesterday," 51
MacDermot, Galt, 513
Machaut, Guillaume de, 86, 97–99
    Je puis trop bien, 98
    Notre Dame Mass, 98–99
    rediscovery of, 377
Madame Butterfly (Puccini), 264, 346, 348
Madamina ("Catalogue Aria") from *Don Giovanni* (Mozart), 226–228
Madonna and Child with Two Angels, The (Lippi), 104
Madrigal, Renaissance, 112–113
Maeterlinck, Maurice, 392
Magic Flute, The (Mozart), 219, 220
Magical Mystery Tour (Beatles), 522
Mahler, Gustav, 262, 264, 365–369
    biographical sketch, 365
    The Boy's Magic Horn (Des Knaben Wunderhorn), 366
    brass instruments in orchestra, 264
    compositions, style, form and technique, 366–369
    as conductor composer, 268
    as director of New York Philharmonic Orchestra, 366
    The Song of the Earth (Das Lied von der Erde), 366
    Symphony No. 1 in D Major, Third Movement, 367–369(LO)
    Symphony No. 8 ("Symphony of a Thousand"), 366
Major scale:
    church mode and, 88, 120
    described, 57–59

key signatures, 569
and minor scale, twentieth-century use of, 381
Majority, The (Ives), 380
Mallarmé, Stéphane, 387, 389, 392
Mandolin, Romantic and twentieth-century use of, 366, 475
Manon Lescaut (Puccini), 346
Maple Leaf Rag (Joplin), 487–488
Marche slave (Tchaikovsky), 319
Marenzio, Luca, 112
Margrave of Brandenburg, 129
Maria Theresa, Empress, 216
Marimba, described, 24
Marriage of Figaro, The (Mozart), 218–220, 229
Maru-Bihag (Shankar), 547–549
    melodic forms of, 547
"Mary Had a Little Lamb," notation of, 43
Mascagni, Pietro, 346
Mashed Potato, The (rock dance), 520
Mass:
    in B Minor (Bach), 158–160
    Notre Dame (Machaut), 98–99
    Palestrina and, 108–110
    Pope Marcellus (Palestrina), 109–110
    Renaissance, 108–110, 159
Mass in B Minor (Bach), 158–160
    and Renaissance Masses, compared, 159
Mass Ordinary, described, 98
Mastersingers of Nuremburg, The (Wagner), 359
Mayuri, described, 531
Mbira ("thumb piano"):
    described, 535–536
    pictured, 537
Measure, defined, 37
Measured rhythm, 94–96
Meck, Nadishda von:
    Debussy and, 389
    Tchaikovsky and, 318
Medici, Marie de', 139
Medieval church modes, 88–90
    Debussy use of, 391
Medieval music, 84–99
    chant, notation of, 90
    church modes, 88, 391
    church music, 84, 87–90, 93–96, 98–99
    Danse Royale, 91
    in fourteenth century ("new art"), 96–99
    Gregorian chant (*see* Gregorian chant)
    and instruments, use of, 84, 91, 92
    Mass Ordinary, 98
    Notre Dame Mass, 98–99
    organum, 93–96
    and polyphony, development of, 93–96
    Renaissance and, compared, 105–106
    Romanticism and, 258
    School of Notre Dame, 94–96
    secular, 91–92, 96–98
    sociocultural elements in, 84–86
    twentieth-century rediscovery of, 377

584

Meeting, The (Fragonard), 185
Melodic curve, defined, 48
Melodic minor, defined, 59*n.*
Melody, 47–52
    Baroque, 121
    in bebop, 503
    Classical, 188
    defined, 48
    "fixed" (*cantus firmus*), 95
    Indian principles of (raga), 544–545
    in Ives work, 452–455
    in jazz, 485
    nationalism and, 311–316
    in non-Western music, 530, 544–545
    Renaissance, 106
    in rock music, 517
    Romantic preference for, 262
    in twentieth-century music, 384
    (*See also* Twelve-tone system)
Membranophones:
    defined, 530
    uses of, 536, 538, 541
    (*See also* Drums; Percussion instru-
        ments; *specific instruments*)
"Memphis Blues" (Handy), 488
Mendelssohn, Felix, 155, 262, 295–301
    biographical sketch of, 295
    Concerto for Violin and Orchestra in E
        Minor, Op. 64, 297–301(LO)
    as conductor-composer, 268, 295
    Elijah, 295
    Hebrides Overture (*Fingal's Cave*), 297,
        302
    Italian Symphony, 297
    A Midsummer Night's Dream, 319
        Overture, 295
    music of, 297–301
    portrait of, 296
    Scotch Symphony, 297
    Songs Without Words, 297
    Trio in D Minor for Violin, Cello, and
        Piano, 297
Mendelssohn, Moses, 295
Menotti, Gian Carlo, 385
Menuetto (*see* Minuet and trio)
Mephisto Waltz (Liszt), 291
Merchant of Venice, The (Shakespeare), 103
Merriam, Alan P., 533
Messiaen, Olivier:
    influenced by Indian music, 376
    serialism and, 463
Messiah (Handel), 172, 174, 176–181
    "And the glory of the Lord shall be re-
        vealed," 180
    "Hallelujah Chorus," 67–68(LO), 177
Meter:
    in Bartók works, irregular, 444
    in cool jazz, 506
    in Copland works, changing, 457
    defined, 37
    in Gregorian chant, absent, 87–88

    in Indian raga, 545
    notation, 47
    patterns, 37–38
    in post-1950 jazz, 505
    and twentieth-century rhythmic innova-
        tions, 382–383, 446
Meter signature, 47
Metrical modulation, defined, 468
Metronome, described, 40
Metropolitan Opera:
    broadcasts, 385
    Mahler as conductor of, 366
Mezzo forte *(mf)*, defined, 5
Mezzo piano *(mp)*, defined, 5
Mezzo-soprano (voice):
    described, 10
    modern vocalise for, 475
    operatic categories of, 137
Michelangelo Buonarroti, 103
Microtones:
    electronic music and, 466
    in non-Western music, 530
Middle Ages, 79, 84–99
    Romanticism and, 258
    sociocultural background, 84–86
    (*See also* Medieval music)
Middle C, 41, 43
Midsummer Night's Dream, A (Men-
    delssohn), 295, 319
    Overture, 295
Milhaud, Darius:
    *The Creation of the World (La Création du
        monde)*, 377
    jazz and, 480
"Military" Symphony No. 100 (Haydn), 212
Miller, Glen, 497
Minor scale:
    church mode and, 88, 120
    described, 59–60
    key signatures, 569
    and major scale, twentieth-century use
        of, 381
    types of, 59*n.*
Minton's Playhouse, bebop and, 502
Minuet and trio (minuet), 201–302
    examples of, 202–203(LO), 215, 233–
        234(LO)
    in twelve-tone system, 397
Missa solemnis ("Solemn Mass")
    (Beethoven), 242, 244
Mitamba Yalagala Kumchuzi, 542
Mixed-media presentations, 466–467
Modes, 88–90, 115, 508
    Aeolian and Dorian, examples of, 88
    [*See also* Church modes; Scale(s)]
Modulation:
    defined, 61
    metrical, defined, 468
    in Romantic music, 265
Moldau, The (Vltava) (Smetana), 264,
    323–325(LO)

    as program music, 264, 301
    as tone poem, 303
Molto, defined, 39
Moments musicaux ("Musical Moments")
    (Schubert), 273
Monet, Claude, 387, 388
Monk, Thelonious, 502
Monkey, the (rock dance), 520
Monophonic texture:
    defined, 62–63
    examples of, 66–68, 88–90
    Gregorian chant as, 87
Monteverdi, Claudio, 118, 141–143
    *Coronation of Poppea (L'incoronazione di
        Poppea)*, 141
    Orfeo, 139, 141–143
Morley, Thomas, 111, 113–114
Morrison, Jim, 513
Morton, Ferdinand "Jelly Roll," 493
Moses and Aron (Schoenberg), 418
Motet, Renaissance, 106–108
Motion pictures, scores for, 386
Motives (fragments), described, 195
"Motown" music, described, 512
Mouthpiece for brass instruments, 23
Movement, defined, 124
Mozart, Wolfgang Amadeus, 187, 216–
    238
    Abduction from the Seraglio, The, 218
    and Beethoven, 242–244
    biographical sketch of, 216–219
    Brahms and, 332
    as Classical composer, 187, 189–191,
        193–194, 196–197, 202–203,
        205–207
    and Classical concerto, 220, 234–237(LO)
    composition forms, style, and
        techniques, 219–238
    Concerto for Clarinet, K. 622, 220
    Così fan tutte, 220
    Don Giovanni, 219–230
    Eine kleine Nachtmusik, K. 525 ("A Little
        Night Music"), Minuet, 202–
        203(LO)
    and Haydn, 196, 210, 212, 218, 221
    The Magic Flute, 219, 220
    The Marriage of Figaro, 218–220, 229
    Piano Concerto in D Minor, K. 466, 207,
        220, 234–238(LO)
    portrait of, 217
    Requiem, 219, 283
    Symphony No. 40 in G Minor, K. 550,
        196–198(LO), 220, 230–234(LO)
Mridangam (tabla), described, 547
Music director, role of, in Baroque period,
    125
Music drama (Wagnerian), described,
    359–360, 389
Music notation (*see* Notation)
Music for Strings, Percussion and Celeste (Bar-
    tók), 378, 444

585

Music for the Theatre (Copland), 456
Musical form [*see* Form(s)]
Musical instruments (*see* Instruments)
"Musical saw," defined, 475
Musical texture (*see* Texture)
Musicians:
  "classical" and jazz, compared, 484
  social status of: in Baroque period, 123,
    125–128
    in Classical period, 191–193
    in Hitler's Germany, 386, 442
    (*See also* Nazism)
    in Middle Ages, 84, 88, 91
    in Renaissance, 102–103, 105, 111
    in twentieth century, 384–386
    (*See also specific names*)
Mussorgsky, Modest:
  biographical sketch of, 313
  Boris Godunov, 313–316, 409
  classical rock and, 515
  Night on Bald Mountain, 313
  Pictures at an Exhibition, 302, 313
  "The Russian Five" and, 312, 313
Mute:
  for brass instruments, 22, 24
  for string instruments, 15
My Country (Má Vlast) (Smetana), 323

Nabucco (Verdi), 339
Napoleonic Wars, Romantic music and,
  311
Nashville Grand Ole Opry, 512
Nationalism:
  and exoticism, in Romantic music,
    263–264
  and folk music, 263, 312–313, 318,
    322–324, 444–446
  leading composers affected by, 312
  in nineteenth-century music, 311–316
  in Romantic music (*see* Romantic music,
    nationalism in)
  Russian music and, 312–313
Natural sign, 44
Nazism, impact on music and musicians,
  312, 386, 415, 424, 439, 442, 462, 469
NBC Symphony Orchestra, 385
Neobaroque (*see* Neoclassicism)
Neoclassical style:
  in art, example of, 186
  described, 184, 186
Neoclassicism:
  in art and literature, 397
  composers reflective of, 396–397
  features of, in *Symphony of Psalms*
    (Stravinsky), 410
  Romanticism as rebellion against, 258
  in twentieth century, described, 396–
    397, 410
"New art" (*ars nova*), 96–99
New Journal of Music, Schumann and, 280

New Orleans (Dixieland) style, 480, 482,
    493–497
  described, 493
  examples of, 490, 495–496(LO)
  front line in ensemble, 493–494
  (*See also* Jazz)
New World Symphony (Symphony No. 9 in E
    Minor) (Dvořák), 326–331(LO)
New York Philharmonic Orchestra, 13, 14
  Bernstein as conductor, 385
  Mahler as director, 366
Newton, Sir Isaac, 118, 184
Nicolai, Philipp, 164
"Night music":
  Bartók and, 444
  described, 449
Night on Bald Mountain (Mussorgsky), 313
Night Pieces (Schumann), 280
Nijinsky, Vaslav, 398
Nketia, J. H. Kwabena, 535
Nocturne, defined, 285
Nocturne in E-flat Major, Op. 9, No. 2
    (Chopin), 285–286
Nolde, Emil, 413
  (*See also* Expressionism)
Nonsense syllables in rock music, 516
Non troppo, defined, 39
Non-Western music, 528–554
  African (*see* African music)
  improvisation in, 73, 529, 543
  Indian (*see* Indian classical music)
  instruments for, 529–530, 535–541,
    546–547, 549–550
  Japanese (*see* Koto music)
  melody in, 530, 544–545
  notation of, 528
  oral tradition of, 528
  rhythm in, 530–531
  texture in, 530–531
  and Western music, interaction
    between, 531
  (*See also specific nations*)
Notation, 41–47
  defined, 41
  in fourteenth century, 96
  of jazz, difficulty of, 485
  of medieval chant, 90
  in non-Western music, 528
  of pitch, 41–44
  of rhythm, 44–46
  for *Sprechstimme,* 418
Note, defined, 42
Note-against-note style, 94
Notre Dame Mass (Machaut), 86, 98–99
Notre Dame polyphony, examples of,
    95–96
Notre Dame School, 94–95
Nuages (Clouds) (Debussy), 390
Nude Descending the Staircase No. 2
    (Duchamp), 375
Nutcracker, The (Tchaikovsky), 70, 319

Nutcracker Suite, the (Tchaikovsky), 70, 319
  Dance of the Reed Pipes, 70–71(LO)

Oberto (Verdi), 338
Oboe, described, 18, 19
Octave, described, 3–4
"Ode to Joy," (Schiller), 243
Oedipus Rex (Stravinsky), 400
Of Mice and Men (Copland), 456
"Old Adam's Fall" (*Durch Adams Fall*)
    (Bach), 155
Oliver, Joseph "King," 493, 494
  Armstrong and, 496
  Dippermouth Blues, 490, 495–496(LO)
114 Songs (Ives), 452
Opera:
  Baroque (*see* Baroque opera)
  by Beethoven, 244
  by Berg, 427–438
  by Berlioz, 305
  characters, range of, 136
  comic (*buffo*), 192–193, 219–230
  by Debussy, 390, 392
  defined, 135
  elements of, 135–138
  grand, age of, 260, 338–365
  by Handel, 173–176
  by Mozart, 218–230
  nationalistic, example of, 313–316
  and oratorio, compared, 172
  overture, defined, 138
  by Puccini, 346–356
  rock, 513
  Royal Academy of Music, 173
  by Schoenberg, 418
  by Tchaikovsky, 319
  Venetian, 140
  by Verdi, 319, 340–346
  voice categories for, 136–137
  by Wagner, 357–365
  (*See also specific composers and opera titles*)
Opera and Drama (Wagner), 358
Opera of the Nobility, The, 173
Opus, defined, 7*n.*
Oratorio:
  advantages of, 174
  Baroque, 172, 174–181
  Classical, 211, 212
  described, 172
  Handel and, 174–181
  origins of, 172
Orchestra:
  Baroque, 123
  Classical, 189–190
    and Romantic, compared, 264
  conducted by Wagner, 357
  for *Fantastic Symphony* (Berlioz), 305–
    310
  Indonesian (gamelan), 530
  instrumental distribution in, 13

instrumental sections in standard, 13, 123, 189–190, 264–265
Mahler use of, 366
neoclassical features of, 410
opera, 138
in *Requiem* (Berlioz), 305
for *Rite of Spring* (Stravinsky), 407
in Romantic music, 264–265
seating plan (sample), 14
Tchaikovsky treatment of, 319
twentieth-century tone color of, 378
in Wagnerian opera, 360
(See also specific orchestra)
Orchestral Piece, Op. 10, No. 3 (Webern), 378
Orchestral score *(see* Score)
Orchestration:
by Berlioz, 305–310
in Romantic music, 264–265
Orfeo (Monteverdi), 139, 141–143
Organ:
in Baroque period, 122
described, 28, 30
history of, 30
in Middle Ages, 84
Organ Fugue in G Minor ("Little" Fugue) (Bach), 133–135
Organum, 93–96
defined, 93
Original Dixieland Band, 480
Ornaments (embellishments), 73
Ory, Kid, 496
Ostinato:
defined, 383–384
role of, examples of, 422–423
Stravinsky use of, 400, 410
Otello (Verdi), 319, 340
Ottoboni, Cardinal, 148
Our Town (Copland), 456–457
Overture:
concert, 302
French, 161
to opera, described, 138
Overture 1812 (Tchaikovsky), 302, 319

Paganini, Niccolò:
Liszt piano transcriptions of works of, 288
as virtuoso, 268
Pagliacci, I ("The Clowns") (Leoncavallo), 348
Pagodes (Debussy), 376
Palestrina, Giovanni Pierluigi da, 108–110
Pope Marcellus Mass, 109–110
Parallel chords:
in African music, 535
described, in Debussy works, 391
Paris as music and art center, 282, 288
Paris International Exhibition of 1889, 376, 389, 391

Paris Opera, Wagner and, 359
Parker, Charlie "Bird", 480, 503–505(LO)
bebop and, 502
KoKo, 503
Perhaps, 490, 504–505(LO)
Parker, Horatio, 450
"Parlor piano," 12
Parsifal (Wagner), 359
Passacaglia *(see* Ground bass)
Patronage:
aristrocratic, 103, 125–129, 139, 153, 173–174, 191–194, 209–211, 216, 218, 240, 241
church, 103, 125–128, 153–154
in eighteenth century, 191–194, 209–212
Esterházy family and, 209–211
of Haydn, 209–212
Mme. von Meck and, 318, 389
and middle-class market, growth of, 192–194, 207–208, 267–268
opera-house, commecial, 126–127
town, 126–127
(See also Musicians, social status of)
Pavarotti, Luciano, 11
Pedal point (organ point), defined, 133
Pedals, piano, 28
Pegs of violin, 14–15
Pelléas et Mélisande (Debussy), 390, 392
Penderecki, Krzysztof:
Dies irae, 469
electronic music and, 466
St. Luke Passon, 469
Threnody for the Victims of Hiroshima, 469–470(LO)
Pentatonic scale:
Debussy use of, 376, 391–392
described, 392
in koto music, 552
Peppermint Lounge, dances associated with, 521
Percussion instruments:
in African music, 28, 530, 532–541
Bartók use of, 444
in Classical orchestra, 190
classification and descriptions of, 11, 13, 24–28
Copland use of, 457
of definite and indefinite pitch, 24
distribution in orchestra, 13
Ionisation (Varèse) for, 471
in jazz and rock, 28, 480, 482, 485, 494, 498, 503, 515
Stravinsky use of, 401–405, 409
in twentieth-century music, 372, 378
(See also Membranophones; *specific instruments)*
Performance, 73–78
conductor, 75, 77
evaluation of, 78
performer and, 73–75
recorded and live, 77–78

Performer, 73–75
jazz and "classical," compared, 484
operatic, 135–136
Renaissance effect on, 105
(See also specific names)
Pergolesi, Giovanni Battista, 400
Perhaps (Parker), 490, 504–505(LO)
Peri, Jacopo, 139
Pérotin:
Alleluya Nativitas, 95–96
rediscovery of, 377
Petrushka (Stravinsky), 381, 386, 398, 400–402
Opening Scene, 403–405(LO)
"Petrushka chord," defined, 401
Philharmonische Konzerte, 268
Philips Radio Corporation, 471
Philomel for soprano, recorded soprano, and synthesized tape (Babbitt), 473
Phrases, defined, 48
Pianissimo *(pp)*, defined, 5
Piano, 3, 7, 12, 28
accompaniment, in art songs, 273
Bartók use of, 444
Chopin and, 283–287
in Classical era, 189, 220, 243
damper pedal, 28, 395
described, 28–29
development, 28
"electric," 464, 475, 476, 505, 515
as harpsichord replacement, 189
history, 28
improvements, 265
innovations by Debussy, 391, 395–396
Liszt and, 288, 290
pedals, described, 28
percussive use of, 378
in Romantic era, 265, 266, 268, 273, 283–287, 288, 290
seven-tone scale on, 4
as status symbol, 12
toy, as unconventional instrument, 475, 476
Piano *(p)*, defined, 5
Piano Concerto (Carter), 468
Piano Concerto (Copland), 377
Piano Concerto in D Minor, K. 466 (Mozart), 207, 220, 234–238(LO)
Piano Concerto in E-flat Major (Liszt), 266
Piano Concerto No. 1 in B-flat Minor (Tchaikovsky), 319
Piano Piece No. 11 (Stockhausen), 464
Piano Quintet in A Major *("Trout")* (Schubert), Fourth Movement, 278–279(LO)
Piano rags *(see* Joplin, Scott; Ragtime)
Piano Sonata in B-flat Minor (Chopin), 283
Piano Sonata in C Minor, Op. 13 *(Pathétique)* (Beethoven), 244–247
Piano trio, defined, 208
Piano Variations (Copland), 456

Picasso, Pablo, 370, 375
  Les Demoiselles d'Avignon, 405–407
  as influence, 372
  as neoclassicist, 397
Piccolo:
  in Classical symphonies, 243
  described, use of, 18, 19
  in Romantic music, 265, 266, 306
Picture with White Border, No. 173 (Kandinsky), 376
Pictures at an Exhibition (Mussorgsky-Ravel), 313
  classical rock version of, 514–515
  as program music, 302
Pierrot lunaire, Op. 21 ("Moonstruck Pierrot") (Schoenberg), 417–418
Pipe organ (*see* Organ)
Pique Dame (The Queen of Spades) (Tchaikovsky), 319
Pissaro, Camille, 387
Pitch:
  defined, 2
  definite and indefinite, 3–4, 24
  notation, 41–44
  organization [*see* Chord(s); Key; Tonal system]
  and tension, 14
  in twentieth century, 372
Pitch inflections in jazz, variety of, 484
Pitch range:
  defined, 4
  and register, 12
  in Romantic music, 266
  of voices, 4, 10, 136–137
Pitch regulation of brass instruments, 24
Pizzicato:
  Bartók use of, 444–445
  defined, 15
Planer, Minna (Wagner, Minna Planer), 357
Platters, The, 512
Plectra on harpsichord, 30
Plucked-string instruments:
  non-Western, 529, 546–547, 549–550
  Western, 17–18, 91–92, 113, 114, 265
  (*See also specific instruments*)
Poco più animato, defined, 336
Poe, Edgar Allan, 258
Poème électronique ("Electronic Poem") (Varèse), 466, 470–472(LO)
Poet's Love (Schumann), 270, 280
"Pointillist" music, 462
Polonaise, defined, 287
Polonaise in A-flat Major, Op. 53 (Chopin), 287
Polychords:
  Copland use of, 457
  described, examples of, 379–380, 408
Polyphonic texture:
  in Bach works, 155
  in Classical music, 184

described, 63–64
examples of, 66–68(LO), 109, 110, 334–338
in late-Baroque music, 121
in Mahler works, 366
medieval development of, 93–96, 98–99
in Pope Marcellus Mass (Palestrina), 109–110
of Renaissance music, 105–106, 114–115
in sonata-form development, 195
Polyphony:
  defined, 63–64
  medieval development of, 93–96
  (*See also* Polyphonic texture)
Polyrhythm:
  Copland use of, 457
  defined, 383
  in Ives's work, 452–455
  in *Petrushka* (Stravinsky), 402
Polytonality:
  defined, 381
  in Ives' work, 452–455
Pope Marcellus Mass (Palestrina), 109–110
Porgy and Bess (Gershwin), 377
Postlude in art song, 269
Pre-Classical period, defined, 184
Prelude:
  chorale, 163
  and fugue, 133
  opera, 6–7(LO), 138
  short piano piece, 7(LO), 55–56
Prelude in C Minor for Piano, Op. 28, No. 20 (Chopin), 7(LO)
Prelude in C Minor from *The Well-Tempered Clavier, Book 2* (Bach), 71–72(LO)
Prelude in E Minor for Piano, Op. 28, No. 4 (Chopin), 55–56(LO)
Prelude to Act III (*Lohengrin*) (Wagner), 6–7(LO), 138
Prelude to "The Afternoon of a Faun" (Prélude à "L'Après-midi d'un faune") (Debussy), 390–391, 393–394(LO)
Préludes, Les (Liszt), 290–291, 303
Preludes for piano, Book I (Debussy) (see *The Sunken Cathedral*)
Premonitions (Vorgefühle) from *Five Pieces for Orchestra*, Op. 16 (Schoenberg), 421–422
Presley, Elvis, 512, 519
  pictured, 514
Pressure drum, 539, 541
Prestissimo, defined, 39
Presto, defined, 39
Primitivism, 399
  defined, examples of, 407
  The Rite of Spring (Stravinsky) as example, 400

Printing, invention of, 102
  impact on Renaissance music, 102, 111
Program, defined, 301
Program music:
  of Berlioz, 301, 305–310
  described, 264, 301
  form, 302–303
  Liszt innovations in, 290–291, 302–303
  of Mahler, 366–369
  orchestral, forms of, 302
  Romantic, 264, 290–291, 301–310
  of Smetana, 264, 301
  symphonic poem, 302–303
  of Tchaikovsky, 264, 301–302
Program symphony, defined, 302
Progression, defined, 52
Prokofiev, Sergei:
  Classical Symphony, 377
  Lieutenant Kije, 386
  Russian Ballet and, 398
Prompter, role of, 137
Prussia, King of, and Handel, 173
Prussian Academy of Arts (Berlin), 415
Psychedelic rock, 513
Puccini, Giacomo, 346–356
  biographical sketch, 346
  La Bohéme, 346, 348–356
  Madame Butterfly, 264, 346, 348
  Manon Lescaut, 346
  portrait of, 347
  Tosca, 346
  Turandot, 346, 348
Pulcinella (Stravinsky) as neoclassical work, 397
  from Pergolesi themes, 400
Purcell, Henry, 33, 118, 127, 143–147
  Britten use of theme, 377
  Dido and Aeneas, 144–147
  rediscovery of, 377
Pushkin, Alexander, 313
Putnam's Camp, Redding, Connecticut from *Three Places in New England* (Ives), 454–455

Quadruple meter:
  Brandenburg Concerto No. 5 in D Major (Bach), First Movement as example, 130–131
  defined, 38
  notation, 47
Quadruple stop, defined, 15
Quantz, Johann, 125
Questions on Nature (Gideon), 474
Quintuple meter, defined, 38

Radio broadcasts:
  effects on music world, 385
  rock spread through, 520

Raga:
  defined and illustrated, 544–545
  example of, 547–549
Raga rock, 513
Ragtime, 373, 485–488
  defined, 482, 485, 487
  elements of: in Copland works, 456
    in Ives' works, 452
    in Stravinsky works, 377
  Joplin innovations in, 487–488
  rhythms, use of, 400
"Ragtime" from *The Soldier's Tale*
    (Stravinsky), 377
Rake's Progress, The (Stravinsky), 400
Rameau, Jean-Philippe, 127
Range (*see* Pitch range)
Ravel, Maurice:
  Daphnis et Chloé, 386
  Debussy and, compared as impres-
    sionists, 392
  jazz and, 480
  Pictures at an Exhibition arranged by, 313
  Russian Ballet and, 398
Recapitulation:
  defined, 194–195
  described, 196
  examples of, 198, 232–233(LO), 236–
    237(LO), 246, 251(LO), 299,
    322(LO), 328(LO), 447
Recitative:
  accompanied, described, 170
  and aria, by Puccini, 346
  defined, 137
  development of, 139
  examples of, 146–147, 164, 168
  secco (dry), defined, 168
  Tu se' morta from *Orfeo* (Monteverdi),
    142–143
Recorder:
  described, 21, 22
  in Renaissance ricercar music, 115
  resurgent use of, 12
Recording:
  dubbing and, 77
  and live performances, 77–78
  long-playing, effects of, 118, 385, 462
  multitrack, 520
  rock music, 520
  twentieth-century repertory, 77, 385
Reed, woodwind, defined, 22
Reflections in the Water (Reflets dans l'eau)
    (Debussy), 390
Register:
  bass, first use of, 105
  defined, 12
  use of, by Webern, 440
Rembrandt van Rijn, 118
Renaissance Mass, 106, 108–110, 159
Renaissance music, 102–115
  choral, 103, 106–110
  composers of, 105

Elizabethan, 111–114
instrumental, 114–115
Josquin des Prez and, 106–108
lute song, 113–114
madrigal, 112–113
Mass, 106, 108–110, 159
medieval and, compared, 105–106
motet, 106–108
Palestrina and, 108–110
rhythm and melody of, 106
sacred, 106–110
secular, 110–115
society and, 102–105
texture of, 105–106
twentieth-century rediscovery of, 377
word-music relationships, 105
Renoir, Auguste, 387
Repeat sign, 195, 201
Repetition as form technique, 49–51,
    68–69
Requiem (Berlioz), 305
Requiem (Mozart), 219, 283
Resolution, defined, 53
Rests, types and notation of, 46
Retrograde:
  example of, 473
  in fugue, defined, 133
  in twelve-tone composition, 419–420
Retrograde inversion, defined, 419–420
Rhapsody in Blue (Gershwin), 377
Rhine Gold, The (Wagner), 267, 358
Rhythm, 35–40
  in African music, 533–534
  in Babbitt works, 473–474
  Baroque, 121
  in Bartók works, 444
  in bebop style, 503
  blues, 490
  Classical, 188
  defined, 36–37
  dotted, 45–46, 165–166
    in *forlana*, 469
  fourteenth-century innovations in, 96
  innovations in, by Stravinsky, 400–401,
    405, 407
  in Ives's works, 452–453
  in jazz, 480–482, 485
  measured, first notation of, 94–95
  and medieval polyphony, 94–96
  nationalism and, 311–316
  in non-Western music, 530–531
  notation of, 44–46
  in post-1950 music, 467, 505
  Renaissance, 106
  in rock music, 516–517
  triplet, example of, 247
  twentieth-century innovations in, 372,
    382–384, 392
Rhythm and blues, 488, 512
Rhythm section in jazz ensemble, de-
    scribed, 482, 494, 503

Ricercar, defined, 115
Ricercar in the Twelfth Mode (Gabrieli),
    115
Rienzi (Wagner), 357
Riff, defined, 498
Rigoletto (Verdi), 339, 341–346
  La donna è mobile ("Woman is fickle") and
    Quartet, 341–346
  story of, 341
Rimbaud, Arthur, 389
Rimsky-Korsakov, Nikolai, 264, 312, 313
  Russian Easter Overture, 311
  Scheherazade, 264
  Stravinsky as student of, 397
  (*See also* "Russian Five, The")
Rinaldo (Handel), 173
Ring of the Nibelung, The (Wagner), 358–
    365
  The Rhine Gold, 267, 358
  Siegfried, 358–359
  *The Twilight of the Gods (Götterdäm-
    merung)*, 359–365
  The Valkyrie, 358
Risoluto, defined, 468
Ritardando, defined, 39
Rite of Spring, The (Le Sacre du printemps)
    (Stravinsky), 372, 383, 385, 399,
    405–409
  elements of, 407
  orchestration for, 407
  rhythmic innovations in, 383
Ritornello:
  defined, 129
  examples of, 129–131, 151, 166–167
Ritornello form:
  concerto grosso and, 128–131(LO),
    157–158
  described, 129
  examples of, 129–131(LO), 151, 166–
    167
"Rock Around the Clock" (Bill Haley and
    the Comets), 512, 517
Rock group, described, 515
Rock music, 51, 53, 512–525
  American society and, 517–521
  Beatles and, 512, 513, 522–525
  dancing and, 520–521
  diversity of 1960s styles, 513
  Dylan and, 513, 514, 517
  electronic music and, 464
  elements of, 515–517
  influences on, 512
  and jazz ("jazz rock"), 506
  jazz influenced by, 508
  of mid-1950s, 512
  of 1960s, 513
  recordings and, 520
  rhythm, 516, 517
  rhythm-and-blues style and, 512
  singing styles in, 516
  as theatrical events, 519

589

Rock music:
tone colors in, 515–516
Woodstock, festival of, 518
Rock 'n' Roll:
leading performers of, 512
records, 520
Rock performers, theatrics of, 519
See also specific names)
Rococo style, described, 184–185
Rodeo (Copland), 456
Rokudan (Kengyō), 552
Rolling Stones, 512, 514
Beatles and, 512
Romantic love in Romantic music, 263
Romantic music, 79, 258–369
art song, 269–277, 279–282, 332–334
Berlioz and, 303–310
Brahms and, 332–338
Chopin and, 283–287
and Classical, compared, 258, 262–267
composers and their public, 267–268
Dvořák and, 325–331
elements of, 262–267
exoticism in, 263–264
Liszt and, 288–295
literature and, importance of, 263
Mendelssohn and, 295–301
nationalism in, 263–264, 285–287, 290,
311–316, 318, 322–325(LO),
325–331(LO), 338–340, 359–364
orchestra for, 264–265
program music, 264, 290–291, 301–310
Puccini and, 346–356
Schubert and, 270–279
Schumann and, 279–283
Smetana and, 322–325
sociocultural background, 258–261,
267–268
style characteristics, 262–267
subjects of, 263
Tchaikovsky and, 316–322
Verdi and, 338–345
Wagner and, 357–365
Romanticism:
in art and literature, 258, 261
Middle Ages and, 258
in music, described, 258–267
(*See also* Romantic music)
Romeo and Juliet (Berlioz), 305
Romeo and Juliet, Overture-Fantasy
(Tchaikovsky), 76, 264, 301, 316,
319–322(LO)
orchestral score, sample of, 76
as program music, 301
Rondo, 203–204(LO)
defined, 203
example of, 203–204, 246, 247
reinterpreted by Bartók, 444
Ronstadt, Linda, 514, 516
Ross, Diana, 512
Rouen Cathedral (Monet), 388

Round:
Frère Jacques as, 367–369
imitation and, 64
Row, twelve-tone (*see* Tone row)
Royal Academy of Music, 173
Rubato:
described, 266
use of, 285
Rubens, Peter Paul, 118, 119
Rudolf, Archduke of Austria, 241
Ruggles, Carl, 453
Russian Ballet (Diaghilev), 385–386, 398
Petrushka for, 401
Russian Easter Overture (Rimsky-Korsakov),
311
"Russian Five, The," 312–313
Tchaikovsky and, 318
Russian Revolution (1919), effect on
Stravinsky, 399

St. Cyr, Johnny, 496
"St. Louis Blues" (Handy), 488
St. Luke Passion (Penderecki), 469
St. Matthew Passion (Bach), 155
conducted by Mendelssohn, 295
St. Petersburg Carnival, 401
Salomon, Johann Peter, 210
"Salomon Symphonies" (Haydn), 210–212
Sand, George, 283
Sansa (see *Mbira*)
Sarabande, 160
Sarod, described, 547
"Satin Doll" (Ellington), 500
Saturday Night Fever (movie), disco and,
521
Saul (Handel), 174
Saxophone:
in bebop, 502
Coltrane and, 506–509
described, 21, 22
in jazz, 482
in swing, 497
Sayn-Wittgenstein, Princess Carolyne,
Liszt and, 290
Scale(s), 3–4, 57–61, 381–382
chromatic, 60–61, 265, 391–392
defined, 57
five-tone (*see* Pentatonic scale)
Indian raga, 544–545
major, 57–59, 88, 120, 380–381
minor, 59–60, 88, 120, 380–381
seven-tone, 4
twelve-tone, 4
whole-tone, 392, 417
(*See also* Church mode; Twelve-tone system
Scat singing, described, 496
Scenes of Childhood (Kinderscenen)
(Schumann), 280
Scheherazade (Rimsky-Korsakov), 264

Scherzo:
defined, 202
example of, 253–254(LO), 293
Schiller, Johann Christoph Friedrich, 243
Schoenberg, Arnold, 415–426
atonal works of, 414, 417–418, 421–
423(LO)
atonality and, 417–418
biographical sketch of, 415–416
Brahms influence on, 382
Chamber Symphony, Op. 9, 417
as expressionist composer, 413, 415
Five Piano Pieces, Op. 23, 418
Five Pieces for Orchestra, Op. 16, 414, 417,
421–423(LO)
Fourth String Quartet, Op. 37, 386, 418
Gurre-Lieder ("Songs of Gurre"), 417
on Ives, 452
Mahler and, 366
Moses and Aron, 418
music of, 373, 382, 386, 415–426
Piano Concerto, Op. 42, 418
Pierrot lunaire, Op. 21 ("Moonstruck
Pierrot"), 417–418
portrait of, 416
as refugee, 386
rhythmic innovations of, 382, 422
Serenade, Op. 24, 418
Suite for piano, Op. 25, 418, 419
A Survivor from Warsaw, Op. 46, 414,
418, 424–426
twelve-tone system developed by, 382,
418–421, 461–462
twelve-tone works of, 386, 414, 418, 419,
424–426
Variations for Orchestra, 418
Verklärte Nacht ("Transfigured Night"),
417
Violin Concerto, Op. 36, 418
Webern as student of, 438–439
School of Notre Dame, 94–95
Schubert, Franz, 262, 270–279
biographical sketch of, 270–271
economics of, 268
"The Erlking" *(Erlkönig),* 271, 273–276
and Goethe texts, song-settings for, 271,
273–277
"Gretchen at the Spinning Wheel," 271
Heidenröslein ("The Wild Rose"), 276–
277
music of, 271–279
Piano Quintet in A Major *("Trout"),* 273,
278–279(LO)
portrait of, 272
songs, 269, 271, 273–277
Symphony in C Major *("Great"),* 273,
295
Symphony No. 8 in B Minor *(Unfinished),* 273
Die Winterreise ("The Winter Journey"),
270

"Schubertiads," 271
Schuller, Gunther, 506
Schumann, Clara Wieck, 280
    Brahms and, 332–334
    portrait of, 281
Schumann, Robert, 262, 279–282
    biographical sketch of, 279–280
    Brahms and, 332
    Carnaval as program music, 302
    on Chopin, 263
    composition forms, styles, techniques, 280–282
    Dichterliebe ("Poet's Love"), 270, 280
    as music critic, 268
    on Schubert, 273
    as song composer, 269
    song cycles by, 280
    Träumerei ("Dreaming") from *Kinderscenen (Scenes of Childhood)*, Op. 15, 282
    as virtuoso, 279
Score:
    defined, 77
    electronic, 464
    for motion pictures, 386
    from *Romeo and Juliet* (Tchaikovsky), 76
Scotch Symphony (Mendelssohn), 297
Scott, Sir Walter, 258
Seasons, The (Haydn), 211, 212
Secco recitative, defined, 168
Second Piano Sonata ("Concord, Mass. 1840–60") (Ives), 453
Septuple meter, defined, 38
Sequence, defined, 51
Serenade, defined, 202
Serenade, Op. 24 (Schoenberg), 418
Serenade in A (Stravinsky), 381
Serial organization (*see* Serialism)
Serial technique, 418*n.*
    (*See also* Twelve-tone system)
Serialism:
    Babbitt and, 473
    defined, proponents of, 463
    electronic music and, 464
Seven tones in Western scale, 4
Sextuple meter, defined, 38
Sexual openness in rock songs, 519–520
Sgt. Pepper's Lonely Hearts Club Band (Beatles), 522–525
    recording process, 520
Shakahachi, defined, 552
Shake, the (rock dance), 520
Shakespeare, William, 102–103, 112
    As You Like It, 113–114
    Berlioz use of, 303–304
    inspiration of, in Romantic music, 319–320
    use of, for operatic libretti, 340
Shamisen, defined, 552
Shankar, Ravi, 543, 547–549
    Maru-Bihag raga by, 547–549
Sharp sign, 43

Shastri, Shyama, 544
Shelley, Mary, 258
Shema Yisroel ("Hear, O Israel") from *A Survivor from Warsaw*, Op. 46 (Schoenberg), 424–426
Shostakovich, Dimitri, 449
Shultal, defined, 545
Sibelius, Jean, 311, 312
Side drum (snare drum), described, 24, 25
Siegfried (Wagner), 358–359
Silence (rests), notation of, 46
"Simple Gifts" (Trad.):
    Copland variations on, 458, 460
    as theme-and-variation example, 460
Sinatra, Frank, 497
Singing:
    African styles of, 535
    methods (Western) of, 110
    in non-Western cultures, 529
Single-reed woodwinds, examples of, 22
Sitar:
    described, 546–547
    in rock groups, 516
Six Dances in Bulgarian Rhythm (Bartók), 383
Slavonic Dances (Dvořák), 311
Sleep of Reason Breeds Monsters, The (Goya). 258
Sleeping Beauty (Tchaikovsky), 319
Smetana, Bedřich:
    The Bartered Bride, 323
    biographical sketch of, 322–323
    Má Vlast (My Country), 323
    The Moldau (Vltava), 264, 301, 303, 323–325(LO)
    as musical nationalist, 312, 322–325
Smith, Bessie, 488, 490–492
Smithson, Harriet (Berlioz, Harriet Smithson), 303–304
Smithsonian Collection of Classic Jazz, A, 480*n.*, 501, 506, 508
Snare drum, described, 24, 25
Social protest (*see* Expressionism)
Société des Concerts du Conservatoire, 268
Society for Private Musical Performances in Vienna, 427
Soldier's Tale, The (L'Histoire du soldat) (Stravinsky), 378, 399
    ragtime and tango rhythms in, 400
Soli Deo Gloria (Bach), 153
Solo concerto, 150
Sonata:
    Baroque, defined, 148
    Beethoven and development of, 243–244
    chamber and church, 148
    classical, 194–198(LO)
    defined, 190
    examples of, 149, 197–198, 244–247
    piano, 243–247
    sonata form and, defined, 194

    trio, 148–149
    for violin and piano, 208
Sonata-allegro form (*see* Sonata form)
Sonata da camera (chamber sonatas), 148
Sonata da chiesa (church sonatas), 148
Sonata for Flute, Cello, Oboe, and Harpsichord (Carter), 377, 467–469
Sonata for solo violin (Bartók), 443
Sonata for Two Pianos and Percussion (Bartók), 444
Sonata form:
    Beethoven and, 243–247
    Classical, defined, 194–198
        concerto, 207, 234–237(LO)
        symphony, 205, 213, 230–233(LO), 249–252(LO), 254
    defined, 194
    examples of, 197–198, 221, 235–237(LO), 245, 254–255(LO), 298–301(LO), 320–322(LO), 326–328(LO), 446–448(LO)
    in Mozart opera overture, 221
    reinterpreted by Bartók, 444–448, 450
    Stravinsky and, compared with Classical, 409
Sonata-rondo form:
    described, 203
    example, 216, 237
Song (*see* Art song; Lute song)
Song cycles:
    Ancient Voices of Children (Crumb), 475–477
    described, 270
    in koto music, 552
    Questions on Nature (Gideon), 474–475
    Romantic, 270
    of Schubert, 270
    of Schumann, 270, 280
Song from Angola, form of, 541
Song of the Earth, The (Das Lied von der Erde) (Mahler), 366
"Song of the Plovers" (*Chikori No Kyoku*) (Yoshizawa Kengyō), 553
Songs Without Words (Mendelssohn), 297
"Sophisticated Lady" (Ellington), 500
Soprano, 10
    operatic categories of, 136–137
    Wagnerian, 360
Sorcerer's Apprentice, The (Dukas), 303
Soul music:
    musicians, 512
    rhythm-and-blues and, 512
Sound:
    defined, 2
    directional aspect of, 466
    "liberation of," 465–466
    properties of, 2–9
Sounds and the Perfumes Swirl in the Evening Air, The (Les Sons et les parfums tournent dans l'air du soir) (Debussy), 360
Sousa, John Philip, 454

"Special Theory of Relativity," (Einstein), 372

Sprechstimme:
defined, 418
use of, 424, 428

Springsteen, Bruce, 514
Staccato, defined, 48
Staff, defined, 42
Stalinism, revolt against, effect on music, 469
"Star-Spangled Banner, The," 2–3
Starr, Ringo, 522

Steps:
half and whole, 57–60
and leaps, melodic, 48

Stern, Isaac, 74

Stockhausen, Karlheinz:
Etude II, electronic score of, 465
Piano Piece No. 11, 464
serialism and, 463, 464

Stopping a string, defined, 15

Stops:
pipe organ, 30
string (double, triple, quadruple), 15

Storyville, jazz home, 493
(*See also* Jazz; New Orleans style)
Strauss, Richard, 303, 377, 413, 421
Till Eulenspiegel, 303

Stravinsky, Igor, 397–413
ballet music of, 398–409
biographical sketch, 397–399
on Debussy, 393
The Firebird, 8, 398
Firebird Suite, 7–8(LO)
music of, 373, 377–379, 381–383, 396–413
as neoclassicist composer, 396–397
Oedipus Rex, 400
Petrushka, 381, 386, 398, 400, 401–405(LO)
Picasso sketch of, 398
Pulcinella, 397, 400
"Ragtime" from *The Soldier's Tale,* 377, 400
The Rake's Progress, 400
as refugee, 386
rhythmic innovations of, 400–401, 405, 407
The Rite of Spring (Le Sacre du printemps), 372, 383, 385, 399, 405–409
Russian Ballet and, 398
Serenade in A, 381
The Soldier's Tale (L'Histoire du soldat), 378, 399, 400
Symphony of Psalms, 397, 400, 409–413
twelve-tone system adopted by, 400
The Wedding (Les Noces), 378
work habits of, 399

Strayhorn, Billy, 500
Street, Dresden (Kirchner), 414
Stretto, defined, 133

String instruments:
in Classical orchestra, 190
classified and described, 11, 14–18
distribution in orchestra, 13
non-Western (*see* Chordophones; Koto; Sitar)

String quartet:
Bartók and, 444, 445
Beethoven and, 203–204(LO), 243
Classical, 190, 194, 208
described, 190, 194, 208
Haydn and, 212

String Quartet (Debussy), 390
String Quartet in C Minor, Op. 18, No. 4 (Beethoven), 203–204(LO)
String Quartet No. 1 (Carter), 467
String section, defined, 14
String quintet, defined, 208
Strings of violin, described, 14–15

Strophic song (form):
defined, 269
examples of, 113–114, 276–277
modified, 270

Style:
chronology in relation to, 556–561
defined, 79
periods, 79–80

Subdominant chord, defined, 489

Subject (fugue):
described, 131–132
example of, 134
variation techniques, 133

Suite:
Appalachian Spring (Copland) as example, 380, 456, 458–460
Baroque, 160–162, 397
defined, 160

Suite for piano, Op. 25 (Schoenberg), 418, 419
Suite (Overture) No. 3 in D Major (Bach), 161–163
Summer, Donna, 514
Summer Morning by a Lake: Colors (The Changing Chord) from *Five Pieces for Orchestra,* Op. 16 (Schoenberg), 421
Sunken Cathedral, The (La Cathédrale engloutie) from *Preludes* for Piano (Debussy), 387, 391, 395–396
Supremes, The, Motown music and, 512
"Surprise" Symphony No. 94 in G Major (Haydn), 199–201(LO), 212
Survivor from Warsaw, A, Op. 46 (Schoenberg), 414, 418, 424–426
Shema Yisroel ("Hear, O Israel"), 424–426
Süssmayr, Franz, 219
Swan Lake (Tchaikovsky), 319
Swieten, Baron Gottfried van, 221

Swing:
arrangements, 497–498, 500
band, instrumental organization of, 497

Ellington and, 480, 497, 499–502
forms, 499, 501–502(LO)
improvisation in, 498
and New Orleans jazz, compared, 497
percussion, 498
riffs, 498–500

Symbolism:
impressionism and, in music, 387–396
in literature, 387, 389
musical, in *Wozzeck,* 428–438

Symbolist poets, French, 387, 389, 392

Symphonic poem (tone poem):
by Debussy, 393–394(LO)
described, 290–291, 302–303
examples of, 290–291, 302–303, 313, 323–325(LO), 393–396(LO)
Liszt as creator of, 290–291, 303

Symphonie fantastique (Fantastic Symphony) (Berlioz), 263, 288, 301, 302, 304–310

Symphony:
Classical, elements of, 205–206, 230–234
defined, 190
"dramatic," of Berlioz, 305
eighteenth- and nineteenth-century, compared in length, 266
neoclassical meaning of, 410
program, defined, 302

Symphony No. 1 in D Major (Mahler), Third Movement, 367–369(LO)
Symphony No. 3 (*Eroica*) (Beethoven), 240, 242
Symphony No. 4 (Tchaikovsky), 319
Symphony No. 5 (Tchaikovsky), 319
Symphony No. 5 in C Minor, Op. 67 (Beethoven), 242, 247–255(LO)
Symphony No. 6 (*Pastoral*) (Beethoven), 241, 243
as program music, 302
Symphony No. 6 (*Pathétique*) (Tchaikovsky), 318, 319
as program music, 302
Symphony No. 8 ("Symphony of a Thousand") (Mahler), 366
Symphony No. 8 in B Minor (*Unfinished*) (Schubert), 273
Symphony No. 9 (*Choral*) (Beethoven), 242
Symphony No. 9 in E Minor, "From the New World" (Dvořák), 326–331(LO)
Symphony No. 40 in G Minor, K. 550 (Mozart), 196–198(LO), 220, 230–234(LO)
Fourth Movement, 196–198(LO)
Symphony No. 41 in C (*Jupiter*) (Mozart), 230
Symphony No. 94 in G Major (Surprise) (Haydn), 199–201(LO)
Symphony No. 100 (*Military*) (Haydn), 212
Symphony No. 101 (*Clock*), (Haydn), 212
Symphony No. 103 in E-flat Major (*Drum Roll*) (Haydn), 212–216

592

Symphony in C Major *(Great)* (Schubert), 273, 295
Symphony in F-sharp Minor *(Farewell)* (Haydn), 210
Symphony of Psalms (Stravinsky), 397, 400, 409–413
  neoclassical features of, 410
Syncopation:
  in Beethoven works, 242
  defined, 38
  example of, 233(LO)
  fourteenth-century development of, 96
  in jazz, 39, 382, 480, 482, 485, 487
  in ragtime, 487–488
  in Tchaikovsky works, 320
Synthesizers, electronic: Babbitt as composer for, 32, 465, 473–474
  Buchla, 32
  compositions for, 473
  described, 32–33
  in jazz compositions, 505
  method for using, 473–474
  Moog, 32
  RCA Mark II, 31, 32, 473
  in rock music, 515

Tabla, described, 547
Tabors, defined, 91
Tag (coda), described, 495
Tailpiece of violin, 14–15
Take Five (Brubeck), 506
Tala system, defined and illustrated, 545
"Talking drums" in African music, 533, 536, 538
Tambourine, described, 24, 27
Tambura:
  as accompaniment, 547
  defined, 544
Tam-tam (gong), defined, 24, 27
Tannhäuser (Wagner), 359
Tape recorder, Varèse use of, 470–472
  (*See also* Recording; Tape studio as composing tool)
Tape studio as composing tool, 31–32, 464, 472, 520
Taped sounds, electronic music and, 464
  (*See also* Synthesizers, electronic)
Tate, Nahum, 144
Tchaikovsky, Peter Ilyich, 262, 316–322
  ballet music, 319
  biographical sketch, 316–318
  composition style, form and technique, 318–322
  "Dance of the Reed Pipes" from the *Nutcracker Suite*, 70–71(LO)
  Eugene Onegin, 319
  individuality of, 263
  Marche slave, 319
  The Nutcracker, 70, 319
  The *Nutcracker Suite*, 70–71(LO), 319

Overture 1812, 302, 319
  personal finances of, 268
  Piano Concerto No. 1 in B-flat Minor, 319
  Pique Dame (The Queen of Spades), 319
  portrait of, 317
  Romeo and Juliet, Overture-Fantasy, 76, 264, 301, 316, 319–322(LO)
  Sleeping Beauty, 319
  Swan Lake, 319
  Symphony No. 4, 319
  Symphony No. 5, 319
  Symphony No. 6 *(Pathétique)*, 302, 318, 319
  Violin Concerto, 319
Tegotomono, defined, 552
Television:
  effect on music and society, 385
  effects on musical style since 1950, 461
Tempo, 39–40
  defined, 39
  indications, 39
  in Romantic music, 266
Ten Commandments, The (Bach), 155
Tenor (voice), 10
  heroic ("helden"), 360
  operatic categories of, 137, 360
Tension:
  example of, 248
  and pitch, 14
Ternary form [*see* A B A Ternary form]
Terraced dynamics, 121–122
Texier, Rosalie, 390
Texture, 62–68
  in African music, 535
  Baroque, 122
  changes of, 65–68
  Classical, 188
  of Copland works, 457
  defined, 62
  homophonic, 64–65
  in koto music, 552–553
  monophonic, 62–63
  nationalism and, 311–316
  in non-Western music, 530–531
  polyphonic, 63–64
  Renaissance, 105–106
  Webern and, 440
Thematic transformation, described, 266–267
Theme(s):
  contrasting, in Classical music, 190
  defined, 51
  Haydn development of, 212
Theme-and-variation form:
  Brahms as master of, 334–338
  in Classical period, described, 199–201(LO)
  defined, 199
  examples of, 199–201(LO), 214–215, 251–253(LO), 278–279(LO), 292–294, 335–337, 360

jazz improvisation as, 484
  example of, 504–505(LO)
  in koto music, 552
  in Renaissance music, 114
  (*See also* Ground bass)
Third of May (Goya), 192
Third Piano Concerto (Bartók), 443
Third stream jazz style, 506
Third Symphony (Ives), 452
Thirteenth-century music, *Danse Royale*, 91
  (*See also* Medieval music)
Three Compositions for Piano (Babbitt), 473
Three-minute "sound barrier" for 78 records, 500
Three-part form [*see* A B A ternary form]
Three Places in New England (Ives), 453
  Putnam's Camp, Redding, Connecticut, 454–455
Threnody for the Victims of Hiroshima (Penderecki), 469–470(LO)
Throne of St. Peter (Bernini), 116
Through-composed form:
  defined, 269–270
  example of, 274–276
Tibetan prayer stone, as unconventional instrument, 475
Tie, defined, 46
Till Eulenspiegel (Strauss), 303
Timbre (*see* Tone color)
Time signature, defined, 47
Timpani (kettledrums), 24–25
  Bartók use of, 444
  described, 25
  in *Fantastic Symphony* (Berlioz), 306, 308
  (*See also* Percussion instruments)
Tolstoy, Leo, 312
Tommy (Townshend), 513
Tonal gravity [*see* Key (tonality)]
Tonal system:
  non-Western, 530, 535, 544, 552–553
  rhythm and, twentieth-century innovations in, 382–384
  of Schoenberg, 415
  traditional, 56–62, 372–373, 381
  twentieth-century approaches to, 372–373, 379–382, 391–392, 399–401, 417–421, 463–464, 466
  (*See also* Atonality; Key; Twelve-tone system)
Tonality (*see* Key)
Tone, defined, 3
Tone cluster(s):
  defined, 380
  electronic music and, 466
  in Ives work, 452
  in Penderecki works, 469–470(LO)
Tone color:
  Baroque, 123
  Bartók use of, 444
  Classical, 189–190

Tone color:
    in Crumb music, 475–477
    in Debussy music, 390–393
    described, 2, 5–6
    and harmonic series, 568–569
    of harpsichord, 468
    as impressionistic characteristic, 390
    of instruments, 12
    in jazz, 482, 484
    in Mahler music, 366
    melody built of, 439
    in Mozart music, 230
    nationalism and, 311–316
    in post-1950 jazz, 505
    and register, 12
    in rock music, 515–516
    Romantic, 264–265
    Stravinsky innovations in, 400–401, 408, 412
    twentieth-century, 378
    uses of, 5–6
    Webern and, 439–440
    woodwind, in Mozart music, 220
Tone-color melody *(Klangfarbenmelodie)*:
    described, 421, 462
    in Schoenberg and Webern works, 439, 440
"Tone language," 533
Tone poem (*see* Symphonic poem)
Tone row (set, series):
    in Babbitt works, 473–474
    Copland use of, 458
    defined, 418
    examples of, 419, 420, 426
    forms, 419–420
    Webern use of, 440
Tonic (keynote), 57, 381
Tonic key (home key), defined, 62
Tosca (Puccini), 346
Toscanini, Arturo, 385
Tosto che ll'alba ("As soon as the dawn") (Gherardello da Firenze), 96–97
Totem and Taboo (Freud), 407
Toulouse-Lautrec, 390
Townshend, Peter, 513
Toy piano, as unconventional instrument, 475, 476
Transcendental Études (Liszt), 288
"Transfigured Night" *(Verklärte Nacht)* (Schoenberg), 417
Träumerei ("Dreaming") from *Kinderscenen (Scenes of Childhood)*, Op. 15 (Schumann), 282
Traviata, La (Verdi), 339–340
Treatise on Modern Instrumentation and Orchestration (Berlioz), 265
Treble clef, 42
Treemonisha (Joplin), 487
Tremolo, defined, 18
Triad, 54–55, 379–380
    defined, 54

dominant, 54, 381
    to tonic, 55
    medieval, 95
    tonic, 54, 57, 60, 381
        major and minor, 60
    twentieth-century alternatives to, 379–380
Triangle:
    described, 24, 27
    in Liszt concerto, 291
    in Romantic music, 265
Trill, defined, 130
Trio:
    minuet and, defined, 201–203
    piano, defined, 208
    sonata, defined, 148
Trio in D Minor for Violin, Cello, and Piano (Mendelssohn), 297
Trio sonata (form):
    defined, 148
    example of, 149
Trio Sonata in E Minor, Op. 3, No. 7 (Corelli), 149
Triple meter:
    defined, 38
    Eine Kleine Nachtmusik (Mozart), Third Movement(LO) as example, 202–203
    notation, 47
Triple stop, defined, 15
Triplet:
    defined, 46
    examples of, 255, 274, 292–294
Tristan and Isolde (Wagner), 359
    atonality in, 382
Tristano, Lennie, 506
Triumphes of Oriana, The, 112–113
Trojans, The (Berlioz), 305
Trombone:
    Classical use of, 189, 243
    current uses, 23–24
    described, 22
    first use in symphony, 248
    in jazz, 482
    in Romantic music, 264, 306, 361, 368
Troubadours and *trouvères*, 91
"Trout, The" *(Die Forelle)* (Schubert), 273
"Trout" Quintet (Schubert), 273, 278–279(LO)
Trovatore, Il (Verdi), 339
Trumpet:
    Armstrong and, 496–497
    Baroque, described, 123
    in Baroque music, 161
    in Classical music, 189–190, 200, 235, 249, 252
    Davis and, 504–505
    described, 22–24
    in jazz, 482, 496–502
    in Romantic music, 264, 298, 306, 361, 363

Tu se' morta from *Orfeo* (Monteverdi), 142–143
Tuba:
    current uses of, 23–24
    described, 22
    "Wagner," 360
Tuning systems:
    equal temperament, Bach and, 157
    koto, 549–550
Turandot (Puccini), 346, 348
Turner, William, 261
Tutsi (of Rwanda), 533
Tutti, defined, 128
Twelfth mode, defined, 115
Twelve-bar blues:
    in bebop, 503
    chord progression of, 495
    described, 489–490
    Parker use of, 504–505(LO)
    in rock music, 517
Twelve-tone system:
    advantages of, 462
    Babbitt and, 473–474
    described, 382
    developed by Schoenberg, 415, 418–421
    diversity within, 462
    extensions of, 463–467
    increased use of, after 1950, 461–463
    neoclassicism and, 397
    principles of, 382, 418–421
    as "serial technique," 418*n.*
    serialism as extension of, 463
    Stravinsky adoption of, 399, 461
    Webern and, 438–442
Twelve tones in Western scale, 4
    [*See also* Scale(s)]
Twentieth-century music, 372–477
    American themes and composers, 450–460
    art movements and, 372, 374–376, 387–389, 396, 400, 405–407, 413, 414
    atonality and, 382, 417–418, 421–423, 427, 439, 440
    Baroque influences on, 377
    Bartók and, 442–450
    Berg and, 427–438
    chance music and, 463–464
    characteristics of, 378–384
    chord structures in, 379–382, 391–392, 395–396
    Copland and, 456–460
    Debussy and, 389–396
    electronic music and, 464–467, 470–474
    expressionism in, 413–414, 421–442
    and French symbolist poetry, 387, 389–393
    harmony in, 379–380
    impressionism and, 387–393

influences on, 372–377
Ives and, 450–455
jazz rhythms in, 377, 382, 400, 480
"liberation of sound," 465–466
major composers of, 373
melody, 384
mixed media, 467
neoclassicism and. 396–397, 410
performance difficulties, 453
as revolution in musical language, 372
rhythm, 382–384
Schoenberg and, 415–426
serialism, 463
society and, 384–386
Stravinsky and, 397–413
styles, 1900–1950, 372–373
styles since 1950, 461–467
stylistic diversity of, 373, 376–389
tonal systems, 380–382
tone color, 378
twelve-tone system and (*see* Twelve-tone system)
Webern and, 438–442
Twilight of the Gods, The (*Götterdämmerung*) (Wagner), 359–365
Twist, the (rock dance), 520
Two-part form [*see* A B (binary) form]
Tyagaraja, Swami, 544

Unanswered Question, The for Chamber Orchestra (Ives), 453–454
"Unfinished" Symphony (Schubert), 273
Unison:
  defined, 63
  examples of, 67–68(LO), 89
Unity of mood, Baroque, 121, 124, 155
University of California in Los Angeles (UCLA), Schoenberg at, 416
Unsquare Dance (Brubeck), 40, 504
Upbeat, defined, 38

Valkyrie, The (Wagner), 358
Valves (brass-instrument), described, 24
Varèse, Edgard, 470–472
  Ionisation, 28, 378, 471
  "liberation of sound" add, 465
  pictured, 471
  Poème électronique ("Electronic Poem"), 466, 470–472(LO)
Variation:
  as form technique, 69
  theme and (*see* Theme-and-variation form)
Variations for Orchestra (Carter), 468
Variations for Orchestra (Schoenberg), 418
Variations on a Theme by Haydn (Brahms), 334–338
Verdi, Giuseppe, 262, 338–346
  Aïda, 340

biographical sketch of, 338–340
  Falstaff, 340
  Macbeth, 319
  music of, 340–346
  Nabucco, 339
  nationalism and, 311–312, 338–339
  Oberto, 338
  Otello, 319, 340
  portrait of, 339
  Rigoletto, 339, 341–346
  La Traviata, 339–340
  Il Trovatore, 339
Verismo (realism), described, 346–348
Verklärte Nacht ("Transfigured Night") (Schoenberg), 417
Verlaine, Paul, 387, 392
Verrett, Shirley, 11
Vibraphone:
  described, 24
  in jazz, 482
Vibration frequency, defined, 3
  (*See also* Pitch)
Vibrato, defined, 5
Victoria, Queen, 295
Vienna as major music center, 193–194, 208–209, 218–219, 238, 241
Vienna Opera:
  Mahler as director, 365
  Wagner and, 359
Vienna Philharmonic Orchestra, 365
Vienna Workers' Symphony Concerts, 438
Vietnam War, rock music and, 520
Vina, described, 546–547
Vinci, Leonardo da, 102
Viol, described, 115
Viola, described, 14, 16
Violin, 3, 5, 11, 14–18
  construction of, 14–15
  Corelli use of, 149
  electrified, 464
  technique, Corelli influence on, 148
  Vivaldi and, 150
Violin Concerto (Berg), 427
Violin Concerto, Op. 36 (Schoenberg), 418
Violin Concerto (Tchaikovsky), 319
Violin and Grapes (Picasso), 370
Violoncello, 14, 16
  in jazz, 505, 506
Virgil, 144
Virtuoso:
  Bach as, 153
  Beethoven as, 240
  conductor, 75, 77
  defined, 74
  Liszt as, 268, 288
  Mozart as, 220
  Paganini as, 268
  performer, defined, 73–74, 206–207
  Schumann (Clara) as, 332
  Schumann (Robert) as, 279
  singer, operatic, 140

Vision and Prayer for soprano and synthesized accompaniment (Babbitt), 473
Vivace, defined, 39
Vivaldi, Antonio, 118, 127, 128, 150–152
  biographical sketch, 150
  Concerto Grosso in A Minor, Op. 3, No. 8, 150–152
  "The Harmonic Whim" (*L'Estro armonico*), 150
  rediscovery of, 377
Vocal music:
  in African cultures, 532, 535
  of Babbitt, 473
  of Bach, 153, 155, 158–160, 162–171
  Baroque, 135–147, 162–181
  of Beethoven, 244
  Classical, 188, 192, 218–230
  of Crumb, 475–477
  of Gideon, 474–475
  of Handel, 172–181
  of Ives, 452–453
  of Mahler, 366
  medieval, 84, 87–92
  of Monteverdi, 141–143
  in non-Western cultures, 529, 532, 535, 552
  of Purcell, 143–147
  Renaissance, 105–114
  of Schubert, 273–277
  of Schumann, 280–282
  of Webern, 439
  (*See also specific types*)
Vocal technique in non-Western cultures, 529
Vocalise, defined, 475
Voice ranges, 4, 10
  operatic categories of, 136–137
Voiles (*Sails*) (Debussy), 392
Voltaire, 184

Wachet auf, ruft uns die Stimme ("Awake, a Voice Is Calling Us") from Cantata No. 140 (Bach), 163–171
Wagner, Cosima Liszt von Bülow, 290, 359
Wagner, Minna Planer, 357
Wagner, Richard, 8, 262, 357–365, 377, 382, 389, 392, 413, 417
  art theories, writing on, 359
  biographical sketch, 357–359
  Brahms and, 333–334
  comments on great composers, 304
  essays by, 358
  influenced b y Beethoven, 357
  "leitmotif" as musical idea, 360–361, 364
  librettos by, 358
  Liszt influence on, 291
  Lohengrin, Prelude to Act III, 6–7(LO), 138

Wagner, Richard:
  The Mastersingers of Nuremberg, 359
  music of, 359–365
  "music drama" concept, 359–360, 389
  nationalism and, 359
  Parsifal, 359
  personal character of, 359
  personal finances of, 268
  portrait of, 358
  The Rhine Gold, 267, 358
  Rienzi, 357
  The Ring of the Nibelung, 358–365
  Schoenberg influenced by, 415
  Siegfried, 358–359
  Tannhäuser, 359
  Tristan and Isolde, 359, 382
  as twentieth-century influence, 377, 389
  The Twilight of the Gods (Götterdämmerung), 359–365
  "unending melody" concept, 360
  The Valkyrie, 358
Wagner tuba, 360
Wagnerian Review, The (La Revue Wagnérienne), 389
Wagnerian soprano, 360
Wagnerian (heroic) tenor, 360
Walter, Bruno, Mahler as supporter of, 366
Waltz, 38, 307
War and peace (Tolstoy), 312
Warsaw Ghetto, 424
Watteau, Antoine, 184
Weber, Constanze, 218
Webern, Anton, 373, 438–442
  biographical sketch, 438–439
  Five Pieces for Orchestra, Op. 10, 414, 440–442(LO)
  influence of, 462
  influenced by Mahler, 366
  music of, 439–442
  as music historian, 377
  Orchestral Piece, Op. 10, No. 3, 378

as Schoenberg disciple, 415
Stravinsky and, 400
Wedding, The (Les Noces) (Stravinsky), 378
Weelkes, Thomas, 112–113
Weimar, Duke of, 153
Weisgall, Hugo, 461
Well-Tempered Clavier, The (Bach), 71–72(LO), 157
"What Shall We Do with the Drunken Sailor?" as Dorian mode example, 88
"When Johnny Comes Marching Home" as Aeolian mode example, 88
Whitman, Walt, 258
Who, The (rock group), 513
Whole step, defined, 57
Whole-tone scale:
  described, 392
  Schoenberg use of, 417
Wieck, Clara (*see* Schumann, Clara Wieck)
Williams, Cootie, 501
Wind instruments (*see* Aerophones; Brass instruments; Woodwind instruments)
Winterreise, Die ("The Winter Journey") (Schubert), 270
Wonder, Stevie, 512, 514
Wooden Prince, The (Bartok), 442
Woodstock (film), 518
Woodstock Music and Art Fair, 518
Woodwind instruments, 11, 13, 18–23
  in Classical orchestra, 190
  Debussy use of, 391, 394
  described, 18–23
  distribution in orchestra, 13
  double- and single-reed, 22
  Romantic composers use of, 265
  in twentieth-century music, 400–413
Word-music relationship:
  in art song, Romantic, 269
  in Baroque music, 124, 179
  in Debussy works, 392
  in Purcell works, 143–144
  in Renaissance music, 105, 111

Word-painting:
  described, 105, 111
  example of, 112, 179
  Monteverdi use of, 143
Wordsworth, William, 258, 259
World War I:
  effects on artists and musicians, 399, 400, 413, 452
  expressionism and, 413
  nationalism and, 390
World War II:
  effects on artists and musicians, 386, 399, 469
  (*See also* Nazism)
  music since, 461–467
Woyzeck (Büchner), 427
Wozzeck (Berg), 414, 427–438
  forms and symbolic techniques in, 428–429
  libretto sections from, 430–438
  self-contained compositions in, 428

Xylophone, 24, 26
  in African music, 535–546
  described, 26

Yellow Submarine (movie), 522
"Yesterday" (Lennon and McCartney), 51–52
Yesteryears (Vergangenes) from *Five Pieces for Orchestra,* Op. 16 (Schoenberg), 422–423(LO)
Yoshida, Fusako, 551
Young, Lester, 497, 503
Young Person's Guide to the Orchestra, A, Op. 32 (Britten), 33–34, 377

Zen Buddhism, influence of, 464